THE OFFICIAL PRICE GUIDE

FINE ART

THE OFFICIAL®
PRICE GUIDE TO
FINE ART

SECOND EDITION

Rosemary and Michael McKittrick

House of Collectibles • New York

Important Notice. The artists' prices in this guide are based on *McKittrick's Art Price Guide* database. All of the information, including valuations, in this book has been compiled from the most reliable sources, and every effort has been made to eliminate errors and questionable data. Nevertheless, the possibility of error, in a work of such immense scope, always exists. The publisher will not be held responsible for losses which may occur in the purchase, sale, or other transaction of items because of information contained herein. Readers who feel they have discovered errors are invited to *write* and inform us, so they may be corrected in subsequent editions. Those seeking further information on the topics covered in this book are advised to refer to the complete line of *Official Price Guides* published by the House of Collectibles.

Published by: House of Collectibles
                     201 East 50th Street
                     New York, New York 10022

Distributed by Ballantine Books, a division of Random House, Inc., New York, and simultaneously in Canada by Random House of Canada Limited, Toronto.

Cover design by Kristine V. Mills
Cover painting by Jasper Francis Cropsey (*Autumn on the Hudson River, 1860*), courtesy of the Granger Collection.

Manufactured in the United States of America

Library of Congress Catalog Card Number 92-75368

ISBN: 0-876-37909-9

Second Edition: February 1993

10 9 8 7 6 5 4 3 2 1

To our children, Erin and Jordan. To my mother, Alice O'Connor, who, through her illness, is teaching me the meaning of the word courage.

"You gain strength, courage and confidence by every experience in which you really stop to look fear in the face. You are able to say to yourself, 'I lived through this horror. I can take the next thing that comes along.' ...You must do the thing you think you cannot do."

— *Eleanor Roosevelt*

"This is the true joy in life: that being used for a purpose recognized by yourself as a mighty one; that being a force of nature instead of a feverish, selfish, little clod of ailments and grievances complaining that the world will not devote itself to making you happy...

I want to be thoroughly used up when I die — for the harder I work the more I live. I rejoice in life for its own sake. Life is no brief candle to me. It is a sort of splendid torch which I've got a hold of for the moment and I want to make it burn as brightly as possible before handing it on to future generations."

— *George Bernard Shaw*

Contents

Acknowledgments

A special thank you to our editor, Stephen Sterns, who believed in and encouraged this project from the beginning.

The book would not exist without the help of our staff Cliff Gallagher and Jean De Grazia. Their commitment and quality of work over the years have made a real contribution.

We want to also thank the auction houses who provided the catalogs for this book. Without their support we could not have done this project. A complete list of auction houses is included in the book.

THE OFFICIAL®
PRICE GUIDE TO
FINE ART

Market Overview

Economic conditions certainly affect auction sales around the country, but to say the art market is not affected by the worldwide recession would be simplistic. At the same time, however, sales continue, and both the high and medium level paintings of good quality, especially those not recently on the market, continue to sell strongly.

Traditional areas of art, like Old Master paintings, show particular growth. At Sotheby's auction house in New York, the January and May 1992 sale results for Old Masters totaled $30 million. For example, there was a magnificent *Still Life of Flowers* by Jan van Huysum in excellent condition that had not been available for sale in fifty years. Prior to the auction, the painting was estimated to sell for up to $2 million. It sold for $3.52 million. At Christie's auction house, thirty-one Old Master paintings, dating from the fourteenth to seventeenth centuries, were sold on behalf of the J. Paul Getty Museum, realizing a total of $3.3 million.

Eight Impressionist and Modern paintings sold for over $1 million in the summer sale at Christie's, including works by Chagall, Manet, Mondrian, Renoir, and Toulouse-Lautrec. Andy Warhol's masterwork, *210 Coca-Cola Bottles,* became the most expensive Contemporary painting sold in 1992 when it realized $2.09 million. The market was also strong for Latin American paintings, American paintings, and Oriental works of art.

Having been in the art and appraisal business ourselves for fourteen years, we have seen firsthand the fluctuations in the market, but we still contend buying and selling at auction is a good route to go.

In this book there are over 53,000 auction sale results from sixty U.S. auction houses. The houses were chosen because of their catalog sales and because we believe they were a good representation of the market in the United States. The book covers every painting sold over $100 and includes works of art from Old Masters to Contemporary that sold during a two-year period.

Almost all of the art price guides available today report prices attained through auction, not prices asked by private dealers. With auction prices, the reader will get a much more objective measure of value. What someone pays for a work of art tells us a lot more about that work of art than the price advertised does.

3

Learn Before You Spend

People often ask us: How do I get started with collecting art? Begin by looking at paintings as much as you can. Go to galleries, museums, auctions; study the art . Decide what styles you like the most, and in the case of auctions, determine what the paintings are selling for. Most art auctions have previews a day or two before the sale, where you can look at the art close-up, and the sale catalog will provide estimates on the paintings you are interested in. These estimates are ranges placed on the items by the auction houses to give buyers a sense of value.

The people we have seen who are the most successful with art investments are people who specialize in a particular area. These individuals learn as much as they can about their chosen area, like Impressionism, or Contemporary art, nineteenth-century paintings, etc. In the field of art, like most fields, knowledge is power. Most of us have paid for our education in this field through the mistakes we have made. Being a generalist in the art field when large sums of money are at stake can be dangerous. Learn! Learn! Learn!

Invest in price guides. Most people in the art business and many hobbyists, appraisers, and collectors use price guides. They are an invaluable tool in giving you an objective measure of what art is selling for around the country. You would not go to school without books, and serious art enthusiasts rarely go shopping without price guides.

What Determines Value in Art

Quality is the most important factor in determining the value of a painting. You can develop an eye for quality through observation. Contrary to what some people believe, you are not necessarily born with an eye for art.

Condition is the second most important factor in determining the value of an art work or antique. Ideally, the best way to purchase a work of art is in its original condition. The less that has been done to an antique painting the better.

The medium of a work of art plays a part in the value. Generally, oil paintings are the most valuable, then watercolors and drawings and prints. However, there are countless exceptions to this rule of thumb.

The size of a painting affects its value. We have seen many wonderful paintings that were huge sell at auction for much less than you might guess because they were too large for most homes. The ideal size for a painting is 24 inches in height by 36 inches in width. This is the size that would fit above most sofas and fireplaces.

Another important point in assessing value is whether a painting bears the artist's signature or monogram. Without a signature, most paintings have limited value. Once again there are exceptions. Old Master paintings often were not signed. The same is true of primitive folk art paintings, and many of these works sell for large sums.

Seeing an artist listed in a price guide is an important distinction as well. What this tells you is that this artist has a track record. His works are desirable enough to be sold at auction. You can see the price ranges his work sells for, and in terms of buying, you have an objective measure of value. Why pay more than you have to? This is another example where knowledge is power.

Supply and demand factors are critical, too. After the death of Andy Warhol, his work and personal belongings got really hot. We attended the preview for the sale of his personal collection of furniture, watches, cookie jars, etc. Everyone wanted some memorabilia from the Warhol collection. Many of the items sold for much more than they were worth, just because they belonged to him.

Fakes and Forgeries

The point here is to be careful. Even the most knowledgeable people get fooled sometimes. Our advice is that if there is some real doubt about the authenticity of a work of art, pass it by! It is a lot harder to get a refund on a painting that is a fake than it is not to purchase it in the first place.

As appraisers, we have had the unpleasant experience of informing clients that a painting they paid thousands for is a fake and probably worth only a hundred dollars. No one wants this kind of problem. Fortunately, the opposite also happens where someone has purchased a work of art for a small amount of money and it turns out to be worth much more.

Beware of bargains! If you are purchasing art from a gallery or an antique dealer, make sure you are confident in their credibility. If you are buying at auction, find out what the auction house's terms are for selling. The terms of sale are usually listed in the front of the auction catalog. If you don't understand the terms, ask questions.

One of the benefits of buying art at the major auction houses in New York is that in most cases they guarantee works painted after 1870 to be authentic. This kind of expertise is comforting in an art market that contains some shark-infested waters.

Purchase and learn how to use a blacklight. They are inexpensive and are excellent tools for seeing what has been done to a painting. The pigments in modern-day paints fluoresce. Old pigments fluoresce faintly if not at all. Modern pigments are usually mixed with titanium white and will fluoresce much more vividly. Holding a blacklight on the reverse side of a painting will also spot any canvas repairs. This becomes very noticeable when a painting is examined under a blacklight, and in this way most restoration work will be revealed. In restoration, old varnish on a painting will retard fluorescence. As varnish is removed, the fluorescence of the pigments below will start to show so that the removal progress can be gauged. Sometimes a signature has been added, which indicates that there is a real problem with this work of art. Other times the painting may just have a little touch up here and there. This kind of restoration can be expected in a hundred-year-old painting, and if it is done well, it does not affect the overall value much. If there is extensive restoration, this will severely affect the value.

Much of what you need to learn will occur through observation. After looking at the fronts and backs of hundreds of paintings, many facets of determining authenticity will become obvious.

Another area of concern is bronze sculpture. Many of these nineteenth - and early twentieth - century beauties are being recast with the utmost precision. They are beautiful but not old. If someone loves bronzes and cannot afford the $2,000 and up to buy one, then an alternative exists. They look authentic and cost a fraction of the original. Unfortunately, there are unethical dealers who know these bronzes are not authentic but still attempt to sell them as period pieces. At the same time, there are dealers who think these bronzes are authentic and pass them off as originals as well. The market can become a real mine field!

Once again much information is available through observation. A hundred-year-old bronze is going to have some wear. Turn the bronze upside down. If the base looks new with no scratches, start to wonder. Original bronzes will often have some type of foundry mark on them, very often on the base somewhere. This tells you where the bronze was cast. Also, the less expensive recasts do not have the detail of the originals.

How Much to Pay

We have been asked the question: How much should I spend on a painting? In terms of investment we often suggest $5,000 and up as the quality level desirable on the market for oil paintings. This is a reasonable range if potential resale value in the future is important. With bronze sculpture we recommend $2,000 and up. With regard to drawings, watercolors and prints around $1,000 is a solid price to pay. Within these price ranges, there is a great deal of variability, and how much should be spent on art will depend on the buyer's finances and whether the art is purchased for personal enjoyment or investment potential.

Where to Buy

You have to start somewhere! The first consideration to buying art is whether this is a work of art you really like. You are the one who has to live with it, and it makes sense to live with pieces you love. Also, down the road when it is time for resale, if you find out your work of art is not worth much more than what you paid for it, you can exercise the option to hang onto it. Although much of what we purchase is for resale down the line, we have a number of paintings in our own collection that will remain there just because we really enjoy them. Their resale value is of small importance to us.

You might want to look into the local and regional auctions in your area. This is a good place to get your feet wet and at the same time study the market. Attend the auctions a few times before you buy so that you have some sense of how things go, and speak to other people at the auction about their experiences buying from this au on house.

Other places to buy are antiques shops, flea markets, household sales, art shows, and galleries. Once again, establish some kind of relationship with the seller. Unfortunately, there are many unscrupulous people out there who would be glad to take your money and take advantage of you at the same time. Start slowly and carefully. If you have any doubts about the seller or the work of art, pass it by. There will be other paintings to buy. Very few times in our career have we walked away from something and truly regretted it.

Most of all, have fun with collecting. Living with and having the opportunity to purchase works of art is a real privilege. Art represents all that is good and positive about human beings. It is a real gift to share with our families as well. I got so much enjoyment recently out of watching our one-year-old son in the living room standing pensively in front of one of my favorite paintings. Art can be for everybody.

Rosemary McKittrick

How to Use This Book

All of the artists are listed in alphabetical order by last name. The first name is given along with nationality, birth, and death date, when known. Four mediums are listed by initial: D=Drawing, P=Painting, S=Sculpture, W=Watercolor. Current price range is then listed: Low, Mean, and High. The selling prices are averaged to arrive at the mean figures. When only one price is listed, then you can assume only one painting sold for that artist during the two-year period. If all three prices are the same, then two paintings sold at the same price. This does happen in this book.

Authenticity and Representation of Artists' Names

The following are examples of the terminology used in this guide.

1. AACHEN, Johann von
   In the opinion of the auction house the work is by the artist named.
2. AACHEN, Johann von (Attrib.) or (Att.)
   Probably a work by the artist, but less certainty as to the authorship is expressed than in the preceding category.
3. AACHEN, Johann von (Studio) or (St.)
   A work by an unknown artist in the studio of the artist, which could or could not have been done under the artist's direction.
4. AACHEN, Johann von (School), (Sch.), or (Sc.)
   A work by an unknown painter who was a pupil of the artist.
5. AACHEN, Johann von (Circle) or (Cir.)
   A work by an as yet unidentified but distinct hand closely associated with the named artist, but not necessarily his pupil.
6. AACHEN, Johann von (Style)
   A work by a painter working in the artist's style, but not necessarily his pupil.
7. AACHEN, Johann von (Follower) or (Foll.)
   A work by a painter working in the artist's style, but not necessarily his pupil.
8. AACHEN, Johann von (Manner) or (Mann.)
   A work in the style of the artist, and of a later date.
9. AACHEN, Johann von (After) or (Aft.)
   A copy of a known work of an artist.
10. AACHEN, Johann von (Et al.)
    A work by the artist named and also by one or more identified artists.

Auction Houses

Sanford Alderfer Auction Center; Hatfield, PA
Abandoned Acres Auction Gallery; New Castle, PA
Altermann & Morris Art Gallery; Houston, TX
F.O. Bailey; Portland, ME
Barridoff Galleries; Portland, ME
Bruce Collins Seaboard Action Gallery; Eliot, ME
Jeffery Burchard; St. Petersburg, FL
Richard A. Bourne Co., Inc.; Hyannis, MA
Braswell Galleries; Norwalk, CT
Butterfield & Butterfield; San Francisco, CA
Christie's; New York, NY
Christie's East; New York, NY
Chicago Art Galleries, Inc.; Chicago, IL
Clearing House Auction Galleries, Inc.; Wethersfield, CT
Douglas Auctioneers; South Deerfield, MA
DeCaro Auction Sales; Seaford, DE
Dunning's Auction Service; Elgin, IL
William Doyle Galleries; New York, NY
DuMouchelles; Detroit, MI
Robert C. Eldred Co., Inc.; East Dennis, MA
Frank H. Boos Gallery; Bloomfield Hills, MI
Freeman/Fine Arts; Philadelphia, PA
Morton M. Goldberg Auction Galleries, Inc.; New Orleans, LA
Garth's Auctions; Delaware, OH
Grogan & Co.; Boston, MA
Guernsey's; New York, NY
Hanzel Galleries; Chicago, IL
Habsburg Feldman, Inc.; New York, NY
Willis Henry Auctions; Marshfield, MA
Leslie Hindman Auctioneers; Chicago, IL
Illustration House, Inc.; New York, NY
James R. Bakker; Cambridge, MA
Litchfield Auction Gallery; Litchfield, CT
Louisiana Auction Exchange; Baton Rouge, LA
Mystic Fine Arts; Mystic, CT
David W. Mapes, Inc. Auctioneers; Vestal, NY
John Moran Auctioneers & Appraisers; Pasadena, CA
Nadeau Auction Gallery; Colchester, CT
Neal Alford Company; New Orleans, LA
Northeast Auctions; Hampton, NH
Pettigrew Auction Gallery; Colorado Springs, CO
Provincetown Art Association & Museum; Provincetown, MA
Roan, Inc. Auction Gallery; Cogan Station, PA
Charles M. Russell Auction; Great Falls, MT
Royal York Auction Gallery; Pittsburgh, PA
Sotheby's; New York, NY
Sotheby's Arcade; New York, NY
Schrager Auction Galleries; Milwaukee, WI
Selkirk's; St. Louis, MO
Philip C. Shute Gallery; West Bridgewater, MA
Robert W. Skinner; Bolton, MA
C.G. Sloan & Co., Inc.; North Bethesda, MD
Don Treadway; Cincinnati, OH
Weschler's; Washington, DC
Gustave J.S. White Auctioneer; Newport, RI
Winter Associates, Inc.; Plainville, CT
Wolf's Gallery; Cleveland, OH
Young Fine Arts Gallery, Inc.; N. Berwick, ME

		Current Price Range		
		Low	Mean	High

		Low	Mean	High
AACHEN, Johann von (Attrib.) German (1552 - 1615)	D			$1,320
AACHEN, Johann von (Circle) German (1552 - 1615)	P	$2,750	$4,125	$5,500
AALTEN, Jacques van American (1907 -)	D			$16,500
AARONS, George American (1896 - 1980)	S			$5,500
ABAD, J. Gomez Spanish (19th -)	P			$187
ABADES, Juan M. Spanish (1862 -)	P	$9,350	$11,825	$14,300
ABADIE-LANDEL, Pierre French (20th -)	W			$220
ABAKANOWICZ, Magdelena (20th -)	P			$7,975
ABARTAUIL, (?)	P			$215
ABBATE, Niccolo dell (Circle) Italian (1512 - 1571)	D			$1,650
ABBE DE SAINT-NON, Jean C. French (1727 - 1791)	D			$2,200
ABBEMA, Louise French (1858 - 1927)	P	$990	$1,425	$1,860
ABBEY, Edwin A. American (1852 - 1911)	D	$1,210	$2,668	$3,300
	W	$550	$2,475	$4,400
ABBEY, Edwin A. (Manner) American (1852 - 1911)	P			$303
ABBOTT, Yarnall American (1870 - 1938)	P	$138	$727	$1,650
ABBRESCIA, Joe American (20th -)	P			$400
ABDELL, Doug (20th -)	S	$1,100	$2,475	$3,850
ABDY, Rowena	P	$6,050	$9,625	$13,200

D=Drawing, P=Painting, S=Sculpture, W=Watercolor

		Current Price Range		
		Low	Mean	High

		Low	Mean	High
ABDY, Rowena American (1887 - 1945)	*W*			$605
ABEL, Frank American (19th - 20th)	*P*			$990
ABEL-BOULINEAU, N. French (20th -)	*P*			$10,450
ABERCROMBIE, Gertrude American (1909 -)	*P*			$605
ABIATTI, F. Italian (19th -)	*P*			$193
ABIERI, Gino (?)	*P*			$220
ABIETA, James American (20th -)	*P*			$2,640
ABOUVARD, European (19th -)	*P*			$2,090
ABRAM, European (19th -)	*P*			$1,870
ABRAMOVITZ, Albert Russian (1879 - 1963)	*D* *P*			$165 $1,210
ABRAMS, Lucien American (1870 - 1941)	*P*	$1,650	$2,292	$2,750
ABREU, Mario Venezuelan (1918 -)	*P*	$6,600	$6,875	$7,150
ABRIL, Ben American (1923 -)	*P*	$413	$614	$990
ABRY, Leon E. A. Belgian (1857 - 1905)	*P*			$6,600
ACCARISI, Lodovico (?)	*P*			$550
ACCONCI, Vito American (1940 -)	*D*			$11,000
ACEVEDO, Manvel H. (20th -)	*P*			$275
ACEVES, Gustavo Mexican (1957 -)	*D*	$2,750	$2,915	$3,080

D=Drawing, P=Painting, S=Sculpture, W=Watercolor

		Current Price Range		
		Low	Mean	High

ACEXES, T.	*P*			$550
Spanish (19th - 20th)				
ACHEFF, William	*D*			$1,320
American (1947 -)	*P*	$13,200	$15,400	$16,500
ACHENBACH, Andreas	*P*			$8,250
German (1815 - 1910)	*W*	$125	$530	$935
ACHENBACH, Oswald	*D*			$1,650
German (1827 - 1905)	*P*	$715	$21,904	$55,000
ACHESON, Alice S.	*P*			$1,293
American (1895 -)				
ACHESON, Georgina E.	*P*			$440
American (20th -)				
ACHTSCHELLINCK, Lucas	*P*			$24,200
Flemish (1626 - 1699)				
ACKER, Edna L.	*P*			$165
American (20th -)				
ACKERMAN,	*P*			$110
(?)				
ACKERSON, Floyd G.	*P*	$248	$422	$550
American (1883 -)				
ACQUA, Cesare dell	*P*			$4,675
Austrian (1821 - 1904)				
ACQUIVITO,	*P*			$165
Italian (20th -)				
ADAM, Edouard	*P*			$3,850
French (1847 - 1922)				
ADAM, Emil	*P*			$2,750
German (1843 - 1866)				
ADAM, Franz	*P*			$44,000
German (1815 - 1886)				
ADAM, Joseph	*P*	$825	$972	$1,210
British (1842 - 1896)				
ADAM, Julius	*P*	$11,550	$24,200	$42,350
German (1852 - 1913)				

D=Drawing, P=Painting, S=Sculpture, W=Watercolor

		Current Price Range		
		Low	Mean	High
ADAM, Richard B.	*P*			$5,500
German (1873 - 1936)				
ADAM, William	*P*	$413	$702	$990
American (1846 - 1931)				
ADAMS, Charles P.	*P*	$440	$3,231	$8,800
American (1858 - 1942)	*W*	$303	$528	$990
ADAMS, Chauncey	*P*			$770
American (1895 -)				
ADAMS, Ed	*P*			$1,540
(19th -)				
ADAMS, J. H.	*P*			$1,650
American (?)				
ADAMS, Jeff	*P*			$1,760
(20th -)				
ADAMS, John C.	*P*	$1,100	$7,150	$13,200
British (1840 - 1906)				
ADAMS, John O.	*P*			$17,600
American (1851 - 1927)				
ADAMS, John Q.	*P*			$38,500
Austrian (1874 - 1933)				
ADAMS, John S.	*P*			$1,540
European (20th -)				
ADAMS, John W.	*D*			$450
American (1874 - 1925)				
ADAMS, Kenneth M.	*P*			$578
American (1897 - 1966)				
ADAMS, Philip	*P*			$660
(1881 -)				
ADAMS, Robert	*S*			$770
(20th -)				
ADAMS, Wayman	*P*			$4,125
American (1883 - 1959)				
ADAMS, Willis S.	*W*			$165
American (1844 - 1921)				
ADAMSON, John	*P*			$5,500
British (19th -)				

D=Drawing, P=Painting, S=Sculpture, W=Watercolor

		Current Price Range		
		Low	Mean	High

ADAN, Louis	*P*	$13,200	$18,975	$24,750
French (1839 - 1937)				
ADANDE, G.	*D*			$165
European (19th -)				
ADDISON, Byron K.	*S*			$3,850
American (1937 -)				
ADDY, Alfred	*P*	$220	$238	$275
American (19th - 20th)	*W*	$121	$141	$165
ADEMA, Gerhardus J.	*P*			$660
Dutch (1898 -)				
ADLER, Edmund	*P*	$4,400	$5,610	$7,920
German (1871 - 1957)				
ADLER, Jankel	*D*	$880	$1,540	$2,200
Polish (1895 - 1949)	*P*			$29,700
	W			$4,400
ADLER, Jules	*P*			$5,500
French (1865 - 1952)				
ADLER, Oscar F.	*P*			$1,760
American (19th - 20th)				
ADNET, Francoise	*P*			$550
French (1924 -)				
ADOLPHE, Albert Jean	*P*	$1,100	$1,155	$1,210
American (1865 - 1940)				
ADOLPHE, Albert Jean (Attrib.)	*P*			$880
American (1865 - 1940)				
ADOMEIT, George G.	*P*			$138
American (1879 -)				
ADRIAENSSEN, Alexander	*P*			$7,700
Dutch (1587 - 1661)				
ADRIAN, M.	*P*			$6,050
German (19th -)				
ADRIANI, Camillo	*P*	$550	$1,155	$1,760
American (19th - 20th)				
ADRIEN, Camille	*P*			$33,000
French (1834 - 1901)				

D=Drawing, P=Painting, S=Sculpture, W=Watercolor

		Current Price Range		
		Low	Mean	High

		Low	Mean	High
ADRION, Lucien French (1889 - 1953)	P	$1,650	$4,116	$9,900
AELST, Pieter C. van Dutch (1502 - 1550)	P	$60,500	$82,500	$104,500
AELST, Pieter C. van (Attrib.) Dutch (1502 - 1550)	P	$8,800	$28,600	$48,400
AELST, Pieter C. van (Circle) Dutch (1502 - 1550)	P	$2,750	$11,825	$20,900
AELST, Pieter C. van (Studio) Dutch (1502 - 1550)	P	$11,000	$18,700	$26,400
AELST, Willem van (Attrib.) Dutch (1626 - 1683)	P			$15,400
AENVANCK, Theodor van Flemish (1633 - 1690)	P			$44,000
AERTSEN, Pieter Dutch (1507 - 1575)	P	$13,200	$50,600	$88,000
AERTSEN, Pieter (Attrib.) Dutch (1507 - 1575)	P			$28,600
AFFLECK, William British (1869 -)	W	$2,860	$10,780	$18,700
AFON, Nicolas American (20th -)	P	$495	$523	$550
AFRICANO, Nicholas American (1948 -)	D	$1,430	$1,650	$1,870
	P	$2,970	$17,889	$52,250
	S			$41,250
	W			$3,190
AFRO (BASALDELLA), Italian (1912 -)	D	$8,800	$25,850	$35,750
	P	$5,775	$86,295	$253,000
	W	$6,050	$7,425	$8,800
AFSARY, Cyrus American (1940 -)	P	$2,800	$6,900	$11,000
AGAM, Yaacov Israeli (1928 -)	S	$495	$9,474	$19,800
	W	$4,125	$4,675	$5,225

D=Drawing, P=Painting, S=Sculpture, W=Watercolor

| | | Current Price Range | | |
		Low	Mean	High
AGARD, Charles J. (1900 -)	*P*			$4,400
AGNEW, Clark American (19th - 20th)	*P*			$5,500
AGNEW, William American (19th - 20th)	*P*			$121
AGOSTINELLI, French (20th -)	*P*			$880
AGOSTINI, Guido Italian (19th -)	*P*	$1,650	$2,475	$3,300
AGOSTINI, Peter American (1913 -)	*W*			$990
AGOSTINI, Tony French (1916 -)	*P*	$825	$1,073	$1,320
AGRASOT Y JUAN, Joaquim Spanish (1836 - 1907)	*P* *W*			$88,000 $286
AGRICOLA, Christoph L. (Circle) German (1667 - 1719)	*P*			$1,320
AGUILAR, Homero (19th -)	*P*	$1,650	$2,915	$4,180
AGUIRRE, Luis Ecuadorian (1946 -)	*P*	$330	$372	$413
AGUIRRE, Tomas C. Spanish (1857 -)	*P*			$3,850
AHEARN, John American (20th -)	*P* *S*	$2,750	$5,555	$8,800 $7,700
AHL, Henry C. American (1905 -)	*P*			$2,475
AHL, Henry H. American (1869 - 1946)	*P* *W*	$138	$390	$1,103 $220
AHLBORN, August W. J. German (1796 - 1857)	*P*			$6,050
AHLBORN, Emil American (20th -)	*P*	$440	$440	$440

D=Drawing, P=Painting, S=Sculpture, W=Watercolor

		Current Price Range		
		Low	Mean	High
AHORN, John	*W*			$110
British (20th -)				
AICHLEIN, T.	*W*			$110
European (20th -)				
AIKEN, Charles A.	*P*	$165	$317	$468
American (1872 - 1965)	*W*	$165	$193	$220
AIKEN, Mary H.	*P*			$770
American (20th -)				
AILKEN, J.	*P*			$358
American (19th -)				
AINSLEY, Dennis	*P*	$220	$391	$550
American (20th -)				
AINSLIE, R. St. John (Attrib.)	*P*			$4,950
British (? - 1908)				
AIRY, Anna	*P*			$17,050
British (20th -)				
AITKEN, John E.	*W*			$413
British (1881 - 1957)				
AITKIN, Harry C.	*P*			$413
American (20th -)				
AIVAZOVSKY, Ivan C.	*P*	$51,700	$55,000	$58,300
Russian (1817 - 1900)				
AIVAZOVSKY, Ivan C. (Attrib.)	*P*			$7,150
Russian (1817 - 1900)				
AIZELIN, Eugene A.	*S*			$3,520
French (1821 - 1902)				
AIZPIRI, Paul	*P*	$4,400	$42,232	$115,500
French (1919 -)	*W*	$2,420	$6,435	$10,450
AJDUKIEWICZ, Thaddeus von	*P*	$2,475	$8,388	$14,300
Polish (1852 -)				
AKELEY, Carl	*S*	$1,100	$6,160	$18,700
American (1864 - 1926)				
AKERMAN, A.	*P*			$495
(20th -)				

D=Drawing, P=Painting, S=Sculpture, W=Watercolor

		Current Price Range		
		Low	Mean	High

		Low	Mean	High
AKERS, Roger	P			$605
American (1940 -)				
AKERS, Vivian M.	P	$440	$2,224	$5,500
American (1886 -)				
AL TISSIMO, Cristofano (Attrib.)	P			$5,500
Italian (16th - 17th)				
ALAJALOV, Constantin	P	$825	$1,458	$2,090
American (1900 -)				
ALASKAN SCHOOL 19C,	P			$12,100
American (19th -)				
ALAZZO, F.P.	P			$303
Italian (19th - 20th)				
ALBANI, Francesco	D			$8,250
Italian (1578 - 1660)				
ALBANI, Francesco (Attrib.)	D	$2,970	$3,685	$4,400
Italian (1578 - 1660)				
ALBANI, Francesco (Circle)	P	$3,850	$11,275	$18,700
Italian (1578 - 1660)				
ALBAREDE, Andre-Rene	P			$770
French (20th -)				
ALBERIA, A.	P			$2,860
(19th -)				
ALBEROLA, Jean-Michel	P			$2,200
(20th -)				
ALBERS, Josef	P	$550	$62,205	$198,000
American (1888 - 1976)				
ALBERT, Arthur	D	$440	$972	$1,870
American (1919 - 1987)	P	$550	$1,568	$2,860
ALBERT, E. Maxwell	P	$440	$4,620	$12,100
American (1890 -)				
ALBERT, Ernest	P	$495	$6,519	$16,500
American (1857 - 1946)	W			$825
ALBERT, Hermann	P			$2,970
(20th -)				

D=Drawing, P=Painting, S=Sculpture, W=Watercolor

		Current Price Range		
		Low	Mean	High
ALBERT, Jose J.	*P*			$11,000
Spanish (19th -)				
ALBERT, Karl	*P*	$523	$564	$605
American (1911 -)				
ALBERTI, Cherubino	*D*	$11,000	$12,100	$13,200
Italian (1553 - 1615)				
ALBERTOLLI, Fiscondo	*D*			$330
(?)				
ALBERTS, W. J.	*P*			$660
American (20th -)				
ALBINSON, Dewey	*P*			$3,300
American (1898 -)				
ALBRIGHT, Adam E.	*P*	$121	$11,678	$63,800
American (1862 - 1957)				
ALBRIGHT, Henry J.	*P*	$550	$825	$1,100
American (1887 - 1951)				
ALBRIGHT, Herman O.	*D*			$825
American (1876 - 1944)				
ALBRIGHT, Ivan Le L.	*W*			$2,750
American (1897 -)				
ALBRIGHT, John A.	*P*	$330	$733	$935
American (20th -)				
ALBRIZZIO, Conrad	*P*			$523
American (1894 -)				
ALBRO, Maxine	*P*			$1,320
American (1903 - 1966)				
ALCALAY, Albert	*D*			$880
American (20th -)				
ALCAZAR, Luis P. (Circle)	*P*			$5,500
Spanish (1747 - 1799)				
ALCAZAR Y RUIZ, Manuel	*P*			$15,400
Spanish (19th -)				
ALDAN, Erma van	*P*			$110
European (20th -)				
ALDERTON, Henry A.	*P*	$413	$564	$715
American (1896 - 1961)				

D=Drawing, P=Painting, S=Sculpture, W=Watercolor

		Current Price Range		
		Low	Mean	High
ALDIN, Cecil	*W*			$9,900
British (1870 - 1930)				
ALDIN, Cecil (Attrib.)	*W*			$385
British (1870 - 1930)				
ALDINE, Mark	*P*	$385	$2,881	$8,250
Italian (1917 -)				
ALDRICH, Clarence N.	*W*			$275
American (1893 - 1953)				
ALDRICH, George A.	*P*	$495	$2,124	$4,840
American (1872 - 1941)				
ALDRIDGE, F. J.	*W*			$1,100
British (1850 - 1933)				
ALDRIN, Anders G.	*P*	$385	$2,328	$4,125
American (1889 - 1970)				
ALECHINSKY, Pierre	*D*	$4,950	$11,825	$18,700
Belgian (1927 -)	*P*	$29,700	$157,929	$330,000
	S			$935
	W			$66,000
ALEXANDER, Clifford G.	*P*	$770	$1,540	$2,310
American (1870 - 1954)				
ALEXANDER, Francesca	*D*			$3,850
American (1837 - 1917)	*P*			$4,180
ALEXANDER, Francis	*P*			$660
American (1800 - 1880)				
ALEXANDER, Henry	*P*			$12,100
American (1860 - 1895)	*W*			$770
ALEXANDER, John	*D*			$3,300
American (1945 -)	*P*	$1,320	$10,956	$25,300
ALEXANDER, John W.	*P*	$20,900	$32,267	$49,500
American (1856 - 1915)				
ALEXANDROFF, J. A.	*P*			$2,090
Russian (1837 -)				

D=Drawing, P=Painting, S=Sculpture, W=Watercolor

		Current Price Range		
		Low	Mean	High
ALFANI, Domenico	P			$49,500
Italian (16th -)				
ALFINITO,	P			$715
(?)				
ALICHIN, Harry	P			$935
(20th -)				
ALIGNY, Claude	P			$1,650
French (1798 - 1871)				
ALIX, Gabriel	P			$247
(?)				
ALKE, Elizabeth	P			$578
American (1877 - 1938)				
ALKEN, Henry	P	$3,960	$6,380	$8,800
British (19th - 20th)				
ALKEN, Henry (School)	P			$770
British (19th - 20th)				
ALKEN, Samuel	P	$2,750	$8,993	$19,800
British (1784 -)				
ALKEN, Samuel (Style)	P	$880	$963	$1,045
British (1784 -)				
ALKEN, SR., Henry T.	D	$4,950	$4,950	$4,950
British (1785 - 1851)	P	$3,025	$41,608	$143,000
	W	$660	$770	$880
ALKEN, SR., Henry T. (Follower)	P	$1,430	$2,090	$2,750
British (1785 - 1851)				
ALKEN, SR., Henry T. (Manner)	P			$1,100
British (1785 - 1851)				
ALLAN, Archibald R.	P	$1,210	$1,210	$1,210
British (1878 - 1959)				
ALLAN, David (Follower)	P			$1,980
Scottish (1744 - 1796)				
ALLAN, M.	P			$1,155
British (19th -)				
ALLAN, R. W.	P			$825
British (19th -)				

D=Drawing, P=Painting, S=Sculpture, W=Watercolor

		Current Price Range		
		Low	Mean	High

		Low	Mean	High
ALLBON, Charles F.	*W*			$715
British (19th -)				
ALLEAUME, Ludovic	*P*			$4,950
French (1859 -)				
ALLEGRAIN, Etienne (School)	*P*			$2,640
French (1644 - 1736)				
ALLEN, Anne H.	*P*			$220
American (1858 -)				
ALLEN, Boyd	*W*			$440
American (20th -)				
ALLEN, Charles C.	*P*	$385	$866	$1,100
American (1886 - 1950)				
ALLEN, Courtney	*D*			$125
American (1896 - 1969)	*P*			$880
ALLEN, Douglas	*W*	$495	$523	$550
American (20th -)				
ALLEN, F. V.	*P*			$358
(?)				
ALLEN, Frank L.	*W*			$138
American (1884 -)				
ALLEN, Frederick W.	*S*			$6,600
American (1888 - 1961)				
ALLEN, Greta	*P*			$110
American (1881 -)				
ALLEN, Harry	*P*			$385
British (20th -)				
ALLEN, John H.	*P*	$275	$317	$358
American (1866 - 1935)				
ALLEN, Junius	*P*	$2,530	$3,190	$3,850
American (1896 - 1962)				
ALLEN, Marion B.	*P*	$715	$1,430	$3,025
American (1862 - 1941)				
ALLEN, Thomas	*D*			$7,700
American (1849 - 1924)	*P*	$990	$2,237	$4,400

D=Drawing, P=Painting, S=Sculpture, W=Watercolor

		Current Price Range		
		Low	Mean	High
ALLIEVI, Fernando	*D*	$2,640	$3,520	$4,400
Argentina (1954 -)				
ALLIS, A. S.	*P*			$358
American (20th -)				
ALLIS, C. Harry	*P*	$165	$502	$1,320
American (? - 1938)				
ALLIS, Genevieve	*W*			$154
(?)				
ALLORI, Alessandro	*P*			$110,000
Italian (1535 - 1607)				
ALLORI, Alessandro (Circle)	*D*	$6,050	$6,188	$6,325
Italian (1535 - 1607)				
ALLORI, Alessandro (School)	*P*	$2,860	$3,520	$4,180
Italian (1535 - 1607)				
ALLORI, Alessandro (Workshop)	*P*			$52,800
Italian (1535 - 1607)				
ALLORI, Angelo de (Manner)	*P*			$1,870
Italian (1503 - 1572)				
ALLORI, Cristofano	*P*	$1,760	$1,980	$2,200
Italian (1577 - 1621)				
ALLSTON, Washington (Attrib.)	*P*			$2,200
American (1779 - 1843)				
ALLTER, M.	*P*			$935
French (19th - 20th)				
ALLUSTANTE, Joaquin P.	*P*			$4,070
Spanish (19th -)				
ALMA-TADEMA, Laura T.	*P*			$22,000
British (1852 - 1909)				
ALMA-TADEMA, Sir Lawrence	*D*	$330	$4,693	$13,200
British (1836 - 1912)	*P*	$110,000	$141,167	$176,000
ALMQUIST, Olaf	*D*			$248
American (19th -)				
ALONSO-PERES, Carlos	*P*			$6,050
Spanish (19th - 20th)				
ALORDA Y PEREZ, Ramon	*W*			$1,870
Spanish (19th -)				

D=Drawing, P=Painting, S=Sculpture, W=Watercolor

		Low	Current Price Range Mean	High
ALOTT, Robert French (19th -)	P			$2,200
ALOTT, Rudolf French (19th - 20th)	P			$6,600
ALOUNANY, (?)	S			$220
ALPHONSE, L. V. American (19th -)	P			$1,045
ALSINA, J. French (20th -)	P	$1,540	$1,870	$2,200
ALSKOV, N. American (20th -)	P			$330
ALSTON, Abbey British (1864 -)	P			$11,000
ALSTON, Frank H. American (1913 -)	P W			$660 $743
ALT, Franz von (Attrib.) Austrian (1821 - 1914)	D			$3,300
ALT, Rudolf von Austrian (1812 - 1905)	W			$20,900
ALTAMIRANO, Arturo P. (20th -)	P	$2,200	$4,125	$6,050
ALTHAUS, Fritz British (19th - 20th)	W			$303
ALTO, American (19th -)	P			$275
ALTOON, John American (1925 - 1969)	D	$358	$1,267	$4,675
ALTSON, Abbey British (19th - 20th)	P	$2,200	$8,983	$22,000
ALVAR (SUNOL), Spanish (1935 -)	S			$440
ALVAREZ, Luis Spanish (1836 - 1901)	P	$9,900	$25,575	$41,250
ALVAREZ, Mabel	P	$440	$2,090	$3,025

D=Drawing, P=Painting, S=Sculpture, W=Watercolor

		Current Price Range		
		Low	Mean	High

ALVAREZ, Mabel	W			$440
American (1891 - 1985)				
AMADIO,	W			$303
American (20th -)				
AMADO Y BERNARDET, Ramon	P			$825
Spanish (1844 - 1888)				
AMAN-JEAN, Edmond F.	D			$27,500
French (1860 - 1935)	P	$1,650	$17,050	$46,750
AMAN-JEAN, Edmond F. (Attrib.)	D			$605
French (1860 - 1935)				
AMARAL, Antonio H.	P	$2,750	$15,675	$28,600
Brazilian (1935 -)				
AMARATICO, Joseph	W			$715
American (1931 - 1986)				
AMAT, Frederic	P			$4,400
(20th -)				
AMAT, Jose	P			$3,300
Spanish (1883 -)				
AMATO, Luigi	P			$605
Italian (20th -)				
AMBROGIANI, Pierre	P			$2,850
French (1907 -)	W			$880
AMBROIS, Jules F. A.	P			$2,420
(19th -)				
AMEGLIO, Merio	P	$1,045	$4,516	$8,800
French (1897 - 1970)				
AMEN, Irving	P			$193
American (1918 -)				
AMENOFF, Gregory	P	$1,870	$11,110	$17,600
American (1948 -)	W			$3,850
AMERICAN SCHOOL,	P	$1,018	$1,819	$4,070
American (?)	S			$2,750
AMERICAN SCHOOL,	P	$1,018	$1,059	$1,100

D=Drawing, P=Painting, S=Sculpture, W=Watercolor

		Current Price Range		
		Low	Mean	High

		Low	Mean	High
AMERICAN SCHOOL,	*S*			$3,300
American (18th - 19th)				
AMERICAN SCHOOL,	*D*			$1,100
American (19th - 20th)	*P*	$1,100	$3,543	$13,200
AMERICAN SCHOOL 18C,	*P*	$1,045	$1,994	$3,850
American (18th -)				
AMERICAN SCHOOL 19C,	*D*	$1,400	$2,405	$3,410
American (19th -)	*P*	$550	$4,335	$93,500
	S	$1,210	$2,837	$4,400
	W	$1,000	$1,512	$2,310
AMERICAN SCHOOL 20C,	*D*	$1,650	$1,760	$1,870
American (20th -)	*P*	$275	$2,545	$8,250
	S	$1,760	$1,815	$1,870
	W	$1,760	$2,805	$3,850
AMES, Ezra	*P*			$3,520
American (1768 - 1836)				
AMES, Jessie	*P*			$220
American (19th - 20th)	*W*			$220
AMES, May	*P*			$330
American (19th -)				
AMICK, Robert W.	*P*			$2,200
American (1879 - 1969)	*W*	$248	$367	$605
AMIE, F. L.	*P*			$165
American (20th -)				
AMIGOMI, Pietro	*D*			$2,475
Italian (20th -)				
AMIGONI, Jacopo	*P*	$12,100	$32,175	$52,250
Italian (1675 - 1752)				
AMIGONI, Jacopo (Attrib.)	*P*			$4,180
Italian (1675 - 1752)				
AMIGONI, Jacopo (Circle)	*D*			$275

D=Drawing, P=Painting, S=Sculpture, W=Watercolor

		Current Price Range		
		Low	Mean	High
AMIGONI, Jacopo (Circle)	*P*	$2,200	$2,805	$3,410
Italian (1675 - 1752)				
AMMAN, Jost	*D*			$825
German (1539 - 1591)				
AMORONGEN, V.	*P*			$605
European (19th -)				
AMOROSI, Antonio	*P*			$44,000
Italian (1660 - 1736)				
AMOROSI, Antonio (Circle)	*P*			$1,980
Italian (1660 - 1736)				
AMORSOLO, Fernando	*P*	$2,750	$4,235	$5,775
Philippino (20th -)				
AMSDEN, William K.	*P*			$990
American (20th -)				
AMSTERDAM SCHOOL 17C,	*P*			$96,250
Dutch (17th -)				
AMYOT, C. G.	*P*			$2,750
French (19th -)				
ANCILLOTTI, T. (Attrib.)	*P*			$2,900
Italian (19th -)				
ANDERS, Ernest	*P*			$1,705
German (1845 - 1911)				
ANDERSEN, Carl C.	*P*			$24,200
Danish (1849 - 1906)				
ANDERSON, Abraham A.	*P*			$248
American (1847 - 1940)				
ANDERSON, Carolyn	*P*	$250	$500	$750
American (20th -)				
ANDERSON, Doris	*W*	$450	$473	$495
American (20th -)				
ANDERSON, Douglas	*P*	$1,650	$2,200	$2,750
British (20th -)				
ANDERSON, E. A.	*P*			$110
American (1900 -)				
ANDERSON, G. W.	*P*			$1,650
American (20th -)				

D=Drawing, P=Painting, S=Sculpture, W=Watercolor

		Current Price Range	
	Low	Mean	High

		Low	Mean	High
ANDERSON, Grace	*P*			$110
American (20th -)				
ANDERSON, Harold N.	*P*			$1,870
American (1894 - 1973)	*W*			$523
ANDERSON, Harry	*W*			$853
American (1906 -)				
ANDERSON, James B.	*P*			$248
British (1886 - 1938)				
ANDERSON, Joel R.	*D*			$275
American (1905 - 1971)				
ANDERSON, Ken	*D*			$440
American (20th -)				
ANDERSON, Laurie	*P*			$1,760
American (1947 -)				
ANDERSON, Mary	*S*			$220
American (20th -)				
ANDERSON, Neil	*W*			$770
(20th -)				
ANDERSON, Oscar	*P*	$110	$454	$880
American (1873 -)				
ANDERSON, Ronald	*D*			$138
American (1886 - 1926)				
ANDERSON, Victor C.	*D*			$688
American (1882 - 1937)	*P*	$3,300	$4,400	$5,500
	W			$165
ANDERSON, Walter	*W*			$2,310
American (1903 - 1965)				
ANDERSON, William (Attrib.)	*P*			$495
British (1757 - 1837)				
ANDRADE, Mary	*P*			$413
(20th -)				
ANDRE, Albert	*P*	$9,020	$24,497	$44,000
French (1869 - 1954)	*W*	$605	$743	$880

D=Drawing, P=Painting, S=Sculpture, W=Watercolor

		Current Price Range		
		Low	Mean	High
ANDRE, Carl	S	$18,700	$95,700	$198,000
American (1935 -)				
ANDREA, John de	P			$49,500
American (1941 -)	S			$12,100
ANDREA, Mariano	P			$715
(20th -)				
ANDREINI, Ferinando	S			$16,500
Italian (1843 -)				
ANDREIS, Alex de	P	$440	$2,013	$5,280
Belgian (19th -)				
ANDREJEVIC, Milet	P	$3,300	$3,575	$3,850
Yugoslavian (1925 -)				
ANDREOTTI, Federico	P	$6,050	$23,953	$66,000
Italian (1847 - 1930)				
ANDREW,	P			$154
(?)				
ANDREW, Richard	D			$440
American (1867 - 1934)				
ANDREW, Robert	P			$187
American (19th -)				
ANDREWS,	P			$850
(?)				
ANDREWS,	P			$165
American (20th -)				
ANDREWS, Benny	P			$1,210
American (1930 -)	S			$935
ANDREWS, Eliphalat F.	P			$5,390
American (1833 - 1915)				
ANDREWS, G.	P			$275
American (20th -)				
ANDREWS, Henry	P	$2,200	$2,310	$2,420
British (1816 - 1898)				
ANDREWS, James	W			$605
American (19th -)				

D=Drawing, P=Painting, S=Sculpture, W=Watercolor

		Current Price Range		
		Low	Mean	High

ANDREWS, Roger	*W*			$165
(20th -)				
ANDREY, James	*S*			$1,210
French (20th -)				
ANDRIESSEN, Hendrick	*P*			$253,000
Flemish (? - 1655)				
ANDRIESSEN, J. & A. (Attrib.)	*P*			$22,000
Dutch (18th - 19th)				
ANDRIEU, Mathurin	*P*			$1,650
American (20th -)				
ANDRUS,	*P*			$138
(?)				
ANESI, Paolo	*P*			$31,900
Italian (1700 - 1761)				
ANGELI, A.	*P*			$358
Italian (20th -)				
ANGELICO, Fra (After)	*P*			$358
Italian (1387 - 1455)				
ANGELLIS, Pieter (School)	*P*			$715
Flemish (1685 - 1734)				
ANGELUCCIO, Attributed	*P*			$13,200
Italian (17th -)				
ANGENOT, O.	*P*			$248
French (19th -)				
ANGLADA-CAMARASA, Hermen	*P*			$50,600
Spanish (1873 - 1959)				
ANGLADE, Gaston	*P*	$550	$1,167	$2,200
French (1854 - 1919)				
ANGLO-DUTCH SCHOOL,	*P*			$1,210
(18th -)				
ANGO, Jean-R.	*D*			$4,400
French (18th -)				
ANGOLO DEL MORO, Battista	*D*	$660	$3,718	$8,250
Italian (1514 - 1575)				
ANGRAND, Charles (Attrib.)	*P*			$1,100
French (1854 - 1926)				

D=Drawing, P=Painting, S=Sculpture, W=Watercolor

		Current Price Range		
		Low	Mean	High
ANGUIANO, Raul	*P*			$4,125
Mexican (1915 -)				
ANIVITTI, Filippo	*P*	$1,760	$2,860	$4,400
Italian (1876 -)	*W*	$1,320	$1,833	$2,090
ANNIGONI, Pietro	*D*			$660
Italian (1900 -)				
ANSDELL, Richard	*P*	$8,800	$78,100	$198,000
British (1815 - 1885)				
ANSDELL, Richard (Attrib.)	*P*			$1,870
British (1815 - 1885)				
ANSHUTZ, Thomas P.	*P*			$9,900
American (1851 - 1912)	*W*	$1,100	$2,017	$3,300
ANTES, Horst	*P*	$605	$46,076	$71,500
German (1936 -)				
ANTHONISEN, George R.	*S*			$1,045
American (?)				
ANTHONY, Carol	*S*			$2,200
(20th -)				
ANTOINE, Robert	*P*			$330
(?)				
ANTONIANI, Pietro	*P*			$52,800
Italian (1740 - 1805)				
ANTONINI,	*D*			$4,950
Italian (?)				
ANTONIO, Cristobal di	*P*			$2,200
Spanish (19th -)				
ANTRAL, Louis R.	*P*			$2,750
French (1895 - 1940)				
ANTUNES, Nemesis	*P*	$2,200	$3,300	$4,400
Chilean (1918 -)				
ANTWERP SCHOOL 16C,	*P*	$4,675	$23,879	$44,000
Belgian (16th -)				
ANTWERP SCHOOL 17C,	*P*	$3,300	$3,850	$4,400
Belgian (17th -)				

D=Drawing, P=Painting, S=Sculpture, W=Watercolor

		Low	Mean	High
			Current Price Range	

		Low	Mean	High
ANTWERP SCHOOL 18C,	*P*			$37,400
Belgian (18th -)				
ANUSKIEWICZ, Richard	*P*	$1,650	$5,506	$13,200
American (1930 -)				
APOL, Louis	*P*	$2,200	$2,420	$2,640
Dutch (1850 -)	*W*			$1,760
APPEL, Charles P.	*P*	$1,650	$2,081	$2,475
American (1877 -)				
APPEL, Charles P. (Attrib.)	*P*			$660
American (1877 -)				
APPEL, Karel	*P*	$7,150	$35,186	$110,000
Dutch (1921 -)	*S*	$3,575	$11,110	$22,000
	W	$12,100	$18,013	$30,250
APPEL, Karel (After)	*S*			$7,700
Dutch (1921 -)				
APPERLEY, George O. W.	*P*			$29,700
British (1884 - 1961)				
APPERT, George	*P*	$2,090	$2,475	$2,860
(19th -)				
APPIAN, Adolphe	*P*			$1,650
French (1818 - 1898)				
APPIAN, Louis	*D*			$2,420
French (1862 - 1896)				
APPLEGATE, M. E.	*P*			$275
American (19th - 20th)				
APSHOVEN, Thomas van	*P*	$9,900	$11,000	$12,100
Flemish (1622 - 1664)				
APT, Charles	*P*	$275	$440	$605
American (1933 -)				
ARAGONESE SCHOOL 15C,	*P*			$5,500
(15th -)				
ARAKAWA, Shusaku	*P*	$6,600	$87,450	$176,000
Japanese (1936 -)	*S*			$126,500

D=Drawing, P=Painting, S=Sculpture, W=Watercolor

		Current Price Range		
		Low	Mean	High

ARAKAWA, Shusaku	*W*			$4,180
Japanese (1936 -)				
ARAPOFF, Alexis	*P*	$1,210	$3,355	$5,500
Russian (1904 - 1948)				
ARAUJO, Carlos	*P*			$7,700
Brazilian (1950 -)				
ARAUJO, Emanuoel	*P*			$13,200
(20th -)				
ARCHER, T. V.	*P*			$220
American (19th - 20th)				
ARCHIMBOLDO, Giuseppe (Foll)	*P*			$15,400
Italian (16th -)				
ARCHIPENKO, Alexander	*D*	$3,850	$12,650	$24,200
Russian (1887 - 1964)	*S*	$41,250	$101,000	$253,000
ARCHIPENKO, Alexander (Att.)	*D*			$523
Russian (1887 - 1964)				
ARCIERI, Charles F.	*P*			$11,000
American (1885 -)				
ARCOS Y MEGALDE, Santiago	*W*			$1,540
Chilean (1865 - 1912)				
ARDEN, H.	*P*			$248
(?)				
ARDEN, V.	*P*			$385
Belgian (19th -)				
ARDISSONE, Yolande	*P*	$660	$1,467	$2,200
French (1872 -)				
ARDON, Mordecai	*P*			$47,300
Israeli (1896 -)				
ARELLANO, Juan de	*P*	$9,900	$256,300	$715,000
Spanish (1614 - 1676)				
ARELLANO, Juan de (Circle)	*P*			$2,640
Spanish (1614 - 1676)				
ARELLANO, Juan de (Manner)	*P*			$2,750
Spanish (1614 - 1676)				
ARELLANO, Juan de (School)	*P*			$9,350
Spanish (1614 - 1676)				

D=Drawing, P=Painting, S=Sculpture, W=Watercolor

		Current Price Range		
		Low	Mean	High

		Low	Mean	High
ARENTZ, Josef M.	*P*	$275	$303	$358
American (1903 - 1969)				
ARERA,	*P*			$8,800
French (19th -)				
ARESTI, Carlos	*P*			$6,050
Chilean (1941 -)				
ARGYROS, Oumbertos	*P*	$9,900	$11,000	$12,100
Greek (1877 - 1963)				
ARIAS, Gessa y	*P*			$880
Spanish (1840 - 1920)	*P*			$825
ARIENTIA, Gustavo L.	*P*			$3,300
(?)				
ARIKHA, Avigdor	*D*			$2,750
(1929 -)				
ARIO, V.	*W*			$121
(?)				
ARIOLLA, Fortunato	*P*			$27,500
American (1827 - 1872)				
ARIZA, Gonzalo	*P*	$5,500	$16,867	$25,300
Colombian (1912 -)				
ARLT, Paul T.	*W*			$303
American (1914 -)				
ARMAN, Charles	*D*	$5,775	$41,388	$77,000
French (1928 -)	*P*	$18,700	$56,581	$71,500
	S	$9,350	$72,294	$363,000
ARMAND-DUMARESQ, Edouard	*P*			$1,760
French (1826 - 1895)				
ARMER, Ruth	*P*			$660
American (1896 - 1977)	*W*			$468
ARMFIELD, Edward	*P*	$578	$2,781	$7,700
British (19th - 20th)				
ARMFIELD, Edward (Attrib.)	*P*			$1,650
British (19th - 20th)				

D=Drawing, P=Painting, S=Sculpture, W=Watercolor

| | | Current Price Range | | |
		Low	Mean	High
ARMFIELD, George British (1840 - 1875)	*P*	$550	$3,878	$16,500
ARMFIELD, George (Attrib.) British (1840 - 1875)	*P*	$880	$1,925	$2,970
ARMFIELD, George (Circle) British (1840 - 1875)	*P*			$1,650
ARMFIELD, George (Manner) British (1840 - 1875)	*P*	$990	$1,283	$1,650
ARMFIELD, Maxwell A. American (1881 - 1972)	*P*			$19,800
ARMIN, Emil Austrian (1895 - 1983)	*W*	$220	$321	$468
ARMINGTON, Caroline American (1875 - 1939)	*P*			$330
ARMINGTON, Frank M. Canadian (1876 - 1940)	*P*			$3,740
ARMITAGE, Kenneth British (1916 -)	*S*	$1,870	$15,806	$49,500
ARMITAGE, Thomas L. British (19th - 20th)	*P*			$33,000
ARMLEDER, John (20th -)	*P*	$14,300	$23,100	$27,500
ARMOR, Charles American (1844 -)	*P*			$2,420
ARMS, John T. American (1887 - 1953)	*D*	$440	$633	$825
ARMSTRONG, Carolyn F. American (1910 -)	*P*			$358
ARMSTRONG, David American (1836 - 1918)	*W*	$3,520	$3,850	$4,180
ARMSTRONG, William W. Canadian (1822 - 1914)	*P*	$600	$1,520	$3,080
ARNALD, George British (1763 - 1841)	*P*			$14,300
ARNEGGER, Alois Austrian (1879 - 1967)	*P*	$248	$2,353	$4,950

D=Drawing, P=Painting, S=Sculpture, W=Watercolor

		Current Price Range		
		Low	Mean	High

ARNEGGER, G. (?)	*P*			$275
ARNESON, Robert American (1930 -)	*S*	$935	$9,171	$18,700
ARNEST, Bernard American (20th -)	*P*			$303
ARNETT, J. A. Dutch (19th - 20th)	*P*			$1,100
ARNOLD, (?)	*P*			$220
ARNOLD, B. & J. American (20th -)	*P*			$440
ARNOLD, Bill American (20th -)	*D*			$330
ARNOLD, E. American (20th -)	*P*			$1,320
ARNOLD, Edward American (1824 - 1866)	*P*			$44,000
ARNOLD, F. (?)	*P*			$250
ARNOLD, Howard W. American (1903 -)	*D*			$110
ARNOLD, J. American (20th -)	*P*	$138	$372	$605
ARNOLD, James American (20th -)	*P*			$1,100
ARNOLD, John American (20th -)	*P*			$825
ARNOLD, P. J. American (20th -)	*P*			$468
ARNOLD, Reginald E. British (1853 - 1938)	*P*			$18,700
ARNOLD-KAISER, Bernita American (?)	*P*			$6,600
ARNOLDI, Charles	*D*			$6,600

D=Drawing, P=Painting, S=Sculpture, W=Watercolor

		Current Price Range		
		Low	Mean	High
ARNOLDI, Charles	*P*	$11,550	$17,508	$23,100
American (1946 -)	*W*	$440	$1,458	$2,475
ARNOUX, Michel	*P*			$3,850
French (1833 - 1877)				
ARNULL, George	*P*	$5,500	$10,450	$15,400
British (19th -)				
ARONSON, Boris	*S*			$1,100
(20th -)				
ARONSON, David	*S*			$468
American (1923 -)				
AROSTEGUI, A.	*D*			$110
Spanish (20th -)				
ARP, Jean	*D*	$3,300	$8,983	$13,200
French (1887 - 1966)	*S*	$2,090	$188,714	$990,000
	W			$7,700
ARP, Jean (After)	*S*	$3,850	$5,225	$6,600
French (1887 - 1966)				
ARP, Jean (Et al.)	*P*			$605
French (19th - 20th)				
ARPA Y PEREA, Jose	*P*	$4,400	$4,813	$5,225
Spanish (1862 - 1903)				
ARPA Y PEREA, Jose (Attrib.)	*P*			$1,980
Spanish (1862 - 1903)				
ARPS, Bernardus (Attrib.)	*P*			$990
Dutch (1865 - 1938)				
ARRANTS, Shirley	*D*	$450	$885	$1,320
American (20th -)	*P*			$2,090
ARRIETA, Jose A.	*P*	$30,800	$34,650	$38,500
Mexican (1802 - 1879)				
ARTHUR, Reginal	*P*			$4,180
British (19th -)				
ARTHURS, Stanley M.	*P*	$1,320	$3,153	$6,600
American (1877 - 1950)				

D=Drawing, P=Painting, S=Sculpture, W=Watercolor

		Current Price Range		
		Low	Mean	High

ARTIGUE, Albert E.	*P*			$8,800
French (19th - 20th)				
ARTOIS, Jacques de (Attrib.)	*P*			$6,600
(1613 -)				
ARTSCHWAGER, Richard	*D*	$1,870	$8,621	$14,300
American (1924 -)	*P*	$18,700	$131,300	$990,000
	S	$17,600	$138,050	$308,000
ARTZ,	*P*			$1,980
(19th -)				
ARTZ, Constant	*P*			$3,080
Dutch (1870 - 1951)	*W*			$4,400
ARTZ, David A. C.	*D*			$468
Dutch (1837 - 1890)	*P*			$8,250
ARTZYBASHEFF, Boris	*D*			$700
American (1899 - 1965)				
ARUFFT, Luis	*P*			$5,500
American (?)				
ASH CAN SCHOOL 20C,	*P*			$1,320
American (20th -)				
ASHBROOK, Paul	*P*			$935
American (1867 -)				
ASHLEY, Clifford W.	*P*			$2,200
American (1881 - 1947)				
ASHLEY, Frank	*D*	$2,750	$3,355	$3,960
American (1920 -)	*W*			$1,100
ASHTON, Frederico	*P*			$825
Italian (1836 -)				
ASHTON, Sir John W.	*P*			$660
British (1881 - 1963)				
ASHTON, William	*P*			$550
British (19th - 20th)				
ASKENAZY, Maurice	*P*			$8,800
American (1888 - 1951)				

D=Drawing, P=Painting, S=Sculpture, W=Watercolor

		Current Price Range		
		Low	Mean	High
ASKEVOLD, Anders M.	*P*	$2,200	$7,425	$12,650
Swedish (1834 - 1900)				
ASSELYN, Jan	*P*			$25,300
French (1610 - 1652)				
ASSELYN, Jan (Circle)	*P*	$6,050	$10,025	$14,000
French (1610 - 1652)				
ASSERETO, Gioacchino	*P*			$110,000
Italian (1600 - 1649)				
ASSETTO, Franco	*P*			$770
Italian (1911 -)				
AST, Balthasar van	*P*	$275,000	$605,000	$935,000
Dutch (1590 - 1656)				
AST, Balthasar van (Manner)	*P*	$1,100	$1,265	$1,430
Dutch (1590 - 1656)				
ASTI, Angelo	*P*	$550	$3,438	$7,700
French (1847 - 1903)				
ASTON, Charles R.	*W*			$143
British (1832 - 1908)				
ASTUDILLO, Ever	*D*			$1,100
Lat. Amer. (20th -)				
ATALAYA, Enrique	*P*			$13,200
Spanish (19th - 20th)				
ATCHISON, Joseph A.	*W*			$165
British (20th -)				
ATHERTON, John	*W*	$400	$420	$440
American (1900 - 1952)				
ATKINSON, Howard	*P*			$248
American (20th -)				
ATKINSON, John	*P*			$990
British (19th -)				
ATL, Dr.	*D*	$8,250	$10,083	$11,000
Mexican (1875 - 1964)	*P*	$22,000	$45,192	$72,600
ATLAN, Jean	*P*			$58,850
French (1913 - 1960)				
ATRIJGAJEFF, Nikolaj A.	*P*			$2,750
Russian (1823 - 1892)				

D=Drawing, P=Painting, S=Sculpture, W=Watercolor

		Current Price Range		
		Low	Mean	High

ATTAVIANI, S.	*P*			$121
Italian (20th -)				
ATTENDU, Antoine F.	*P*			$2,750
French (19th - 20th)				
ATWOOD, Gilbert	*P*			$468
American (19th -)				
ATWOOD, Robert	*P*	$440	$640	$880
American (1892 -)				
AUBERT, Jean E.	*P*			$6,325
French (1824 - 1906)				
AUBERT, Rene Raymond L.	*P*			$2,200
French (20th -)				
AUBLET, Albert	*P*			$44,000
French (1851 - 1938)				
AUBRY, Emile	*P*	$468	$1,554	$2,640
French (1880 - 1964)				
AUBRY, Emile (Attrib.)	*P*			$935
French (1880 - 1964)				
AUCELLO, Salvatore	*P*			$110
American (1903 -)				
AUCHENBACH, Oswald	*P*			$6,600
German (1827 - 1905)				
AUCK, R. E.	*P*			$935
(?)				
AUCLAIR, Andre	*P*			$440
French (20th -)				
AUDUBON, John J.	*D*			$3,300
American (1785 - 1851)				
AUDUBON, John J. (Attrib.)	*P*			$303
American (1785 - 1851)				
AUDUBON, John W.	*P*	$3,850	$12,375	$20,900
American (1812 - 1868)				
AUDY, Jonny	*W*			$8,250
French (19th -)				
AUERBACH, Frank	*D*			$4,400

D=Drawing, P=Painting, S=Sculpture, W=Watercolor

		Current Price Range		
		Low	Mean	High

AUERBACH, Frank	*P*			$660,000
British (1931 -)				
AUGE, Philippe	*P*	$523	$1,476	$2,970
European (20th -)				
AUGERO, F.	*P*			$1,980
Italian (19th -)				
AUGUR, David	*W*			$165
American (19th -)				
AUGUSTE, Robert J.	*S*			$20,900
French (1789 - 1850)				
AUGUSTI, Cesare	*P*			$3,300
Italian (19th -)				
AUGUSTINE, L.	*P*			$770
(19th - 20th)				
AUKELL, T.	*W*			$110
European (20th -)				
AULT, George C.	*D*			$3,080
American (1891 - 1948)	*P*	$10,725	$32,863	$55,000
AURELI, Giuseppe	*W*	$715	$4,801	$9,900
Italian (1858 - 1929)				
AUS, Carol	*P*			$770
Norwegian (1868 -)				
AUSSANDON, Joseph N. H.	*P*			$242,000
French (1836 -)				
AUSTEN, Alexander	*P*	$880	$1,073	$1,320
British (19th - 20th)				
AUSTEN, R. S.	*P*	$440	$458	$475
British (19th -)				
AUSTEN, Winifred	*W*			$1,870
British (19th - 20th)				
AUSTIN, Darrel	*P*	$440	$605	$770
American (1907 -)				
AUSTRIAN, Ben	*P*	$154	$2,866	$14,000
American (1870 - 1921)	*W*			$1,500

D=Drawing, P=Painting, S=Sculpture, W=Watercolor

		Current Price Range	
	Low	Mean	High

		Low	Mean	High
AUSTRIAN SCHOOL 15C,	*P*			$9,350
Austrian (15th -)				
AUSTRIAN SCHOOL 18C,	*P*	$1,210	$5,170	$8,250
Austrian (18th -)				
AUSTRIAN SCHOOL 19C,	*P*	$1,320	$5,060	$11,000
Austrian (19th -)	*S*			$1,073
	W			$3,300
AUTIO, Rudy	*S*	$5,280	$20,240	$35,200
(20th -)				
AVAL, E.	*P*	$110	$124	$138
American (19th - 20th)				
AVATI, James	*P*			$200
(1912 -)				
AVED, Jacques A.	*P*			$11,000
American (1702 - 1766)				
AVED, Jacques A. (Circle)	*P*			$440
American (1702 - 1766)				
AVED, Jacques A. (School)	*P*			$1,980
American (1702 - 1766)				
AVEDISIAN, Edward	*P*	$110	$570	$1,320
American (1936 -)				
AVERCAMP, Hendrick (Circle)	*D*			$6,050
Dutch (1585 - 1663)				
AVERESH,	*D*			$440
(?)				
AVERY, Kenneth N.	*P*			$6,600
American (1882 -)				
AVERY, Milton	*D*	$1,650	$3,384	$7,700
American (1893 - 1965)	*P*	$1,045	$44,201	$198,000
	W	$1,760	$20,517	$68,750
AVERY, Milton (Attrib.)	*W*			$1,870
American (1893 - 1965)				
AVERY, Sally	*P*	$495	$1,485	$2,475
American (20th -)				

D=Drawing, P=Painting, S=Sculpture, W=Watercolor

		Current Price Range		
		Low	Mean	High
AVIANI, Francesco (Attrib.)	*P*			$11,000
Italian (?)				
AVIGNON SCHOOL 16C,	*P*	$8,250	$15,125	$22,000
French (16th -)				
AVISON, George	*P*	$468	$839	$1,210
American (1885 -)				
AVONT, Pieter van	*P*			$4,620
Flemish (1600 - 1632)				
AXENTOWICZ, Theodor	*P*			$38,500
Polish (1859 - 1938)				
AYRTON, Michael	*S*	$3,960	$4,455	$4,950
British (1921 - 1975)				
AYUSAWA, Leman	*W*			$193
Flemish (1597 - 1681)				
AZACETA, Luis C.	*D*			$3,575
Cuban (1942 -)				
AZUZ, David	*W*			$3,520
Israeli (1941 -)				
BAADSGAARD, Alfrida	*P*			$3,575
Danish (1839 - 1912)				
BABAYEV, Rasim	*P*			$5,280
Russian (1927 -)				
BABB, John S.	*W*	$24,750	$28,875	$33,000
British (20th -)				
BABCOCK, R. Lloyd	*P*			$358
American (1897 - 1981)				
BABCOCK, William P.	*D*			$193
American (1826 - 1899)				
BABUREN, Dirck van	*P*	$2,090	$23,045	$44,000
Dutch (17th -)				
BACARDY, Don	*W*			$16,500
(20th -)				
BACCARD, Joseph	*P*			$578
(?)				
BACCHI, Cesare	*P*			$3,300
Italian (20th -)				

D=Drawing, P=Painting, S=Sculpture, W=Watercolor

		Current Price Range		
		Low	Mean	High
BACCI, Edmondo	*P*	$1,650	$2,255	$2,860
Italian (1913 -)				
BACH, Elvira	*P*			$8,800
(20th -)				
BACH, Guido	*P*			$2,860
German (1828 - 1905)				
BACH, Otto	*P*			$17,600
Danish (1839 - 1914)				
BACHELDER, Jonathan B.	*W*			$138
American (1825 - 1894)				
BACHELIER, Jean Jacques	*P*			$121,000
French (1724 - 1806)				
BACHENIN, Valeri	*P*			$3,520
Russian (1943 -)				
BACHER, Otto	*D*			$275
American (1856 - 1909)				
BACHMANN, Karl	*W*			$495
Hungarian (1874 - 1924)				
BACHMANN, Max	*S*			$6,600
American (1862 - 1921)				
BACHRACH-BARRE, Helmut	*P*			$1,650
German (1898 -)				
BACK, Joseph W.	*P*			$193
American (1899 - 1970)				
BACKER, Jacob A.	*D*			$36,300
Dutch (1608 - 1651)	*P*			$9,900
BACKER, Jacob A. (Circle)	*P*			$10,450
Dutch (1608 - 1651)				
BACKMANSSON, Hugo	*P*			$770
Danish (1860 - 1953)				
BACKUS, A. E.	*P*			$4,950
(?)				
BACKVIS, Francois	*P*	$4,950	$12,375	$19,800
French (19th -)				
BACON, Charles R.	*P*	$220	$2,035	$3,850
American (1868 - 1913)				

D=Drawing, P=Painting, S=Sculpture, W=Watercolor

		Current Price Range		
		Low	Mean	High
BACON, Francis	*P*	$1.870M	$4.276M	$6.270M
British (1909 -)				
BACON, Frank L.	*P*			$440
(1815 - 1898)				
BACON, Henry	*D*			$715
American (1839 - 1912)	*P*	$660	$5,298	$9,900
	W	$220	$886	$1,980
BACON, I. L.	*P*			$605
American (19th -)				
BACON, Irving R.	*P*	$220	$403	$550
American (1875 - 1962)				
BACON, M. A.	*P*			$1,320
(?)				
BACON, Peggy	*D*	$495	$605	$770
American (1895 -)	*P*			$3,850
BACON, Peggy (Circle)	*D*			$330
American (1895 -)				
BACSKAY, Bela	*P*			$110
Polish (1860 - 1933)				
BADGER, C. H.	*P*			$330
American (20th -)				
BADGER, James W.	*P*			$1,320
American (19th -)				
BADGER, Joseph (Attrib.)	*P*			$1,430
American (19th -)				
BADGER, S. F. M.	*P*	$6,600	$9,717	$13,200
American (19th - 20th)				
BADIN, Jean J.	*P*			$15,400
French (1843 -)				
BADURA, Benjamin	*P*			$725
American (?)				
BADURA, Bernard	*D*	$370	$485	$600
American (1896 -)				
BAECHLER, Donald	*P*	$4,400	$9,763	$17,600

D=Drawing, P=Painting, S=Sculpture, W=Watercolor

		Current Price Range		
		Low	Mean	High

BAECHLER, Donald	*S*			$33,000
American (20th -)				
BAEDER, John	*D*			$3,850
American (1938 -)	*P*			$27,500
	W			$27,500
BAEN, Jan de (Circle)	*P*			$7,700
Dutch (1673 - 1700)				
BAER, Jo	*P*	$63,800	$67,650	$71,500
American (1929 -)				
BAGG, Henry H.	*P*	$132	$585	$1,320
American (1852 - 1928)				
BAGLEY, Ralph L.	*P*			$495
American (1913 -)				
BAGLIONE, Cavaliere G.	*D*			$1,430
Italian (1571 - 1644)				
BAHIEU, Jules G.	*P*	$770	$1,265	$1,760
Belgian (19th -)				
BAIL, Franck A.	*P*	$5,500	$10,450	$15,400
French (1858 - 1924)				
BAIL, Joseph	*P*	$1,320	$14,124	$33,000
French (1862 - 1921)				
BAILEY, Clayton	*S*			$2,090
American (20th -)				
BAILEY, Forest R.	*P*			$176
American (20th -)				
BAILEY, Frederick V.	*P*	$9,900	$13,200	$16,500
British (19th -)				
BAILEY, George H.	*P*			$3,850
American (19th -)				
BAILEY, Thomas	*P*	$132	$197	$248
American (1875 - 1935)	*W*	$110	$147	$176
BAILEY, Walter A.	*P*	$352	$589	$825
American (1894 -)				
BAILEY, William	*D*	$248	$15,524	$30,800

D=Drawing, P=Painting, S=Sculpture, W=Watercolor

BAILEY

		Current Price Range		
		Low	Mean	High
BAILEY, William	*P*	$132,000	$174,167	$253,000
American (1902 -)				
BAILLY, David (Attrib.)	*P*			$7,700
Dutch (1584 -)				
BAILLY, J. B.	*S*			$2,640
(?)				
BAILY, C.	*W*			$385
American (1866 - 1951)				
BAIN, Marcel A.	*P*			$8,800
French (1878 - 1937)				
BAIRD, Nathaniel H.	*P*	$935	$3,768	$6,600
British (1865 -)				
BAIRD, William B.	*P*	$1,980	$3,163	$4,950
American (1847 -)				
BAIZE, Wayne	*D*			$1,650
(1943 -)				
BAJ, Enrico	*P*	$2,200	$17,820	$29,700
Italian (1924 -)	*S*	$2,970	$12,173	$26,400
BAKER, Bryant	*S*			$550
American (1881 - 1970)				
BAKER, Ernest	*P*			$2,530
American (19th -)				
BAKER, Frederick Van V.	*P*	$220	$275	$330
American (1876 -)				
BAKER, George H.	*D*			$220
American (1878 - 1943)	*P*	$550	$2,613	$4,675
BAKER, George O.	*P*			$1,650
American (1882 -)				
BAKER, Lester	*W*			$275
(20th -)				
BAKER, Lucy	*S*			$1,320
(20th -)				
BAKER, Max	*W*	$220	$234	$248
American (20th -)				

D=Drawing, P=Painting, S=Sculpture, W=Watercolor

		Current Price Range		
		Low	Mean	High

		Low	Mean	High
BAKER, O. F.	*P*			$385
American (19th - 1869)				
BAKER, Ralph	*W*	$605	$688	$770
American (1908 - 1976)				
BAKER, Samuel C.	*P*			$1,100
American (1874 - 1964)				
BAKER, Thomas	*P*			$3,300
English (1809 - 1869)				
BAKER, William	*P*			$605
American (1859 - 1886)				
BAKHUYZEN, Alexandre H.	*P*			$3,300
Dutch (1830 -)				
BAKHUYZEN, Gerardina J. van de	*P*			$5,610
Dutch (1826 - 1895)	*W*	$1,100	$5,023	$12,100
BAKHUYZEN, Hendrick van de S.	*P*			$28,600
Dutch (1795 - 1860)				
BAKHUYZEN, Ludolf	*P*	$2,640	$14,548	$44,000
Dutch (1631 - 1708)				
BAKHUYZEN, Ludolf (Attrib.)	*P*	$2,640	$2,970	$3,300
Dutch (1631 - 1708)				
BAKHUYZEN, Ludolf (Manner)	*P*			$660
Dutch (1631 - 1708)				
BAKHUYZEN, Ludolf (School)	*P*			$6,050
Dutch (1631 - 1708)				
BAKST, Leon	*D*			$2,475
Russian (1866 - 1924)	*P*			$5,500
BALASSI, Mario	*P*			$11,000
Italian (1604 - 1667)				
BALCH, Georgia	*P*			$358
American (1888 -)				
BALCIAR, Gerald	*S*	$770	$770	$770
American (20th -)				
BALCKE, Robert	*P*			$275
German (1860 -)				

D=Drawing, P=Painting, S=Sculpture, W=Watercolor

		Current Price Range		
		Low	Mean	High
BALDASSARRE, Antonio	*P*			$165
Italian (20th -)				
BALDESSARI, John	*D*			$52,800
American (1931 -)				
BALDI, Lazzaro	*D*			$1,650
Italian (17th - 18th)				
BALDRIDGE, Cyrus L.	*W*			$1,210
American (1889 -)				
BALE, Charles T.	*P*	$385	$2,049	$5,225
British (19th -)				
BALE, Edwin R. J.	*P*			$605
British (1842 -)				
BALE, Thomas C.	*P*			$902
British (19th -)				
BALEN, Hendrik van	*P*	$16,500	$20,625	$24,750
Flemish (1575 - 1632)				
BALESTRA, Antonio	*D*			$495
Italian (1666 - 1740)	*P*	$20,900	$29,333	$46,200
BALESTRIERI, Lionello	*P*	$3,300	$12,833	$18,700
Italian (1872 - 1958)				
BALGARD, A.	*P*			$385
French (19th -)				
BALINK, Hendricus	*P*			$550
(?)				
BALL, Adrien J. V.	*P*			$4,675
Belgian (1824 - 1882)				
BALL, Alice L.	*W*	$358	$358	$358
American (1870 - 1942)				
BALL, L. Clarence	*P*	$220	$660	$1,100
American (1858 - 1915)	*W*			$413
BALL, T. C.	*P*			$150
(?)				
BALL, Thomas	*P*			$440
American (1819 - 1911)	*S*	$3,300	$20,625	$55,000

D=Drawing, P=Painting, S=Sculpture, W=Watercolor

		Current Price Range		
		Low	Mean	High

		Low	Mean	High
BALL, Thomas Watson	*P*	$165	$248	$385
American (1863 - 1934)	*W*			$110
BALL, Wilfred	*W*			$121
British (1853 - 1917)				
BALLA, Giacomo	*D*	$44,000	$69,667	$154,000
Italian (1871 -)	*P*	$3,300	$1.051M	$4.400M
	S	$2,200	$317,350	$632,500
	W	$24,750	$411,583	$660,000
BALLANTYNE, John	*P*	$825	$5,913	$11,000
British (1815 - 1897)				
BALLANTYNE, Keith	*P*			$1,540
(?)				
BALLARD, Richard	*P*			$880
(20th -)				
BALLAVOINE, Jules F.	*P*	$1,430	$9,641	$35,200
French (19th -)				
BALLESIO, Federico	*P*			$16,500
Italian (19th -)	*W*			$6,600
BALLIN-CRAMER, Florence	*P*			$605
American (1884 -)				
BALLINGALL, Alexander	*W*			$550
British (19th -)				
BALLINGER, Harry	*P*	$248	$550	$825
American (1892 -)				
BALLIO, H. C.	*P*			$165
Italian (19th -)				
BALLIQUANT,	*P*			$2,310
French (19th -)				
BALLOWE, Marcia	*P*	$550	$1,320	$1,760
American (20th -)	*W*			$1,500
BALTEN, Pieter (Attrib.)	*P*			$176,000
Flemish (1525 - 1598)				

D=Drawing, P=Painting, S=Sculpture, W=Watercolor

		Current Price Range		
		Low	Mean	High
BALTHUS,	*D*	$14,300	$131,267	$319,000
French (1908 -)	*P*	$550,000	$1.320M	$2.090M
BALZRE,	*P*			$165
(?)				
BAMBERGER, Gustave	*D*			$165
German (1860 -)				
BAMFYLDE, Coppelstone W.	*P*			$1,320
British (? - 1791)				
BANCEL, Louis	*S*			$1,320
French (1926 -)				
BANCHIERI, Giuseppe	*P*			$110
Italian (1927 -)				
BANCROFT, Milton H.	*P*			$605
American (1867 - 1947)	*W*			$1,100
BANDECK, Fritz M.	*P*			$1,650
German (19th - 20th)				
BANDINELLI, Baccio	*D*	$19,800	$31,900	$44,000
Italian (1493 - 1560)				
BANG, L.	*P*			$468
(19th -)				
BANGE, A.	*P*			$385
(?)				
BANISTER, Patti	*P*			$358
American (?)				
BANITT, J.	*P*			$231
British (19th - 20th)				
BANKS, B.	*P*			$198
American (20th -)				
BANKS, Niewley	*D*			$132
(?)				
BANKS, Robert	*W*	$1,320	$1,430	$1,540
British (19th -)				
BANNARD, Walter D.	*P*	$770	$1,491	$2,860
American (1931 -)				

D=Drawing, P=Painting, S=Sculpture, W=Watercolor

		Current Price Range		
		Low	Mean	High
BANNISTER, Alice H.	*W*			$193
American (17th - 18th)				
BANNISTER, Patti	*P*	$275	$385	$495
American (20th -)	*S*			$605
BAQUERO, Mariano	*W*			$41,250
Spanish (19th -)				
BAR, Bonaventure de (Circle)	*P*			$14,300
French (1700 - 1729)				
BARABAN-CAHAGNET, Blanche	*P*			$1,210
French (20th -)				
BARAIN, J.	*P*			$825
(?)				
BARANYA, Gustov L. von	*P*			$7,700
Hungarian (1886 - 1938)				
BARATTI, Filippo	*P*			$4,070
Italian (19th - 20th)				
BARAU, Emile	*P*			$1,870
French (1851 - 1930)				
BARBAGELATA, Giovanni	*P*			$22,000
Italian (1484 - 1508)				
BARBARINI, Emil	*P*			$3,960
Austrian (1855 - 1930)				
BARBARINI, Franz	*P*	$1,870	$3,190	$5,500
Austrian (1804 - 1873)				
BARBASAN, Mariano	*P*			$38,500
Spanish (1864 - 1924)				
BARBAULT, Jean (Circle)	*P*	$990	$2,558	$4,125
French (1705 - 1766)				
BARBEDIENNE, F.	*S*	$330	$550	$770
(?)				
BARBER, Alfred R.	*P*			$18,700
British (19th -)				
BARBER, Alice	*W*			$550
American (1858 - 1932)				
BARBER, C. J.	*P*			$2,200
(19th -)				

D=Drawing, P=Painting, S=Sculpture, W=Watercolor

		Current Price Range		
		Low	Mean	High

BARBER, George	*P*			$1,760
American (1910 -)				
BARBER, H.	*P*			$605
(?)				
BARBER, John J. (Attrib.)	*P*			$1,100
American (1840 -)				
BARBER, Sam	*P*	$176	$748	$1,320
American (?)				
BARBIER, Georges	*W*	$3,300	$3,410	$3,520
American (1882 -)				
BARBIER, Jean-Jacques le	*D*			$2,200
French (1738 - 1826)	*P*			$28,600
	W			$5,225
BARBIER, Nicolas F.	*D*			$1,375
French (1768 - 1826)				
BARBIERI, Francesco (Manner)	*D*			$550
Italian (17th -)				
BARBIERI, Giovanni F.	*D*	$11,000	$37,086	$82,500
Italian (1591 - 1666)				
BARBIERI, Giovanni F. (Attrib.)	*D*			$7,700
Italian (1591 - 1666)				
BARBIERI, Giovanni F. (Circle)	*D*			$2,090
Italian (1591 - 1666)				
BARCELO, Miguel	*D*			$14,300
(20th -)	*S*			$16,500
BARCHUS, Eliza	*P*	$220	$659	$1,760
American (1857 - 1959)				
BARCLAY, J.	*W*			$1,210
(19th -)				
BARCLAY, McClelland	*P*	$495	$2,552	$6,000
American (1891 - 1943)	*S*	$413	$647	$880
BARDONE, Guy	*P*	$110	$1,760	$3,520
French (1927 -)				

D=Drawing, P=Painting, S=Sculpture, W=Watercolor

		Current Price Range		
		Low	Mean	High

BARDONE, Paris (Attrib.)	*P*			$99,000
Italian (1500 - 1571)				
BARDWELL, Thomas	*P*	$4,125	$5,088	$6,050
British (? - 1780)				
BARE, E.	*P*			$5,280
French (19th -)				
BAREAU, Georges	*S*			$4,125
French (1866 -)				
BARENGER, James	*P*			$3,960
British (1745 - 1813)				
BARGER, John	*P*			$3,800
American (1953 -)				
BARIG, L.	*P*			$523
European (19th -)				
BARILARI, Enrique	*P*			$8,250
Argentina (1931 -)				
BARILE, Xavier J.	*P*	$110	$330	$550
American (1891 -)				
BARILLOT, Eugene	*S*			$1,760
French (?)				
BARILLOT, Leon	*P*			$4,950
French (1844 - 1929)				
BARK, Jared	*S*			$1,100
American (1944 -)				
BARKER, Benjamin (Attrib.)	*P*			$5,225
British (1776 - 1838)				
BARKER, George	*P*			$385
American (1882 - 1965)	*W*			$385
BARKER, J. P.	*P*			$440
(19th -)				
BARKER, John	*P*			$1,100
British (18th - 19th)				
BARKER, John J.	*P*	$193	$1,857	$3,520
British (19th -)				
BARKER, John J. (Attrib.)	*P*			$880
British (19th -)				

D=Drawing, P=Painting, S=Sculpture, W=Watercolor

		Current Price Range		
		Low	Mean	High

		Low	Mean	High
BARKER, Thomas J.	*P*			$14,300
British (1815 - 1882)				
BARKER, Wright	*P*	$3,300	$4,693	$5,500
British (1941 -)				
BARKER OF BATH, Joseph	*P*			$4,400
British (19th -)				
BARKER OF BATH, Thomas	*P*	$1,100	$3,850	$7,150
British (1769 - 1847)				
BARLACH, Ernst	*D*	$6,600	$8,342	$11,000
German (1870 -)	*S*	$38,500	$57,750	$77,000
BARLAND, Adam	*P*			$5,500
British (19th -)				
BARLEIGH, Sydney R.	*W*			$880
American (1853 - 1931)				
BARLOW,	*P*			$1,430
(?)				
BARLOW, Francis	*D*			$3,300
British (1626 - 1704)				
BARLOW, John N.	*P*	$880	$1,474	$2,200
American (1861 - 1917)				
BARLOW, Myron	*D*	$495	$1,100	$2,200
American (1873 - 1937)	*P*	$3,850	$14,850	$38,500
BARNABE, Duilio	*P*	$1,100	$5,771	$12,100
Italian (1914 - 1961)				
BARNARD, Edward	*P*	$3,190	$3,685	$4,180
American (1855 - 1909)				
BARNARD, George G.	*S*	$2,200	$3,080	$3,960
American (1863 - 1938)				
BARNES, Edward C.	*P*	$715	$953	$1,320
British (1856 - 1882)				
BARNES, Ernest H.	*P*	$121	$764	$2,090
American (1873 -)				
BARNES, Frank	*P*			$6,050
New Zealander (19th - 20th)				

D=Drawing, P=Painting, S=Sculpture, W=Watercolor

		Current Price Range		
		Low	Mean	High
BARNES, Gertrude	*P*			$1,650
American (1865 -)				
BARNES, S.	*P*			$330
British (19th -)				
BARNETT, Isa	*P*	$110	$454	$798
American (1924 -)	*W*	$325	$342	$358
BARNETT, Les	*W*	$715	$758	$800
American (20th -)				
BARNEY, Frank A.	*P*	$303	$495	$770
American (1862 -)				
BARNOIN, Henri A.	*P*	$5,500	$8,983	$12,100
French (1882 -)				
BARNSLEY, J. Macdonald	*P*	$1,430	$2,365	$3,300
Canadian (1861 - 1929)				
BAROCCI, Federico (After)	*P*			$6,325
Italian (1526 - 1612)				
BAROCCI, Federico (Attrib.)	*D*			$13,200
Italian (1526 - 1612)				
BAROCCI, Federico (Circle)	*D*			$1,870
Italian (1526 - 1612)				
BAROCCI, Federico (Follower)	*P*			$3,575
Italian (1526 - 1612)				
BARON, Charles H.	*P*			$3,080
(?)				
BARON, Henri	*P*	$1,760	$2,970	$4,180
French (1816 - 1885)	*W*			$275
BARONE, Antonio	*P*			$413
American (1889 -)				
BARONE, Antonio (Attrib.)	*P*			$880
American (1889 -)				
BARR, Allan	*P*			$385
British (19th - 20th)				
BARR, William	*P*	$275	$2,235	$4,400
American (1867 - 1933)				

D=Drawing, P=Painting, S=Sculpture, W=Watercolor

		Current Price Range		
		Low	Mean	High
BARRAGAN, Luis	*P*			$3,300
Lat. Amer. (20th -)				
BARRANTI, P.	*S*			$1,650
Italian (20th -)				
BARRAU, Laureano	*P*			$55,000
Spanish (1864 -)				
BARRAUD, Francois	*P*			$3,025
Swiss (1899 - 1934)				
BARRAUD, Henry	*P*			$44,000
British (1811 - 1874)				
BARRAUD, William	*P*	$8,800	$26,767	$51,700
British (1810 - 1850)				
BARRE, Martin	*P*			$24,200
French (1924 -)				
BARREDA, Ernesto	*P*	$2,860	$5,522	$8,800
French (1927 -)				
BARRERA, Antonio	*P*	$7,150	$12,210	$16,500
Colombian (1948 -)				
BARRETT, Elizabeth H.	*P*			$220
American (1863 -)	*W*			$110
BARRETT, Oliver G.	*P*	$303	$349	$385
American (20th -)				
BARRETT, Robert D.	*W*			$275
American (1903 -)				
BARRETT, W. J.	*P*			$743
(?)				
BARRETT, William S.	*W*	$248	$399	$550
American (1854 - 1927)				
BARRETT, SR., George	*P*			$46,200
(? - 1784)				
BARRIAS, Louis E.	*S*	$10,450	$17,875	$24,750
French (1841 - 1905)				
BARRIE, Erwin S.	*P*	$220	$495	$770
American (1886 -)				
BARRIENTOS, I.	*W*			$193
Spanish (19th - 20th)				

D=Drawing, P=Painting, S=Sculpture, W=Watercolor

		Current Price Range		
		Low	Mean	High

		Low	Mean	High
BARRIOS, Armando	*P*			$17,600
Venezuelan (1920 -)				
BARRITT, Robert C.	*P*			$660
American (1898 -)				
BARRON, Grace	*P*			$132
American (1903 -)	*W*			$143
BARRON, Hugh	*P*			$2,420
British (1745 - 1791)				
BARROW, Edith	*W*			$550
American (20th -)				
BARROW, John D.	*P*			$2,860
American (?)				
BARROW, Julian	*P*			$770
American (20th -)				
BARRY, Gerard	*P*	$120	$253	$385
American (1864 -)				
BARSE, JR., George R.	*P*			$8,250
American (1861 - 1938)				
BARSOTTI, Hercules	*P*			$6,600
Brazilian (1914 -)				
BARSTOW, G. M.	*P*			$660
American (19th -)				
BARTA, Montserrat	*P*			$440
Spanish (20th -)				
BARTELL, Ira	*P*			$660
(20th -)				
BARTENBACH, H.	*P*	$413	$413	$413
(?)				
BARTHE, Richmond	*S*			$1,925
American (1901 - 1989)				
BARTHELEMY, Raymond	*S*			$1,320
(?)				
BARTHOLOMEW, William N.	*W*			$220
American (1856 - 1919)				
BARTHOWLOWSKI, Johannes	*P*	$110	$121	$132
American (19th - 20th)				

D=Drawing, P=Painting, S=Sculpture, W=Watercolor

		Current Price Range		
		Low	Mean	High
BARTLE, Sara N.	P	$275	$413	$550
American (20th -)				
BARTLETT, Clarence D.	P			$495
American (1860 -)				
BARTLETT, Dana	P	$770	$2,420	$5,500
American (1882 - 1957)	W	$1,320	$1,595	$1,870
BARTLETT, Frederic C.	P			$1,210
American (1873 - 1951)				
BARTLETT, Gray	P			$715
American (1885 - 1951)				
BARTLETT, Jennifer	D	$6,600	$7,975	$9,350
American (1941 -)	P	$15,400	$73,920	$137,500
	S			$2,530
BARTLETT, L.	P			$715
(?)				
BARTLETT, Paul W.	S	$715	$7,847	$22,000
American (1865 - 1925)				
BARTLETT, William H. (Attrib.)	P			$1,540
British (1858 -)				
BARTLINO, E. T.	P			$138
American (20th -)				
BARTOLI, Jacques	P			$2,090
French (1920 -)				
BARTOLINI, Federico	P			$49,500
Italian (19th - 20th)	W	$3,025	$5,088	$7,150
BARTOLINI, Lorenzo (Attrib.)	D			$1,650
Italian (1777 - 1850)				
BARTOLO, Andrea di	P			$74,250
Italian (? - 1428)				
BARTOLOMMEO, Fra (Attrib.)	D			$46,750
Italian (1472 - 1517)				
BARTON, Donald	P	$605	$1,306	$1,870
American (1903 - 1934)				

D=Drawing, P=Painting, S=Sculpture, W=Watercolor

| | | Current Price Range | | |
		Low	Mean	High
BARTON, Harry	*P*			$110
American (20th -)				
BARTON, Loren	*W*			$770
American (1893 - 1975)				
BARTSCH, Ernst L.	*P*			$715
American (19th - 20th)				
BARTSCH, Walter F.	*P*			$250
(20th -)				
BARUCCI, Pietro	*P*	$3,850	$11,550	$27,500
Italian (1845 - 1917)				
BARWIG, Franz	*S*			$4,180
Austrian (1868 -)				
BARYE, Alfred	*S*	$660	$3,493	$11,000
French (19th -)				
BARYE, Antoine	*D*			$88,000
French (1795 - 1875)	*P*	$2,200	$3,025	$3,850
	S	$220	$4,888	$38,500
	W			$8,250
BARYE, Antoine (After)	*S*	$220	$781	$1,760
French (1795 - 1875)				
BARZANTI, Licinio	*P*			$880
(?)				
BASCHENIS, Evaristo (Circle)	*P*			$88,000
Italian (1617 - 1677)				
BASCHENIS, Evaristo (Follower)	*P*			$22,000
Italian (1617 - 1677)				
BASCHENIS, Evaristo (Studio)	*P*			$99,000
Italian (1617 - 1677)				
BASCOMB, Ruth H.	*D*			$5,775
(19th -)				
BASELITZ, Georg	*D*	$8,800	$24,420	$39,600
American (1938 -)	*P*	$110,000	$333,208	$797,500
	W	$4,620	$10,074	$17,600

D=Drawing, P=Painting, S=Sculpture, W=Watercolor

		Current Price Range		
		Low	Mean	High

		Low	Mean	High
BASING, Charles	W			$220
American (1865 - 1933)				
BASKERVILLE, Charles	W			$825
American (1896 -)				
BASKIN, Leonard	D	$165	$809	$1,540
American (1922 -)	S	$165	$5,570	$19,800
	W	$990	$1,238	$1,485
BASOLI, Antonio	D	$3,850	$4,400	$4,950
Italian (1774 - 1848)				
BASQUIAT, Jean-Michel	D	$3,410	$19,563	$52,250
(1960 -)	P	$3,300	$113,300	$440,000
	S	$3,850	$130,868	$319,000
	W	$8,800	$12,650	$18,700
BASSANO, Jacopo	D			$9,900
Italian (16th -)	P	$49,500	$244,750	$440,000
BASSANO, Jacopo (Attrib.)	P			$4,400
Italian (16th -)				
BASSANO, Jacopo (Circle)	D			$770
Italian (16th -)				
BASSANO, Leandro	P			$15,400
Italian (1557 - 1622)				
BASSANO, Leandro (Circle)	P			$3,025
Italian (1557 - 1622)				
BASSANO, JR., Fran. (Foll)	P	$6,600	$41,800	$77,000
Flemish (1549 - 1592)				
BASSEN, Bartolomeus (Et al.)	P			$49,500
(16th - 17th)				
BASSEPORTE, Madeleine F.	W			$16,500
French (1701 - 1780)				
BASSETT, Raveau	P	$2,200	$3,919	$6,600
American (1897 - 1981)				
BASTERT, Nicolas	P			$2,310
Dutch (1854 - 1939)				

D=Drawing, P=Painting, S=Sculpture, W=Watercolor

		Current Price Range		
		Low	Mean	High
BASTIANI, Lazzaro di J.	P			$52,250
Italian (1425 - 1512)				
BASTIDA, Joaquin S.	P	$5,775	$108,694	$297,000
Spanish (1863 - 1923)				
BASTIDE, P.	S			$2,750
French (19th -)				
BASTIEN, Alfred T. J.	P	$3,300	$3,575	$3,850
Belgian (1873 - 1955)				
BASTIEN-LEPAGE, Jules	P			$9,900
French (1848 - 1884)				
BASTON, Andre	P			$1,540
French (19th -)				
BATAIL, Jean	P			$200
(20th -)				
BATCHELLER, Frederick S.	P	$990	$1,966	$4,400
American (1837 - 1889)				
BATE, Francis	P			$440
British (1858 -)				
BATE, Rutledge	W			$523
American (1891 -)				
BATEMAN, Robert	D			$6,050
British (19th -)				
BATES, David	P	$3,960	$6,292	$8,250
British (1840 - 1921)	W	$1,320	$1,668	$1,925
BATES, David (Et al.)	P			$2,750
British (1840 - 1921)				
BATES, Dewey	P			$385
American (1851 - 1891)				
BATES, Gladys	S			$1,980
(1896 -)				
BATES, Kenneth	P	$330	$633	$1,045
American (1904 -)				
BATES, R. E.	P			$110
(?)				
BATON, Claude	P			$2,090
French (20th -)				

D=Drawing, P=Painting, S=Sculpture, W=Watercolor

		Current Price Range		
		Low	Mean	High

		Low	Mean	High
BATONI, Pompeo (Circle) Italian (1708 - 1787)	*P*			$12,100
BATOWJKI, Stanislas K. (19th -)	*P*			$3,520
BATTACHI, A. Italian (19th -)	*S*			$2,200
BATTAGLIA, Alessandro Italian (1870 - 1940)	*W*			$1,540
BATTAGLIA, C. Bompiani Italian (19th -)	*W*	$440	$2,516	$4,675
BATTEN, John D. (1860 - 1932)	*D*			$200
BATTI, Leon Italian (19th -)	*S*			$2,750
BATTISTA, Giovanni Italian (1858 - 1925)	*W*	$187	$520	$880
BATTLES, Blake D. American (1887 - 1972)	*W*			$330
BAUCHANT, Andre French (1873 - 1958)	*P*	$4,950	$18,219	$34,100
BAUDESSON, Nicolas French (17th -)	*P*			$7,700
BAUDIT, Amadee Swiss (1825 - 1890)	*P*			$1,980
BAUDRY, Paul French (1828 - 1886)	*P*	$1,650	$1,925	$2,200
BAUER, Carl F. Austrian (1879 - 1954)	*P*			$4,950
BAUER, Marius A. J. Dutch (1867 - 1932)	*P*			$1,100
BAUER, Rudolf German (1889 - 1954)	*D*	$1,650	$3,025	$4,400
	P	$30,800	$55,550	$93,500
	W	$3,740	$5,647	$7,150
BAUER, W. C. American (?)	*W*			$770

D=Drawing, P=Painting, S=Sculpture, W=Watercolor

		Current Price Range		
		Low	Mean	High

		Low	Mean	High
BAUER, William	*P*			$440
(?)				
BAUER-RADNAY, Elizabeth de	*W*			$2,970
American (1897 - 1972)				
BAUERLE, Karl W. F.	*P*			$13,200
German (1831 - 1912)				
BAUERMEISTER, Mary	*P*	$12,100	$13,567	$16,500
(20th -)	*S*			$9,900
BAUGIN, Lubin	*P*			$71,500
French (1612 - 1633)				
BAUM, Carl	*P*			$5,500
American (19th -)				
BAUM, Walter E.	*D*	$250	$525	$1,000
American (1884 - 1956)	*P*	$130	$2,726	$19,800
	W	$176	$907	$2,200
BAUM, Walter E. (Attrib.)	*P*	$176	$253	$330
American (1884 - 1956)				
BAUMANN, Gustave	*P*			$220
American (1881 -)	*S*			$1,760
BAUMANN, Ida	*P*			$9,900
Swiss (1864 -)				
BAUMANN, Karl H.	*P*			$10,450
American (1911 - 1984)	*W*			$2,475
BAUMEISTER, Mary	*S*			$5,060
(20th -)				
BAUMEISTER, Willi	*P*			$110,000
German (1889 - 1955)				
BAUMER, S.	*P*			$413
(?)				
BAUMES, Amedee	*P*			$5,500
French (1820 -)				
BAUMGARTNER, H.	*P*	$1,760	$5,720	$13,200
German (19th -)				

D=Drawing, P=Painting, S=Sculpture, W=Watercolor

		Current Price Range		
		Low	Mean	High
BAUMGARTNER, J. Jay	W	$880	$990	$1,100
American (1885 - 1946)				
BAUMGARTNER, Johann (Att)	P			$6,600
German (1712 - 1761)				
BAUMGARTNER, Peter	P			$38,500
German (1834 - 1911)				
BAUMGARTNER, Warren W.	D			$660
American (1894 - 1963)	W	$330	$495	$715
BAUMGRAS, Peter	P	$200	$650	$1,100
American (1827 - 1904)				
BAUMHOFFER, Walter	P	$880	$3,245	$6,600
American (1904 -)				
BAUR, Johann W.	W	$6,050	$7,242	$7,975
French (? - 1640)				
BAURGENIS, J. A.	W			$110
American (19th -)				
BAUTER, C.	P			$2,310
(?)				
BAXTER, B.	P			$165
(?)				
BAXTER, Bertha E.	P			$385
American (19th -)				
BAXTER, Robert	P			$1,200
(?)				
BAXTER, JR., Elijah	P			$1,540
American (1849 - 1939)				
BAYARD, Clifford A.	P			$193
American (1892 - 1934)				
BAYEU, Ramon	P			$57,200
(?)				
BAYEU Y SUBIAS, Francisco (Att)	P			$11,000
Spanish (1734 - 1795)				
BAYLINSON, A. S.	P			$6,820
American (1882 - 1950)				
BAYNE, Walter M.	P			$3,300
British (1795 - 1859)				

D=Drawing, P=Painting, S=Sculpture, W=Watercolor

		Current Price Range		
		Low	Mean	High

		Low	Mean	High
BAZAINE, Jean	*D*			$1,540
French (1904 -)	*P*			$15,400
	W			$1,100
BAZANE, A. P.	*W*			$138
(19th - 20th)				
BAZILE, Castera	*P*			$1,430
Haitian (1923 - 1965)				
BAZILLE, Frederic (Attrib.)	*D*			$1,210
French (1841 - 1870)				
BAZIOTES, William	*D*	$2,200	$7,315	$23,100
American (1912 - 1963)	*P*	$28,600	$121,642	$385,000
	W	$12,100	$19,250	$26,400
BAZZANI, Giuseppe	*P*			$63,250
Italian (1690 - 1769)				
BAZZARO, Leonardo	*P*			$5,500
Italian (1853 - 1937)				
BEACH, Chester	*S*			$440
American (1881 - 1956)				
BEACH, Thomas	*P*	$1,100	$10,267	$22,000
British (1738 - 1806)				
BEACON, Susan	*P*			$165
(19th - 20th)				
BEAL, Gifford	*P*	$2,475	$11,092	$28,600
American (1879 - 1956)	*W*	$1,650	$2,787	$3,630
BEAL, Helen H.	*W*			$605
American (20th -)				
BEAL, Jack	*P*	$9,350	$14,438	$27,500
American (1931 -)				
BEAL, Reynolds	*D*	$150	$942	$4,400
American (1867 - 1951)	*P*	$850	$8,205	$38,500
	W	$220	$1,517	$6,875
BEALE, Mary (Attrib.)	*P*			$1,100
British (1632 - 1697)				

D=Drawing, P=Painting, S=Sculpture, W=Watercolor

		Current Price Range		
		Low	Mean	High
BEALES, Isaac B.	W			$121
American (1866 -)				
BEALL, Cecil C.	P	$220	$495	$770
American (1892 - 1967)	W	$165	$358	$550
BEAMAN, Gamafiel	P	$220	$385	$550
American (19th -)				
BEAMAN, William	P			$550
(19th - 20th)				
BEAN, Caroline van Hook	W	$715	$1,742	$2,750
American (20th -)				
BEAR, Jessie B.	P			$3,575
American (20th -)				
BEARD, Carolyn	S			$468
American (20th -)				
BEARD, James H.	P	$2,200	$6,394	$8,525
American (1814 - 1893)				
BEARD, William	P	$2,310	$5,412	$7,700
American (1825 - 1900)				
BEARDEN, Romare	D	$1,320	$2,090	$2,860
American (1914 - 1988)	P			$13,200
	S	$5,500	$30,957	$66,000
	W			$8,800
BEARDINOSE, W.	P			$451
(?)				
BEARDSLEY, Aubrey V.	D			$165
British (1872 - 1898)				
BEARDSLEY, Aubrey V. (Attrib.)	D			$330
British (1872 - 1898)				
BEARE, George	P			$37,400
British (18th -)				
BEATON, Cecil	W	$715	$1,656	$3,300
British (1904 - 1980)				
BEAUBIEN, A. J.	P			$770
American (20th -)				

D=Drawing, P=Painting, S=Sculpture, W=Watercolor

		Current Price Range	
	Low	Mean	High

		Low	Mean	High
BEAUBRUN, Charles (Attrib.)	*P*			$6,600
French (1604 - 1692)				
BEAUBRUN, Charles (Circle)	*P*			$4,180
French (1604 - 1692)				
BEAUBRUN, Charles (School)	*P*			$1,100
French (1604 - 1692)				
BEAUCHAMP, Robert	*P*	$825	$1,733	$2,640
American (1923 -)				
BEAUDIN, Andre	*S*			$5,500
French (1895 - 1979)				
BEAUDOUIN, Frank	*P*			$990
American (20th -)				
BEAUDUIN, Jean	*P*	$1,980	$4,803	$9,350
Belgian (1851 - 1916)				
BEAUFRERE, Adolphe	*W*			$2,860
French (1876 - 1960)				
BEAUGUREAU, Francis H.	*D*	$330	$550	$770
American (1920 -)	*P*	$825	$1,540	$3,300
	W			$1,650
BEAUMONT, Arthur	*P*	$138	$836	$1,870
American (1879 - 1956)	*W*			$1,100
BEAUMONT, Charles	*P*			$825
American (19th -)				
BEAUMONT, Claudio F.	*D*			$2,860
Italian (1694 - 1766)				
BEAUMONT, G. de	*P*			$412
European (19th - 20th)				
BEAUMONT, T. D.	*P*			$253
(?)				
BEAUQUESNE, Wilfred C.	*P*	$1,430	$3,190	$5,500
French (1847 - 1913)				
BEAUREGARD, Donald	*P*			$220
American (1884 - 1915)				
BEAUX, Cecilia	*D*			$3,300

D=Drawing, P=Painting, S=Sculpture, W=Watercolor

		Current Price Range		
		Low	Mean	High

		Low	Mean	High
BEAUX, Cecilia	*P*			$8,250
American (1863 -)				
BEAVIS, Richard	*P*	$2,860	$4,730	$6,600
British (1824 - 1896)				
BECHER, Arthur	*P*			$1,430
(?)				
BECHER, Bernd and Hilla	*D*			$35,200
(20th -)				
BECHI, Luigi	*P*	$9,900	$20,900	$31,900
Italian (1830 - 1919)				
BECHTLE, Robert	*P*			$19,800
American (1932 -)	*W*	$6,600	$7,700	$8,800
BECK, Augustus W.	*W*			$1,100
American (?)				
BECK, Carol	*P*			$264
American (19th - 20th)				
BECK, E.	*S*			$2,530
(19th -)				
BECK, I. F.	*P*			$11,000
(19th -)				
BECK, J. Augustus	*W*			$220
American (19th - 20th)				
BECK, Joel	*P*			$1,100
(20th -)				
BECK, Johannes (Style)	*P*			$3,850
European (18th - 19th)				
BECK, Rosemary	*P*			$660
American (?)				
BECKER, C.	*P*			$275
(?)				
BECKER, Carl G. L.	*P*			$468
American (?)				
BECKER, Frederick	*P*	$220	$676	$990
American (1888 - 1953)	*W*	$121	$398	$770

D=Drawing, P=Painting, S=Sculpture, W=Watercolor

		Current Price Range		
		Low	Mean	High

BECKER, W.	P			$1,045
British (19th - 20th)				
BECKERS, Franz	P			$990
Dutch (1898 - 1983)				
BECKET, Maria J.	D			$330
American (? - 1904)	P	$358	$647	$935
BECKETT, Charles E.	P			$385
(?)				
BECKHOFF, Harry	W	$375	$593	$990
American (1901 - 1979)				
BECKLEY, Bill	S			$880
(20th -)				
BECKMAN, Jessie M.	P			$770
American (1856 - 1929)				
BECKMAN, William	D	$3,850	$15,492	$38,500
(20th -)				
BECKMANN, Max	D	$715	$12,573	$24,200
German (1884 - 1950)	P			$528,000
BECKWITH, Arthur	P	$358	$1,091	$2,475
American (1860 - 1930)				
BECKWITH, James C.	D			$990
American (1852 - 1917)	P	$825	$4,039	$10,450
	W			$3,300
BECQUEREL, A. V.	S			$880
French (19th - 20th)				
BEDA, Francesco	P			$46,200
Italian (1840 - 1900)				
BEDINEFIELD,	P			$880
(?)				
BEE, Lonie	P			$1,900
American (1902 -)				
BEECHER, Amariah D.	P			$1,650
American (1839 -)				

D=Drawing, P=Painting, S=Sculpture, W=Watercolor

		Current Price Range		
		Low	Mean	High

BEECHER, F. H.	P			$193
(?)				
BEECHEY, Richard B.	P			$6,600
British (1808 - 1895)				
BEECHEY, Sir William	P	$3,025	$5,363	$7,700
British (1753 - 1839)				
BEECHEY, Sir William (Attrib.)	P	$1,100	$7,700	$14,300
British (1753 - 1839)				
BEECHEY, Sir William (Circle)	P			$3,850
British (1753 - 1839)				
BEECHEY, Sir William (School)	P	$3,300	$3,650	$4,000
British (1753 - 1839)				
BEEKMAN, H. R.	P			$1,100
(?)				
BEELER, Joe Neil	P	$4,125	$5,638	$7,150
American (1931 -)	S	$1,650	$2,842	$4,125
BEELT, Cornelis	P			$13,200
Dutch (1660 - 1702)				
BEER, John	P			$2,475
British (19th - 20th)				
BEERS, Jan van	P	$3,300	$3,850	$4,950
Belgian (1852 - 1927)				
BEERS, Julia H.	P	$110	$248	$385
American (1835 - 1913)				
BEERSTRATEN, Jan A.	P			$7,150
Dutch (1622 - 1666)				
BEERT I, Osias	P	$110,000	$506,000	$902,000
Flemish (1622 - 1678)				
BEEST, Albert van	P	$4,400	$9,533	$15,400
American (1820 - 1860)				
BEFANI, Achille F.	P			$4,950
Italian (1832 - 1906)				
BEGA, C. (Attrib.)	P			$523
European (19th -)				
BEGA, Cornelis P.	P	$2,200	$30,067	$60,500
Dutch (1631 - 1664)				

D=Drawing, P=Painting, S=Sculpture, W=Watercolor

		Current Price Range		
		Low	Mean	High

BEGEYN, Abraham J. (Attrib.) Dutch (1637 - 1697)	*P*			$1,650
BEGUINE, Michael L. French (1855 - 1929)	*S*			$1,870
BEHMER, Marcus German (1879 - 1958)	*D*			$385
BEHNCKE, Nile (?)	*W*			$220
BEHR, Carel J. Dutch (1812 - 1895)	*P*			$3,740
BEICH, Joachim F. (Circle) German (1665 - 1748)	*P*			$11,000
BEICH, Mary (?)	*P*			$715
BEIL, C. A. Canadian (20th -)	*S*			$990
BEIRHALS, Otto (?)	*P*			$8,250
BEL-GEDDES, Norman (20th -)	*W*	$2,530	$2,860	$3,080
BELARDINELLI, A. Italian (1922 -)	*P*	$165	$207	$248
BELEM, Orozio Brazilian (20th -)	*P*			$265
BELENOK, Pyotr Russian (1938 -)	*S*	$1,760	$2,310	$2,860
BELGIAN SCHOOL, Belgian (19th - 20th)	*P*	$1,980	$4,290	$6,600
BELGIAN SCHOOL 19C, Belgian (19th -)	*P*			$2,640
BELIMBAU, Adolfo Italian (1845 -)	*P*			$1,320
BELING, Helen American (1914 -)	*S*			$440
BELKNAP, Zedekiah (Attrib.) American (1781 - 1858)	*P*			$5,500

D=Drawing, P=Painting, S=Sculpture, W=Watercolor

		Current Price Range		
		Low	Mean	High
BELL, Arthur G.	*W*			$660
British (19th -)				
BELL, Caroline	*P*	$248	$391	$605
American (20th -)				
BELL, Cecil C.	*P*	$1,650	$4,180	$8,800
American (1906 - 1970)	*W*			$990
BELL, Charles	*P*	$38,500	$115,500	$187,000
American (20th -)	*W*			$14,300
BELL, Clara L.	*P*			$2,970
American (1886 -)				
BELL, Edward A.	*P*	$5,500	$9,167	$13,200
American (1862 - 1953)				
BELL, Elizabeth	*P*			$165
American (20th -)				
BELL, George C.	*W*			$1,430
American (19th -)				
BELL, John	*P*			$4,400
British (19th -)				
BELL, Larry	*D*			$1,430
American (20th -)	*S*			$4,950
BELL, Stuart H.	*P*			$1,045
British (1823 - 1896)				
BELLANGE, Joseph L. H.	*D*			$330
French (1800 - 1866)	*P*	$2,250	$15,550	$52,250
	W			$385
BELLANGER, Camille-F.	*P*	$9,350	$73,425	$137,500
French (1853 - 1923)				
BELLANGER, Georges	*P*			$6,600
French (1847 - 1918)				
BELLANO, A.	*P*			$9,350
Italian (19th -)				
BELLE, Alexis-S (Attrib.)	*P*			$1,210
French (1674 - 1734)				

D=Drawing, P=Painting, S=Sculpture, W=Watercolor

		Current Price Range		
		Low	Mean	High
BELLE, Marcel	*P*			$3,300
French (20th -)				
BELLEI, Gaetano	*P*	$2,750	$3,575	$4,400
Italian (1857 - 1922)				
BELLENGE, Michel B.	*P*			$12,100
French (1726 - 1793)				
BELLER, Alvin J.	*W*			$248
American (1902 - 1968)				
BELLERMAN, Ferdinand	*P*			$49,500
German (1814 - 1889)				
BELLET, Auguste E.	*P*	$3,300	$4,950	$6,600
French (? - 1911)				
BELLEUSE, Albert E. C.	*S*	$990	$4,107	$7,150
French (1824 - 1887)				
BELLEUSE, D. Carriere	*P*			$2,200
(?)				
BELLEUSE, Pierre C.	*D*			$1,320
(19th -)				
BELLEVOIS, Jacob (Circle)	*P*			$5,500
Dutch (1621 - 1675)				
BELLI, Giovacchino	*D*	$770	$2,489	$4,950
Italian (1756 - 1822)	*P*			$4,950
BELLIAS, Richard	*P*	$550	$1,375	$2,200
French (1921 -)				
BELLIN, Barbara	*P*			$550
American (20th -)				
BELLINI, Giovanni	*P*			$352,000
Italian (1430 - 1516)				
BELLINI, Giovanni (Attrib.)	*P*			$71,500
Italian (1430 - 1516)				
BELLINI, Giovanni (Circle)	*P*			$7,700
Italian (1430 - 1516)				
BELLINI, Giovanni (School)	*P*	$3,300	$7,700	$14,300
Italian (1430 - 1516)				
BELLINI, S.	*P*			$220
Italian (18th - 19th)				

D=Drawing, P=Painting, S=Sculpture, W=Watercolor

		Current Price Range		
		Low	Mean	High

BELLIS, Daisy M. American (1887 -)	*P*	$165	$371	$660
BELLIS, Hubert Belgian (1831 - 1902)	*P*			$19,800
BELLMER, Hans French (1902 -)	*D*			$3,960
	S			$2,640
	W			$7,150
BELLOTTI, Pietro Italian (1627 - 1700)	*P*			$34,100
BELLOTTI, Pietro (Circle) Italian (1627 - 1700)	*P*			$2,200
BELLOTTO, Bernardo Italian (1724 - 1780)	*P*			$1.870M
BELLOTTO, Bernardo (After) Italian (1724 - 1780)	*P*			$93,500
BELLOTTO, Bernardo (Studio) Italian (1724 - 1780)	*P*	$35,200	$89,467	$192,500
BELLOWS, Albert F. American (1829 - 1883)	*P*	$1,540	$19,003	$39,600
	W			$2,090
BELLOWS, George American (1882 - 1925)	*D*	$1,183	$46,328	$220,000
	P	$13,200	$158,125	$407,000
	S			$22,000
BELLOWS, George (Attrib.) American (1882 - 1925)	*P*			$385
BELLROCK, Watson (Et al.) American (20th -)	*W*			$275
BELLUCCI, Antonio Italian (1654 - 1726)	*P*			$60,500
BELNET, G. American (20th -)	*P*			$330
BELTRAN-MASSES, Federico Spanish (1885 -)	*P*			$7,975
BELVEDERE, Andrea (School) Italian (1642 - 1723)	*P*			$18,700

D=Drawing, P=Painting, S=Sculpture, W=Watercolor

		Current Price Range		
		Low	Mean	High
BEMBO, Giovanni F.	*P*			$63,800
Italian (16th -)				
BEMEL, Sebastian (Attrib.)	*W*			$1,870
German (1743 - 1796)				
BEMELMENS, Ludwig	*W*			$715
German (20th -)				
BEMESDERFER, J. K.	*P*			$303
American (20th -)				
BEMISH, R. Hills	*W*	$154	$207	$275
American (19th - 20th)				
BEMMEL, Pieter von	*P*			$4,400
German (1685 - 1754)				
BEN-ZION,	*P*			$468
American (20th -)				
BENDA, Wladyslaw T.	*D*	$660	$990	$1,320
American (1873 - 1948)	*W*			$660
BENDER, Bill	*P*			$1,320
American (1920 -)				
BENDINER, Alfred	*W*			$110
American (1899 -)				
BENDIXEN, Siegfried-D.	*W*			$1,980
German (1786 - 1864)				
BENDIXEN, Siegfried-D. (Attrib.)	*P*			$1,045
German (1786 - 1864)				
BENEDETTI, Andrea	*P*			$121,000
Italian (17th -)				
BENEDITO-VIVES, Manuel	*P*			$4,400
Spanish (1875 - 1963)				
BENEDUCCI,	*D*			$154
Italian (20th -)				
BENEDUCE, Antimo (Attrib.)	*W*			$100
American (1900 -)				
BENEKER, Gerrit A.	*D*	$330	$453	$575
American (1882 - 1934)	*P*	$550	$3,974	$7,920

D=Drawing, P=Painting, S=Sculpture, W=Watercolor

| | | Current Price Range | | |
		Low	Mean	High
BENGLIS, Lynda	*P*	$1,540	$13,068	$20,900
American (1941 -)	*S*	$5,225	$6,692	$8,800
BENGSTON, Billy A.	*S*			$1,100
American (20th -)				
BENHOLD,	*P*			$2,860
(20th -)				
BENLLIURE Y GIL, Jose	*P*	$55,000	$83,600	$165,000
Spanish (1855 - 1914)				
BENLLIURE Y GIL, Juan A.	*P*			$36,300
Spanish (1884 - 1901)				
BENN, Ben	*P*	$990	$1,964	$4,180
American (1884 - 1983)	*W*	$550	$1,320	$2,090
BENNER, Emmanuel M.	*P*			$29,700
French (1873 - 1965)				
BENNES, J.	*S*			$2,640
(19th -)				
BENNET, W.	*P*			$495
American (19th - 20th)				
BENNETT, Dorothy E.	*W*			$330
American (20th -)				
BENNETT, Frank M.	*P*	$1,320	$4,473	$7,150
British (1874 - 1953)				
BENNETT, Harry	*P*			$400
(1925 -)				
BENNETT, Ruth M.	*W*			$330
American (1899 - 1960)				
BENNETT, Thomas	*P*			$303
(?)				
BENNETT-BROWN, Mae	*P*			$770
American (20th -)				
BENNETTI, M.	*W*			$110
European (20th -)				
BENOIS, Alexandre	*D*			$1,430
Russian (1870 - 1960)	*W*	$1,100	$1,595	$1,870

D=Drawing, P=Painting, S=Sculpture, W=Watercolor

		Current Price Range		
		Low	Mean	High

BENSA, Alexander C. de (Attrib.)	P			$4,950
Austrian (1820 - 1902)				
BENSA, C.	W			$935
Italian (19th -)				
BENSCO, Charles J.	W			$413
American (1894 - 1960)				
BENSELL, George F.	P	$1,100	$1,503	$1,870
American (1837 - 1879)				
BENSO, Giulio	D	$1,320	$3,410	$5,500
Italian (17th -)				
BENSON, Ambrosius	P	$9,900	$13,200	$16,500
Flemish (? - 1550)				
BENSON, Ambrosius (Circle)	P	$22,000	$28,600	$35,200
Flemish (? - 1550)				
BENSON, Ambrosius (Follower)	P			$41,250
Flemish (? - 1550)				
BENSON, Eugene	P	$4,125	$6,142	$8,800
American (1839 - 1908)				
BENSON, Frank W.	D	$385	$4,382	$8,250
American (1862 - 1951)	P	$41,800	$171,508	$583,000
	W	$1,760	$13,994	$30,800
BENSON, M.	P			$248
American (20th -)				
BENSON, Nesbitte	P			$193
American (20th -)				
BENSON, Townley	P			$440
(19th - 20th)				
BENSON, Tressa E.	P	$1,650	$2,063	$2,475
American (1896 -)				
BENTALL,	S	$110	$130	$149
(20th -)				
BENTLEY, A.	P			$275
(?)				
BENTLEY, Claude	P			$825
American (20th -)				

D=Drawing, P=Painting, S=Sculpture, W=Watercolor

		Current Price Range		
		Low	Mean	High
BENTLEY, Jack	*P*			$440
American (20th -)				
BENTLEY, John W.	*P*	$4,400	$9,350	$14,300
American (1880 -)				
BENTLEY, Lester W.	*P*	$165	$715	$1,320
American (1908 -)				
BENTLEY, Rachel	*W*			$275
American (1894 -)				
BENTON, Harry S.	*P*			$143
American (1877 -)				
BENTON, Rita P.	*P*			$132
American (?)				
BENTON, Thomas Hart	*D*	$110	$1,623	$6,875
American (1889 - 1975)	*P*	$2,200	$144,153	$1.540M
	S			$9,680
	W	$1,320	$15,400	$57,200
BENUVENUTI, Eugenio	*W*	$193	$378	$550
Italian (19th - 20th)				
BENZONI, Giovanni M.	*S*			$330,000
Italian (1809 - 1873)				
BERAIN, Jean	*D*			$20,900
French (1640 - 1711)				
BERARD, Christian	*D*	$1,650	$4,675	$8,800
French (1902 - 1949)	*W*	$5,500	$7,288	$9,075
BERAUD, Jean	*P*	$19,800	$325,531	$2.860M
French (1849 - 1936)				
BERCHEM, Nicolaes	*D*			$3,520
Dutch (1620 - 1683)	*P*			$2,750
BERCHEM, Nicolaes (Circle)	*P*	$2,475	$4,538	$6,600
Dutch (1620 - 1683)				
BERCHEM, Nicolaes (Manner)	*P*	$1,100	$3,561	$5,225
Dutch (1620 - 1683)				
BERCHERE, Narcisse	*P*	$1,210	$2,457	$3,410
French (1819 - 1891)				

D=Drawing, P=Painting, S=Sculpture, W=Watercolor

		Current Price Range		
		Low	Mean	High

		Low	Mean	High
BERCHMANS, Emile Belgian (1867 -)	*D*			$2,420
BERCKHEYDE, Gerrit A. (Attrib.) Dutch (1638 - 1698)	*P*			$5,775
BERCKHEYDE, Gerrit A. (Circle) Dutch (1638 - 1698)	*D*			$7,150
BERCKMANS, Charles Belgian (19th -)	*P*			$1,650
BERCOT, Paul French (20th -)	*P*			$330
BEREA, Dimitri Rumanian (1908 - 1975)	*P*			$440
BERESFORD, Frank British (19th - 20th)	*P*			$550
BERG, Anna Swedish (1875 - 1950)	*P*			$1,980
BERG, Floyd American (20th -)	*P*			$110
BERG, Ralph American (20th -)	*S*	$1,200	$2,217	$3,850
BERG, Ro (20th -)	*P*			$6,050
BERG, Willem van den (?)	*D*	$165	$165	$165
BERGAMINI, Francesco Italian (1815 - 1883)	*P*	$5,390	$7,113	$8,800
BERGE, Edward American (1876 - 1924)	*S*	$825	$3,135	$5,720
BERGEN, C German (19th -)	*P*			$7,700
BERGEN, Dirck van Dutch (1645 - 1690)	*D*			$550
BERGEN, Dirck van (Attrib.) Dutch (1645 - 1690)	*P*			$660
BERGEN, Fritz (Attrib.) German (1857 -)	*P*			$110

D=Drawing, P=Painting, S=Sculpture, W=Watercolor

		Low	Mean	High
		\multicolumn{3}{c}{Current Price Range}		

		Low	Mean	High
BERGER, Ernst Austrian (1857 - 1919)	*P*			$11,000
BERGER, Nick American (20th -)	*W*	$550	$550	$550
BERGERON, Eugene French (19th -)	*P*			$2,090
BERGHAAST, Jan European (20th -)	*P*			$138
BERGHE, Charles A. van den Belgian (1798 - 1853)	*P*			$27,500
BERGHE, Christoffel van den (17th -)	*P*			$60,500
BERGLER, Joseph Austrian (1753 - 1829)	*P*			$5,500
BERGMAN, Anna (20th -)	*P*			$2,640
BERGMAN, R. P. Austrian (20th -)	*S*			$385
BERGMANN, Julius H. German (1861 - 1940)	*P*			$6,600
BERGNER, Yosl (Et al.) Israeli (20th -)	*P*			$1,210
BERGSTROM, Charles J. American (20th -)	*P*			$660
BERINGER, John E. American (?)	*P*			$150
BERINGUIER, Eugene French (1874 - 1949)	*P*			$11,000
BERJON, Antoine (Attrib.) French (1754 - 1843)	*P*			$7,700
BERKE, Ernest American (1921 -)	*S*			$3,300
BERKE, Hubert American (1908 - 1979)	*W*			$193
BERKELEY, Stanley French (1855 - 1909)	*P*			$82,500

D=Drawing, P=Painting, S=Sculpture, W=Watercolor

		Current Price Range		
		Low	Mean	High
BERKES, Antal	*P*	$330	$990	$1,650
Hungarian (1874 - 1938)				
BERKES, Antal (Attrib.)	*P*	$575	$813	$1,050
Hungarian (1874 - 1938)				
BERKMAN, Aaron	*W*			$385
American (1900 -)				
BERKOWITZ, Leon	*P*			$3,575
American (20th -)				
BERLANT, Tony	*P*			$7,700
(20th -)	*S*	$990	$7,458	$17,600
BERMAN, Cotelle R.	*P*			$248
American (20th -)				
BERMAN, Eugene	*D*	$440	$1,259	$4,400
Russian (1899 - 1972)	*P*	$2,090	$5,038	$10,450
	S			$1,870
	W	$770	$2,330	$7,700
BERMAN, Eugene (Manner)	*P*			$825
Russian (1899 - 1972)				
BERMAN, Leonid	*P*	$990	$3,163	$6,600
Russian (1898 -)				
BERMAN, Peter	*P*			$165
British (20th -)				
BERMAN, Saul	*P*			$7,150
American (19th - 20th)	*W*			$1,760
BERMAN, W. E.	*P*	$2,090	$2,200	$2,310
American (19th -)				
BERMAN, Wallace	*S*	$6,050	$6,325	$6,600
(20th -)				
BERMUDEZ, Cundo	*P*	$5,500	$10,670	$19,800
Cuban (1914 -)	*W*			$2,200
BERNABA, S	*P*			$220
(?)				

D=Drawing, P=Painting, S=Sculpture, W=Watercolor

		Current Price Range		
		Low	Mean	High

		Low	Mean	High
BERNADOTTE OF SWEDEN, E.	P			$33,000
Swedish (1865 - 1947)				
BERNARD, Auguste-Henri	P			$825
French (20th -)				
BERNARD, Emile	D	$303	$537	$770
French (1868 - 1941)	P	$3,080	$83,518	$286,000
BERNARD, Jean Joseph	D	$660	$1,210	$2,200
French (1740 -)				
BERNARD, Joseph	P			$6,820
French (1864 - 1933)				
BERNATH, Aurel	P			$935
Hungarian (1895 -)				
BERNATH, Sandor	W			$1,870
American (1892 -)				
BERNAY, B.	P			$165
(?)				
BERND, Lucile	P			$358
(?)				
BERNE-BELLECOUR, Etienne	D			$550
French (1838 - 1910)	P	$2,640	$11,830	$66,000
BERNEDE, Pierre E.	P			$3,575
French (1820 -)				
BERNEKER, Lewis F.	P			$275
American (? - 1876)	W			$110
BERNEKER, Louis	P	$550	$3,844	$24,200
American (1872 - 1937)				
BERNEKER, Maud	P			$1,045
American (1882 -)				
BERNI, Antonio	D			$3,300
Argentine (1905 - 1981)	P			$33,000
BERNIER, Geo.	P			$880
Belgian (1862 - 1918)				
BERNINGER, Edmund	P			$13,200
German (1843 -)				

D=Drawing, P=Painting, S=Sculpture, W=Watercolor

		Current Price Range		
		Low	Mean	High

		Low	Mean	High
BERNINGHAUS, Charles	P	$660	$688	$715
American (1905 -)				
BERNINGHAUS, Oscar E.	P	$1,430	$17,136	$38,500
American (1874 - 1952)				
BERNINI, Gian. (Follower)	D			$5,500
Italian (1598 - 1680)				
BERNSTEIN, Theresa	P	$550	$2,930	$7,150
American (1895 -)				
BERNT, Rudolf	W			$550
Austrian (1844 -)				
BERONNEAU, Andre	P			$743
French (20th -)				
BEROUD, Louis	P			$187,000
French (1852 - 1930)				
BERRESFORD, Virginia	W			$165
American (1904 -)				
BERRIDGE, John	P			$1,100
British (1740 - 1804)				
BERROCAL, Miguel	P	$880	$917	$990
Spanish (1933 -)	S	$308	$1,854	$12,100
BERRUGUETE, Alonso (Circle)	P			$3,300
Spanish (1486 - 1561)				
BERRY, Carroll T.	D			$154
American (1886 - 1978)	P			$275
BERRY, Nathanial	P	$770	$1,063	$1,210
American (1859 -)				
BERRY, Patrick V.	P	$385	$921	$1,485
American (1852 - 1922)				
BERSON, Adolph	P			$358
American (1880 - 1970)				
BERT, Paul	W			$248
(?)				
BERTAULD,	P			$1,980
(?)				

D=Drawing, P=Painting, S=Sculpture, W=Watercolor

		Current Price Range		
		Low	Mean	High

		Low	Mean	High
BERTAUX, Jacques	P			$49,500
French (18th - 19th)				
BERTE, Allard	P	$175	$184	$193
(?)				
BERTHELEMY, Jean-Simon	P			$181,500
French (1743 - 1811)				
BERTHELEMY, YOUNGER, Ant.	P			$12,100
French (1631 - 1669)				
BERTHELSEN, Johann	D			$1,045
American (1883 - 1969)	P	$358	$2,679	$7,975
BERTHOLD, Joachim	S			$1,980
(?)				
BERTHOT, Jake	D			$660
American (20th -)	P	$770	$3,608	$8,250
BERTIN, Alexandre	P			$3,850
French (19th -)				
BERTINI, L.	P			$2,200
Austrian (1843 - 1932)				
BERTINIZZI, G.	W			$132
Italian (20th -)				
BERTIOLI, Frank	P			$165
British (19th -)				
BERTOIA, Harry	P			$19,800
American (1915 - 1978)	S	$1,650	$12,311	$30,800
BERTOLD, C.	P			$440
Swiss (20th -)				
BERTOLINGRANDE, E.	P			$825
Italian (19th - 20th)				
BERTON, Louis	P			$18,700
French (19th -)				
BERTRAM, Abel	P	$1,980	$5,390	$8,800
French (1871 - 1954)				
BERTRAND, Mary	P			$550
(?)				

D=Drawing, P=Painting, S=Sculpture, W=Watercolor

		Current Price Range		
		Low	Mean	High

		Low	Mean	High
BERTRAND, Paulin A. French (1852 - 1940)	*P*	$7,150	$9,350	$11,000
BERTSHINGER, Marie E. Swiss (1807 - 1890)	*P*			$605
BERTZIK, A. (?)	*P*			$2,475
BERZANO, E. (?)	*P*			$100
BERZEVIZY, Julius American (1875 -)	*P*			$605
BESCHEY, Balthasar Flemish (1708 - 1776)	*P*	$2,200	$6,600	$11,000
BESCHEY, Balthasar (Style) Flemish (1708 - 1776)	*P*			$770
BESJI, G. (19th -)	*S*	$825	$1,082	$1,320
BESNARD, Albert French (1849 - 1934)	*D* *P*	$4,620	$6,710	$8,800 $19,800
BESS, Forrest American (1911 -)	*P*			$4,180
BESSE, Raymond French (1899 -)	*P*			$413
BESSER, Arne American (1935 -)	*P*			$1,980
BESSIRE, Dale American (1892 -)	*P*			$1,210
BESSON, Charles A. French (19th -)	*P*			$2,200
BESSONOF, Boris Russian (19th - 20th)	*P*	$6,600	$7,150	$7,700
BEST, Arthur W. American (1859 - 1935)	*P*	$633	$1,190	$2,090
BEST, David American (20th -)	*P*			$605
BEST, Hans German (19th - 20th)	*P*			$4,400

D=Drawing, P=Painting, S=Sculpture, W=Watercolor

| | | Current Price Range | | |
		Low	Mean	High
BEST, Harry C.	*P*	$523	$816	$1,320
American (1863 - 1936)				
BEST, Mary Ellen	*D*	$2,750	$8,250	$17,600
British (1809 - 1891)				
BESTSON, C. (Attrib.)	*P*			$495
(?)				
BETHERS, Ray	*P*			$605
American (1902 -)				
BETTINGER, Hoyland B.	*P*			$715
American (1890 - 1934)				
BETTINGER, Paul	*P*	$825	$853	$880
American (20th -)				
BETTS, Anna W.	*P*	$990	$2,087	$3,520
American (19th - 20th)				
BETTS, E. F.	*P*			$6,050
American (20th -)				
BETTS, Harold H.	*P*	$220	$733	$1,100
American (1881 - 1961)				
BETTS, Louis	*P*	$825	$6,456	$27,500
American (1873 - 1961)				
BETTS, Virginia B.	*P*	$275	$440	$605
American (20th -)				
BETZEVIZY, J.	*P*			$770
American (20th -)				
BEUL, Frans de	*P*			$2,475
Dutch (1849 - 1919)				
BEUL, Laurent de	*P*	$770	$2,457	$5,500
Belgian (1821 - 1872)				
BEURDELEY, Alfred E. L.	*S*			$1,870
(?)				
BEUYS, Joseph	*D*	$4,950	$7,150	$9,350
German (1921 -)	*P*	$1,925	$62,356	$121,000
	S	$66,000	$118,800	$242,000
BEVERLOO, Carneille G. V	*W*			$330
Belgian (1922 -)				

D=Drawing, P=Painting, S=Sculpture, W=Watercolor

		Current Price Range		
		Low	Mean	High
BEVORT, G.	P			$193
Dutch (1926 -)				
BEVORT, Jean	P	$413	$523	$660
Dutch (20th -)				
BEYER, Ed	P			$880
(1820 - 1865)				
BEYSCHLAG, Robert	P	$6,600	$8,067	$9,900
German (1838 - 1903)				
BEZOMBES, Roger	P	$880	$3,135	$5,775
(1913 -)				
BIALA, Janice	P			$715
American (20th -)				
BIANCHI, Isidoro	P			$99,000
Italian (1602 - 1690)				
BIANCHI, Mose	P			$44,000
Italian (1840 - 1904)				
BIANCHI, Pietro	P			$11,000
Italian (1694 - 1740)				
BIANCHI, Troller	P			$220
(?)				
BIANCHINI, C.	P	$1,540	$2,695	$3,850
Italian (19th -)				
BIANCHINI, E.	P	$440	$770	$1,100
Italian (19th -)				
BIANCHINI, V.	P	$550	$1,210	$2,420
Italian (19th -)				
BIARD, Francois A.	P			$165,000
French (1799 - 1882)				
BIBER-TALUGITZKI,	P			$1,045
German (19th -)				
BIBERSTEIN, Franz	P			$358
American (1850 - 1930)				
BIBERSTEIN, Franz (Attrib.)	P			$105
American (1850 - 1930)				
BIBIENA, Ferdinando (Circle)	D			$1,760
Italian (1657 - 1743)				

D=Drawing, P=Painting, S=Sculpture, W=Watercolor

		Current Price Range		
		Low	Mean	High
BIBIENA, Guiseppe G.	*D*	$1,650	$7,333	$18,700
Italian (1696 - 1756)				
BICKERSTAFF, George	*P*	$330	$520	$825
American (1897 - 1954)				
BICKERSTAFF, George (Attrib.)	*P*	$200	$225	$250
American (1897 - 1954)				
BICKFORD, Nelson N.	*S*			$440
American (1846 - 1943)				
BICKNELL, Albion H.	*P*	$220	$1,447	$4,400
American (1837 - 1915)				
BICKNELL, Evelyn M.	*P*	$275	$468	$660
American (1857 - 1936)	*W*	$193	$303	$413
BICKNELL, Frank A.	*P*	$880	$5,335	$24,200
American (1866 - 1943)				
BICKNELL, William H.W.	*D*			$330
American (20th -)				
BIDAULD, Jean J. X.	*P*			$8,800
French (1758 - 1846)				
BIDDLE, George	*D*			$132
American (1885 - 1973)	*P*	$770	$2,713	$7,700
	W			$193
BIDLO, Mike	*P*	$2,420	$7,111	$19,800
(20th -)				
BIDWELL, Mary W.	*P*			$2,530
American (19th -)				
BIE, Louis	*P*			$495
French (19th -)				
BIEDERMAN, James	*D*			$4,400
(20th -)				
BIEDERMANN-ARENDTS, Her.	*P*			$3,300
German (1855 -)				
BIEGAS, Boleslas	*S*	$4,400	$8,800	$13,200
Polish (1877 - 1954)				
BIEGEL, Peter	*P*			$7,700
British (1913 -)				

D=Drawing, P=Painting, S=Sculpture, W=Watercolor

| | | Current Price Range | | |
		Low	Mean	High
BIEHLE, August F.	*P*			$2,970
American (1885 - 1979)				
BIELEFELD, Otto	*P*			$220
American (20th -)				
BIENVETU, Gustave	*P*	$5,500	$8,250	$11,000
French (19th - 20th)				
BIERDMAN, James	*S*			$7,920
(20th -)				
BIERHALS, Otto	*D*			$352
(1879 -)	*P*			$330
BIERSTADT, Albert	*P*	$550	$153,795	$2.640M
American (1830 - 1902)	*W*	$3,080	$11,990	$20,900
BIERSTADT, Albert (After)	*P*			$880
American (1830 - 1902)				
BIERSTADT, Albert (Attrib.)	*P*			$2,200
American (1830 - 1902)				
BIERSTADT, Albert (Manner)	*P*			$3,190
American (1830 - 1902)				
BIESE, Karl	*P*			$440
German (1863 -)				
BIESEL, Charles	*P*			$550
(1865 - 1945)				
BIESEL, Fred	*P*			$880
American (1893 -)				
BIEVRE, Marie de	*P*			$52,250
Belgian (1865 -)				
BIGARI, Vittorio M.	*D*	$1,540	$4,033	$7,700
Italian (1692 - 1776)	*P*	$3,850	$18,425	$33,000
BIGAUD, Wilson	*P*			$990
Italian (1931 -)				
BIGELOW,	*P*			$198
(?)				
BIGELOW, Charles A.	*D*			$303

D=Drawing, P=Painting, S=Sculpture, W=Watercolor

		Current Price Range		
		Low	Mean	High

BIGELOW, Charles A.	*P*			$440
American (20th -)				
BIGELOW, Daniel F.	*P*	$110	$858	$1,705
American (1823 - 1910)				
BIGELOW, Mary	*P*			$248
(20th -)				
BIGG, William R.	*P*			$468
British (1755 - 1828)				
BIGG, William R. (Attrib.)	*P*			$8,250
British (1755 - 1828)				
BIGGI, Felice F. (Circle)	*P*			$4,675
Italian (17th -)				
BIGGS, Geoffrey	*W*			$138
American (1908 -)				
BIGGS, T.	*P*			$303
(?)				
BIGGS, Walter	*P*	$660	$4,840	$11,000
American (1886 - 1968)	*W*			$1,650
BIHAN, D. L.	*P*			$6,050
British (1850 -)				
BILCOQ, Marie M. A.	*P*			$12,100
French (1755 - 1838)				
BILIVERTI, Giovanni	*D*			$15,400
Italian (1576 - 1644)	*P*			$3,575
BILL, Max	*P*	$23,100	$30,800	$46,200
Swiss (1908 -)	*S*	$825	$16,372	$46,750
BILLET, Etienne	*P*			$9,350
French (1821 - 1888)				
BILLET, Leon	*P*			$1,100
French (19th -)				
BILLINGS, Hammat (Et al.)	*S*			$3,520
American (19th - 20th)				
BILLINGS, Hammatt	*D*			$715
American (1816 - 1874)				

D=Drawing, P=Painting, S=Sculpture, W=Watercolor

		Current Price Range		
		Low	Mean	High

BILLINGS, Henry J.	P			$1,320
American (1894 -)				
BILLOTTE, Leon J.	P			$1,760
French (1815 -)				
BILLOU, Paul L.	P			$440
French (1821 -)				
BILS, Raymond	P			$275
French (20th -)				
BILTIUS, Jacobus	P			$38,500
Dutch (17th -)				
BIMMERMANN, Ceasar	P	$4,950	$9,625	$14,300
German (19th -)				
BINCK, Georges	P			$880
European (19th -)				
BINDER, Alois	P	$605	$1,293	$1,980
German (19th -)				
BINDER, Erwin	S			$1,210
(?)				
BINDER, John	P	$330	$385	$440
American (20th -)				
BINET, Georges	P	$3,520	$5,500	$7,480
French (1865 - 1949)				
BINET, Victor J.	P			$4,950
French (1849 - 1924)				
BINGHAM, George C.	P	$990	$5,088	$11,000
American (1811 - 1879)				
BINGHAM, James R.	P			$715
(20th -)				
BINKS, John	P			$1,320
(?)				
BINKS, Reuben W.	W			$550
British (1934 -)				
BINOIT, Peter	P			$60,500
German (17th -)				
BINTKOWSKI, W.	P			$2,750
Russian (19th - 20th)				

D=Drawing, P=Painting, S=Sculpture, W=Watercolor

		Current Price Range		
		Low	Mean	High
BIODI, Nicola (Attrib.) Italian (19th -)	*P*			$2,420
BIONDETTI, A. Italian (19th -)	*W*			$248
BIONDO, Giovanni del Italian (15th -)	*P*			$181,500
BIORN, Emil American (1864 -)	*P*			$385
BIRCH, Craig I. American (20th -)	*P*			$600
BIRCH, Reginald American (1856 - 1943)	*D*	$138	$244	$350
BIRCH, Samuel J. L. British (1869 - 1955)	*P*	$3,850	$8,525	$13,200
BIRCH, Thomas American (1779 - 1851)	*P*	$1,155	$12,018	$39,600
BIRCH, Thomas (Attrib.) American (1779 - 1851)	*P*	$3,850	$3,850	$3,850
BIRCH, William R. (Attrib.) American (1755 - 1834)	*P*			$770
BIRCHALL, William M. British (19th - 20th)	*W*			$1,540
BIRDSALL, Amos American (1865 -)	*P*	$220	$330	$440
BIRDSALL, Bryon American (20th -)	*W*	$660	$1,326	$3,300
BIRDSEY, American (20th -)	*W*			$275
BIRK, C. American (20th -)	*P*			$880
BIRKS, E. British (19th -)	*P*			$770
BIRLEY, Oswald N.Zealand (1880 - 1979)	*P*			$5,500
BIRNEY, William V. American (1858 - 1909)	*P*	$715	$3,933	$7,150

D=Drawing, P=Painting, S=Sculpture, W=Watercolor

		Low	Mean	High
BIRO, Geza Hungarian (1919 -)	P	$193	$2,572	$4,950
BIROLLI, Renato Italian (1906 - 1959)	P	$1,045	$12,888	$34,100
BIRREN, Joseph P. American (1865 - 1933)	P	$550	$2,764	$6,600
BIRT, J. British (19th -)	P			$303
BIRTLES, Harry British (19th -)	P			$880
BISBEE, Ezra (19th -)	P			$880
BISBING, Henry S. American (1849 - 1933)	P			$440
BISCHOFF, Franz A. American (1864 - 1929)	P	$176	$7,005	$38,500
	W	$605	$1,082	$1,650
BISHOP, A. F. American (19th -)	P			$825
BISHOP, Brooke American (20th -)	P			$935
BISHOP, Isabel American (1902 -)	D	$825	$2,283	$3,740
	P			$3,300
BISHOP, Richard E. American (1887 - 1975)	P	$330	$2,178	$13,750
BISHOP, Richard E. (Attrib.) American (1887 - 1975)	P			$110
BISON, Giuseppe B. Italian (1762 - 1844)	D			$1,320
BISPHAM, Henry C. American (1841 - 1882)	P	$1,320	$9,057	$16,500
BISSCHOP, Abraham Dutch (1670 - 1730)	P			$126,500
BISSCHOP, Jan de Dutch (1628 - 1671)	D	$3,300	$4,400	$5,500

D=Drawing, P=Painting, S=Sculpture, W=Watercolor

| | | Current Price Range | | |
		Low	Mean	High
BISSELL, George Edwin	*S*	$1,430	$3,190	$4,950
American (1839 - 1920)				
BISSET, C.	*P*			$550
French (19th - 20th)				
BISSIER, Jules	*P*	$15,400	$22,413	$33,000
German (1893 - 1965)	*W*	$13,200	$19,360	$26,400
BISSON, Edouard	*P*	$1,980	$4,290	$6,600
French (1856 -)				
BISSON, Lucienne	*P*	$880	$1,137	$1,650
French (20th -)				
BISTTRAM, Emil	*D*	$358	$3,786	$8,800
American (1895 - 1976)	*P*	$4,620	$18,205	$52,800
	W	$2,200	$2,888	$3,575
BITKHALIM, N.	*P*			$440
Scandinavian (20th -)				
BITNEY, Bye	*P*	$4,900	$5,888	$6,875
American (20th -)				
BITTAR, Pierre	*P*			$7,700
French (?)				
BITTER, Ary	*S*			$1,870
French (1883 - 1960)				
BITTINGER, Charles	*P*	$468	$894	$1,320
American (1879 - 1970)				
BIU, Hing	*P*			$440
(?)				
BIVA, Henri	*P*	$6,050	$12,513	$22,000
French (1848 - 1928)				
BIXBEE, William J.	*P*	$220	$754	$2,090
American (1850 - 1921)	*W*	$248	$367	$468
BIZZELLI, Giovanni	*D*			$4,400
Italian (1556 - 1612)				
BJAMORN, Thomas	*W*			$440
American (?)				

D=Drawing, P=Painting, S=Sculpture, W=Watercolor

		Current Price Range	
		Low	Mean	High

		Low	Mean	High
BJORGE, Ken	S	$715	$933	$1,150
American (20th -)				
BJORGUM, N.	P			$220
European (20th -)				
BJORN, Emil	P			$143
American (?)				
BJULF, S. C.	P			$220
Danish (20th -)				
BJURSTROM, David	D	$495	$498	$500
American (20th -)				
BLAAS, Eugen de	P	$15,400	$97,680	$286,000
Austrian (1843 - 1932)				
BLAAS, Julius von	P			$2,750
Austrian (1845 - 1922)				
BLACHE, Christian V.	P	$1,100	$1,650	$2,200
Danish (1838 -)				
BLACK, Francois	S			$1,540
Polish (1881 -)				
BLACK, La Verne N.	P	$9,075	$12,788	$16,500
American (1887 - 1939)				
BLACK, Mae	P	$110	$152	$193
American (1932 -)				
BLACK, N.	W	$198	$198	$198
(?)				
BLACK, Olive	P	$825	$3,682	$11,000
American (1868 - 1948)				
BLACKBURN, Morris A.	D			$275
American (1902 - 1979)	P	$413	$633	$908
	W			$935
BLACKLOCK, Thomas B. (Attrib.)	P			$825
British (1863 - 1903)				
BLACKMAN, Walter	P	$1,210	$2,530	$3,850
American (1847 - 1928)				
BLACKMORE, Arthur E.	P			$1,430
American (1854 - 1921)				

D=Drawing, P=Painting, S=Sculpture, W=Watercolor

		Current Price Range		
		Low	Mean	High

BLACKTON, James S.	P			$6,325
American (1875 - 1941)				
BLAGDEN, Allen	P			$1,320
American (19th - 20th)				
BLAINE, Mahlon	D	$110	$200	$330
American (20th -)	W			$110
BLAINE, Nell	P			$2,860
American (1922 -)	W			$660
BLAIR, Mark	P			$2,420
(20th -)				
BLAIR, Robert N.	W			$220
American (1912 -)				
BLAIR-BRUCE, William	P			$4,125
Canadian (1859 - 1906)				
BLAIS, Jean C.	W			$17,600
(?)				
BLAKE, Buckeye	D			$330
American (20th -)	P			$600
BLAKE, George	W			$286
American (20th -)				
BLAKE, Leo B.	P	$622	$1,824	$3,850
American (1887 - 1976)				
BLAKE, Ralph A.	P			$2,200
American (1847 - 1919)				
BLAKE, Thomas C.	P			$165
American (20th -)				
BLAKELOCK, Ralph A.	D			$990
American (1847 - 1919)	P	$440	$4,543	$49,500
BLAKELOCK, Ralph A. (Attrib.)	P	$330	$1,173	$3,575
American (1847 - 1919)				
BLAKELOCK, Ralph A. (Manner)	P	$325	$795	$1,265
American (1847 - 1919)				
BLAKELY, Dudley	P			$880
American (1902 -)				

D=Drawing, P=Painting, S=Sculpture, W=Watercolor

		Current Price Range		
		Low	Mean	High

		Low	Mean	High
BLAMPIED, Edmund	*W*			$1,540
British (1886 - 1966)				
BLANCH, Arnold	*P*	$1,650	$1,953	$2,420
American (1896 - 1968)	*W*			$440
BLANCH, Lucille	*P*			$3,960
American (1895 -)				
BLANCHARD, Antoine	*P*	$248	$2,677	$10,450
French (20th -)				
BLANCHARD, Antoine (Attrib.)	*P*			$165
French (20th -)				
BLANCHARD, Antoine (Manner)	*P*			$154
French (20th -)				
BLANCHARD, Blanche	*W*			$1,650
American (19th - 20th)				
BLANCHARD, Emile	*P*			$220
American (?)				
BLANCHARD, Jacques	*P*			$7,700
French (1600 - 1638)				
BLANCHARD, Marie	*P*			$418,000
Spanish (1881 - 1932)				
BLANCHARD, Remy	*P*			$715
(20th -)				
BLANCHE, Jacques E.	*D*			$15,400
French (1861 - 1942)	*P*	$7,700	$41,014	$77,000
BLANCHET, Thomas	*P*			$13,200
French (1614 - 1689)				
BLANCO, Dionisio	*P*	$1,650	$3,369	$6,050
(20th -)				
BLANDFORD, Curtis	*P*			$330
American (19th -)				
BLANEY, Dwight	*P*			$1,650
American (1865 - 1944)	*W*			$825
BLANT & DAVID, Julien le & L.	*D*			$220
French (1851 - 1936)				

D=Drawing, P=Painting, S=Sculpture, W=Watercolor

		Current Price Range		
		Low	Mean	High
BLARENBERGE, Henri J. van	*W*			$9,900
French (1741 - 1826)				
BLASCO, V.	*P*			$193
European (20th -)				
BLASHFIELD, Edwin H.	*D*	$385	$1,815	$2,860
American (1848 - 1936)	*P*	$550	$7,443	$18,700
BLASS, Charlotte L.	*P*			$550
American (1908 -)	*W*			$200
BLASS, Rico	*P*			$248
American (20th -)				
BLATAS, Arbit	*P*	$495	$1,084	$1,760
American (1908 -)				
BLATHAM, Elizabeth	*P*			$110
American (?)				
BLATTIER, B.	*P*			$1,210
(?)				
BLAUVELT, Charles F.	*P*	$1,870	$2,127	$2,310
American (1824 - 1900)				
BLAUVELT, Charles F. (Attrib.)	*P*			$935
American (1824 - 1900)				
BLAVIER, E.	*S*	$523	$578	$660
French (19th -)				
BLAYLOCK, Ted	*P*			$800
American (20th -)				
BLAZEBY, J.	*P*			$3,300
British (19th -)				
BLECKNER, Ross	*P*	$23,100	$56,306	$165,000
American (20th -)	*W*	$5,500	$11,000	$14,300
BLEEKER, Uwe	*P*			$770
Dutch (20th -)				
BLEKER, Dirck	*P*			$34,100
Dutch (1622 - 1672)				
BLENNER, Carle J.	*P*	$193	$4,471	$16,500
American (1864 - 1952)				

D=Drawing, P=Painting, S=Sculpture, W=Watercolor

		Current Price Range		
		Low	Mean	High

		Low	Mean	High
BLES, Herri M. de	*P*	$99,000	$203,500	$308,000
Flemish (1480 - 1550)				
BLEULER, Johann L.	*W*	$1,870	$3,108	$4,950
Swiss (1792 - 1850)				
BLEY, Willebrordus	*P*			$385
Dutch (20th -)				
BLIEK, Pieter	*P*			$275
Dutch (1812 - 1853)				
BLINKS, Thomas	*P*	$7,150	$25,644	$60,500
British (1860 - 1912)				
BLISS, Robert	*P*	$220	$408	$660
American (1925 -)				
BLOCH, Albert	*P*			$27,500
American (1882 - 1951)				
BLOCH, Julius T.	*D*			$330
American (1888 - 1966)	*P*	$770	$1,050	$1,320
	W			$110
BLOCH, Maurice E.	*W*	$385	$495	$605
American (1916 - 1989)				
BLODGETT, Walton	*W*	$132	$220	$358
American (1908 - 1964)				
BLOEMAERT, Abraham	*D*	$8,800	$15,033	$18,700
Dutch (1564 - 1651)				
BLOEMAERT, Abraham (Circle)	*P*			$19,800
Dutch (1564 - 1651)				
BLOEMAERT, Adriaen	*P*			$7,150
Dutch (1609 - 1666)				
BLOEMAERT, Pseudo H.	*P*			$44,000
Dutch (17th -)				
BLOEMEN, Jan F. van	*P*	$3,520	$12,687	$44,000
Flemish (1662 - 1749)				
BLOEMEN, Jan F. van (Circle)	*P*			$3,300
Flemish (1662 - 1749)				
BLOEMEN, Pieter van	*P*	$4,950	$8,525	$12,100
Flemish (1657 - 1720)				

D=Drawing, P=Painting, S=Sculpture, W=Watercolor

		Current Price Range		
		Low	Mean	High

BLOEMEN, Pieter van (Circle) Flemish (1657 - 1720)	*P*			$2,200
BLOEMERS, Arnoldus Dutch (1786 - 1844)	*P*			$35,750
BLOMBERG, W. American (19th -)	*P*			$440
BLOMMERS, Bernardus J. Dutch (1845 - 1914)	*P*	$2,530	$11,257	$28,600
BLOMMERS, Bernardus J. (After) Dutch (1845 - 1914)	*P*			$468
BLOND, Marcel (?)	*P*	$150	$163	$175
BLONDEL, George F. (1730 - 1791)	*D*			$3,960
BLONDEL, Merry J. French (1781 - 1853)	*P*	$1,980	$20,790	$39,600
BLONDIN, Charles French (20th -)	*P*	$110	$271	$550
BLOODGOOD, Morris American (1845 - 1920)	*P*	$193	$1,439	$3,410
BLOOM, Hyman American (1913 -)	*D*	$550	$605	$660
	P	$1,320	$5,060	$8,800
	W			$1,760
BLOOMER, Hiram R. American (1845 - 1911)	*P*			$385
	W			$248
BLOOMFIELD, Harry British (19th -)	*P*			$2,420
BLOSER, Florence P. American (1889 - 1935)	*P*			$715
BLOSSOM, David (1927 -)	*W*			$175
BLOWER, David H. American (1901 -)	*W*	$275	$743	$1,210
BLUEMNER, Oscar F.	*D*	$110	$625	$3,850

D=Drawing, P=Painting, S=Sculpture, W=Watercolor

		Current Price Range	
	Low	Mean	High

		Low	Mean	High
BLUEMNER, Oscar F.	P			$286,000
American (1867 - 1938)	W	$605	$1,962	$3,850
BLUHM, Norman	P	$1,650	$13,805	$46,200
American (1920 -)				
BLUM, Charles	S			$880
American (19th -)				
BLUM, Edith	P			$3,300
American (20th -)				
BLUM, Robert F.	D	$7,150	$25,575	$44,000
American (1857 - 1903)	P	$26,400	$32,450	$38,500
	W	$11,000	$27,500	$44,000
BLUMBERG, O. Muller	P			$110
American (20th -)				
BLUME, Peter	D	$330	$2,090	$3,080
American (1906 -)				
BLUMENSCHEIN, Ernest	D			$550
American (1874 - 1960)	P	$9,900	$37,217	$79,750
	W	$660	$1,650	$2,640
BLYTH, R. Henderson	P			$1,650
British (1919 -)				
BLYTHE, David G.	P	$15,000	$38,530	$60,500
American (1815 - 1865)				
BOBBETT, C. A.	W			$1,870
(19th -)				
BOBIER, Michael	W			$121
American (20th -)				
BOBLEDIJK, Felicien	P			$121
Dutch (1876 - 1964)				
BOCCHI, Faustino (Attrib.)	P			$5,280
Italian (1659 - 1742)				
BOCCHI, Faustino (Circle)	P			$30,800
Italian (1659 - 1742)				
BOCCHI, Faustino (Follower)	D			$2,530
Italian (1659 - 1742)				

D=Drawing, P=Painting, S=Sculpture, W=Watercolor

		Current Price Range		
		Low	Mean	High
BOCCIONI, Umberto	*P*			$60,500
Italian (1882 - 1916)	*S*			$605,000
BOCHMAN, C. L.	*P*			$440
American (19th - 20th)				
BOCHNER, Mel	*D*			$8,250
American (1940 -)	*W*	$3,520	$3,850	$4,180
BOCK, Frederick W.	*P*	$1,100	$1,760	$2,420
American (1876 -)				
BOCK, Richard W.	*S*			$7,150
American (19th -)				
BOCK, Theophile de	*P*	$1,980	$3,117	$5,280
Dutch (1851 - 1904)				
BOCKLIN, Arnold	*P*			$1,650
Swiss (1827 - 1901)				
BODDINGTON, Edwin H.	*P*	$385	$633	$880
British (19th -)				
BODDINGTON, Henry J.	*P*	$6,600	$7,883	$9,350
British (1811 - 1865)				
BODDINGTON, J.	*P*			$525
(?)				
BODEMANN, Willem	*P*	$440	$2,420	$4,400
Dutch (1806 - 1880)				
BODENMULLER, Alphons	*P*	$1,980	$3,410	$4,840
German (1847 - 1886)				
BODILY, Sheryl L.	*P*			$350
American (20th -)				
BODIN, A.	*P*			$1,870
(19th -)				
BODLEY, Josselin R.	*P*	$121	$418	$715
British (1893 -)				
BODNAR, Bertalan	*P*			$110
American (20th -)				
BODWELL, A. V.	*P*	$110	$193	$275
American (20th -)				

D=Drawing, P=Painting, S=Sculpture, W=Watercolor

		Current Price Range	
	Low	Mean	High

		Low	Mean	High
BOE, J. Scandinavian (20th -)	*P*			$440
BOECKHORST, Jan van German (1605 - 1668)	*P*			$4,400
BOEH, H. British (19th -)	*P*			$935
BOEHNER, Alexander European (20th -)	*P*			$825
BOEL, Pieter (Circle) Flemish (1622 - 1674)	*P*			$7,150
BOEMM, Ritta Hungarian (1868 -)	*W*			$413
BOER, Dutch (19th -)	*P*			$605
BOER, John P. D. American (19th - 20th)	*P*	$330	$358	$385
BOERS, Marianne American (1945 -)	*D* *W*			$715 $2,750
BOESE, Henry American (?)	*P*	$1,870	$2,695	$3,520
BOESEN, Johannes Danish (1847 - 1916)	*P*			$880
BOETTI, Aligherio Italian (1940 -)	*P*	$3,520	$6,160	$8,800
BOEZIEK, Bern European (20th -)	*P*			$193
BOFILL, Antoine Spanish (19th - 20th)	*S*			$1,430
BOGART, George H. American (1864 - 1944)	*P*	$908	$1,554	$2,200
BOGDANI, Jakob Hungarian (1660 - 1724)	*P*	$28,600	$43,450	$57,750
BOGDANOV-BJELSKY, Nikolai Russian (1868 - 1945)	*P*			$8,800
BOGER, (?)	*S*			$880

D=Drawing, P=Painting, S=Sculpture, W=Watercolor

| | | Current Price Range | | |
		Low	Mean	High
BOGERT, George H.	*P*	$358	$999	$1,815
American (1864 - 1944)				
BOGERT, George H. (Attrib.)	*P*			$150
American (1864 - 1944)				
BOGGIO, Emilio	*P*	$8,800	$18,700	$28,600
Venezuelan (1857 - 1920)				
BOGGS, Frank M.	*P*	$1,100	$15,033	$49,500
American (1855 - 1926)	*W*	$688	$2,070	$4,400
BOGGS, William B.	*W*			$440
American (1809 - 1875)				
BOGH, Carl H.	*D*			$3,300
Danish (1827 - 1893)	*P*			$13,200
BOGHOSIAN, Varujan	*P*	$3,520	$10,010	$16,500
American (1926 -)				
BOGMAN, Hermanus C.	*P*			$605
Dutch (1861 - 1921)				
BOHANNAH, Charles	*P*	$138	$183	$264
American (1910 - 1981)				
BOHDE, George W.	*P*			$1,100
American (?)				
BOHLAND, Gustave	*S*			$1,320
Austrian (1897 - 1959)				
BOHLER, Joe	*W*	$850	$1,898	$2,860
American (20th -)				
BOHM, C. Curry	*P*	$660	$935	$1,210
American (1894 -)				
BOHM, Max B.	*P*	$330	$440	$550
American (1868 - 1923)				
BOHM, Pal	*P*			$2,860
Hungarian (1839 - 1905)				
BOHROD, Aaron	*D*	$400	$558	$715
American (1907 -)	*P*	$1,100	$3,314	$7,700
	W	$605	$2,035	$6,600

D=Drawing, P=Painting, S=Sculpture, W=Watercolor

		Current Price Range		
		Low	Mean	High

		Low	Mean	High
BOHROD, Aaron (Attrib.)	P	$1,900	$1,960	$2,020
American (1907 -)				
BOICHARD, Jean A. H. (Attrib.)	P			$3,080
French (1817 -)				
BOILAUGES, Fernand	P	$660	$798	$935
(?)				
BOILLEAU, Philip	P			$1,375
American (1864 - 1917)				
BOILLY, Jules	D			$880
French (1796 - 1874)				
BOILLY, Jules (Attrib.)	D			$1,100
French (1796 - 1874)				
BOILLY, Louis L.	P	$7,150	$15,950	$33,000
French (1761 - 1845)				
BOILLY, Louis L. (Attrib.)	P			$3,300
French (1761 - 1845)				
BOILLY, Louis L. (Circle)	P			$30,800
French (1761 - 1845)				
BOISROND, Francois	P	$1,100	$1,705	$2,310
French (1959 -)				
BOISSIER, Gaston M. E.	P			$35,200
French (19th - 20th)				
BOIT, Edward D.	P			$6,600
American (1840 - 1916)	W	$495	$578	$660
BOITARD, Francois	D			$990
French (1670 - 1715)				
BOIZARD, C. V.	P	$1,650	$1,705	$1,760
French (?)				
BOL, Ferdinand	D			$60,500
Dutch (1616 - 1680)	P	$9,350	$38,913	$99,000
BOL, Ferdinand (Attrib.)	P			$5,500
Dutch (1616 - 1680)				
BOL, Ferdinand (Manner)	P	$2,750	$17,325	$31,900
Dutch (1616 - 1680)				

D=Drawing, P=Painting, S=Sculpture, W=Watercolor

		Current Price Range	
	Low	Mean	High

		Low	Mean	High
BOL, Ferdinand (School)	*P*			$4,180
Dutch (1616 - 1680)				
BOL, Hans	*P*	$4,400	$29,700	$55,000
Dutch (1534 - 1593)				
BOLAND, Charles	*P*			$18,700
European (19th -)				
BOLDINI, Giovanni	*D*	$165,000	$308,000	$451,000
Italian (1841 - 1931)	*P*	$5,500	$389,889	$852,500
	W	$57,750	$86,625	$115,500
BOLDINI, Giovanni (Attrib.)	*W*			$350
Italian (1841 - 1931)				
BOLE, Jeanne	*P*			$17,600
French (19th -)				
BOLINGER, Franz J.	*P*	$303	$386	$468
American (20th -)				
BOLINGER, Truman	*S*	$385	$1,018	$1,650
American (1944 -)				
BOLLES, Ida R.	*P*			$605
American (? - 1951)				
BOLLING, Leslie G.	*S*			$4,675
American (1898 -)				
BOLMER, M. De Forest	*P*			$880
American (1854 - 1910)				
BOLOGNA, Giovanni (After)	*S*	$440	$880	$1,320
Italian (1529 - 1608)				
BOLOGNESE SCHOOL 16C,	*P*	$2,420	$6,857	$9,350
Italian (16th -)				
BOLOGNESE SCHOOL 17C,	*D*	$1,430	$15,510	$46,750
Italian (17th -)	*P*	$1,540	$5,657	$11,000
	W			$10,450
BOLOGNESE SCHOOL 18C,	*D*	$3,300	$7,700	$12,100
Italian (18th -)	*P*	$1,320	$5,239	$11,000
BOLOTOWSKY, Ilya	*P*	$4,400	$10,218	$19,800
Russian (1907 -)				

D=Drawing, P=Painting, S=Sculpture, W=Watercolor

		Current Price Range		
		Low	Mean	High
BOLTANSKI, Christian	*P*			$22,000
French (1944 -)				
BOLTRAFFIO, Giovanni A.	*P*			$121,000
Italian (1467 - 1516)				
BOMBLED,	*P*			$385
(?)				
BOMBOIS, Camille	*P*	$3,520	$22,342	$121,000
French (1883 -)				
BOMMEL, Elias P. van	*P*	$14,300	$29,150	$44,000
Dutch (1819 - 1890)				
BOMPARD, Maurice	*P*	$2,200	$2,310	$2,420
French (1857 - 1936)				
BOMPIANI, Augusto	*W*			$132
Italian (1852 - 1930)				
BOMPIANI, Roberto	*P*	$1,100	$3,300	$5,500
Italian (1821 - 1908)				
BONAMY, Philippe	*P*			$990
French (20th -)				
BONAR, James K.	*P*			$3,850
American (1864 -)				
BONAVIA, Carlo	*P*	$11,000	$93,500	$176,000
Italian (18th -)				
BONCART, Gaston H.	*P*			$358
French (20th -)				
BOND, Douglas	*D*			$550
(20th -)				
BOND, James	*P*			$875
British (19th - 20th)				
BONDELL, C.	*P*			$660
(?)				
BONE, Muirhead	*D*	$385	$440	$495
British (1876 - 1953)	*W*			$715
BONECHI, Matteo	*P*			$2,750
Italian (17th -)				
BONEVARDI, Marcelo	*P*	$5,500	$14,392	$24,200

D=Drawing, P=Painting, S=Sculpture, W=Watercolor

		Current Price Range		
		Low	Mean	High

		Low	Mean	High
BONEVARDI, Marcelo	S	$8,800	$15,538	$22,000
Argentine (1929 -)				
BONFIELD, George	P			$605
American (1802 - 1898)				
BONFIELD, George (Attrib.)	P			$220
American (1802 - 1898)				
BONFIELD, William van de V.	P			$1,430
American (19th -)				
BONFILS, Gaston	P			$605
French (19th -)				
BONFORT, Vernet	P	$193	$424	$880
French (1934 -)				
BONGART, Sergei	P			$1,100
American (20th -)				
BONHAM, Horace	P			$28,600
American (1835 - 1892)				
BONHEUR, Isidore J.	S	$715	$10,037	$38,500
French (1827 - 1901)				
BONHEUR, Isidore J. (After)	P	$193	$647	$1,100
French (1827 - 1901)	S	$248	$1,801	$2,860
BONHEUR, Juliette Peyrol	P			$2,200
French (1830 - 1891)				
BONHEUR, Rosa	P	$3,520	$15,437	$63,250
French (1822 - 1899)	S	$880	$1,953	$2,750
	W			$231,000
BONHEUR, Rosa (After)	P			$1,320
French (1822 - 1899)				
BONHEUR, Rosa (School)	P			$440
French (1822 - 1899)				
BONHOMME, Leon	W			$1,870
(20th -)				
BONINGTON, Richard P.	W	$798	$3,149	$5,500
British (1801 - 1828)				
BONINGTON, Richard P. (Attrib.)	P	$715	$1,595	$2,475
British (1801 - 1828)				

D=Drawing, P=Painting, S=Sculpture, W=Watercolor

		Current Price Range		
		Low	Mean	High

		Low	Mean	High
BONINGTON, Richard P. (Manner)	P			$550
British (1801 - 1828)				
BONINGTON, Richard P. (Style)	P			$1,650
British (1801 - 1828)				
BONIROTE, Pierre	P			$6,600
French (1811 - 1891)				
BONITO, Giuseppe	P	$6,600	$135,667	$352,000
Italian (1705 - 1789)				
BONN, J. W.	P			$358
Dutch (19th -)				
BONNAR, James K.	P	$330	$1,221	$2,860
American (1885 - 1961)	W	$1,045	$1,183	$1,320
BONNARD, Pierre	D	$605	$15,204	$99,000
French (1867 - 1947)	P	$52,250	$946,535	$5.500M
	S	$9,900	$10,450	$11,000
	W	$4,675	$22,596	$33,000
BONNAT, Leon J. F.	P	$8,800	$13,200	$17,600
French (1834 - 1922)				
BONNEMAISON, Jules de	P			$8,250
French (1809 -)				
BONNY, J.	P			$330
(19th -)				
BONO, Primitif	P			$1,320
Italian (19th -)				
BONOMICI, Lionel	P			$935
Italian (20th -)				
BONONE, Carlo (Attrib.)	P			$17,600
Italian (1569 - 1632)				
BONTECOU, Lee	D			$1,760
American (1931 -)	P			$1,650
	S	$1,045	$15,015	$22,000
BONVICINO, Alessandro	P			$60,500
Italian (1498 - 1554)				

D=Drawing, P=Painting, S=Sculpture, W=Watercolor

		Current Price Range		
		Low	Mean	High
BONVIN, Francois	*P*			$9,625
French (1817 - 1887)				
BOOG, Carle M.	*P*	$220	$4,785	$9,350
American (1877 - 1967)				
BOOGAARD, Frank	*P*			$4,620
American (?)				
BOOGAARD, Willem J.	*P*	$1,430	$6,976	$15,400
Dutch (1842 - 1887)				
BOOK, Harry M.	*P*			$1,200
American (1879 - 1953)				
BOOM, Karel	*P*			$1,980
Dutch (1858 -)				
BOONEN, Arnold	*P*			$1,650
Dutch (1669 - 1729)				
BOOTH, Cameron	*P*			$2,250
American (1892 -)				
BOOTH, Franklin	*D*			$715
American (1874 - 1948)	*P*			$330
	W	$248	$3,874	$7,500
BOOTH, George	*D*			$413
American (1926 -)				
BORACK, Stan	*P*	$275	$550	$935
American (1927 -)	*W*			$385
BORCHARDT, Hans	*P*			$330
German (1865 -)				
BORCHERS, Dean	*S*			$275
American (20th -)				
BORDIGNON, Noe	*P*	$16,500	$18,150	$19,800
Italian (1841 - 1920)				
BORDONE, Paris (After)	*P*			$1,870
Italian (1500 - 1571)				
BOREIN, Edward	*D*	$250	$2,143	$6,050
American (1873 - 1945)	*W*	$2,750	$15,159	$41,800

D=Drawing, P=Painting, S=Sculpture, W=Watercolor

		Current Price Range		
		Low	Mean	High

		Low	Mean	High
BOREIN, Edward (Manner)	*W*			$165
American (1873 - 1945)				
BOREN, James	*D*			$1,320
American (1921 -)	*P*			$4,950
	W	$1,045	$3,483	$7,370
BORES, Francisco	*D*	$1,045	$1,403	$1,760
Spanish (1898 - 1972)	*P*	$2,420	$57,970	$132,000
BORG, Carl O.	*D*			$1,980
American (1879 - 1947)	*P*	$550	$7,975	$41,250
	W	$578	$3,215	$13,200
BORGES, Jacobo	*P*	$18,700	$36,850	$66,000
Venezuelan (1931 -)				
BORGLUM, Elizabeth J.	*P*			$660
American (1848 - 1922)				
BORGLUM, John G. de la M.	*S*	$2,200	$17,050	$38,500
American (1871 - 1941)				
BORGLUM, Solon	*S*	$6,600	$34,375	$110,000
American (1868 - 1922)				
BORIE, Adolphe	*P*	$1,100	$2,200	$3,300
American (1877 - 1934)				
BORIONE, Bernard L.	*P*	$1,210	$1,650	$1,980
French (1865 -)	*W*			$3,575
BORISSOVA, Aimee L.	*P*			$1,100
French (19th - 20th)				
BORKOWSKI, Jozef	*P*			$220
Polish (20th -)				
BORMAN, Johannes	*P*			$40,700
Dutch (17th -)				
BORMEL, Eugene	*S*			$2,310
German (1858 -)				
BORNARTH, Mary S.	*P*			$176
American (?)				

D=Drawing, P=Painting, S=Sculpture, W=Watercolor

		Current Price Range		
		Low	Mean	High
BOROFSKY, Jonathan	*D*			$6,050
American (1942 -)	*P*	$220	$19,938	$46,750
	S			$18,700
BORONDA, Lester	*P*	$523	$1,073	$1,650
American (1886 - 1951)				
BOROTHA,	*P*			$248
American (20th -)				
BORRANI, Giovanni	*P*			$1.650M
Italian (1842 - 1931)				
BORRANI, Odoardo	*P*	$52,800	$103,400	$154,000
Italian (1834 - 1905)				
BORRIS, Albert	*P*			$358
American (19th -)				
BORROMINI, Francesco	*D*			$88,000
Italian (1599 - 1667)				
BORROW, J. C.	*P*			$330
American (19th - 20th)				
BORSELEN, Jan W. van	*P*			$2,090
Dutch (1825 - 1892)				
BORSTEIN, Elena	*P*			$8,250
(20th -)				
BORTNYIK, Sandor	*W*			$17,600
(20th -)				
BORTOLUZZI, Camillo	*P*	$2,200	$2,475	$2,750
Italian (1868 - 1933)				
BORTSOME, Fillippo	*W*			$770
European (19th -)				
BOS, George van den	*P*	$2,475	$3,506	$4,950
Belgian (1853 - 1911)				
BOSA, Louis	*P*	$440	$1,144	$2,310
American (1905 - 1981)				
BOSBOOM, Johannes	*D*			$1,540
Dutch (1817 - 1891)				
BOSCARATTI, Felice (Attrib.)	*P*			$8,800
Italian (1721 - 1807)				

D=Drawing, P=Painting, S=Sculpture, W=Watercolor

		Current Price Range		
		Low	Mean	High

		Low	Mean	High
BOSCOLI, Andrea Italian (? - 1606)	*D*	$1,980	$9,240	$16,500
BOSCOLI, Andrea (Attrib.) Italian (? - 1606)	*D*			$605
BOSCOLI, Andrea (Circle) Italian (? - 1606)	*D*			$550
BOSE, Norma American (1898 - 1949)	*W*			$110
BOSELLI, Felice Italian (1650 - 1732)	*P*			$24,200
BOSELLI, Felice (Circle) Italian (1650 - 1732)	*P*			$8,800
BOSKERCK, Robert W. van American (1855 - 1932)	*P*	$990	$2,554	$5,500
BOSLEY, Frederick A. American (1881 - 1941)	*P*			$2,310
BOSMAN, C. Dutch (19th - 20th)	*P*			$385
BOSMAN, Richard American (1944 -)	*P*	$4,950	$6,875	$8,800
BOSS, Homer American (1820 - 1916)	*P*			$440
BOSSCHAERT, Jean B. Flemish (1667 - 1746)	*P*			$42,900
BOSSCHAERT, Jean B. (Circle) Flemish (1667 - 1746)	*P*			$9,350
BOSSCHE, Balthasar van den Flemish (1681 - 1715)	*P*	$11,550	$13,017	$15,400
BOSSE, Abraham French (1602 - 1676)	*D*			$1,650
BOSSE, Meta French (1870 -)	*P*			$468
BOSSHART, Ernest Swiss (1879 - 1951)	*P*			$330
BOSSUET, Francois A. Belgian (1800 - 1889)	*P*	$8,250	$15,675	$23,100

D=Drawing, P=Painting, S=Sculpture, W=Watercolor

		Current Price Range		
		Low	Mean	High
BOSTON, Frederick J.	*P*	$193	$1,359	$4,400
American (1855 - 1932)				
BOSTON, Frederick J. & Joseph H.	*P*			$1,320
American (19th - 20th)				
BOSTON, Joseph H.	*P*	$330	$9,664	$45,100
American (1901 - 1954)				
BOSTON SCHOOL,	*P*			$468
American (?)				
BOSWELL, Jessie	*P*			$220
(?)				
BOTELLO, Angel	*P*	$2,090	$13,490	$31,900
Spanish (1913 - 1986)	*S*			$1,320
BOTERO, Fernando	*D*	$5,000	$47,119	$231,000
Colombian (1932 -)	*P*	$8,250	$186,742	$715,000
	S	$19,800	$148,800	$462,000
	W	$3,520	$40,187	$88,000
BOTH, Andries Dirksz.	*D*	$1,870	$9,423	$14,300
Dutch (1612 - 1650)				
BOTH, Jan	*P*			$88,000
Dutch (1615 - 1652)				
BOTH, Jan (Attrib.)	*D*			$7,150
Dutch (1615 - 1652)				
BOTH, Jan (School)	*P*			$4,180
Dutch (1615 - 1652)				
BOTKE, Jessie A.	*P*	$880	$10,450	$27,500
American (1883 - 1971)	*W*	$495	$880	$1,100
BOTKIN, Henry A.	*P*	$495	$1,348	$2,200
American (1896 -)				
BOTT, E. F.	*P*			$1,210
American (19th -)				
BOTTICELLI, Sandro (Circle)	*P*			$82,500
Italian (1444 - 1510)				
BOTTICELLI, Sandro (School)	*P*			$66,000
Italian (1444 - 1510)				

D=Drawing, P=Painting, S=Sculpture, W=Watercolor

		Current Price Range		
		Low	Mean	High

		Low	Mean	High
BOTTICELLI, Sandro (Studio)	*P*			$55,000
Italian (1444 - 1510)				
BOTTICINI, Francesco	*P*			$35,750
Italian (1446 - 1497)				
BOTTINELLI, Antonio	*S*			$2,200
Italian (1827 - 1898)				
BOTTO, Otto	*P*			$440
American (1903 -)				
BOTTON, Jean de	*D*			$715
French (1898 - 1978)	*P*	$220	$657	$1,100
BOTTOS, Peter D.	*P*			$138
American (1935 -)				
BOUAT, H.	*P*			$11,000
(?)				
BOUCHARD, Marie C.	*P*			$385
(?)				
BOUCHARDON, Edma (Attrib.)	*D*	$660	$3,080	$5,500
French (1698 - 1762)				
BOUCHE, Louis	*P*	$150	$543	$935
American (1896 - 1969)				
BOUCHE, Louis-Alexandre	*P*			$3,300
French (1838 - 1911)				
BOUCHENE, Dimitri	*D*	$220	$490	$715
(20th -)	*P*	$220	$605	$1,540
	W	$198	$621	$3,080
BOUCHER, Alfred	*P*	$165	$6,683	$13,200
French (1865 - 1934)	*S*	$3,850	$6,325	$8,800
BOUCHER, Francois	*D*	$2,090	$52,239	$159,500
French (1703 - 1770)	*P*	$11,000	$289,667	$726,000
BOUCHER, Francois & Studio	*P*	$77,000	$207,167	$385,000
French (1703 - 1770)				
BOUCHER, Francois (After)	*P*	$275	$2,152	$6,050
French (1703 - 1770)				

D=Drawing, P=Painting, S=Sculpture, W=Watercolor

		Current Price Range		
		Low	Mean	High

		Low	Mean	High
BOUCHER, Francois (Attrib.)	*D*			$2,750
French (1703 - 1770)				
BOUCHER, Francois (Circle)	*D*	$605	$12,953	$25,300
French (1703 - 1770)	*P*	$2,200	$6,600	$11,000
BOUCHER, Francois (Follower)	*D*			$6,325
French (1703 - 1770)				
BOUCHER, Francois (Manner)	*D*			$220
French (1703 - 1770)	*P*	$468	$5,399	$10,450
BOUCHER, Francois (School)	*P*	$3,300	$4,033	$4,400
French (1703 - 1770)				
BOUCHER, Francois (Studio)	*P*			$22,000
French (1703 - 1770)				
BOUCHER, Francois (Style)	*P*	$1,650	$11,275	$20,900
French (1703 - 1770)				
BOUCHOR, Joseph F.	*P*			$2,090
French (1853 - 1937)				
BOUCKHORST, Jan van	*D*			$16,500
Dutch (1588 - 1631)				
BOUCLE, Pierre	*P*			$60,500
Flemish (1610 - 1673)				
BOUDEWYNS, Adriaen F. (Attrib.)	*P*	$2,200	$2,585	$2,970
Belgian (1644 - 1711)				
BOUDEWYNS, Adriaen F. (Circle)	*P*			$9,350
Belgian (1644 - 1711)				
BOUDEWYNS, Adriaen F. (Et al)	*P*			$14,300
Belgian (17th - 18th)				
BOUDIN, Eugene	*D*	$6,600	$13,750	$27,500
French (1824 - 1898)	*P*	$19,800	$261,816	$1.540M
	W	$2,860	$21,560	$44,000
BOUDIN, Eugene (Attrib.)	*P*			$3,520
French (1824 - 1898)				
BOUDIN, Eugene (Style)	*W*			$412
French (1824 - 1898)				

D=Drawing, P=Painting, S=Sculpture, W=Watercolor

		Current Price Range		
		Low	Mean	High

BOUGH, Sam	*P*	$605	$2,211	$4,400
British (1822 - 1878)				
BOUGH, Sam (Attrib.)	*P*			$1,320
British (1822 - 1878)				
BOUGHTON, George H.	*D*			$550
American (1833 - 1905)	*P*	$468	$7,759	$24,200
	W			$2,200
BOUGUEREAU, William A.	*P*	$16,500	$90,903	$242,000
French (1825 - 1905)				
BOUGUEREAU, William A. (Sc.)	*P*			$4,180
French (1825 - 1905)				
BOUILLIERE,	*P*	$220	$262	$303
(20th -)				
BOUILLON, Michel	*P*	$303	$19,876	$41,800
(17th -)				
BOUILLON, Michel (Circle)	*P*			$16,500
(17th -)				
BOULANGER, Graciela R.	*P*	$6,600	$11,092	$14,300
Bolivian (1935 -)				
BOULANGER, Gustave C. R.	*P*	$16,500	$24,750	$33,000
French (1824 - 1888)				
BOULARD, Auguste	*P*			$550
French (1825 - 1897)				
BOULIER, Lucien	*D*			$825
French (1890 - 1964)				
BOULLEE, Louis E. (Circle)	*D*			$275
French (1728 - 1799)				
BOULLOGNE, Bon (Circle)	*P*			$2,860
French (17th - 18th)				
BOULLOGNE, Louis de	*D*			$33,000
French (1654 - 1733)				
BOULTON, Joseph L.	*S*			$275
American (1896 -)				
BOUN, V.	*P*			$770
American (19th -)				

D=Drawing, P=Painting, S=Sculpture, W=Watercolor

		Low	Mean	High
			Current Price Range	

		Low	Mean	High
BOUNDEY, Burton	P			$660
American (1879 - 1962)				
BOUQUET, Andre	P			$935
French (1897 -)				
BOURDELLE, Emile A.	D			$1,320
French (1861 - 1929)	S	$660	$130,827	$1.760M
BOURDON, Sebastian (Attrib.)	P			$20,900
French (1616 - 1671)				
BOURDON, Sebastian (Circle)	P			$3,300
French (1616 - 1671)				
BOURDON, Sebastian (Follower)	D			$990
French (1616 - 1671)				
BOURGAIN, Gustave	P			$99,000
French (? - 1921)				
BOURGEOIS, Douglas	P			$2,200
American (20th -)				
BOURGEOIS, Eugene	P			$4,620
French (1855 - 1909)				
BOURGEOIS, Louise	S			$4,675
American (1911 - 1957)				
BOURGEOIS-BORGEX, Louis	P			$2,640
French (1873 -)				
BOURGES, Pauline-Elise	P			$1,925
French (1838 - 1910)				
BOURGUIGNON, Jacques (Cir.)	P			$1,320
French (15th -)				
BOURNE, Gertrude	W	$330	$779	$1,210
American (1897 - 1962)				
BOURNE, Jean B. C.	P			$935
French (19th -)				
BOURNET, Gertrude Beals	W			$275
French (20th -)				
BOUT, Pieter	P			$3,850
Flemish (1658 - 1702)				
BOUT, Pieter (Et al.)	P	$13,200	$15,400	$17,600
Flemish (1658 - 1702)				

D=Drawing, P=Painting, S=Sculpture, W=Watercolor

		Current Price Range		
		Low	Mean	High

BOUTELLE, Dewitt C.	*P*			$17,600
American (1817 - 1884)				
BOUTELLE, G.	*P*			$303
(?)				
BOUTER, Cornelis	*P*	$1,870	$4,392	$7,150
Dutch (1888 - 1966)				
BOUTER, Pieter	*P*			$935
Dutch (1887 - 1968)				
BOUTERWEK, Friedrich	*P*			$20,900
German (1806 - 1867)				
BOUTHOORN,	*W*			$193
Dutch (1916 -)				
BOUTS, Albert	*P*			$38,500
Dutch (1454 - 1549)				
BOUTTATS, Jacob (Circle)	*P*			$12,100
Flemish (18th -)				
BOUTTATS, Jacob (Manner)	*P*			$880
Flemish (18th -)				
BOUTTATS, ELDER, Frederik	*P*			$19,800
Flemish (? - 1661)				
BOUUAERT,	*P*			$275
(?)				
BOUVARD, Antoine	*P*	$2,420	$6,243	$12,100
French (? - 1956)				
BOUVARD, Hughes de	*P*	$3,300	$3,740	$4,400
Austrian (1879 - 1959)				
BOUVARD, Noel A.	*P*			$2,475
French (1912 - 1975)				
BOUYSSOU, Jacques	*P*			$2,750
French (1926 -)				
BOWDOIN, Harriete	*P*			$990
American (? - 1947)				
BOWEN, Benjamin J.	*P*	$523	$1,857	$3,190
American (1859 - 1930)				
BOWEN, H. L.	*S*			$110
American (20th -)				

D=Drawing, P=Painting, S=Sculpture, W=Watercolor

		Current Price Range		
		Low	Mean	High
BOWEN, John	P			$880
(?)				
BOWEN, Paul	P			$1,870
(20th -)	S			$2,000
BOWER, Alexander	P			$358
American (1875 - 1952)	W	$275	$289	$303
BOWER, J.	D	$220	$248	$275
British (19th - 20th)				
BOWERS, George N.	P			$1,980
American (1849 - 1909)				
BOWES, Betty M.	W			$193
American (20th -)				
BOWIE, Frank Louville	P	$303	$640	$990
American (1856 - 1936)				
BOWLER, Joseph	P			$1,500
(1928 -)				
BOWMAN, M. E.	P			$770
American (19th - 20th)				
BOWSER, David B.	P			$20,900
American (1820 - 1900)				
BOXER, Stanley	P			$3,520
American (1926 -)				
BOYCE, George P.	D			$13,200
British (1826 - 1897)				
BOYD, John R.	D			$1,045
American (1884 -)				
BOYD, Rutherford	D			$248
American (1884 - 1951)	P	$550	$3,575	$6,600
BOYD, S.	P			$275
British (19th -)				
BOYDEN, Dwight F.	P	$275	$303	$330
American (1860 - 1933)				
BOYE, Abel D.	P			$3,300
French (1864 - 1934)				

D=Drawing, P=Painting, S=Sculpture, W=Watercolor

		Current Price Range		
		Low	Mean	High

BOYER, Fred J.	*S*	$2,800	$3,050	$3,300
American (20th -)				
BOYHAN, Matthew	*P*			$495
American (20th -)				
BOYLE, A.	*P*			$495
British (19th -)				
BOYLE, Charles W.	*P*			$4,400
American (1861 - 1925)				
BOYLE, George A.	*P*			$550
British (19th -)				
BOYLE, James N.	*W*			$358
American (1931 -)				
BOYLE, John J.	*S*			$19,800
American (1851 - 1917)				
BOYLE, Neil	*P*	$1,300	$1,400	$1,500
American (20th -)				
BOYS, Thomas S. (Attrib.)	*W*			$825
British (1803 - 1874)				
BOZE, Honore	*P*			$16,500
British (1830 - 1908)				
BOZE, Joseph (Attrib.)	*D*			$5,500
French (1744 - 1826)				
BOZZALLA, Giuseppe	*P*			$2,750
Italian (1874 - 1958)				
BOZZATO, A.	*P*			$264
(?)				
BRAADE, H.	*P*			$275
Dutch (20th -)				
BRABAZON, Hercules B.	*W*	$550	$825	$1,320
British (1821 - 1906)				
BRABAZON, Hercules B. (Attrib.)	*W*			$110
British (1821 - 1906)				
BRABE, Dosio	*P*			$330
(?)				
BRACHO Y MURILLO, Jose M.	*P*			$33,000
Spanish (19th -)				

D=Drawing, P=Painting, S=Sculpture, W=Watercolor

		Current Price Range		
		Low	Mean	High
BRACHT, Eugen	*P*			$3,520
Swiss (1842 - 1921)				
BRACK, Emil	*W*			$2,860
German (1860 - 1905)				
BRACKEN, Clio H.	*S*			$3,300
American (1870 - 1925)				
BRACKENBURG, Richard	*P*			$18,700
(1650 - 1702)				
BRACKER, M. Leone	*D*	$138	$152	$165
American (1885 - 1937)				
BRACKETT, Sidney L.	*D*			$330
American (19th -)	*P*	$358	$1,656	$2,750
BRACKETT, Walter M.	*P*			$2,970
American (1823 - 1919)				
BRACKMAN, David	*W*			$6,600
British (19th -)				
BRACKMAN, Robert	*D*	$220	$1,183	$1,760
American (1898 - 1980)	*P*	$1,045	$3,031	$8,800
BRACONY, Leopold	*S*			$8,800
Italian (19th - 20th)				
BRACQUEMOND, Felix	*W*			$4,400
French (1833 - 1914)				
BRACQUEMOND, Pierre	*P*			$880
French (20th -)				
BRACY, A. E.	*P*	$165	$461	$825
American (20th -)				
BRADBURY, Bennett	*P*	$275	$656	$1,320
American (20th -)				
BRADBURY, E. H.	*P*			$550
British (19th -)				
BRADBURY, Gideon E.	*P*	$715	$2,283	$3,850
American (1833 - 1904)				
BRADDON, Charles	*P*			$1,760
American (1906 -)				

D=Drawing, P=Painting, S=Sculpture, W=Watercolor

		Current Price Range		
		Low	Mean	High

		Low	Mean	High
BRADDON, Charles (Attrib.)	*P*			$110
American (1906 -)				
BRADESH, Alvah	*P*			$1,100
(?)				
BRADFORD, C. H.	*P*			$303
American (?)				
BRADFORD, Dean	*P*			$990
American (20th -)				
BRADFORD, William	*D*	$550	$1,925	$3,300
American (1827 - 1892)	*P*	$1,540	$23,130	$60,500
BRADFORD, William (School)	*P*			$440
American (1827 - 1892)				
BRADLEY, Anne C.	*P*			$550
American (1884 -)				
BRADLEY, E. G.	*P*	$193	$289	$385
British (19th -)				
BRADLEY, Mabel	*P*			$358
American (?)				
BRADNER, Karl	*P*			$605
(?)				
BRADSHAW, George A.	*P*			$175
American (1880 -)				
BRADSHAW, Glen	*P*			$440
American (20th -)				
BRADY, Robert	*S*			$4,950
(20th -)				
BRAEKELEER, Adriaan de	*P*	$15,400	$19,250	$23,100
Belgian (1818 - 1904)				
BRAIL, Archille J. T.	*P*			$38,500
French (19th -)				
BRAITH, Anton	*P*	$1,155	$17,078	$33,000
German (1836 - 1905)				
BRAKENBURGH, Richard	*P*			$4,950
Dutch (1650 - 1702)				
BRALEY, Clarence E.	*D*	$220	$403	$660

D=Drawing, P=Painting, S=Sculpture, W=Watercolor

		Current Price Range		
		Low	Mean	High
BRALEY, Clarence E.	P	$193	$633	$990
American (19th -)	W	$110	$202	$275
BRAMER, Leonard	P			$33,000
Dutch (1595 - 1674)				
BRAMER, Leonard (Circle)	W			$1,320
Dutch (1595 - 1674)				
BRAMHALL, W. T.	P			$1,100
American (19th -)				
BRANCACCIO, Carlo	P	$5,500	$29,975	$115,500
Italian (1861 - 1920)				
BRANCACCIO, Giovanni	P	$1,100	$1,100	$1,100
Italian (1903 -)				
BRANCUSI, Constantin	D	$19,800	$70,400	$121,000
Rumanian (1876 - 1957)	P	$38,500	$211,750	$385,000
	S	$330,000	$5.793M	$8.800M
BRANCUSI, Constantin (Et al.)	D			$143,000
Rumanian (20th -)				
BRAND, Johann C. (Attrib.)	P			$990
Austrian (1722 - 1795)				
BRAND, Myra	P			$660
American (19th -)				
BRANDAO, Wilson	P	$2,860	$3,190	$3,520
Panamanian (1950 -)				
BRANDEIS, Antonietta	P	$1,650	$6,985	$16,500
Bohemian (1849 -)				
BRANDES,	P	$1,540	$1,540	$1,540
German (19th -)				
BRANDI, Domenico	P			$8,250
Italian (1683 - 1736)				
BRANDI, Giacinto	P	$1,320	$11,110	$20,900
Italian (1623 - 1691)				
BRANDI, Giacinto (Circle)	P			$1,540
Italian (1623 - 1691)				
BRANDIEN, Carl W.	P			$1,320
American (20th -)				

D=Drawing, P=Painting, S=Sculpture, W=Watercolor

	Current Price Range		
	Low	Mean	High

		Low	Mean	High
BRANDMULLER, Gregor (Attrib.)	P			$770
Swiss (1661 - 1690)				
BRANDNER, Carl C.	P			$880
American (1808 -)				
BRANDNER, Karl	P	$303	$1,041	$2,640
American (1898 - 1961)				
BRANDRIFF, George K.	P	$385	$862	$1,430
American (1890 - 1936)				
BRANDT,	P			$715
German (19th - 20th)				
BRANDT, Carl	P			$5,500
Swedish (? - 1930)	W			$385
BRANDT, Carl L.	P	$275	$1,678	$3,080
American (1831 - 1905)				
BRANDT, S. Kielland	P			$1,403
Danish (19th - 20th)				
BRANDT, Warren	P			$1,210
American (1918 -)				
BRANGWYN, Sir Frank	D			$523
British (1867 - 1943)	P			$41,800
	W	$1,980	$3,630	$5,280
BRANK, Rockwell	P	$220	$473	$950
American (20th -)				
BRANNAN, Sophie	P	$138	$509	$880
American (20th -)	S			$1,540
BRANNON, M. E. (Et al.)	D			$220
American (20th -)				
BRANSOM, Paul	D	$193	$422	$950
American (1885 - 1979)	P			$550
	W			$1,100
BRANWHITE, Charles	P			$1,100
British (1817 - 1880)	W			$1,210

D=Drawing, P=Painting, S=Sculpture, W=Watercolor

		Current Price Range		
		Low	Mean	High

		Low	Mean	High
BRAQUAVAL, Louis	*P*	$1,650	$3,025	$4,400
French (1856 - 1919)				
BRAQUE, Georges	*D*	$19,800	$86,113	$253,000
French (1882 - 1963)	*P*	$99,000	$1.371M	$4.675M
	S	$990	$36,713	$132,000
	W	$44,000	$273,625	$660,000
BRASHER, Rex	*W*			$715
American (1869 - 1960)				
BRASILIER, Andre	*P*	$13,200	$115,133	$225,500
French (1929 -)				
BRASZ, Arnold F.	*P*			$550
American (1888 - 1966)	*W*			$660
BRATBY, John	*P*	$495	$1,678	$2,860
British (1924 -)				
BRAUER, Ferdinand	*D*	$138	$248	$468
German (1870 - 1940)				
BRAUN, Maurice	*P*	$303	$9,421	$35,750
American (1877 - 1941)	*W*			$440
BRAUN, Maurice (Attrib.)	*P*	$880	$1,375	$1,870
American (1877 - 1941)				
BRAUNER, Victor	*D*			$27,500
French (1903 - 1966)	*P*	$82,500	$112,750	$132,000
	W	$24,200	$24,750	$25,300
BRAUNTUCH, Troy	*D*	$715	$5,005	$9,350
American (1954 -)				
BRAVO, Claudio	*D*	$3,850	$37,400	$66,000
Chilean (1936 -)	*P*	$12,100	$74,507	$148,500
	S			$15,400
	W			$4,400
BRAY, Arnold	*P*	$303	$544	$990
American (20th -)				

D=Drawing, P=Painting, S=Sculpture, W=Watercolor

		Current Price Range	
	Low	Mean	High

		Low	Mean	High
BRAY, Jan de Dutch (1627 - 1697)	*P*			$7,150
BRAY, Jan de (Follower) Dutch (1627 - 1697)	*P*			$1,980
BRAY, Salomon de Dutch (1597 - 1664)	*P*			$19,800
BRAYER, Yves French (1907 -)	*P*	$1,100	$13,933	$28,600
BREACH, E. R. British (1868 - 1886)	*P*			$4,125
BREAKSPEARE, William A. British (19th -)	*P*	$1,210	$2,255	$3,300
BREANSKI, Alfred de British (1852 - 1928)	*P*	$660	$10,784	$39,600
BREANSKI, Alfred de (Attrib.) British (1852 - 1928)	*P*			$550
BREANSKI, Gustav de British (19th -)	*P*	$1,320	$1,540	$1,760
BREANSKI, JR., Alfred de British (1877 - 1957)	*P*	$1,100	$3,108	$4,950
BRECHER, Samuel American (1897 -)	*P*			$880
BRECKENRIDGE, Hugh H. American (1870 - 1937)	*P*	$523	$624	$825
BREDAEL, Jans F. van (Attrib.) Flemish (1686 - 1750)	*P*			$14,300
BREDAEL, Josef van Flemish (1688 - 1739)	*P*			$12,100
BREDAEL, Pieter van (Circle) Flemish (1629 - 1719)	*P*			$17,600
BREDIN, R. Sloan American (1881 - 1933)	*P*	$7,150	$14,575	$22,000
BREDOW, A. German (19th - 20th)	*P*			$330
BREE, Joseph Van Dutch (19th - 20th)	*P*			$2,860

D=Drawing, P=Painting, S=Sculpture, W=Watercolor

		Current Price Range	
	Low	Mean	High

BREEDE, Alex	P			$1,430
American (19th -)				
BREEDWELD, H.	P			$550
European (?)				
BREEN, Adam van (Attrib.)	P			$8,800
Dutch (17th -)				
BREEN, James T.	P	$110	$248	$385
American (19th - 20th)				
BREENBERGH, Barth. (Circle)	P			$4,400
Dutch (1599 - 1659)				
BREEVORT, James R.	P			$1,760
American (1832 - 1918)	W			$330
BREHM, George	D	$225	$374	$523
American (1878 - 1966)	P			$900
	W			$358
BREHM, Worth	D			$165
American (1883 - 1928)				
BREITNER, George H.	P			$1,210
Dutch (1957 - 1923)	W			$28,600
BREKELENKAMP, Quiryn	P	$16,500	$22,550	$28,600
Dutch (1620 - 1668)				
BREKELENKAMP, Quiryn (Att.)	P			$5,775
Dutch (1620 - 1668)				
BREKELENKAMP, Quiryn (Cir.)	P			$7,700
Dutch (1620 - 1668)				
BREKELENKAMP, Quiryn (Sc.)	P			$1,100
Dutch (1620 - 1668)				
BRELL, J. Peru	P			$8,800
Spanish (19th -)				
BREMEN, Meyer von	P	$2,750	$32,136	$77,000
German (1813 - 1886)				
BREMEN, Meyer von (Style)	P			$2,750
German (1813 - 1886)				

D=Drawing, P=Painting, S=Sculpture, W=Watercolor

		Current Price Range	
	Low	Mean	High

		Low	Mean	High
BRENDEKILDE, Hans A.	*P*			$19,800
Danish (1857 - 1920)				
BRENEISER, Stanley G.	*W*			$275
American (1890 -)				
BRENNER, Carl C.	*P*	$385	$3,438	$7,150
American (1838 - 1888)				
BRENNER, F. S.	*P*			$550
American (20th -)				
BRENNER, Victor D.	*S*	$110	$1,348	$3,740
American (1871 - 1924)				
BRENNIR, Carl	*P*			$2,200
British (1850 - 1920)				
BRERETON, James	*P*	$1,100	$1,155	$1,210
British (?)				
BRERETON, Robert (Style)	*P*			$4,950
British (1835 - 1847)				
BRETE,	*S*			$550
(?)				
BRETLAND, Thomas	*P*			$7,700
British (1802 - 1874)				
BRETON, Andre	*W*	$6,050	$6,600	$7,150
French (20th -)				
BRETON, Jacqueline	*W*			$4,180
(?)				
BRETON, Jules	*P*	$13,200	$241,700	$1.650M
French (1827 - 1905)				
BRETON, Paul E.	*S*			$1,760
French (1868 - 1933)				
BRETT, Donald	*P*			$220
(?)				
BRETT, Dorothy E.	*P*			$11,000
American (1883 - 1977)				
BRETT, Harold M.	*P*	$450	$885	$1,320
American (1880 - 1955)	*W*			$715
BREU, ELDER, Jorg	*P*			$13,200
German (1475 - 1537)				

D=Drawing, P=Painting, S=Sculpture, W=Watercolor

		Current Price Range		
		Low	Mean	High

		Low	Mean	High
BREUER, H. A.	P			$110
(?)				
BREUER, Henry J.	P	$800	$1,752	$3,025
American (1860 - 1932)	W			$468
BREUER, T.	S			$770
(?)				
BREULL, Hugo	P			$330
American (1854 - 1910)				
BREVOORT, James Renwick	P	$935	$3,589	$9,350
American (1832 - 1918)				
BREWER, Adrian L.	P			$660
American (1891 - 1956)				
BREWER, John	W			$770
British (18th - 19th)				
BREWER, Nicholas R.	P	$165	$1,452	$4,400
American (1857 - 1949)				
BREWERTON, George D.	D	$330	$944	$1,650
American (1820 - 1901)	P	$770	$1,898	$3,025
BREWSTER, Anna R.	D			$220
American (1870 - 1952)	P	$110	$623	$2,310
	W			$935
BREWSTER, G. Douglas	D			$1,540
American (?)				
BREWSTER, Julia	W			$110
American (20th -)				
BREWSTER, JR., John	P			$77,000
(?)				
BREYDAEL, Karel	P			$4,675
Flemish (1678 - 1733)				
BRIANCHON, Maurice	P	$14,300	$50,325	$88,000
French (1899 - 1979)				
BRIANTE, Ezelino	P			$1,210
Italian (1901 - 1970)				

D=Drawing, P=Painting, S=Sculpture, W=Watercolor

		Current Price Range	
	Low	Mean	High

		Low	Mean	High
BRICHARD,	*P*			$550
American (20th -)				
BRICHER, Alfred T.	*D*	$385	$1,243	$2,475
American (1837 - 1908)	*P*	$1,760	$27,386	$82,500
	W	$495	$11,040	$52,800
BRICHER, Alfred T. (Attrib.)	*P*	$880	$5,390	$9,900
American (1837 - 1908)				
BRICKDALE, Eleanor F.	*W*	$4,950	$5,775	$6,600
British (1871 - 1945)				
BRIDGE, P. J. A.	*W*			$248
(19th - 20th)				
BRIDGE, W. B.	*W*	$935	$1,073	$1,210
(19th -)				
BRIDGES, Charles (Attrib.)	*P*			$4,125
British (18th -)				
BRIDGES, Fidelia	*W*	$275	$3,060	$9,900
American (1835 - 1924)				
BRIDGMAN, Frederick A.	*P*	$385	$47,873	$418,000
American (1847 - 1928)				
BRIGANTI, Nicolas	*P*	$440	$1,320	$2,200
American (1895 -)	*W*			$165
BRIGGS, Austin	*D*			$600
American (1909 - 1973)	*P*			$400
	W			$935
BRIGGS, Lela M.	*P*			$138
American (1896 -)				
BRIGGS, Lucius A.	*W*	$330	$495	$715
American (1852 - 1931)				
BRIGHT, Harry	*P*			$1,980
British (1814 - 1873)	*W*	$688	$1,059	$1,430
BRIGNONI, Serge	*P*			$26,400
Swiss (1903 -)				

D=Drawing, P=Painting, S=Sculpture, W=Watercolor

		Current Price Range		
		Low	Mean	High

		Low	Mean	High
BRIL, Paul	*D*			$15,400
Flemish (1554 - 1626)	*P*	$11,000	$51,700	$88,000
BRIL, Paul (Follower)	*D*			$2,750
Flemish (1554 - 1626)				
BRIL, Paul (School)	*P*			$3,080
Flemish (1554 - 1626)				
BRILLOUIN, Louis-Georges	*P*			$2,090
French (1817 - 1893)				
BRINDISI, Remo	*P*	$3,410	$3,410	$3,410
Italian (1918 -)				
BRINDLE, Melbourne	*P*			$4,400
American (1906 -)				
BRINK, Guido	*S*			$825
American (20th -)				
BRINLEY, Daniel P.	*D*			$138
American (1879 - 1963)	*P*			$4,620
BRIONI,	*P*			$138
(20th -)				
BRIOSCHI, Carlo	*P*			$1,595
Italian (1826 - 1895)				
BRISCOE, Franklin	*D*			$440
American (1844 - 1903)	*P*	$605	$2,365	$5,500
BRISCOE, Franklin (Attrib.)	*P*			$220
American (1844 - 1903)				
BRISSOT DE WARVILLE, Felix S.	*P*			$2,310
French (1818 - 1892)				
BRISTOL, John B.	*P*	$440	$2,774	$9,130
American (1826 - 1909)				
BRISTOW, Edmund	*P*	$1,760	$6,380	$11,000
British (1787 - 1876)				
BRISTOW, Edmund (Attrib.)	*P*	$798	$3,149	$5,500
British (1787 - 1876)				
BRITISH SCHOOL,	*P*	$1,045	$2,078	$5,500
British (?)				

D=Drawing, P=Painting, S=Sculpture, W=Watercolor

		Current Price Range		
		Low	Mean	High
BRITISH SCHOOL,	*P*			$1,100
British (17th - 18th)				
BRITISH SCHOOL,	*P*	$1,320	$3,383	$6,050
British (18th - 19th)				
BRITISH SCHOOL,	*D*			$1,045
British (19th - 20th)	*P*	$825	$1,713	$2,970
	W			$1,760
BRITISH SCHOOL 16C,	*P*	$4,950	$8,525	$12,100
British (16th -)				
BRITISH SCHOOL 17C,	*P*	$2,860	$9,240	$25,300
British (17th -)				
BRITISH SCHOOL 18C,	*P*	$1,045	$5,410	$33,000
British (18th -)	*W*			$5,775
BRITISH SCHOOL 19C,	*P*	$1,045	$2,540	$9,350
British (19th -)	*S*			$1,210
	W	$1,100	$3,864	$9,625
BRITISH SCHOOL 20C,	*P*			$1,100
British (20th -)				
BRITO, Ramon V.	*P*	$6,600	$7,975	$9,350
Venezuelan (1927 -)				
BRITTAN, Charles E.	*W*			$605
British (1870 -)				
BRIULLOY, Aleksandr	*W*			$303
Russian (1798 - 1877)				
BRIZZI, Francesco	*P*			$2,200
Italian (1574 - 1623)				
BROAD, J. K.	*W*			$303
American (20th -)				
BROCHART, Constant J.	*D*	$1,650	$3,025	$4,400
French (1816 - 1899)				
BROCK, Thomas	*S*			$1,210
British (1847 - 1922)				
BROCKLEHURST, S.	*W*	$165	$220	$275
European (?)				

D=Drawing, P=Painting, S=Sculpture, W=Watercolor

		Current Price Range		
		Low	Mean	High
BROCKMAN, Ann	*P*			$110
American (1899 - 1943)				
BRODERS,	*P*	$523	$695	$853
(?)				
BRODERSON, Charles	*W*			$275
(20th -)				
BRODERSON, Morris	*D*			$1,760
American (20th -)	*P*	$1,650	$1,650	$1,650
	W	$880	$2,090	$3,300
BRODHEAD, George H.	*W*			$176
American (1860 -)				
BRODNEY, Edward	*P*			$165
American (20th -)				
BROE, Vern	*P*	$385	$850	$1,870
American (20th -)				
BROECK, Elias van den	*P*	$33,000	$57,750	$82,500
Dutch (1650 - 1708)				
BROEMEL, Carl W.	*P*			$165
American (1891 -)	*W*	$121	$556	$990
BROGI, Gino	*P*			$330
Italian (20th -)				
BROITOUVAHL, R.	*P*			$385
European (20th -)				
BROMBERG,	*P*			$220
American (20th -)				
BROMLEY, Frank C.	*P*	$605	$1,054	$2,200
American (19th -)				
BROMLEY, John W.	*P*			$2,310
British (19th -)				
BROMLEY, Valentine W.	*P*			$1,650
British (1848 - 1877)				
BROMLEY, William	*P*			$9,350
British (19th -)				
BRON, Aghille	*P*			$1,320
French (19th - 20th)				

D=Drawing, P=Painting, S=Sculpture, W=Watercolor

		Current Price Range		
		Low	Mean	High

		Low	Mean	High
BRONSON, Clark	*S*	$2,750	$4,167	$7,000
American (1939 -)				
BRONZINO, Angelo (Circle)	*P*	$2,200	$15,400	$28,600
Italian (1503 - 1572)				
BRONZINO, Angelo (Follower)	*P*			$14,300
Italian (1503 - 1572)				
BROODTHAERS, Marcel	*S*			$77,000
Belgian (1924 - 1976)				
BROOK, Alexander	*D*			$468
American (1898 - 1980)	*P*	$275	$2,173	$6,380
BROOKE, Joseph	*P*			$3,575
British (18th -)				
BROOKE, Richard N.	*P*	$495	$784	$1,210
American (1847 - 1920)				
BROOKER, Harry	*P*	$8,800	$13,750	$18,700
British (20th -)				
BROOKES, Samuel M.	*P*	$3,960	$7,003	$9,900
American (1816 - 1892)				
BROOKS, Adele R.	*P*			$550
American (1873 -)				
BROOKS, Alden F.	*P*	$220	$275	$330
American (1840 -)	*W*			$193
BROOKS, Cora	*P*			$100
American (20th -)				
BROOKS, Henry	*P*			$495
American (1898 -)				
BROOKS, Henry H.	*P*	$165	$638	$1,210
American (20th -)				
BROOKS, J. B.	*P*			$2,750
(?)				
BROOKS, Jacob	*P*			$1,100
British (1877 -)				
BROOKS, James	*D*			$1,870
American (1906 -)	*P*	$7,150	$24,750	$41,250

D=Drawing, P=Painting, S=Sculpture, W=Watercolor

		Current Price Range		
		Low	Mean	High
BROOKS, James	*W*			$2,310
American (1906 -)				
BROOKS, Maria	*P*			$110,000
British (19th -)				
BROOKS, Nicholas A.	*P*	$935	$7,659	$26,400
American (19th - 20th)				
BROOKS, Richard E	*S*			$770
American (1865 - 1919)				
BROOKS, Thomas	*P*			$71,500
British (1818 - 1891)				
BROOKS, Victoria	*P*	$121	$121	$121
(?)				
BROSE, Carl	*S*			$3,300
German (1880 -)				
BROSE, Morris	*S*	$715	$812	$908
(20th -)				
BROSHARD,	*P*			$825
French (20th -)				
BROTMAN, Lisa	*D*			$220
American (20th -)				
BROUGGA, P.	*P*			$350
(20th -)				
BROUGIER, Adolphe	*P*			$2,475
German (1870 -)				
BROUILLET, Pierre A.	*P*			$104,500
French (1857 - 1914)				
BROULOWSKY, L & N	*P*			$2,310
(?)				
BROUWER, Adriaen (After)	*P*			$770
Flemish (1606 - 1638)				
BROUWER, Adriaen (Circle)	*P*	$3,190	$5,445	$7,700
Flemish (1606 - 1638)				
BROUWER, Gien	*P*			$715
Dutch (20th -)				
BROUX, Silas (Attrib.)	*P*			$750
French (19th - 20th)				

D=Drawing, P=Painting, S=Sculpture, W=Watercolor

| | Current Price Range | | |
	Low	Mean	High
BROWER, K. (Attrib.) P			$400
Dutch (20th -)			
BROWERES, A. D. O. P			$3,080
(19th -)			
BROWN, Alexander P	$1,210	$2,035	$2,860
British (1849 - 1922) W			$385
BROWN, Anna W. P	$193	$427	$660
American (19th - 20th)			
BROWN, Arnesby P			$358
British (1866 - 1955)			
BROWN, Arthur W. D	$225	$292	$358
American (1881 - 1966)			
BROWN, B. L. P			$385
American (19th -)			
BROWN, Benjamin P	$605	$7,472	$26,400
American (1865 - 1942) W	$825	$935	$1,045
BROWN, Byron P			$2,100
American (1907 - 1961) S			$1,200
W			$1,320
BROWN, C. P. P			$1,045
American (?)			
BROWN, Carlyle P			$990
American (20th -) W	$385	$995	$1,980
BROWN, Carroll P			$220
American (20th -) W			$3,850
BROWN, Charles (Attrib.) P			$275
American (1848 -)			
BROWN, Clinton P			$220
(20th -)			
BROWN, Douglas W			$330
American (1904 -)			
BROWN, Elmore W			$110
American (1899 - 1968)			

D=Drawing, P=Painting, S=Sculpture, W=Watercolor

| | | Current Price Range | | |
		Low	Mean	High
BROWN, Francis F.	*P*	$110	$337	$1,155
American (1891 -)				
BROWN, Frank A.	*P*	$660	$770	$880
American (1876 -)				
BROWN, Fred C.	*P*			$8,800
American (19th - 20th)				
BROWN, G.	*P*			$440
American (19th -)				
BROWN, George E.	*P*	$2,750	$4,400	$6,050
American (1871 - 1946)	*W*			$193
BROWN, George L.	*D*			$2,090
American (1814 - 1889)	*P*	$770	$9,209	$49,500
	W	$358	$1,366	$2,090
BROWN, George L. (Attrib.)	*P*			$1,650
American (1814 - 1899)	*W*			$220
BROWN, Harley	*D*	$1,320	$1,795	$1,980
American (1939 -)	*P*			$1,980
BROWN, Harrison B.	*P*	$220	$1,720	$5,225
American (1831 - 1915)				
BROWN, Horace	*P*	$143	$432	$935
American (1876 -)				
BROWN, Howell C.	*P*			$450
American (1880 -)				
BROWN, Hugh B.	*P*			$358
British (19th - 20th)				
BROWN, J. G.	*P*	$3,960	$25,117	$66,000
Scottish (18th - 19th)				
BROWN, J. G. (Attrib.)	*W*			$220
Scottish (18th - 19th)				
BROWN, James	*D*	$1,870	$11,743	$18,700
American (20th -)	*P*	$14,300	$62,608	$159,500
	S	$3,300	$8,360	$14,300

D=Drawing, P=Painting, S=Sculpture, W=Watercolor

		Current Price Range		
		Low	Mean	High
BROWN, James F.	*P*			$4,675
American (19th - 20th)				
BROWN, Joan	*P*	$468	$2,028	$6,050
American (20th -)				
BROWN, John A.	*D*	$1,540	$5,390	$16,500
American (1844 - 1902)	*P*			$3,080
	W			$275
BROWN, John G.	*D*	$1,045	$3,548	$6,050
American (1831 - 1913)	*P*	$880	$17,802	$82,500
	W			$2,860
BROWN, John G. (After)	*D*			$193
American (1831 - 1913)				
BROWN, John L.	*P*	$2,200	$14,850	$27,500
French (1829 - 1890)	*W*			$303
BROWN, Judy	*S*	$110	$220	$330
American (20th -)				
BROWN, Marnell	*P*			$950
American (20th -)				
BROWN, Mather	*P*			$495
American (1761 - 1831)				
BROWN, Paul	*D*	$165	$904	$4,125
American (1871 - 1944)	*W*			$4,125
BROWN, R. Woodley	*P*	$1,320	$1,320	$1,320
British (19th -)				
BROWN, Reynold	*P*			$132
American (20th -)				
BROWN, Robert A.	*P*			$1,980
British (19th -)				
BROWN, Roger	*P*	$1,100	$16,170	$28,600
American (1941 -)	*S*			$8,800
BROWN, Roy H.	*P*	$385	$454	$523
American (1879 - 1956)				

D=Drawing, P=Painting, S=Sculpture, W=Watercolor

		Current Price Range		
		Low	Mean	High
BROWN, Sonia G.	*S*			$1,100
American (1890 -)				
BROWN, W. Warren	*P*	$303	$1,128	$1,650
Canadian (1881 -)				
BROWN, Walter F.	*P*			$1,650
American (1853 - 1929)	*W*			$248
BROWN, William B.	*P*	$523	$1,329	$2,750
British (1831 - 1909)				
BROWN, William M.	*P*	$3,300	$15,321	$35,200
American (1828 - 1898)				
BROWN, William M. (After)	*P*			$550
American (1828 - 1898)				
BROWN, William M. (Attrib.)	*P*			$330
American (1828 - 1898)				
BROWN, Woodley	*P*			$660
British (19th -)				
BROWNE, Byron	*D*	$220	$1,595	$4,125
American (1907 - 1961)	*P*	$1,430	$6,689	$22,000
	W	$578	$2,045	$4,400
BROWNE, Charles F.	*P*	$440	$2,794	$7,150
American (1859 - 1920)				
BROWNE, Dorothea S.	*P*			$715
American (20th -)				
BROWNE, George E.	*D*			$248
American (1871 - 1946)	*P*	$165	$1,087	$4,400
	W	$330	$697	$880
BROWNE, George E. (Attrib.)	*P*			$275
American (1871 - 1946)				
BROWNE, Hablot K.	*D*			$2,750
British (1815 - 1882)	*W*	$176	$5,038	$9,900
BROWNE, Henriette	*P*			$15,400
French (1829 - 1901)				

D=Drawing, P=Painting, S=Sculpture, W=Watercolor

		Current Price Range		
		Low	Mean	High

BROWNE, Margaret F.	D			$110
American (1884 - 1972)	P	$110	$316	$605
BROWNE, Matilda	P			$4,400
American (1869 - 1947)	W			$660
BROWNE, W. H.	P			$880
(19th -)				
BROWNELL, Charles D.	P			$8,250
American (1822 - 1909)				
BROWNELL, Franklin	P			$825
American (1857 -)	W			$110
BROWNLOW, George W.	P			$3,575
British (1835 - 1876)				
BROWNSCOMBE, Jennie A.	P			$6,050
American (1851 - 1936)	W	$550	$880	$1,210
BROZIK, Wenceslas	P	$1,320	$8,507	$39,600
Bohemian (1851 - 1901)				
BRUCE, Edward	P			$3,300
American (1879 - 1943)				
BRUCE, Joseph A.	P			$990
American (1838 - 1908)				
BRUCE, Tom H.	P			$110
British (19th - 20th)				
BRUCE, William	P			$6,600
American (19th - 20th)				
BRUCK, H.	P			$450
(?)				
BRUCKER, Edmund	P			$2,420
American (1912 -)				
BRUCKMAN, Lodewyk	P	$440	$1,164	$3,080
American (1903 -)				
BRUEGHEL, Abraham (School)	P			$3,960
Flemish (1631 - 1690)				
BRUEGHEL, ELDER, Jan	P	$99,000	$1.067M	$2.035M
Flemish (1568 - 1625)				

D=Drawing, P=Painting, S=Sculpture, W=Watercolor

		Current Price Range		
		Low	Mean	High
BRUEGHEL, ELDER, Jan (Att)	*P*			$2,090
Flemish (1568 - 1625)				
BRUEGHEL, ELDER, Jan (Mann)	*P*	$578	$9,089	$17,600
Flemish (1568 - 1625)				
BRUEGHEL, ELDER, Jan (Style)	*P*			$1,320
Flemish (1568 - 1625)				
BRUEGHEL, YOUNGER, Jan	*P*	$30,800	$189,860	$550,000
Flemish (1601 - 1678)				
BRUEGHEL, YOUNGER, Jan (Aft.)	*P*			$27,500
Flemish (1601 - 1678)				
BRUEGHEL, YOUNGER, Jan (Att.)	*P*			$28,600
Flemish (1601 - 1678)				
BRUEGHEL, YOUNGER, Jan (Cir)	*P*			$16,500
Flemish (1601 - 1678)				
BRUEGHEL, YOUNGER, Pieter	*P*	$33,000	$974,380	$2.970M
Flemish (1564 - 1637)				
BRUEHLER, Herm	*W*			$413
American (20th -)				
BRUEL, Harold	*W*			$550
(?)				
BRUEL, Hugo	*W*	$220	$825	$1,430
American (1854 - 1910)				
BRUESTLE, Bertram G.	*P*	$440	$1,526	$3,300
American (1902 - 1939)				
BRUESTLE, George M.	*P*	$440	$1,818	$6,600
American (1872 - 1939)				
BRUFF, Joseph G.	*D*			$715
(1804 - 1889)				
BRUGAIROLLES, Victor	*P*			$3,028
French (1869 -)				
BRUGO, Guiseppe	*P*			$1,100
Italian (19th - 20th)	*W*			$495
BRUIN, C. K.	*P*			$176
(?)				
BRUKMAN, Lodewyk	*P*			$990
(1903 -)				

D=Drawing, P=Painting, S=Sculpture, W=Watercolor

		Current Price Range		
		Low	Mean	High

BRULE, Vincent	P			$605
American (?)				
BRULERE, J. C.	P			$110
(?)				
BRULLOFF, Alexandre	W			$220
Russian (1798 - 1877)				
BRUN, Louis A. (Style)	P	$523	$1,197	$1,870
Swiss (1758 - 1815)				
BRUNEAU, Adrien	W			$715
French (19th - 20th)				
BRUNER, P.	P			$935
European (19th -)				
BRUNERY, Francois	P	$17,600	$20,350	$23,100
Italian (19th - 20th)				
BRUNERY, Marcel	P			$10,450
French (20th -)				
BRUNET-HOUARD, Pierre A.	P			$5,060
French (? - 1922)				
BRUNI, G. L.	P			$176
(20th -)				
BRUNIN, Leon	P			$1,980
Belgian (1861 - 1949)				
BRUNINI, C.	S			$3,300
(?)				
BRUNISH, Fred	P			$165
American (20th -)				
BRUNNER, A. F.	P	$2,090	$2,090	$2,090
(?)				
BRUNNER, F. Sands	P	$550	$1,325	$2,100
American (1886 -)				
BRUNO, Zach	S			$1,650
American (20th -)				
BRUSH, George de F.	D			$880
American (1855 - 1941)	P	$2,750	$4,675	$6,600
	W			$330

D=Drawing, P=Painting, S=Sculpture, W=Watercolor

		Current Price Range	
	Low	Mean	High

BRUSH, George de F. (Attrib.)	*P*			$154
American (1855 - 1941)				
BRUSKIN, Grisha	*P*			$39,600
Russian (1945 -)				
BRUTON, Margaret	*P*			$715
American (1894 - 1983)				
BRUTT, Ferdinand	*P*			$1,045
(?)				
BRUYERE, Elise	*P*			$16,500
French (1776 - 1842)				
BRUYN, Bartholom. (Circle)	*P*			$19,800
German (1530 - 1607)				
BRUYN, Cornelis-Johannes	*P*			$22,000
Dutch (19th -)				
BRUYN, ELDER, Barthel	*P*			$33,000
German (1493 - 1555)				
BRUYN, ELDER, Barthel (Attrib.)	*P*			$11,000
German (1493 - 1555)				
BRUYN, ELDER, Barthel (Circle)	*P*			$11,000
German (1493 - 1555)				
BRUZZI, Stefano	*P*			$44,000
Italian (1835 - 1911)				
BRYAN, Mary T.	*P*			$220
American (20th -)				
BRYAN, Rick	*S*			$600
American (20th -)				
BRYANT, Everett L.	*P*	$605	$4,455	$12,100
American (1864 - 1945)				
BRYERS, Duane	*P*	$2,530	$3,740	$4,950
American (1911 -)				
BRYNJOLF, Jorgen	*P*			$110
Danish (1931 -)				
BRYYN, Barthel	*P*			$18,700
German (1493 - 1555)				
BUBARNIK, A. Gyula	*P*			$2,090
Hungarian (20th -)				

D=Drawing, P=Painting, S=Sculpture, W=Watercolor

		Current Price Range		
		Low	Mean	High

		Low	Mean	High
BUCH, H.C.	*P*			$303
American (20th -)				
BUCHBINDER, Simeon	*P*			$7,150
German (19th -)				
BUCHET, Gustave	*P*			$6,325
(?)				
BUCHHOLZ, Erich	*P*			$60,500
German (1891 -)	*W*			$1,650
BUCHTA, Anthony	*P*			$825
American (20th -)				
BUCHTERKIRCH, Armin	*W*	$138	$234	$330
American (1859 -)				
BUCK, Claude	*P*	$523	$812	$1,100
American (1890 -)				
BUCK, William	*P*	$2,750	$14,410	$33,000
American (1840 - 1880)				
BUCKHOLZ, Fred	*D*			$440
(20th -)				
BUCKLER, Charles E.	*P*	$275	$629	$1,375
American (1869 -)				
BUCKLEY, Charles F.	*W*			$715
British (1841 - 1869)				
BUCKLEY, John M.	*P*	$605	$1,183	$1,760
American (1891 - 1958)				
BUCKLEY, Stephen	*P*			$6,325
British (1944 -)				
BUCKLIN, William S.	*P*			$330
American (1851 - 1928)	*W*	$110	$429	$825
BUCKSTONE, Frederick	*P*			$1,650
British (19th -)				
BUDELL, Ada	*D*			$385
American (1873 -)				
BUDELL, Hortense	*P*			$275
American (1884 -)				

D=Drawing, P=Painting, S=Sculpture, W=Watercolor

		Current Price Range		
		Low	Mean	High

		Low	Mean	High
BUDELOT, Phillipe French (18th - 19th)	*P*			$2,200
BUECHE, Johann (Attrib.) German (19th - 20th)	*P*			$880
BUECKL, Heinrich (?)	*P*			$2,200
BUEHR, George American (1905 -)	*D*			$143
BUEHR, Karl A. American (1886 -)	*P*	$605	$2,090	$3,575
BUENGIORNO, D. (?)	*P*			$825
BUENO, Antonio Italian (1918 -)	*P*			$5,500
BUFF, Conrad American (1886 - 1975)	*P*	$1,430	$3,449	$11,000
	W	$358	$889	$1,210
BUFFET, Amedee French (1869 - 1934)	*P*			$2,090
BUFFET, Bernard French (1928 -)	*D*	$3,850	$16,932	$39,600
	P	$30,500	$205,208	$797,500
	S			$1,760
	W	$24,200	$58,300	$99,000
BUFFIN, Carlos French (19th - 20th)	*P*			$22,000
BUGATTI, Rembrandt French (1885 - 1916)	*S*	$38,500	$82,500	$126,500
BUGGIANI, Paolo (20th -)	*P*			$110
BUGIARDINI, Giulio Italian (1475 - 1554)	*P*			$99,000
BUGZESTER, Max (?)	*P*	$1,045	$1,128	$1,210
BUHLER, Augustus W. American (1853 - 1920)	*P*	$1,100	$1,595	$2,090

D=Drawing, P=Painting, S=Sculpture, W=Watercolor

		Current Price Range		
		Low	Mean	High

		Low	Mean	High
BUHLER, Augustus W. (Attrib.)	*W*			$633
American (1853 - 1920)				
BUHLMANN, R.	*P*			$187
Swiss (19th -)				
BUHLMAYER, F.	*P*			$1,100
German (19th -)				
BUICK, J.	*P*			$495
British (18th -)				
BUKILL, G.	*S*			$1,210
American (19th - 20th)				
BUKILL, G. (Attrib.)	*S*			$5,500
American (19th - 20th)				
BULAND, Jean E.	*P*			$82,500
French (1852 - 1927)				
BULL, Charles L.	*D*	$248	$394	$660
American (1874 - 1932)	*W*	$935	$1,540	$2,310
BULLEID, George L.	*W*			$7,150
British (1858 - 1911)				
BULLOCK, Edith	*P*			$1,045
British (? - 1911)				
BULMAN, Orville	*P*			$550
American (20th -)				
BULTHUIS, Jan (Attrib.)	*D*			$660
Dutch (1750 - 1801)				
BUNCE, William G.	*P*			$1,100
American (1840 - 1916)				
BUNCH, C. V.	*P*			$715
Scandinavian (20th -)				
BUNDT, L.	*P*			$220
European (19th - 20th)				
BUNDY, E. W.	*P*			$2,090
British (19th -)				
BUNDY, Gilbert	*W*	$121	$185	$248
American (1911 - 1955)				
BUNDY, Horace	*P*			$2,420
(?)				

D=Drawing, P=Painting, S=Sculpture, W=Watercolor

		Current Price Range		
		Low	Mean	High

		Low	Mean	High
BUNDY, John E.	*P*	$605	$1,815	$2,420
American (1853 - 1933)	*W*	$413	$532	$660
BUNN, George	*P*	$2,090	$4,345	$6,600
British (19th -)				
BUNNER, Andrew F.	*P*			$3,850
American (1841 - 1897)	*W*	$303	$702	$1,100
BUNNIK, Jan van	*P*			$5,500
Dutch (1654 - 1727)				
BUNNIK, Jan van (Circle)	*P*			$770
Dutch (1654 - 1727)				
BUNNY, Rupert C. W.	*P*	$11,000	$126,500	$242,000
Australian (1864 - 1947)				
BUONGIORNO, C.	*P*			$275
(?)				
BUONO, J. S.	*P*			$605
Italian (19th - 20th)				
BURBANK, Addison B.	*P*			$1,045
American (1895 -)				
BURBANK, Elbridge A.	*P*	$935	$2,174	$4,675
American (1858 - 1947)				
BURBANK, William E.	*P*			$660
American (1866 - 1922)				
BURCH, Alice	*P*	$165	$286	$715
American (1909 - 1975)				
BURCHARD, Pablo	*P*			$7,150
Chilean (1876 -)				
BURCHFIELD, Charles E.	*D*	$165	$1,120	$2,090
American (1893 - 1967)	*W*	$660	$44,890	$143,000
BURDICK, Horace R.	*D*	$165	$220	$275
American (1844 - 1942)	*P*	$110	$209	$303
	W	$193	$479	$1,155
BURDICK, Horace R. (Attrib.)	*P*			$220
American (1844 - 1942)				

D=Drawing, P=Painting, S=Sculpture, W=Watercolor

		Current Price Range		
		Low	Mean	High

		Low	Mean	High
BUREN, Raeburn van	*P*			$138
(1891 -)				
BURFIELD, James M.	*P*			$990
British (19th -)				
BURG, H. S. S.	*P*			$220
(?)				
BURGDORFF, Ferdinand	*P*	$935	$1,421	$3,300
American (1881 - 1975)	*W*	$605	$1,705	$3,300
BURGER, Carl	*W*			$330
American (?)				
BURGER, Fritz	*P*			$660
German (1867 -)				
BURGER, Willy F.	*P*			$495
German (1882 - 1964)				
BURGERS, Hendricus J.	*P*	$3,300	$11,000	$18,700
Dutch (1834 - 1899)				
BURGESS, Emma A.	*P*			$330
(19th - 20th)				
BURGESS, John B.	*P*	$495	$3,823	$7,150
British (1830 - 1897)				
BURGESS, John B. (Attrib.)	*P*			$1,320
British (1830 - 1897)				
BURGESS, Ruth P.	*P*	$523	$537	$550
American (? - 1934)				
BURGH, Cornelis J. van der	*P*			$14,300
Dutch (1640 -)				
BURGHART, C.	*P*	$1,320	$1,705	$2,090
American (19th - 20th)				
BURGUM, John	*P*			$1,870
American (?)				
BURKE, Adriaen von	*P*			$550
(?)				
BURKE, Patrick	*P*			$1,320
(20th -)				
BURKERT, Robert (Attrib.)	*D*			$100
American (20th -)				

D=Drawing, P=Painting, S=Sculpture, W=Watercolor

| | | Current Price Range | | |
		Low	Mean	High
BURKHARD, Henri	P			$1,650
American (1892 -)				
BURKHARDT, Giovanni	P			$523
(?)				
BURKHARDT, Hans	D	$385	$715	$1,045
American (1904 -)	P			$440
BURLEIGH, Charles H. H.	P			$24,200
British (1875 - 1956)				
BURLEIGH, Sidney R.	W	$330	$1,052	$2,200
American (1853 - 1931)				
BURLIN, Harry Paul	P	$1,760	$1,870	$1,980
American (1886 - 1969)	W			$495
BURLINGAME, Charles A.	P	$495	$1,348	$2,200
American (1860 - 1931)				
BURLINGAME, Dennis M.	P			$1,100
American (1901 -)				
BURLINGAME, Sheila H.	S			$26,400
American (1893 - 1969)				
BURLIUK, David	P	$660	$10,050	$275,000
American (1882 - 1967)	S			$52,250
	W	$308	$1,301	$5,500
BURMEISTER, Paul	P			$3,960
German (1847 -)				
BURNE-JONES, Sir Edward C.	D	$3,025	$21,542	$39,600
British (1833 - 1898)				
BURNETTE, M.	P	$935	$1,018	$1,100
American (20th -)				
BURNS, E.	P			$440
(19th -)				
BURNS, J.	P			$4,400
American (19th -)				
BURNS, Mark	S			$1,650
(20th -)				

D=Drawing, P=Painting, S=Sculpture, W=Watercolor

		Current Price Range		
		Low	Mean	High

		Low	Mean	High
BURNS, Maurice K.	P			$2,640
American (20th -)				
BURNS, Milton J.	D			$880
American (1853 - 1933)	P			$5,280
BURNS, Paul C.	W			$350
American (1910 -)				
BURNS, Raymond	P			$138
American (20th -)				
BURNS, Robert	P			$303
American (20th -)				
BURNS-WILSON, Robert	W			$990
American (1851 - 1916)				
BURNSIDE,	P			$209
(20th -)				
BURNSIDE, Cameron	W			$770
American (1887 - 1952)				
BURPEE, William P.	D	$220	$715	$990
American (1846 -)	P			$2,750
	W	$303	$344	$385
BURR, Alexander H.	P			$4,950
British (1837 - 1899)				
BURR, George B.	P	$385	$2,548	$5,500
American (1876 - 1939)				
BURR, George E.	P			$6,050
American (1859 - 1939)	W	$495	$605	$715
BURR, Harold S.	P	$330	$385	$440
American (1889 - 1973)				
BURR, John	P	$1,540	$2,145	$2,750
British (1831 - 1893)				
BURR, Saxton	P	$248	$350	$550
American (1889 - 1973)				
BURR, Saxton (Attrib.)	P			$743
American (1889 - 1973)				

D=Drawing, P=Painting, S=Sculpture, W=Watercolor

		Current Price Range		
		Low	Mean	High
BURRAS, Thomas of Leeds	*P*			$13,200
British (19th -)				
BURRELL, Alfred R.	*P*			$550
American (1877 - 1952)				
BURRI, Alberto	*S*	$55,000	$264,000	$473,000
Italian (1915 -)				
BURRIDGE, Walter W.	*P*			$1,100
American (1857 -)	*W*			$165
BURRILL, JR., E.	*P*			$495
American (19th - 20th)				
BURRINGTON, Arthur A.	*P*			$7,700
British (1856 - 1925)				
BURRISS, R. Hal	*D*			$275
American (1892 -)	*W*	$220	$669	$880
BURRITT, Edwin	*P*			$440
(?)				
BURROUGHS, A. Leicester	*P*			$2,860
British (19th -)				
BURT, Charles T.	*P*	$1,210	$1,650	$2,090
British (1823 - 1902)				
BURT, Maria E.	*W*			$825
British (19th - 20th)				
BURTON, Frederick W.	*P*			$1,100
British (1816 - 1900)				
BURTON, Scott	*S*	$16,500	$17,600	$18,700
American (20th -)				
BURY, Pol	*S*			$29,700
(20th -)				
BUSA, Peter	*P*	$220	$248	$275
American (20th -)				
BUSCH, Clarence F.	*P*	$248	$1,169	$2,090
American (1887 -)				
BUSCH, Hans	*W*			$4,290
American (20th -)				

D=Drawing, P=Painting, S=Sculpture, W=Watercolor

		Current Price Range		
		Low	Mean	High

		Low	Mean	High
BUSCH, S. van den	*D*			$1,650
Belgian (19th - 20th)				
BUSCHER, Franz	*P*			$3,300
American (19th -)				
BUSH, Jack	*P*	$15,400	$46,567	$66,000
Canadian (1909 -)				
BUSH, Norton	*P*	$1,100	$1,888	$3,025
American (1834 - 1894)				
BUSQUETS, Jean	*P*	$468	$708	$935
French (20th -)				
BUSSE, Gustave	*D*			$176
(?)				
BUSSIERE, Gaston	*P*			$8,800
French (1862 - 1929)				
BUSSON, Charles	*P*			$4,400
French (1822 - 1908)				
BUTIN, Ulysee	*P*	$440	$1,100	$1,760
French (1837 - 1883)				
BUTINONE, Bernardino	*P*			$39,600
Italian (1436 - 1507)				
BUTLER, Charles E.	*P*	$220	$372	$523
British (1864 - 1918)				
BUTLER, Courtland	*P*	$1,045	$1,128	$1,210
(1871 -)				
BUTLER, Frank	*P*			$165
(20th -)				
BUTLER, Herbert E.	*P*			$1,100
British (19th -)				
BUTLER, Howard R.	*D*	$358	$454	$550
American (1856 - 1934)	*P*	$385	$2,228	$7,150
BUTLER, James	*P*			$495
American (20th -)				
BUTLER, Lady Elizabeth S.	*P*			$1,100
British (19th -)				
BUTLER, Mary	*P*	$138	$401	$1,540

D=Drawing, P=Painting, S=Sculpture, W=Watercolor

| | | Current Price Range | | |
		Low	Mean	High
BUTLER, Mary	W	$121	$143	$165
American (1865 - 1946)				
BUTLER, Phillip A.	P	$330	$779	$1,650
American (19th -)				
BUTLER, Reg	S	$6,050	$12,452	$22,000
British (1913 -)				
BUTLER, Rozel O.	P	$2,200	$3,410	$6,600
American (20th -)				
BUTLER, Theodore E.	D	$358	$729	$1,100
American (1861 - 1936)	P	$350	$20,200	$33,000
BUTLER, Thomas	P	$6,050	$36,025	$66,000
British (18th -)				
BUTMAN, Frederick A.	P			$5,500
American (1820 - 1871)				
BUTTER, Tom	P			$8,250
(20th -)	S	$3,300	$5,775	$7,700
BUTTERFIELD, Deborah	P	$27,500	$28,050	$28,600
American (1949 -)	S	$49,500	$50,050	$50,600
BUTTERFIELD, W. Cortland	P			$550
American (20th -)				
BUTTERI, Giovanni M.	P			$20,900
Italian (? - 1606)				
BUTTERS, Charles	W			$231
(?)				
BUTTERSWORTH, James E.	P	$4,510	$52,477	$242,000
American (1817 - 1894)				
BUTTERSWORTH, James E. (Att)	P			$4,400
American (1817 - 1894)				
BUTTERSWORTH, Thomas	P	$12,650	$28,417	$48,400
British (1768 - 1842)				
BUTTERSWORTH, JR., Thomas	P			$8,800
British (19th -)				
BUTTNER, Hans	P	$3,300	$3,850	$4,400
German (19th -)				

D=Drawing, P=Painting, S=Sculpture, W=Watercolor

		Current Price Range		
		Low	Mean	High

BUTTON, Albert P.	*P*	$303	$758	$1,430
American (1872 -)	*W*			$275
BUTTS, Kathleen V.	*P*			$800
American (20th -)				
BUXTON,	*W*			$165
American (20th -)				
BUYCK, Edward P.	*P*			$165
American (1868 -)				
BUYTEWECH, Willem P. (Circle)	*P*			$16,500
Dutch (16th - 17th)				
BUZIO, Lidya	*S*			$3,740
(20th -)				
BUZZELLI, Joseph A.	*P*			$660
American (1907 -)				
BYARS, James Lee	*S*			$9,350
(20th -)				
BYE, Ranulph	*W*			$375
American (1916 -)				
BYLERT, Jan van (Attrib.)	*P*			$31,900
Dutch (1603 - 1673)				
BYNE, Arthur	*W*			$275
American (1884 - 1935)				
BYRD, Gibson (Attrib.)	*P*	$200	$312	$475
American (20th -)	*W*			$250
BYRD, Henry	*P*			$2,090
American (?)				
BYRNES, Harry	*P*			$440
(?)				
BYRUM, R. H.	*P*			$275
(?)				
CABAILLOT, Louis S.	*P*			$2,750
French (1810 -)				
CABALLERO, Luis	*D*	$2,750	$5,317	$9,900
Colombian (1943 -)	*P*			$2,200

D=Drawing, P=Painting, S=Sculpture, W=Watercolor

		Current Price Range		
		Low	Mean	High

		Low	Mean	High
CABALLERO, Luis Colombian (1943 -)	W			$2,750
CABALLERO, Maximo Spanish (19th -)	P	$14,300	$16,500	$20,900
CABANEL, Alexandre French (1824 - 1889)	P	$7,150	$11,275	$15,400
CABANEL, Alexandre (Attrib.) French (1824 - 1889)	P			$1,980
CABEL, Adrian van der (School) French (1631 - 1695)	P			$1,650
CABOT, Edward C. American (1818 - 1901)	W	$165	$284	$358
CABOT, W. Channing (1868 - 1932)	P	$165	$234	$303
CABRADA, V. Spanish (20th -)	P			$110
CABRERA, Miguel Mexican (18th -)	P	$8,800	$10,450	$12,100
CABRERA, Ricardo L. Spanish (1864 - 1950)	P			$9,900
CABUZEL, Auguste H. French (1836 -)	P			$9,350
CABZULANI, Luigi Italian (19th -)	P			$1,100
CACCIARELLI, Victor Italian (19th -)	W	$1,320	$1,320	$1,320
CACCIERELLI, Umberto Italian (19th -)	P			$3,080
CACHOUD, Felix (?)	P			$990
CACHOUD, Francois C. French (1866 - 1943)	P	$2,200	$5,225	$13,200
CADENASSO, Guiseppe American (1858 - 1918)	D P	$1,650 $1,320	$1,870 $5,708	$2,090 $18,700
CADES, Giuseppi (Attrib.) Italian (1750 - 1799)	D			$2,475

D=Drawing, P=Painting, S=Sculpture, W=Watercolor

		Current Price Range		
		Low	Mean	High

		Low	Mean	High
CADMUS, Paul	D	$1,320	$7,678	$23,100
American (1904 -)	P	$5,500	$78,375	$154,000
CADORET, Michel	W			$1,430
French (1912 -)				
CADY, Arthur	W			$358
American (20th -)				
CADY, F.	P			$330
American (20th -)				
CADY, Harrison	P			$2,200
American (1877 - 1970)	W			$330
CADY, Henry B.	P			$4,620
American (?)				
CADY, Henry N.	P	$385	$674	$1,320
American (1849 -)	W	$248	$431	$825
CADY, Sam	P	$550	$550	$550
American (1943 -)				
CAESAR, Doris	S			$468
American (1892 - 1971)				
CAFE, Thomas W.	P			$1,430
British (1856 -)				
CAFFE, Nino	P	$1,650	$5,449	$12,100
Spanish (1909 - 1975)				
CAFFERTY, James H.	D			$385
American (1819 - 1869)	P	$770	$2,173	$3,575
CAFFIERI, Hector	W			$12,100
British (1847 - 1932)				
CAFFIERI, Jean J. (Manner)	S			$11,000
French (1678 - 1775)				
CAFFYN, Walter W.	P	$1,760	$3,355	$4,950
British (1845 - 1898)				
CAGLI, Corrado	P			$3,850
Italian (1910 -)				
CAGLIANI, Louis	D			$770

D=Drawing, P=Painting, S=Sculpture, W=Watercolor

		Current Price Range		
		Low	Mean	High

		Low	Mean	High
CAGLIANI, Louis Italian (20th -)	P	$132	$204	$248
CAGNACCI, Guido Italian (1601 - 1681)	P			$55,000
CAGNIART, Emile French (1851 - 1911)	P			$7,700
CAHOON, Charles D. American (1861 - 1951)	P	$550	$3,758	$30,800
CAHOON, Charles D. (Attrib.) American (1861 - 1951)	P			$990
CAHOON, Martha American (1905 -)	P	$330	$1,932	$7,425
CAHOON, Ralph American (1910 - 1982)	P W	$1,925	$6,625	$13,200 $935
CAILLE, Leon E. French (1836 - 1907)	P	$1,210	$2,489	$4,125
CAILLEBOTTE, Gustave French (1840 - 1894)	D P	$330,000	$584,375	$577,500 $715,000
CAIN, Auguste N. French (1822 - 1894)	S	$143	$2,409	$7,700
CAIN, Georges French (1856 - 1919)	P	$4,400	$4,675	$4,950
CALABRIA, Ennio Italian (20th -)	P	$1,320	$1,815	$2,310
CALAME, Alexandre (Attrib.) Swiss (1810 - 1864)	P			$1,430
CALANDRUCCI, Giacinto Italian (1646 - 1707)	D			$605
CALBET, Antoine French (1860 - 1944)	P			$550
CALCAR, Jan S. von Dutch (1499 - 1546)	P			$6,050
CALDECOTT, Randolph British (1846 - 1886)	D			$137,500

D=Drawing, P=Painting, S=Sculpture, W=Watercolor

		Current Price Range		
		Low	Mean	High

		Low	Mean	High
CALDER, Alexander	*D*	$550	$15,151	$55,000
American (1898 - 1976)	*P*	$25,300	$44,894	$66,000
	S	$3,520	$234,043	$2.090M
	W	$1,980	$13,760	$30,800
CALDER, Alexander (After)	*S*	$1,870	$4,091	$7,700
American (1898 - 1976)				
CALDER, Alexander (Attrib.)	*W*			$1,045
American (1898 - 1976)				
CALDERON, Charles C.	*P*			$3,575
French (19th -)				
CALDERON, Philip H.	*P*			$1,265
British (1833 - 1898)				
CALDINI, A.	*P*			$275
Italian (20th -)				
CALDWELL, Georgia	*P*	$121	$207	$358
American (1867 - 1946)				
CALHOUN, Frederick D.	*P*			$248
American (1883 -)				
CALICE, R.	*P*			$550
French (19th -)				
CALICOTT,	*D*			$468
(?)				
CALIFANO, E.	*P*	$165	$262	$358
(?)				
CALIFANO, John	*P*	$165	$1,810	$14,300
American (1864 - 1924)				
CALIFORNIA SCHOOL 20C,	*P*			$1,650
American (20th -)				
CALIGA, Isaac H.	*D*			$220
American (1857 -)	*P*	$1,100	$1,393	$1,760
CALLAHAN, Kenneth	*W*			$385
American (1906 -)				
CALLAWAY, William F.	*P*			$413
British (19th -)				

D=Drawing, P=Painting, S=Sculpture, W=Watercolor

| | | Current Price Range | | |
		Low	Mean	High
CALLE, Paul	*D*			$4,510
(1928 -)	*P*			$55,000
CALLERY, Mary	*S*			$605
(?)				
CALLET, Antoine F. (Attrib.)	*P*			$330
French (1741 - 1823)				
CALLOT, Jacques	*D*	$20,900	$25,300	$29,700
French (1592 - 1635)				
CALLOT, Jacques (Circle)	*D*			$2,310
French (1592 - 1635)				
CALLOW, George	*P*			$660
British (?)				
CALLOW, John	*P*			$2,310
British (1822 - 1878)				
CALLOW, William	*P*	$3,080	$3,300	$3,520
British (1812 - 1908)				
CALMELET, Hedwig	*W*	$358	$358	$358
French (1814 -)				
CALOGERO, Jean	*P*	$220	$468	$935
Italian (1922 -)				
CALOSCI, Arturo	*P*			$1,430
Italian (1855 - 1926)				
CALRAET, Abraham van	*P*	$11,000	$16,500	$22,000
Dutch (1642 - 1722)				
CALS, Adolphe F.	*P*			$1,980
French (1810 - 1880)				
CALVAERT, Dionisio	*D*			$10,450
Flemish (1540 - 1619)				
CALVAERT, Dionisio (Attrib.)	*P*			$7,700
Flemish (1540 - 1619)				
CALVELLI, Fillip	*P*	$138	$193	$248
Italian (20th -)				
CALVERT, Henry	*P*			$2,750
British (1798 -)				
CALVES, G.	*P*	$1,000	$1,150	$1,300
European (19th -)				

D=Drawing, P=Painting, S=Sculpture, W=Watercolor

		Current Price Range		
		Low	Mean	High
CALVES, Leon	P	$1,320	$1,540	$1,760
French (1848 -)				
CALVI, Jacopo A.	D			$770
Italian (1740 - 1815)				
CALVI, Lazzaro (Attrib.)	D			$7,150
Italian (1502 - 1603)				
CALVIN, E. P.	W			$110
(?)				
CALYDAT & VARTAN, G. & A.	W			$121
(?)				
CALYO, Nicolino	P			$3,520
(1799 - 1884)				
CALZADA, Humberto	P	$4,400	$4,675	$4,950
Cuban (1944 -)				
CAMACHO, Jorge	P	$2,475	$4,263	$6,050
Cuban (1934 -)				
CAMARGO, Sergio de	S			$6,600
Lat. Amer. (20th -)				
CAMASSEI, Andrea (Attrib.)	P			$33,000
Italian (1601 - 1648)				
CAMBIASO, Luca	D	$1,870	$7,132	$12,100
Italian (1527 - 1585)				
CAMBIASO, Luca (Attrib.)	D			$2,200
Italian (1527 - 1585)				
CAMBIASO, Luca (Circle)	D	$660	$853	$1,045
Italian (1527 - 1585)				
CAMBIASO, Luca (Follower)	D			$2,860
Italian (1527 - 1585)				
CAMBIER, Guy	P	$715	$1,788	$2,860
Belgian (?)				
CAMERINO, Arcangelo di Cola da	P			$1.100M
Italian (15th -)				
CAMERON, David Y.	P	$825	$1,018	$1,210
Scottish (1865 - 1945)				
CAMERON, Donald	P	$550	$770	$990
Scottish (19th -)				

D=Drawing, P=Painting, S=Sculpture, W=Watercolor

		Current Price Range		
		Low	Mean	High

		Low	Mean	High
CAMERON, Douglas (?)	P			$303
CAMERON, E. American (20th -)	P			$715
CAMOIN, Charles French (1879 - 1965)	D			$5,500
	P	$1,650	$21,962	$71,500
CAMP, Jeffrey American (20th -)	P			$825
CAMPAGNA, Girolamo (Attrib.) Italian (18th -)	S			$9,900
CAMPAGNOLA, Domenico (Foll) Italian (1484 - 1550)	D			$1,320
CAMPAGNOLA, Enrico Italian (1911 -)	P			$330
CAMPBELL, Charles American (1905 -)	P			$220
CAMPBELL, David (20th -)	D			$1,100
CAMPBELL, Edmund J. (20th -)	W			$150
CAMPBELL, Francis (Et al.) American (20th -)	D			$1,320
CAMPBELL, H. European (19th - 20th)	P	$319	$352	$385
CAMPBELL, L. British (19th -)	W			$303
CAMPBELL, Laurence A. American (20th -)	P			$990
CAMPBELL, R. American (20th -)	P			$1,100
CAMPBELL, Scott British (19th - 20th)	P			$523
CAMPBELL, Steven British (1946 -)	P	$9,350	$15,714	$19,800
	W			$3,850

D=Drawing, P=Painting, S=Sculpture, W=Watercolor

		Current Price Range		
		Low	Mean	High

		Low	Mean	High
CAMPBELL, William	*P*			$523
(19th -)				
CAMPI, Bernardino (Attrib.)	*P*			$104,500
Italian (1522 - 1592)				
CAMPI, Giulio (Attrib.)	*P*			$13,200
Italian (1500 - 1572)				
CAMPI, Giulio (Workshop)	*D*			$2,200
Italian (1500 - 1572)				
CAMPIDOGLIO, Michele (Att.)	*P*			$46,200
Italian (1610 - 1670)				
CAMPIGLI, Massimo	*P*	$99,000	$162,250	$242,000
Italian (1895 - 1971)	*W*			$19,800
CAMPO, Francisco P. Del	*P*			$29,700
Spanish (1837 - 1897)				
CAMPO, Frederico Del	*D*			$523
Peruvian (19th - 20th)	*P*	$55,000	$141,167	$198,000
	W			$2,420
CAMPOLMI, S.	*P*			$28,600
Italian (19th -)				
CAMPOS, Florencio	*P*	$9,900	$10,175	$10,450
Argentine (1891 - 1959)	*W*			$9,350
CAMPOTOSTO, Henry	*P*			$1,650
Belgian (? - 1910)				
CAMPOTOSTO, Octavio	*P*	$1,045	$1,128	$1,210
Belgian (19th -)				
CAMUS, Blanche	*P*			$16,500
French (20th -)				
CANALETTO, Antonio	*D*			$16,500
Italian (1697 - 1768)	*P*	$1.595M	$6.297M	$11.000M
CANALETTO, Antonio (Circle)	*P*			$137,500
Italian (1697 - 1768)				
CANALETTO, Antonio (Manner)	*P*	$2,640	$14,204	$38,500
Italian (1697 - 1768)				

D=Drawing, P=Painting, S=Sculpture, W=Watercolor

		Current Price Range		
		Low	Mean	High

		Low	Mean	High
CANALETTO, Antonio (School) Italian (1697 - 1768)	P	$5,500	$22,471	$38,500
CANALETTO, Antonio (Studio) Italian (1697 - 1768)	P	$55,000	$126,500	$198,000
CANCIO, Carlos Lat. Amer. (20th -)	P			$6,600
CANDIA, Domingo Lat. Amer. (20th -)	P	$9,900	$10,175	$10,450
CANDIDA, Alfredo (After) (?)	P			$660
CANEDALLE, R. American (?)	P			$1,100
CANELLA, A. (?)	W			$468
CANEVARI, Carlo Italian (1922 -)	P	$248	$427	$605
CANINI, Giovanni A. (Attrib.) Italian (1617 - 1666)	D			$3,520
CANNELLA, Pizzi Italian (20th -)	P	$16,500	$18,150	$19,800
CANOVA, Antonia (After) Italian (1757 - 1822)	S			$2,475
CANTAGALLINA, Remigio Italian (1582 - 1630)	D			$1,980
CANTAGALLINA, Remigio (Cir.) Italian (1582 - 1630)	D			$660
CANTARINI, Simone Italian (1612 - 1648)	D	$4,180	$4,565	$4,950
CANTARINI, Simone (Attrib.) Italian (1612 - 1648)	D			$1,980
CANTATORE, Domenico (?)	P			$1,320
CANTI, (?)	P			$185
CANTINEAU, Virgile Belgian (19th -)	P			$303

D=Drawing, P=Painting, S=Sculpture, W=Watercolor

		Current Price Range		
		Low	Mean	High

		Low	Mean	High
CANTU, Federico	P	$770	$1,595	$2,420
Mexican (1908 -)				
CANTWELL, James	P			$220
American (19th - 20th)				
CANU, Yvonne	P	$1,155	$1,788	$2,420
French (1921 -)				
CAPLAN, Jerry L.	S			$495
(1922 -)				
CAPLES, Robert C.	P			$220
American (1908 - 1979)				
CAPONE, Gaetano	P	$770	$3,056	$13,200
Italian (1845 - 1920)				
CAPORALI, Bartolomeo (Attrib.)	P			$74,800
Italian (1420 -)				
CAPP, Al	D	$176	$281	$385
American (1909 -)	P	$550	$2,008	$6,050
CAPPELLI, Pietro	P			$4,400
Italian (? - 1724)				
CAPPIELLO, Leonetto	P			$2,750
French (1875 - 1942)				
CAPPIELLO, Suzanne	P			$2,475
French (20th -)				
CAPRILE, Vincenzo	D			$330
Italian (1856 - 1936)				
CAPRON, Jean-Pierre	P	$358	$970	$1,650
French (1921 -)				
CAPUTO, Ulisse	P			$4,400
Italian (1872 - 1948)				
CARA, Henry	P			$770
Australian (?)				
CARABAIN, Jacques F.	P	$12,100	$15,950	$19,800
Belgian (1834 - 1892)				
CARABAIN, Victor	P			$2,200
Belgian (19th - 20th)				
CARACCIOLO, Giovanni	P	$5,775	$63,388	$121,000
Italian (1570 - 1637)				

D=Drawing, P=Painting, S=Sculpture, W=Watercolor

		Current Price Range		
		Low	Mean	High

		Low	Mean	High
CARACH, W. A. (?)	P			$1,265
CARAUD, Joseph French (1821 - 1905)	P	$16,500	$17,050	$17,600
CARAVAGGIO, Michel. (Foll) Italian (1573 - 1610)	P			$935
CARBOULD, Alfred (?)	P			$1,650
CARDENAS, Agustin Cuban (1927 -)	S	$5,500	$21,588	$44,000
CARDENAS, Juan Colombian (1939 -)	P			$18,700
CARDENAS, Santiago Columbian (1937 -)	P			$10,450
CARDI, Lodovico C. Italian (1559 - 1613)	P			$132,000
CARDI, Lodovico C. (Attrib) Italian (1559 - 1613)	P			$4,400
CARDON, Claude British (19th -)	W			$1,100
CARDONA, Juan Spanish (19th - 20th)	P			$19,800
CARDONE, G. American (20th -)	P			$110
CARDOSSI, Professor Vittorio Italian (19th - 20th)	S			$99,000
CARDUCCI, Adolfo Italian (1901 -)	P			$1,540
CARELL, Florence (?)	P			$468
CARELLI, Consalve Italian (1818 - 1900)	P	$3,080	$11,990	$20,900
CARELLI, Gabriel Italian (1820 - 1880)	W	$1,100	$1,375	$1,650
CARELLI, Giuseppe Italian (1858 - 1921)	P	$2,200	$2,420	$2,640

D=Drawing, P=Painting, S=Sculpture, W=Watercolor

		Current Price Range		
		Low	Mean	High

CAREY, H.	P			$825
American (19th -)				
CARGNEL, Vittore A.	P			$770
Italian (1872 - 1931)				
CARIANI, Giovanni	P	$14,300	$84,150	$154,000
Italian (15th -)				
CARIANI, Varaldo J.	P			$440
(?)				
CARILLO, Lilia	P			$5,225
Mexican (1930 -)				
CARL, Ewan B.	P			$660
American (19th -)				
CARLANDI, Onorato	W	$550	$743	$935
Italian (1848 - 1939)				
CARLES, Arthur B.	D	$110	$1,414	$2,640
American (1882 - 1952)	P	$1,800	$16,745	$38,500
	W	$523	$1,197	$1,870
CARLES, Arthur B. (School)	P			$220
American (1882 - 1952)				
CARLETON, Anne	P			$1,540
American (1878 - 1968)				
CARLETTI, Alicia	W			$2,200
Argentina (1946 -)				
CARLEVARIJS, Luca	P			$93,500
Italian (1665 - 1731)				
CARLIER, Modeste	P			$6,380
Belgian (1820 - 1878)				
CARLIN, James	P			$605
(?)				
CARLIN, John	P	$2,750	$2,860	$2,970
American (1813 - 1891)				
CARLISLE, John	W			$825
British (19th -)				
CARLISLE, S.	W			$440
British (18th - 19th)				

D=Drawing, P=Painting, S=Sculpture, W=Watercolor

		Current Price Range		
		Low	Mean	High
CARLSEN, Dines	*P*	$605	$5,019	$18,700
American (1901 - 1966)				
CARLSEN, Flora B.	*P*			$275
American (1878 -)				
CARLSEN, Soren E.	*P*	$825	$13,678	$66,000
American (1853 - 1932)	*W*			$3,850
CARLSEN, Soren E. (After)	*P*			$275
American (1853 - 1932)				
CARLSEN, Soren E. (Manner)	*P*			$770
American (1853 - 1932)				
CARLSON, Carl A.	*W*	$138	$284	$440
American (20th -)				
CARLSON, E.	*D*			$165
American (20th -)				
CARLSON, John F.	*D*			$1,045
American (1875 - 1947)	*P*	$605	$8,548	$41,800
CARLSON, Ken	*P*			$6,050
American (20th -)				
CARLSON, M.	*P*			$143
(?)				
CARLSON, Oscar	*P*			$165
American (1895 -)				
CARLSSON, E. F.	*P*			$220
Swedish (19th - 20th)				
CARMASSI, Arturo	*P*			$1,633
Italian (1925 -)				
CARMICHAEL, John W.	*P*	$963	$5,813	$13,200
British (1800 - 1868)				
CARMICHAEL, John W. (Attrib.)	*P*			$2,200
British (1800 - 1868)				
CARMIENCKE, John H.	*P*	$3,300	$4,583	$7,150
American (1810 - 1867)				
CARMODY, Anne	*P*			$440
American (20th -)				

D=Drawing, P=Painting, S=Sculpture, W=Watercolor

		Current Price Range	
	Low	Mean	High

		Low	Mean	High
CARNEVARI, Carlo (20th -)	*P*			$1,650
CARNICERO, Antonio Spanish (1748 - 1814)	*P*			$57,750
CARNIER, H. French (19th - 20th)	*P*	$374	$407	$440
CARNOT, Paul French (20th -)	*P*			$440
CARO, Anthony British (1924 -)	*S*	$28,600	$47,422	$77,000
CARO-DELVAILLE, Henry French (1876 - 1926)	*P*	$8,800	$11,000	$13,200
CAROLUS-DURAN, Emile A. French (1838 - 1917)	*P*	$18,700	$212,850	$407,000
CARON, Antoine Italian (1521 - 1599)	*D*			$60,500
CARON, Henry French (19th - 20th)	*P*			$1,430
CARON, P. French (20th -)	*P*			$1,430
CARONE, Nicolas American (1917 -)	*P*			$138
CAROSELLI, Angelo (After) Italian (1585 - 1652)	*P*			$1,980
CAROSELLI, Angelo (Attrib.) Italian (1585 - 1652)	*P*			$20,900
CAROT, Jean B. French (1796 - 1875)	*P*	$220,000	$473,000	$704,000
CAROTO, Giovan F. Italian (1480 - 1555)	*D*			$88,000
CARPEAUX, Jean B. French (1827 - 1875)	*S*	$8,800	$16,775	$24,200
CARPEAUX, Jean B. (After) French (1827 - 1875)	*S*	$4,125	$9,763	$15,400
CARPENTER, A. R. British (19th -)	*P*			$660

D=Drawing, P=Painting, S=Sculpture, W=Watercolor

		Current Price Range		
		Low	Mean	High

CARPENTER, Ellen M. American (1836 - 1909)	*P*			$220
CARPENTER, Fred G. American (1882 - 1965)	*P*	$825	$1,298	$2,420
CARPENTER, H. J. American (20th -)	*W*			$138
CARPENTER, Louise M. American (1876 - 1963)	*P*	$1,100	$1,320	$1,540
CARPENTER, Margaret British (1793 - 1872)	*P*			$4,950
CARPENTER, Margaret (Attrib.) British (1793 - 1872)	*P*			$3,025
CARPENTERO, Henri J. G. Belgian (1820 - 1874)	*P*			$1,210
CARPENTIER, Evariste Belgian (1845 - 1922)	*P*			$22,000
CARPENTIER, Madeleine European (19th -)	*P*			$1,980
CARPENTIERS, Adrien (? - 1778)	*P*			$3,575
CARPI, Girolamo da Italian (1501 - 1556)	*D*			$2,200
CARR, J. C. American (19th - 20th)	*P*			$370
CARR, Lyell American (1857 - 1912)	*P*	$880	$1,943	$3,410
CARR, Michael C. American (1881 -)	*P*			$385
CARR, Samuel S. American (1837 - 1908)	*P*	$935	$13,933	$82,500
CARRA, Carlo Italian (1881 - 1966)	*S*			$385,000
CARRACCI, Annibale Italian (1560 - 1609)	*D*			$19,800
CARRACCI, Annibale (Attrib.) Italian (1560 - 1609)	*D*			$743

D=Drawing, P=Painting, S=Sculpture, W=Watercolor

		Current Price Range		
		Low	Mean	High

		Low	Mean	High
CARRACCI, Annibale (Circle)	*D*	$2,530	$5,940	$9,350
Italian (1560 - 1609)				
CARRACCI, Annibale (Follower)	*D*			$2,860
Italian (1560 - 1609)				
CARRACCI, Annibale (Manner)	*P*			$1,650
Italian (1560 - 1609)				
CARRACCI, Lodovico	*P*			$27,500
Italian (1555 - 1619)				
CARRACCI, Lodovico (School)	*D*			$4,400
Italian (1555 - 1619)				
CARRADO,	*P*			$187
(?)				
CARRARA,	*S*			$1,650
(?)				
CARRAVAGGIO, Polidoro da	*D*			$550
Italian (1492 - 1543)				
CARREE, Michiel	*D*			$3,520
Dutch (1657 - 1747)	*P*	$1,320	$4,318	$7,150
CARRENO, Mario	*D*			$6,600
Cuban (1913 -)	*P*	$7,700	$54,285	$286,000
	W			$13,200
CARRICK, John M.	*P*			$44,000
British (19th -)				
CARRIER-BELLEUSE, Albert E.	*D*			$44,000
French (1824 - 1887)	*S*	$1,320	$3,011	$4,675
CARRIER-BELLEUSE, Louis R.	*P*	$7,700	$9,075	$10,450
French (1848 - 1913)				
CARRIER-BELLEUSE, Pierre	*D*	$7,700	$17,050	$27,500
French (1851 - 1932)				
CARRIERA, Rosalba (Follower)	*D*	$1,650	$5,225	$8,800
Italian (1675 - 1757)				
CARRIERE, Eugene	*D*			$165
French (1849 - 1906)	*P*	$3,300	$9,075	$19,800

D=Drawing, P=Painting, S=Sculpture, W=Watercolor

		Current Price Range		
		Low	Mean	High

		Low	Mean	High
CARRILLO, Lilia (?)	P			$5,280
CARRINGTON, James Y. British (1857 - 1892)	P			$2,090
CARRINGTON, Leonora British (1917 -)	D	$770	$1,956	$3,850
	P	$17,600	$44,950	$132,000
	S	$4,950	$6,600	$8,250
	W	$5,500	$6,669	$9,350
CARROLL, Beryl American (20th -)	W	$110	$171	$231
CARROLL, Georgia (?)	D			$176
CARROLL, John American (1892 - 1959)	D			$121
	P	$275	$1,338	$2,420
CARROLL, Lawrence (20th -)	P			$16,500
CARSMAN, Jon American (20th -)	P			$1,430
CARSON, Frank American (1881 -)	P	$495	$3,190	$7,975
CARSON, W. A. American (20th -)	P	$121	$279	$468
CARTER, Charles M. American (1853 - 1929)	P	$138	$207	$275
CARTER, Clarence H. American (1904 - 1981)	P	$3,850	$21,175	$38,500
	S			$1,540
	W	$550	$1,283	$2,200
CARTER, Dennis M. American (1827 - 1881)	P			$4,620
CARTER, Gary American (1939 -)	D	$1,320	$1,360	$1,400
	P	$3,300	$5,042	$6,600
	S			$4,620

D=Drawing, P=Painting, S=Sculpture, W=Watercolor

		Current Price Range		
		Low	Mean	High
CARTER, Hugh	*W*			$1,265
British (1837 - 1903)				
CARTER, Pruett	*P*	$1,200	$1,958	$2,475
American (1891 - 1955)	*W*			$193
CARTER, R. H.	*W*			$1,540
European (20th -)				
CARTER, Raymond	*P*			$1,210
(? - 1939)				
CARTER, Sydney	*P*			$4,400
British (19th -)	*W*	$138	$413	$688
CARTER, William	*D*			$825
American (1905 -)	*W*			$770
CARTER, William S.	*P*			$1,210
American (1909 -)	*W*			$440
CARTIER, Jacques	*P*			$4,400
French (20th -)				
CARTIER, Thomas F.	*S*			$1,100
French (1879 -)				
CARTWRIGHT, W. P.	*P*			$220
British (19th -)				
CARUSO, Bruno	*P*			$660
Italian (1927 -)				
CARUSO, Enrico	*D*			$468
Italian (1873 - 1921)				
CARVER, Franklin H.	*P*			$275
American (20th -)				
CASALIS, G. (Attrib.)	*P*			$275
Italian (19th -)				
CASANODAY, Arcadio	*P*			$7,700
Spanish (19th -)				
CASANOVA, A.	*W*			$990
(19th -)				
CASANOVA, Emilio	*P*			$110
(20th -)				

D=Drawing, P=Painting, S=Sculpture, W=Watercolor

		Low	Mean	High
		Current Price Range		

		Low	Mean	High
CASANOVA, Francesco	P			$12,100
Italian (1727 - 1802)				
CASANOVA, Francesco (Circle)	P			$2,475
Italian (1727 - 1802)				
CASARINI, P.	P			$220
Italian (20th -)				
CASCELLA, Michele	P	$2,750	$9,350	$14,300
Italian (1892 - 1989)	W	$1,045	$3,039	$7,700
CASCIARO, Giuseppe	P	$4,400	$8,250	$11,000
Italian (1863 - 1941)				
CASE, Edmund E.	P	$935	$1,331	$1,870
American (1840 - 1919)				
CASE, Richard	P			$3,600
(?)				
CASER, Ettore	P	$550	$843	$1,320
Italian (1880 - 1944)				
CASH, Herbert	P	$110	$275	$440
American (19th - 20th)				
CASHWAN, Samuel A.	S			$550
American (1900 -)				
CASILE, Alfred	P			$6,050
French (1848 - 1909)				
CASILEAR, John W.	D			$5,500
American (1811 - 1893)	P	$550	$7,794	$39,600
	W			$6,600
CASILEAR, John W. (Attrib.)	P			$1,045
American (1811 - 1893)				
CASIMIR, Laurent	P			$165
Haitian (20th -)				
CASINELLI, Victor	W	$176	$865	$2,310
American (1865 - 1961)				
CASOLANI, Alessandro (Attrib.)	D			$3,025
Italian (1552 - 1606)				
CASS, George N.	P	$2,750	$2,860	$2,970
American (1806 - 1882)				

D=Drawing, P=Painting, S=Sculpture, W=Watercolor

		Current Price Range		
		Low	Mean	High

		Low	Mean	High
CASSANA, Giovanni A.(Attrib.)	P			$22,000
Italian (1658 - 1720)				
CASSANA, Niccolo (Attrib.)	P			$16,500
Italian (1659 - 1714)				
CASSANI, D.	P			$330
Italian (19th - 20th)				
CASSATT, Mary	D	$3,300	$496,467	$3.850M
American (1844 - 1926)	P	$286,000	$1.457M	$3.080M
	W			$41,800
CASSATT, Mary (Attrib.)	W			$1,980
American (1844 - 1926)				
CASSELL, Frank	P			$825
(19th -)				
CASSELLI, Henry	D	$4,400	$6,588	$11,000
American (1946 -)				
CASSIDY, Gerald	P	$5,500	$11,550	$19,800
American (1879 - 1934)				
CASSIDY, Ira D. G.	P			$16,500
American (1879 - 1934)	W			$6,050
CASSIERS, Henry	P			$2,750
Belgian (1858 - 1944)	W			$495
CASSIGNEUL, Jean P.	D			$60,500
French (20th -)				
CASTAGNOLA, Gabriele	P	$4,125	$4,263	$4,400
Italian (1828 - 1883)				
CASTAIGNE, Jean Andre	P	$798	$1,699	$2,600
French (1860 - 1930)				
CASTALDO, Amaylia	P	$110	$165	$220
American (1906 -)				
CASTAN, Pierre J. E.	P			$4,125
French (1817 - 1892)				
CASTANEDA, Alfredo	P	$3,300	$17,631	$44,000
Mexican (1938 -)	S			$4,400

D=Drawing, P=Painting, S=Sculpture, W=Watercolor

		Current Price Range		
		Low	Mean	High

		Low	Mean	High
CASTANEDA, Felipe	*S*	$3,300	$7,975	$15,400
Mexican (1933 -)				
CASTANO, G.	*P*			$660
Mexican (20th -)				
CASTANO, John	*P*			$1,320
(1896 - 1978)				
CASTEELS, Pieter	*P*			$45,100
Flemish (1684 - 1749)				
CASTEL,	*P*			$523
French (20th -)				
CASTEL, Moshe	*P*	$3,300	$6,710	$11,000
Israeli (1909 -)				
CASTELLANI, Enrico	*P*			$19,800
Italian (1930 -)				
CASTELLANOS, Julio	*D*			$2,530
Lat. Amer. (?)	*P*			$3,080
CASTELLI, Bartolomeo	*P*			$55,000
Italian (18th -)				
CASTELLI, Luciano	*P*			$7,700
(20th -)	*W*			$5,280
CASTELLO, Giovanni B. (Circle)	*P*			$7,700
Italian (1547 - 1637)				
CASTELLO, Valerio	*P*	$159,500	$629,750	$1.100M
Italian (1625 - 1659)				
CASTELLO, Valerio (Attrib.)	*D*			$1,100
Italian (1625 - 1659)				
CASTELLO, Valerio (Style)	*P*			$3,300
Italian (1625 - 1659)				
CASTELLON, Frederico	*D*			$275
American (1914 -)				
CASTER, James	*P*			$770
American (20th -)				
CASTEX-DEGRANGE, Adolphe L.	*P*	$2,200	$5,500	$8,800
French (1840 -)				

D=Drawing, P=Painting, S=Sculpture, W=Watercolor

		Current Price Range		
		Low	Mean	High

		Low	Mean	High
CASTIGLIONE, Giovanni B.	*D*			$104,500
Italian (1616 - 1670)	*P*	$4,675	$38,088	$71,500
CASTIGLIONE, Giovanni B. (Aft)	*D*			$935
Italian (1616 - 1670)				
CASTIGLIONE, Giuseppe	*P*			$31,900
Italian (19th - 20th)				
CASTILLO, Jorge	*P*	$6,380	$10,395	$14,300
Spanish (20th -)	*W*			$3,300
CASTLE, Wendell	*S*			$132,000
American (20th -)				
CASTLEDEN, George F.	*P*			$248
American (1869 - 1945)				
CASTLEDON, C. E.	*P*			$132
European (19th - 20th)				
CASTOLDI, Gugliemo	*P*	$550	$2,677	$4,400
Italian (1852 -)				
CASTRES, C. P.	*P*			$275
(?)				
CASTRES, Edouard	*P*			$22,000
Swiss (1838 - 1902)				
CASWELL, Helen	*P*			$138
(20th -)				
CATALAN, Ramos	*P*	$120	$272	$468
S.American (20th -)				
CATALAN SCHOOL 15C,	*P*			$35,200
Spanish (15th -)				
CATANO, F.	*W*			$440
(?)				
CATES, J.	*P*			$385
American (19th -)				
CATHELIN, Bernard	*P*	$550	$14,259	$34,100
French (1919 -)				
CATLIN, George	*P*	$15,400	$208,633	$539,000
American (1796 - 1872)				

D=Drawing, P=Painting, S=Sculpture, W=Watercolor

		Current Price Range		
		Low	Mean	High
CATOK, Lottie M.	W			$165
American (20th -)				
CATS, Jacob	D	$880	$3,337	$6,050
Dutch (1741 - 1799)				
CATTI, Michele	P			$440
Italian (1855 - 1914)				
CAUCHOIS, Eugene H.	P	$770	$8,910	$20,900
French (1850 - 1911)				
CAUCHOIS, Eugene H. (Attrib.)	P			$1,320
French (1850 - 1911)				
CAUHOIS, H.	P			$1,430
Dutch (20th -)				
CAULDWELL, Leslie G.	P			$523
American (1861 - 1941)				
CAULLERY, Louis de	P	$13,200	$17,600	$22,000
Flemish (16th - 17th)				
CAULLERY, Louis de (Circle)	P			$3,850
Flemish (16th - 17th)				
CAUSSIN, Marque L.	S			$1,100
French (?)				
CAVAILLES, Jules	P			$6,050
French (1901 -)				
CAVALCANTE, Lito	P			$2,750
Brazilian (1926 -)				
CAVALCANTI, Emiliano di	D	$1,210	$2,970	$4,400
Brazilian (1897 - 1976)	P	$38,500	$53,625	$66,000
	W			$1,650
CAVALERI, Ludovicio	P			$1,980
Italian (1867 - 1942)				
CAVALIERE, Alik	S			$2,860
(?)				
CAVALLINO, Bernardo	P			$1.925M
Italian (1622 - 1654)				
CAVALLINO, Bernardo (Circle)	P			$15,400
Italian (1622 - 1654)				

D=Drawing, P=Painting, S=Sculpture, W=Watercolor

		Current Price Range		
		Low	Mean	High

CAVALLON, Giorgio	*P*	$15,400	$44,458	$99,000
American (1906 -)				
CAVALLORI, L.	*P*			$385
Italian (19th -)				
CAVANAUGH, Robert M.	*S*			$880
American (20th -)				
CAVE, Jules C.	*P*			$4,400
French (1859 -)				
CAVEDONE, Giacomo	*D*			$6,600
Italian (1577 - 1660)				
CAVEDONE, Giacomo (Attrib.)	*D*			$5,500
Italian (1577 - 1660)				
CAVIEDES, Hipolito H.	*P*			$7,150
Spanish (1902 -)				
CAWSE, John	*P*			$1,650
British (1779 - 1862)				
CAWTHORNE, Neil	*P*	$330	$5,015	$14,300
British (1936 -)				
CAYEUX,	*W*			$385
French (19th -)				
CAZASSUS,	*P*			$440
French (1923 -)				
CAZIN, Jean C.	*D*			$165
French (1841 - 1901)	*P*	$963	$1,887	$3,520
CAZIN, Jean C. (Attrib.)	*P*			$4,620
French (1841 - 1901)				
CECCARELLI, Naddo	*P*			$407,000
Italian (14th -)				
CECCOBELLI, Bruno	*P*	$3,300	$5,500	$7,700
(20th -)				
CELESTI, Andrea	*P*			$30,800
Italian (1637 - 1706)				
CELIO, Gaspare (Attrib.)	*D*			$2,750
Italian (16th - 17th)				
CELIS, Perez	*P*	$4,180	$8,745	$13,200
Argentine (1939 -)				

D=Drawing, P=Painting, S=Sculpture, W=Watercolor

		Current Price Range		
		Low	Mean	High
CELMINS, Vija	D	$19,800	$21,450	$23,100
Russian (20th -)				
CELOMMI, Pasquale	P	$2,970	$2,970	$2,970
Italian (1860 -)				
CELOS, Julien	P			$1,100
Belgian (1884 - 1953)				
CELOSTIN,	P			$770
(?)				
CEMIN, Saint Clair	S	$2,200	$24,338	$57,750
(20th -)				
CENIC,	P			$150
French (?)				
CENTURION, Emilio	P			$2,475
Argentine (1894 - 1970)				
CEPEDA, Ender	P			$4,400
Venezuelan (1945 -)				
CERAMANO, Charles F.	P	$550	$4,081	$6,325
Belgian (1829 - 1909)				
CERCONE, Ettore	P			$13,200
Italian (1850 - 1896)				
CERES,	P			$2,640
(?)				
CERIA, Edmond	P			$1,100
French (1884 - 1955)				
CERNI, Leopold	W			$110
French (19th -)				
CERNY, Charles	P			$358
(20th -)				
CERQUOZZI, Mich. (Et al.)	P			$42,900
Italian (17th -)				
CERQUOZZI, Michelangelo (Cir)	P			$3,300
Italian (1602 - 1660)				
CERQUOZZI, Michelangelo (Sc)	P			$5,500
Italian (1602 - 1660)				
CERUTI, Giacomo	P			$20,900
Italian (18th -)				

D=Drawing, P=Painting, S=Sculpture, W=Watercolor

		Current Price Range		
		Low	Mean	High

CESAR,	*S*	$28,600	$55,000	$82,500
French (1921 -)	*W*			$3,300
CESARE, Giuseppe (Circle)	*P*			$3,575
Italian (1568 - 1640)				
CESARINI, Pier L.	*P*	$110	$138	$165
Italian (20th -)				
CESPEDES, Lucas	*P*			$187
Spanish (20th -)				
CESTARO, Jacopo	*P*			$13,200
Italian (?)				
CEULEN, Cornelis J. van	*P*	$9,350	$17,600	$41,800
British (1593 - 1664)				
CEULEN, Cornelis J. van (Circle)	*P*	$2,750	$3,025	$3,300
British (1593 - 1664)				
CEZANNE, Paul	*D*	$19,800	$33,733	$55,000
French (1839 - 1906)	*P*	$319,000	$3.292M	$11.550M
	W	$55,000	$177,100	$357,500
CHAB, Victor	*P*			$4,125
Argentina (1930 -)	*S*			$17,600
CHABAS, Maurice	*P*	$5,225	$9,763	$14,300
French (1862 - 1947)				
CHABAS, Paul E.	*P*	$2,090	$7,645	$13,200
French (1869 - 1937)	*W*	$468	$1,224	$1,980
CHABELLARD, J. Charles	*P*			$8,800
French (19th - 20th)				
CHABRIER, G. L.	*P*			$550
(?)				
CHABRIER, Nathalie	*D*	$165	$165	$165
French (1932 -)				
CHADBOURN, A.	*P*			$385
American (20th -)				
CHADBOURNE, Lester E.	*P*	$303	$427	$550
American (1901 - 1971)				

D=Drawing, P=Painting, S=Sculpture, W=Watercolor

		Current Price Range		
		Low	Mean	High
CHADEAYNE, Robert	P			$990
American (1897 -)				
CHADWICK, Lynn	D	$3,025	$3,713	$4,400
British (1914 -)	S	$3,850	$22,605	$60,500
	W			$1,650
CHADWICK, William	P	$688	$8,335	$27,500
American (1879 - 1962)				
CHAFFEE, Oliver	P	$385	$1,018	$1,650
American (1881 - 1944)	W	$225	$382	$523
CHAFFEE, Samuel R.	D			$303
American (19th - 20th)	P			$523
	W	$110	$388	$1,045
CHAGALL, Marc	D	$1,980	$72,796	$682,000
French (1887 - 1985)	P	$231,000	$1.927M	$14.850M
	S			$385,000
	W	$7,700	$289,987	$935,000
CHAGALL, Marc (Attrib.)	W			$4,070
French (1887 - 1985)				
CHAILLOUX, Robert	P			$385
French (1913 -)				
CHALEYE, Jean	P			$6,050
French (1878 - 1960)				
CHALFANT, Jefferson D.	P			$24,200
American (1856 - 1931)				
CHALIAPIN, Boris	D			$198
American (20th -)				
CHALLICE, Annie J.	P			$1,430
British (19th -)				
CHALON, Henry B.	P	$9,900	$24,200	$38,500
British (1770 - 1849)				
CHALON, Henry B. (Attrib.)	P			$13,200
British (1770 - 1849)				

D=Drawing, P=Painting, S=Sculpture, W=Watercolor

		Current Price Range		
		Low	Mean	High

		Low	Mean	High
CHALON, J. J. (?)	P			$1,760
CHALON, Louis French (1866 -)	P			$4,400
CHAMBERLAIN, C. H. American (20th -)	P			$220
CHAMBERLAIN, John American (1927 -)	P	$4,950	$29,480	$71,500
	S	$7,700	$98,136	$253,000
CHAMBERLAIN, Norman S. American (1887 - 1961)	P	$248	$633	$1,100
CHAMBERLIN, Frank T. American (1873 - 1961)	P	$550	$1,247	$2,090
	W			$550
CHAMBERS, Charles E. American (1883 - 1941)	P	$660	$1,290	$1,800
CHAMBERS, George British (1803 - 1840)	P			$2,200
CHAMBERS, George (Attrib.) British (1803 - 1840)	P			$5,225
CHAMBERS, J. K. American (19th -)	P			$825
CHAMBERS, Richard E. E. Irish (1863 - 1944)	W	$110	$220	$413
CHAMBERS, Thomas American (1841 -)	P	$525	$703	$880
CHAMBERS, Thomas (Manner) American (1841 -)	P			$1,430
CHAMPAIGNE, Philippe de Flemish (1602 - 1674)	P			$3,080
CHAMPAIGNE, Philippe de (Cir) Flemish (1602 - 1674)	P			$2,640
CHAMPAIGNE, Philippe de (Foll) Flemish (1602 - 1674)	P			$2,200
CHAMPAIGNE, Philippe de (Sc) Flemish (1602 - 1674)	P			$1,540

D=Drawing, P=Painting, S=Sculpture, W=Watercolor

		Current Price Range		
		Low	Mean	High

		Low	Mean	High
CHAMPLIN, Ada B.	*P*	$1,980	$2,090	$2,200
American (1875 - 1950)				
CHAMPNEY, B.	*P*			$1,320
(?)				
CHAMPNEY, Benjamin	*P*	$330	$3,288	$14,300
American (1817 - 1907)	*W*			$1,980
CHAMPNEY, Benjamin (Attrib.)	*P*	$165	$640	$1,650
American (1817 - 1907)				
CHAMPNEY, Benjamin (School)	*P*	$110	$343	$935
American (1817 - 1907)				
CHAMPNEY, James W.	*D*	$495	$1,953	$5,720
American (1843 - 1903)	*P*	$248	$1,576	$3,850
	W	$165	$3,332	$8,250
CHAN, Eddie	*W*	$358	$654	$950
American (?)				
CHANCRIN, Rene	*P*			$1,100
French (20th -)				
CHANDLER,	*D*	$110	$215	$319
American (19th -)	*W*			$413
CHANDLER, Christy	*P*			$1,650
American (?)				
CHANDLER, George W.	*D*			$440
American (20th -)				
CHANDLER, Joseph (Attrib.)	*P*			$15,000
American (1813 - 1880)				
CHANEY, Lester J.	*P*	$116	$727	$1,870
American (1907 -)				
CHANEY, William H.	*P*			$770
American (1821 - 1903)				
CHANNING, Norwood	*P*			$4,400
British (19th -)				
CHANTEAU, Alphonse	*W*			$110
American (?)				

D=Drawing, P=Painting, S=Sculpture, W=Watercolor

		Current Price Range		
		Low	Mean	High

		Low	Mean	High
CHAPAUD, Marc	*P*	$110	$413	$715
French (1914 -)				
CHAPELAIN-MIDY, Roger	*P*			$6,325
French (1904 -)				
CHAPIN, Bryant	*P*	$385	$4,062	$13,200
American (1859 - 1927)	*W*			$330
CHAPIN, C. H.	*P*	$385	$468	$550
American (19th - 20th)				
CHAPIN, Charles E.	*D*			$770
American (19th - 20th)				
CHAPIN, Charles E. (Attrib.)	*W*			$175
American (19th - 20th)				
CHAPIN, Francis	*P*	$176	$350	$523
American (1899 - 1965)	*W*	$275	$468	$660
CHAPIN, Francis (Attrib.)	*P*			$176
American (1899 - 1965)				
CHAPIN, James	*D*			$550
American (1887 -)				
CHAPIN, Lucy G.	*P*			$110
American (? - 1939)				
CHAPLEAU, Eugene J. A.	*P*			$550
French (1882 -)				
CHAPLIN, Charles	*D*	$1,155	$3,328	$5,500
French (1825 - 1891)	*P*	$4,400	$26,228	$71,500
	W			$3,850
CHAPMAN, Carleton T.	*P*	$550	$3,797	$22,000
American (1860 - 1926)	*W*	$165	$248	$330
CHAPMAN, Charles S.	*P*	$440	$1,719	$4,950
American (1879 - 1962)				
CHAPMAN, Conrad W.	*P*			$15,400
American (1842 - 1910)	*W*			$7,700
CHAPMAN, Conrad W. (Attrib.)	*P*			$1,600
American (1842 - 1910)				

D=Drawing, P=Painting, S=Sculpture, W=Watercolor

		Current Price Range		
		Low	Mean	High
CHAPMAN, Cyrus-Durand	*D*	$110	$125	$154
American (1856 - 1918)	*P*	$110	$802	$2,970
	W	$110	$138	$165
CHAPMAN, F. W.	*P*			$220
American (20th -)				
CHAPMAN, Frederich	*P*			$248
American (1818 - 1891)				
CHAPMAN, H. E.	*P*			$165
American (20th -)				
CHAPMAN, John (Et al.)	*D*			$990
American (19th - 20th)				
CHAPMAN, John F.	*P*			$413
American (19th -)				
CHAPMAN, John G.	*P*			$880
American (1808 - 1889)				
CHAPMAN, John L.	*P*	$1,650	$3,263	$5,500
American (1839 - 1905)				
CHAPMAN, Minerva	*P*			$1,650
American (1858 -)				
CHAPN, Henri	*S*			$550
French (1833 - 1891)				
CHAPOVAL, Youla	*W*			$1,650
French (1919 - 1951)				
CHAPPEL, Alonzo	*P*			$4,400
American (1820 - 1885)				
CHAPPELL, Reuben	*P*	$385	$2,108	$3,520
British (1870 - 1940)				
CHAPY, R.	*S*			$935
European (19th -)				
CHARCHOUNE, Serge	*P*	$2,310	$25,795	$77,000
Russian (1888 - 1975)				
CHARDIN, Camille (Style)	*P*			$1,540
French (1841 -)				
CHARLEMONT, Eduard	*P*	$7,150	$8,250	$10,450
French (1846 - 1906)				

D=Drawing, P=Painting, S=Sculpture, W=Watercolor

		Current Price Range		
		Low	Mean	High

		Low	Mean	High
CHARLES, James	P			$27,500
British (1851 - 1906)				
CHARLESON, Malcolm D.	P	$660	$660	$660
Canadian (1888 -)				
CHARLET, Frantz	P	$13,200	$20,900	$28,600
Belgian (1862 - 1928)				
CHARLET, Nicola T.	D			$165
French (1792 - 1845)	P			$5,500
CHARLOT, Jean	D	$138	$138	$138
French (1898 - 1979)	P	$1,320	$10,780	$28,600
	W			$3,850
CHARLOT, Louis	P			$1,430
(?)				
CHARMAN, Frederick M.	W	$110	$317	$550
American (1894 - 1986)				
CHARMAN, Rodney	P			$1,320
American (20th -)				
CHARMY, Emilie	P			$4,180
French (1877 - 1974)				
CHARNAY, Armand	P			$14,300
French (1884 - 1916)				
CHARON,	P			$1,540
(?)				
CHARON, Guy	P	$2,860	$3,135	$3,410
French (1927 -)				
CHARPENTIER, Jean B.	P			$22,000
French (18th - 19th)				
CHARPIN, Albert	P	$660	$660	$660
French (1842 - 1924)				
CHARPIN, F.	P			$990
European (?)				
CHARRAT,	P			$550
French (20th -)				
CHARRETON, Victor	P	$9,900	$34,772	$77,000
French (1864 - 1937)				

D=Drawing, P=Painting, S=Sculpture, W=Watercolor

		Current Price Range		
		Low	Mean	High

		Low	Mean	High
CHARTON, Ernest	P			$49,500
French (1815 - 1877)				
CHARTRAND, Esteban	P	$3,520	$3,960	$4,400
Lat. Amer. (1825 - 1889)				
CHARTRAUD, A.	P			$605
Spanish (19th - 20th)				
CHASE, Francis	P			$165
American (? - 1955)				
CHASE, Frank S.	P	$358	$2,633	$8,250
American (1886 - 1958)				
CHASE, Jessie K.	P			$1,650
American (1879 - 1970)				
CHASE, Joseph	P	$121	$215	$303
American (1878 - 1965)				
CHASE, Louisa	D			$1,870
American (1951 -)	P	$2,860	$8,510	$16,500
CHASE, Marian (Attrib.)	W			$165
British (1844 - 1905)				
CHASE, Sidney M.	P	$1,650	$3,813	$7,700
American (1877 -)				
CHASE, Susan B.	W			$165
American (20th -)				
CHASE, William M.	D	$1,760	$529,509	$2.200M
American (1849 - 1916)	P	$9,900	$99,905	$1.100M
CHASE, William M. (Attrib.)	P	$550	$3,850	$7,150
American (1849 - 1916)				
CHASSELAT, Pierre	D			$9,900
French (1753 - 1814)				
CHASSERIAU, Theodore	P			$286,000
French (1819 - 1856)	W			$13,200
CHASSON, Pierre	P			$1,430
French (20th -)				
CHATELET, Claude L.	D			$12,100

D=Drawing, P=Painting, S=Sculpture, W=Watercolor

| | | Current Price Range | | |
		Low	Mean	High
CHATELET, Claude L.	*P*			$44,000
French (1753 - 1794)	*W*	$3,025	$5,363	$7,700
CHATELET, Claude L. (Attrib.)	*P*	$6,325	$18,563	$30,800
French (1753 - 1794)				
CHATTAWAY, William	*S*			$3,300
British (1927 -)				
CHATTERTON, Clarence	*P*	$3,850	$7,370	$16,500
American (1880 - 1973)	*W*	$440	$578	$715
CHATWICK, F.	*P*			$550
(19th -)				
CHAUDET, Antoine D. (After)	*S*			$7,150
French (19th -)				
CHAVANNES,	*P*			$110
Haitian (20th -)				
CHAVANNES, Pierre P. de	*D*			$4,180
French (1824 - 1898)				
CHAVET, Victor J.	*P*			$1,540
French (1822 - 1906)				
CHAVEZ, Gerardo	*P*			$13,200
Lat. Amer. (20th -)				
CHAVEZ, Jose de	*P*			$10,450
Spanish (19th -)				
CHAVIER, Jusepe L. de (Attrib.)	*P*	$9,350	$32,175	$55,000
Spanish (?)				
CHEADLE, H.	*P*			$385
British (1852 -)				
CHEEK, C. R.	*P*			$440
American (20th -)				
CHELMINSKI, Jan van	*P*	$2,200	$4,153	$6,050
Polish (1851 - 1925)				
CHELMONSKI, Josef	*P*			$8,800
Polish (1850 - 1914)				
CHEMIAKIN, Mihail	*D*	$1,320	$2,530	$3,740
Russian (1943 -)				

D=Drawing, P=Painting, S=Sculpture, W=Watercolor

| | | Current Price Range | | |
		Low	Mean	High
CHEMIN, Joseph V.	S	$1,100	$1,788	$2,475
French (1825 - 1901)				
CHEN, Hilo	P			$3,850
American (20th -)	W	$495	$1,031	$1,650
CHENEY, Harold W.	P	$220	$968	$2,750
American (1889 - 1946)				
CHENEY, Philip	P			$110
American (1887 -)				
CHENEY, Russell	P	$193	$703	$1,650
American (1881 - 1945)				
CHENOWETH,	P			$495
(?)				
CHERET, Jules	D	$605	$633	$660
French (1836 - 1932)	P			$14,300
CHERON, Louis	D	$2,200	$2,200	$2,200
French (1655 - 1715)				
CHERRY, Kathryn	P	$358	$702	$1,045
American (1880 - 1931)				
CHERUBINI, Andrea	P			$275
Italian (19th -)				
CHERUBINI, Carlo	P			$1,210
Italian (1897 -)				
CHESTER, E.	P	$220	$303	$385
American (19th -)				
CHESTNUT, Billy D.	W			$1,760
American (20th -)				
CHETCUTI, John	W			$330
(20th -)				
CHEVALIER, Nicholas	P			$13,200
British (19th -)				
CHEVALIER, Peter	D			$880
(20th -)	P			$9,350
CHEVILLIARD, Vincent J.	P			$6,600
French (1841 -)				

D=Drawing, P=Painting, S=Sculpture, W=Watercolor

		Current Price Range		
		Low	Mean	High

		Low	Mean	High
CHEVIOT, Lilian	*P*	$2,640	$4,895	$7,150
British (20th -)				
CHEVOLLEAU, Jean	*P*			$3,850
French (1924 -)				
CHI, Chen	*W*			$963
Chinese (1912 -)				
CHI-CHUNG, Hu	*P*			$220
American (20th -)				
CHIA, Sandro	*D*	$3,300	$21,221	$51,700
Italian (1946 -)	*P*	$7,700	$66,122	$126,500
	S	$11,000	$37,950	$110,000
	W			$23,100
CHIALIVA, Luigi	*P*	$4,950	$10,725	$16,500
Swiss (1842 - 1914)	*W*			$3,850
CHIARA, Alan	*W*			$468
American (20th -)				
CHICAGO, Judy	*D*			$2,640
American (1930 -)				
CHICHESTER, Cecil	*P*	$125	$336	$523
American (1891 - 1963)				
CHIDLAW, Paul	*P*	$220	$1,230	$2,200
(20th -)	*W*			$193
CHIERICI, Gaetano	*P*	$13,200	$147,840	$297,000
Italian (1838 - 1920)				
CHIHULY, Dale	*S*	$3,300	$8,525	$12,100
(20th -)				
CHILD, Edwin B.	*P*			$2,310
American (1868 - 1937)				
CHILD, Robert C.	*D*			$193
American (1872 -)	*P*			$715
CHILDS, Elias	*P*			$2,310
British (19th -)				

D=Drawing, P=Painting, S=Sculpture, W=Watercolor

		Current Price Range		
		Low	Mean	High
CHILLMAN, Philip E.	*P*			$550
American (1841 -)				
CHIMENTI, Jacopo	*D*			$3,630
Italian (1554 - 1640)	*P*			$2,750
CHINESE SCHOOL,	*P*			$2,750
Chinese (19th - 20th)				
CHINESE SCHOOL 19C,	*P*	$2,200	$4,081	$8,750
Chinese (19th -)	*W*			$15,400
CHINGANO,	*D*			$110
(20th -)				
CHINNERY, George	*D*	$935	$2,228	$3,520
British (1748 - 1847)				
CHIPARUS, Demetre H.	*S*	$2,750	$7,333	$13,200
Rumanian (1914 - 1933)				
CHIPARUS, Demetre H. (After)	*P*			$165
Rumanian (1914 - 1933)	*S*			$1,650
CHIRIACKA, Ernest	*P*	$330	$1,430	$2,530
American (1920 -)	*W*			$523
CHIRICO, Giorgio de	*D*	$5,500	$22,275	$46,750
Italian (1888 - 1978)	*P*	$9,350	$676,913	$5.280M
	W	$6,050	$100,283	$269,500
CHIRICO, V. Colombo da	*W*			$3,080
European (19th -)				
CHIRIS, Peter S.	*P*			$495
(?)				
CHITTENDEN, Alice B.	*P*	$248	$5,276	$17,600
American (1859 - 1944)				
CHITTENDEN, Alice B. (Attrib.)	*P*			$605
American (1859 - 1944)				
CHMIELINSKI, W. T.	*P*	$275	$578	$880
Polish (19th - 20th)				
CHO, Chang Young	*P*			$660
Japanese (20th -)				

D=Drawing, P=Painting, S=Sculpture, W=Watercolor

		Current Price Range		
		Low	Mean	High
CHOATE, Nathaniel	S			$5,500
American (1899 - 1965)				
CHOCARNE-MOREAU, Paul	P	$2,750	$7,957	$16,500
French (1855 - 1931)				
CHOCHON, Andre	P	$220	$385	$550
French (20th -)				
CHODOWIECKI, Daniel (Circle)	D			$990
German (1726 - 1801)				
CHOH, Lou	P			$110
(?)				
CHOULTSE, Ivan	P	$7,700	$7,883	$8,250
Russian (20th -)				
CHRISTENSEN, Anthonore	P			$4,400
Danish (1849 - 1926)				
CHRISTENSEN, Dan	P	$440	$1,408	$4,400
American (1942 -)				
CHRISTENSEN, Ronald J.	P			$165
American (20th -)				
CHRISTENY,	P			$880
European (20th -)				
CHRISTIAN, G	P			$1,210
Scandinavian (19th -)				
CHRISTIANSEN, Dan	D			$715
(20th -)				
CHRISTIANSEN, Nils H.	P			$605
Swedish (1876 - 1903)				
CHRISTIE, A. B.	P			$115
(?)				
CHRISTO,	D	$28,600	$88,367	$132,000
Rumanian (1935 -)	P	$12,100	$56,637	$214,500
	S	$17,600	$62,354	$143,000
	W			$71,500
CHRISTUS, Petrus (Style)	P			$6,600
Flemish (15th - 16th)				

D=Drawing, P=Painting, S=Sculpture, W=Watercolor

		Current Price Range		
		Low	Mean	High
CHRISTY, F. Earl	*D*			$2,475
American (?)				
CHRISTY, Howard C.	*D*	$605	$5,121	$9,900
American (1872 - 1952)	*P*	$523	$14,385	$35,200
	W	$605	$5,929	$18,700
CHRONISTER, R. J.	*W*			$385
(?)				
CHRYSSA,	*P*	$4,620	$6,600	$8,580
American (1933 -)	*S*	$2,750	$17,875	$33,000
CHUIKOV, Ivan	*P*	$15,400	$39,443	$90,200
Russian (1935 -)				
CHURCH, Frederick E.	*P*	$14,300	$1.498M	$8.250M
American (1826 - 1900)				
CHURCH, Frederick E. (Attrib)	*P*			$3,630
American (1826 - 1900)				
CHURCH, Frederick S.	*D*			$1,650
American (1842 - 1924)	*P*	$825	$4,228	$7,150
	W	$1,650	$1,815	$1,980
CHURCHILL, Alfred	*P*	$110	$303	$495
American (1864 -)				
CIA, Reysoria	*S*			$330
(?)				
CIAPPA, B.	*P*			$297
(?)				
CIAPPA, Carlo	*P*			$2,200
Italian (19th - 20th)				
CIAPPI, V.	*P*			$440
Italian (20th -)				
CIARDI, Beppe	*P*			$9,020
Italian (1875 - 1932)				
CICERI, Eugene	*D*			$165
French (1813 - 1890)	*W*	$1,430	$1,595	$1,760

D=Drawing, P=Painting, S=Sculpture, W=Watercolor

| | | Current Price Range | |
	Low	Mean	High
CIDONCHA, Rafael *P*			$3,300
Spanish (1952 -)			
CIGE, Theo van *P*			$110
American (20th -)			
CIGNANI, Carlo (Attrib.) *D*			$1,650
Italian (1628 - 1719)			
CIGNANI, Carlo (Circle) *P*	$1,870	$4,620	$6,600
Italian (1628 - 1719)			
CIKOVSKY, Nicolai *D*			$990
American (1894 - 1934) *P*	$358	$1,386	$2,970
CILFONE, Gianni *P*			$330
American (1908 -)			
CIMAROLI, Giovanni B. *P*			$3,300
Italian (18th -)			
CIMAROLI, Giovanni B. (Attrib.) *P*			$2,200
Italian (18th -)			
CIMIOTTI, Gustave *P*	$275	$697	$1,540
American (1875 - 1929) *W*			$140
CINALLI, Ricardo *D*			$4,400
Argentina (1948 -)			
CINGOLI, Messer Ulisse S. da *D*			$25,300
(?)			
CINISELLI, G. *S*			$2,420
Italian (19th -)			
CIPPER, Giacomo F. *P*			$11,000
Italian (18th -)			
CIPPER, Giacomo F. (Attrib.) *P*			$4,400
Italian (18th -)			
CIPRIANI, A. *S*	$770	$1,045	$1,540
Italian (19th -)			
CIPRIANI, Giovanni B.(Attrib.) *D*			$2,090
Italian (1727 - 1785) *P*			$8,800
CIPRIANI, J. A. *S*			$1,100
Italian (?)			

D=Drawing, P=Painting, S=Sculpture, W=Watercolor

		Current Price Range		
		Low	Mean	High
CIPRIANI, Nazzareno	P			$4,400
Italian (1843 - 1925)				
CIPRICO, Margurite	P			$1,100
American (1891 - 1973)				
CIRCIGNANO, Niccolo	D			$16,500
Italian (1519 - 1591)				
CIRINO, Antonio	P	$550	$1,737	$4,180
American (1889 - 1983)				
CIRY, Michael	P	$3,410	$3,777	$4,400
French (1919 - 1944)				
CITTADINI, Pier F.	P			$17,600
Italian (1613 - 1681)				
CITTADINI, Pier F. (Attrib.)	P			$41,800
Italian (1613 - 1681)				
CIVITICO, Bruno	P			$413
American (1942 -)				
CLAEISSINS II, Pieter (Attrib.)	P			$22,000
Flemish (1532 - 1623)				
CLAESSENS, Antoine (Circle)	P			$8,800
Flemish (15th -)				
CLAESZ, Aert	P			$170,500
Dutch (1498 - 1564)				
CLAESZ, Anthony	P			$28,600
Dutch (1592 - 1635)				
CLAESZ, Pieter	P			$60,500
Dutch (1590 - 1661)				
CLAGHORN, Joseph C.	P	$440	$1,357	$2,200
American (1869 - 1947)	W	$495	$787	$1,430
CLAIR, Charles	P	$1,100	$3,300	$5,500
French (19th - 20th)				
CLAIRE, Auguste J.	P			$3,850
French (19th - 20th)				
CLAIRE, Vincent	P			$2,750
European (1855 - 1925)				
CLAIRIN, Georges J.	P			$5,280
French (1843 - 1919)				

D=Drawing, P=Painting, S=Sculpture, W=Watercolor

		Current Price Range		
		Low	Mean	High

		Low	Mean	High
CLAIRIN, Pierre-Eugene	P			$2,750
French (20th -)				
CLAPHAM, Mark	P	$5,500	$6,325	$7,150
American (20th -)				
CLAPP, William	D	$275	$394	$468
American (1879 - 1954)	P	$523	$4,681	$12,100
	W			$578
CLARA, Jose	D	$1,320	$1,760	$2,200
Spanish (1878 -)	W			$1,100
CLARE, George	P	$1,210	$1,320	$1,430
British (19th -)	W			$880
CLARE, Oliver	P	$352	$1,942	$4,400
British (1853 - 1927)				
CLARE, Vincent	P	$1,870	$4,868	$8,800
British (1855 - 1925)				
CLARIN, George J. V.	D			$303
French (1843 - 1919)				
CLARK, Albert	P			$3,300
British (19th -)				
CLARK, Allan	S	$550	$660	$770
American (1896 - 1950)				
CLARK, Alson S.	P	$990	$4,421	$13,200
American (1876 - 1949)				
CLARK, Benton	P	$825	$2,933	$9,075
American (1895 - 1964)				
CLARK, C. A.	P			$413
American (19th - 20th)				
CLARK, C. Myron	P	$110	$792	$2,475
American (1876 - 1925)	W	$110	$220	$468
CLARK, David	W			$440
(20th -)				
CLARK, Eliot C.	D	$110	$173	$440

D=Drawing, P=Painting, S=Sculpture, W=Watercolor

		Current Price Range		
		Low	Mean	High
CLARK, Eliot C.	P	$150	$1,499	$9,900
American (1883 - 1980)	W			$120
CLARK, Frederick H.	P			$1,980
American (? - 19th)				
CLARK, George M.	P			$165
American (?)				
CLARK, Homer	P	$385	$536	$687
American (19th - 20th)				
CLARK, James	P			$15,400
British (19th - 20th)				
CLARK, James L.	S	$1,100	$4,538	$7,700
American (1883 - 1957)				
CLARK, L. M.	P			$550
(?)				
CLARK, Matt	P			$220
American (1903 - 1972)	W	$138	$223	$400
CLARK, Noel H.	P			$110
American (20th -)				
CLARK, P.	W			$990
American (19th -)				
CLARK, Roland	W			$165
American (1874 -)				
CLARK, S.	P			$303
(?)				
CLARK, W. W.	P			$935
British (20th -)				
CLARK, Walter A.	P	$440	$1,370	$5,500
American (1848 - 1917)				
CLARK, William	P	$660	$880	$990
British (19th -)				
CLARKE, Emery	P			$1,700
(?)				
CLARKE, John C.	P	$1,870	$4,840	$12,100
American (1937 -)				

D=Drawing, P=Painting, S=Sculpture, W=Watercolor

		Current Price Range		
		Low	Mean	High

		Low	Mean	High
CLARKE, Joseph C.	*W*			$1,100
British (19th - 20th)				
CLARKSON, S.	*P*			$248
American (?)				
CLAUDE, Eugene	*P*			$5,720
French (1841 - 1922)				
CLAUDEL, Camille	*S*			$110,000
French (? - 1943)				
CLAUS, William A. J.	*P*	$230	$361	$550
American (20th -)				
CLAUSADES, Pierre de	*P*			$1,100
(?)				
CLAUSELL, Joaquin	*P*	$17,600	$23,100	$28,600
Mexican (1866 - 1935)				
CLAUSEN, Franciska	*W*	$12,100	$13,750	$15,400
Danish (20th -)				
CLAUSEN, George	*P*	$1,430	$72,215	$143,000
British (1852 - 1944)	*W*			$660
CLAUSEN, William	*P*			$440
American (20th -)				
CLAVE, Antoni	*D*	$8,250	$35,888	$77,000
Spanish (1913 -)	*P*	$44,000	$113,667	$187,000
	S	$5,720	$26,004	$49,500
	W	$15,400	$33,978	$66,000
CLAVEL, Joseph L.	*P*			$440
French (1850 - 1923)				
CLAVER, Francois	*P*			$550
French (1918 -)				
CLAXTON, Marshall	*P*			$2,200
British (1811 - 1881)				
CLAY, Jordan	*P*	$1,650	$1,825	$2,000
American (20th -)				
CLAYES, Berthe des	*D*			$825

D=Drawing, P=Painting, S=Sculpture, W=Watercolor

		Current Price Range	
	Low	Mean	High
CLAYES, Berthe des W			$770
American (1877 - 1968)			
CLAYS, Paul J. P	$633	$6,105	$17,600
Belgian (1819 - 1900) W			$880
CLAYS, Paul J. (Attrib.) P			$1,650
Belgian (1819 - 1900)			
CLAYTON, P			$413
(?)			
CLAYTON, J. Hughes W			$1,100
British (19th - 20th)			
CLAYTON, W. P			$275
British (19th -)			
CLEARY, Shirley W	$450	$567	$700
American (20th -)			
CLEAVE, Joe van W			$935
American (20th -)			
CLEEMPUT, Paul P			$275
American (19th -)			
CLEENEWERCK, Henry P			$770
Belgian (19th -)			
CLEM, Rovert V. W			$413
American (20th -)			
CLEMENS, Paul D			$880
American (1911 -) P	$550	$4,950	$8,800
CLEMENT, Serge P			$495
(?)			
CLEMENT-RENE, Paul-Henri P			$935
French (20th -)			
CLEMENTE, Francesco D	$1,100	$36,004	$66,000
Italian (1952 -) P	$35,200	$149,661	$286,000
S			$198,000
W	$7,700	$28,539	$63,250
CLEMENTS, George H. W			$303
(1854 - 1935)			

D=Drawing, P=Painting, S=Sculpture, W=Watercolor

		Current Price Range		
		Low	Mean	High
CLEMINSON, Robert	P	$880	$1,430	$2,090
British (19th -)				
CLERCK, Hendrick (Follower)	P			$3,080
Flemish (1570 - 1629)				
CLERGET, Hubert	W			$880
French (1818 - 1899)				
CLERICI, Fabrizio	W			$2,090
Italian (1913 -)				
CLERISSEAU, Charles-L.	D			$11,000
French (1721 - 1820)	P			$24,200
CLERISSEAU, Charles-L. (Att.)	D			$440
French (1721 - 1820)				
CLESINGER, Jean B.	S	$1,375	$7,324	$17,600
French (1814 - 1883)				
CLESSE, Louis	P			$1,760
Belgian (1889 - 1961)				
CLEVE, Cornelis van	P			$35,200
Flemish (16th -)				
CLEVE, Joos van (Circle)	P			$110,000
Dutch (1485 - 1540)				
CLEVE, Joos van (Manner)	P			$1,100
Dutch (1485 - 1540)				
CLEVE, ELDER, Martin (Foll.)	P			$17,600
Flemish (1527 - 1581)				
CLEVELY, John	W			$1,540
British (1747 - 1786)				
CLIME, Winfield S.	P	$220	$1,063	$2,640
American (1881 - 1958)	W	$165	$358	$550
CLINEDINSDT, B. West	W			$170
American (1859 -)				
CLINEDINST, K. P.	W			$165
American (20th -)				
CLINEDINST, May S.	P	$248	$248	$248
American (1859 - 1931)				

D=Drawing, P=Painting, S=Sculpture, W=Watercolor

		Current Price Range		
		Low	Mean	High

		Low	Mean	High
CLINGER, Robert	*P*	$220	$578	$935
American (20th -)				
CLINT, Alfred	*W*			$198
British (1807 - 1883)				
CLODION, Claude M. (After)	*S*	$715	$1,296	$2,420
French (1738 - 1814)				
CLOSE, Chuck	*D*	$15,400	$15,950	$16,500
American (1940 -)	*W*	$19,800	$53,900	$88,000
CLOSKY,	*P*			$1,210
(20th -)				
CLOSSON, William B.	*D*			$440
American (1848 - 1926)	*P*	$330	$1,881	$5,500
	W			$138
CLOUET, Francois (Circle)	*P*	$5,500	$13,750	$33,000
French (? - 1572)				
CLOUET, Jean (School)	*P*	$660	$1,155	$1,650
French (1486 - 1541)				
CLOUGH, Forest	*P*			$193
American (1909 -)				
CLOUGH, George L.	*P*	$770	$2,475	$7,700
American (1824 - 1901)				
CLOUGH, Prunella	*P*			$2,970
British (1919 -)				
CLOUGH, Stanley T.	*P*			$248
American (1905 -)				
CLOVIO, Giulio	*D*			$19,800
Italian (1498 - 1578)				
CLOWES, Daniel	*P*			$11,000
British (1790 - 1835)				
CLUSMANN, William	*P*			$3,960
American (1859 - 1927)	*W*	$440	$1,210	$1,980
CLYMER, John	*P*	$715	$16,953	$75,000
American (1907 -)				

D=Drawing, P=Painting, S=Sculpture, W=Watercolor

		Current Price Range		
		Low	Mean	High

		Low	Mean	High
CLYMER, John	*P*	$468	$1,052	$1,375
British (1944 -)				
COALE, Griffith B.	*P*			$2,200
American (1890 - 1950)				
COATES, Edmund C.	*P*	$770	$2,017	$5,280
American (1816 - 1871)				
COATES, Edmund C. (Attrib.)	*P*			$440
American (1816 - 1871)				
COATES, Randolph	*P*			$3,080
American (1891 -)				
COBB, Cyrus	*P*			$110
American (1834 - 1903)	*S*			$193
COBB, Darius	*P*	$165	$710	$1,760
American (1834 - 1919)				
COBB, Henry I.	*P*			$220
American (1859 - 1931)				
COBBETT, Edward J.	*P*			$3,080
British (1815 - 1899)				
COBELLE, Charles	*P*	$275	$1,155	$2,420
French (1902 -)				
COBO, Chema	*D*			$11,000
(20th -)				
COBURN, Frank	*P*	$1,100	$2,457	$3,520
American (1866 - 1931)				
COCCAPANI, Sigismondo (Att.)	*P*			$5,500
Italian (1583 - 1642)				
COCCHI, E. G.	*P*			$220
(?)				
COCCO, Francesco di	*W*			$303
Italian (1900 -)				
COCCORANTE, Leonardo (Cir.)	*P*			$110,000
Italian (18th -)				
COCCORANTE, Leonardo (Sc.)	*P*			$8,800
Italian (18th -)				
COCHERILL, Elizabeth	*W*			$110
British (19th -)				

D=Drawing, P=Painting, S=Sculpture, W=Watercolor

		Current Price Range		
		Low	Mean	High

COCHIN, JR., Charles (Mann.)	*D*			$825
French (1715 - 1790)				
COCHRAN, Allen D.	*P*	$450	$2,094	$8,250
American (1888 -)				
COCHRAN, George	*W*			$385
American (1848 - 1935)				
COCHRANE, Josephine	*P*			$248
American (20th -)				
COCHS, J. H.	*P*			$605
American (19th - 20th)				
COCK, C.	*S*			$9,900
(19th -)				
COCK, Jan de	*P*			$71,500
Flemish (15th - 16th)				
COCK, Xavier de	*P*			$9,900
Belgian (1818 - 1896)				
COCKCROFT,	*P*			$715
(20th -)				
COCTEAU, Jean	*D*	$468	$4,048	$38,500
French (1889 - 1963)	*P*			$2,860
	S	$2,200	$4,730	$7,700
CODAZZI, Viviano	*P*	$14,300	$25,667	$31,900
Italian (1603 - 1672)				
CODAZZI, Viviano (Attrib.)	*P*	$3,300	$15,033	$22,000
Italian (1603 - 1672)				
CODAZZI, Viviano (Circle)	*P*			$7,700
Italian (1603 - 1672)				
CODAZZI, Viviano (Et al.)	*P*			$60,500
Italian (17th -)				
CODAZZI, Viviano (Follower)	*P*			$10,450
Italian (1603 - 1672)				
CODDE, Pieter	*P*			$110,000
Dutch (1599 - 1678)				
CODDE, Pieter (School)	*P*			$3,300
Dutch (1599 - 1678)				

D=Drawing, P=Painting, S=Sculpture, W=Watercolor

		Current Price Range		
		Low	Mean	High

		Low	Mean	High
CODMAN, John A.	P			$1,870
American (1824 - 1886)				
CODRON, Jef	P			$7,150
French (19th -)				
COE, Ethel	W			$193
American (1880 - 1938)				
COE, Helen A.	P			$165
(?)				
COELLO, Alonso S. (Attrib.)	P			$33,000
Spanish (1531 - 1588)				
COELLO, Alonso S. (Follower)	P			$12,100
Spanish (1531 - 1588)				
COELLO, Alonso S. (School)	P			$2,200
Spanish (1531 - 1588)				
COELLO, Alonso S. (Studio)	P			$52,250
Spanish (1531 - 1588)				
COENDERS, Johan F. E.	P			$440
Dutch (1913 - 1945)				
COENE, Jean B.	P			$8,800
Flemish (1805 -)				
COENE, Jean B. (Attrib.)	P			$2,310
Flemish (1805 -)				
COENE, Jean B. (Et.al.)	P			$13,200
Flemish (19th -)				
COENRAEDS, Ferdinand	W			$385
American (19th -)				
COESSIN DE LA FOSSE, Charles	P	$1,540	$3,795	$6,050
French (1829 - 1900)				
COFFERMANS, Marcellus	P	$19,800	$27,500	$35,200
Flemish (16th -)				
COFFERMANS, Marcellus (Attrib)	P			$14,300
Flemish (16th -)				
COFFIN, Esther L.	D			$105
American (?)				
COFFIN, Hannah	W			$3,300
American (1795 -)				

D=Drawing, P=Painting, S=Sculpture, W=Watercolor

		Current Price Range		
		Low	Mean	High
COFFIN, W. Haskell	*D*			$440
American (1878 - 1941)	*P*	$688	$949	$1,210
COFFIN, William A.	*P*			$6,820
American (1855 - 1926)				
COFFMAN, P. (Attrib.)	*W*			$525
American (20th -)				
COGGESHALL, John I.	*W*	$154	$207	$275
American (1856 - 1927)				
COGGESHALL, K. M.	*P*			$110
American (20th -)				
COGNIET, Leon	*P*			$30,250
French (1794 - 1880)				
COGSWELL, William	*P*			$248
American (1819 - 1903)				
COHEN, Anna H.	*P*			$358
American (20th -)				
COHEN, Bernard	*P*			$330
British (1933 -)				
COHEN, Frederick E.	*P*			$660
(?)				
COHEN, Isabel	*P*			$600
American (1867 -)				
COHEN, Lewis	*P*			$1,320
American (1857 - 1915)				
COHN, Harold	*P*			$110
British (1928 -)				
COHN, William	*P*			$220
(20th -)				
COIGNARD, James	*P*	$825	$2,035	$3,960
French (1925 -)				
COIGNARD, Louis	*P*			$1,650
French (1810 - 1883)				
COL, Jan D.	*P*			$28,600
Belgian (1822 - 1900)				
COLACICCO, Salvatore	*P*			$715
Italian (20th -)				

D=Drawing, P=Painting, S=Sculpture, W=Watercolor

		Current Price Range		
		Low	Mean	High

COLAMA, Sta.	*S*			$303
(?)				
COLB, F.	*P*			$220
American (20th -)				
COLBRIT, Philip S.	*P*			$495
American (20th -)				
COLBURN, Elanor	*P*			$440
American (1866 - 1939)				
COLBY, George E.	*W*	$110	$124	$138
American (1859 -)				
COLE,	*P*			$121
American (?)				
COLE, Alphaeus P.	*P*	$495	$2,017	$3,905
American (1876 -)				
COLE, Blanche D.	*P*			$440
American (1869 -)				
COLE, E.	*P*			$138
British (19th -)				
COLE, G.	*P*	$330	$1,705	$3,080
British (19th -)				
COLE, George F.	*P*	$2,090	$10,945	$19,800
British (1833 - 1893)				
COLE, Joseph F.	*P*	$330	$1,667	$3,520
American (1837 - 1892)				
COLE, Lyman E.	*P*			$3,300
(19th -)				
COLE, Philip T.	*P*			$1,540
British (19th -)				
COLE, T.	*P*	$165	$179	$193
British (20th -)				
COLE, Thomas	*D*			$16,500
American (1801 - 1848)	*P*	$1,017	$119,872	$330,000
COLE, Thomas (After)	*P*	$550	$843	$1,320
American (1801 - 1848)				
COLE, Thomas (Attrib.)	*D*			$193
American (1801 - 1848)				

D=Drawing, P=Painting, S=Sculpture, W=Watercolor

		Current Price Range		
		Low	Mean	High

		Low	Mean	High
COLE, Thomas C.	*P*			$3,080
American (1888 - 1976)				
COLEMAN, Charles C.	*D*	$880	$908	$935
American (1840 - 1928)	*P*	$110	$8,209	$18,700
	W			$6,600
COLEMAN, Enrico	*P*			$440
Italian (1846 - 1911)	*W*	$385	$5,863	$10,450
COLEMAN, F.	*P*			$1,870
Italian (1851 -)				
COLEMAN, G.	*W*			$770
American (?)				
COLEMAN, Glen O.	*P*			$5,775
American (1887 - 1932)				
COLEMAN, Harvey B.	*P*	$660	$770	$880
American (1884 - 1959)				
COLEMAN, Loring W.	*P*			$468
American (20th -)				
COLEMAN, Mary D.	*P*	$468	$514	$550
American (1894 - 1945)				
COLEMAN, Michael	*P*	$110	$4,108	$16,500
American (1946 -)	*W*			$5,500
COLEMAN, Ralph P.	*P*			$138
American (1892 - 1968)				
COLEMAN, Samuel	*D*			$121
American (1832 - 1920)	*W*			$715
COLEMAN, William S.	*P*	$1,980	$6,556	$10,450
British (1829 - 1904)				
COLI, Giovanni (Et al.)	*P*			$68,200
Italian (16th - 17th)				
COLIN, Gustav H.	*D*			$880
French (1828 - 1910)	*P*			$1,650
COLINET, Claire J. R.	*S*	$605	$8,553	$16,500
French (19th -)				

D=Drawing, P=Painting, S=Sculpture, W=Watercolor

		Current Price Range		
		Low	Mean	High

		Low	Mean	High
COLINSON, J.	*P*			$220
British (19th -)				
COLINUS, Emile	*P*			$495
French (1884 - 1966)				
COLKETT, Samuel D. (Attrib.)	*P*			$2,420
British (1806 - 1863)				
COLLANTES, Francisco (School)	*P*			$3,080
Spanish (1599 - 1656)				
COLLE, G. R.	*W*			$605
Italian (19th -)				
COLLIER,	*P*			$176
(?)				
COLLIER, C. Myles	*P*			$385
American (1836 -)				
COLLIER, Evert	*P*			$4,400
Dutch (? - 1702)				
COLLIER, Evert (Attrib.)	*P*			$13,200
Dutch (? - 1702)				
COLLIER, Grace	*P*			$550
American (20th -)				
COLLIER, John	*P*	$3,520	$11,825	$29,700
British (1850 - 1934)				
COLLIN, Bernard	*W*			$770
Swiss (1896 - 1979)				
COLLIN, Louis J. R.	*P*	$3,300	$20,350	$37,400
French (1850 - 1916)				
COLLIN, Raphael	*P*			$5,280
French (1850 - 1916)				
COLLINA, Alberto	*W*			$550
Italian (19th -)				
COLLINS, Amelia	*W*			$110
American (20th -)				
COLLINS, Arthur B.	*P*			$578
European (19th - 20th)				
COLLINS, C. L.	*P*			$440
American (19th -)				

D=Drawing, P=Painting, S=Sculpture, W=Watercolor

		Current Price Range	
	Low	Mean	High

COLLINS, Charles	*W*			$550
British (19th -)				
COLLINS, Earl	*P*			$1,100
American (1925 -)				
COLLINS, J. R.	*P*			$770
British (19th -)				
COLLINS, James	*P*			$660
(19th -)				
COLLINS, John	*P*			$413
British (19th -)				
COLLINS, William	*P*	$2,475	$4,162	$7,150
British (1788 - 1847)				
COLLINSON, James	*P*	$6,600	$33,550	$60,500
British (1825 - 1881)				
COLLO, E.	*P*			$1,100
(20th -)				
COLMAN, James	*P*			$825
(?)				
COLMAN, Roi C.	*P*	$303	$792	$1,210
American (1884 - 1945)				
COLMAN, Samuel	*D*	$193	$1,111	$3,520
American (1832 - 1920)	*P*	$4,400	$19,800	$35,200
	W	$248	$990	$1,980
COLOGERO, Jean	*P*	$303	$358	$413
Italian (1922 -)				
COLOMANUS, M.	*P*	$715	$1,045	$1,375
British (19th - 20th)				
COLOMBEL, Nicolas	*P*			$4,400
French (1644 - 1717)				
COLOMBIAN SCHOOL 19C,	*P*			$30,800
Colombian (19th -)				
COLOMBO, J.	*S*			$3,025
Italian (19th -)				
COLOMBO, R.	*S*	$990	$1,100	$1,210
European (19th -)				

D=Drawing, P=Painting, S=Sculpture, W=Watercolor

		Current Price Range		
		Low	Mean	High

		Low	Mean	High
COLOMBO, Virgilio	*W*			$605
Italian (19th -)				
COLONELLI-SCIARRA, Salvatore	*P*			$115,500
Italian (18th -)				
COLSON, Chester	*P*			$495
American (?)				
COLT, John N. (Attrib.)	*P*	$300	$450	$600
American (20th -)				
COLT, Morgan	*P*			$2,250
American (1876 - 1926)				
COLTMAN, Ora	*P*	$400	$515	$660
American (1858 - 1940)				
COLUCCI, Gio	*P*	$550	$788	$1,210
Italian (20th -)	*S*			$495
COLUNGA, Alejandro	*P*	$1,870	$10,074	$22,550
Mexican (1948 -)	*S*	$1,980	$3,328	$4,675
COLVILLE, George	*P*			$550
British (19th -)	*W*			$275
COLVIN,	*P*			$1,320
(19th -)				
COLWAY, James	*W*	$1,320	$1,540	$1,760
(20th -)				
COMAN, Charlotte	*P*	$880	$1,870	$2,640
American (1833 -)				
COMBAS, Robert	*D*			$3,080
(20th -)	*P*	$11,000	$13,200	$14,300
COMERRE, Leon F.	*P*	$4,675	$17,256	$30,250
French (1850 - 1916)				
COMERRE-PATON, Jaqueline	*P*			$13,200
French (1859 -)				
COMMARIEUX, Raymond	*D*			$6,820
French (18th -)				
COMMUNAL, Joseph V.	*P*			$5,500
French (19th - 20th)				

D=Drawing, P=Painting, S=Sculpture, W=Watercolor

		Current Price Range		
		Low	Mean	High

		Low	Mean	High
COMP, Norm	*P*			$1,000
American (20th -)				
COMPARD, Emile	*D*			$110
French (1900 - 1977)				
COMPRIS, Maurice	*P*			$1,210
American (1885 - 1939)				
COMPTE, Victor Le	*P*			$2,090
French (1856 - 1920)				
COMPTE-CALIX, Francois	*P*			$7,700
French (1813 - 1880)				
COMPTON, Edward H.	*W*	$935	$1,073	$1,210
British (1881 -)				
COMPTON, Winifred W.	*P*	$110	$124	$138
American (20th -)				
CONANT, Lucy S.	*P*			$3,575
American (1867 - 1921)	*W*			$275
CONATI, L.	*P*			$110
(?)				
CONDAMY, Charles F. de	*W*			$990
French (19th -)				
CONDO, George	*D*	$2,200	$4,253	$7,700
American (20th -)	*P*	$2,860	$28,862	$93,500
	S			$5,500
	W	$1,100	$3,850	$6,600
CONDORA,	*S*			$1,430
French (19th -)				
CONE, Marvin D.	*P*	$5,500	$12,650	$19,800
American (1891 - 1965)				
CONEGLIANO, Cima da (Studio)	*P*			$30,800
Italian (15th -)				
CONELY, William B.	*P*			$990
American (1849 - 1909)				
CONGDON, Anne R.	*P*			$1,100

D=Drawing, P=Painting, S=Sculpture, W=Watercolor

		Current Price Range		
		Low	Mean	High

		Low	Mean	High
CONGDON, Anne R.	*W*	$550	$743	$935
American (1873 - 1958)				
CONGDON, Thomas R.	*P*			$330
American (1862 - 1917)				
CONGDON, William	*P*			$825
American (1912 -)				
CONINXLOO, Gillis van (Circle)	*D*			$1,650
Flemish (1544 - 1607)				
CONKLIN, Jessie	*P*	$110	$183	$220
American (20th -)				
CONLON, James	*P*			$193
American (1894 -)				
CONNARD, Philip	*P*			$14,300
British (1875 - 1958)				
CONNAVALE, Robert	*P*			$385
(20th -)				
CONNAWAY, Jay H.	*P*	$303	$1,454	$3,080
American (1893 - 1970)				
CONNELL, C. W.	*W*			$220
American (?)				
CONNELL, Edwin	*P*	$3,410	$3,493	$3,575
American (1859 -)				
CONNELL, Sybil H.	*P*			$880
(?)				
CONNELLY, Chuck	*P*	$2,750	$6,783	$14,300
American (1956 -)				
CONNER, Bruce	*S*	$9,350	$12,283	$15,400
American (1933 -)				
CONNER, John A.	*P*	$303	$610	$1,540
American (1932 -)				
CONNER, John R.	*P*	$798	$6,449	$12,100
American (1869 - 1952)				
CONNER, McCauley	*W*			$950
(1891 - 1943)				
CONNER, Paul	*P*			$1,320
American (1881 - 1968)				

D=Drawing, P=Painting, S=Sculpture, W=Watercolor

		Current Price Range		
		Low	Mean	High
CONNOR, Charles	P			$4,125
American (1857 -)				
CONNRAD, Phillip	P	$880	$1,100	$1,320
British (1876 - 1958)				
CONREY, Lee F.	D			$220
American (1883 -)				
CONROY, George T.	P			$330
French (20th -)				
CONSAGRA, Pietro	S	$2,090	$10,798	$33,000
(20th -)				
CONSTABLE, John	D	$1,018	$1,279	$1,540
British (1776 - 1837)				
CONSTABLE, John (Follower)	P			$3,850
British (1776 - 1837)				
CONSTABLE, John (School)	P	$165	$633	$1,100
British (1776 - 1837)				
CONSTABLE, William	D	$165	$293	$385
American (1783 - 1861)	W	$138	$506	$1,045
CONSTANT, Benjamin	P	$3,080	$4,840	$6,600
French (1845 - 1902)				
CONSTANT, David A.	P			$5,500
(?)				
CONSTANT, J.	S			$121
French (20th -)				
CONSTANTIN, S.	P	$358	$999	$2,200
American (20th -)				
CONSTANTINE, George H.	W			$1,980
(?)				
CONSTANTINI,	W			$880
Italian (19th -)				
CONTEMPORARY SCHOOL,	P			$1,540
(20th -)				
CONTENT, Dan	P			$2,200
American (1902 -)				
CONTI,	W			$220
(?)				

D=Drawing, P=Painting, S=Sculpture, W=Watercolor

		Current Price Range		
		Low	Mean	High
CONTI, Antonio	D			$3,025
Italian (18th -)				
CONTI, Bernardino dei	P			$24,200
Italian (1450 - 1525)				
CONTI, Francesco (Circle)	P			$7,700
Italian (1681 - 1760)				
CONTI, Gino E.	P			$468
American (1900 -)				
CONTI, Primo	P	$2,750	$3,575	$4,400
Italian (1900 -)				
CONTI, Tito	P	$715	$1,705	$3,520
Italian (1842 - 1924)				
CONTINENTAL SCHOOL,	P	$1,045	$1,458	$1,870
European (?)				
CONTINENTAL SCHOOL,	P	$248	$1,549	$3,190
European (18th - 19th)				
CONTINENTAL SCHOOL,	D	$1,320	$1,375	$1,430
European (19th - 20th)	P	$1,100	$1,980	$3,300
CONTINENTAL SCHOOL 18C,	P	$1,045	$3,331	$10,450
European (18th -)				
CONTINENTAL SCHOOL 19C,	P	$358	$3,768	$24,750
European (19th -)	S	$2,530	$10,615	$18,700
CONTINENTAL SCHOOL 20C,	P	$1,100	$2,624	$7,150
European (20th -)	W	$1,210	$1,833	$2,310
CONTWAY, Bruce & Kathy	S			$850
American (20th -)				
CONTWAY, Jay	S	$990	$1,670	$2,420
American (20th -)				
CONTWAY, Kathy	S			$1,210
American (20th -)				
CONTWAY, Ross	S			$1,350
American (20th -)				
CONWAY, Fred	W	$220	$550	$880
American (1900 - 1972)				

D=Drawing, P=Painting, S=Sculpture, W=Watercolor

		Current Price Range		
		Low	Mean	High

		Low	Mean	High
CONWAY, John S.	*P*	$3,520	$4,785	$6,050
American (1852 - 1925)				
CONYDON, Thomas R.	*W*			$165
(?)				
COOGEN, Jay	*P*			$121
(?)				
COOK, Ebenezer W.	*W*			$6,050
British (1843 -)				
COOK, George E.	*P*			$303
American (? - 1930)				
COOK, Gladys E.	*D*			$165
American (1899 -)	*P*	$358	$372	$385
COOK, Howard	*D*	$880	$6,857	$18,700
American (1901 -)				
COOK, Howard (Et al.)	*D*			$715
American (20th -)				
COOK, J. A.	*W*			$330
(?)				
COOK, John A.	*W*	$110	$421	$825
American (1870 - 1936)				
COOK, Otis	*P*			$1,210
American (20th -)				
COOKE, Charles A.	*P*			$440
British (1878 -)				
COOKE, Edward W.	*P*			$3,575
British (1811 - 1880)	*W*			$1,540
COOKE, G.	*P*			$770
British (19th -)				
COOKE, George	*P*			$4,950
American (1793 - 1849)				
COOKE, John	*P*			$8,250
British (19th - 20th)				
COOKE, Roger	*P*			$1,000
American (20th -)				

D=Drawing, P=Painting, S=Sculpture, W=Watercolor

		Current Price Range	
		Low	Mean	High

		Low	Mean	High
COOKESLEY, Margaret M. British (19th -)	*P*			$3,520
COOL, Delphine de French (1830 -)	*P*			$13,200
COOLE, Brian American (19th -)	*P*	$413	$1,235	$2,200
COOLE, Brian (Attrib.) American (19th -)	*P*	$1,375	$1,513	$1,650
COOLIDGE, Cassius M. American (1844 - 1934)	*P*	$1,430	$2,915	$4,400
COOLIDGE, John E. American (1882 - 1947)	*P*			$110
COOLIDGE, Rosamond American (1884 -)	*P*			$220
COOMANS, Diana Belgian (19th -)	*P*			$2,200
COOMANS, Pierre O. J. Belgian (1816 - 1889)	*P*	$2,420	$4,098	$6,600
COOMBS, Delbert D. American (1850 - 1938)	*P* *W*	$138	$1,107	$2,200 $330
COOMBS, William J. American (20th -)	*P*			$605
COONEY, Fanny (Et al.) American (19th - 20th)	*D*			$1,540
COOPER, A. D. American (19th -)	*P*	$385	$921	$2,200
COOPER, Abraham British (1787 - 1868)	*P*	$2,200	$9,900	$17,600
COOPER, Abraham (Attrib.) British (1787 - 1868)	*P*			$1,650
COOPER, Alfred H. British (1864 - 1929)	*W*			$495
COOPER, Alice American (19th - 20th)	*S*			$2,200
COOPER, Astley D. M. American (1865 - 1924)	*P*	$275	$477	$770

D=Drawing, P=Painting, S=Sculpture, W=Watercolor

		Low	Current Price Range Mean	High
COOPER, Colin C.	D			$715
American (1856 - 1937)	P	$523	$18,048	$77,000
	W	$495	$3,383	$14,300
COOPER, Edwin	P			$4,400
British (1785 - 1833)				
COOPER, Emma L.	P	$2,200	$4,125	$6,050
American (1860 - 1920)				
COOPER, Fred	D			$175
American (1883 - 1962)				
COOPER, Mario	W			$275
American (1905 -)				
COOPER, Richard	P			$523
(?)				
COOPER, Rita	P	$825	$1,018	$1,210
Dutch (20th -)				
COOPER, Thomas G.	P			$1,540
British (19th -)				
COOPER, Thomas S.	D			$220
British (1803 - 1902)	P	$605	$5,294	$14,300
COOPER, Thomas S. (Attrib.)	P	$1,430	$1,925	$2,420
British (1803 - 1902)				
COOPER, William H.	P	$495	$1,018	$1,540
British (1903 -)				
COOPER, William S.	P			$3,740
British (19th -)				
COOPSE, Pieter	P			$35,750
Dutch (? - 1677)				
COPE, Charles W.	W			$385
British (1811 - 1890)				
COPE, George	P			$3,850
American (1855 - 1929)				
COPE, J. Fisher	P			$110
American (20th -)				
COPELAND, Alfred B.	P	$330	$871	$1,760
American (1840 - 1909)				

D=Drawing, P=Painting, S=Sculpture, W=Watercolor

		Current Price Range		
		Low	Mean	High

		Low	Mean	High
COPELAND, Charles	W			$2,310
American (1858 -)				
COPELAND, Joseph F.	W			$413
American (1872 -)				
COPLEY, John S.	D			$19,800
American (1737 - 1815)				
COPLEY, John S. (After)	P			$2,750
American (1737 - 1815)				
COPLEY, Robert	P			$6,600
(20th -)				
COPLEY, William	D	$330	$385	$440
American (1919 -)	P	$990	$5,940	$19,800
	S			$7,700
COPP, William S.	P	$550	$660	$770
American (1891 -)				
COPPEDGE, Fern I.	P	$3,080	$6,689	$12,100
American (1888 - 1951)				
COPPIN, John	P	$115	$326	$660
American (1904 -)				
COPPINI, G.	P			$1,100
Italian (19th -)				
COQUES, Gonzales (School)	P			$825
Flemish (1614 - 1684)				
CORADAL-GUGAT, Frances	W			$165
(20th -)				
CORAY, Sharon T.	P	$800	$913	$990
American (20th -)				
CORBELL, H.	P			$220
American (?)				
CORBELLINI, Luigi	P	$330	$947	$3,190
French (1901 - 1968)				
CORBETT, Josephine G.	P			$1,650
American (?)				
CORBINO, Jon	D	$2,200	$2,310	$2,420

D=Drawing, P=Painting, S=Sculpture, W=Watercolor

| | | Current Price Range | | |
		Low	Mean	High
CORBINO, Jon	*P*	$1,430	$1,430	$1,430
American (1905 - 1964)	*W*	$660	$880	$1,100
CORBOULD, Aster	*P*			$1,650
British (19th -)				
CORBUSIER, Le	*D*			$5,500
French (1887 - 1965)	*S*			$44,000
	W			$20,900
CORCHON Y DIAQUE, Federico	*P*			$6,600
Spanish (19th -)				
CORCOS, Vittorio M.	*P*	$13,200	$36,520	$66,000
Italian (1859 - 1933)				
CORCOS, Vittorio M. (Attrib.)	*P*			$13,200
Italian (1859 - 1933)				
CORDERO, Francisco	*P*	$4,180	$5,115	$6,050
Mexican (19th -)				
CORDERO, Jose V.	*P*			$16,500
Spanish (1848 - 1922)	*W*			$14,300
CORDIER, H.	*P*			$880
French (19th -)				
CORDREY, Earl	*W*	$138	$236	$550
American (1902 - 1977)				
CORDREY, John	*P*			$4,950
British (18th - 19th)				
COREILL, Michael	*W*			$193
American (20th -)				
CORELLI, Augusto	*W*	$880	$1,137	$1,430
Italian (1853 -)				
CORENZIO, Belisario	*W*			$8,800
Italian (1558 - 1640)				
COREY, Bernard	*P*			$330
(20th -)				
CORINTH, Lovis	*D*	$880	$880	$880
German (1858 - 1925)				

D=Drawing, P=Painting, S=Sculpture, W=Watercolor

		Current Price Range		
		Low	Mean	High

		Low	Mean	High
CORMON, Fernand A. P.	P	$1,320	$15,107	$27,500
French (1845 - 1924)				
CORNEAU, Eugene	P			$990
French (1894 - 1976)				
CORNEILLE,	P			$170,500
Belgian (1922 -)	W	$4,620	$10,523	$18,700
CORNEILLE, Michel	D			$17,600
French (1642 - 1708)				
CORNEILLE DE LYON, (School)	P			$5,500
Flemish (? - 1574)				
CORNEJO, Francisco	P			$660
American (? - 1963)				
CORNELIUS,	P			$2,200
European (19th -)				
CORNELL, Jeffrey	D			$150
(1945 -)				
CORNELL, Joseph	D			$17,600
American (1903 - 1973)	P	$28,600	$152,411	$495,000
	S	$9,350	$37,327	$176,000
CORNER, Thomas	P	$1,870	$2,695	$3,520
American (1865 - 1938)				
CORNIL, Gaston	P			$23,100
French (1883 -)				
CORNOYER, Paul	D	$523	$779	$1,100
American (1864 - 1923)	P	$880	$11,250	$35,200
CORNU, Pierre	P			$6,050
French (1895 -)				
CORNWELL, Dean	D			$330
American (1892 - 1960)	P	$715	$1,689	$3,025
CORONA, Leonardo (Attrib.)	D			$7,700
Italian (1561 - 1605)				
CORONEL, Pedro	P	$8,250	$38,343	$88,000

D=Drawing, P=Painting, S=Sculpture, W=Watercolor

		Current Price Range		
		Low	Mean	High
CORONEL, Pedro	*W*			$6,050
Mexican (1923 - 1985)				
CORONEL, Rafael	*D*	$2,475	$2,819	$3,850
Mexican (1932 -)	*P*	$1,760	$21,321	$143,000
COROT, Jean B. C.	*D*	$688	$5,844	$11,000
French (1796 - 1875)	*P*	$38,500	$253,642	$880,000
COROT, Jean B. C. (Manner)	*P*	$935	$2,365	$3,960
French (1796 - 1875)				
COROT, Jean B. C. (School)	*P*			$2,310
French (1796 - 1875)				
COROT, Jean B. C. (Style)	*P*			$605
French (1796 - 1875)				
CORPORA, Antonio	*P*	$8,250	$8,525	$8,800
Italian (1909 -)				
CORRADI, Konrad	*W*	$1,980	$3,300	$4,620
Swiss (1813 - 1878)				
CORRADINI, C.	*P*			$2,200
Italian (19th -)				
CORREA, Benito R.	*P*	$3,520	$8,103	$14,300
Chilean (1880 - 1964)				
CORREA, Juan	*P*			$22,000
Mexican (18th -)				
CORREA, Raphael	*P*			$3,300
South American (19th - 20th)				
CORREGGIO, Antonio (After)	*P*			$1,870
Italian (1489 - 1534)				
CORREGGIO, L.	*P*			$385
(?)				
CORRIER, J.	*P*			$138
French (20th -)				
CORRODI, Hermann D.	*P*	$2,860	$14,242	$33,000
Italian (1844 - 1905)				
CORRODI, Salomon	*W*			$2,310
Swiss (1810 - 1892)				

D=Drawing, P=Painting, S=Sculpture, W=Watercolor

		Current Price Range		
		Low	Mean	High

		Low	Mean	High
CORSI, Sante	*P*	$9,900	$10,450	$11,000
Italian (19th -)				
CORSICA, Felix C.	*P*			$660
(20th -)				
CORT, Hendrik F. de	*P*			$9,900
Dutch (1742 - 1810)				
CORTAZZ,	*W*			$770
American (20th -)				
CORTE, Gabriel de la	*P*			$132,000
(1648 - 1694)				
CORTE, H. de	*P*			$715
Belgian (20th -)				
CORTES, Edouard	*P*	$1,540	$17,518	$44,000
French (1882 - 1969)	*W*			$3,630
CORTESE, Guglielmo	*D*			$1,925
Italian (1628 - 1679)				
CORTONE, Pietro (Attrib.)	*D*			$770
Italian (1596 - 1669)				
CORVI, Domenico (Circle)	*P*			$5,500
Italian (1721 - 1803)				
CORWIN, Charles Abel	*D*			$3,300
American (1857 - 1938)	*P*	$880	$4,494	$16,500
CORZAS, Francisco	*P*	$5,225	$38,304	$71,500
Mexican (1936 -)	*W*	$2,200	$2,750	$3,300
COSENZA, Guiseppe	*P*			$3,850
Italian (1847 -)				
COSGROVE, Jack	*D*			$330
American (20th -)				
COSIKCKI, Catherine W.	*P*			$110
(?)				
COSSIERS, Jan	*P*			$5,500
Flemish (1600 - 1671)				
COSSIERS, Jan (Attrib.)	*P*			$18,700
Flemish (1600 - 1671)				

D=Drawing, P=Painting, S=Sculpture, W=Watercolor

| | | Current Price Range | | |
		Low	Mean	High
COSSON, Marcel	P	$3,025	$11,722	$22,000
French (19th - 20th)				
COSTA, Emanuele	P			$990
Italian (1875 -)				
COSTA, Giovanni	P	$4,400	$9,350	$14,300
Italian (1833 - 1903)				
COSTA, Lorenzo (Circle)	P			$9,900
Italian (1460 - 1535)				
COSTA, Olga	D			$1,320
German (1913 -)	P	$14,300	$23,650	$33,000
	W	$4,840	$7,663	$11,000
COSTA, Oreste	P	$1,980	$11,957	$26,400
Italian (1851 -)				
COSTANTINO,	P			$605
(?)				
COSTANZI, Placido	P			$23,100
Italian (16th - 17th)				
COSTE, E.	P			$187
(?)				
COSTE, Jean B.	W			$2,090
French (18th - 19th)				
COSTELLO,	P			$165
American (?)				
COSTIGAN, John E.	P	$3,025	$4,180	$6,050
American (1888 - 1972)	W	$605	$1,788	$2,970
COSWAY, Richard	P			$7,700
British (1742 - 1821)				
COSWAY, Richard (Manner)	P			$990
British (1742 - 1821)				
COT, Pierre A.	P			$99,000
French (1837 - 1883)				
COTES, Francis	D	$4,950	$6,050	$7,150
British (1725 - 1770)	P			$2,090

D=Drawing, P=Painting, S=Sculpture, W=Watercolor

		Current Price Range		
		Low	Mean	High

		Low	Mean	High
COTES, Francis (Attrib.) British (1725 - 1770)	*P*	$880	$1,448	$2,200
COTES, Francis (Circle) British (1725 - 1770)	*P*	$1,320	$1,430	$1,540
COTHARIN, Kate Leah (?)	*D*	$165	$216	$275
COTSWORTH, Staats American (1908 -)	*P* *W*			$358 $110
COTTET, Charles French (1863 - 1924)	*P*	$660	$2,255	$3,850
COTTINGHAM, Robert American (1935 -)	*D* *P* *W*	$1,650 $23,100	$2,483 $36,064	$3,300 $71,500 $9,350
COTTON, John W. American (1868 - 1931)	*W*	$330	$440	$550
COTTON, Ross American (20th -)	*P*			$198
COUGHLIN, Mildred (1895 -)	*W*			$165
COULDREY, Horatio H. British (1832 - 1893)	*P*			$5,500
COULDREY, Horatio H. (Attrib.) British (1832 - 1893)	*P*			$248
COULON, George D. French (1914 -)	*W*	$605	$2,063	$3,520
COULON, George D. (Attrib.) French (1914 -)	*P*			$2,200
COULTER, William A. American (1849 - 1936)	*P*	$1,760	$6,026	$15,400
COULTOU, After (?)	*S*			$1,980
COUMON, J. French (20th -)	*P*			$550
COUPER, William American (1853 - 1942)	*S*	$1,650	$2,365	$3,080

D=Drawing, P=Painting, S=Sculpture, W=Watercolor

		Current Price Range		
		Low	Mean	High

		Low	Mean	High
COUR, Hidela (?)	*P*			$121
COURBET, Gustave French (1819 - 1877)	*P*	$1,100	$347,008	$715,000
COURBET, Gustave (Et al.) French (19th -)	*P*			$44,000
COURBET, Gustave (Manner) French (1819 - 1877)	*P*			$1,045
COURBET, Gustave (Studio) French (1819 - 1877)	*P*			$33,000
COURS, A. American (1950 -)	*P*	$198	$209	$220
COURTAT, Louis French (? - 1909)	*P*	$8,250	$10,725	$13,200
COURTOIS, Gustave C. E. French (1853 - 1924)	*P*	$1,540	$13,273	$33,000
COURTOIS, Jacques (Attrib.) French (1621 - 1676)	*P*	$2,090	$2,420	$2,750
COURTOIS, Jacques (Circle) French (1621 - 1676)	*P*	$5,500	$5,638	$5,775
COURVOISIER, Jules Swiss (1884 -)	*D*			$880
COUSE, Eanger I. American (1866 - 1936)	*D* *P* *W*	 $220	 $15,749	$440 $49,500 $6,600
COUSTOU, French (19th -)	*S*	$1,210	$2,118	$3,025
COUTAUD, Lucien (20th -)	*W*	$2,200	$2,860	$3,520
COUTOURIER, Rene French (20th -)	*P*			$715
COUTTS, Alice American (?)	*P*			$4,400
COUTTS, Gordon American (1880 - 1937)	*P*	$550	$2,145	$4,180

D=Drawing, P=Painting, S=Sculpture, W=Watercolor

		Current Price Range		
		Low	Mean	High
COUTURE, Thomas	D	$1,540	$4,180	$8,250
French (1815 - 1879)	P	$2,200	$11,000	$19,800
COUTURIE, Ninette	P	$990	$1,045	$1,100
American (19th - 20th)				
COUTURIER, Philibert L.	P			$16,500
French (1823 - 1901)				
COUVER, Jan van	P			$880
British (19th - 20th)	W			$193
COUWENBERGH, Christiaan van	P	$44,000	$52,250	$60,500
Dutch (1604 - 1667)				
COVARRUBIAS, Miguel	D	$2,200	$4,730	$7,700
Mexican (1904 - 1957)	W	$2,200	$5,016	$8,250
COVERLEY, A. V.	P			$440
British (1901 -)				
COW, J.	P			$468
(19th -)				
COWAN, John	W	$2,750	$5,506	$8,525
American (1920 -)				
COWDERY, Eva	P	$990	$2,970	$4,950
American (19th - 20th)				
COWELL, Joseph G.	D			$110
American (1886 -)				
COWLAND, Alice C.	W			$770
American (20th -)				
COWLES, Russell	P			$660
American (1887 -)				
COX, Albert S.	P	$605	$1,568	$2,750
American (1863 - 1920)				
COX, David	P	$605	$3,328	$6,050
British (1783 - 1859)	W	$935	$3,108	$5,280
COX, Frank	P			$935
American (19th -)				
COX, Garstin	P	$440	$1,540	$2,750
British (1892 - 1933)				

D=Drawing, P=Painting, S=Sculpture, W=Watercolor

		Current Price Range		
		Low	Mean	High

		Low	Mean	High
COX, George J. American (1884 - 1946)	P			$825
COX, Lyda American (1881 -)	P			$165
COX, Palmer American (1840 - 1924)	D	$110	$1,118	$3,080
COX, Timmy American (20th -)	P			$1,430
COX, Walter A. British (1862 -)	D			$165
COX, JR., David (After) British (1809 - 1885)	P			$880
COXE, Reginald C. American (1855 -)	P			$3,025
COXIE, Michiel (Attrib.) Flemish (1603 -)	P			$7,700
COYPEL, Charles A. French (1694 - 1752)	D P	$1,100 $9,900	$3,025 $39,325	$4,950 $77,000
COYPEL, Noel N. French (1628 - 1707)	D			$6,600
COYPEL, Noel N. (After) French (1628 - 1707)	P			$2,860
COYPEL, Noel N. (Circle) French (1628 - 1707)	P			$7,700
COYPEL, Noel N. (Studio) French (1628 - 1707)	P			$23,100
COZENS, Alexander British (1717 - 1786)	D			$2,090
COZZA, Francesco Italian (1605 - 1682)	P	$60,500	$67,375	$74,250
COZZENS, Frederick S. American (1856 - 1928)	W	$660	$1,538	$2,640
CRADOCK, Marmaduke British (1660 - 1717)	P			$3,300
CRAESBEECK, Joos van Flemish (1606 - 1654)	P	$660	$15,180	$29,700

D=Drawing, P=Painting, S=Sculpture, W=Watercolor

		Current Price Range		
		Low	Mean	High
CRAESBEECK, Joos van (Attrib.)	P	$5,500	$5,775	$6,050
Flemish (1606 - 1654)				
CRAGG, Tony	S	$20,900	$37,950	$55,000
(20th -)				
CRAIG,	P			$1,100
(?)				
CRAIG, Anderson	P	$330	$330	$330
American (20th -)				
CRAIG, Charles	P	$100	$877	$1,650
American (1846 - 1931)				
CRAIG, Frank	P			$2,310
British (1874 - 1918)	W			$1,400
CRAIG, Henry R.	P	$330	$1,760	$3,190
Irish (1916 - 1984)				
CRAIG, Thomas B.	P	$413	$1,414	$3,740
American (1849 - 1924)	W	$165	$521	$1,100
CRAIG, William	W			$770
European (19th -)				
CRALI, Tullio	P			$3,080
Italian (20th -)				
CRAM, Allen G.	P	$1,045	$1,045	$1,045
American (1886 - 1947)				
CRAMER, Ernest	P			$165
American (20th -)				
CRAMER, Helene	P			$6,875
German (1844 -)				
CRAMER, Konrad	P	$16,500	$20,350	$24,200
German (1888 -)				
CRAMPTON, W. J.	P			$880
British (19th -)				
CRANACH, ELDER, Lucas	P	$88,000	$341,000	$715,000
German (1472 - 1553)				
CRANACH, ELDER, Lucas (After)	P			$550
German (1472 - 1553)				

D=Drawing, P=Painting, S=Sculpture, W=Watercolor

		Current Price Range		
		Low	Mean	High

		Low	Mean	High
CRANACH, ELDER, Lucas (Att.)	*P*			$90,750
German (1472 - 1553)				
CRANACH, ELDER, Lucas (Mann)	*P*			$4,950
German (1472 - 1553)				
CRANACH, ELDER, Lucas (Sc.)	*P*			$3,300
German (1472 - 1553)				
CRANACH, ELDER, Lucas (St.)	*P*			$14,300
German (1472 - 1553)				
CRANACH, YOUNGER, Lucas	*P*	$15,400	$29,700	$44,000
German (1515 - 1586)				
CRANCH, Christopher P.	*P*	$990	$1,687	$2,200
American (1813 - 1892)				
CRANDELL, Bradshaw	*D*	$193	$622	$1,100
American (1896 - 1966)				
CRANE, Alan H.	*W*	$165	$193	$220
American (1901 -)				
CRANE, Fred	*P*			$468
American (1847 - 1915)				
CRANE, Robert Bruce	*P*	$605	$7,454	$42,900
American (1857 - 1934)	*W*	$330	$344	$358
CRANE, Robert Bruce (Attrib.)	*P*	$220	$385	$550
American (1857 - 1934)	*W*			$680
CRANE, Walter	*D*			$770
British (1845 - 1915)	*P*	$30,800	$207,900	$385,000
CRANE, Wilbur	*P*			$220
American (1875 -)				
CRASKE, Leonard	*S*			$27,500
American (1882 - 1950)				
CRATZ, Benjamin	*P*			$880
American (1888 -)				
CRAVETT, A. M.	*W*			$154
American (19th -)				
CRAWFORD, A. L.	*P*			$248
American (19th - 20th)				

D=Drawing, P=Painting, S=Sculpture, W=Watercolor

		Current Price Range		
		Low	Mean	High

		Low	Mean	High
CRAWFORD, Brunette H.	*P*			$770
American (1876 - 1956)				
CRAWFORD, J.	*P*			$6,820
American (19th -)				
CRAWFORD, Lanson H.	*W*			$440
American (20th -)				
CRAWFORD, Mckennon	*P*			$523
Canadian (20th -)				
CRAWFORD, Ralston	*P*	$22,000	$51,333	$82,500
American (1906 - 1977)	*W*			$7,700
CRAWFORD, T.	*P*			$187
American (20th -)				
CRAWFORD, Thomas	*S*			$44,000
American (1813 - 1857)				
CRAWFORD, Wendell	*D*			$750
American (20th -)				
CRAWLEY,	*P*			$275
Irish (19th -)				
CRAWLEY, Ida J.	*P*			$1,100
American (1867 -)				
CRAYER, Caspar de	*P*			$27,500
Flemish (1584 - 1669)				
CRAYER, Caspar de (Attrib.)	*P*	$13,200	$22,000	$30,800
Flemish (1584 - 1669)				
CREE, James	*W*			$935
American (1867 - 1951)				
CREEFT, Jose de	*S*	$1,320	$3,080	$6,600
Spanish (1884 -)				
CREIFELDS, Richard	*P*	$275	$509	$880
American (1853 - 1939)	*W*			$550
CREMONINI, Leonardo	*P*	$4,620	$9,873	$19,800
Italian (1925 -)				
CRESPI, Daniele (Attrib.)	*D*			$6,600
Italian (1590 - 1630)				

D=Drawing, P=Painting, S=Sculpture, W=Watercolor

		Current Price Range		
		Low	Mean	High

CRESPI, Giuseppe M. Italian (1665 - 1747)	*D*			$52,250
CRESPI, Giuseppe M. (Attrib.) Italian (1665 - 1747)	*P*			$24,200
CRESPI, Luigi (Circle) Italian (1710 - 1779)	*P*			$1,100
CRESWICK, Thomas British (1811 - 1869)	*P*	$935	$1,718	$2,500
CRETI, Donato Italian (1671 - 1749)	*D*	$1,650	$10,175	$18,700
CRETI, Donato (Attrib.) Italian (1671 - 1749)	*P*			$28,600
CRETI, Donato (Circle) Italian (1671 - 1749)	*D* *P*			$3,575 $11,000
CRETI, Donato (Follower) Italian (1671 - 1749)	*D*			$605
CREWE, Thomas British (19th -)	*D*			$330
CRILEY, Theodore M. American (1880 - 1930)	*P*	$1,760	$2,365	$2,970
CRIPPI, Roberto American (1921 - 1972)	*S*			$6,325
CRISP, G. British (20th -)	*P*			$770
CRISS, Francis American (1901 - 1973)	*P*			$4,400
CRISTADORO, Charles American (?)	*S*			$19,800
CRISTALL, Joshua British (1767 - 1847)	*W*			$110
CRITE, Allan R American (1910 -)	*D*			$495
CRIVELLI, Angelo M. Italian (17th - 18th)	*P*			$8,800
CRIVELLI, Vittorio Italian (15th -)	*P*			$36,300

D=Drawing, P=Painting, S=Sculpture, W=Watercolor

		Current Price Range		
		Low	Mean	High

		Low	Mean	High
CRIVELLONE, (Attrib.)	*P*			$9,900
(?)				
CROCIFISSI, Simone Dei	*P*			$484,000
Italian (1330 - 1399)				
CROCIFISSI, Simone Dei (Manner)	*P*			$4,180
Italian (1330 - 1399)				
CROCKER,	*P*			$248
American (19th -)	*W*			$220
CROCKER, Charles M. K.	*P*	$468	$1,476	$3,300
American (1877 - 1950)				
CROCKER, J. Denison	*P*			$1,320
American (1823 -)				
CROCKETT, S. D.	*P*			$1,980
British (1806 - 1865)				
CROCKWELL, Douglas	*P*			$3,300
American (1904 - 1968)				
CROEGAERT, Georges	*P*	$8,250	$25,850	$88,000
French (1848 -)				
CROFT, Arthur	*W*			$715
British (1828 -)				
CROME, John B.	*P*	$3,300	$3,575	$3,850
British (1794 - 1842)				
CROMWELL, Joane	*P*	$110	$382	$660
American (? - 1966)				
CROOKS, Ron	*P*	$700	$1,100	$1,500
American (20th -)				
CROOS, Anthony J. van	*P*	$1,980	$14,593	$28,600
Dutch (1606 - 1622)				
CROOS, Anthony J. van (Attrib.)	*P*			$10,450
Dutch (1606 - 1622)				
CROOS, Pieter van der	*P*	$9,350	$15,125	$20,900
Dutch (1610 - 1701)				
CROPSEY, Jasper F.	*D*			$9,900
American (1823 - 1900)	*P*	$2,475	$42,018	$209,000

D=Drawing, P=Painting, S=Sculpture, W=Watercolor

| | | Current Price Range | | |
		Low	Mean	High
CROPSEY, Jasper F.	*W*	$1,760	$10,450	$26,400
American (1823 - 1900)				
CROPSEY, Jasper F. (Attrib.)	*P*			$2,090
American (1823 - 1900)				
CROPSEY, Jasper F. (Manner)	*P*			$176
American (1823 - 1900)				
CROSBY, Raymond M.	*P*			$1,210
American (20th -)				
CROSMAN, John H.	*P*	$880	$1,678	$2,475
American (20th -)				
CROSS, Amy	*W*			$275
American (1865 - 1939)				
CROSS, Anson K.	*P*	$330	$1,082	$1,980
American (1862 - 1944)				
CROSS, Henri-E.	*D*			$935
French (1856 - 1910)	*P*	$264,000	$494,083	$660,000
	W	$1,210	$13,112	$30,800
CROSS, Henry H.	*P*	$1,210	$8,844	$20,900
American (1837 - 1918)				
CROSS, Penni Anne	*D*			$3,575
American (1939 -)				
CROSS, Sally	*P*			$1,100
American (1874 - 1950)				
CROSS, JR., Watson	*W*	$121	$994	$2,200
American (1918 -)				
CROTTI, Jean	*P*			$2,640
French (1878 - 1958)				
CROUCH, A.	*P*			$825
British (19th -)				
CROW, Gonzalo E.	*P*	$9,350	$12,306	$18,700
Ecuadoran (1936 -)				
CROWELL, Lucius	*P*			$1,073
American (1911 - 1988)				
CROWLEY, David B.	*P*			$110
American (20th -)				

D=Drawing, P=Painting, S=Sculpture, W=Watercolor

| | | Current Price Range | |
	Low	Mean	High
CROWLEY, J. M. D			$1,870
(19th -)			
CROWNINSHIELD, Frederic P			$3,025
American (1845 - 1918)			
CROWTHER, H. P			$523
British (20th -)			
CROXFORD, Thomas Swainson P			$303
(?)			
CROZIER, William S	$1,650	$1,925	$2,200
British (20th -)			
CRUICKSHANK, William P			$495
British (1844 - 1922) W	$880	$1,540	$2,200
CRUIKSHANK, George W	$660	$798	$935
British (1792 - 1878)			
CRUISE, Aluyk B. W	$9,350	$9,717	$9,900
American (1909 - 1988)			
CRUYS, Cornelis P			$49,500
Dutch (17th -)			
CRUZ-DIEZ, Carlos P	$9,900	$16,500	$23,100
Venezuelan (1923 -)			
CRUZET, S. P			$220
(?)			
CRYAN, Steven W			$385
(?)			
CUARTAS, Gregorio P	$1,100	$3,575	$6,050
Mexican (1938 -) W	$770	$853	$935
CUATRI, Frederico P			$770
Mexican (20th -)			
CUBELLS, Salvador M. P			$44,000
Spanish (19th -)			
CUBELLS Y RUIZ, Enrique M. P			$11,000
Spanish (1874 - 1917)			
CUBLEY, Henry H. P	$605	$825	$1,045
British (19th - 20th)			

D=Drawing, P=Painting, S=Sculpture, W=Watercolor

		Current Price Range		
		Low	Mean	High
CUCARO,	P			$193
American (20th -)				
CUCCHI, Enzo	D	$5,225	$7,931	$15,400
Italian (1950 -)	P	$14,300	$68,888	$121,000
	S	$6,600	$6,875	$7,150
CUCUEL, Edward	P	$8,250	$30,388	$41,800
American (1879 -)				
CUEVAS, C.	P			$440
Spanish (20th -)				
CUEVAS, Jose L.	D	$495	$2,310	$3,520
Mexican (1934 -)	P			$2,475
	W	$3,520	$5,078	$8,250
CUGAT, Frances C.	P			$165
American (1893 -)				
CUGAT, Xavier	P			$935
Argentina (20th -)				
CULBERTSON, Josephine	P	$605	$963	$1,320
American (1852 - 1939)				
CULLIN, Isaac J.	P			$24,750
American (19th - 20th)				
CULVER, Charles	P			$275
American (1908 - 1967)	W	$770	$1,014	$1,540
CULVERHOUSE, Johann M.	P	$1,045	$4,614	$9,900
American (1849 - 1891)				
CUMING, Beatrice	P	$1,210	$2,585	$3,960
American (1903 - 1975)				
CUMMING, Arthur	P	$770	$1,173	$1,540
American (19th -)	W	$165	$303	$550
CUMMINGS, Marjorie	W			$660
American (20th -)				
CUMMINGS, Melvin E.	S			$550
American (1876 - 1936)				

D=Drawing, P=Painting, S=Sculpture, W=Watercolor

		Current Price Range		
		Low	Mean	High

CUNEO, Rinaldo	P			$2,750
American (1877 - 1939)				
CUNNINGHAM, John W.	P			$660
American (? - 1903)				
CUNNINGHAM, Roger	P			$155
American (?)				
CUNNINGHAM, Theodore St. A.	W			$105
American (1899 -)				
CUPRIEN, Frank W.	P	$468	$1,826	$8,800
American (1871 - 1948)				
CURFI, S.	P			$825
French (19th - 20th)				
CURLER, T.	P	$220	$220	$220
(20th -)				
CURNOCK, James	W			$2,475
British (1839 -)				
CURRADI, Francesco	D	$1,430	$4,290	$7,150
Italian (1570 - 1661)				
CURRADI, Francesco (After)	P			$28,600
Italian (1570 - 1661)				
CURRAN, Charles C.	D			$1,100
American (1861 - 1942)	P	$1,320	$23,214	$99,000
CURRIE, Mrs. S. C.	P			$550
British (19th -)				
CURRIER, Cyrus B.	P			$550
American (1868 - 1946)				
CURRIER, J. Frank	D			$1,430
American (1843 - 1909)				
CURRIER, Mary Ann	D	$22,000	$31,625	$41,250
(20th -)				
CURRIER, Walter B.	P	$550	$633	$715
American (1879 - 1934)				
CURRY, John S.	D			$18,700
American (1897 - 1946)	P	$16,500	$49,500	$82,500

D=Drawing, P=Painting, S=Sculpture, W=Watercolor

		Current Price Range		
		Low	Mean	High
CURRY, John S.	*W*	$1,320	$5,060	$8,800
American (1897 - 1946)				
CURRY, John S. (Attrib.)	*P*			$495
American (1897 - 1946)				
CURTIN, Thomas	*P*			$660
(19th - 20th)				
CURTIS, Alice M.	*P*			$1,760
American (1847 - 1911)				
CURTIS, C.	*W*			$418
(?)				
CURTIS, Hughes	*S*			$660
American (20th -)				
CURTIS, Leland	*P*	$550	$1,181	$1,700
American (1897 -)	*W*			$275
CURTIS, M. P.	*P*			$127
(?)				
CURTIS, Roger	*P*			$303
American (20th -)				
CURTIS, William F.	*P*	$1,100	$3,300	$5,500
American (1873 -)				
CURTIUS, Boudewijn D.	*W*			$303
Dutch (1804 - 1856)				
CURZON, Paul A. de	*P*			$16,500
French (1820 - 1895)				
CUSACHS Y CUSACHS, Jose C.	*P*	$770	$53,669	$137,500
Spanish (1851 - 1908)				
CUSHING, Lily	*W*			$550
European (19th - 20th)				
CUSHING, Val	*S*	$770	$1,650	$2,530
(20th -)				
CUSHMAN, Alice	*W*			$110
American (1854 -)				
CUSHMAN, M. J.	*W*	$165	$193	$220
American (19th -)				
CUSTER, Edward L.	*P*			$1,650
French (1837 - 1880)				

D=Drawing, P=Painting, S=Sculpture, W=Watercolor

		Current Price Range		
		Low	Mean	High
CUSTIS, Eleanor P.	W	$220	$533	$1,100
American (1897 - 1983)				
CUSTODIS, Hieronimus (Circle)	P			$7,700
Flemish (16th -)				
CUTLER, Edward J.	P			$248
(?)				
CUTTING, Francis H.	P	$333	$579	$825
American (1872 - 1964)				
CUYP, Aelbert	P	$18,700	$32,350	$46,000
Dutch (1620 - 1691)				
CUYP, Aelbert (Attrib.)	P			$4,750
Dutch (1620 - 1691)				
CUYP, Aelbert (Circle)	P			$4,950
Dutch (1620 - 1691)				
CUYP, Aelbert (Manner)	P	$154	$9,310	$25,300
Dutch (1620 - 1691)				
CUYP, Aelbert (School)	P			$1,815
Dutch (1620 - 1691)				
CUYP, Benjamin G.	P	$3,300	$16,913	$35,200
Dutch (1612 - 1652)				
CUYP, Jacob G. (Attrib.)	P			$3,025
Dutch (1594 - 1651)				
CUYP, Jacob G. (Circle)	P			$2,200
Dutch (1594 - 1651)				
CUZCO SCHOOL,	P			$6,050
(?)				
CUZCO SCHOOL 18C,	P	$2,200	$3,300	$4,400
(18th -)				
CYGAN, Z.	P			$715
Polish (20th -)				
CYGNE, E. J.	P			$385
French (20th -)				
CYRSKY, Frank	P			$1,980
American (20th -)				
CZACHORSKI, Ladislas de	P			$8,800
Polish (1850 - 1911)				

D=Drawing, P=Painting, S=Sculpture, W=Watercolor

		Low	Mean	High
		Current Price Range		
CZECHOWSKI, Alice (Attrib.)	*P*			$150
American (20th -)				
CZERNUS, Tibor	*P*	$4,950	$9,900	$14,850
(20th -)				
D'ACOSTA, Hy. Walker	*P*			$7,150
Spanish (19th -)				
D'AIRE, Paul	*S*			$1,540
(?)				
D'ALESSARDI, Michele	*S*			$1,320
American (?)				
D'ANCONA, Nicola de (Circle)	*P*			$18,700
Italian (?)				
D'ANDREA, Bernard	*W*	$110	$380	$650
American (1923 -)				
D'ANTY, Henry	*P*	$550	$1,100	$1,650
French (1910 -)				
D'ANVERS, Cavalier	*P*			$4,950
(1678 - 1733)				
D'AOUST, Enrique	*P*			$3,850
Mexican (20th -)				
D'ARCANGELO, Alan	*D*			$990
(20th -)	*P*	$2,090	$11,880	$18,150
D'ARPINO, Cavaliere (Circle)	*P*			$1,540
Italian (16th - 17th)				
D'ARTHOIS, Jacques (Circle)	*P*	$1,650	$7,975	$14,300
Flemish (1613 -)				
D'ASCENZO, Nicola	*P*	$303	$367	$430
American (1871 -)	*W*	$220	$321	$385
D'AVENNES, Emile P.	*D*	$1,100	$1,650	$2,200
European (19th -)				
D'AVIGNON, Nicolas M. (Attrib.)	*P*			$11,000
(1606 - 1668)				
D'EAUBONNE, Louis-Lucien	*P*			$3,410
French (1834 - 1894)				

D=Drawing, P=Painting, S=Sculpture, W=Watercolor

		Current Price Range		
		Low	Mean	High
D'ENTRAYGUES, Charles B.	P	$7,700	$31,167	$77,000
French (1851 -)				
D'ESPAGNAT, Georges	D	$440	$1,705	$2,970
French (1870 - 1950)	P	$6,050	$43,539	$198,000
	W	$440	$1,503	$2,750
D'HONDECOETER, Gillis C.	P	$22,000	$57,750	$93,500
Dutch (1575 - 1638)				
D'HONDECOETER, Melchior	P			$242,000
(1639 - 1695)				
D'ILLIERS, Gaston	S	$660	$1,595	$2,420
French (1876 -)				
D'LEON, Omar	P	$3,080	$3,190	$3,300
Nicaraguan (1929 -)				
D'ORSI, A.	S			$880
(?)				
D'OTEMAR, Marie A. E. M.	P			$825
French (19th -)				
DA COSTA, Milton	P			$15,400
Brazilian (1915 -)				
DA MOLIN, Oreste	P			$2,750
Italian (1856 - 1921)				
DABO, Leon	D			$2,970
American (1868 - 1960)	P	$110	$7,280	$25,200
DADD, Richard (Attrib.)	P			$8,800
British (1851 - 1929)				
DADO,	P	$13,200	$17,967	$22,000
Yugoslavia (1933 -)				
DAELE, Casimir van den	P			$2,860
Belgian (1818 - 1880)				
DAEN, Lindsay	S			$935
American (1923 -)				
DAGGETT, Grace E.	P			$220
American (1867 -)				
DAGGY, Augustus	P			$440
American (1858 - 1942)				

D=Drawing, P=Painting, S=Sculpture, W=Watercolor

		Current Price Range		
		Low	Mean	High

		Low	Mean	High
DAGGY, Richard	*W*			$220
American (1892 -)				
DAGNAN-BOUVERET, Pascal A.	*P*			$4,400
French (1852 - 1929)				
DAGNAUX, Albert M. A.	*P*			$550,000
French (1861 - 1933)				
DAGONET, Ernest	*S*			$2,200
French (19th -)				
DAHL, C.	*P*			$264
Norwegian (19th - 20th)				
DAHL, Hans A.	*P*	$275	$4,538	$8,800
Norwegian (1849 - 1937)	*W*			$1,980
DAHL, J.	*P*			$6,050
Danish (19th -)				
DAHL, Johannes S.	*P*			$2,420
German (1827 - 1902)				
DAHL, Michael	*P*	$1,100	$1,100	$1,100
Swedish (1656 - 1743)				
DAHL, Michael (Attrib.)	*P*			$5,500
Swedish (1656 - 1743)				
DAHL, Michael (Circle)	*P*			$6,600
Swedish (1656 - 1743)				
DAHL, Siegwald	*P*			$25,300
German (1827 - 1902)				
DAHLAGER, Jules	*P*	$770	$2,647	$13,200
American (20th -)				
DAHLGREEN, Charles W.	*P*	$660	$1,279	$2,090
American (1864 - 1955)				
DAHLGREN, Carl	*P*	$825	$1,526	$2,750
American (1841 - 1920)	*W*			$330
DAHN, Walter	*P*			$15,400
(20th -)				
DAINGERFIELD, Elliott	*P*	$715	$3,410	$7,700
American (1859 - 1932)	*W*	$165	$257	$303

D=Drawing, P=Painting, S=Sculpture, W=Watercolor

		Current Price Range		
		Low	Mean	High

		Low	Mean	High
DAINI, Augusto	*W*	$880	$1,870	$2,860
Italian (19th -)				
DAIO, David	*P*			$1,320
(20th -)				
DAKEN, Sidney T.	*P*	$275	$626	$880
American (1876 - 1935)				
DALBY, David	*P*			$17,600
British (1794 - 1836)				
DALBY, John	*P*	$4,070	$5,885	$7,700
British (19th -)				
DALBY, Joshua	*P*			$30,250
British (19th -)				
DALEN, Anton van	*D*			$330
Dutch (1927 -)	*P*			$550
DALEY, William & Catherine	*S*			$3,850
(20th -)				
DALI, Louis	*P*			$1,210
French (20th -)				
DALI, Salvador	*D*	$2,860	$46,886	$253,000
Spanish (1904 - 1989)	*P*	$2,310	$769,110	$4.070M
	S	$2,640	$44,834	$143,000
	W	$1,210	$77,929	$231,000
DALLIN, Cyrus E.	*S*	$275	$8,811	$33,000
American (1861 - 1944)				
DALMATIAN SCHOOL 14C,	*P*			$14,300
(14th -)				
DALMATIAN SCHOOL 17C,	*P*			$2,860
(17th -)				
DALOU, Aime	*S*	$550	$10,230	$25,300
French (1838 - 1902)				
DALOU, Aime (After)	*S*			$660
French (1838 - 1902)				
DALTON, William B.	*W*			$550
(?)				

D=Drawing, P=Painting, S=Sculpture, W=Watercolor

		Current Price Range		
		Low	Mean	High

		Low	Mean	High
DALVIT, Oskar	P			$880
Swiss (1911 -)				
DALYRYMPLE, Amy F.	W			$550
American (19th - 20th)				
DAM, Vu Cao	P	$385	$440	$495
Indochina (1908 -)				
DAMM, Johan F.	P			$13,200
Danish (1820 - 1894)				
DAMME, E. van	P			$770
Belgian (1853 -)				
DAMOYE, Pierre E.	P	$1,320	$11,896	$35,200
French (1847 - 1916)				
DAMPIER, William	P	$275	$523	$770
American (1910 - 1985)				
DAMROW, Charles	P			$440
American (1916 -)				
DAMSCHROEDER, Jan J. M.	P	$1,705	$3,726	$6,050
German (1825 - 1905)				
DANA, C. G.	P			$660
American (19th - 20th)				
DANA, William P.	D			$495
American (1833 - 1927)				
DANBY, James F.	P	$523	$2,462	$4,400
British (1816 - 1875)				
DANBY, Mrs. E. R.	P			$825
British (19th -)				
DANBY, Thomas	P			$1,100
British (1818 - 1886)				
DANDE, Y.	P			$220
(?)				
DANDINI, Pietro	P			$35,200
Italian (1646 - 1712)				
DANDINI, Pietro (Circle)	P			$8,800
Italian (1646 - 1712)				
DANERI, Eugenio	P			$6,600
Argentina (1891 - 1970)				

D=Drawing, P=Painting, S=Sculpture, W=Watercolor

		Current Price Range		
		Low	Mean	High

		Low	Mean	High
DANFORTH, Charles A.	P			$605
American (19th -)				
DANIELL, William	W	$1,650	$2,750	$3,300
British (1769 - 1837)				
DANIELL, William S.	P	$440	$482	$523
American (1865 - 1933)	W	$550	$770	$990
DANIELS, Elmer H.	P			$275
American (1905 -)				
DANIELS, F. H.	P			$385
(20th -)				
DANIELS, George F.	P			$2,750
American (1821 -)				
DANISH SCHOOL,	P			$8,800
Danish (?)				
DANISH SCHOOL 19C,	P			$8,800
Danish (19th -)				
DANITZ, W.	P			$110
American (20th -)				
DANLOUX, Henri P.	P	$14,850	$92,675	$170,500
French (1753 - 1809)				
DANLOUX, Henri P. (Circle)	P	$1,045	$3,273	$5,500
French (1753 - 1809)				
DANN, Frode N.	W			$5,225
American (1892 -)				
DANNENBERG, Alice	P			$1,320
Russian (1861 -)				
DANNER, Sara K.	P	$550	$1,375	$2,200
American (1894 - 1969)				
DANSAERT, Leon	P			$5,280
Belgian (1830 - 1909)				
DANTON, JR., F.	P			$7,700
American (19th -)				
DANTZIG, M.	P			$1,320
American (20th -)				
DANZ, Robert	P			$35,200
German (1841 -)				

D=Drawing, P=Painting, S=Sculpture, W=Watercolor

| | | Current Price Range | | |
		Low	Mean	High
DAPHNIS, Nassos	*P*	$1,870	$2,145	$2,420
Greek (1914 -)	*S*			$4,620
DARBOVEN, Hanne	*D*			$7,150
German (1941 -)				
DARET, Ernesto (Attrib.)	*P*			$20,900
Italian (17th -)				
DARGAUD, P. J. V.	*S*			$440
(?)				
DARGE, Fred	*P*			$385
American (1900 -)				
DARGELAS, Andre Henri	*P*			$11,000
French (1828 - 1906)				
DARLEY, Felix O.	*D*	$275	$1,659	$6,050
American (1822 - 1888)	*W*	$495	$963	$1,430
DARLEY, Felix O. (Et al.)	*D*			$990
American (19th -)				
DARLEY, Jane C. (Attrib.)	*P*			$770
American (1807 - 1877)				
DARLING, Wilder M.	*P*			$1,210
American (1856 -)				
DARLING, Wilder M. (Attrib.)	*D*			$165
American (1856 -)				
DARLING, William S.	*P*	$715	$770	$825
American (1882 - 1963)				
DARONDEAU, Stanislas H. B.	*P*			$1,210
French (1807 - 1841)				
DARRAH, Sophie T.	*P*			$248
American (19th - 20th)				
DARRIEUX, Charles Renee	*P*			$825
French (1879 -)				
DARRO, Peter	*P*			$330
American (20th -)				
DARROW, Titus H.	*P*			$1,540
(20th -)				

D=Drawing, P=Painting, S=Sculpture, W=Watercolor

		Current Price Range		
		Low	Mean	High

		Low	Mean	High
DARRU, Louise	P			$6,050
French (19th -)				
DART, Richard P.	P			$22,000
American (1916 -)				
DASBURG, Andrew	P	$37,400	$79,200	$121,000
American (1887 - 1979)	W			$18,700
DASTUGUE, Maxime	P			$6,600
French (19th -)				
DAUB, Matthew	W			$440
(?)				
DAUBIGNY, Charles F.	D			$7,700
French (1817 - 1878)	P	$495	$26,838	$85,250
DAUBIGNY, Charles F. (Attrib.)	P			$825
French (1817 - 1878)				
DAUBIGNY, Karl	P	$1,430	$6,854	$20,900
French (1846 - 1886)				
DAUCHOT, Gabriel	P	$523	$1,249	$1,980
French (1927 -)				
DAUDIN, Henry C.	P			$4,400
French (1861 -)				
DAUGHERTY, James H.	D	$200	$1,095	$2,090
American (1889 - 1974)	P	$3,520	$14,960	$26,400
DAUMIER, Honore	D			$8,250
French (1808 - 1879)	P	$154,000	$627,000	$1.100M
	S			$12,100
DAUMIER, Jean	P			$440
(?)				
DAUX, Charles E.	P			$19,800
French (1817 - 1888)				
DAVENPORT, W. S.	P			$358
American (19th - 20th)				
DAVEY, Randall	P	$825	$5,145	$13,200

D=Drawing, P=Painting, S=Sculpture, W=Watercolor

| | | Current Price Range | | |
		Low	Mean	High
DAVEY, Randall	*S*			$715
American (1887 - 1964)	*W*			$1,100
DAVID, Gerard	*P*			$33,000
Flemish (1460 - 1523)				
DAVID, Hermine	*P*			$3,850
French (1886 - 1971)	*W*	$165	$193	$220
DAVID, Jacques L.	*D*			$18,700
French (1748 - 1825)				
DAVID, Jacques L. (After)	*D*			$8,800
French (1748 - 1825)	*P*			$6,600
DAVID, Jacques L. (School)	*D*			$770
French (1748 - 1825)				
DAVID, Michael	*P*			$5,500
(20th -)				
DAVID, Pierre J.	*S*			$1,320
French (1788 - 1856)				
DAVID, School	*P*			$2,200
Flemish (1450 - 1523)				
DAVID, Stanley S.	*P*	$8,800	$12,100	$15,400
American (19th -)				
DAVIDSON, Charles G.	*W*	$121	$143	$165
American (1866 - 1965)				
DAVIDSON, Clara D.	*P*	$176	$1,848	$3,520
American (1874 -)				
DAVIDSON, Daniel P.	*P*			$660
Scottish (20th -)				
DAVIDSON, Herbert	*P*	$275	$688	$1,100
(?)				
DAVIDSON, Jo	*D*	$825	$963	$1,210
American (1883 - 1952)	*P*	$495	$633	$770
	S	$715	$4,461	$12,100
DAVIDSON, Jo (Et al.)	*D*			$1,430
American (19th - 20th)				

D=Drawing, P=Painting, S=Sculpture, W=Watercolor

		Current Price Range		
		Low	Mean	High

		Low	Mean	High
DAVIDSON, Julian O.	*D*			$605
American (1853 - 1893)				
DAVIDSON, R. A.	*P*			$605
American (20th -)				
DAVIDSON, Thomas E.	*P*			$176
American (?)				
DAVIE, Alan	*P*	$3,850	$48,950	$93,500
British (1920 -)	*W*			$2,090
DAVIES, Albert W.	*P*			$132
(?)				
DAVIES, Arthur B.	*D*	$138	$1,036	$5,500
American (1862 - 1928)	*P*	$220	$5,243	$24,200
	W	$198	$2,187	$6,050
DAVIES, Arthur B. (Attrib.)	*P*			$330
American (1862 - 1928)				
DAVIES, Edward	*P*			$495
British (1843 - 1912)				
DAVIES, Harold C.	*W*			$990
American (1891 - 1976)				
DAVIES, James H.	*P*	$1,540	$1,540	$1,540
British (1848 -)				
DAVIES, Ken	*P*			$3,850
American (1925 -)	*W*			$880
DAVIES, William S.	*W*			$1,430
American (1826 - 1901)				
DAVIHOT,	*P*			$825
French (20th -)				
DAVILA, Fernando	*P*			$3,300
American (1935 -)				
DAVILA, Jose A.	*P*	$3,300	$10,267	$22,000
Venezuelan (1935 -)				
DAVIS, Alexander J.	*D*			$880
American (19th -)				

D=Drawing, P=Painting, S=Sculpture, W=Watercolor

| | | Current Price Range | | |
		Low	Mean	High
DAVIS, Arthur	*P*			$3,740
British (19th -)				
DAVIS, Charles F.	*P*			$1,430
British (19th - 20th)				
DAVIS, Charles H.	*D*			$2,860
American (1856 - 1933)	*P*	$1,210	$2,823	$5,280
DAVIS, Debby	*P*	$330	$825	$1,320
(20th -)	*S*			$330
DAVIS, Floyd	*D*			$578
American (1896 - 1966)	*W*			$165
DAVIS, Frank R.	*P*			$209
American (20th -)				
DAVIS, Gene	*D*			$715
American (1920 -)	*P*	$1,870	$6,508	$16,500
DAVIS, Gladys Rockmore	*D*			$440
American (1901 - 1967)	*P*	$303	$3,266	$6,600
DAVIS, J. E.	*P*	$143	$223	$303
American (19th - 20th)				
DAVIS, Jack	*D*			$250
(?)				
DAVIS, John S.	*P*			$6,600
British (1804 - 1045)				
DAVIS, L. E.	*P*			$303
(?)				
DAVIS, Leonard M.	*P*	$413	$578	$770
American (1864 - 1938)				
DAVIS, M. A.	*P*			$550
American (19th -)				
DAVIS, Marsha	*W*	$350	$740	$1,375
American (20th -)				
DAVIS, Richard B.	*P*	$33,000	$47,667	$66,000
British (1782 - 1854)				

D=Drawing, P=Painting, S=Sculpture, W=Watercolor

		Current Price Range		
		Low	Mean	High

		Low	Mean	High
DAVIS, Ron	P	$6,050	$12,650	$16,500
American (1937 -)	S	$605	$908	$1,210
	W			$4,950
DAVIS, S. C.	P			$165
American (19th -)				
DAVIS, Stan	P	$4,510	$7,058	$9,625
American (1942 -)				
DAVIS, Stark	P			$990
American (1885 -)	W			$1,540
DAVIS, Stuart	D	$4,950	$36,850	$68,750
American (1894 - 1964)	P	$41,800	$324,867	$880,000
	W	$8,800	$44,660	$88,000
DAVIS, Theodore R.	D	$275	$715	$1,045
American (1840 - 1894)				
DAVIS, Vestie E.	P	$495	$495	$495
American (1904 - 1978)				
DAVIS, W. H.	P	$880	$3,887	$7,700
British (19th -)				
DAVIS, W. T.	P			$633
American (20th -)				
DAVIS, Warren	P	$193	$3,592	$13,200
American (1865 - 1928)	W			$39,600
DAVIS, William M.	P	$275	$2,292	$4,400
American (1829 - 1920)	W			$3,300
DAVIS, William R.	P			$5,775
American (20th -)				
DAVISON, Wilfred P.	D			$495
American (19th - 20th)	P	$1,100	$1,320	$1,540
DAVISSON, Homer G.	W			$193
American (1866 -)				
DAVOL, Edith	P	$110	$257	$330
American (20th -)				

D=Drawing, P=Painting, S=Sculpture, W=Watercolor

		Current Price Range		
		Low	Mean	High

		Low	Mean	High
DAVOL, Joseph B.	*P*	$550	$825	$1,100
American (1864 - 1923)				
DAVY, W.	*P*			$440
(19th -)				
DAWES, Dexter B.	*D*			$385
American (1872 -)				
DAWES, Edwin	*W*			$440
American (1872 - 1934)				
DAWN, Giordiani	*P*			$935
(?)				
DAWSON, Arthur	*P*			$550
British (1858 -)				
DAWSON, E.	*P*			$220
(?)				
DAWSON, Henry	*P*	$1,980	$7,920	$15,400
British (1811 - 1878)				
DAWSON, Henry (Attrib.)	*P*			$1,870
British (1811 - 1878)				
DAWSON, Jack	*P*	$220	$220	$220
(20th -)				
DAWSON, John W.	*W*			$110
American (1888 -)				
DAWSON, Manierre	*P*			$57,750
American (1887 - 1969)				
DAWSON, Montague	*P*	$2,860	$29,850	$176,000
British (1895 - 1973)	*W*	$15,400	$16,500	$17,600
DAWSON, Montague (Attrib.)	*P*			$24,200
British (1895 - 1973)	*W*			$440
DAWSON-WATSON, Dawson	*P*	$1,375	$2,658	$4,510
American (1864 - 1939)				
DAY, Clarence C.	*P*			$193
American (19th - 20th)				
DAY, Francis	*P*	$468	$6,717	$13,200
American (1863 -)				

D=Drawing, P=Painting, S=Sculpture, W=Watercolor

		Current Price Range		
		Low	Mean	High

DAY, G. F.	*P*			$7,150
British (19th -)				
DAY, Herbert J.	*P*			$110
American (20th -)				
DAY, Larry	*P*			$1,650
American (20th -)				
DAY, Mabel	*P*			$303
American (1884 -)				
DAYEZ, Georges	*P*	$660	$2,933	$5,500
French (1907 -)				
DAYMUDE, Gene	*P*	$220	$348	$550
American (1925 -)				
DE BANFIELD,	*W*			$330
(20th -)				
DE BEUL, Laurent	*P*			$2,090
Belgian (19th -)				
DE BIEVRE, Marie	*P*			$5,500
Belgian (1865 -)				
DE BLAS, E.	*P*			$660
European (19th -)				
DE BLOIS, Francois B.	*P*			$715
Canadian (19th - 20th)				
DE BOEVER, Jean F.	*P*			$3,575
Belgian (1872 - 1949)				
DE BOUCK, T.	*W*			$110
Dutch (19th - 20th)				
DE CAMP, Joseph	*P*	$14,850	$24,475	$34,100
American (1858 - 1923)				
DE COCK,	*P*			$2,750
European (19th -)				
DE CUVILLON, Louis R.	*W*			$440
French (1848 -)				
DE FAVANNE, Henri-Antoine	*D*			$770
French (? - 1752)				
DE FEO, Charles	*W*			$300
American (?)				

D=Drawing, P=Painting, S=Sculpture, W=Watercolor

		Current Price Range		
		Low	Mean	High
DE FER, Edward (?)	P			$4,620
DE FOREST, Henry J. Canadian (1860 - 1924)	P			$2,475
DE FOREST, Roy (20th -)	D W	 $4,400	 $5,133	$4,400 $6,050
DE HAVEN, Franklin American (1856 - 1934)	P	$220	$1,770	$4,125
DE KLYN, Charles American (20th -)	P	$248	$459	$605
DE LACY, Charles J. British (?)	P			$1,100
DE LEULE, (19th -)	P			$165
DE LIVRE, (?)	W			$523
DE LUMMEN, Emile V. M. (1827 - 1890)	W			$660
DE MERS, Joe American (1910 - 1984)	P W			$500 $578
DE MONTALANT, I. O. French (19th -)	P			$275
DE NIRO, Robert (20th -)	D			$660
DE PAUW, Robert (19th -)	W			$110
DE POIX, Hugh (?)	P			$1,430
DE RETZ, Eudes A. F. French (19th -)	P			$2,420
DE ROME, Albert T. American (1885 - 1959)	P			$1,320
DE SIMONE, (19th -)	P			$3,520

D=Drawing, P=Painting, S=Sculpture, W=Watercolor

		Current Price Range	
	Low	Mean	High

		Low	Mean	High
DE VITY, A.	*P*			$248
Italian (20th -)				
DE VITY, Emilio	*P*			$132
Italian (1886 - 1964)				
DEAKIN, Edwin	*P*	$1,100	$3,581	$8,250
American (1838 - 1923)	*W*	$187	$1,254	$2,860
DEAN, Abner	*W*			$385
American (1910 -)				
DEAN, Peter	*P*	$605	$963	$1,320
American (20th -)				
DEAN, Walter	*P*	$220	$1,303	$3,575
American (1854 - 1912)				
DEARTH, Henry	*P*	$1,100	$1,943	$2,530
American (1864 - 1918)				
DEAS, Charles	*P*	$165,000	$165,000	$165,000
American (1818 - 1867)				
DEAS, Charles (School)	*P*			$7,700
American (1818 - 1867)				
DEASET, H.	*P*			$220
American (20th -)				
DEBAT-PONSON, Edouard B.	*P*	$9,350	$18,150	$25,300
French (1847 - 1913)				
DEBEUL, Armand	*P*			$1,100
Belgian (1874 -)				
DEBEUL, H.	*P*			$4,675
Belgian (19th -)				
DEBLOCK, Eugenius F.	*P*			$770
American (19th -)				
DEBLOIS, Francois B.	*P*	$605	$1,008	$1,650
Canadian (1829 - 1913)				
DEBRAS, Louis	*P*	$880	$1,128	$1,375
French (1820 - 1899)				
DEBRE, Olivier	*P*			$50,600
French (1920 -)				
DEBROCK, Eugene	*P*	$1,100	$1,320	$1,540
(19th -)				

D=Drawing, P=Painting, S=Sculpture, W=Watercolor

		Current Price Range		
		Low	Mean	High
DEBRUCKNER, W.	P	$303	$427	$550
American (19th - 20th)				
DEBUT, D.	S			$6,820
French (19th -)				
DECAMP,	P	$358	$454	$550
American (?)				
DECAMP, Ralph	P	$1,200	$1,755	$2,310
American (1858 - 1936)				
DECAMPS, Alexandre G.	P	$3,025	$3,905	$5,280
French (1803 - 1860)	W			$550
DECANDDER, S.	P			$5,500
Belgian (19th -)				
DECHAMP, A.	P	$358	$496	$633
(20th -)				
DECHAR, Peter	P			$2,750
(20th -)				
DECKER, Cornelis G.(Attrib.)	P			$5,225
Dutch (? - 1678)				
DECKER, Joseph	P	$19,800	$314,600	$759,000
American (1853 - 1924)	W			$550
DECKER, Robert M.	P	$220	$248	$275
American (1847 -)				
DECKLEMANN, Andreas	P			$2,970
German (1820 - 1882)				
DECOB, G.	W			$468
British (19th - 20th)				
DEDECKER, Thomas	P			$800
American (20th -)				
DEDUAL, Lucien F.	P			$440
Canadian (20th -)				
DEERING, Roger	P			$440
American (1904 -)				
DEFAUX, Alexandre	P	$3,575	$5,638	$7,700
French (1826 - 1900)				

D=Drawing, P=Painting, S=Sculpture, W=Watercolor

		Low	Mean	High
		Current Price Range		

		Low	Mean	High
DEFIZE, Alfred Belgian (19th - 20th)	P			$1,430
DEFONTE, Edmond A. French (1862 -)	P			$1,045
DEFOREST, Lockwood American (1850 - 1932)	P			$110
DEFOREST, Roy (20th -)	P	$3,300	$13,200	$23,100
DEFREGGER, Franz von German (1835 - 1921)	P	$7,700	$38,225	$68,750
DEGANO, Munez (20th -)	P			$275
DEGAS, Edgar French (1834 - 1917)	D	$10,450	$1.190M	$7.975M
	P	$47,300	$1.223M	$3.850M
	S	$28,600	$234,676	$687,500
DEGAS, Edgar (After) French (1834 - 1917)	S	$1,760	$2,255	$2,750
DEGAVERE, Carnella American (1877 - 1955)	P			$468
DEGROSSI, Adelchi Italian (19th -)	W	$303	$399	$495
DEGROUX, Charles Belgian (1825 - 1870)	P			$550
DEHASPE, Francois Belgian (1874 -)	P			$935
DEHAVEN, Franklin American (1856 - 1934)	P	$1,045	$1,334	$1,760
DEHAVEN, Hugh (20th -)	P			$275
DEHN, Adolf A. American (1895 - 1968)	P	$578	$2,649	$6,050
	W	$440	$2,773	$10,450
DEIKE, Clara American (20th -)	P	$605	$1,128	$1,650
DEJOINER, Oscar D. American (1860 - 1924)	P			$1,100

D=Drawing, P=Painting, S=Sculpture, W=Watercolor

		Current Price Range		
		Low	Mean	High
DEJUINNE, Francois L.	*P*			$33,000
French (1786 - 1844)				
DEL MUE, Maurice A.	*P*	$1,045	$1,183	$1,320
American (1878 - 1955)				
DEL PEZZO, Lucio	*P*			$7,700
(20th -)				
DELABRIERRE, Paul Edouard	*S*	$495	$1,623	$3,575
French (1829 - 1912)				
DELACOUR, G.	*P*			$138
American (20th -)				
DELACROIX, Auguste A. (Attrib.)	*P*			$715
French (1809 - 1868)				
DELACROIX, Eugene	*D*	$1,100	$14,102	$52,800
French (1798 - 1863)	*P*	$11,000	$1.114M	$5.500M
	W	$4,950	$14,740	$38,500
DELACROIX, Eugene (Style)	*P*			$5,500
French (1798 - 1863)				
DELACROIX, Henry	*P*			$2,640
French (1845 - 1929)				
DELACROIX, Paul	*P*	$440	$440	$440
European (19th -)				
DELACY, Charles J.	*P*			$440
British (20th -)				
DELAGE, Pierre	*P*	$770	$2,035	$3,300
French (19th -)				
DELAHAYE, Louis	*P*			$6,050
French (19th -)				
DELANCE, Paul L.	*P*			$5,500
French (1848 - 1924)				
DELANEY, Joseph (Attrib.)	*P*			$1,265
American (1904 -)				
DELANO, Gerard Curtis	*P*			$550
American (1890 - 1972)				
DELANOY, Jacques	*P*			$6,050
French (1820 - 1890)				

D=Drawing, P=Painting, S=Sculpture, W=Watercolor

		Current Price Range		
		Low	Mean	High

		Low	Mean	High
DELAROCHE, B.	*P*			$550
French (19th -)				
DELAROCHE, Hippolyte P. (Cir.)	*P*			$1,925
French (1797 - 1856)				
DELARUE, L.	*P*			$798
(?)				
DELASALLE, Angele	*P*			$990
French (19th -)				
DELATTRE, Henri	*P*			$8,800
French (1801 - 1876)				
DELAUNAY, Jules E.	*D*			$3,520
French (1828 - 1891)	*P*			$4,400
DELAUNAY, Jules E. (Attrib.)	*P*			$518
French (1828 - 1891)				
DELAUNAY, Robert	*D*			$9,075
French (1885 - 1941)	*P*			$550,000
	S			$44,000
DELAUNAY, Sonia	*D*			$17,600
French (1885 -)	*P*			$341,000
	W	$1,870	$21,911	$44,000
DELAUNAY, Sonia (After)	*P*			$330
French (1885 -)				
DELBEKE, After	*P*			$495
(?)				
DELBOS, Julius	*P*	$286	$878	$2,200
American (1879 - 1970)	*W*	$193	$303	$550
DELBRIDGE, Thomas J. (Attrib.)	*P*			$220
American (1894 -)				
DELCLOCHE, Paul J.	*P*			$715
Flemish (1716 - 1755)				
DELCOURT, Hector	*W*			$165
American (20th -)				

D=Drawing, P=Painting, S=Sculpture, W=Watercolor

		Low	Current Price Range Mean	High
DELESSARD, Auguste J. French (1827 - 1890)	P			$2,860
DELFF, Cornelis J. Dutch (17th -)	P			$30,800
DELFGAAUW, Gerard J. Dutch (1882 - 1947)	P			$1,650
DELFIN, Victor Lat. Amer. (20th -)	S	$12,100	$15,400	$18,700
DELIMOUX, (20th -)	W			$990
DELISI, Lesa American (20th -)	P			$550
DELISIO, A. Italian (20th -)	P			$550
DELL'ABBATE, Niccolo Italian (16th -)	P			$297,000
DELLENBAUGH, Frederick American (19th -)	P			$13,200
DELLER, Harris (20th -)	S	$308	$363	$418
DELMARLE, Felix French (1936 -)	D	$2,750	$2,750	$2,750
DELOBBE, Alfred French (1835 - 1920)	P	$3,300	$7,700	$12,100
DELOBRE, Emile V. A. French (1873 -)	P			$440
DELOCK, Xaviar French (19th -)	P			$880
DELORME, Louise French (1928 -)	P			$138
DELORT, Charles E. French (1841 - 1895)	P	$5,500	$11,000	$16,500
DELPY, Henri J. French (1877 - 1957)	P			$1,540
DELPY, Hippolyte C. French (1842 - 1910)	P	$6,050	$9,524	$16,500

D=Drawing, P=Painting, S=Sculpture, W=Watercolor

		Current Price Range		
		Low	Mean	High

		Low	Mean	High
DELPY, Lucien V.	P			$825
French (1898 -)				
DELRIEUX, Etienne	W			$330
French (19th -)				
DELSAUX, Jeremie	P			$1,870
Belgian (1852 - 1927)				
DELUC, Gabriel	P			$5,500
French (1850 - 1916)				
DELUCO,	S			$990
Italian (?)				
DELUERMOZ, Henri	P			$5,500
French (1876 - 1943)				
DELVAUX, Paul	P	$605,000	$687,500	$770,000
Belgian (1897 -)				
DELVILLE, Jean	D			$440,000
Belgian (1867 - 1953)				
DEMACHY, Pierre-Antoine	D			$44,000
French (1723 - 1807)				
DEMAINE, Harry	P			$260
American (1880 - 1951)	W	$193	$482	$770
DEMANET, Victor	S			$1,100
French (19th - 20th)				
DEMARNE, Jean L.	P			$22,000
French (1754 - 1829)				
DEMARNE, Jean L. (Attrib.)	P			$5,500
French (1754 - 1829)				
DEMENTER, Jan	P			$578
Dutch (1810 - 1877)				
DEMETROPOULOS, Charles P.	W	$330	$550	$770
American (1912 - 1976)				
DEMEYER, Joseph (Attrib.)	P			$600
Belgian (20th -)				
DEMING, Adelaide	P			$2,750
American (1864 -)	W			$275

D=Drawing, P=Painting, S=Sculpture, W=Watercolor

		Current Price Range		
		Low	Mean	High
DEMING, Edwin W.	P	$550	$3,130	$9,900
American (1860 - 1943)	S			$5,500
	W	$715	$798	$880
DEMOND, F.V.	P			$400
American (1865 - 1951)				
DEMONTE, Bruno	W			$3,080
S. American (20th -)				
DEMONTE, Rosalia	W	$605	$843	$1,045
Brazilian (20th -)				
DEMUTH, Charles H.	D	$550	$2,076	$6,050
American (1883 - 1935)	W	$7,700	$73,663	$275,000
DENAGY, Laszlo	P			$1,210
American (1906 - 1944)				
DENENS, Jan	P			$9,900
Dutch (17th -)				
DENES, Agnes	D			$3,850
(20th -)	W			$2,860
DENEUVILLE, Henry E.	P	$523	$523	$523
French (20th -)				
DENIERE & BELLEUSE, Carrier	S			$660
(?)				
DENIS, Maurice	P	$10,450	$26,217	$46,200
French (1870 - 1943)	W			$2,530
DENISON, Harold	P			$495
American (1887 - 1940)				
DENNER, Balthasar	P			$7,700
German (1685 - 1749)				
DENNING, J.	P			$468
(?)				
DENNINGHOFF, H.	P			$1,760
European (19th -)				
DENNIS, Curt	S			$2,500
American (20th -)				

D=Drawing, P=Painting, S=Sculpture, W=Watercolor

		Current Price Range		
		Low	Mean	High
DENNIS, J.	D			$550
American (19th -)	W			$138
DENNIS, Roger	P	$132	$176	$220
American (1902 -)				
DENNY, Gideon J.	P			$6,050
American (1830 - 1886)				
DENNY, Gideon J. (Attrib.)	P			$880
American (1830 - 1886)				
DENTON, Troy	P			$1,320
American (20th -)				
DENTZ, T.	P			$1,540
American (20th -)				
DEODATO, Esculator	P			$143
Brazilian (20th -)				
DEPACHIERA, Sancha	P			$110
(?)				
DER GARABEDIAN, Giragos	P			$1,100
American (1893 -)				
DERAIN, Andre	D	$1,045	$3,104	$9,350
French (1880 - 1954)	P	$3,575	$114,183	$467,500
	S	$4,180	$5,583	$6,050
	W	$3,080	$3,960	$5,500
DERAIN, Andre (Attrib.)	D			$154
French (1880 - 1954)				
DERBY, William	P			$1,370
British (19th -)				
DERCHEU, Jules A.	S			$1,760
French (1864 - 1912)				
DERENDINGER, C.	P			$1,320
European (19th -)				
DERICKS, Louis	P			$60,500
French (19th -)				
DERO, Roswin	W			$110
American (20th -)				

D=Drawing, P=Painting, S=Sculpture, W=Watercolor

		Current Price Range		
		Low	Mean	High
DERRICK, William R.	*P*	$1,045	$1,668	$2,310
American (1857 - 1941)	*W*			$385
DERRY, Patrick V.	*P*			$990
American (1843 - 1913)				
DERUJINSKY, Gleb W.	*S*	$990	$9,423	$23,100
American (1888 - 1975)				
DERYKE, William	*P*			$6,600
Flemish (1635 - 1699)				
DES, Cornelis de	*P*			$10,450
Flemish (1585 - 1651)				
DESANGES, Louis W.	*P*			$2,200
British (1822 -)				
DESAR, Louis P.	*P*			$4,620
American (1867 - 1952)				
DESAUTY, H.	*P*			$121
European (?)				
DESCHAMPS, Gabriel	*P*	$220	$385	$550
French (1919 -)				
DESCHAMPS, Louis	*P*			$3,520
French (1846 - 1902)				
DESCHAMPS, M.	*P*			$110
American (20th -)				
DESCUBES, A.	*W*	$2,750	$3,135	$3,520
French (19th - 20th)				
DESCUDE, C.	*P*			$550
French (1881 -)				
DESFRICHES, Aignan T.	*D*			$8,250
French (1715 - 1800)				
DESGOFFE, Alexandre	*P*			$8,800
French (1805 - 1882)				
DESGOFFE, Blaise Alexandre	*P*	$8,800	$10,725	$13,200
French (1830 - 1901)				
DESGRANGE, Silmersheima	*W*			$880
French (19th - 20th)				
DESHAYES, Charles F.	*P*	$2,530	$2,695	$2,860
French (1831 -)				

D=Drawing, P=Painting, S=Sculpture, W=Watercolor

		Current Price Range		
		Low	Mean	High

		Low	Mean	High
DESHAYES, Eugene	*P*			$605
French (1828 - 1890)				
DESHAYS DE COLLEVILLE, J.	*D*	$1,925	$9,763	$17,600
French (1729 - 1765)				
DESHON, Robert	*W*			$110
American (20th -)				
DESIDERIO, Monsu	*P*			$19,800
Italian (17th -)				
DESMADRYL, Narcisse E. J.	*P*			$3,575
French (1801 -)				
DESMAREES, George (Circle)	*P*	$6,050	$6,435	$6,820
Swedish (1697 - 1776)				
DESNOYER, Francois	*W*			$2,200
French (1894 - 1972)				
DESPALLARGUES, Pedro	*P*			$44,000
(15th -)				
DESPIAU, Charles	*D*	$193	$647	$1,100
French (1874 - 1946)	*S*	$9,350	$14,575	$19,800
DESPORTES, Alexandre F.	*P*			$286,000
French (1661 - 1743)				
DESPORTES, Alexandre F. (Circle)	*P*			$77,000
French (1661 - 1743)				
DESPORTES, Claude F. (Manner)	*P*			$8,800
French (1695 - 1774)				
DESRAIS, Claude-Louis	*D*	$1,870	$3,080	$3,850
French (1746 - 1816)				
DESSAR, Louis P.	*P*			$413
American (1867 - 1952)				
DESSAR, Louis P. (Attrib.)	*P*			$1,760
American (1867 - 1952)				
DESTREE, Johannes J.	*P*			$1,320
Belgian (1827 - 1888)				
DESVARREUX, James	*P*	$1,100	$2,200	$3,300
American (1847 -)				
DETAILLE, Edouard	*D*	$468	$509	$550

D=Drawing, P=Painting, S=Sculpture, W=Watercolor

		Current Price Range		
		Low	Mean	High
DETAILLE, Edouard	*P*	$4,840	$21,890	$52,800
French (1848 - 1912)	*W*	$1,430	$11,477	$22,000
DETHLOFF, Peter H.	*W*			$132
American (1869 -)				
DETMOLD, Edward J.	*W*			$880
British (? - 1957)				
DETOMMASI, P.	*W*			$110
Italian (19th -)				
DETREVILLE, Richard	*P*	$220	$339	$550
American (1864 - 1929)				
DETREVILLE, Richard (Attrib.)	*P*			$220
American (1864 - 1929)				
DETROY, Leon	*P*			$1,760
French (1857 - 1955)				
DETTI, Cesare A.	*P*	$880	$13,481	$39,600
Italian (1847 - 1914)	*W*	$880	$1,393	$1,980
DETTMANN, Walter	*P*	$220	$660	$1,100
German (20th -)				
DETWILLER, Frederick K.	*P*			$468
American (1882 - 1953)				
DEUBEL, Laura	*W*	$385	$385	$385
American (20th -)				
DEULLY, Eugene A. F.	*P*			$29,700
French (1860 -)				
DEUTSCH, David	*P*	$11,000	$16,500	$22,000
(20th -)				
DEVAGNE,	*P*			$1,100
German (19th -)				
DEVAUX, Jules-Ernst	*P*	$2,640	$3,245	$3,850
French (1837 -)				
DEVEDEUX, Louis	*P*			$17,600
French (1820 - 1874)				
DEVENTER, Willem A.	*P*			$3,850
Dutch (1824 - 1893)				

D=Drawing, P=Painting, S=Sculpture, W=Watercolor

		Current Price Range		
		Low	Mean	High

DEVIS, Thomas A.	*P*			$1,650
British (1763 - 1822)				
DEVIS, Thomas A. (School)	*P*			$3,520
British (1763 - 1822)				
DEVOIS, Arie	*P*			$2,750
Dutch (1631 - 1680)				
DEVOLL, Usher	*P*	$165	$4,644	$30,800
American (1873 - 1941)				
DEVORE, Richard	*S*	$2,420	$3,263	$4,180
(20th -)				
DEVOS, Izaak	*P*			$248
American (19th - 20th)				
DEVRIENT, W.	*D*			$990
European (19th -)				
DEWAAL, John	*P*			$275
American (1864 - 1943)				
DEWEHRT, Friedrich	*P*			$2,200
German (1808 -)				
DEWEY, Charles	*P*			$1,430
American (1849 - 1937)				
DEWING, Thomas W.	*D*			$440
American (1851 - 1938)				
DEWITT, R.	*P*			$2,200
American (19th - 20th)				
DEWOLFE, Wallace l.	*P*			$165
American (1854 - 1930)				
DEYK, V. A.	*P*			$550
Dutch (1701 - 1769)				
DEYNUM, Jean B. (Circle)	*P*			$1,430
Flemish (1620 - 1668)				
DI TITO, Santi	*P*			$15,400
Italian (1536 - 1603)				
DI TITO, Santi (Attrib.)	*P*			$7,150
Italian (1536 - 1603)				
DIAM, Peter	*P*			$990
American (20th -)				

D=Drawing, P=Painting, S=Sculpture, W=Watercolor

		Current Price Range		
		Low	Mean	High

		Low	Mean	High
DIAMOND, Martha (20th -)	P			$1,320
DIAO, David (20th -)	P			$275
DIART, (1856 -)	P			$1,650
DIAZ, Jose Spanish (19th -)	P	$220	$220	$220
DIAZ, Jose (Attrib.) Spanish (19th -)	P			$605
DIAZ DE LA PENA, Narcisse French (1807 - 1876)	P	$330	$13,212	$55,000
DIAZ DE LA PENA, Narcisse (Att.) French (1807 - 1876)	P	$275	$640	$1,320
DIAZ DE LEON, Francisco Mexican (1897 - 1975)	D			$22,000
DIBBETS, Jan (20th -)	D	$14,300	$23,650	$33,000
DIBDIN, Thomas C. British (1810 - 1893)	W			$1,870
DICK, Dorothy American (20th -)	S			$990
DICK, James L. American (1834 - 1868)	P	$1,430	$3,245	$5,060
DICK, W. Lawson British (20th -)	P			$275
DICKINSON, Edwin American (1891 - 1978)	D P	$2,200	$2,750	$3,300 $14,300
DICKINSON, J. Reed American (1844 -)	P			$605
DICKINSON, Preston American (1891 - 1930)	D P	$300	$12,424	$26,400 $71,500
DICKINSON, R. American (20th -)	W			$330

D=Drawing, P=Painting, S=Sculpture, W=Watercolor

		Current Price Range		
		Low	Mean	High

DICKINSON, Sidney E.	*P*			$990
American (1890 -)				
DICKMAN, Charles J.	*P*			$1,045
American (1863 - 1943)				
DICKSEE, Frank	*P*			$4,180
British (1853 - 1928)	*W*			$264,000
DICKSEE, Herbert T.	*D*	$770	$990	$1,210
British (1862 - 1942)	*W*			$7,700
DICKSON, Jane	*P*			$11,000
(20th -)				
DIDDAERT, Henri	*P*			$1,540
Belgian (19th -)				
DIDIER, Jules	*P*	$2,200	$5,225	$8,250
French (1831 - 1892)				
DIDIER-POUGET, William	*P*	$2,475	$3,300	$4,675
French (1864 - 1959)				
DIEBENKORN, Richard	*D*	$5,500	$50,650	$198,000
American (1922 -)	*P*	$30,800	$718,300	$1.760M
	W			$77,000
DIEDRICH, Hunt	*S*			$550
American (1884 - 1953)				
DIEGHAM, Jacob Van	*P*			$1,100
Dutch (19th -)				
DIEHL, Arthur V.	*P*	$165	$785	$2,530
American (1870 - 1929)	*W*			$385
DIELMAN, Frederick	*W*			$6,600
American (1847 - 1935)				
DIELMAN, Pierre E.	*P*			$3,080
Belgian (1800 - 1858)				
DIEPOLD, Maximilian K. von	*P*			$880
German (1873 -)				
DIEPRAAN, A.	*P*			$1,265
Dutch (1622 - 1670)				

D=Drawing, P=Painting, S=Sculpture, W=Watercolor

		Current Price Range		
		Low	Mean	High

		Low	Mean	High
DIERCKX, Pierre J.	P			$1,430
Belgian (1855 -)				
DIERNES, Jan	P			$121
(?)				
DIERS, Ed	P			$440
(?)	W			$440
DIETERLE, Marie	D			$1,100
French (1856 - 1935)	P	$2,200	$6,512	$17,600
DIETRICH, Adelheid	P	$24,200	$34,467	$44,000
American (1827 -)				
DIETRICH, Caspar W. (Circle)	P			$2,970
(?)				
DIETRICH, Christian W. E.	P	$5,225	$17,531	$31,900
German (1712 - 1774)				
DIETTERLIN, Bartholomeus	D			$4,950
French (16th -)				
DIETZ, Feodor	P			$10,765
German (1813 - 1870)				
DIETZ, H. R.	P			$4,125
American (1860 -)				
DIETZER, A.	D			$550
(?)				
DIETZSCH, Barbara R.	W			$16,500
German (1706 - 1783)				
DIEU, Antoine (Circle)	D			$660
French (1662 - 1727)				
DIEUDONNE, Count Jules A.	P			$193
French (19th -)				
DIEVEN, Van	P			$495
(20th -)				
DIGNAN, Mary	P			$880
American (19th -)				
DIJCKMANNS, J.	P			$4,180
European (19th -)				

D=Drawing, P=Painting, S=Sculpture, W=Watercolor

		Current Price Range		
		Low	Mean	High

		Low	Mean	High
DILL, Laddie J.	*P*			$2,090
American (1943 -)				
DILL, Lesley	*S*			$550
(20th -)				
DILL, Ludwig	*P*			$2,750
German (1848 - 1940)				
DILL, Otto	*P*			$7,700
German (1884 - 1957)				
DILLE, J. H.	*W*			$121
American (1820 -)				
DILLENS, Adolf	*P*	$825	$8,663	$16,500
Belgian (1821 - 1877)				
DILLENS, Julien	*S*			$5,500
Belgian (1849 - 1904)				
DILLER, Burgoyne	*D*	$7,150	$13,640	$19,800
American (1906 - 1965)	*P*			$99,000
DILLER, F.	*S*			$1,100
European (19th - 20th)				
DILLON, Frank	*P*			$7,700
British (1823 - 1909)	*W*			$935
DILLON, Julia M.	*P*			$605
American (20th -)				
DIMARE,	*W*			$121
European (19th -)				
DINCKEL, George	*P*			$110
American (1890 -)	*W*	$132	$163	$193
DINE, Jim	*D*	$9,900	$24,593	$46,750
American (1935 -)	*P*	$16,500	$175,500	$660,000
	S	$8,800	$88,978	$154,000
	W	$7,150	$78,169	$385,000
DING, Henri M.	*S*			$2,860
French (1844 - 1898)				

D=Drawing, P=Painting, S=Sculpture, W=Watercolor

		Current Price Range		
		Low	Mean	High
DINGLE, Thomas	P			$1,430
British (19th -)				
DINTTER, Will Von	P			$165
Dutch (20th -)				
DIRANIAN, Serkis	P	$2,750	$5,042	$6,875
Turkish (19th -)				
DIRK, Nathaniel	P			$275
American (1896 - 1961)	W			$550
DISCART, Jean	P			$18,700
French (19th -)				
DISLER, Martin	P			$6,325
Swiss (1949 -)				
DITSCHEINER, Adolf G.	P			$19,800
German (1846 - 1904)				
DITT ZEIGLER, Lee W.	P			$1,210
American (1868 - 1934)				
DITTRICH, R.	S	$5,500	$6,875	$8,250
(19th -)				
DITZLER, T.	P			$660
American (20th -)				
DIVIDSON, Charles G.	W	$248	$262	$275
American (1866 - 1945)				
DIVITA, Frank	S	$850	$1,182	$1,760
American (20th -)				
DIX, Charles (Attrib.)	P	$100	$225	$350
American (20th -)				
DIX, Charles T.	P	$935	$963	$990
American (1838 - 1872)				
DIX, Otto	W	$23,100	$48,675	$74,250
German (1891 -)				
DIXON,	P			$165
American (19th - 20th)				
DIXON, Charles	W	$3,850	$3,850	$3,850
British (1872 - 1934)				
DIXON, Francis	P	$413	$970	$1,760
American (1879 - 1967)				

D=Drawing, P=Painting, S=Sculpture, W=Watercolor

| | | Current Price Range | | |
		Low	Mean	High
DIXON, M. R.	*P*			$2,200
American (19th - 20th)				
DIXON, Maynard	*D*	$385	$2,780	$15,400
American (1875 - 1946)	*P*	$880	$16,816	$49,500
	W	$770	$3,120	$8,800
DIZIANI, Antonio	*P*			$11,000
Italian (1737 - 1797)				
DIZIANI, Antonio (Circle)	*P*			$7,700
Italian (1737 - 1797)				
DIZIANI, Gaspare	*D*	$2,200	$6,325	$10,450
Italian (1689 - 1767)	*P*	$2,200	$13,200	$24,200
DIZIANI, Gaspare (Circle)	*P*			$24,200
Italian (1689 - 1767)				
DIZK, Fos van	*P*			$220
Belgian (19th - 20th)				
DO, Giovanni	*P*			$35,200
Italian (17th -)				
DO, Giovanni (Follower)	*P*			$3,575
Italian (17th -)				
DOAN, Edmund	*P*			$2,475
(?)				
DOBBIN, V. Busby	*W*			$578
European (19th -)				
DOBBS, Anna M.	*P*			$370
(?)				
DOBROWSKY, Josef	*P*			$4,400
Australian (1889 - 1962)				
DOBSON, H. J.	*P*	$880	$963	$1,045
British (1858 - 1928)				
DOBSON, William C. T.	*P*			$4,400
British (1817 - 1898)				
DOBUZJINSKY, Mstislav	*W*	$660	$770	$880
Russian (1875 - 1957)				
DOCH, F. van den	*P*			$1,100
European (19th - 20th)				

D=Drawing, P=Painting, S=Sculpture, W=Watercolor

		Current Price Range		
		Low	Mean	High

		Low	Mean	High
DODD, Mark D. American (1888 -)	*P*			$165
DODD, Robert British (1748 - 1816)	*P*			$3,080
DODGE, Chester American (1880 -)	*D*			$110
DODGE, Frances F. American (1878 -)	*P*			$330
DODGE, John W. American (1807 - 1893)	*W*	$165	$242	$319
DODGE, Mary de Leftwich American (19th -)	*P*			$330
DODGE, William de L. American (1867 - 1935)	*P* *W*	$550 $440	$4,400 $1,650	$8,250 $4,180
DOERING, Paul American (19th - 20th)	*P*			$358
DOESBURG, Theo van Dutch (1883 - 1931)	*P*	$88,000	$126,500	$165,000
DOESJEAN, Adriaan Dutch (1740 - 1817)	*D*			$4,400
DOHANOS, Stevan American (1907 -)	*P* *W*	$3,600 $413	$5,100 $1,110	$6,600 $1,760
DOIKER, E. European (19th -)	*W*			$440
DOILLON, Maydeleine French (20th -)	*P*			$385
DOKOUPIL, Jiri (20th -)	*P*	$5,775	$6,738	$7,700
DOLAN, American (19th - 20th)	*P*			$468
DOLAN, G.H. American (?)	*P*			$220
DOLBY, Joshua E. A. British (19th -)	*P*			$440

D=Drawing, P=Painting, S=Sculpture, W=Watercolor

		Low	Mean	High
		Current Price Range		
DOLCI, Carlo Italian (1616 - 1686)	*P*	$121,000	$940,500	$1.760M
DOLCI, Carlo (After) Italian (1616 - 1686)	*P*	$440	$2,633	$4,950
DOLCI, Carlo (Follower) Italian (1616 - 1686)	*P*			$1,100
DOLCI, Carlo (School) Italian (1616 - 1686)	*P*			$440
DOLE, William (20th -)	*S*	$935	$1,705	$2,475
DOLEY, Peter American (1907 -)	*P*	$385	$623	$990
DOLICE, Leon American (20th -)	*D* *P* *W*	$220	$367	$578 $1,210 $195
DOLINSKY, Nathan American (1890 -)	*P*			$165
DOLL, Anton German (1826 - 1887)	*P*	$4,400	$12,100	$17,600
DOLLMAN, John C. British (1851 - 1934)	*P*	$14,300	$27,500	$40,700
DOLPH, John H. American (1835 - 1903)	*P*	$1,540	$4,855	$11,000
DOMELA, Cesar Dutch (1900 -)	*S*			$1,870
DOMENCH, Pla Spanish (1917 -)	*P*			$1,375
DOMERGUE, Emile J. French (1879 -)	*P*			$550
DOMERGUE, Jean-Gabriel French (1889 - 1962)	*P*	$4,620	$22,440	$52,250
DOMINGO, F. (?)	*P*			$385
DOMINGO, Roberto Spanish (1867 -)	*D*			$880

D=Drawing, P=Painting, S=Sculpture, W=Watercolor

		Current Price Range		
		Low	Mean	High
DOMINGUEZ, Oscar	*P*			$176,000
Spanish (1906 - 1958)				
DOMINICIS, Achille De	*W*	$495	$550	$605
Italian (19th -)				
DOMINIQUE, John A.	*P*	$248	$578	$1,320
American (1893 -)				
DOMMERSEN, Pieter C.	*P*			$2,200
Dutch (1834 - 1903)				
DOMMERSEN, William	*P*			$1,650
Dutch (? - 1927)				
DOMOTO, Hisao	*P*	$6,600	$11,733	$22,000
Japanese (20th -)				
DONA, Lydia	*P*	$550	$3,163	$7,700
American (20th -)				
DONADONI, Stefano	*W*	$165	$642	$990
Italian (1844 - 1911)				
DONAGHY, John	*P*			$1,100
American (1838 - 1931)				
DONAHUE, Vic	*P*			$935
American (20th -)				
DONALD, John M.	*P*			$6,600
British (1819 - 1858)				
DONALDSON, J. B.	*W*			$154
(?)				
DONAT, F. R.	*P*			$1,870
Belgian (19th -)				
DONATI, Enrico	*P*	$3,850	$7,731	$17,600
American (1909 -)				
DONATI, Lazzaro	*D*			$440
Italian (20th -)	*P*	$550	$623	$715
DONCK, Gerard (Attrib.)	*P*			$46,200
Flemish (17th -)				
DONCKER, Herman M. (Circle)	*P*			$1,540
Dutch (1620 - 1656)				
DONDUCCI, Giovanni A.	*P*			$5,500
Italian (1575 - 1655)				

D=Drawing, P=Painting, S=Sculpture, W=Watercolor

		Current Price Range		
		Low	Mean	High

DONGEN, Dionys van	*P*			$4,400
Dutch (1748 - 1819)				
DONGEN, Guus van	*P*			$495
Dutch (1878 - 1946)				
DONGEN, Kees van	*D*	$4,180	$15,400	$24,200
French (1877 - 1968)	*P*	$17,600	$658,900	$1.760M
	W	$7,150	$43,358	$93,500
DONNELLY,	*W*			$110
American (20th -)				
DONNELLY, Crawford F.	*P*			$220
American (20th -)				
DONOHO, Ruger	*P*	$330	$935	$1,540
American (1857 - 1916)				
DONOUY, Alexandre	*P*			$20,900
French (1757 - 1841)				
DONOVAN, John A.	*P*			$193
American (1871 - 1941)				
DOORN, J. van	*P*	$440	$1,045	$1,980
Dutch (19th - 20th)				
DOOYEWARD,	*P*			$935
American (19th - 20th)				
DORAZIO, Piero	*P*			$440
Italian (1927 -)	*W*			$880
DORCY, Albert	*P*			$220
French (19th -)				
DORE, Gustave	*D*			$154
French (1832 - 1883)	*P*	$12,100	$192,363	$605,000
	S			$12,100
	W			$1,760
DORENZ, D.	*P*			$220
European (20th -)				
DORIAN, E.	*P*	$220	$234	$248
American (?)				

D=Drawing, P=Painting, S=Sculpture, W=Watercolor

		Current Price Range		
		Low	Mean	High

		Low	Mean	High
DORICK, Van V. (?)	P	$385	$385	$385
DORINSON, V. A. European (19th - 20th)	P			$908
DORION, C. S. (19th - 20th)	P	$275	$660	$1,045
DORLEANS, Raymond Haitian (20th -)	P			$385
DORN, Vincent American (20th -)	P			$110
DOSSO, Amico F. del (?)	P			$7,700
DOU, Gerrit Dutch (1613 - 1675)	P			$330,000
DOU, Gerrit (After) Dutch (1613 - 1675)	P			$660
DOU, Gerrit (Circle) Dutch (1613 - 1675)	P			$495
DOU, Gerrit (Style) Dutch (1613 - 1675)	P			$550
DOUGHERTY, Park C. American (1867 -)	P	$385	$399	$413
DOUGHERTY, Paul American (1877 - 1947)	P	$825	$3,434	$8,800
DOUGHTY, Thomas American (1793 - 1856)	P	$5,720	$16,654	$28,600
DOUGHTY, Thomas (Attrib.) American (1793 - 1856)	P	$550	$2,750	$4,950
DOUGLAS, American (?)	W	$110	$154	$303
DOUGLAS, Earl G. American (1879 - 1954)	P			$880
DOUGLAS, Edward A. S. British (19th -)	P			$1,430
DOUGLAS, Edwin British (1848 - 1914)	P			$27,500

D=Drawing, P=Painting, S=Sculpture, W=Watercolor

		Current Price Range		
		Low	Mean	High

		Low	Mean	High
DOUGLAS, Edwin (Attrib.)	*P*			$110
British (1848 - 1914)				
DOUGLAS, James	*W*			$1,320
Scottish (19th -)				
DOUGLAS, Sir William F.	*P*			$8,250
Scottish (1822 - 1891)				
DOUGLAS, Walter	*P*	$220	$677	$990
American (1864 -)				
DOUON, C. S.	*P*			$165
American (19th -)				
DOVE, Arthur	*D*			$770
American (1880 - 1946)	*P*	$55,000	$155,833	$319,000
	W	$4,180	$8,195	$14,300
DOVE, Benjamin	*P*			$358
American (20th -)				
DOW, Arthur W.	*P*	$1,100	$20,614	$46,200
American (1857 - 1922)				
DOW, John (Attrib.)	*P*			$385
American (1770 - 1862)				
DOW, William J.	*P*	$110	$232	$495
American (1899 - 1973)	*W*	$110	$182	$303
DOWALSKOFF, J.A.	*D*			$11,000
Russian (19th -)				
DOWNES, Duke	*P*			$110
British (19th - 20th)				
DOWNES, Rackstraw	*D*			$4,180
(20th -)	*P*			$25,300
DOWNIE, John P.	*P*			$4,730
British (1871 - 1945)				
DOWNING, Peter	*P*			$385
Canadian (1922 -)				
DOWNING, Thomas	*P*	$880	$1,507	$2,420
American (20th -)				

D=Drawing, P=Painting, S=Sculpture, W=Watercolor

		Current Price Range		
		Low	Mean	High
DOWNMAN, John (Circle)	*P*			$1,650
British (1750 - 1824)				
DRACH, Sophia	*P*			$495
(?)				
DRAGO,	*P*			$440
Yugoslavian (1943 -)	*S*			$220
DRAIN, Elizabeth	*P*			$110
(?)				
DRAKE, C. A.	*P*			$358
British (19th -)				
DRAKE, Peter	*P*			$3,300
(20th -)				
DRAKE, R.	*P*			$495
American (20th -)				
DRAKE, Will H.	*W*			$1,650
American (1856 - 1926)				
DRAKE, William A.	*P*			$2,090
American (1891 - 1964)				
DRAPER, George	*P*			$165
American (20th -)				
DRAPER, J. E.	*W*	$248	$344	$440
American (20th -)				
DRAPER, William F.	*P*	$121	$171	$220
American (1912 -)				
DRASSER,	*P*			$2,860
(?)				
DRAVER, Orrin	*P*	$495	$660	$825
(?)				
DRAYTON, Grace	*D*			$1,700
American (1872 - 1936)				
DREGER, I.	*P*			$440
(?)				
DREIER, Dorothea	*P*			$165
American (1870 - 1923)				
DREIER, Katherine	*P*	$3,850	$7,700	$14,300

D=Drawing, P=Painting, S=Sculpture, W=Watercolor

		Current Price Range		
		Low	Mean	High

DREIER, Katherine	*W*			$1,210
American (1877 - 1952)				
DREIN, Maud	*P*			$413
American (19th - 20th)				
DREISBACH, Clarence I.	*P*			$135
American (?)				
DREUX, Alfred de (Attrib.)	*P*			$12,100
French (1810 - 1860)				
DREUX, Alfred de (Circle)	*P*			$6,600
French (1810 - 1860)				
DREW, Clement	*P*	$440	$5,060	$8,800
American (1806 - 1889)				
DREW, Clement (Attrib.)	*P*			$6,050
American (1806 - 1889)				
DREW, Elbert G.	*P*	$165	$165	$165
American (?)				
DREW, George W.	*P*	$220	$1,081	$3,025
American (1875 -)				
DREWES, Werner	*P*	$2,090	$4,125	$5,280
American (1899 -)				
DREYFUS, Bernard	*P*	$2,640	$3,520	$4,400
Nicaraguan (1946 -)				
DRIAN,	*D*			$2,475
European (20th -)	*S*			$4,400
DRIBEN, Peter	*P*			$2,000
(?)				
DRIELST, Egbert van	*D*			$3,300
Dutch (1746 - 1818)	*P*			$44,000
DRINKARD, David	*P*	$1,980	$2,227	$2,500
American (1948 -)				
DRISCOLE, M. A.	*P*			$275
(19th -)				
DRISCOLL, Robert E.	*W*			$220
American (20th -)				

D=Drawing, P=Painting, S=Sculpture, W=Watercolor

		Current Price Range		
		Low	Mean	High

		Low	Mean	High
DRISLER, (?)	W			$341
DRITTLES, (?)	P			$110
DRIVIER, Leon E. French (1878 - 1951)	S			$2,090
DROBNY, C. (?)	P			$248
DROLLING, Martin French (1752 - 1817)	P	$12,100	$24,017	$46,750
DROLLING, Martin (Attrib.) French (1752 - 1817)	P			$220
DROLLING, Martin (Circle) French (1752 - 1817)	P			$1,760
DROOCHSLOOT, Joost C. Dutch (1586 - 1666)	P			$9,900
DROST, Willem Dutch (17th -)	P			$38,500
DROUAIS, Francois (Attrib.) French (1727 - 1775)	P			$1,980
DROUAIS, Francois (Circle) French (1727 - 1775)	P			$4,400
DROUAIS, Francois (Follower) French (1727 - 1775)	P			$2,750
DROUAIS, Francois (Studio) French (1727 - 1775)	P			$9,350
DROUAIS, Jean-Germain French (1763 - 1788)	D			$3,300
DROUIN & PETIT, J. & E. (19th -)	P			$2,640
DROUOT, Edouard French (1859 - 1945)	S	$1,320	$2,457	$3,300
DROUOT, Edouard (After) French (1859 - 1945)	S			$715
DROWN, William S. American (? - 1915)	P	$193	$1,219	$2,750

D=Drawing, P=Painting, S=Sculpture, W=Watercolor

		Current Price Range		
		Low	Mean	High
DRUMMOND, J.	*P*			$660
European (?)				
DRURY, Herbert R.	*P*	$413	$454	$495
American (1873 -)				
DRURY, William	*D*			$110
American (1888 -)	*P*			$330
DRYER, Nancy	*D*			$121
American (1903 -)				
DRYSDALE,	*W*			$275
Australian (19th - 20th)				
DRYSDALE, Alexander John	*P*	$330	$1,177	$3,300
American (1870 - 1934)	*W*	$248	$1,162	$4,125
DU CHATTEL, Fredericus J. van	*W*			$1,980
Dutch (1856 -)				
DU FRENES, Rudolf H.	*P*			$12,100
(?)				
DU PASSAGE, Arthur M. G.	*S*	$7,700	$17,050	$26,400
French (1838 - 1900)				
DU VAUNES, A.	*P*			$440
American (19th - 20th)				
DUBAUT, Pierre-Olivier	*W*			$1,210
French (1886 - 1968)				
DUBBELS, Hendrik-Jacobsz	*P*			$11,000
Dutch (1620 - 1676)				
DUBIC, Abner	*P*			$550
Haitian (20th -)				
DUBOIS,	*P*	$1,210	$2,668	$4,125
French (18th -)	*S*			$121
DUBOIS, Arsene	*P*			$6,600
French (19th -)				
DUBOIS, Maurice P.	*P*			$4,400
French (20th -)				
DUBOIS, Simon	*D*			$935
Flemish (1632 - 1708)				

D=Drawing, P=Painting, S=Sculpture, W=Watercolor

		Current Price Range		
		Low	Mean	High

		Low	Mean	High
DUBOIS, Yvonne (?)	*P*			$2,750
DUBOURG, Louis F. Dutch (1693 - 1775)	*D*			$1,320
DUBRAY-BESNARD, Charlotte G. French (1855 -)	*S*			$60,500
DUBREUIL, Victor American (19th -)	*P*	$8,800	$11,000	$13,200
DUBUCAND, Alfred French (1828 -)	*S*	$495	$1,714	$3,300
DUBUFE, Edouard L. French (1820 - 1883)	*P*			$6,600
DUBUFE, Edouard L. (Attrib.) French (1820 - 1883)	*P*			$880
DUBUFFET, Jean French (1901 - 1985)	*D*	$9,350	$30,650	$187,000
	P	$14,300	$840,200	$5.170M
	S	$10,450	$182,334	$907,500
	W	$44,000	$91,850	$143,000
DUCCI, Italian (20th -)	*P*			$110
DUCHAMP, Marcel French (1887 - 1968)	*D*			$9,900
	P	$6,600	$47,300	$88,000
	S	$35,750	$37,125	$38,500
DUCHAMP, Suzanne French (1889 - 1963)	*P*			$2,420
DUCHAMP-VILLON, Raymond French (1876 - 1918)	*S*	$46,750	$693,917	$1.100M
DUCHEMIN, Victoire French (19th -)	*P*			$1,870
DUCHOISELLE, (19th -)	*S*			$1,540
DUCK, Jacob Dutch (1600 - 1660)	*P*			$15,400

D=Drawing, P=Painting, S=Sculpture, W=Watercolor

		Current Price Range		
		Low	Mean	High

DUCKWORTH, Ruth (20th -)	*S*	$660	$2,821	$8,800
DUCOIN, A. European (19th - 20th)	*P*			$2,200
DUDER, Douglas (1887 - 1964)	*P*			$385
DUDLEY, Frank V. American (1868 -)	*P*			$2,530
DUDLEY, L.A. (?)	*P*			$143
DUESBERRY, Joellyn (20th -)	*D*			$4,125
DUESSEL, Henry A. American (19th - 20th)	*P*	$550	$596	$660
DUFAUG, G. A. French (19th -)	*P*			$20,900
DUFF, John T. American (?)	*P*			$1,320
DUFFART, (?)	*P*			$385
DUFFAUT, Prefete Haitian (1929 -)	*P*	$550	$2,283	$6,600
DUFNER, Edward American (1871 - 1957)	*P*	$3,520	$44,495	$220,000
DUFNER, Edward (Attrib.) American (1871 - 1957)	*P*			$550
DUFOUR, Bernard French (1922 -)	*P*	$330	$2,640	$4,950
DUFRESNE, Charles French (1876 - 1938)	*P*	$2,420	$7,700	$17,600
DUFY, Jean French (1888 - 1964)	*D*	$121	$1,207	$6,050
	P	$1,430	$24,493	$52,250
	W	$2,310	$11,271	$25,300
DUFY, Raoul	*D*	$1,320	$13,232	$55,000

D=Drawing, P=Painting, S=Sculpture, W=Watercolor

		Current Price Range		
		Low	Mean	High
DUFY, Raoul	*P*	$8,470	$310,738	$1.815M
French (1877 - 1953)	*S*			$35,750
	W	$1,430	$109,493	$341,000
DUGEN, A.van	*P*			$1,320
Dutch (1878 - 1946)				
DUGHET, Gaspard	*P*	$1,540	$2,833	$4,125
French (1615 - 1675)				
DUGHET, Gaspard (Attrib.)	*P*			$7,700
French (1615 - 1675)				
DUGHET, Gaspard (Circle)	*P*	$5,280	$21,076	$52,800
French (1615 - 1675)				
DUGHET, Gaspard (Follower)	*D*			$825
French (1615 - 1675)	*P*			$1,980
DUGHET, Gaspard (School)	*P*			$1,320
French (1615 - 1675)				
DUJARDIN, Karel	*P*	$4,400	$12,100	$19,800
Dutch (1622 - 1678)				
DUJARDIN, Karel (After)	*D*			$495
Dutch (1622 - 1678)				
DUJARDIN, Karel (Attrib.)	*P*			$4,400
Dutch (1622 - 1678)				
DUKE, Alfred	*P*			$5,500
British (19th -)				
DULAC, A.	*P*			$440
(?)				
DULAC, Edmund	*D*	$8,250	$8,250	$8,250
French (1882 -)	*W*	$6,875	$23,815	$39,600
DULL, John	*D*			$248
American (1859 - 1949)	*W*	$125	$165	$220
DULMAN, Erasmus B. van	*P*			$578
Dutch (20th -)				
DULUARD, Hippolyte-Francois	*P*			$880
French (1871 -)				

D=Drawing, P=Painting, S=Sculpture, W=Watercolor

		Current Price Range		
		Low	Mean	High

		Low	Mean	High
DUMAIGE, Henri	*S*	$2,475	$2,475	$2,475
French (1830 - 1888)				
DUMIER, H.	*P*			$150
(20th -)				
DUMMER, H. Boylston	*P*	$248	$559	$990
American (1878 - 1945)				
DUMOND, Frank V.	*D*	$1,100	$4,675	$8,250
American (1865 - 1951)	*P*	$138	$3,004	$6,600
DUMOND, Frank V. (Manner)	*P*			$165
American (1865 - 1951)				
DUMONT, Edme	*S*			$2,750
French (1722 - 1775)				
DUMONT, Pierre	*P*	$7,150	$10,863	$14,300
French (1884 - 1936)				
DUMONT, Rene	*P*	$880	$1,210	$1,540
French (19th -)				
DUMOULIN,	*P*			$825
Belgian (19th -)				
DUNBAR, Harold C.	*P*	$220	$593	$1,540
American (1882 - 1953)	*W*			$385
DUNCAN, Andres J.	*P*			$495
Dutch (? - 1834)				
DUNCAN, Edmund	*W*			$1,210
British (19th -)				
DUNCAN, Edward	*W*			$715
British (1803 - 1882)				
DUNCAN, Geraldine B.	*P*			$1,100
American (1883 - 1972)				
DUNCAN, Rodger	*W*			$990
(20th -)				
DUNCAN, Scott	*P*			$165
American (20th -)				
DUNCANSON, Robert	*P*	$1,870	$2,732	$4,125
American (19th -)				

D=Drawing, P=Painting, S=Sculpture, W=Watercolor

		Current Price Range	
	Low	Mean	High

		Low	Mean	High
DUNCKHAM, H. British (19th -)	*P*			$770
DUNHAM, Carroll (20th -)	*D*	$4,400	$32,450	$60,500
	P	$5,500	$20,625	$38,500
	W	$8,800	$20,533	$44,000
DUNINGTON, Albert American (19th -)	*P*			$880
DUNLAP, Mary S. American (1846 -)	*P*	$523	$523	$523
DUNLAY, Thomas R. American (20th -)	*P*	$1,100	$3,575	$6,050
DUNLOP, Marian American (20th -)	*W*			$138
DUNLOP, Roland British (20th -)	*P*			$1,650
DUNN, Harvey T. American (1884 - 1952)	*P*	$550	$15,033	$24,750
DUNNING, Lois American (20th -)	*P*			$358
DUNNING, Robert S. American (1829 - 1905)	*P*	$880	$16,445	$39,600
DUNNINGTON, A. British (19th -)	*P*			$1,100
DUNOYER DE SEGONZAC, And. French (1884 - 1974)	*D*	$1,980	$6,903	$19,800
	P	$14,300	$20,900	$27,500
	W			$1,650
DUNSMORE, John W. American (1865 - 1945)	*P*			$275
DUNTON, W. Herbert American (1878 - 1936)	*P*	$19,800	$25,300	$30,800
	W			$578
DUPAIN, Edmund L. French (1847 -)	*P*			$6,600
DUPLESSIS, J. S. French (19th -)	*P*			$605

D=Drawing, P=Painting, S=Sculpture, W=Watercolor

		Current Price Range		
		Low	Mean	High
DUPOND, Marcel	*P*			$303
French (1907 - 1954)				
DUPONT, Gainsborough	*P*	$880	$990	$1,100
British (1754 - 1797)				
DUPONT, Gainsborough (Att)	*P*	$1,650	$2,787	$3,850
British (1754 - 1797)				
DUPONT, Louis	*P*			$1,650
French (19th -)				
DUPRAT, Albert F.	*P*			$1,540
French (1882 -)				
DUPRE, Francois	*P*			$248
French (1803 - 1871)				
DUPRE, Henri	*P*			$330
(?)				
DUPRE, Jules	*P*	$825	$7,913	$22,000
French (1811 - 1889)				
DUPRE, Jules (Attrib.)	*D*			$1,870
French (1811 - 1889)	*P*	$1,320	$1,797	$2,420
DUPRE, Julien	*P*	$1,870	$35,009	$170,500
French (1851 - 1910)				
DUPRE, Victor	*P*	$7,700	$10,588	$12,100
French (1816 - 1879)				
DUPUIS, Pierre	*P*			$1,650
French (1833 -)				
DUPUIS, Pierre (Attrib.)	*P*	$550	$21,817	$38,500
French (1610 - 1682)				
DUPUY, L.	*P*			$1,045
French (19th -)				
DUPUY, Paul M.	*P*	$33,000	$49,500	$66,000
French (1869 - 1949)				
DURA, Gaetano	*W*			$1,870
Italian (19th -)				
DURAN, Francesca (Attrib.)	*P*			$1,045
Spanish (19th -)				
DURAND, Asher B.	*D*			$3,850

D=Drawing, P=Painting, S=Sculpture, W=Watercolor

| | | Current Price Range | | |
		Low	Mean	High
DURAND, Asher B.	P	$16,500	$31,680	$60,500
American (1796 - 1886)	W			$523
DURAND, Asher B. (Attrib.)	D			$523
American (1796 - 1886)	P			$2,860
DURAND, John	P	$1,155	$1,348	$1,540
(?)				
DURAND-BRAGER, Jean B. H.	P	$2,310	$3,355	$4,620
French (1814 - 1879)				
DURAND-HENRIOT, P.	P			$550
(?)				
DURAND-SIKES, Lucy	D			$150
(?)				
DURANT, Albert	P	$253	$1,652	$4,400
French (1886 - 1941)				
DURANT, D.	P			$660
(20th -)				
DURANTI, R.	P			$275
Swiss (19th -)				
DURASKY, M. M.	P			$154
(?)				
DURAUT,	P			$440
European (?)				
DUREAU, George	D			$990
(?)				
DUREN, Terence R.	W	$770	$1,018	$1,100
American (1907 - 1968)				
DURENCEAU, Andre	P	$650	$875	$1,100
(?)				
DURENNE, Eugene A.	P			$17,600
French (1860 - 1944)				
DURET, Fransisque-Joseph	S			$6,325
French (1804 - 1865)				
DUREVIL, Michel	P	$1,320	$2,998	$4,675
French (20th -)				

D=Drawing, P=Painting, S=Sculpture, W=Watercolor

	Current Price Range		
	Low	Mean	High

DUREY, Rene	*P*			$3,850
French (1890 - 1959)				
DURGIN, Lyle	*P*			$1,650
American (19th - 20th)				
DURHAM, Darrow P.	*P*			$413
American (1890 - 1960)				
DURHAM, Joseph	*P*			$605
British (1814 - 1877)	*S*			$2,860
DURIEUX, Caroline	*D*			$2,640
American (1896 - 1989)				
DURNAD, Elias W.	*P*			$3,080
American (19th -)				
DURRIE, George H.	*P*	$82,500	$243,833	$385,000
American (1820 - 1863)				
DURRIE, George H. (Att.)	*P*			$3,850
American (1820 - 1863)				
DURRIE, George H. (Mann.)	*P*			$231
American (1820 - 1863)				
DURRIE, John	*P*			$19,800
American (?)				
DURSUT,	*P*			$165
(?)				
DURU, Jean B.	*P*			$49,500
French (18th -)				
DURUY, P.	*W*			$550
French (19th - 20th)				
DUSART, Cornelis	*D*			$19,800
Dutch (1660 - 1704)	*P*			$18,700
DUSART, Cornelis (Attrib.)	*D*			$990
Dutch (1660 - 1704)	*P*			$12,100
DUSART, Cornelis (Manner)	*P*			$440
Dutch (1660 - 1704)				
DUSSEK, Eduard A.	*P*			$1,430
Hungarian (1871 -)				

D=Drawing, P=Painting, S=Sculpture, W=Watercolor

		Current Price Range	
		Low	Mean	High

		Low	Mean	High
DUTCH SCHOOL, Dutch (?)	*P*			$2,090
DUTCH SCHOOL, Dutch (18th - 19th)	*P*	$2,310	$6,270	$8,800
DUTCH SCHOOL, Dutch (19th - 20th)	*P*			$1,485
DUTCH SCHOOL 17C, Dutch (17th -)	*D*	$1,210	$3,344	$10,450
	P	$1,100	$18,116	$187,000
DUTCH SCHOOL 18C, Dutch (18th -)	*D*	$2,310	$3,768	$5,225
	P	$550	$5,990	$30,250
DUTCH SCHOOL 19C, Dutch (19th -)	*P*	$1,265	$2,321	$5,775
DUTCH SCHOOL 20C, Dutch (20th -)	*P*			$6,600
DUTEURTRE, Pierre E. French (1911 -)	*P*	$660	$866	$1,100
DUTILLIEU, Jef Belgian (1876 - 1960)	*P*			$1,375
DUTTLIE, H. Dutch (20th -)	*P*			$605
DUVAL, European (19th -)	*P*			$1,540
DUVAL, Constant L. French (1877 -)	*P*			$2,200
DUVENECK, Frank American (1848 - 1919)	*P*			$2,310
DUVENECK, Frank (Attrib.) American (1848 - 1919)	*P*			$1,210
DUVENECK, Frank (Style) American (1848 - 1919)	*P*			$242
DUVENT, Charles J. French (1867 - 1940)	*P*			$49,500
DUVERGER, Theophile E. French (1821 -)	*P*			$23,100

D=Drawing, P=Painting, S=Sculpture, W=Watercolor

		Current Price Range		
		Low	Mean	High
DUVIEUX, Henri	P	$550	$3,795	$9,350
French (19th -)				
DUVIVIER,	D			$1,650
(19th -)	W	$1,540	$1,650	$1,760
DUX, Alexander	P			$375
American (20th -)				
DUYSTER, Willem C. (Attrib.)	P			$46,750
Dutch (1598 - 1635)				
DWIGHT-BENTON,	P			$660
American (1834 -)				
DWYER, Anna	W			$600
American (20th -)				
DYCK, Philip van	P			$8,250
Flemish (1680 - 1753)				
DYCK, Sir Anthony van	D			$231,000
Flemish (1599 - 1641)	P	$176,000	$275,000	$374,000
DYCK, Sir Anthony van (After)	P	$523	$2,837	$4,180
Flemish (1599 - 1641)				
DYCK, Sir Anthony van (Attrib)	P			$60,500
Flemish (1599 - 1641)				
DYCK, Sir Anthony van (Circle)	P	$1,100	$2,338	$3,575
Flemish (1599 - 1641)				
DYCK, Sir Anthony van (Foll.)	D			$660
Flemish (1599 - 1641)	P			$5,775
DYCK, Sir Anthony van (School)	P	$1,760	$7,656	$18,700
Flemish (1599 - 1641)				
DYCK, Sir Anthony van (Studio)	P	$9,350	$125,675	$242,000
Flemish (1599 - 1641)				
DYCK, Sir Anthony van (Style)	P			$1,320
Flemish (1599 - 1641)				
DYCZKOWSKI, Eugene	P			$7,700
(?)				
DYE, Clarkson	P	$495	$1,173	$2,750

D=Drawing, P=Painting, S=Sculpture, W=Watercolor

		Current Price Range		
		Low	Mean	High
DYE, Clarkson	S			$1,600
American (1869 - 1955)				
DYER, Anthony H.	P			$935
American (1872 - 1943)	W	$165	$613	$1,540
DYER, Harry W.	P			$303
American (1871 -)	W			$248
DYER, Marion	W			$578
American (19th - 20th)				
DYF, Marcel	P	$2,420	$8,617	$16,500
French (1899 - 1985)				
DYK, Anton von	P			$1,210
Dutch (20th -)				
DYKE, Samuel P.	P			$990
American (19th -)				
DYKMAN, C. H.	P			$220
Dutch (19th -)				
DYKMAN, Howard	P			$110
American (?)				
DYNASTY, Qajar	P			$16,500
Persian (18th -)				
DYNES, John	P			$550
(20th -)				
DYVARG,	P			$440
European (19th -)				
DZIGURSKI, Alex	P	$440	$1,276	$3,300
American (1910 -)				
DZUBAS, Friedel	P	$1,100	$13,683	$33,000
German (1915 -)				
D'AGOTY, Pierre E. G.	P			$3,850
French (1775 - 1871)				
EADIE, Robert	W			$5,735
British (1877 - 1954)				
EAGLES, John	W			$990
British (1783 - 1855)				

D=Drawing, P=Painting, S=Sculpture, W=Watercolor

		Current Price Range		
		Low	Mean	High

		Low	Mean	High
EAKINS, Thomas	P	$19,800	$92,400	$165,000
American (1844 - 1916)	W			$3.520M
EAMES, Charles	S			$715
American (20th -)				
EARHART, John F.	P	$165	$492	$1,320
American (1853 - 1938)				
EARL, George	P	$1,320	$24,053	$71,500
British (19th -)				
EARL, Jack	S			$2,090
(20th -)				
EARL, Maud	P	$2,970	$11,193	$17,600
British (1864 - 1943)				
EARL, Percy	P	$8,800	$13,200	$17,600
British (20th -)				
EARLE, Lawrence C.	P	$248	$1,362	$2,475
American (1845 - 1921)	W	$990	$1,375	$1,760
EARLE, Ralph (Attrib.)	P	$2,310	$5,280	$8,250
American (1751 - 1801)				
EARLY, Miles J.	P	$165	$187	$209
American (20th -)				
EARNIST, Florence R.	P			$660
American (20th -)				
EAST, Barbara	W			$1,700
American (20th -)				
EAST, H.	P			$1,540
British (19th -)				
EAST, Sir Alfred	P	$1,100	$3,806	$12,100
British (1849 - 1913)				
EASTLAKE, Charles	D			$1,650
British (1793 - 1865)	P			$660
EASTMAN, William J.	P	$105	$498	$880
American (1881 - 1950)	W	$116	$124	$132
EASTWOOD, Raymond J.	P			$1,100
American (1898 -)				

D=Drawing, P=Painting, S=Sculpture, W=Watercolor

		Current Price Range		
		Low	Mean	High

		Low	Mean	High
EATON, Alfred J. American (19th -)	P			$165
EATON, Charles H. American (1850 - 1937)	P			$1,320
EATON, Charles W. American (1857 - 1937)	P W	$413 $440	$2,135 $1,128	$6,050 $1,980
EATON, Elliott American (20th -)	W	$495	$848	$1,200
EATON, I.F. American (19th -)	W	$138	$289	$440
EATON, M. Elizabeth (?)	P			$303
EBE, B. (?)	S			$303
EBEL, H. (19th -)	W			$220
EBERHARD, Heinrich German (1884 -)	P	$110	$1,815	$2,530
EBERLE, Abastenia St. Leger American (1878 - 1942)	S	$3,080	$10,601	$30,800
EBERT, Anton Austrian (1845 - 1896)	P			$7,700
EBERT, Carl German (1821 - 1885)	P	$110	$5,665	$8,250
EBERT, Charles H. American (1873 - 1959)	P	$4,400	$14,300	$24,200
EBHARD, G. American (19th -)	P			$330
EBNER, Lajos D. Hungarian (1850 - 1934)	P			$1,980
EBURT, Emanuel (Attrib.) (?)	D			$1,650
ECHENA, Jose (Attrib.) Spanish (1845 -)	W			$1,300
ECKART, Lissy (?)	S			$352

D=Drawing, P=Painting, S=Sculpture, W=Watercolor

		Current Price Range	
	Low	Mean	High

		Low	Mean	High
ECKBERG, John E.	*P*			$413
American (20th -)				
ECKEN, Charles V.	*P*			$1,650
Belgian (19th -)				
ECKENBRECHER, Themistocles	*P*			$3,300
German (1842 -)				
ECKERMANS, Alice	*P*			$1,980
European (19th - 20th)				
ECKERSBURG, Christoffer-W.	*P*			$1,540
Danish (1783 - 1853)				
ECKERT, Henri-Ambrose	*P*			$4,125
German (1807 - 1840)				
ECKHARDT, Edris	*P*			$220
American (1904 -)	*S*	$110	$574	$935
EDAM, E.	*P*			$1,870
(?)				
EDDIS, Eden U. (Attrib.)	*P*			$880
British (1812 - 1901)				
EDDY, Don	*P*			$60,500
American (20th -)				
EDDY, H.	*P*			$275
(?)				
EDDY, W.	*P*			$1,760
British (19th -)				
EDE, F. C. V.	*W*			$138
Dutch (20th -)				
EDE, Frederic	*P*	$2,530	$3,190	$3,850
American (1865 - 1907)				
EDEL, Albert	*P*	$200	$225	$250
(?)				
EDEN, John	*S*			$220
(20th -)				
EDIE, Stuart C.	*P*			$825
American (1908 -)				
EDLICH, Stephan	*P*	$935	$3,135	$4,400

D=Drawing, P=Painting, S=Sculpture, W=Watercolor

		Current Price Range		
		Low	Mean	High
EDLICH, Stephan	S	$880	$2,514	$5,500
American (20th -)				
EDMONDS, Francis W.	P	$16,500	$17,050	$17,600
American (1800 - 1863)				
EDMONDSON, Edward	P			$1,540
(19th -)				
EDMONDSON, William	P			$468
American (1868 -)				
EDRIDGE, Henry	D	$550	$1,540	$2,420
British (1769 - 1821)	W			$880
EDVARDO, Jorge	P			$11,000
Brazilian (1936 -)				
EDWARD,	P			$175
(?)				
EDWARDS, George W.	D	$150	$240	$330
American (1869 - 1950)	P	$880	$1,815	$2,750
	W			$3,300
EDWARDS, Harry C.	D			$176
American (1868 - 1922)	P	$220	$825	$1,430
EDWARDS, J.	P	$825	$825	$825
British (19th -)				
EDWARDS, Lionel	P	$303	$1,029	$2,090
American (20th -)	W			$4,950
EDWARDS, M. E.	P			$2,750
(?)				
EDWARDS, Stanley	P			$385
American (20th -)				
EDWARDS, Sydeham T.	P			$9,075
British (1768 - 1819)				
EDZARD, Dietz	P	$660	$6,133	$18,700
German (1893 - 1963)				
EDZGERADZE, Giya	P			$13,200
Russian (1953 -)				

D=Drawing, P=Painting, S=Sculpture, W=Watercolor

		Current Price Range		
		Low	Mean	High

		Low	Mean	High
EECKHOUT, Gerbrand van den	*P*			$88,000
Dutch (1621 - 1674)				
EERTVELT, Andries van	*P*	$8,250	$26,125	$44,000
Flemish (1590 - 1652)				
EGERTON, Daniel T.	*P*	$660	$14,153	$26,400
British (? - 1842)				
EGGENHOFER, Nick	*D*	$700	$1,130	$1,540
American (1897 -)	*W*	$1,100	$4,073	$9,350
EGGERT, Sigmund	*P*			$715
German (1839 - 1896)				
EGGINGTON, Frank	*W*			$330
British (1908 -)				
EGGLESTON, Benjamin	*P*	$275	$2,328	$7,700
American (1867 - 1937)				
EGLAN, Max	*P*	$880	$977	$1,073
American (1825 -)				
EHNINGER, John W.	*P*			$330
American (1827 - 1889)				
EHREN, Susus F. von	*W*	$110	$116	$121
American (1865 - 1957)				
EHRENBERG, Wilhelm van	*P*			$9,900
Dutch (1630 - 1676)				
EHRET, Georg D.	*D*			$3,300
German (1710 - 1770)				
EHRET, Georg D. (After)	*W*			$165
German (1710 - 1770)				
EHRHART, Samuel D.	*D*			$550
British (19th -)				
EHRIG, William C.	*P*			$385
(20th -)				
EICHHLOTZ, Rebecca	*P*			$935
American (19th - 20th)				
EICHHOLTZ, Jacob (Attrib.)	*P*			$2,310
(?)				
EICHINGER, Erwin	*P*			$11,000
Austrian (19th -)				

D=Drawing, P=Painting, S=Sculpture, W=Watercolor

		Current Price Range		
		Low	Mean	High

EICHINGER, Oswald German (1915 -)	*P*	$880	$935	$990
EICHINGER, Otto Austrian (1922 -)	*P*	$385	$532	$770
EICHNER, Laurits C. (?)	*S*			$440
EICHNER, W. American (20th -)	*P*			$385
EICHOLTZ, Jacob American (1776 - 1842)	*P*			$2,200
EICHSTAEDT, Rudolph German (1857 - 1924)	*P*			$3,300
EICKELBERG, William H. Dutch (1845 - 1920)	*P*			$2,475
EIDSON, Scott American (20th -)	*W*	$110	$214	$770
EIENARD, E. French (20th -)	*S*			$550
EILSHEMIUS, Louis M. American (1864 - 1942)	*D*			$330
	P	$220	$1,712	$5,500
	W			$770
EILSHEMIUS, Louis M. (Attrib.) American (1864 - 1942)	*W*			$165
EISELE, Charles C. American (20th -)	*P*			$1,870
EISEN, Charles D. French (1720 - 1778)	*D*			$3,960
EISEN, Francois Flemish (1695 - 1778)	*P*			$13,200
EISEN, Francois (Attrib.) Flemish (1695 - 1778)	*P*			$31,900
EISENDIECK, Suzanne German (1908 -)	*P*	$468	$3,677	$11,550
EISENHUT, Ferencz Hungarian (1857 - 1903)	*P*			$33,000

D=Drawing, P=Painting, S=Sculpture, W=Watercolor

		Current Price Range		
		Low	Mean	High

EISENSCHITZ, Willy	*P*	$1,045	$1,485	$1,760
French (1889 - 1974)				
EISLER, Georg	*P*	$935	$1,403	$1,870
Austrian (1939 -)				
EISMANN, Johann A. (Attrib.)	*P*			$14,300
German (1604 - 1698)				
EITEL, Jacques	*P*			$385
French (1926 -)				
EKBLAG, K. F.	*P*			$385
American (19th - 20th)				
EKENAES, Jahn	*P*	$7,700	$14,850	$22,000
Norwegian (1847 - 1920)				
EKMAN, Stan	*P*	$330	$431	$523
American (20th -)	*W*			$275
ELASIS, Ed	*S*			$660
(?)				
ELDRED, Lemuel	*D*			$330
American (1848 - 1921)	*P*	$1,210	$3,664	$7,150
ELDRIDGE, Marion	*P*			$1,210
American (20th -)				
ELGOOD, George S.	*W*			$330
British (1851 - 1943)				
ELIAERTS, Jean-Francois	*P*			$57,750
Belgian (1761 - 1848)				
ELIASOPH, Paula	*P*			$3,850
American (1895 - 1983)				
ELKINS, Henry A.	*P*	$550	$2,283	$5,500
American (1847 - 1884)				
ELKINS, Henry A. (Attrib.)	*P*	$550	$550	$550
American (1847 - 1884)				
ELLE, Ferdinand (Attrib.)	*P*			$3,575
Flemish (1580 - 1637)				
ELLENSHAW, Peter	*P*			$4,950
(20th -)				

D=Drawing, P=Painting, S=Sculpture, W=Watercolor

		Current Price Range		
		Low	Mean	High

		Low	Mean	High
ELLINGER, R. American (19th -)	*P*			$110
ELLIS, Edwin British (1841 - 1895)	*W*			$440
ELLIS, Fremont American (1897 -)	*P*	$3,630	$8,608	$11,000
ELLIS, Paul H. European (19th - 20th)	*W*			$1,320
ELLIS, Russ (?)	*W*			$275
ELLIS, Tristram J. British (1844 - 1922)	*W*			$330
ELLIS, W. E. British (19th -)	*P*			$1,045
ELLISON, Julius M. American (1909 -)	*W*			$275
ELLSWORTH, Clarence A American (1885 - 1961)	*P* *W*			$990 $193
ELLSWORTH, Edyth G. American (20th -)	*P*	$110	$317	$523
ELLSWORTH, Eleanor American (19th -)	*P*			$385
ELLSWORTH, James S. (Attrib.) (?)	*W*			$4,840
ELLSWORTH, L.M.A. (19th -)	*P*			$550
ELLWOOD, Evelyn (20th -)	*P*			$2,200
ELSHEIMER, Adam Flemish (1578 - 1610)	*P*			$450,000
ELSHEIMER, Adam (Attrib.) Flemish (1578 - 1610)	*P*			$1,430
ELSHEIMER, Adam (Circle) Flemish (1578 - 1610)	*P*	$1,870	$10,340	$22,000
ELSLEY, Arthur J. British (1861 -)	*P*			$104,500

D=Drawing, P=Painting, S=Sculpture, W=Watercolor

		Low	Mean	High
		Current Price Range		
ELTEN, Hendrik-Dirk van	*P*	$770	$2,357	$6,600
American (1829 - 1904)				
ELTING, N.D.	*P*			$275
American (19th -)				
ELVEN, Pierre H. T.	*P*	$3,575	$26,538	$49,500
Dutch (1828 - 1908)				
ELVEN, Pierre H. T. (Attrib.)	*P*			$990
Dutch (1828 - 1908)				
ELVEN, Teater Van	*P*			$1,650
Dutch (19th - 20th)				
ELWELL, D. Jerome	*P*	$110	$591	$1,430
American (1857 - 1912)	*W*			$275
ELY, Donald H.	*P*			$413
American (20th -)				
ELY, Letitia M.	*D*	$100	$105	$110
American (?)				
ELZINGRE, Edouard	*D*			$1,045
Swiss (20th -)				
EMANUEL, Frank L.	*P*	$440	$578	$715
British (1865 - 1948)				
EMBRY, Norris	*P*	$770	$1,348	$1,980
(20th -)				
EMERIC, V. W.	*P*			$440
French (20th -)				
EMERSON, Charles	*D*			$275
American (1874 - 1922)	*P*			$138
EMERSON, Edith	*P*	$193	$547	$900
American (1888 -)				
EMERSON, Louis	*P*	$275	$509	$743
American (20th -)				
EMERSON, William O.	*P*			$385
American (1856 -)				
EMERY, James	*P*			$110
American (19th -)				

D=Drawing, P=Painting, S=Sculpture, W=Watercolor

		Current Price Range		
		Low	Mean	High

		Low	Mean	High
EMIG, Adolph P.	*W*			$550
American (20th -)				
EMILE, Nicolet G.	*P*			$275
Belgian (1856 - 1921)				
EMMONS, Alexander H.	*P*			$198
American (1816 - 1879)				
EMMONS, Alexander H. (Attrib.)	*P*			$770
American (1816 - 1879)				
EMMONS, Dorothy S.	*P*	$715	$1,878	$4,180
American (1891 -)				
EMMS, John	*P*	$715	$9,209	$38,500
British (1843 - 1912)	*W*			$2,310
EMMS, John (Manner)	*P*			$2,475
British (1843 - 1912)				
EMPOLI, Jacopo da (After)	*P*			$990
Italian (1554 - 1640)				
EMPOLI, Jacopo da (Attrib.)	*D*			$2,475
Italian (1554 - 1640)				
ENCKE, Fedor	*P*	$303	$4,684	$10,450
German (1851 -)				
ENDER, Axel H.	*P*	$4,400	$14,300	$24,200
Norwegian (1853 - 1920)				
ENDER, Edouard	*P*			$1,430
Australian (1822 - 1883)				
ENDER, Thomas	*P*			$2,420
Austrian (1793 - 1875)				
ENDERS, Frank	*P*			$358
American (19th - 20th)				
ENGELHARDT, Edna P.	*P*	$770	$880	$990
American (19th - 20th)				
ENGELHARDT, Georg	*P*			$11,000
German (1823 - 1883)				
ENGL, Hugo (Attrib.)	*P*			$413
Australian (1852 -)				
ENGLE, Harry L.	*P*	$220	$697	$1,430
American (19th - 20th)				

D=Drawing, P=Painting, S=Sculpture, W=Watercolor

	Current Price Range		
	Low	Mean	High

		Low	Mean	High
ENGLEHART, John J.	P			$330
American (20th -)				
ENGLEHART, Joseph J.	P			$413
American (1867 - 1915)				
ENGLEMANN, E.J.	P			$126
(?)				
ENGLES, Leo	P			$1,375
Belgian (1882 - 1952)				
ENGLISH, Frank F.	W	$100	$1,279	$3,300
American (1854 - 1922)				
ENGLISH, H. C.	P			$440
American (20th -)				
ENGLISH, Mabel B.	P			$770
American (1861 -)				
ENGMAN, Harald	P			$468
Swedish (20th -)				
ENJOLRAS, Delphin	D			$8,250
French (1857 -)				
ENNEKING, John J.	P	$605	$6,685	$52,800
American (1841 - 1916)				
ENNEKING, Joseph E.	P	$825	$2,178	$6,490
American (? - 1946)				
ENNEKING, Joseph E. (Attrib.)	P			$248
American (? - 1946)				
ENNESS, Augustus W.	W			$165
British (?)				
ENNIS,	P			$1,760
Belgian (19th - 20th)				
ENNIS, George P.	P	$1,210	$2,860	$4,950
American (1884 - 1936)	W	$330	$1,485	$4,400
ENNIS, Gladys A.	P			$275
American (19th - 20th)				
ENRIQUEZ, Carlos	P	$4,400	$4,950	$6,050
(20th -)				
ENSEL, H.	P			$495
(?)				

D=Drawing, P=Painting, S=Sculpture, W=Watercolor

		Current Price Range		
		Low	Mean	High
ENSER, John F.	*P*	$358	$367	$385
American (1898 -)				
ENSOR, James	*D*			$34,100
Belgian (20th -)	*P*	$60,500	$132,000	$264,000
ENWRIGHT, J. J.	*P*	$110	$500	$1,128
American (19th - 20th)				
ENZINGER, H.	*P*			$2,090
(?)				
EPP, Rudolf	*P*	$3,850	$14,080	$30,800
German (1834 - 1910)				
EPPERLY, R. R.	*P*			$132
(?)				
EPPINK, Norman	*P*			$6,600
American (1906 -)				
EPSTEIN, Henri	*P*			$5,720
Polish (1892 -)				
EPSTEIN, Jehudo	*P*			$825
Polish (1870 - 1946)				
EPSTEIN, Sir Jacob	*D*	$1,100	$1,760	$2,420
British (1880 - 1959)	*S*	$3,850	$7,937	$12,100
	W	$1,100	$1,980	$2,860
ERDELY, Francis de	*D*	$385	$908	$1,430
American (1904 - 1959)	*P*	$5,500	$9,900	$14,300
ERDMAN, Don	*P*			$358
American (?)				
ERDMAN, Otto	*P*	$3,300	$22,275	$41,250
German (1834 - 1905)				
ERDOSSY, Bella	*P*	$495	$633	$770
Hungarian (1871 -)				
ERGAMIAN, Sarka	*P*	$385	$495	$605
(?)				
ERGGELET, Paula (Baroness)	*W*			$303
Austrian (19th - 20th)				

D=Drawing, P=Painting, S=Sculpture, W=Watercolor

		Current Price Range		
		Low	Mean	High
ERICSON, David	P			$605
American (1873 - 1946)				
ERNI, Hans	P	$10,450	$13,750	$16,500
Swiss (1909 -)				
ERNST, Jimmy	P	$1,045	$1,348	$1,650
American (1920 -)	S			$2,860
	W	$1,430	$1,797	$2,200
ERNST, Max	D	$3,520	$51,205	$170,500
German (1891 - 1976)	P	$27,500	$237,875	$687,500
	S	$6,600	$29,095	$82,500
ERNST, Max (After)	S			$5,500
German (1891 - 1976)				
ERNST, Rudolf	P	$16,500	$71,706	$132,000
Austrian (1854 - 1932)				
ERTE,	D			$3,575
Russian (1892 -)	S			$3,190
	W	$4,400	$11,479	$19,800
ERTZ, Edward F.	P	$413	$867	$1,320
American (1862 -)				
ERUBELLIN, J.	P			$14,300
French (19th -)				
ES, Jacob van	P			$66,000
Flemish (17th -)				
ESCHARD, Charles	W			$550
French (1748 - 1810)				
ESCHKE, Wilhelm B. H.	P			$2,640
German (1823 - 1900)				
ESCOBAR, Marisol	S			$6,050
(20th -)				
ESCOSURA, Ignacio L.	P			$2,750
Spanish (19th -)				
ESCURIAZ., Diego L. de	D			$5,225
Spanish (16th -)				

D=Drawing, P=Painting, S=Sculpture, W=Watercolor

		Current Price Range		
		Low	Mean	High

		Low	Mean	High
ESCURIAZ., Diego L. de (Attrib.)	*W*			$3,025
Spanish (16th -)				
ESPINO, Richard	*P*			$770
American (1888 - 1954)				
ESPINOSA, Jeronimo J. de	*P*			$20,900
Spanish (1600 - 1680)				
ESPINOSA, Professor	*P*			$1,980
Spanish (19th - 20th)				
ESPOY, Angel	*P*	$715	$2,127	$4,675
American (1869 - 1962)				
ESSEN, Johannes van	*P*			$2,200
Dutch (1854 -)	*W*			$1,035
ESSIG, George E.	*W*	$130	$644	$1,760
American (1838 - 1919)				
ESTALL, Walter C.	*P*			$523
British (1857 - 1897)				
ESTE, Francesco B. da	*P*			$37,400
Italian (18th - 19th)				
ESTE, Gaudi	*S*	$4,620	$8,910	$13,200
Venezuelan (1947 -)				
ESTES, A. Fowles	*P*			$275
American (20th -)				
ESTES, Florence	*P*			$660
(?)				
ESTES, Richard	*P*	$33,000	$221,833	$539,000
American (1936 -)	*W*	$1,100	$25,300	$49,500
ESTEVE Y MARQUES, Augustin	*P*	$44,000	$60,500	$77,000
Spanish (1753 - 1809)				
ESTEY, A. Genevieve	*P*			$248
American (19th - 20th)				
ETCHEVERRY, Hubert D.	*P*			$30,800
French (1867 - 1950)				
ETNIER, Stephen	*P*			$1,980
American (1903 -)				

D=Drawing, P=Painting, S=Sculpture, W=Watercolor

		Current Price Range		
		Low	Mean	High
ETROG, Sorel	*S*	$1,100	$11,594	$35,750
Rumanian (1933 -)				
ETTELUM, A.	*P*			$165
(?)				
ETTING, Emlen	*P*			$1,760
American (1905 -)				
ETTY, William	*P*	$1,045	$8,986	$38,500
British (1787 - 1849)				
ETTY, William (Attrib.)	*P*			$1,100
British (1787 - 1849)				
EUBANKS, Tony	*P*	$2,420	$4,640	$6,000
American (1939 -)				
EULER, Carl	*P*			$1,320
German (1815 -)				
EURICH, Richard	*P*	$3,520	$5,335	$7,150
British (1903 -)				
EUROPEAN SCHOOL,	*P*			$1,705
European (?)				
EUROPEAN SCHOOL,	*P*			$2,310
European (19th - 20th)				
EUROPEAN SCHOOL 18C,	*P*	$1,320	$1,639	$2,090
European (18th -)				
EUROPEAN SCHOOL 19C,	*P*	$1,100	$2,242	$6,050
European (19th -)	*S*			$1,980
	W			$1,760
EUROPEAN SCHOOL 20C,	*P*			$2,310
European (20th -)	*S*			$1,100
EUSTON, J. Howard	*P*	$110	$371	$1,210
American (1892 -)	*W*	$110	$243	$468
EVANS, Bruce	*P*			$660
American (20th -)				
EVANS, De Scott	*P*	$2,860	$7,986	$19,800
American (1847 - 1898)				

D=Drawing, P=Painting, S=Sculpture, W=Watercolor

		Current Price Range		
		Low	Mean	High
EVANS, Donald	W			$12,100
American (20th -)				
EVANS, Edith G.	P			$429
American (20th -)				
EVANS, Grace L.	D			$2,200
American (1877 -)	P			$660
EVANS, Jessie B.	P	$715	$715	$715
American (1866 - 1954)				
EVANS, Joe	P			$4,620
American (1857 - 1898)				
EVE, Jean	P			$4,950
French (1900 - 1968)				
EVERDINGEN, Allaert van	D	$5,720	$7,957	$9,350
Dutch (1621 - 1675)	W			$440
EVERDINGEN, Cesar van	P	$8,800	$147,400	$286,000
Dutch (1646 -)				
EVEREN, Jay Van	W			$2,090
American (?)				
EVERGOOD, Miles	P			$550
(?)				
EVERGOOD, Philip	D	$550	$1,238	$2,640
American (1901 - 1973)	P	$825	$6,557	$24,200
	W	$1,320	$2,585	$3,850
EVERS, J.	P			$1,760
American (1797 - 1884)				
EVERSEN, Adrianus	P	$4,180	$13,719	$24,200
Dutch (1818 - 1897)				
EVRARD, Paula	P			$6,600
Belgian (1876 - 1927)				
EWALD, Marion	D			$165
American (1910 - 1944)	P	$138	$606	$1,073
EWING,	P			$220
American (20th -)				

D=Drawing, P=Painting, S=Sculpture, W=Watercolor

		Current Price Range		
		Low	Mean	High

		Low	Mean	High
EWING, Harris (?)	P			$990
EWING, R. A. American (20th -)	P			$495
EXNER, F. (?)	P			$413
EXTER, Alexandra (20th -)	W	$2,310	$2,585	$2,860
EYBERGEN, Johanna G. van Dutch (1865 - 1950)	P			$3,080
EYCK, Caspar van Dutch (1613 - 1673)	P			$7,150
EYCKEN, Charles van den Belgian (1859 - 1923)	P	$3,850	$17,207	$52,800
EYDEN, William A. American (1859 -)	P	$220	$825	$1,155
EYFELLS, Eyjolfur J. Danish (20th -)	P			$500
EZGANIAN, S. (?)	P			$330
FABBI, Alberto Italian (1858 - 1906)	P			$4,400
FABBI, Fabbio Italian (1861 - 1946)	P W	$6,600 $770	$17,463 $1,467	$41,250 $2,200
FABER, Jean French (20th -)	P			$385
FABER DU FAUR, Otto von German (1828 - 1901)	P			$13,200
FABION, John American (20th -)	S			$330
FABRES Y COSTA, Antonio Spanish (1854 -)	P W			$29,700 $2,200
FABRI-CANTI, Jose French (20th -)	P	$660	$4,785	$12,650

D=Drawing, P=Painting, S=Sculpture, W=Watercolor

		Current Price Range		
		Low	Mean	High
FABRIS, Pietro	W	$23,100	$27,225	$31,900
Italian (18th -)				
FABRITIUS DE TENG, Frederik	P			$8,800
Danish (1781 - 1849)				
FACCINI, Pietro	D			$29,700
Italian (1560 - 1602)				
FAED, John	P			$3,850
British (1820 - 1902)				
FAED, JR., James	P			$770
British (1857 - 1920)				
FAES, Pieter (Attrib.)	P			$20,900
Belgian (1750 - 1814)				
FAGEN, Robert (Attrib.)	P			$1,650
British (1745 - 1816)				
FAGG, Arthur J.	P			$2,310
British (19th -)				
FAGGI, Alfeo	D			$248
American (1885 -)				
FAGOTTO, H.	S			$2,090
(?)				
FAGUAYS, Pierre le	S	$605	$1,293	$1,980
(?)				
FAHAN, Edward W.	P	$1,650	$1,815	$1,980
American (1920 -)				
FAHNESTOCK, Wallace W.	P	$440	$440	$440
American (1877 -)				
FAHRINGER, Carl	D			$275
Austrian (1874 - 1952)	W			$990
FAIN, Yonia	P			$440
(20th -)				
FAIRCHILD, Elizabeth N.	P			$990
American (20th -)				
FAIRFIELD, Hannah	P			$10,340
(19th -)				
FAIRINETTI, C.	P			$1,540
Italian (19th - 20th)				

D=Drawing, P=Painting, S=Sculpture, W=Watercolor

		Current Price Range		
		Low	Mean	High
FAIRMAN, Frances	*P*	$3,575	$7,288	$11,000
British (1836 - 1923)				
FAIRMAN, James	*P*	$550	$5,628	$11,000
American (1826 - 1904)				
FAISTENBERGER, Anton (Attrib)	*P*			$8,250
Austrian (1663 - 1708)				
FAISTENBERGER, Anton (Circle)	*P*			$4,950
Austrian (1663 - 1708)				
FAIVRE, Justin	*P*			$275
American (1902 -)	*W*			$990
FALANGE, Enrico	*P*	$675	$1,163	$1,650
(17th -)				
FALANGER, M.	*P*			$165
(?)				
FALBE, Joachim M.	*P*			$1,430
German (1709 - 1782)				
FALCIATORE, Filippo	*P*			$121,000
Italian (18th -)				
FALCONE, Aniello (Follower)	*P*			$7,975
Italian (1607 - 1656)				
FALCONER, John M.	*P*			$880
American (1820 - 1903)	*W*			$1,045
FALCONET, Etienne-M. (After)	*S*			$660
French (1716 - 1791)				
FALCONET, Pierre E.	*D*			$24,200
French (1741 - 1791)				
FALERO, Luis R.	*P*	$13,200	$17,050	$20,900
Spanish (1851 - 1896)				
FALES, L.	*W*			$743
(?)				
FALGUIERE, Jean A. J.	*S*			$6,050
French (1831 - 1900)				
FALK, Robert	*P*			$198
British (1886 - 1958)				

D=Drawing, P=Painting, S=Sculpture, W=Watercolor

		Current Price Range		
		Low	Mean	High

FALKENBERG, Richard	*P*			$220
German (1875 -)				
FALL, George	*W*			$275
British (1848 - 1925)				
FALL RIVER SCHOOL,	*P*			$2,530
American (19th -)				
FALLOLA, Robert	*P*			$880
Spanish (1867 -)				
FALLS, Charles B.	*D*			$500
American (1874 - 1960)				
FALTER, John	*P*	$200	$2,020	$7,150
American (1910 - 1982)	*W*			$650
FANCELLI, Pietro (Attrib.)	*D*			$440
Italian (1764 - 1850)				
FANFANI, Enrico	*P*			$11,000
Italian (19th -)				
FANFARISI,	*S*			$935
(?)				
FANGEL, Maud T.	*D*			$850
American (?)				
FANGH, Maler D.	*W*			$275
Austrian (20th -)				
FANNEN, J.				$330
(?)				
FANNING, William S.	*P*			$605
American (1887 -)				
FANTIN-LATOUR, Henri	*D*	$2,750	$5,775	$8,800
French (1836 - 1904)	*P*	$12,100	$405,642	$1.870M
FANTIN-LATOUR, Henri (Attrib.)	*P*	$2,750	$8,875	$15,000
French (1836 - 1904)				
FANTIN-LATOUR, Victoria D.	*P*			$49,500
French (1840 - 1926)				
FARAI, Gennaro	*P*			$715
Italian (1879 - 1958)				

D=Drawing, P=Painting, S=Sculpture, W=Watercolor

		Current Price Range		
		Low	Mean	High

		Low	Mean	High
FARASYN, Edgard	*P*	$1,760	$7,480	$13,200
Belgian (1858 - 1938)				
FARBER, Manny	*P*	$165	$413	$660
American (20th -)				
FARINATI, Paolo	*D*	$715	$5,583	$10,450
Italian (1524 - 1606)				
FARLEY, Richard B.	*P*	$440	$779	$1,018
American (1875 - 1951)				
FARM, Gerald	*P*			$3,575
American (1935 -)				
FARMER, Edna	*W*			$550
American (20th -)				
FARNDON, Walter	*P*	$990	$2,838	$4,950
American (1876 - 1964)				
FARNHAM, Ammi Merchant	*P*	$193	$468	$825
American (1846 - 1922)				
FARNHAM, Sally James	*S*	$1,210	$17,820	$49,500
American (1876 - 1943)				
FARNI, Tebaldo	*P*			$440
Italian (19th -)				
FARNSWORTH, Alfred V.	*W*			$990
American (1858 - 1908)				
FARNSWORTH, Ethel N.	*P*	$248	$331	$413
American (1873 -)				
FARNSWORTH, Jerry	*P*	$220	$333	$660
American (1895 - 1983)				
FARNUM, H. Cyrus	*P*	$605	$788	$880
American (1866 - 1925)				
FARNY, Henry F.	*D*			$18,700
American (1847 - 1916)	*P*	$1,815	$3,383	$4,950
	S			$770
	W	$29,700	$118,067	$203,500
FARQUHARSON, Joseph	*P*			$2,200
British (1846 - 1935)				

D=Drawing, P=Painting, S=Sculpture, W=Watercolor

		Current Price Range		
		Low	Mean	High

		Low	Mean	High
FARR, Helen American (1908 -)	P			$880
FARRE, Henri American (1871 - 1934)	P	$1,980	$2,787	$4,400
FARRER, Henry American (1843 - 1903)	P W	$605	$4,308	$11,000 $18,700
FARRIER, Edgar G. British (1827 - 1902)	P			$3,300
FARRINGTON, E. British (19th -)	P			$688
FARSKY, Otto American (19th - 20th)	P	$193	$693	$1,540
FARWELL, (?)	P			$105
FASCE, F. Italian (19th -)	S W			$26,400 $468
FASSETT, Koffe H. (?)	P			$358
FASSETT, Truman American (1885 -)	P			$3,850
FASSIN, Nicolas H. J. de Flemish (1728 - 1811)	P			$13,200
FATORI, (?)	S			$1,650
FAULEY, Albert American (1858 - 1919)	P			$880
FAULKNER, Charles (19th - 20th)	P			$1,430
FAULKNER, Frank British (20th -)	P	$2,750	$5,225	$7,700
FAURE, Amandus German (1874 - 1931)	P	$138	$330	$440
FAURNIER, Alex French (19th - 20th)	P			$1,870

D=Drawing, P=Painting, S=Sculpture, W=Watercolor

		Current Price Range		
		Low	Mean	High

		Low	Mean	High
FAUSETT, William D.	*W*			$468
American (1913 -)				
FAVAI, Gennardo	*P*	$715	$949	$1,183
Italian (1879 - 1958)				
FAVE, Paul	*P*			$2,200
French (19th - 20th)				
FAVORY, Andre	*P*			$4,180
French (1888 - 1937)				
FAVRETTO, Giacomo	*P*	$11,000	$16,775	$22,550
Italian (1849 - 1887)				
FAVRETTO, Giacomo (Attrib.)	*P*			$7,700
Italian (1849 - 1887)				
FAVRINI, Eduardo	*P*			$385
Italian (1913 -)				
FAWCETT, Robert	*D*			$100
American (1903 - 1967)	*W*	$330	$800	$1,300
FAWCUS, Margaret	*W*			$413
American (19th -)				
FAWKES, Guy	*P*			$1,540
(?)				
FAWLER, W.B.	*P*			$286
(?)				
FAY, Arlene H.	*D*	$1,800	$2,573	$3,410
American (20th -)	*P*	$550	$825	$1,100
FAY, Redmond	*P*			$450
American (19th -)				
FAYRAL,	*S*			$660
(?)				
FEBVRE, Edouard	*P*	$825	$1,403	$1,980
French (20th -)				
FECHIN, Nicolai	*P*	$23,100	$100,729	$176,000
American (1881 - 1955)				
FECHIN, Nicolai (Attrib.)	*P*			$1,045
American (1881 - 1955)				

D=Drawing, P=Painting, S=Sculpture, W=Watercolor

		Current Price Range		
		Low	Mean	High

		Low	Mean	High
FEDER, Adolphe	*P*	$1,980	$2,420	$2,860
French (1886 - 1945)				
FEDERICO, Cavalier M.	*P*			$385
Italian (1884 -)				
FEDERICO, Michele	*P*			$1,100
Italian (1884 -)				
FEDERICO & MOUTON, Al & J.	*P*			$138
American (20th -)				
FEDERLE, Helmut	*D*			$1,320
(20th -)				
FEDOROWSKY, S.	*P*			$440
Russian (20th -)				
FEHDMER, Eugene	*P*			$1,980
Dutch (19th -)				
FEHER, Joseph	*P*	$385	$1,128	$1,870
American (1908 -)				
FEHERVARI,	*P*			$165
(?)				
FEILLET, A.	*P*			$495
French (19th -)				
FEININGER, Lyonel	*D*	$4,950	$16,775	$44,000
German (1871 - 1956)	*P*	$60,500	$237,417	$495,000
	W	$8,800	$22,447	$33,000
FEININGER, Lyonel (Attrib.)	*W*			$660
German (1871 - 1956)				
FEININGER, Theodore L.	*P*			$880
American (1910 -)				
FEINSTEIN, Sam	*P*			$825
(?)				
FELGUEREZ, Manuel	*P*	$5,500	$7,425	$9,350
Mexican (1928 -)	*S*			$220
FELICIAN, H.	*P*			$2,860
Italian (19th -)				
FELIX, K. E.	*P*	$468	$656	$1,210
German (20th -)				

D=Drawing, P=Painting, S=Sculpture, W=Watercolor

		Current Price Range		
		Low	Mean	High

		Low	Mean	High
FERNEKES, Max (Attrib.) American (20th -)	*D*	$145	$178	$240
FERNELEY, JR., John (Attrib.) British (1815 - 1862)	*P*			$1,760
FERNELEY, JR., John (Manner) British (1815 - 1862)	*P*			$6,050
FERNELEY, SR., John British (1781 - 1860)	*P*	$5,500	$72,279	$308,000
FERNIE, John American (?)	*W*	$110	$152	$193
FERRANTI, Carlo Italian (19th -)	*W*	$825	$1,302	$1,760
FERRARA, Jackie (20th -)	*S*			$16,500
FERRARA, Joe American (20th -)	*P*	$900	$2,150	$3,300
FERRARI, A. Italian (20th -)	*P*			$2,200
FERRARI, G. Italian (19th -)	*S*			$1,430
FERRARI, Gregorio de Italian (1644 - 1726)	*D*			$990
FERRARI, Lorenzo de Italian (1680 - 1744)	*D* *P*			$1,650 $30,800
FERRARI, Virginio American (20th -)	*S*	$110	$578	$1,045
FERREN, John American (1905 - 1970)	*P* *W*	$1,100	$3,894	$7,150 $1,650
FERRER, Joaquin Lat. Amer. (20th -)	*P*			$1,870
FERRER-COMAS, Edouard Spanish (19th -)	*P*			$16,500
FERRI, Ciro Italian (1634 - 1689)	*D*			$4,950

D=Drawing, P=Painting, S=Sculpture, W=Watercolor

		Current Price Range		
		Low	Mean	High
FERRI, Ciro (Attrib.)	*P*			$3,300
Italian (1634 - 1689)				
FERRI, Ciro (Follower)	*D*			$440
Italian (1634 - 1689)				
FERRIER, James	*W*			$1,650
British (19th -)				
FERRIERES, Martin	*P*			$990
French (19th -)				
FERRIS, Jean L.G.	*P*	$13,750	$15,125	$16,500
American (1863 -)	*W*			$110
FERRIS, R. D.	*P*			$2,640
American (19th -)				
FERRISS, Laura	*W*			$880
American (19th -)				
FERRITER, Clare	*S*			$193
(20th -)				
FERRONE, Gianfranco	*P*			$220
Italian (1927 -)				
FERRONI, E.	*P*			$440
(?)				
FERRUZZA, F.	*P*			$150
(?)				
FERY, John	*P*	$935	$1,784	$2,860
American (1865 - 1935)				
FERY, John (Attrib.)	*P*	$900	$1,313	$1,750
American (1865 - 1935)				
FESENMAIER, Helene	*S*			$715
(20th -)				
FETI, Domenico (Attrib.)	*P*			$14,300
Italian (1589 - 1624)				
FETI, Domenico (Manner)	*P*			$2,200
Italian (1589 - 1624)				
FETT, William F.	*W*			$165
American (1918 -)				
FETTERS, N. J.	*P*			$990
(?)				

D=Drawing, P=Painting, S=Sculpture, W=Watercolor

		Current Price Range		
		Low	Mean	High

FETTING, Rainer	*P*	$14,300	$23,980	$34,100
(20th -)	*W*			$6,050
FEUDEL, Arthur	*D*			$193
American (1857 -)	*P*			$715
	W			$275
FEUDEL, Constantin	*P*			$1,100
German (1860 -)				
FEUERMAN, Carole J.	*P*	$23,100	$29,425	$35,750
(20th -)				
FEYEN, Jacques E.	*P*			$1,210
French (1815 - 1908)				
FEYEN-PERRIN, August	*P*	$6,600	$8,250	$9,900
French (1826 - 1888)				
FIAMMINGO, Paolo (Circle)	*P*	$3,300	$3,850	$4,400
Flemish (1540 - 1596)				
FICHEL, Benjamin E.	*P*			$3,520
French (1826 - 1895)				
FICHERELLI, Felice (Circle)	*P*			$5,500
Italian (1605 - 1660)				
FICHT, C. O.	*P*			$550
American (19th -)				
FIDLER, Anton	*P*			$11,000
Austrian (19th -)				
FIDLER, Harry	*P*			$4,675
British (20th -)				
FIDRIT, Charles A.	*P*			$24,200
French (1881 - 1927)				
FIEDLER, K.	*P*			$330
German (19th -)				
FIELD, E. Loyal	*P*	$165	$1,004	$2,640
American (1856 - 1914)	*W*	$220	$303	$385
FIELD, Erastus S.	*P*	$3,850	$11,825	$19,800
American (1807 - 1900)				

D=Drawing, P=Painting, S=Sculpture, W=Watercolor

		Low	Mean	High
		\multicolumn{3}{c}{Current Price Range}		

		Low	Mean	High
FIELD, Frances (?)	*D*			$440
FIELD, Freke British (19th -)	*P*	$35,200	$46,475	$57,750
FIELDING, Anthony Copley British (1787 - 1855)	*W*	$550	$968	$1,760
FIELDING, Ernest British (19th -)	*P*			$2,750
FIELDING, G. British (19th -)	*P*			$990
FIENE, Ernest American (1894 - 1966)	*P* *W*	$660 $385	$4,652 $468	$28,600 $550
FIERAVINO, Francesco (Circle) Italian (1640 -)	*P*			$3,080
FIERAVINO, Francesco (School) Italian (1640 -)	*P*			$1,650
FIERRO, Pancho (19th -)	*W*			$3,850
FIESOLE, Fra A. da Italian (1387 - 1455)	*S*			$1,650
FIESOLE, Fra A. da (Attrib.) Italian (1387 - 1455)	*P*			$26,400
FIEUX, Robert American (20th -)	*P*			$715
FIGARI, Pedro Uruguayan (1861 - 1938)	*P*	$5,500	$28,182	$82,500
FIGARO, Charles (?)	*P*			$935
FIGINO, Ambrogio Italian (1548 - 1608)	*D*			$1,650
FIGURA, Hang Austrian (20th -)	*P*			$275
FILATOV, Nikolai Russian (1951 - 1984)	*P*			$16,500
FILIPPELLI, Cafiero (1889 -)	*P*			$880

D=Drawing, P=Painting, S=Sculpture, W=Watercolor

		Current Price Range		
		Low	Mean	High
FILLERUP, Peter M.	*S*	$302	$1,531	$2,750
American (1953 -)				
FILLIARD, Ernest	*W*			$358
French (19th - 20th)				
FILLON, Arthur	*P*			$1,760
(?)				
FILOSA, Giovanni	*W*			$8,800
Italian (1850 - 1935)				
FINCH, Marjorie	*P*			$385
American (1907 -)				
FINCK, Hazel	*P*			$8,800
American (1894 -)				
FINCKEN, James H.	*P*			$220
American (1860 - 1943)				
FINDLAY, J. L.	*P*			$600
(?)				
FINDLEY, G. H.	*W*			$110
British (19th -)				
FINES, Eugene F.	*P*			$1,980
French (1826 -)				
FINI, Leonor	*D*	$880	$1,839	$4,620
Italian (1908 -)	*P*	$605	$55,202	$154,000
	W	$1,540	$3,200	$6,600
FINK, Aaron	*P*			$2,090
(20th -)				
FINTOF,	*P*			$138
Dutch (19th -)				
FIORAVANTI, Ugo	*P*			$220
Italian (20th -)				
FIORENTINO, L.	*W*			$330
Italian (20th -)				
FIOT, Maximilien	*S*			$2,420
French (1886 - 1953)				
FIRKELBACH, Laszlo	*P*			$220
Hungarian (20th -)				

D=Drawing, P=Painting, S=Sculpture, W=Watercolor

| | | Current Price Range | | |
		Low	Mean	High
FIRMIN-GIRARD, Marie F. French (1838 - 1921)	P	$9,350	$16,225	$23,100
FISCHER, Anton O. American (1882 - 1962)	P	$605	$1,569	$3,600
FISCHER, Carl Danish (19th - 20th)	P	$550	$1,100	$1,650
FISCHER, Joel (20th -)	S			$15,400
FISCHER, L. American (20th -)	P			$495
FISCHER, Ludwig H. German (1848 - 1915)	P	$468	$4,026	$12,100
FISCHER, Paul Danish (1860 - 1934)	P			$9,900
FISCHL, Eric American (1948 -)	D	$7,150	$9,717	$11,000
	P	$11,000	$147,070	$715,000
	W	$49,500	$50,875	$52,250
FISH, G. G. American (19th -)	D			$275
FISH, Janet American (1938 -)	D	$5,500	$12,375	$19,800
	P	$44,000	$74,250	$104,500
FISHER, Alvan American (1792 - 1863)	P			$4,400
FISHER, Alvan (School) American (1792 - 1863)	P			$605
FISHER, Anna S. American (? - 1942)	P			$2,473
FISHER, Anton O. American (?)	P			$1,320
FISHER, Ben Welsh (? - 1939)	P			$330
FISHER, D.A. American (19th -)	P	$110	$152	$248
	W			$110

D=Drawing, P=Painting, S=Sculpture, W=Watercolor

		Current Price Range		
		Low	Mean	High

		Low	Mean	High
FISHER, Eliza C.	*P*			$605
American (1871 - 1959)				
FISHER, Elizabeth C.	*P*			$110
American (1910 -)				
FISHER, Harrison	*W*	$413	$3,364	$8,800
American (1875 - 1934)				
FISHER, Horace	*P*	$6,050	$6,325	$6,600
British (? - 1893)	*W*	$110	$168	$220
FISHER, Hugo A.	*P*	$248	$454	$660
American (1867 - 1916)	*W*	$193	$963	$2,860
FISHER, Hugo M.	*P*	$468	$1,884	$3,300
American (1876 -)				
FISHER, Joshua	*W*			$935
British (1859 -)				
FISHER, Paul	*W*			$2,860
Mexican (?)				
FISHER, Samuel M.	*P*			$15,400
British (1860 - 1939)				
FISHER, Vernon	*P*	$17,600	$23,650	$35,750
American (1943 -)				
FISHER, William	*P*			$825
American (1890 -)				
FISHER, William M.	*P*	$385	$1,306	$3,575
American (1841 - 1923)				
FISHER-CLAY, Elizabeth C.	*P*	$440	$788	$990
American (1871 - 1959)				
FISK, Edward	*P*			$250
(?)				
FISKE, Gertrude	*P*	$578	$15,586	$52,800
American (1879 - 1961)				
FISKE, Harry T.	*P*			$248
American (20th -)				
FITGER, Arthur H.	*P*			$8,800
German (1840 - 1909)				

D=Drawing, P=Painting, S=Sculpture, W=Watercolor

		Current Price Range		
		Low	Mean	High
FITLER, William C.	P	$660	$1,265	$1,870
American (1857 - 1915)	W	$275	$843	$1,760
FITZGERALD, Edmond J.	P	$605	$1,293	$1,980
American (1912 -)				
FITZGERALD, Eugenia T.	P			$825
American (19th - 20th)				
FITZGERALD, M.	P			$303
(?)				
FITZGIBBONS, James	P			$165
American (19th - 20th)				
FJAESTAD, Gustav E.	P			$17,600
Swedish (1868 - 1949)				
FLACK, Audrey	D			$5,500
American (1931 -)	P	$33,000	$57,200	$104,500
FLAGG, H. Peabody	P	$165	$424	$715
American (1859 -)	W	$165	$275	$385
FLAGG, James M.	D	$350	$795	$1,320
American (1877 - 1960)	P	$1,600	$2,037	$2,860
	W	$990	$1,416	$2,200
FLAGG, James M. (Attrib.)	W			$935
American (1877 - 1960)				
FLAGG, Jared B.	P			$3,080
American (1820 - 1899)				
FLAHERY, J. J.	P			$578
American (20th -)				
FLAMENG, Francois	P	$3,300	$23,833	$49,500
French (1856 - 1923)				
FLAMM, Albert	P			$22,000
German (1823 - 1906)				
FLANAGAN, Barry	P			$26,400
British (1941 -)				
FLANDRIN, Jules	P			$660
French (1871 - 1947)				

D=Drawing, P=Painting, S=Sculpture, W=Watercolor

| | | Current Price Range | | |
		Low	Mean	High
FLAVELLE, G. H.	W	$165	$266	$413
European (19th -)				
FLAVIN, Dan	D	$9,900	$10,450	$11,000
American (1933 -)	S	$550	$76,381	$231,000
FLAVIN, Dan & Sonja	P			$11,000
American (20th -)				
FLECK, Joseph	P	$5,500	$12,100	$18,700
American (1893 -)				
FLEGEL, George	P			$1.980M
German (16th - 17th)				
FLEMING, A.	P	$605	$788	$1,100
British (20th -)				
FLEMING, Hulan	P	$1,500	$3,750	$6,000
American (20th -)				
FLEMISH SCHOOL,	P			$7,150
Flemish (?)				
FLEMISH SCHOOL,	P			$1,320
Flemish (18th - 19th)				
FLEMISH SCHOOL 16C,	P	$1,650	$8,106	$17,600
Flemish (16th -)				
FLEMISH SCHOOL 17C,	D	$880	$4,510	$13,200
Flemish (17th -)	P	$1,100	$6,651	$33,000
FLEMISH SCHOOL 18C,	D			$2,640
Flemish (18th -)	P	$1,100	$5,518	$46,200
FLEMISH SCHOOL 19C,	P	$1,320	$2,057	$3,300
Flemish (19th -)				
FLESCH, Joanne	P			$650
American (20th -)				
FLETCHER, E.	P	$248	$537	$825
American (19th - 20th)				
FLETCHER, Edwin	P			$935
British (1857 - 1945)				
FLETTRICH, Leonard	P			$275
(?)				

D=Drawing, P=Painting, S=Sculpture, W=Watercolor

| | | Current Price Range | | |
		Low	Mean	High
FLEURANT, Louisane-Saint	*P*			$110
Haitian (20th -)				
FLEURY, Francois A. L.	*P*			$2,475
French (1804 - 1858)				
FLEURY, G.	*P*			$330
American (20th -)				
FLIEHER, Karl	*W*			$220
European (19th - 20th)				
FLINCK, Govaert	*P*	$23,100	$213,033	$407,000
Dutch (1615 - 1660)				
FLINCK, Govaert (Circle)	*P*			$9,020
Dutch (1615 - 1660)				
FLINCK, Govaert (Manner)	*P*			$30,250
Dutch (1615 - 1660)				
FLINT, Savile	*P*			$358
British (19th - 20th)				
FLINT, Sir William R.	*D*	$880	$7,002	$15,400
British (1880 - 1969)	*P*			$11,000
	W	$1,100	$28,949	$99,000
FLOCH, Joseph	*P*			$3,520
American (1895 -)				
FLOCKENHAUS, Heinz	*P*			$2,200
German (20th -)				
FLOOD, Daro	*S*	$770	$3,200	$13,200
American (20th -)				
FLORENTINE SCHOOL 14C,	*P*			$8,250
Italian (14th -)				
FLORENTINE SCHOOL 15C,	*P*	$6,050	$12,925	$19,800
Italian (15th -)				
FLORENTINE SCHOOL 16C,	*D*	$1,320	$1,998	$2,475
Italian (16th -)	*P*	$2,090	$3,933	$5,775
	W			$29,700
FLORENTINE SCHOOL 17C,	*D*	$1,100	$1,613	$2,200

D=Drawing, P=Painting, S=Sculpture, W=Watercolor

		Current Price Range		
		Low	Mean	High

		Low	Mean	High
FLORENTINE SCHOOL 17C, Italian (17th -)	*P*	$2,475	$3,713	$4,950
FLORENTINE SCHOOL 19C, Italian (19th -)	*P*			$1,980
FLORENTINE SCHOOL 20C, Italian (20th -)	*P*			$880
FLORES, Spanish (20th -)	*P*	$110	$385	$660
FLORES, Pedro V. Spanish (1897 -)	*P*			$2,090
FLORIAN, Walter American (1878 - 1909)	*P*	$440	$440	$440
FLORIS, Frans Flemish (1516 - 1570)	*P*	$33,000	$52,250	$71,500
FLORIS, Frans (Follower) Flemish (1516 - 1570)	*P*			$6,600
FLORSHEIM, Richard American (1916 -)	*P*			$275
FLORY, Arthur American (20th -)	*P*	$440	$729	$1,018
FLORY, Phoebe American (20th -)	*W*			$110
FLOYD, Harry American (20th -)	*P*			$220
FLUCKE, Harold American (20th -)	*P*			$275
FOERSTER, Herbert American (20th -)	*P*	$110	$257	$413
FOGARTY, Thomas American (1873 - 1938)	*D*	$248	$482	$715
FOGGINI, Giovanni B. (Circle) Italian (1652 - 1725)	*D*			$385
FOGILSON, American (20th -)	*W*			$165
FOGLER, Doris (20th -)	*P*			$605

D=Drawing, P=Painting, S=Sculpture, W=Watercolor

		Current Price Range		
		Low	Mean	High
FOLDES, (20th -)	*D*			$1,980
FOLEY, (?)	*P*			$825
FOLINSBEE, John F.	*D*			$220
American (1892 - 1972)	*P*	$2,090	$7,010	$14,300
FOLLETT, Foster	*P*			$1,430
American (1872 -)				
FOLTZ, J.G.	*W*			$121
American (1879 - 1961)				
FOLTZ, Philipp (Attrib.)	*P*			$4,950
German (1825 - 1877)				
FON, Jade	*W*			$413
American (1911 - 1983)				
FONECHE, A.	*P*			$4,400
French (20th -)				
FONSECA, Gonzalo	*S*			$47,300
Lat. Amer. (20th -)				
FONSELL,	*P*			$660
American (19th -)				
FONSSAGRIVES-PENN, Lisa	*S*			$8,250
(20th -)				
FONT, Constatin	*P*			$6,050
French (1890 -)				
FONTAINE, Thomas S. la	*P*	$6,600	$21,175	$35,750
British (1915 -)				
FONTAINEBLEAU, School	*D*			$7,700
French (16th -)	*P*			$1,540
FONTAINES, Andre des	*D*			$6,600
French (1869 -)				
FONTANA, Lavinia	*P*			$12,100
Italian (1525 - 1587)				
FONTANA, Lavinia (Circle)	*P*			$16,500
Italian (1525 - 1587)				

D=Drawing, P=Painting, S=Sculpture, W=Watercolor

		Current Price Range		
		Low	Mean	High

FONTANA, Lucio	*S*	$23,100	$29,700	$36,300
Italian (1899 - 1968)				
FONTANAROSA, Lucien	*P*			$1,320
French (1912 - 1975)				
FONTANESI, Francesco	*D*			$495
Italian (1751 - 1795)				
FONTAYNE, Rene	*P*			$220
French (19th - 20th)				
FONTENA, A.	*P*			$121
(?)				
FONTENAY, Andre	*P*			$4,950
French (1913 -)				
FONTYN, Pieter	*P*			$1,210
Dutch (1773 - 1839)				
FOORD, Fritz	*P*			$330
(20th -)				
FOOTE, Mary	*P*			$1,045
American (19th -)				
FOOTE, Will Howe	*P*	$440	$4,767	$9,900
American (1874 - 1965)				
FORABOSCO, Gerolamo	*P*			$6,600
Italian (1675 -)				
FORAIN, Jean-Louis	*D*	$248	$2,783	$7,150
French (1852 - 1931)	*P*	$4,950	$17,402	$44,000
	S			$1,100
	W			$1,100
FORAIN, Jean-Louis (Attrib.)	*P*			$825
French (1852 - 1931)				
FORBES, Charles	*P*	$248	$537	$880
American (1860 -)	*W*			$100
FORBES, Edwin	*D*	$935	$4,785	$12,100
American (1839 - 1895)	*P*	$3,300	$5,500	$7,700
	W	$770	$1,650	$3,300

D=Drawing, P=Painting, S=Sculpture, W=Watercolor

		Current Price Range		
		Low	Mean	High
FORBES, Leyton	*W*	$138	$972	$2,420
British (19th - 20th)				
FORBES, Stanhope	*P*	$2,200	$19,030	$63,250
British (1857 - 1947)				
FORBES, Stanhope (Attrib.)	*P*			$13,200
British (1857 - 1947)				
FORBES, Stanhope (Et al.)	*W*			$825
British (1857 - 1947)				
FORD, Dale	*P*			$2,860
American (20th -)				
FORD, Gordon O.	*P*			$13,200
(20th -)				
FORD, Henry C.	*P*			$7,700
American (1828 - 1894)	*W*			$1,540
FORD, James	*P*			$220
(20th -)				
FORD, Lauren	*P*			$30,800
American (1891 - 1973)				
FORD, William O.	*P*			$880
British (19th -)	*W*			$660
FOREAU, Louis H.	*P*			$880
French (1866 - 1910)				
FOREST, Lockwood de	*P*			$880
American (1850 - 1932)				
FOREST, Pierre	*P*	$935	$2,530	$4,125
French (1881 - 1971)				
FORESTER, Herbert	*P*	$143	$233	$358
American (20th -)				
FORETT, Pierre	*P*			$1,100
French (20th -)				
FORG, Gunther	*P*	$16,500	$32,267	$41,800
German (20th -)	*W*	$46,200	$60,500	$74,800
FORKNER, Edgar	*W*	$110	$163	$248
American (? - 1945)				

D=Drawing, P=Painting, S=Sculpture, W=Watercolor

		Current Price Range		
		Low	Mean	High

FORNAIROS, E.	*P*			$825
(19th -)				
FORNIK, F.	*S*			$440
(?)				
FORREST, Grace B. de	*P*			$4,290
American (1897 -)				
FORRESTER, Alfred H.	*D*			$1,045
British (1804 - 1872)				
FORSTER, B.	*P*			$578
American (19th -)				
FORSTER, G.	*P*			$2,420
(19th -)				
FORSTER, George	*P*	$3,520	$5,418	$7,700
American (19th -)				
FORSTER, John	*P*			$743
American (1925 -)				
FORSTER, W.	*W*			$578
(?)				
FORSYTH, William	*W*			$2,860
American (1854 - 1935)				
FORSYTHE, J. E.	*W*			$1,650
American (20th -)				
FORT, Curtis	*S*	$495	$536	$550
American (20th -)				
FORTE, Luca	*P*			$88,000
Italian (18th -)				
FORTE, Luca (Manner)	*P*			$35,200
Italian (18th -)				
FORTE, Luigi	*P*			$550
Italian (20th -)				
FORTE, Vicente	*P*			$4,620
Lat. Amer. (20th -)				
FORTESS, Karl	*P*			$330
American (1907 -)				
FORTI, Eduardo	*P*			$22,000
Italian (19th -)				

D=Drawing, P=Painting, S=Sculpture, W=Watercolor

| | | Current Price Range | | |
		Low	Mean	High
FORTI, Ettore	P	$14,300	$24,640	$49,500
Italian (19th -)				
FORTINI, A.	P			$770
Italian (20th -)				
FORTINY,	S			$1,210
(?)				
FORTIZ,	P			$110
(?)				
FORTUNE, E. Carlton	D	$880	$1,815	$2,750
American (1885 - 1969)	P	$3,575	$5,088	$6,600
FORTUNY Y CARBO, Mariano	D			$2,200
Spanish (1838 - 1874)	P			$1,760
	W			$14,300
FOSCHI, Francesco	P			$60,500
Italian (16th -)				
FOSCHI, Francesco (School)	P	$1,100	$1,485	$1,870
Italian (16th -)				
FOSS, Oliver	P			$385
(20th -)				
FOSSATI, Domenico	D			$3,025
Italian (1743 - 1784)				
FOSSE, Charles A. C. de la	P			$8,250
French (1829 -)				
FOSSE, Charles de la	P			$715
Italian (1636 - 1713)				
FOSSOUX, Claude	P	$1,210	$1,210	$1,210
French (20th -)				
FOSTER, Agnes	W	$110	$168	$275
American (19th - 20th)				
FOSTER, Alice	P			$468
American (19th -)				
FOSTER, Ben	P	$440	$1,862	$4,500
American (1852 - 1926)	W	$495	$523	$550

D=Drawing, P=Painting, S=Sculpture, W=Watercolor

		Current Price Range	
		Low	Mean	High

		Low	Mean	High
FOSTER, Ben (Attrib.)	*P*			$165
American (1852 - 1926)				
FOSTER, Charles	*P*	$303	$418	$550
American (1850 - 1931)				
FOSTER, J.B.	*W*			$121
American (20th -)				
FOSTER, James	*P*			$825
(?)				
FOSTER, Miles B.	*W*			$660
British (1825 - 1899)				
FOSTER, Will	*P*	$468	$976	$1,650
American (1882 - 1953)				
FOSTER, Willet	*P*			$385
American (1885 - 1940)				
FOUCQUIER, Jacques	*P*			$4,400
(? - 1659)				
FOUJITA, Tsuguharu	*D*	$2,200	$56,295	$286,000
Japanese (1886 - 1968)	*P*	$33,000	$781,948	$6.050M
	W	$27,500	$87,686	$154,000
FOULKE, B. F.	*P*			$110
(20th -)				
FOULKES, Lynn	*D*			$1,980
American (1935 -)	*S*	$990	$1,595	$2,200
FOULQUIER, Francois J.	*D*			$1,650
French (1744 - 1789)				
FOUNTAIN, Grace R.	*P*			$715
American (1857 - 1942)				
FOUNTAINBLEAU SCHOOL,	*P*			$3,520
French (?)				
FOURIE, Albert A.	*P*			$8,800
French (1854 -)				
FOURNIER, Alexis J.	*P*	$523	$1,843	$3,850
American (1865 - 1948)	*W*	$550	$642	$825

D=Drawing, P=Painting, S=Sculpture, W=Watercolor

| | | Current Price Range | | |
		Low	Mean	High
FOURNIER, Alfred	*W*			$275
French (1872 - 1924)				
FOURTANE, Loyola	*W*			$523
American (20th -)				
FOWLER, A. C.	*P*			$660
(20th -)				
FOWLER, Daniel	*W*	$193	$193	$193
Canadian (1810 - 1894)				
FOWLER, Dorothy	*S*	$2,100	$2,100	$2,100
American (20th -)				
FOWLER, E. L.	*W*	$160	$160	$160
(?)				
FOWLER, Frank	*P*	$2,860	$2,860	$2,860
American (1852 - 1910)				
FOWLER, Robert	*P*	$605	$2,878	$6,600
Scottish (1853 - 1926)				
FOWLER, Trevor T.	*P*	$3,025	$3,025	$3,025
American (19th -)				
FOWZER, J.	*P*	$550	$550	$550
American (19th - 20th)				
FOX,	*P*	$193	$193	$193
(?)				
FOX, Charles J.	*P*	$1,430	$1,430	$1,430
French (19th -)				
FOX, Dorothy	*W*	$350	$350	$350
(?)				
FOX, Ernest R.	*P*	$1,650	$1,650	$1,650
British (19th -)				
FOX, G. B.	*P*			$660
(20th -)				
FOX, G. B.	*P*	$633	$1,164	$1,430
British (19th -)				
FOX, Henry	*W*	$275	$358	$440
British (1860 -)				
FOX, J.	*P*			$550
(19th -)				

D=Drawing, P=Painting, S=Sculpture, W=Watercolor

		Current Price Range		
		Low	Mean	High

		Low	Mean	High
FOX, R. Atkinson	*P*	$220	$468	$715
American (1860 -)				
FOXHORN,	*W*			$110
British (19th -)				
FOY, Frances F.	*P*			$110
(1890 -)				
FRAGIACOMO, Pietro	*P*			$4,125
Italian (1856 - 1922)				
FRAGONARD, Alexandre E.	*P*			$33,000
French (1780 - 1850)				
FRAGONARD, Jean H.	*D*			$297,000
French (1732 - 1806)	*P*			$352,000
FRAGONARD, Jean H. (After)	*P*			$1,540
French (1732 - 1806)				
FRAGONARD, Jean H. (Attrib.)	*P*			$77,000
French (1732 - 1806)				
FRAGONARD, Jean H. (Circle)	*D*	$990	$55,495	$110,000
French (1732 - 1806)	*P*			$13,200
FRAGONARD, Jean H. (Manner)	*P*			$1,100
French (1732 - 1806)				
FRAGONARD, Jean H. (School)	*P*	$2,090	$9,295	$16,500
French (1732 - 1806)				
FRAHM, A.	*P*			$1,760
American (?)				
FRAILLE, Alfonso	*P*	$110	$303	$468
Spanish (20th -)				
FRAILLION, Paul	*P*			$1,430
French (19th - 20th)				
FRAMPTON, Edward R.	*P*			$12,100
British (1872 - 1923)				
FRANCA, Manuel de (Attrib.)	*P*			$413
American (19th -)				
FRANCE, Eurilda L.	*P*	$330	$3,960	$8,800
American (1865 - 1931)				

D=Drawing, P=Painting, S=Sculpture, W=Watercolor

| | | Current Price Range | | |
		Low	Mean	High
FRANCE, Jessie	*P*	$220	$296	$330
American (1862 -)	*W*	$138	$172	$193
FRANCES, Emilio Sala y	*P*			$4,400
Spanish (1850 - 1910)				
FRANCES, Esteban	*W*			$6,820
Spanish (1937 -)				
FRANCESCHINI, Marco Antonio	*P*			$1,540
Italian (1648 - 1729)				
FRANCESCHINI, Mariano de	*P*	$2,420	$4,510	$6,600
Italian (1849 - 1896)	*W*	$550	$1,100	$1,650
FRANCHEVILLE, Clemence	*P*			$2,420
French (1875 -)				
FRANCHI, Pietro	*S*			$5,060
Italian (19th -)				
FRANCHINI, Antonio	*P*	$1,760	$1,760	$1,760
Italian (19th -)	*S*			$121,000
FRANCHOYS, Peter	*P*			$6,600
Dutch (1606 - 1681)				
FRANCIA, Giacomo	*P*	$24,200	$36,850	$49,500
Italian (1486 - 1557)				
FRANCIA, Il	*P*			$407,000
Italian (1450 - 1517)				
FRANCIS, John F.	*P*	$3,740	$54,552	$264,000
American (1808 - 1886)	*W*			$330
FRANCIS, John J.	*W*	$220	$284	$413
American (1889 -)				
FRANCIS, Sam	*P*	$7,150	$197,466	$1.870M
American (1923 -)	*S*			$20,900
	W	$17,600	$162,250	$550,000
FRANCIS, Thomas E.	*P*			$1,650
British (1899 - 1912)				
FRANCISCI, Anthony de	*S*	$495	$4,198	$9,900
American (1887 - 1964)				

D=Drawing, P=Painting, S=Sculpture, W=Watercolor

		Current Price Range		
		Low	Mean	High

		Low	Mean	High
FRANCISCO, John B.	*P*	$990	$1,496	$2,090
American (1863 - 1931)	*W*	$825	$1,719	$2,613
FRANCKEN II, Frans	*P*	$4,400	$17,160	$38,500
Flemish (1581 - 1642)				
FRANCKEN II, Frans (Circle)	*P*			$2,200
Flemish (1581 - 1642)				
FRANCKEN II, Frans (Follower)	*P*			$4,675
Flemish (1581 - 1642)				
FRANCKEN II, Frans (Manner)	*P*			$3,850
Flemish (1581 - 1642)				
FRANCKEN III, Frans	*P*	$2,200	$6,967	$10,450
Flemish (1607 - 1667)				
FRANCO, Giacomo (Circle)	*D*			$660
Italian (1550 - 1620)				
FRANCO, Giovanni B. (Follower)	*P*			$8,800
Italian (1510 - 1580)				
FRANCO, Siron	*P*	$5,280	$6,893	$8,250
Brazilian (1947 -)				
FRANCOIS,	*P*			$4,675
French (19th -)				
FRANCOIS, Joseph C.	*P*			$2,640
Belgian (1851 - 1949)				
FRANCOIS, Pierre J. C.	*P*			$16,500
Belgian (1759 - 1851)				
FRANCUCCI, Innocenzo	*P*	$18,700	$19,250	$19,800
Italian (1494 - 1550)				
FRANDZEN, Eugene M.	*P*	$550	$1,063	$1,540
American (1893 -)	*W*	$303	$344	$385
FRANK, Gerald	*P*	$495	$1,630	$2,640
American (1889 -)				
FRANK, Josef	*P*			$1,100
European (19th -)				
FRANK, Mary	*S*	$220	$4,015	$7,150
(20th -)				

D=Drawing, P=Painting, S=Sculpture, W=Watercolor

| | | Current Price Range | | |
		Low	Mean	High
FRANK-WILL,	D			$7,700
French (1900 - 1951)	P	$3,740	$12,683	$24,200
	W	$1,210	$3,142	$5,500
FRANKE, Albert	P	$1,430	$3,826	$6,050
German (1860 - 1924)				
FRANKENSTEIN, Curt	P			$468
American (20th -)				
FRANKENSTEIN, Godfrey N.	P			$2,970
American (1820 - 1873)				
FRANKENSTEIN, Godfrey N. (Att)	P			$1,650
American (1820 - 1873)				
FRANKENTHAL SCHOOL,	P			$3,850
(17th -)				
FRANKENTHAL SCHOOL, 17C,	P			$4,950
(17th -)				
FRANKENTHALER, Helen	P	$9,350	$121,000	$715,000
American (1928 -)	W			$13,200
FRANKFORT, Edward	P			$1,650
Dutch (1864 - 1920)				
FRANKLIN, E. G.	P			$495
(?)				
FRANKLIN, John	P			$550
American (20th -)				
FRANQUE, Joseph (Attrib.)	P			$13,200
French (1774 - 1833)				
FRANQUELIN, Jean A.	P			$93,500
French (1798 - 1839)				
FRANQUINET, Eugene	P			$1,210
American (1865 - 1940)				
FRANZEN, August	P			$6,600
American (1863 - 1938)	W			$2,200
FRASCASSI, Cesare (Attrib.)	D			$1,100
Italian (1838 - 1868)				

D=Drawing, P=Painting, S=Sculpture, W=Watercolor

| | | Current Price Range | | |
		Low	Mean	High
FRASER, Alexander	P	$1,760	$3,355	$4,950
British (1786 - 1865)				
FRASER, Emma B.	D			$110
American (1881 -)				
FRASER, James E.	S	$358	$2,328	$9,900
American (1876 - 1953)				
FRASER, Malcolm	D	$220	$286	$352
American (1869 - 1949)	P	$110	$248	$385
FRASER, Thomas D.	P			$1,650
American (1885 - 1955)				
FRATIN, Christophe	S	$1,210	$3,654	$7,150
French (1800 - 1864)				
FRATIN, Christophe (After)	S			$1,320
French (1800 - 1864)				
FRAZAR, H. F.	W			$303
American (19th - 20th)				
FRAZIER, C. James	P	$4,400	$5,737	$7,480
American (1944 -)				
FRAZIER, Kenneth	P			$19,800
American (1867 - 1949)				
FREAS, Kelly	W			$193
American (?)				
FREDENTHAL, David	W			$3,080
(20th -)				
FREDERICI, T.	P			$1,100
(19th -)				
FREDERICK, Frank G.	P			$330
(19th - 20th)				
FREDERICK, George	P			$1,430
British (19th -)				
FREDERICKS, Ernest	P	$110	$306	$770
American (1877 -)				
FREDERICKS, Marshall	S			$990
(?)				
FREDI, Bartolo di	P			$121,000
(?)				

D=Drawing, P=Painting, S=Sculpture, W=Watercolor

		Current Price Range		
		Low	Mean	High
FREDOU, Jean-Martial	D			$4,950
French (? - 1795)				
FREEDLANDER, Arthur R.	D			$193
American (1875 - 1940)	P			$660
FREEDLY, Elizabeth	P			$155
American (?)				
FREELAND, David	W			$138
Scottish (20th -)				
FREEMAN, A.	P			$138
American (19th -)				
FREEMAN, Daniel W.	P			$880
(20th -)				
FREEMAN, Don	P	$2,200	$7,700	$13,200
American (1908 - 1978)				
FREER, Frederick	P	$9,350	$9,350	$9,350
American (1849 - 1908)	W	$825	$990	$1,155
FREEZOR, George A.	P	$1,045	$2,448	$3,850
British (19th -)				
FREILICHER, Jane	D			$1,045
American (20th -)				
FREMIET, Emmanuel	S	$528	$2,598	$11,000
French (1824 - 1910)				
FREMIET, Emmanuel (After)	S			$1,650
French (1824 - 1910)				
FREMINET, Martin	D			$82,500
French (1567 - 1619)				
FREMLIN, Gwen	W			$220
American (?)				
FRENCH, Daniel C.	S			$3,520
American (1850 -)				
FRENCH, Frank	P			$1,760
American (1850 - 1933)				
FRENCH SCHOOL,	P	$1,073	$2,232	$3,630
French (?)	S	$1,430	$2,127	$2,860

D=Drawing, P=Painting, S=Sculpture, W=Watercolor

		Current Price Range		
		Low	Mean	High

		Low	Mean	High
FRENCH SCHOOL,	*S*			$1,045
French (17th - 18th)				
FRENCH SCHOOL,	*D*			$1,788
French (18th - 19th)	*P*	$1,650	$2,241	$2,970
FRENCH SCHOOL,	*P*			$1,650
French (19th - 20th)				
FRENCH SCHOOL 16C,	*P*	$1,100	$24,750	$82,500
French (16th -)				
FRENCH SCHOOL 17C,	*D*	$1,925	$3,438	$4,950
French (17th -)	*P*	$1,210	$15,217	$99,000
FRENCH SCHOOL 18C,	*D*	$1,045	$4,150	$24,220
French (18th -)	*P*	$1,100	$7,194	$35,750
	W	$1,980	$5,033	$10,450
FRENCH SCHOOL 19C,	*D*	$1,430	$1,650	$1,870
French (19th -)	*P*	$440	$5,811	$57,750
	W			$1,265
FRENCH SCHOOL 20C,	*D*			$1,320
French (20th -)	*P*	$1,210	$7,887	$28,600
	W			$1,320
FRENZEL, Oscar	*P*			$2,750
German (1855 -)				
FRENZENY, P.	*P*			$275
American (19th -)				
FRERE, Charles T.	*P*	$1,760	$16,294	$82,500
French (1814 - 1888)				
FRERE, Pierre Edouard	*P*	$468	$9,689	$23,100
French (1819 - 1886)				
FRERE, Theodore	*P*			$3,520
French (20th -)				
FRERICHS, William C. A.	*P*	$880	$4,310	$10,450
American (1829 - 1905)				

D=Drawing, P=Painting, S=Sculpture, W=Watercolor

		Current Price Range		
		Low	Mean	High

		Low	Mean	High
FRERICHS, William C. A. (Att.)	P	$550	$1,595	$4,400
American (1829 - 1905)				
FRESNAYE, Roger de la	D	$1,320	$25,410	$49,500
French (1885 - 1925)	W	$24,750	$26,125	$27,500
FREUND, Harry L.	P			$990
American (1905 - 1979)				
FREWNHUPER, Thomas	S			$550
(?)				
FREY, Joseph	P	$605	$869	$1,210
American (1892 - 1977)				
FREY, Viola	S			$24,200
(20th -)				
FREY, Wilhelm	P			$1,320
German (1826 - 1911)				
FREYBERG, Conrad	P	$1,760	$6,930	$12,100
German (1842 -)				
FREYBERG, Edgar	P			$330
American (20th -)				
FREYE, William	P			$770
(1812 - 1872)				
FRICK, Paul de	P			$880
French (1864 - 1935)				
FRIEBERT, Joseph (Attrib.)	P			$3,450
American (20th -)				
FRIED, Pal	D	$550	$715	$880
Hungarian (1914 -)	P	$143	$1,186	$2,530
FRIED, Pal (Attrib.)	P	$685	$1,078	$1,350
Hungarian (1914 -)				
FRIEDEBERG, Pedro	S			$1,430
Mexican (1937 -)				
FRIEDENTHAL, David	W			$1,210
American (1914 - 1958)				
FRIEDLANDER, Friedrich	P	$2,200	$3,575	$4,950
Austrian (1825 - 1901)				

D=Drawing, P=Painting, S=Sculpture, W=Watercolor

		Current Price Range		
		Low	Mean	High

FRIEDLANDER, Maurice	*W*			$110
American (1899 -)				
FRIEDLINGER, J.	*P*			$1,650
European (19th -)				
FRIEDMAN, Arnold	*P*			$2,310
American (1879 - 1946)				
FRIEDRICH, H.	*P*			$275
(?)				
FRIEDRICH, M. G.	*P*	$165	$605	$1,430
American (20th -)				
FRIELICHER, Jane	*P*			$28,600
American (1924 -)				
FRIES, Charles A.	*P*	$385	$1,386	$3,300
American (1854 - 1940)				
FRIESE, Richard B. L.	*P*			$3,025
German (1854 -)				
FRIESEKE, Frederick C.	*D*			$2,970
American (1874 - 1939)	*P*	$33,000	$130,121	$440,000
	W			$6,050
FRIESZ, Emile Othon	*D*	$440	$752	$1,045
French (1879 - 1949)	*P*	$1,320	$69,792	$440,000
	W	$1,650	$1,980	$2,200
FRIGERIO, Raffaele	*P*	$187	$466	$825
Italian (19th - 20th)				
FRILL, A.	*S*			$990
(19th -)				
FRIND, August	*P*			$24,200
Austrian (1852 - 1924)				
FRINK, Elizabeth	*S*			$12,100
British (1930 -)				
FRIPP, Charles E.	*D*	$138	$303	$468
British (1854 - 1906)				
FRISCH,	*P*			$770
Dutch (19th -)				

D=Drawing, P=Painting, S=Sculpture, W=Watercolor

		Current Price Range		
		Low	Mean	High
FRISCH, J. C.	*P*	$550	$1,265	$1,980
German (19th -)				
FRISHMUTH, Harriet W.	*S*	$1,980	$22,237	$143,000
American (1880 - 1980)				
FRISHMUTH, Harriet W. (After)	*S*			$550
American (1880 - 1980)				
FRISON, Gustave	*W*			$204
(?)				
FRISTRUP, Niels	*P*			$13,750
Danish (1837 - 1909)				
FRITH, William P.	*P*	$715	$2,585	$4,400
British (1819 - 1909)				
FRITH, William P. (Attrib.)	*P*			$605
British (1819 - 1909)				
FRITZ, Charles	*P*	$1,500	$1,685	$1,870
American (20th -)				
FRITZ, E. M.	*P*			$175
(?)				
FRITZ, Henry E.	*P*			$550
American (1875 -)				
FRITZEL, Wilhelm	*P*			$4,400
German (1870 -)				
FROELICH, Paul	*P*			$385
American (1897 - 1968)				
FROMANTIOU, Hendrik de	*P*			$22,000
Dutch (1633 - 1694)				
FROMENTIN, Eugene	*D*			$1,760
French (1820 - 1876)	*P*	$700	$40,450	$99,000
FROMKES, Maurice	*P*			$2,200
American (1872 - 1931)				
FROMUTH, Charles H.	*D*			$770
American (1861 - 1937)				
FRONTIERO, Paul	*P*			$110
American (20th -)				
FROQIZ, Ettore R.	*W*			$468
Italian (19th -)				

D=Drawing,   P=Painting,   S=Sculpture,   W=Watercolor

		Current Price Range		
		Low	Mean	High

		Low	Mean	High
FROSCHL, Carl	*D*			$2,860
German (1848 -)				
FROST, Arthur B.	*D*	$330	$805	$1,650
American (1851 - 1928)	*P*			$3,850
	W	$1,045	$32,650	$85,250
FROST, Arthur B. (Attrib.)	*W*	$880	$1,210	$1,540
American (1851 - 1928)				
FROST, F.	*P*	$770	$853	$935
American (?)				
FROST, George A.	*P*	$413	$1,146	$1,980
American (1843 -)				
FROST, John	*D*	$660	$715	$770
American (1890 - 1937)	*P*	$1,210	$2,668	$4,125
FROST, John (Attrib.)	*P*			$1,045
American (1890 - 1937)				
FROST, William E.	*P*			$4,400
British (19th -)				
FROTHINGHAM, James (Attrib.)	*P*	$1,100	$1,210	$1,320
American (1786 - 1864)				
FRUGE, Nestor	*P*			$110
American (1914 -)				
FRY, Elizabeth	*P*			$330
American (20th -)				
FRY, John H.	*W*			$495
American (?)				
FRY, Mary L. F.	*W*			$303
American (1908 -)				
FRY, William	*P*			$880
British (19th - 20th)				
FRYER, C. W.	*P*			$209
(?)				
FUCHS, Bernie	*W*			$1,100
(1932 -)				
FUCHS, Brenda	*P*			$116
American (20th -)				

D=Drawing, P=Painting, S=Sculpture, W=Watercolor

		Current Price Range		
		Low	Mean	High

		Low	Mean	High
FUCHS, Emil	S			$935
American (1866 - 1929)				
FUCHS, Richard	P			$1,650
German (1852 -)				
FUECHSEL, Hermann	P	$1,650	$11,396	$40,700
American (1833 - 1915)				
FUENTE, Manuel	S	$17,600	$19,250	$20,900
Lat. Amer. (20th -)				
FUENTES, Giorgio	D	$1,430	$1,540	$1,650
Italian (1756 - 1821)				
FUERTES, Louis A.	D	$400	$805	$1,210
American (1874 - 1927)	P			$2,860
	W	$4,675	$11,917	$18,700
FUES, Christian	P			$2,200
German (1772 - 1836)				
FUGER, Friedrich H.	D			$1,210
German (1751 - 1818)	P			$22,000
FUHR, Ernest	D			$700
American (1874 - 1933)				
FUKUI, Ryonosuke	P			$2,310
Japanese (1922 -)				
FULCONIS, Victor L. P.	S			$1,045
French (1851 - 1913)				
FULLER, Alfred	P	$110	$605	$1,320
American (1899 -)				
FULLER, Arthur D.	P	$550	$880	$1,210
American (1889 - 1966)	W			$523
FULLER, George	P	$193	$1,210	$2,750
American (1822 - 1884)				
FULLER, Harvey K.	P			$193
American (20th -)				
FULLER, John	P			$220
(?)				

D=Drawing, P=Painting, S=Sculpture, W=Watercolor

		Current Price Range		
		Low	Mean	High

		Low	Mean	High
FULLER, Richard	*P*	$3,300	$5,225	$7,700
American (1822 - 1871)				
FULLEYLOVE, John	*W*			$660
British (1845 - 1908)				
FULLICK, E.	*P*			$220
American (20th -)				
FULLONTON, Robert	*P*			$303
American (1876 - 1933)				
FULOP, J.	*P*			$275
(?)				
FULOP, Koroly	*P*			$3,300
American (1893 - 1963)	*W*			$3,025
FULTON, Dorothy	*P*			$330
American (20th -)				
FULTON, Fitch	*P*			$1,210
American (20th -)				
FULTON, R.	*D*			$1,210
British (18th -)				
FUNKE, Anton	*P*			$1,980
Dutch (1869 - 1955)				
FUNKE, B.	*P*			$605
German (1902 -)				
FURINI, Francesco	*D*			$18,700
Italian (1604 - 1646)	*P*			$33,000
FURINI, Francesco (Attrib.)	*P*			$9,350
Italian (1604 - 1646)				
FURINI, Francesco (Circle)	*P*			$440
Italian (1604 - 1646)				
FURINI, Francesco (Follower)	*P*			$1,100
Italian (1604 - 1646)				
FURLONG, Charles	*P*	$330	$468	$605
American (1874 -)				
FURNER,	*D*			$110
(19th -)				

D=Drawing, P=Painting, S=Sculpture, W=Watercolor

		Current Price Range		
		Low	Mean	High
FURNIS, Harly	D			$275
British (19th -)				
FURSMAN, Frederick E.	P	$303	$1,802	$3,300
American (1874 - 1943)				
FURSMAN, Frederick E. (Attrib.)	P	$750	$900	$1,050
American (1874 - 1943)				
FURST, August	P	$1,100	$1,788	$2,475
Italian (19th - 20th)				
FUSSELL, Charles L.	P			$2,200
American (1840 - 1909)				
FYT, Jan	P			$60,500
Flemish (1611 - 1661)				
FYT, Jan (Attrib.)	P			$33,000
Flemish (1611 - 1661)				
FYT, Jan (Circle)	P			$8,800
Flemish (1611 - 1661)				
GAAL, Ferenc	P			$770
Hungarian (1891 -)				
GABALLI, A.	P	$138	$193	$248
(20th -)				
GABEL, Kurt	W	$350	$500	$650
American (20th -)				
GABINI,	P			$440
Italian (19th -)				
GABO, Naum	P			$473,000
American (1890 - 1977)				
GABRIEL, F.	P	$1,650	$2,805	$3,850
French (20th -)				
GABRIEL, H.	P			$265
(?)				
GABRIEL, J.	P			$880
Italian (19th -)				
GABRIEL, Paul J. C.	P	$1,760	$1,870	$1,980
Dutch (1828 - 1903)				
GABRIELLE, Rainer Y.	P			$2,090
Hungarian (20th -)				

D=Drawing, P=Painting, S=Sculpture, W=Watercolor

		Current Price Range		
------------------------------------	-	Low	Mean	High
GABRIELLE, Rainer Y. (Attrib.)	P			$1,100
Hungarian (20th -)	W			$150
GABRINI, Pietro	D			$880
Italian (1865 - 1926)	P	$4,620	$9,931	$17,600
	W	$605	$3,149	$7,150
GABRIOL,	P			$165
American (20th -)				
GADSBY, William H.	P			$4,675
British (1844 - 1924)				
GAEL, Barent	P	$7,150	$7,425	$7,700
Dutch (1635 - 1698)				
GAEL, Barent (Attrib.)	D			$1,320
Dutch (1635 - 1698)				
GAERTNER, Carl	P			$440
American (1898 - 1952)				
GAGE, George W.	P	$880	$1,265	$1,650
American (1887 -)				
GAGE, Robert M.	W			$385
American (1892 - 1953)				
GAGEN, Robert F.	W			$2,200
British (1847 - 1926)				
GAGILIARDINI, Julien G.	P			$4,950
French (1846 - 1927)				
GAGNI, P.	P	$303	$468	$660
French (20th -)				
GAGNON, Clarence A.	P			$96,250
Canadian (1882 - 1942)				
GAHMAN, Floyd	P			$715
American (1899 -)				
GAINES, Charles	D			$3,850
(20th -)				
GAINSBOROUGH, Thomas	D			$1,320
British (1727 - 1788)	P	$33,000	$104,500	$176,000

D=Drawing, P=Painting, S=Sculpture, W=Watercolor

		Current Price Range		
		Low	Mean	High

		Low	Mean	High
GAINSBOROUGH, Thomas (Aft) British (1727 - 1788)	P	$275	$578	$880
GAINSBOROUGH, Thomas (Cir) British (1727 - 1788)	P			$8,800
GAINSBOROUGH, Thomas (Foll) British (1727 - 1788)	P			$550
GAINSBOROUGH, Thomas (Sc) British (1727 - 1788)	P			$523
GAISELLE-TAKI, (?)	P			$138
GAISSER, Jacob E. German (1825 - 1899)	P	$2,475	$2,984	$3,850
GAISSER, Max German (1857 - 1922)	P			$3,400
GAISSER, Max (Attrib.) German (1857 - 1922)	P			$605
GAITTI, C. (?)	W			$358
GALE, D. American (19th -)	P			$1,540
GALE, George American (1893 - 1951)	W	$110	$127	$143
GALIEN-LALOUE, Eugene French (1854 - 1941)	D	$6,875	$12,616	$17,600
	P	$4,290	$7,847	$11,000
	W	$6,050	$12,430	$19,800
GALINDEZ, P. Spanish (19th -)	P			$1,430
GALL, Francois French (1912 - 1945)	D			$2,640
	P	$1,760	$5,865	$22,000
GALL, Francois (After) French (1912 - 1945)	P			$165
GALL, Theodore (?)	S			$990
GALLAGHER, Michael (20th -)	P	$2,200	$2,888	$3,575

D=Drawing, P=Painting, S=Sculpture, W=Watercolor

		Current Price Range		
		Low	Mean	High

		Low	Mean	High
GALLAGHER, Sears	*P*			$770
American (1869 - 1955)	*W*	$550	$1,045	$1,540
GALLAGHER, Sherry	*D*			$1,300
American (20th -)	*W*	$1,650	$1,725	$1,800
GALLARD, Michel de	*P*			$3,300
French (20th -)				
GALLATIN, Albert E.	*P*	$880	$8,690	$16,500
American (1882 - 1952)				
GALLEGOS Y ARNOSA, Jose	*P*	$46,200	$56,100	$66,000
Spanish (1859 - 1902)				
GALLET, J.	*P*			$715
(?)				
GALLI, Giuseppe	*P*			$11,000
Italian (1866 - 1953)				
GALLIA, V.	*P*	$660	$743	$825
European (19th - 20th)				
GALLIARI, Bernardino	*D*			$3,850
Italian (1707 - 1794)				
GALLIARI, Giovanni	*D*			$1,650
Italian (1709 - 1790)	*W*	$1,540	$1,540	$1,540
GALLIARI, Giovanni (Attrib.)	*D*	$1,100	$2,200	$3,300
Italian (1709 - 1790)	*W*	$990	$1,045	$1,100
GALLISON, Henry H.	*P*	$440	$743	$1,045
American (1850 - 1910)				
GALLO, Bill	*P*			$550
American (20th -)				
GALLO, Frank	*P*			$7,150
American (1933 -)	*S*	$880	$2,860	$5,500
GALLO, Guiseppe	*P*			$6,325
Italian (20th -)				
GALLO, Vincent	*P*	$2,200	$5,775	$9,900
(20th -)				

D=Drawing, P=Painting, S=Sculpture, W=Watercolor

		Current Price Range		
		Low	Mean	High
GALLON, Robert	*P*	$2,750	$4,879	$7,700
British (1845 - 1925)				
GALLUP & CO., C. H.	*P*			$660
(?)				
GALOFRE Y GIMENEZ, Bald.	*P*			$8,250
Spanish (1849 - 1902)				
GALVAN, Jesus G.	*D*			$2,475
Lat. Amer. (20th -)	*P*	$9,900	$35,750	$71,500
GALVANO,	*S*			$475
(20th -)				
GAMANN, R.	*P*	$193	$207	$220
European (?)				
GAMARRA, Jose	*P*			$17,600
Lat. Amer. (20th -)				
GAMBARA, Lattanzio (Attrib.)	*D*			$880
Italian (1530 - 1574)				
GAMBARINI, Giuseppe	*P*			$5,280
Italian (1680 - 1725)				
GAMBARTES, Leonidas	*S*			$9,350
Lat. Amer. (20th -)				
GAMBLE, John M.	*P*	$1,430	$6,777	$19,800
American (1863 - 1934)				
GAMBLE, Roy C.	*D*	$165	$165	$165
American (1887 -)	*P*	$110	$464	$1,210
	W	$275	$289	$303
GAMBOGI & POCHINI, G. & G.	*S*			$523
European (19th - 20th)				
GAMMELL, Robert H.	*P*	$880	$5,940	$11,000
American (1893 - 1981)				
GAMMERITH, F. L.	*P*			$1,045
German (19th -)				
GAMMIER, J.	*P*			$660
American (20th -)				
GAMPENRIEDER, Karl	*P*			$29,700
German (1860 -)				

D=Drawing, P=Painting, S=Sculpture, W=Watercolor

		Current Price Range		
		Low	Mean	High

		Low	Mean	High
GAMPERT, O. French (19th -)	P			$440
GANDELL, Victor American (1903 - 1977)	P			$385
GANDOLFI, Gaetano Italian (1734 - 1802)	D P	$45,100	$47,300	$3,850 $49,500
GANDOLFI, Gaetano (Manner) Italian (1734 - 1802)	D			$550
GANDOLFI, Mauro Italian (1764 - 1834)	D	$4,620	$7,040	$9,350
GANDOLFI, Ubaldo Italian (1728 - 1781)	D			$15,400
GANNAN, John American (1907 - 1965)	P W			$1,430 $3,960
GANNE, Pierre C. French (20th -)	P			$1,210
GANNE, Yves (20th -)	P W	$209	$473	$880 $715
GANS, E. D. Dutch (1832 - 1874)	P			$1,870
GANSO, Emil American (1895 - 1941)	D P W	$440 $330 $330	$880 $1,482 $963	$1,320 $4,180 $1,760
GANTNER, Bernard French (1930 -)	D			$880
GANZ, Edwin Swiss (1871 -)	P			$4,400
GARABEDIAN, Charles American (1923 -)	P	$2,200	$6,600	$11,000
GARAY Y AREVALO, Manuel Spanish (19th -)	P			$22,000
GARBER, Daniel	D	$230	$2,920	$5,610

D=Drawing, P=Painting, S=Sculpture, W=Watercolor

		Current Price Range		
		Low	Mean	High
GARBER, Daniel	P	$1,980	$34,534	$154,000
American (1880 - 1958)	W			$1,500
GARBO, Raffaellino	P			$47,300
Italian (1476 - 1524)				
GARBO, Raffaellino (Attrib)	P			$68,200
Italian (1476 - 1524)				
GARCIA, D.	D			$1,595
(?)				
GARCIA, Joaquin T.	P	$37,400	$166,972	$550,000
Lat. Amer. (20th -)				
GARCIA, Juan	P			$9,350
Spanish (19th -)				
GARCIA DE MIRANDA, Juan	P			$3,025
Spanish (1677 - 1749)				
GARCIA Y MENCIA, Antonio	W			$6,050
Spanish (19th -)				
GARCIA Y RAMOS, Jose	P	$19,800	$24,200	$28,600
Spanish (1852 - 1912)				
GARCIA Y RODRIGUEZ, Manuel	P	$3,410	$15,046	$33,000
Spanish (1863 - 1925)				
GARDANNE, August	P			$1,925
French (19th -)				
GARDELLI,	P			$605
Italian (20th -)				
GARDET, Georges	S	$880	$1,870	$2,860
French (1863 - 1939)				
GARDEUR,	P			$330
European (?)				
GARDINIER, A. V.	P			$660
European (19th -)				
GARDNER, David (Attrib.)	D	$275	$330	$385
British (19th -)				
GARDNER, Derek	P			$3,300
American (20th -)				
GARDNER, E. B.	P			$110
(?)				

D=Drawing, P=Painting, S=Sculpture, W=Watercolor

		Current Price Range	
	Low	Mean	High

		Low	Mean	High
GARDNER, Sidney V. British (19th - 20th)	P			$605
GARET, Jedd American (20th -)	D P	$385 $110	$1,018 $3,960	$1,650 $19,800
GARIBALDI, Joseph French (1863 -)	P			$6,050
GARINEI, M. (?)	P			$1,045
GARINNI, Michele (20th -)	P			$165
GARLAND, Henry British (19th -)	P			$4,125
GARMAN, Michael American (20th -)	S			$275
GARNER, E. M. European (20th -)	P	$880	$1,045	$1,210
GARNERAY, Jean F. (Attrib.) French (1755 - 1837)	P			$1,650
GARNIER, Jules A. French (1847 - 1889)	P	$5,775	$12,788	$19,800
GARO, John American (20th -)	P			$248
GAROSSA, Heinrich Swiss (1902 -)	P			$660
GARRETA, Raimundo Spanish (1841 - 1920)	P			$132,000
GARRETT, David E. (?)	P			$550
GARRETT, Edmund H. American (1853 - 1929)	W	$385	$427	$468
GARRETTO, Paolo (1903 -)	W			$500
GARRI, Giorgio (Attrib.) Italian (? - 1731)	P			$24,200
GARRIDO, Eduardo L. Italian (1856 - 1949)	P	$2,750	$21,267	$46,750

D=Drawing, P=Painting, S=Sculpture, W=Watercolor

		Current Price Range		
		Low	Mean	High

GARSIDE, Thomas H. Canadian (1906 -)	*D*			$1,370
GARSTON, Gerald (?)	*P*			$2,200
GARTH, John American (1889 - 1971)	*P*	$220	$715	$1,210
GARVARNI, Sulpice G. C. French (1804 - 1866)	*W*			$2,750
GARY, Fred American (?)	*P*			$165
GARZI, Luigi (Attrib.) Italian (1638 - 1721)	*D*			$1,650
GASCARD, Henri French (1635 - 1701)	*P*			$5,500
GASKILL, Thomas F. American (1925 -)	*W*			$154
GASPAR, Miklos (Attrib.) American (1885 - 1946)	*W*			$150
GASPARD, Leon American (1882 - 1964)	*P*	$1,760	$30,103	$275,000
GASPARI, Antonio Italian (1793 -)	*P*			$29,700
GASPARO, Oronzo American (1903 -)	*P*			$715
GASSER, Henry M. American (1909 - 1981)	*P*	$385	$1,516	$3,575
	W	$165	$1,077	$3,960
GASTAVSON, Lealand R. American (1899 - 1966)	*P*			$1,320
GATCH, Lee American (1902 - 1968)	*P*	$880	$3,520	$6,600
	S	$1,980	$3,685	$6,050
GAUCHET, C. French (19th -)	*W*			$330
GAUDEFROY, Alphonse French (1845 - 1936)	*P*			$2,860

D=Drawing, P=Painting, S=Sculpture, W=Watercolor

		Current Price Range	
	Low	Mean	High

		Low	Mean	High
GAUDETT, Raymond	*P*			$550
French (20th -)				
GAUDEZ, Adrien E.	*S*	$880	$1,467	$2,200
French (1845 - 1902)				
GAUDEZ-CHENNEVIERE, Cecile	*W*			$1,980
French (1851 -)				
GAUERMANN, Friedrich	*P*	$14,300	$161,150	$308,000
Austrian (1807 - 1862)				
GAUFFIER, Louis	*P*			$52,250
French (1761 - 1801)				
GAUGENIGL, Ignatz M.	*P*			$2,970
German (1855 - 1932)				
GAUGENIGL, Ignatz M. (Attrib.)	*P*			$3,520
German (1855 - 1932)				
GAUGUIN, Paul	*D*	$18,700	$35,567	$44,000
French (1848 - 1903)	*P*	$77,000	$4.854M	$24.200M
	S	$2,200	$236,107	$1.485M
	W			$77,000
GAUL, Arrah L.	*P*	$275	$289	$303
American (1888 - 1980)				
GAUL, Gilbert	*P*	$880	$4,148	$9,900
American (1855 - 1919)	*W*			$2,200
GAUL, Gustave	*P*			$1,210
Austrian (1836 - 1888)				
GAULEY, Robert D.	*P*	$330	$660	$990
American (1875 -)	*W*			$121
GAULLI, Giovanni B. (Attrib.)	*D*			$7,700
Italian (1639 - 1709)				
GAUME, Henri R.	*P*			$5,720
French (1834 -)				
GAUSS, Eugen	*S*	$660	$1,063	$1,650
American (19th -)				
GAUSSEN, Adolphe	*P*			$770
French (1871 -)				

D=Drawing, P=Painting, S=Sculpture, W=Watercolor

		Current Price Range		
		Low	Mean	High
GAVAGNIN, Giuseppe	P			$7,700
Italian (19th -)				
GAVANI, A.	W			$116
European (20th -)				
GAVARNI, Paul	D			$3,300
French (1804 - 1866)	W			$2,640
GAY, Edward	D			$330
American (1837 - 1928)	P	$550	$2,665	$18,700
GAY, George H.	P	$495	$1,289	$2,420
American (1858 - 1931)	W	$193	$670	$2,750
GAY, Walter	P	$385	$6,421	$22,000
American (1856 - 1937)	W	$2,200	$2,585	$2,860
GAY, Walter (Attrib.)	W			$1,100
American (1856 - 1937)				
GAY, Winckworth	D	$110	$138	$165
American (1821 - 1910)	P	$798	$2,209	$3,080
GAYDISH, Rosamona C.	P			$110
American (20th -)				
GAYRARD, Paul	S			$2,420
French (1807 - 1855)				
GAZE, Harold	W			$1,100
American (20th -)				
GEARHART, Frances	W	$330	$413	$495
American (1869 - 1958)				
GEBELEIN, H.	W			$110
American (20th -)				
GEBLER, Friedrich O.	P			$22,000
German (1838 - 1917)				
GECHTER, Thomas	S	$770	$935	$1,100
(19th -)				
GECHTOFF, Leonid	D	$176	$213	$231
American (19th - 20th)	P	$165	$718	$2,200

D=Drawing, P=Painting, S=Sculpture, W=Watercolor

		Current Price Range		
		Low	Mean	High

		Low	Mean	High
GEDDES, Andrew (Attrib.)	P			$5,500
British (1783 - 1844)				
GEDDES, Ewan	W			$275
Scottish (? - 1935)				
GEDLEK, Ludwig	P	$3,300	$6,188	$7,150
Austrian (1847 -)				
GEER, Mary J.	P			$1,540
(1816 - 1893)				
GEEST, Juliaen F. de	P			$5,500
Flemish (? - 1699)				
GEEST, Wybrand-S. de (Attrib.)	P			$8,800
Dutch (1592 - 1659)				
GEETS, Willem	P			$13,200
Belgian (1838 -)				
GEGOUX, J.	P			$880
(19th -)				
GEHRIG, Jacob	P	$468	$784	$1,100
German (1846 - 1922)				
GEHRING, Louis H.	P	$138	$152	$165
American (1900 -)				
GEHRY, Frank	S			$53,900
(20th -)				
GEIBEL, Casimir	P	$1,210	$2,943	$4,675
German (1839 - 1896)				
GEIBERICH, Oscar	P			$523
American (20th -)				
GEIGER, Richard	P	$935	$1,884	$3,080
Austrian (1870 - 1945)				
GEILLEN, V. H. H.	P			$165
Swiss (19th -)				
GEIS, Joseph W.	P	$165	$179	$193
(1860 - 1935)				
GEISSMAN, Robert	P			$440
American (1909 - 1976)				
GELDER, Aert de	P	$6,600	$17,600	$28,600
Dutch (1645 - 1727)				

D=Drawing, P=Painting, S=Sculpture, W=Watercolor

		Current Price Range		
		Low	Mean	High
GELDER, Lucia M. von	P			$2,420
German (1865 - 1899)				
GELERDTS, Flore	P			$7,700
Belgian (19th - 20th)				
GELHAY, Edouard	P	$1,540	$5,445	$9,350
French (1856 -)				
GELIBERT, Gaston	P			$13,200
French (1850 -)				
GELIBERT, Jules B.	S			$550
French (1834 -)				
GELMUYDEN, R. E.	W			$2,200
Dutch (19th - 20th)				
GEMITO, Vincenzo	S			$9,900
Italian (1852 - 1929)				
GEMPT, Bernard de	P			$8,250
Dutch (1826 - 1879)				
GEN-PAUL,	D	$770	$1,749	$4,180
French (1895 - 1975)	P	$6,050	$15,900	$37,400
	W	$462	$2,820	$5,500
GENDROT, Felix A.	P			$2,200
American (1866 -)				
GENGE, C.	P			$1,760
(19th -)				
GENIN, Lucien	P			$5,500
French (1894 - 1954)	W	$440	$2,503	$6,050
GENIS, Rene	P	$3,300	$3,836	$4,125
French (20th -)				
GENISSON, Jules V.	P			$6,050
Belgian (1805 - 1860)				
GENNARI, ELDER, Benedetto	P	$74,250	$92,125	$110,000
Italian (1570 - 1610)				
GENNARI, YOUNGER, Benedetto	P			$35,200
Italian (1633 - 1715)				
GENOELS, Abraham	D			$2,860
Flemish (1640 - 1723)				

D=Drawing, P=Painting, S=Sculpture, W=Watercolor

		Current Price Range		
		Low	Mean	High
GENOESE SCHOOL 17C,	*D*			$3,300
Italian (17th -)	*P*	$11,000	$11,550	$12,100
GENOESE SCHOOL 18C,	*D*			$1,540
Italian (18th -)				
GENOVES, Juan	*P*	$3,080	$4,840	$6,600
Spanish (1930 -)				
GENTH, Lillian	*P*	$248	$2,594	$9,350
American (1876 - 1953)				
GENTH, Lillian (Attrib.)	*P*			$374
American (1876 - 1953)				
GENTILINI, Franco	*P*			$2,860
Italian (1909 -)				
GENTRY, Michael P.	*P*			$5,000
American (20th -)				
GENZMER, Berthold	*P*			$1,760
German (1858 -)				
GEORGE, Vesper L.	*P*	$303	$3,727	$7,150
American (1865 - 1934)	*W*			$550
GEORGET, C. B.	*P*			$2,310
French (19th -)				
GEORGI, Edwin A.	*W*	$385	$817	$1,540
American (1896 - 1964)				
GEORGI, Otto F.	*P*			$31,900
German (1819 - 1874)				
GERARD, B. (After David)	*P*			$2,200
(?)				
GERARD, Fernand M. E. L.	*D*			$660
French (1856 - 1924)				
GERARD, Francois (After)	*P*			$27,500
French (1760 - 1843)				
GERARD, Lydie	*P*			$275
French (20th -)				
GERARD, Rolf	*P*			$6,325
(?)				

D=Drawing, P=Painting, S=Sculpture, W=Watercolor

		Current Price Range		
		Low	Mean	High
GERARD, Theodore	P	$7,700	$14,520	$33,000
Belgian (1829 - 1895)				
GERGELY, Porge	P			$440
Czechoslovakian (19th - 20th)				
GERHARD, George	P			$330
German (1830 - 1902)				
GERHARDT, C.	P			$358
(?)				
GERHOLD, J.	P			$550
Dutch (19th - 20th)				
GERICAULT, Theodore	D	$11,000	$29,333	$44,000
French (1791 - 1824)	P			$2.420M
GERICAULT, Theodore (Manner)	P			$2,750
French (1791 - 1824)				
GERICAULT, Theodore (School)	P			$1,870
French (1791 - 1824)				
GERMAIN, Jacques	P	$3,080	$6,893	$9,350
French (20th -)				
GERMAIN, Thomas (Attrib.)	D			$1,540
(1763 -)				
GERMAN SCHOOL,	P	$1,045	$11,523	$22,000
German (?)				
GERMAN SCHOOL,	P			$9,900
German (15th - 16th)				
GERMAN SCHOOL,	P			$1,100
German (18th - 19th)				
GERMAN SCHOOL,	P	$1,100	$1,758	$2,475
German (19th - 20th)				
GERMAN SCHOOL 16C,	P	$1,925	$15,046	$33,000
German (16th -)				
GERMAN SCHOOL 17C,	D			$1,210
German (17th -)	P	$2,860	$4,356	$7,150
	W			$4,400
GERMAN SCHOOL 18C,	D	$1,100	$1,320	$1,540

D=Drawing, P=Painting, S=Sculpture, W=Watercolor

		Current Price Range		
		Low	Mean	High

		Low	Mean	High
GERMAN SCHOOL 18C,	*P*	$1,100	$4,360	$17,600
German (18th -)				
GERMAN SCHOOL 19C,	*P*	$825	$2,134	$4,400
German (19th -)				
GERMAN SCHOOL 20C,	*P*	$1,100	$1,650	$2,200
German (20th -)				
GERNAND, M.	*P*			$154
American (20th -)				
GEROME, Francois	*P*	$1,650	$1,980	$2,310
French (20th -)				
GEROME, Jean-Leon	*D*	$550	$2,723	$7,700
French (1824 - 1904)	*P*	$7,150	$373,321	$2.200M
	S	$4,400	$87,725	$440,000
GEROME, Jean-Leon (After)	*P*			$990
French (1824 - 1904)				
GEROME, Jean-Leon (Circle)	*P*			$17,600
French (1824 - 1904)				
GEROME, Jean-Leon (Studio)	*P*			$12,650
French (1824 - 1904)				
GERRY, Samuel L.	*D*			$660
American (1813 - 1891)	*P*	$440	$2,493	$9,350
GERSZO, Gunther	*P*	$3,300	$21,126	$56,100
Mexican (1915 -)	*S*	$6,050	$13,017	$20,900
GERVAIS, Paul J.	*P*			$26,400
French (1859 - 1936)				
GERVEX, Henri	*P*			$3,960
French (1852 - 1929)				
GESNE, Jean V. A. de	*P*			$3,300
French (1834 - 1903)				
GESSI, Francesco (Attrib.)	*P*			$4,400
Italian (1588 - 1649)				
GESSI, Francesco (School)	*P*			$1,430
Italian (1588 - 1649)				

D=Drawing, P=Painting, S=Sculpture, W=Watercolor

		Current Price Range		
		Low	Mean	High
GESSNITZER, Joseph	P			$1,760
Austrian (19th -)				
GESSNITZER, T. C.	P			$2,860
German (19th -)				
GETZ, Don	W			$187
American (20th -)				
GEUILL, M. A.	P			$440
(?)				
GEURIN, Joseph	W			$468
(?)				
GEZA, Peske	P			$1,320
(?)				
GHEERAERTS, YOUNGER, Mar.	P			$4,400
Flemish (1561 - 1635)				
GHEYN, Jacob de (Follower)	D			$2,090
Dutch (1530 - 1582)				
GHEYN, Jacques de (Circle)	D			$6,600
Dutch (1565 - 1629)				
GHIGLION-GREEN, Maurice	P			$1,045
(?)				
GHIKAS, Panos	P			$2,860
(20th -)				
GHIRLANDAIO, Domenico (Mann)	P			$6,050
Italian (1449 - 1494)				
GHIRLANDAIO, Ridolfo	P			$19,800
Italian (1483 - 1561)				
GHISLANDI, Vittore (Attrib.)	P			$7,700
Italian (1655 - 1743)				
GHISOLFI, Giovanni	P			$27,500
Italian (1632 - 1683)				
GHISOLFI, Giovanni (Circle)	P			$3,300
Italian (1632 - 1683)				
GHISOLFI, Giovanni (Follower)	P			$9,900
Italian (1632 - 1683)				
GHISOLFI, Giovanni (Manner)	P			$1,045
Italian (1632 - 1683)				

D=Drawing, P=Painting, S=Sculpture, W=Watercolor

		Current Price Range		
		Low	Mean	High
GHISOLFI, Giovanni (School)	P			$8,250
Italian (1632 - 1683)				
GHIZE, Eleanor de	P			$1,320
American (1896 -)				
GIACOMETTI, Alberto	D	$1,705	$33,647	$68,750
Swiss (1901 - 1966)	P	$605,000	$1.608M	$3.190M
	S	$11,000	$801,972	$4.950M
GIACOMETTI, Alberto & Diego	S	$14,300	$20,167	$26,400
Swiss (20th -)				
GIACOMETTI, Diego	S	$605	$70,457	$462,000
Swiss (1902 -)				
GIACOMOTTI, Felix H.	D			$880
French (1828 - 1909)				
GIACOMUCCI, C.	P			$385
Italian (19th -)				
GIALLI,	P			$1,540
(?)				
GIALLINO, Angelos	W	$605	$4,968	$7,700
Greek (1857 -)				
GIAMMARCO, Camillo	P			$275
Italian (19th - 20th)				
GIAMPETRINO,	P			$13,200
Italian (16th -)				
GIAMPETRINO, (Attributed)	P			$2,750
Italian (16th -)				
GIANI, Felice	P			$605
Italian (1760 - 1823)				
GIANI, Felice (Attrib.)	P			$39,600
Italian (1760 - 1823)				
GIANI, Felice (Circle)	D			$770
Italian (1760 - 1823)				
GIANI, Felice (School)	P			$5,500
Italian (1760 - 1823)				
GIANNI, Gian	P			$11,000

D=Drawing, P=Painting, S=Sculpture, W=Watercolor

		Current Price Range		
		Low	Mean	High
GIANNI, Gian	*W*	$110	$483	$1,216
Italian (19th -)				
GIANNI, H.	*W*			$825
Italian (19th -)				
GIANNI, M.	*W*	$275	$358	$440
Italian (19th -)				
GIANNI, U.	*P*			$110
Italian (19th - 20th)	*W*			$138
GIAQUINTO, Corrado	*P*	$38,500	$188,833	$275,000
Italian (1690 - 1765)				
GIAQUINTO, Corrado (Circle)	*P*			$12,100
Italian (1690 - 1765)				
GIARDIELLO, Giovanni	*P*	$1,540	$1,760	$1,980
Italian (19th - 20th)				
GIARDIELLO, Giuseppe	*P*			$3,850
Italian (19th -)				
GIARDIELLO, J.	*P*			$7,150
Italian (19th - 20th)				
GIBBA, E. V.	*D*			$138
American (?)				
GIBBON, J.	*P*			$468
(?)				
GIBBONS, Arthur	*S*	$3,025	$5,294	$6,600
(20th -)				
GIBBONS, Michael	*P*			$1,400
American (20th -)				
GIBBS, George	*D*			$3,575
American (1870 - 1942)				
GIBBS, J.	*P*			$1,320
American (19th - 20th)				
GIBBS, William W.	*P*			$220
(?)				
GIBERT, Jean A.	*P*			$440
French (1869 -)				
GIBORY, A.	*P*			$1,650
(?)				

D=Drawing, P=Painting, S=Sculpture, W=Watercolor

		Current Price Range	
		Low	Mean	High
---	---	---	---	---

GIBRAN, Kahil	S			$1,870
American (20th -)				
GIBSON, Charles D.	D	$110	$2,709	$8,000
American (1867 - 1944)				
GIBSON, Charles D. (Circle)	D			$193
American (1867 - 1944)				
GIBSON, George	W			$1,760
American (1904 -)				
GIBSON, John	S			$242,000
British (1790 - 1866)				
GIBSON, Thomas	P			$11,000
British (1680 - 1751)				
GIBSON, William Alfred	P			$4,400
British (1850 - 1896)	W			$193
GIDE, Francois	P			$2,750
French (1822 - 1890)				
GIEBERICH, Oscar H.	P			$385
American (1886 -)				
GIES, Joseph W.	P	$303	$724	$1,320
American (1860 - 1935)				
GIESS, W.	P			$495
(?)				
GIFFINGER, R.	P			$4,125
(19th -)				
GIFFORD, Charles H.	P	$330	$6,481	$19,800
American (1839 - 1904)	W	$1,650	$2,145	$3,025
GIFFORD, James	P			$6,050
British (19th -)				
GIFFORD, John	P			$6,600
British (19th -)				
GIFFORD, R. Swain	D			$220
American (1840 - 1905)	P	$2,420	$2,860	$3,300
	W	$330	$568	$825

D=Drawing, P=Painting, S=Sculpture, W=Watercolor

		Current Price Range		
		Low	Mean	High

		Low	Mean	High
GIFFORD, Sanford R.	*D*			$550
American (1823 - 1880)	*P*	$2,420	$41,934	$154,000
	W			$2,310
GIFFORD, Sanford R. (Attrib.)	*P*			$605
American (1823 - 1880)				
GIGNOUX, Regis F.	*P*	$660	$11,234	$34,100
American (1816 - 1882)				
GIGUERE, George	*P*			$550
American (?)				
GIHON, Clarence M.	*P*	$1,100	$2,063	$3,300
American (1871 - 1929)				
GIHOOLY, David	*S*	$1,210	$3,245	$5,280
(20th -)				
GILBERT,	*P*	$468	$624	$935
French (20th -)				
GILBERT, Arthur	*P*	$660	$688	$715
British (1819 - 1895)				
GILBERT, Arthur H.	*P*	$880	$3,614	$18,700
American (1894 - 1970)				
GILBERT, C. Ivar	*P*	$303	$1,142	$1,980
American (20th -)	*W*	$165	$248	$385
GILBERT, Minnie J. (Attrib.)	*P*			$143
(?)	*W*			$121
GILBERT, Octave	*W*			$1,045
French (19th - 20th)				
GILBERT, Sir John	*W*			$770
British (1817 - 1897)				
GILBERT, Terence J.	*P*			$4,400
British (20th -)				
GILBERT, Victor	*P*	$3,300	$9,900	$14,300
French (1847 - 1933)	*W*			$3,300
GILBERT & GEORGE,	*D*	$52,250	$70,583	$104,500

D=Drawing, P=Painting, S=Sculpture, W=Watercolor

		Current Price Range		
		Low	Mean	High

GILBERT & GEORGE,	*P*	$165,000	$181,500	$198,000
British (20th -)	*S*	$35,750	$39,875	$44,000
GILBERT-ROLFE, Jeremy	*W*			$1,760
(20th -)				
GILCHRIST, Philip T.	*P*	$990	$2,145	$3,300
British (1865 - 1956)				
GILCHRIST, JR., William W.	*D*			$413
American (1879 - 1926)	*P*	$248	$12,183	$28,600
	W			$990
GILDER, Robert F.	*P*			$385
American (1856 - 1940)				
GILE, Selden C.	*P*	$770	$2,895	$6,050
American (1877 - 1947)	*W*			$1,320
GILE, Selden C. (Attrib.)	*P*			$3,190
American (1877 - 1947)				
GILES, Evelyn	*D*			$385
American (20th -)				
GILES, Howard	*W*	$110	$138	$165
American (1876 - 1955)				
GILES, J.	*P*			$1,210
British (19th -)				
GILHOOLY, David	*P*			$6,600
American (20th -)	*S*	$550	$2,283	$6,600
GILIOLI, Emile	*S*	$1,650	$5,286	$11,000
French (1911 -)				
GILL, Edmund	*P*			$550
British (1820 - 1894)	*W*			$330
GILL, Frederick	*P*			$110
American (20th -)				
GILL, William	*P*			$3,520
British (19th -)				
GILLEMANS, Jan P. (Et al.)	*P*			$28,600
Flemish (17th -)				

D=Drawing, P=Painting, S=Sculpture, W=Watercolor

		Current Price Range		
		Low	Mean	High

GILLEMANS, ELDER, Jan P.	*P*	$16,500	$22,550	$28,600
Flemish (1618 - 1675)				
GILLEMANS, ELDER, Jan P. (Cir)	*P*			$41,800
Flemish (1618 - 1675)				
GILLES, F.	*W*			$770
European (19th -)				
GILLETT, W. B.	*W*			$303
(?)				
GILLETTE, Lester A.	*P*	$105	$122	$138
American (1855 -)				
GILLIAM, Sam	*W*			$1,980
American (1933 -)				
GILLIG, Jacob	*P*	$1,650	$8,617	$12,100
Dutch (1636 - 1701)				
GILOT, Francoise	*W*			$440
French (1921 -)				
GILPIN, Sawrey	*P*	$11,000	$22,733	$46,200
British (1733 - 1807)				
GILSON,	*P*			$297
British (19th -)				
GILSOUL, Victor O.	*P*			$9,900
Belgian (1867 -)				
GIMENO, Andres	*P*			$1,320
Spanish (1879 -)				
GIMIGNANI, Giacinto	*D*			$1,045
Italian (1611 - 1681)				
GIMIGNANI, Ludovico (Circle)	*P*			$8,800
Italian (1643 - 1697)				
GIMMER, Abel (Manner)	*P*			$1,045
Dutch (1570 - 1619)				
GINNEVER, Charles	*S*	$880	$3,740	$6,600
(20th -)				
GINNS, Lillian E.	*P*			$110
American (?)				
GINTHER, Mary P.	*P*			$500
American (?)				

D=Drawing, P=Painting, S=Sculpture, W=Watercolor

		Current Price Range		
		Low	Mean	High

GIOBBI, Edward	*D*			$1,650
(?)				
GIOJA, Belisario	*P*			$88,000
Italian (1829 - 1906)	*W*	$330	$2,137	$3,300
GIOJA, Edouardo	*W*			$1,540
Italian (1862 -)				
GIOJA, Gaetano	*W*			$165
Italian (? - 1824)				
GIONFRIDDA, Joseph M.	*W*			$275
American (1907 -)				
GIONO, Wilson B.	*P*	$3,300	$4,290	$5,280
Lat. Amer. (20th -)				
GIOR, A.	*P*			$165
Dutch (19th - 20th)				
GIORDANO,	*P*			$198
Italian (?)				
GIORDANO, Felice	*P*	$385	$935	$1,760
Italian (1880 - 1964)				
GIORDANO, Luca	*D*			$4,000
Italian (1632 - 1705)	*P*	$440	$36,135	$88,000
GIORDANO, Luca (Et al.)	*P*			$25,300
Italian (17th - 18th)				
GIORGIONE SCHOOL 16C,	*P*	$2,200	$5,225	$8,250
Italian (16th -)				
GIOVANE, Palma (Attrib.)	*P*			$4,950
Italian (15th - 16th)				
GIOVANNETTI, Vittoria	*P*			$770
Italian (1900 - 1968)				
GIOVANNI, Apollonio de (Attrib.)	*P*			$16,500
Italian (1415 - 1465)				
GIOVANNI, Bartolommeo di	*P*			$90,200
Italian (15th - 16th)				
GIOVATTI,	*P*			$1,100
European (19th -)				

D=Drawing, P=Painting, S=Sculpture, W=Watercolor

		Current Price Range		
		Low	Mean	High
GIPS, Cornelis	*P*			$1,045
(19th -)				
GIRARD,	*P*			$550
European (20th -)				
GIRARDET, Edouard H.	*P*	$825	$2,512	$5,060
Swiss (1819 - 1880)				
GIRARDET, Eugene A.	*P*	$5,500	$27,683	$77,000
French (1853 - 1907)				
GIRARDIN, Frank J.	*P*	$385	$569	$935
American (1856 - 1945)				
GIRARDOT, Ernest G.	*P*			$1,320
British (19th - 20th)				
GIRAUD, Pierre F. G.	*P*			$7,150
French (1806 - 1881)				
GIRIN, David	*P*	$450	$3,398	$13,200
French (1848 - 1917)				
GIRODET-TRIOSON, Anne L.	*P*			$23,100
French (1767 - 1824)				
GIRONELLA, Alberto	*P*			$33,000
Mexican (1929 -)	*S*			$9,350
GIROTTO, Napoleon	*W*			$1,870
European (19th -)				
GISBERT, Antonio	*P*			$52,800
Spanish (1835 -)				
GISH, Delbert	*D*			$220
American (20th -)				
GISSING, R.	*P*			$440
(?)				
GISSON, Andre	*P*	$605	$2,335	$7,425
French (1910 -)				
GIULIO, Romano (Follower)	*D*			$1,540
Italian (1492 - 1546)				
GIUSTI, Guglielo	*W*			$880
Italian (1824 -)				
GJOEDESEN, A.	*P*			$550
Danish (19th - 20th)				

D=Drawing, P=Painting, S=Sculpture, W=Watercolor

| | | Current Price Range | | |
		Low	Mean	High
GLACKENS, William J.	*D*	$330	$3,193	$7,700
American (1870 - 1938)	*P*	$6,600	$97,850	$517,000
GLACKENS, William J. (Attrib.)	*D*	$1,100	$1,224	$1,348
American (1870 - 1938)				
GLADDINGS, Timothy A.	*P*			$4,620
American (1818 - 1864)				
GLADENBECK, H. (Et al.)	*S*			$1,100
(19th -)				
GLAMAN, Eugenie F.	*P*			$495
American (? - 1956)				
GLANSDORFF, Hubert	*P*	$3,025	$4,263	$5,500
Belgian (1877 - 1963)				
GLANTZMAN, Judy	*P*			$1,100
(?)				
GLASCO, Joseph	*P*	$220	$697	$1,320
American (1925 -)	*W*			$770
GLATZ, Oscar	*P*			$1,980
Hungarian (1872 - 1958)				
GLATZER, Simon	*P*			$523
Russian (1890 -)				
GLAUBER, Johannes	*P*			$15,400
Dutch (1646 - 1726)				
GLEASON, Duncan	*P*			$413
American (1881 - 1959)				
GLEITSMAN, Louis A.	*P*	$330	$605	$880
American (1883 - 1970)				
GLEITSMANN, Raphael	*P*	$660	$1,815	$3,850
American (1910 -)	*W*	$440	$862	$1,210
GLEIZES, Albert	*D*	$1,100	$6,600	$12,100
French (1881 - 1953)	*P*	$66,000	$204,875	$467,500
	W			$126,500
GLEN, Robert	*S*			$3,300
(20th -)				

D=Drawing, P=Painting, S=Sculpture, W=Watercolor

| | | Current Price Range | | |
		Low	Mean	High
GLENDENING, Alfred A.	*P*	$8,140	$11,691	$22,000
British (19th -)				
GLENDENING, JR., Alfred A.	*P*			$28,600
British (? - 1907)	*W*	$4,950	$9,625	$14,300
	P	$1,625	$2,738	$3,850
GLENNY, Alice R.	*P*			$1,760
American (1858 -)				
GLERUP, S.	*P*			$3,080
Danish (19th -)				
GLICK, John P.	*S*			$605
(20th -)				
GLICKENSTEIN, Enoch H.	*S*			$550
Russian (1870 - 1942)				
GLINDONI, Henry G.	*P*	$5,500	$7,425	$9,350
British (1852 - 1913)	*W*			$193
GLINTENKAMP, Hendrik	*P*			$1,760
American (1887 - 1946)	*W*			$825
GLOVER, John	*P*	$990	$2,420	$3,850
British (1767 - 1849)				
GLUCK, L.	*D*			$138
(20th -)				
GLUCKMANN, Grigory	*P*	$4,950	$9,396	$15,400
American (1898 - 1973)				
GLYNDON, F.	*P*			$1,540
American (20th -)				
GOATER, Walter H.	*D*			$110
(?)				
GOBBIS, Giuseppe	*P*			$66,000
Italian (18th -)				
GOBER, Robert	*P*			$55,000
(20th -)				
GOBL, Wahl C.	*P*			$935
German (1871 - 1965)				

D=Drawing, P=Painting, S=Sculpture, W=Watercolor

		Current Price Range		
		Low	Mean	High

		Low	Mean	High
GODARD, Gabriel	*P*			$880
(20th -)				
GODCHAUX, Roger	*P*	$6,875	$9,625	$14,300
French (1878 -)				
GODDARD, Margaret	*P*			$1,540
American (1882 -)				
GODDY, A. T.	*P*			$248
American (20th -)				
GODFREY,	*P*			$165
American (20th -)				
GODIN, Raymonde	*P*			$275
Canadian (20th -)				
GODOY, Ant.	*P*			$550
American (20th -)				
GODWARD, John W.	*P*			$46,750
British (1861 - 1922)				
GODWIN, Frances B.	*S*	$330	$440	$550
American (1892 -)				
GODWIN, Karl	*P*			$330
American (1893 -)	*W*			$1,000
GOEBEL, Paul	*P*			$495
American (1877 -)				
GOEDVRIEND, Theo	*P*			$275
Dutch (1879 -)				
GOENUETTE, Norbert	*D*			$14,300
French (1854 - 1894)	*P*			$14,300
GOERG, Edouard	*P*	$6,600	$14,966	$22,000
French (1893 - 1969)				
GOERLICH,	*P*			$1,650
American (19th -)				
GOETSCH, Gustav	*P*			$578
American (1877 - 1967)				
GOETZ, Henri	*D*			$3,575
French (1908 -)	*P*			$2,750

D=Drawing, P=Painting, S=Sculpture, W=Watercolor

		Current Price Range		
		Low	Mean	High
GOETZ, R. V.	P			$1,375
American (20th -)				
GOETZ, S. G.	D			$165
(?)				
GOGH, Vincent van	D	$110,000	$302,500	$418,000
Dutch (1853 - 1890)	P	$407,000	$16.991M	$82.500M
GOINGS, Ralph	P			$77,000
American (1928 -)	W	$9,350	$12,650	$15,400
GOLA, Emilio	P			$935
Italian (1852 - 1923)				
GOLD, Albert	P			$3,300
American (1906 -)				
GOLDBECK,	P			$3,465
(?)				
GOLDBERG, Glenn	P	$880	$13,723	$23,100
(20th -)				
GOLDBERG, Michael	P	$715	$10,138	$25,300
American (1924 -)	S	$1,320	$14,410	$27,500
GOLDEN, Roland	P			$990
American (1931 -)	W	$880	$1,073	$1,265
GOLDIN, Leon	P			$2,200
(20th -)				
GOLDING, Tomas L.	P			$770
Venezuelan (1909 -)				
GOLDSMITH, Wallace	W			$110
American (1873 - 1945)				
GOLDSTEIN, A.	S			$550
American (19th - 20th)				
GOLDSTEIN, Jack	P	$8,800	$17,380	$35,200
(20th -)				
GOLDTHWAITE, Anne	P	$1,760	$2,090	$2,420
American (1875 - 1944)	W			$550

D=Drawing, P=Painting, S=Sculpture, W=Watercolor

		Current Price Range		
		Low	Mean	High

		Low	Mean	High
GOLLINGS, William E.	*P*			$3,300
American (1878 - 1932)	*W*	$2,200	$3,200	$4,200
GOLLMAN, Julius	*P*			$330
German (? - 1898)				
GOLTZ, Walter	*P*	$303	$592	$880
American (1875 - 1956)				
GOLUB, Leon	*P*	$4,180	$10,533	$24,200
American (1922 -)				
GOMERTI, After	*S*			$165
(?)				
GOMEZ, M. A.	*P*	$165	$303	$440
American (20th -)				
GOMEZ Y GIL, Guillermo	*P*			$4,400
Spanish (19th -)				
GONCHAROV, Kolya (Et al.)	*W*			$440
Russian (19th - 20th)				
GONGORA, Leonel	*P*			$138
Mexican (20th -)				
GONTCHAROVA, Natalia	*D*			$14,300
Russian (1881 - 1962)	*P*	$68,200	$132,733	$209,000
	W	$1,980	$2,585	$3,190
GONTIER, Pierre C.	*P*			$4,400
French (19th -)				
GONZAGA, Pietro	*D*			$880
Italian (1751 - 1831)				
GONZALES, Eva	*P*			$154,000
(19th -)				
GONZALES, J.	*P*			$121
(?)				
GONZALES, Roberta	*P*			$440
Spanish (20th -)				
GONZALES, Xavier	*P*			$605
American (1898 -)	*W*			$220

D=Drawing, P=Painting, S=Sculpture, W=Watercolor

| | | Current Price Range | | |
		Low	Mean	High
GONZALEZ, Arthur	*P*			$4,840
(20th -)				
GONZALEZ, Beatriz	*S*			$2,750
Lat. Amer. (20th -)				
GONZALEZ, H.	*P*			$138
Venezuelan (20th -)				
GONZALEZ, Juan A.	*P*			$19,800
Spanish (1842 -)				
GONZALEZ, Julio	*S*	$28,600	$425,920	$1.320M
Spanish (1876 - 1942)				
GOODALE,	*P*			$935
American (20th -)				
GOODALL, Frederick	*P*	$3,300	$63,983	$264,000
British (1822 - 1904)				
GOODALL, Walter	*P*			$3,850
British (19th -)				
GOODELMAN, Aaron J.	*S*			$2,860
American (1890 -)				
GOODES, Edward	*P*			$550
British (19th -)				
GOODMAN, Maude	*P*			$935
British (19th -)				
GOODNOUGH, Robert	*P*	$1,320	$5,256	$18,700
American (1917 -)	*S*	$1,760	$1,980	$2,200
GOODRIDGE, E. (Attrib.)	*P*			$3,850
(1798 - 1882)				
GOODRIDGE, Sarah	*P*			$660
American (1788 - 1853)				
GOODWIN, Albert	*W*	$7,150	$10,725	$14,300
British (1845 - 1932)				
GOODWIN, Arthur C.	*D*	$825	$4,275	$17,600
American (1866 - 1941)	*P*	$550	$11,825	$27,500
	W			$880
GOODWIN, Harry	*P*			$900
British (19th -)				

D=Drawing, P=Painting, S=Sculpture, W=Watercolor

		Current Price Range		
		Low	Mean	High

		Low	Mean	High
GOODWIN, Helen A.	*P*			$660
American (19th - 20th)				
GOODWIN, Karl	*P*			$1,430
American (20th -)				
GOODWIN, Phillip R.	*P*	$220	$4,308	$20,900
American (1882 - 1935)	*W*			$660
GOODWIN, Phillip R. (Et al.)	*P*			$6,500
American (19th - 20th)				
GOODWIN, Richard L.	*P*	$770	$2,585	$5,225
American (1840 - 1910)	*W*	$138	$179	$220
GOODYEAR, Florinda	*P*			$303
(20th -)				
GOOKINS, James F.	*P*			$440
American (1840 - 1906)				
GOOSENS, Josse	*P*			$2,200
German (1876 -)				
GORBATOV, Constantin	*P*	$2,200	$3,850	$5,500
Russian (1876 -)	*W*			$715
GORCHOV, Ron	*P*	$1,540	$2,053	$2,860
American (1930 -)				
GORDON, John	*P*			$220
(20th -)				
GORDON, John W.	*P*	$1,210	$13,970	$23,100
Scottish (1788 - 1864)				
GORDON, John W. (Attrib.)	*P*			$5,500
Scottish (1788 - 1864)				
GORDON, Tania	*P*	$125	$160	$195
(?)				
GORE, Ken	*P*	$440	$1,008	$1,980
(?)				
GORE, William H.	*P*			$11,000
British (20th -)				
GORELICK, B.	*P*			$440
American (20th -)				

D=Drawing, P=Painting, S=Sculpture, W=Watercolor

		Current Price Range		
		Low	Mean	High
GORI,	*P*			$165
(?)				
GORKA, Paul	*P*			$1,155
American (20th -)				
GORKY, Arshile	*D*	$1,320	$29,965	$264,000
American (1905 - 1948)	*P*	$27,500	$173,250	$880,000
	W			$30,250
GORLEY, Philip A.	*P*	$330	$550	$770
Irish (1944 -)				
GORMAN, R. C.	*P*			$4,180
American (1933 -)				
GORP, Henry N. van	*D*			$5,500
French (1756 - 1819)				
GORSON, Aaron H.	*P*	$138	$12,206	$30,800
American (1872 - 1933)				
GORTER, Arnold M.	*P*	$2,200	$5,198	$9,350
Dutch (1866 - 1933)	*W*			$715
GORTZIUS, Geldorp	*P*			$30,800
Flemish (1553 - 1618)				
GORY, Albert	*S*			$3,300
(?)				
GORZU, Norbert	*P*			$175
(?)				
GOSLING, William	*P*			$1,045
British (1824 - 1883)				
GOSMINSKI, Richard	*W*	$220	$234	$248
American (20th -)				
GOSSELIN, Ferdinand J. A.	*P*			$5,500
French (1862 -)				
GOTHELF, Louis	*P*			$523
American (1901 -)				
GOTLIEB, Jules	*W*	$110	$234	$358
American (1897 -)				
GOTTLIEB, Adolph	*D*	$8,800	$11,733	$13,200

D=Drawing, P=Painting, S=Sculpture, W=Watercolor

		Current Price Range		
		Low	Mean	High

GOTTLIEB, Adolph	*P*	$7,700	$100,262	$352,000
American (1903 - 1974)	*W*	$13,200	$44,183	$88,000
GOTTLIEB, Harry	*P*			$1,760
American (1895 -)				
GOTTSCHALK, Max	*P*			$138
American (20th -)				
GOTTWALD, Frederick C.	*P*			$248
American (1860 -)				
GOUBIE, Jean R.	*P*	$2,640	$17,820	$33,000
French (1842 - 1899)				
GOUILLET, Jules	*P*			$4,400
French (1826 -)	*W*			$1,650
GOULD, Alexander C.	*P*			$5,500
British (1870 - 1948)				
GOULD, J. (Et al.)	*D*			$715
American (19th - 20th)				
GOULD, John	*W*			$1,870
American (1906 -)				
GOULD, Walter G.	*W*			$1,760
American (1829 - 1893)				
GOULET, Lorrie	*S*			$660
(20th -)				
GOUPIL, Jules A.	*P*	$3,960	$5,647	$8,800
French (1839 - 1883)				
GOUPIL, Leon L.	*P*			$1,650
French (1834 - 1890)				
GOURDAULT, Pierre	*P*			$2,200
French (1880 - 1915)				
GOURDON, R.	*P*			$550
French (19th -)				
GOURGUE, Jean E.	*P*	$550	$770	$990
Haitian (20th -)				
GOURLET, W. M.	*P*			$935
British (?)				

D=Drawing, P=Painting, S=Sculpture, W=Watercolor

		Low	Current Price Range Mean	High
GOUTMAN, Dolya	P			$165
American (20th -)				
GOVAERTS, Abraham (Circle)	P			$11,000
Flemish (1589 - 1626)				
GOW, Mary L.	P			$104,500
British (1851 - 1929)				
GOWER, George (Follower)	P			$16,500
British (15th - 16th)				
GOYA Y LUCIENTES, F.	D			$715,000
Spanish (1746 - 1828)				
GOYA Y LUCIENTES, F. (Att)	D			$220
Spanish (1746 - 1828)	P			$66,000
GOYA Y LUCIENTES, F. (Foll)	P	$2,750	$3,025	$3,300
Spanish (1746 - 1828)				
GOYEN, Jan van	D	$4,620	$9,988	$28,600
Dutch (1596 - 1665)	P	$28,600	$191,767	$880,000
GOYEN, Jan van (Attrib.)	P	$16,500	$58,667	$132,000
Dutch (1596 - 1665)				
GOYEN, Jan van (Circle)	P	$5,500	$9,900	$14,300
Dutch (1596 - 1665)				
GOZALES, Xavier	P			$110
Mexican (20th -)				
GOZZARD, J. W.	P			$1,430
British (19th -)				
GOZZARD, W.	P			$660
American (19th -)				
GOZZOLI, Benozzo (School)	P			$8,800
Italian (1420 - 1497)				
GRAAT, Berend	P			$8,800
Flemish (1628 - 1709)				
GRABACH, John R.	P	$660	$14,652	$28,600
American (1886 - 1981)	W	$880	$1,723	$2,860
GRABONE, Arnold	P			$605
German (20th -)				

D=Drawing, P=Painting, S=Sculpture, W=Watercolor

		Current Price Range	
	Low	Mean	High

		Low	Mean	High
GRABWINKLER, Paul	*W*			$8,250
Austrian (1880 -)				
GRACEN, Edmond	*P*			$138
American (20th -)				
GRACIANO, Clovis	*D*			$1,100
Brazilian (1907 -)				
GRAEB, Karl G. A.	*P*			$15,400
German (1816 - 1884)				
GRAEGER, Guorun	*P*			$176
European (20th -)				
GRAEME, Colin	*P*			$1,100
British (1858 - 1910)				
GRAETZ, Gordon	*S*			$550
(?)				
GRAF, Carl C.	*P*	$3,300	$3,850	$4,400
American (?)				
GRAF, Ilma	*P*			$1,430
(19th -)				
GRAFF, Anton (Attrib.)	*D*			$1,760
German (1736 - 1813)	*P*			$1,650
GRAFF, Anton (Circle)	*P*			$11,000
German (1736 - 1813)				
GRAFILI, Guglielimo	*S*			$770
Italian (?)				
GRAFTON, Robert W.	*P*			$2,750
American (1876 - 1936)				
GRAGONY,	*P*			$110
French (20th -)				
GRAHAM, Charles	*W*			$6,050
American (1852 - 1911)				
GRAHAM, Clancy	*D*			$330
British (19th -)	*P*			$990
GRAHAM, Donald	*P*			$6,050
American (20th -)				

D=Drawing, P=Painting, S=Sculpture, W=Watercolor

		Current Price Range		
		Low	Mean	High

		Low	Mean	High
GRAHAM, G. W.	*P*			$440
American (19th -)				
GRAHAM, Gloria	*S*			$990
(20th -)				
GRAHAM, John	*D*			$1,320
American (1881 - 1961)	*P*	$3,850	$39,950	$143,000
GRAHAM, Peter	*P*			$7,150
British (1836 - 1921)				
GRAHAM, Robert A.	*P*	$330	$1,210	$2,090
American (1873 - 1946)				
GRAHAM, Robert M.	*P*			$33,000
American (20th -)				
GRAHAM, Thomas A. F.	*P*			$1,980
British (1840 - 1906)				
GRAILLY, Victor de	*P*	$330	$3,447	$8,800
French (1804 - 1889)				
GRAILLY, Victor de (Attrib.)	*P*	$1,320	$2,310	$3,740
French (1804 - 1889)				
GRAILLY, Victor de (Manner)	*P*			$1,540
French (1804 - 1889)				
GRAION, C.	*P*			$385
European (20th -)				
GRAMATKY, Hardie	*W*			$1,045
American (1907 - 1979)				
GRAN, Daniel (Attrib.)	*P*			$3,575
American (1694 - 1757)				
GRANACCI, Francesco	*P*			$71,500
Italian (1477 - 1543)				
GRANCH, John	*P*	$495	$523	$550
(?)				
GRANDGERARD, Lucien H.	*P*			$660
French (1880 - 1965)				
GRANDMAISON, Nickola de	*D*			$4,950
Canadian (1892 - 1978)				
GRANDOLFI, Ubaldo	*D*			$9,350
Italian (1728 - 1781)				

D=Drawing, P=Painting, S=Sculpture, W=Watercolor

		Current Price Range		
		Low	Mean	High

		Low	Mean	High
GRANER, Ernst	W			$880
Austrian (1865 -)				
GRANER Y ARRUFI, Luis	P	$990	$10,753	$18,700
Spanish (1867 - 1929)				
GRANIN,	P			$550
American (20th -)				
GRANT, Catherine H.	P			$495
American (1897 - 1954)				
GRANT, Cecil V.	P			$121
American (1880 -)				
GRANT, Charles H.	P	$303	$509	$715
American (1866 - 1939)				
GRANT, Clement R.	P	$2,200	$3,117	$4,125
American (1849 - 1893)	W			$935
GRANT, Dwinell	D			$1,100
American (20th -)	P	$1,210	$1,430	$1,650
	S			$1,870
GRANT, Edouard R.	P			$1,100
French (19th -)				
GRANT, Eugenia	D			$413
American (20th -)				
GRANT, Frederick M.	P	$330	$1,595	$3,300
American (1886 - 1959)				
GRANT, Gordon	D	$138	$300	$462
American (1875 - 1962)	P	$578	$1,602	$2,860
	W	$350	$1,531	$3,300
GRANT, J. A.	P			$3,850
(?)				
GRANT, J. Jeffrey	W	$523	$564	$605
American (1883 - 1960)				
GRANT, Marthe	P	$935	$1,348	$1,760
(?)				
GRANT, Mimi	P			$660
American (20th -)				

D=Drawing, P=Painting, S=Sculpture, W=Watercolor

		Current Price Range		
		Low	Mean	High
GRANT, William J.	*P*			$17,600
British (1829 - 1866)				
GRASDORP, Willem	*P*			$198,000
Dutch (1678 -)				
GRASS, Karl G.	*W*			$550
Baltic (1767 - 1814)				
GRASSET, Eugene	*W*			$1,100
Swiss (1841 - 1917)				
GRATCHEFF, Alexei	*S*	$1,870	$1,925	$1,980
Russian (19th -)				
GRATCHEV, Georgi I.	*S*			$7,700
Russian (1860 - 1893)				
GRAU, Enrique	*W*			$6,600
Colombian (1920 -)				
GRAU-SALA, Emile	*D*	$9,900	$17,600	$24,200
Spanish (1911 - 1975)	*P*	$8,250	$39,875	$85,250
	W			$16,500
GRAUER, William C.	*W*	$385	$413	$440
American (1896 -)				
GRAVELOT, Hubert	*D*	$935	$12,568	$24,200
French (1699 - 1773)				
GRAVES, Abbott F.	*P*	$880	$19,853	$57,500
American (1859 - 1936)	*W*	$303	$1,107	$2,200
GRAVES, Abbott F. (Attrib.)	*P*			$385
American (1859 - 1936)				
GRAVES, Captain	*P*			$1,650
American (19th -)				
GRAVES, Charles de	*D*			$990
German (17th -)				
GRAVES, Ed	*W*			$413
American (20th -)				
GRAVES, Michael	*D*			$775
American (20th -)				
GRAVES, Morris	*D*	$425	$2,004	$3,300
American (1910 -)				

D=Drawing, P=Painting, S=Sculpture, W=Watercolor

		Current Price Range		
		Low	Mean	High

		Low	Mean	High
GRAVES, Nancy	P	$20,900	$28,875	$44,000
American (1940 -)	S	$27,500	$79,750	$132,000
	W	$14,300	$17,050	$19,800
GRAY, Cedric	P			$165
British (19th - 20th)				
GRAY, Charles A.	P	$110	$733	$1,320
American (1858 - 1923)				
GRAY, Cleve	P	$1,980	$7,590	$13,200
American (1918 -)				
GRAY, G.	P			$1,760
(18th -)				
GRAY, Henry P.	D			$880
American (1869 - 1952)	P			$9,900
	W	$440	$14,040	$30,250
GRAY, Jack L.	P	$1,650	$6,930	$13,200
American (1927 - 1981)				
GRAY, Mary	P			$2,750
American (19th -)				
GRAY, Una	P			$1,100
American (20th -)				
GRAY, William	P	$165	$853	$1,540
British (19th -)				
GRAYSON, L.	P			$605
(19th -)				
GRAZIANI, Ercole (Attrib.)	P			$18,700
Italian (1651 - 1726)				
GREACEN, Edmund W.	P	$8,800	$19,140	$41,800
American (1877 - 1929)				
GREACEN, Nan	P	$165	$754	$1,980
American (1909 -)	W			$14,300
GREASON, William	P	$121	$418	$715
American (1884 -)				
GREATOREX, Eliza P.	P			$3,575
American (1820 - 1897)				

D=Drawing, P=Painting, S=Sculpture, W=Watercolor

		Current Price Range		
		Low	Mean	High
GREATOREX, Katherine H.	P			$11,000
American (?)				
GREAVES, Harry	W	$110	$275	$440
American (1854 - 1919)				
GREAVES, Walter	P			$935
British (1846 - 1930)				
GREB, Nam	S	$330	$825	$1,320
(?)				
GREBBER, Pieter F. de	P			$6,050
Dutch (17th -)				
GRECO, El (Circle)	P			$99,000
Spanish (1547 - 1614)				
GRECO, El (Follower)	P			$2,750
Spanish (1547 - 1614)				
GRECO, El (School)	P	$1,320	$6,710	$12,100
Spanish (1547 - 1614)				
GRECO, El (Studio)	P	$19,800	$23,650	$27,500
Spanish (1547 - 1614)				
GRECO, Emilio	D			$3,300
Italian (1913 -)	S	$28,600	$73,370	$143,000
GRECO, Gennaro (Attrib.)	P			$3,300
Italian (1663 - 1714)				
GREELEY, Russell	D			$110
French (20th -)				
GREEN, Asha	P			$165
American (20th -)				
GREEN, Bernard	P			$1,320
American (1887 - 1951)				
GREEN, Charles	P	$770	$3,693	$8,800
American (1844 - 1899)	W			$880
GREEN, Charles	W	$2,750	$5,207	$8,250
British (1840 - 1898)				
GREEN, E. F. (Attrib.)	P			$4,400
British (19th -)				

D=Drawing, P=Painting, S=Sculpture, W=Watercolor

		Low	Current Price Range Mean	High
GREEN, Frank R. American (1856 - 1940)	P	$138	$414	$558
GREEN, George (20th -)	P			$4,400
GREEN, Gertrude American (1904 -)	P			$1,650
GREEN, J. Barry American (1895 - 1966)	P			$770
GREEN, Roland American (20th -)	W	$1,650	$1,870	$2,090
GREEN, William B. American (1871 - 1945)	P	$105	$585	$2,530
GREENAWAY, Kate British (1846 - 1901)	D	$1,980	$2,090	$2,200
	W	$2,530	$10,065	$17,600
GREENBAUM, Joseph American (1864 - 1940)	P	$660	$1,470	$3,575
GREENBLAT, Rodney A. (20th -)	D			$3,850
	P	$1,650	$7,172	$16,500
	W			$1,870
GREENE, Albert van Neese American (1887 -)	P			$330
	W			$275
GREENE, Edward D. E. (1823 - 1879)	P			$990
GREENE, Gertrude American (1911 - 1956)	S			$3,080
GREENE, H. S. American (20th -)	P			$110
GREENE, J. Barry American (1895 - 1966)	P	$138	$627	$1,045
GREENE, Stephen American (1918 -)	P	$715	$908	$1,100
GREENE, Walter L. American (20th -)	P	$440	$908	$1,375
	W	$385	$413	$440

D=Drawing, P=Painting, S=Sculpture, W=Watercolor

		Current Price Range		
		Low	Mean	High

GREENEVELD, G. European (20th -)	*P*			$825
GREENHILL, John (Attrib.) British (1649 - 1676)	*P*			$1,100
GREENHILL, John (Manner) British (1649 - 1676)	*D*			$303
GREENLEAF, Jacob American (1887 - 1968)	*P*	$440	$940	$2,200
GREENOUGH, Richard S. American (1819 - 1904)	*S*			$1,980
GREENUS, Arthur American (19th -)	*W*			$495
GREENWOOD, George P. British (1850 - 1904)	*P*	$1,650	$1,760	$1,870
GREENWOOD, Joseph H. American (1857 - 1927)	*P*	$468	$2,672	$9,350
GREENWOOD, Marion American (1909 - 1970)	*D*			$413
GREER, A. D. (1904 -)	*P*	$550	$3,025	$5,500
GREER, James E. American (19th - 20th)	*P*			$165
GREEVES, Richard American (19th - 20th)	*S*			$2,640
GREG, British (?)	*P*			$193
GREGG, Paul American (1876 - 1949)	*P*	$132	$315	$440
GREGOIRE, Alexander Haitian (20th -)	*P*			$330
GREGOIRE, Jean-Louis French (1840 - 1890)	*S*			$3,740
GREGOIRE, Jean-Louis (After) French (1840 - 1890)	*S*			$193
GREGOR, Harold American (1929 -)	*P*	$1,650	$1,788	$1,925

D=Drawing, P=Painting, S=Sculpture, W=Watercolor

		Current Price Range		
		Low	Mean	High

GREGORIO, E.	*S*			$385
Mexican (20th -)				
GREGORY, Angela	*P*	$550	$578	$605
American (1903 - 1989)				
GREGORY, Arthur V.	*W*			$1,155
Australian (1862 - 1952)				
GREGORY, Dorothy L.	*P*			$385
American (20th -)				
GREISSINGER, F.	*P*			$165
American (20th -)				
GREITZER, Jack	*P*			$275
American (20th -)				
GRELL, Louis Frederick	*P*			$330
American (1887 - 1960)				
GREMKE, Deidrich H.	*P*	$523	$2,324	$4,125
American (1860 - 1939)				
GRENDE, Janene	*W*	$500	$675	$850
American (20th -)				
GRENIER, Francois	*P*			$1,540
French (1793 - 1867)				
GRENIER, Henry	*P*	$770	$770	$770
French (1922 -)	*W*	$550	$633	$715
GREPPI, A.	*P*			$605
(19th -)				
GRESL, Gary J.	*P*			$220
American (20th -)				
GRESLY, Gabriel (Circle)	*P*			$33,000
French (1712 - 1756)				
GRESPO, Helaine	*P*			$138
(20th -)				
GRESY, Prosper J.	*P*			$990
French (1804 - 1874)				
GRETHA,	*S*			$1,210
(?)				
GRETHOFF, (After)	*S*			$385
(?)				

D=Drawing, P=Painting, S=Sculpture, W=Watercolor

		Low	Mean	High
			Current Price Range	
GRETZNER, Harold	W	$660	$921	$1,100
American (1902 - 1977)				
GREUZE, Jean B.	D	$30,800	$42,717	$57,750
French (1725 - 1805)				
GREUZE, Jean B. (After)	P	$605	$1,045	$1,760
French (1725 - 1805)				
GREUZE, Jean B. (Attrib.)	P	$1,540	$2,145	$2,750
French (1725 - 1805)				
GREUZE, Jean B. (Circle)	P	$2,200	$4,217	$6,050
French (1725 - 1805)				
GREUZE, Jean B. (Manner)	P			$3,025
French (1725 - 1805)				
GREUZE, Jean B. (School)	D			$1,320
French (1725 - 1805)	P			$495
GREVENBROECK, Alessandro	P	$4,400	$8,800	$13,200
Italian (18th -)				
GREY, Steve	W			$110
American (20th -)				
GREYTAK, Don	D	$1,000	$1,050	$1,100
American (20th -)				
GRIBBLE, Bernard F.	P			$880
British (1873 - 1962)				
GRIEG, A.	P			$248
(?)				
GRIFFIER I, Jan	P	$9,350	$13,475	$17,600
Dutch (1652 - 1718)				
GRIFFIN, Arthur	P			$165
American (1931 -)				
GRIFFIN, David	P	$4,000	$5,024	$6,600
American (1952 -)				
GRIFFIN, Delancy	P			$440
American (19th -)				
GRIFFIN, James M.	W			$990
American (1850 - 1931)				
GRIFFIN, Thomas Bailey	P	$355	$1,602	$3,300
American (19th -)				

D=Drawing, P=Painting, S=Sculpture, W=Watercolor

		Current Price Range		
		Low	Mean	High
GRIFFIN, Walter	*D*	$605	$1,412	$2,640
American (1861 - 1935)	*P*	$1,100	$3,554	$8,250
GRIFFITH,	*P*			$1,650
American (20th -)				
GRIFFITH, Conway	*W*			$220
American (1863 - 1924)				
GRIFFITH, E. N.	*P*			$15,400
American (19th -)				
GRIFFITH, Grace Allison	*W*	$715	$1,412	$1,760
American (1885 - 1955)				
GRIFFITH, Louis O.	*P*	$688	$839	$990
American (1875 - 1956)				
GRIFFITH, Marie O.	*P*	$660	$5,537	$12,100
American (20th -)				
GRIFFITH, William A.	*P*			$303
American (1866 - 1940)				
GRIFFITH, William C.	*P*	$110	$149	$220
American (?)				
GRIFFITHS, Harvey R.	*P*			$275
American (20th -)				
GRIFFITHS, O.	*P*			$303
British (19th -)				
GRIFFITHS, W. W. C.	*P*			$220
British (19th - 20th)				
GRIGAR, Otto	*P*			$105
(?)				
GRIGGS, Samuel	*P*	$275	$902	$2,200
American (1827 - 1898)				
GRIGORESCU, Nicolas	*P*			$4,400
Romanian (1838 - 1907)				
GRIGORIEV, Boris	*D*			$1,870
Russian (1866 - 1939)	*W*	$1,045	$1,568	$2,090
GRILLO, John	*P*			$275
American (1917 -)	*W*			$440

D=Drawing, P=Painting, S=Sculpture, W=Watercolor

		Current Price Range		
		Low	Mean	High

		Low	Mean	High
GRILO, Sarah	*P*	$2,200	$5,500	$8,800
Argentine (1921 -)				
GRIMALDI, Giovanni F.	*D*	$2,200	$2,750	$3,300
Italian (1606 - 1681)				
GRIMALDI, Giovanni F. (Attrib.)	*D*			$3,850
Italian (1606 - 1681)				
GRIMES, Frances	*S*			$6,600
American (19th -)				
GRIMM, Paul	*P*	$413	$961	$2,750
American (1891 - 1974)				
GRIMMER, Abel	*P*	$38,500	$52,250	$66,000
Flemish (1573 - 1619)				
GRIMMER, Abel (Attrib.)	*P*			$115,500
Flemish (1573 - 1619)				
GRIMSHAW, John A.	*P*	$25,300	$31,467	$35,000
British (1836 - 1893)				
GRINLING, G.	*P*			$495
British (20th -)				
GRINNELL, George V.	*P*	$440	$605	$770
(? - 1934)				
GRINNELL, Roy	*P*	$1,650	$2,237	$3,300
American (1934 -)	*W*			$165
GRINNELL, Victor	*P*			$303
(?)				
GRIPS, Charles J.	*P*			$9,350
Belgian (1852 - 1920)				
GRIS, Juan	*D*	$6,600	$27,170	$88,000
Spanish (1887 - 1927)	*P*	$77,000	$667,000	$2.640M
	W			$26,400
GRISARD,	*P*			$138
(?)				
GRISET, Ernest	*W*	$165	$193	$220
French (1841 - 1907)				
GRISON, Francois A.	*P*	$1,980	$11,990	$22,000

D=Drawing, P=Painting, S=Sculpture, W=Watercolor

		Current Price Range		
		Low	Mean	High

GRISON, Francois A.	*W*			$1,870
French (1845 - 1914)				
GRISWOLD, Carrie	*W*			$193
American (?)				
GRISWOLD, Casimir C.	*P*			$385
American (1834 - 1918)				
GRISWOLD, Casimir C. (Attrib.)	*P*			$1,870
American (1834 - 1918)				
GRITTEN, Henry C.	*P*			$3,300
British (19th -)				
GRIVAZ, Eugene	*W*			$3,575
French (1852 - 1915)				
GROBON, Francois F.	*P*			$5,500
French (1815 - 1901)				
GROELL, Theophil	*D*			$220
(20th -)				
GROENEVELOLT, Thomas T.	*P*			$1,650
(?)				
GROENEWEGEN, Adrianus J.	*P*			$1,045
Dutch (1874 - 1963)	*W*			$550
GROHE, Glenn	*P*			$385
American (1912 - 1956)				
GROLL, Albert	*P*	$385	$1,054	$2,530
American (1866 - 1952)				
GROLLERON, Paul L.	*P*	$1,045	$6,121	$25,300
French (1848 - 1901)				
GROM-ROTTMAYER, Hermann	*P*			$990
(1877 - 1953)				
GROMAIRE, Marcel	*D*	$770	$6,848	$17,600
French (1892 - 1971)	*P*	$8,250	$42,625	$88,000
GRONDARD, Philippe	*P*			$1,650
French (19th - 20th)				
GRONINGEN, Jan Swart van	*D*			$14,300
Flemish (?)				

D=Drawing, P=Painting, S=Sculpture, W=Watercolor

		Current Price Range		
		Low	Mean	High
GRONLAND, Theude	*P*			$13,200
German (1817 - 1876)				
GROOM, Emily	*P*			$385
American (1876 - 1975)				
GROOME, Esther M.	*P*	$138	$1,994	$3,850
American (? - 1929)				
GROOMS, Red	*D*	$3,575	$33,385	$66,000
American (1937 -)	*P*	$8,800	$26,714	$77,000
	S	$7,700	$12,467	$16,500
	W	$2,750	$12,257	$22,000
GROOT, Frans A. B. de	*P*			$25,300
Dutch (1824 - 1872)				
GROOT, Johannes De	*P*			$2,750
Dutch (1688 -)				
GROOTH, George C.	*P*			$8,800
Russian (1716 - 1749)				
GROPPER, William	*D*	$880	$908	$935
American (1897 - 1977)	*P*	$880	$16,511	$46,200
GROS, Baron Jean L.	*P*	$6,050	$27,867	$52,250
French (1793 - 1870)				
GROSE, D. C.	*P*	$1,320	$1,562	$1,925
American (19th -)				
GROSE, H. E.	*P*			$2,090
American (19th -)				
GROSPERRIN, Claude	*P*			$1,210
Swiss (1936 -)				
GROSS, Chaim	*D*	$220	$1,375	$3,025
American (1904 -)	*P*			$275
	S	$440	$8,779	$37,400
	W	$1,320	$1,540	$1,760
GROSS, Oscar	*P*			$5,500
American (1871 - 1963)				

D=Drawing, P=Painting, S=Sculpture, W=Watercolor

		Current Price Range		
		Low	Mean	High

		Low	Mean	High
GROSS, Sidney	*P*	$220	$358	$495
American (1921 -)				
GROSSENHEIDER, Richard P.	*D*			$2,750
American (1911 - 1975)				
GROSSER, Maurice	*P*			$550
American (19th - 20th)				
GROSSMAN, Morris	*P*	$440	$605	$770
American (20th -)	*W*			$165
GROSSMAN, Nancy	*P*	$5,280	$9,460	$12,100
American (1940 -)				
GROSSMANN, Edwin B.	*P*			$220
American (1887 -)				
GROSVENOR, Robert	*P*			$3,080
American (1937 -)	*S*			$19,800
GROSZ, George	*D*	$1,320	$9,585	$42,900
American (1893 - 1959)	*P*	$6,050	$21,921	$57,750
	W	$1,980	$26,690	$148,500
GROSZ, George (Attrib.)	*W*			$6,050
American (1893 - 1959)				
GROTENRATH, Ruth (Attrib.)	*W*			$105
American (20th -)				
GROUEC, Albertine B.	*P*			$358
French (1896 -)				
GROVE, Maria	*P*			$9,900
Danish (19th -)				
GROVER, Dorothy R.	*P*			$825
American (1908 - 1975)				
GROVER, G. D.	*P*			$605
American (20th -)				
GROVER, Oliver	*P*	$440	$2,151	$9,900
American (1861 - 1927)				
GROVER, Oliver (Attrib.)	*P*			$176
American (1861 - 1927)				

D=Drawing, P=Painting, S=Sculpture, W=Watercolor

		Current Price Range		
		Low	Mean	High

		Low	Mean	High
GRUBE, C. W. (Et al.)	*P*			$198
American (19th -)				
GRUBER, Carl	*W*	$1,100	$1,100	$1,100
Austrian (1803 - 1845)				
GRUBER, Francis	*P*			$71,500
French (1912 - 1948)				
GRUBER, Hans	*P*	$303	$317	$330
German (20th -)				
GRUGER, Frederic R.	*D*	$175	$588	$1,000
American (1871 - 1953)				
GRUGER, Frederic R. (Et al.)	*D*			$770
American (19th - 20th)				
GRULZNY, E.	*P*			$495
German (19th -)				
GRUN, F.	*P*			$2,420
French (19th -)				
GRUN, Jules A.	*P*			$17,600
French (1868 - 1934)				
GRUND, Norbert	*P*			$3,300
Czech. (1717 - 1767)				
GRUND, Norbert (Attrib.)	*P*			$660
Czech. (1717 - 1767)				
GRUNEWALD, Jakob	*P*			$46,200
German (1822 - 1896)				
GRUNWALD, Bela I.	*D*			$138
Hungarian (1867 - 1940)				
GRUNWALD, Charles	*W*			$440
American (?)				
GRUPPE, Charles P.	*P*	$578	$2,815	$13,200
American (1860 - 1940)	*W*	$193	$823	$2,200
GRUPPE, Emile A.	*D*			$137
American (1896 - 1978)	*P*	$358	$3,669	$12,100
	W			$330
GRUPPE, Robert	*P*			$220
American (20th -)				

D=Drawing, P=Painting, S=Sculpture, W=Watercolor

		Current Price Range		
		Low	Mean	High

GRUPPE, Virginia	*W*			$220
American (1907 -)				
GRUPPIO, L.	*P*			$303
Italian (19th - 20th)				
GRUST, F. G.	*P*	$935	$2,237	$3,575
Dutch (19th - 20th)				
GRUTZNER, Eduard von	*P*			$24,200
German (1846 - 1925)				
GSELL, Laurent	*P*			$8,800
French (1860 - 1944)				
GUACCIMANNI, Alessandro	*P*			$24,200
(?)				
GUARDI, Francesco	*D*			$7,700
Italian (1712 - 1793)	*P*	$85,250	$1.262M	$4.510M
GUARDI, Francesco & Giacomo	*D*			$77,000
Italian (18th - 19th)				
GUARDI, Francesco (Attrib.)	*P*	$6,600	$17,710	$41,250
Italian (1712 - 1793)				
GUARDI, Francesco (Circle)	*P*	$2,200	$20,488	$35,750
Italian (1712 - 1793)				
GUARDI, Francesco (Manner)	*P*	$935	$15,748	$88,000
Italian (1712 - 1793)				
GUARDI, Francesco (School)	*P*	$13,200	$25,850	$38,500
Italian (1712 - 1793)				
GUARDI, Giacomo	*P*	$3,080	$40,040	$77,000
Italian (1764 - 1835)				
GUARDI, Giacomo (Attrib.)	*P*	$17,600	$34,925	$52,250
Italian (1764 - 1835)				
GUARDI, Giacomo (Manner)	*D*			$1,870
Italian (1764 - 1835)				
GUARDI, Giacomo (Style)	*W*			$1,100
Italian (1764 - 1835)				
GUARDI, Giovanni A. (School)	*P*			$3,025
Italian (1698 - 1760)				
GUARNIERI, F.	*P*	$303	$454	$715
Italian (20th -)				

D=Drawing, P=Painting, S=Sculpture, W=Watercolor

		Current Price Range		
		Low	Mean	High

		Low	Mean	High
GUASTA, Girolamo B. G. del	*P*			$60,500
Italian (1470 - 1524)				
GUASTAVINO, Clement P. de	*P*	$9,900	$15,033	$17,600
French (19th -)				
GUAYASAMIN, Oswaldo	*D*	$2,640	$2,970	$3,300
Ecuadorian (1919 -)	*P*	$4,950	$7,883	$9,350
GUBIN, Selma	*P*			$1,100
American (1903 - 1974)				
GUDIASHVILI, Lado	*D*			$1,650
(20th -)				
GUDIN, Henriette	*P*			$3,080
French (19th -)				
GUDIN, Jean A.	*P*	$990	$1,018	$1,045
French (1802 - 1880)				
GUE, David J.	*P*			$5,390
American (1836 - 1917)				
GUELDRY, Ferdinand J.	*P*	$4,620	$12,210	$19,800
French (1858 -)				
GUERCINO, Giovanni F.	*D*	$57,750	$67,375	$77,000
Italian (1591 - 1666)	*P*			$71,500
GUERCINO, Giovanni F. (Circle)	*D*			$2,420
Italian (1591 - 1666)				
GUERCINO, Giovanni F. (Foll.)	*D*			$880
Italian (1591 - 1666)				
GUERCINO, Giovanni F. (Manner)	*D*	$352	$396	$440
Italian (1591 - 1666)				
GUERCINO, Giovanni F. (School)	*P*			$15,400
Italian (1591 - 1666)				
GUERIN, Armand	*P*	$220	$1,128	$2,530
Swiss (1913 -)				
GUERIN, Joseph	*P*			$385
(1889 -)				
GUERIN, Jules	*D*	$1,650	$1,833	$1,980
American (1866 - 1946)	*W*	$385	$523	$660

D=Drawing, P=Painting, S=Sculpture, W=Watercolor

		Current Price Range		
		Low	Mean	High

		Low	Mean	High
GUERMACHEFF, Michael	*P*	$413	$1,164	$2,420
Russian (1867 -)				
GUERRA, Archille	*P*			$5,500
Italian (1832 -)				
GUERRA, Carlos	*P*			$550
Lat. Amer. (20th -)				
GUERRERO, Jose	*P*			$1,650
American (1915 -)				
GUERRERO, Luis G.	*P*			$13,200
Mexican (1921 -)				
GUERRESCHI, Giuseppe	*P*	$110	$152	$193
Italian (1929 - 1985)				
GUERRIER, Raymond	*P*			$2,200
French (1920 -)				
GUERTMER, Carl F.	*P*			$358
(19th - 20th)				
GUERY, Arman	*P*			$3,575
French (1850 - 1912)				
GUEYTON,	*S*			$1,430
French (19th -)				
GUGLIELMI, Louis O.	*P*	$15,400	$24,750	$34,100
American (1906 - 1956)				
GUGLIEMI, Luigi	*P*			$1,925
Italian (1804 -)				
GUICHI, L.	*S*			$1,430
(?)				
GUIDI, Giuseppe	*P*			$5,720
Italian (20th -)	*W*			$2,640
GUIGOU, Paul	*P*	$104,500	$178,750	$253,000
French (1834 - 1871)				
GUILLAUME, Albert	*P*			$17,600
French (1973 - 1942)				
GUILLAUME, Georges A.	*D*			$248
French (1852 -)				
GUILLAUMET, Gustave Achille	*P*	$550	$1,925	$3,300
French (1840 - 1887)				

D=Drawing, P=Painting, S=Sculpture, W=Wafercolor

		Current Price Range		
		Low	Mean	High
GUILLAUMIN, Armand	D	$5,500	$21,175	$33,000
French (1841 - 1927)	P	$30,800	$71,050	$143,000
GUILLEMET, Jean B. A.	P	$550	$2,475	$4,400
French (1843 - 1918)				
GUILLEMINET, Claude	P	$1,980	$3,337	$5,170
French (1821 - 1860)				
GUILLONET, Roses	P			$1,430
(?)				
GUILLONNET, Octave Denis V.	P	$2,750	$6,875	$11,000
French (1872 - 1967)				
GUILLOU, Alfred	P	$1,430	$19,250	$52,800
French (19th -)				
GUIRAMAND, Paul	W			$990
French (1926 -)				
GULBRANSSON, Olaf	D			$110
Norwegian (1873 -)				
GUNN, Archie H.	P			$468
American (1863 - 1930)				
GUNTEN, Roger van	P			$11,000
Swiss (1933 -)				
GUNTHER, Georg	P			$2,750
German (1886 -)				
GUPTILL, Arthur L.	P			$220
American (1891 -)				
GURFINKEL, Herman	S			$495
(20th -)				
GURR, Lena	P			$1,100
American (1897 -)				
GURVICH, Jose	P			$12,100
Lithuanian (1927 - 1974)				
GUSCHONIK, F.	P			$4,400
European (20th -)				
GUSSOW, Bernard	D			$440
American (1881 - 1957)	P	$853	$2,774	$6,600

D=Drawing,   P=Painting,   S=Sculpture,   W=Watercolor

		Current Price Range		
		Low	Mean	High

		Low	Mean	High
GUSSOW, Bernard	*W*			$660
American (1881 - 1957)				
GUSSOW, Carl	*P*			$1,540
German (1843 - 1907)				
GUSTAVSON, Leland R.	*D*			$150
American (1899 - 1966)	*P*			$275
	W			$275
GUSTON, Philip	*D*	$6,050	$32,083	$66,000
American (1912 -)	*P*	$52,800	$200,200	$550,000
	W			$29,700
GUTE, Herbert J.	*P*			$1,045
American (1908 - 1977)	*W*			$495
GUTHERZ, Carl	*P*	$1,650	$1,760	$1,870
American (1844 - 1907)				
GUTIERREZ, Ernesto	*P*			$2,200
Italian (19th - 20th)				
GUTIERREZ, F. A.	*W*	$1,980	$2,090	$2,200
(20th -)				
GUTTMAN, Bernhard	*P*			$1,540
German (1869 -)				
GUTTUSO, Renato	*D*			$660
Italian (1912 -)	*P*			$35,200
GUY, Seymour J.	*P*			$23,100
American (1824 - 1910)				
GUYARD, J.	*P*			$275
French (20th -)				
GUYARD, R.	*P*			$495
French (20th -)				
GUYS, Constantin	*D*	$1,045	$1,595	$2,475
French (1802 - 1892)	*W*	$770	$1,485	$2,200
GUZIEWICS, A.	*P*			$440
American (20th -)				

D=Drawing, P=Painting, S=Sculpture, W=Watercolor

		Current Price Range		
		Low	Mean	High
GWATHMEY, Robert	P	$6,600	$12,909	$24,200
American (1903 -)	W			$7,150
GYBERSON, Indiana	P			$138
American (20th -)				
GYROY, Esther	P			$385
Hungarian (1944 -)				
GYSELAAR, M. de	W	$660	$770	$880
(19th -)				
GYSELINCKX, Joseph	P			$3,850
Belgian (19th -)				
GYSELS, Pieter	P			$17,600
Flemish (1621 - 1690)				
GYSELS, Pieter (Circle)	P			$26,400
Flemish (1621 - 1690)				
GYSIN, Brion	W			$495
American (1916 -)				
HAAFT, Cornelia De	P			$935
American (20th -)				
HAAG, Carl	D			$13,200
German (1820 - 1915)				
HAAG, Charles	S			$550
American (1867 - 1933)				
HAAG, Hans J.	P			$1,650
Austrian (1841 -)				
HAAG, Jean P.	P			$3,575
French (19th -)				
HAAGEN, Joris van der	P			$20,900
(1615 - 1669)				
HAANEN, Adriana (Attrib.)	P	$125	$135	$145
Dutch (20th -)				
HAANEN, Casparis	P			$25,300
Dutch (1778 - 1849)				
HAANEN, Cecil van	P			$7,700
Dutch (1844 - 1914)				
HAANEN, George G. van	P	$358	$1,714	$4,125
Dutch (1807 - 1881)				

D=Drawing, P=Painting, S=Sculpture, W=Watercolor

		Current Price Range		
		Low	Mean	High

		Low	Mean	High
HAANEN, Remi van	*P*			$880
German (19th -)				
HAAPANEN, John N.	*P*	$330	$426	$523
American (1891 -)				
HAARDT, J.	*P*			$1,540
Dutch (20th -)				
HAARLEM, Cornelis van	*P*	$9,350	$26,675	$44,000
Dutch (1562 - 1638)				
HAARLEM, Cornelis van (After)	*P*			$5,775
Dutch (1562 - 1638)				
HAAS, Alice P. T. de	*W*	$275	$330	$385
(19th - 20th)				
HAAS, Johannes H. L. de	*P*	$2,200	$2,750	$3,300
Dutch (1832 - 1908)				
HAAS, Mauritz F. de	*P*	$688	$7,202	$35,200
Dutch (1832 - 1895)	*W*			$660
HAAS, Richard	*D*			$2,750
American (1936 -)				
HABENSHADEN,	*D*			$330
(19th -)				
HABERLE, John	*D*			$110
American (1856 - 1933)				
HACKAERT, Jacob P.	*P*			$85,250
German (1737 - 1807)				
HACKER,	*P*			$3,300
American (19th -)				
HACKER, Arthur	*P*			$330
British (1858 - 1919)				
HACKER, Dieter	*P*	$15,400	$15,950	$16,500
(20th -)	*S*			$8,250
	W			$4,400
HACKER, Horst	*P*			$19,800
German (1842 - 1906)				
HACKERT, Jacob P.	*D*	$440	$2,530	$4,620

D=Drawing, P=Painting, S=Sculpture, W=Watercolor

		Current Price Range		
		Low	Mean	High

HACKERT, Jacob P.	*P*	$37,400	$65,450	$93,500
German (1737 - 1807)				
HACKERT, Jacob P. (Circle)	*P*			$8,800
German (1737 - 1807)				
HACKERT, Jacob P. (Follower)	*P*			$2,090
German (1737 - 1807)				
HACKETT, Malcolm	*P*			$825
American (20th -)				
HADDON, David W.	*P*			$880
British (19th -)				
HADDON, L. K.	*P*			$385
British (19th -)				
HADDON, Trevor	*P*	$1,210	$2,530	$3,850
British (1864 - 1941)	*W*	$715	$1,018	$1,320
HADEUSSAL,	*P*			$303
(?)				
HAELSZEL, Johann-Baptist	*P*			$11,000
German (1712 - 1777)				
HAENGER, Max	*P*	$1,155	$1,485	$1,760
German (19th - 20th)				
HAENSBERGEN, Jan van	*P*			$13,200
Dutch (17th -)				
HAENSBERGEN, Willem (Mann.)	*P*			$2,970
Dutch (1680 - 1755)				
HAFFNER, Feliz	*P*			$1,760
French (1818 - 1875)				
HAFNER, Charles A.	*S*	$990	$15,895	$30,800
American (1888 -)				
HAGARTY, James	*P*			$6,600
British (18th -)				
HAGBORG, August W.	*P*			$30,800
Swedish (1852 - 1925)				
HAGEDORN,	*P*			$121
(?)				
HAGEL, Frank	*P*	$1,150	$1,533	$1,800

D=Drawing, P=Painting, S=Sculpture, W=Watercolor

		Low	Mean	High
		\multicolumn{3}{c}{Current Price Range}		
HAGEL, Frank	W	$900	$1,110	$1,320
American (20th -)				
HAGELSTEIN, P.	P			$440
Dutch (? - 1868)				
HAGEMAN, S.	P			$1,540
Dutch (20th -)				
HAGEMANN, Godefroy de	P			$4,125
French (? - 1877)				
HAGEN, A.	P			$413
European (20th -)				
HAGEN, Eduard von	P			$880
German (1834 - 1909)				
HAGERBRUNNER, David	W			$880
American (20th -)				
HAGERUP, Nels	P	$358	$961	$2,475
American (1864 - 1922)				
HAGGERTY, Isabel	P			$2,750
American (20th -)				
HAGHE, Louis	W			$4,620
Belgian (1806 - 1885)				
HAGUE, Joshua A.	P			$660
British (1850 - 1916)				
HAGUE, Maurice S.	P	$138	$248	$303
American (1862 -)				
HAGUE, Michael	W			$2,600
(20th -)				
HAGUE, Raoul	S	$4,620	$13,310	$22,000
American (1905 -)				
HAGYIK, Istvan	P			$220
European (1891 -)				
HAHN, Georg	P			$9,900
German (1841 - 1889)				
HAHN, Gustave A.	P	$1,540	$2,035	$2,530
German (1811 - 1872)				
HAHN, L. A.	P			$468
British (19th -)				

D=Drawing, P=Painting, S=Sculpture, W=Watercolor

		Current Price Range		
		Low	Mean	High

		Low	Mean	High
HAHN, William American (1829 - 1887)	P			$9,130
HAIER, Joseph Austrian (1816 - 1891)	P			$880
HAIG, European (20th -)	P			$303
HAIG, Mabel American (1884 -)	W			$248
HAIGH, Alfred G. British (1870 - 1963)	P			$1,430
HAILMAN, Johanna K. American (1871 -)	P			$220
HAIM, Zigi Ben (?)	P			$605
HAINES, Richard American (1906 -)	P			$440
HAINES, Ted American (20th -)	D	$500	$608	$715
HAITE, G. C. British (1855 -)	P			$330
HAJDU, Etienne French (1907 -)	S	$2,475	$6,168	$17,600
HALAHMY, Oded American (20th -)	S	$825	$1,128	$1,430
HALAUSKA, Ludwig German (1827 - 1882)	P			$8,800
HALBERG, Charles E. American (1855 -)	W			$358
HALBERG-KRAUSS, Fritz German (1874 - 1951)	P	$3,300	$4,143	$5,280
HALE, Ellen Day American (1855 - 1940)	P W	$220	$4,434	$11,000 $1,980
HALE, Lilian W. American (1881 - 1963)	D P	$330 $14,300	$413 $18,700	$495 $22,000

D=Drawing, P=Painting, S=Sculpture, W=Watercolor

		Current Price Range		
		Low	Mean	High

		Low	Mean	High
HALE, Philip L.	D	$1,100	$6,655	$14,300
American (1865 - 1931)	P	$16,500	$27,775	$34,100
HALE, Robert B.	W			$193
(1901 -)				
HALEY, Robert D.	P			$3,025
American (1892 - 1959)				
HALKO, Joe	S	$1,000	$2,330	$4,400
American (20th -)				
HALL, E. W.	P			$187
American (19th -)				
HALL, Edna C.	W			$413
British (1879 - 1979)				
HALL, Emily	P			$550
(20th -)				
HALL, Frederick	P			$68,750
British (1860 - 1948)				
HALL, George Henry	P	$1,540	$2,035	$2,530
American (1825 - 1913)				
HALL, George Henry (Attrib.)	P			$4,400
American (1825 - 1913)				
HALL, H. Tom	W			$450
(1932 -)				
HALL, Harry	P	$5,500	$41,957	$220,000
British (1814 - 1882)				
HALL, Harry (Attrib.)	P			$2,200
British (1814 - 1882)				
HALL, J. E.	P			$110
(?)				
HALL, Lucille	P			$325
American (20th -)				
HALL, Sadie Van Patten	P			$770
American (20th -)				
HALL, Tom	W			$110
American (1879 -)				
HALL, V.	S			$275
(?)				

D=Drawing, P=Painting, S=Sculpture, W=Watercolor

		Current Price Range	
	Low	Mean	High

		Low	Mean	High
HALLAM, J. C. (?)	*P*			$132
HALLBERG, Charles European (19th - 20th)	*P*			$330
HALLE, Noel French (1711 - 1781)	*P*			$20,900
HALLEN, Jan van Dutch (19th -)	*P*			$275
HALLER, G. British (19th -)	*P*			$990
HALLER, Tony European (20th -)	*P*			$413
HALLETT, Hendricks American (1847 - 1921)	*P* *W*	$165	$248	$770 $385
HALLETT, W. American (19th -)	*P*			$385
HALLEY, Peter (20th -)	*P*	$8,250	$75,625	$143,000
HALLMAN, Henry T. American (1904 -)	*P*			$375
HALLOCK, Ruth M. American (? - 1945)	*P*	$176	$336	$495
HALLOWELL, George H. American (1871 - 1926)	*W*	$1,540	$2,970	$4,400
HALLWIG, Oscar American (19th -)	*P*			$495
HALLWORTH, R. American (19th - 20th)	*P*			$330
HALM, George R. (?)	*D*			$220
HALPERT, Samuel American (1884 - 1930)	*P* *W*	$2,750	$2,805	$2,860 $187
HALS, Dirk Dutch (1591 - 1656)	*P*	$16,500	$35,933	$49,500

D=Drawing, P=Painting, S=Sculpture, W=Watercolor

		Current Price Range		
		Low	Mean	High

		Low	Mean	High
HALS, Dirk (Attrib.) Dutch (1591 - 1656)	*P*			$6,050
HALS, Frans (After) Dutch (1580 - 1666)	*P*			$1,430
HALS, Frans (Circle) Dutch (1580 - 1666)	*P*			$1,100
HALS, Frans (Follower) Dutch (1580 - 1666)	*P*	$11,000	$31,625	$52,250
HALS, Harmen-F. Dutch (1611 - 1669)	*P*			$28,600
HALSALL, William F. American (1841 - 1919)	*P*	$550	$1,379	$2,750
HALVERSON, Jean American (20th -)	*W*	$935	$1,142	$1,540
HAM, Gordon R. American (20th -)	*P*			$825
HAMBIDGE, Jay American (1867 - 1924)	*W*			$660
HAMBLEN, Robert (?)	*P*			$275
HAMBOURG, Andre French (1909 -)	*P*	$2,200	$12,143	$33,000
HAMBRIDGE, Jay American (1867 - 1924)	*W*			$1,100
HAMEN Y LEON, Juan van der Spanish (1596 - 1632)	*P*			$550,000
HAMESSE, Adolphe-Jean Belgian (1849 -)	*P*			$440
HAMILTON, Carl W. Austrian (1668 - 1754)	*P*			$8,800
HAMILTON, Edward W. D. American (1864 -)	*W*			$330
HAMILTON, Gavin (School) British (1723 - 1798)	*P*			$1,430
HAMILTON, Gawen British (1697 - 1773)	*P*			$38,500

D=Drawing, P=Painting, S=Sculpture, W=Watercolor

		Current Price Range		
		Low	Mean	High
HAMILTON, Hamilton	P	$110	$2,069	$5,720
American (1847 - 1926)	W	$495	$2,681	$8,800
HAMILTON, Hamilton (Attrib.)	P			$275
American (1847 - 1926)				
HAMILTON, Helen	W			$660
American (?)				
HAMILTON, James	P	$358	$3,988	$14,300
American (1819 - 1878)	W			$413
HAMILTON, John M.	D	$193	$977	$1,760
American (1853 - 1936)	P	$140	$483	$825
HAMILTON, Lillian	W			$275
American (20th -)				
HAMILTON, Robert	P			$468
American (?)				
HAMILTON, Steve	W			$132
(?)				
HAMILTON, Wilbur Dean	P			$8,250
American (1864 -)				
HAMILTON, William (Attrib.)	P			$8,800
British (1751 - 1801)				
HAMILTON, William A.	P			$605
American (1877 -)				
HAMILTON, William R.	P			$330
American (1810 - 1865)				
HAMLIN, Genevieve K.	S			$770
American (1896 -)				
HAMM, Beth C.	W			$193
American (1885 - 1958)				
HAMMAN, Edouard M.	P	$2,750	$2,787	$2,860
French (1850 -)				
HAMME, Alexis van	P	$4,180	$5,885	$8,800
Belgian (1818 - 1875)				
HAMMER, Willam	P			$770
German (1821 - 1889)				

D=Drawing, P=Painting, S=Sculpture, W=Watercolor

		Current Price Range		
		Low	Mean	High

		Low	Mean	High
HAMMERAS, Ralph	*P*			$1,100
American (1939 -)				
HAMMERSHOI, Vilhelm	*P*			$4,620
Danish (1846 - 1916)				
HAMMERSMITH, Paul	*P*			$175
American (1859 - 1937)				
HAMMERSTAD, John O.	*P*	$440	$720	$1,210
American (19th - 20th)				
HAMMOND, Arthur J.	*P*	$110	$422	$880
American (1875 - 1947)	*W*			$165
HAMMOND, John	*P*			$1,155
Canadian (19th - 20th)				
HAMMOND, Richard H.	*P*			$660
American (1854 -)				
HAMON, Roland	*P*	$330	$23,181	$68,750
French (20th -)				
HAMPANITE, E. L.	*P*			$121
(?)				
HAMPE, Ernst H. W.	*P*	$1,320	$1,320	$1,320
German (1806 - 1862)				
HAMPTON, John W.	*P*	$2,310	$4,164	$6,050
American (1918 -)				
HAMSCOM, Trude	*P*			$248
European (20th -)				
HAMZA, Johann	*P*			$1,925
Austrian (1850 - 1927)				
HANAU, Paul Jean	*P*			$1,100
Belgian (1876 - 1933)				
HANAUER, H.	*P*			$110
American (20th -)				
HAND, Orville	*P*			$770
(20th -)				
HAND, Thomas (Attrib.)	*P*			$6,600
British (18th - 19th)				
HANDSON, A.	*P*			$2,090
American (?)				

D=Drawing, P=Painting, S=Sculpture, W=Watercolor

		Current Price Range		
		Low	Mean	High

		Low	Mean	High
HANDVILLE, Robert (1924 -)	*W*			$225
HANGER, Max German (1874 -)	*P*			$2,200
HANICOTTE, Augustin French (1870 - 1957)	*P*			$3,520
HANJE, Dutch (20th -)	*P*			$660
HANKEY, William L. British (1869 - 1952)	*P* *W*	$3,300	$11,917	$16,500 $825
HANKEY, William L. (Attrib.) British (1869 - 1952)	*P*			$13,200
HANKINS, Abraham American (20th -)	*P*	$132	$264	$440
HANKINS, Cornelius H. American (1864 - 1946)	*P*			$440
HANKS, Jarvis American (1799 -)	*P*			$605
HANLEY, B. American (19th - 20th)	*P*			$440
HANLIN, Corna S. (?)	*P*			$385
HANNA, Thomas K. American (1872 - 1957)	*P*			$3,025
HANNAFORT, M. Canadian (20th -)	*P* *W*			$110 $550
HANNAH, Duncan (20th -)	*P*	$2,750	$4,194	$5,500
HANNAUX, Emmanuel French (1855 -)	*S*			$2,750
HANNEMAN, Adriaen Dutch (1601 - 1671)	*P*			$27,500
HANNEMAN, Adriaen (Attrib.) Dutch (1601 - 1671)	*P*			$7,150

D=Drawing, P=Painting, S=Sculpture, W=Watercolor

| | | Current Price Range | | |
		Low	Mean	High
HANNIS,	*P*			$1,540
American (19th -)				
HANNO, Carl von (Attrib.)	*P*	$200	$413	$625
Norwegian (1901 -)				
HANNOT, Jan	*P*			$22,000
Dutch (17th -)				
HANOTEL, Auguste	*P*			$330
European (19th -)				
HANSCH, Anton (Attrib.)	*P*			$2,750
Austrian (1813 - 1876)				
HANSCOM, A. P.	*P*			$138
American (?)				
HANSDORF, George	*P*			$248
(20th -)				
HANSEN, Armin C.	*D*			$715
American (1886 - 1957)	*P*	$1,100	$5,981	$16,500
	W	$413	$844	$1,650
HANSEN, Ejnar	*P*	$468	$763	$1,100
American (1884 - 1965)				
HANSEN, F.	*P*			$880
European (19th - 20th)				
HANSEN, Hans P.	*D*			$385
American (1881 - 1967)				
HANSEN, Herman W.	*P*	$2,475	$32,358	$66,000
Danish (1859 -)				
HANSEN, Leon	*P*			$110
Australian (1918 -)				
HANSEN, Stephen	*P*	$2,640	$2,750	$2,860
American (20th -)				
HANSON, Ann	*D*			$495
American (20th -)				
HANSON, Duane	*P*			$209,000
American (1925 -)				
HANSON, H. (Attrib.)	*P*			$550
(20th -)				

D=Drawing, P=Painting, S=Sculpture, W=Watercolor

		Current Price Range		
		Low	Mean	High

		Low	Mean	High
HANSON, P. (19th -)	*P*			$660
HANSUNG, (?)	*P*			$193
HANUSH, Hubert Scandinavian (19th - 20th)	*P*			$165
HAPPENEN, John N. American (1891 -)	*P*			$1,100
HAPSMANS, M. American (20th -)	*W*			$660
HARBIN, Otto American (19th -)	*P*			$440
HARDEN, William (?)	*P*			$1,045
HARDIME, Pieter Flemish (1677 - 1758)	*P*			$35,200
HARDING, Chester American (1866 - 1937)	*P*			$1,760
HARDING, Chester (After) American (1866 - 1937)	*P*			$220
HARDING, James D. British (1798 - 1863)	*W*	$495	$908	$1,320
HARDING, Robert (20th -)	*W*			$165
HARDTMUTH, C. (19th -)	*P*			$413
HARDWICK, Melbourne H. American (1857 - 1916)	*P* *W*	$138	$399	$1,430 $715
HARDY, Anna E. American (1839 - 1934)	*P*			$990
HARDY, Dewitt American (1940 -)	*W*			$138
HARDY, Dudley British (1865 - 1922)	*W*			$935
HARDY, George American (19th -)	*P*			$1,650

D=Drawing, P=Painting, S=Sculpture, W=Watercolor

		Current Price Range		
		Low	Mean	High
HARDY, Heywood	*P*	$3,850	$15,785	$31,900
British (1842 - 1933)				
HARDY, James	*W*	$660	$770	$880
British (1832 - 1889)				
HARDY, Pat	*W*			$110
American (20th -)				
HARDY, Thomas B.	*W*	$1,485	$2,182	$2,860
British (1842 - 1897)				
HARDY, Walter M.	*W*			$303
American (1877 - 1933)				
HARE, David	*S*			$6,875
American (1917 -)				
HARE, John	*P*	$880	$1,320	$1,760
American (1882 - 1947)	*W*	$138	$354	$605
HARE, Nathaniel (Attrib.)	*P*			$3,850
(?)				
HARE, St. George	*P*			$14,300
British (1857 -)				
HARENYI, R.	*P*			$220
Hungarian (19th - 20th)				
HARGENS, Charles	*P*	$138	$1,857	$3,575
American (1893 -)				
HARGITT, Edward	*P*			$2,090
British (1835 - 1895)				
HARGRAVE, Harry S.	*P*			$715
American (20th -)				
HARGREAVES, Edgar W.	*W*	$302	$474	$935
American (20th -)				
HARING, Keith	*D*	$1,100	$21,905	$49,500
American (1958 -)	*P*	$4,180	$49,231	$148,500
	S	$3,190	$79,499	$231,000
	W	$24,200	$30,433	$39,600
HARING, Keith (Et al.)	*S*			$15,400
American (20th -)				

D=Drawing, P=Painting, S=Sculpture, W=Watercolor

| | | Current Price Range | | |
		Low	Mean	High
HARING & ORR, Keith	*D*			$7,150
American (20th -)				
HARING & OSWALD, Keith	*S*			$10,450
American (20th -)				
HARING AND L.A. 2, Keith	*S*			$1,650
American (20th -)				
HARITONOFF, Nicholas B.	*P*			$8,525
American (1880 - 1944)				
HARKER, Katherine Van Dyke	*P*			$303
American (1872 - 1966)				
HARLAMOFF, Alexei A.	*P*	$7,150	$15,538	$37,400
Russian (19th -)				
HARLES, Victor J.	*P*	$165	$478	$935
American (1894 - 1975)				
HARLOW, George H.	*P*	$5,500	$5,775	$6,050
British (1787 - 1819)				
HARLOW, George H. (Attrib.)	*P*	$550	$880	$1,210
British (1787 - 1819)				
HARLOW, Louis K.	*W*	$110	$269	$550
American (1850 - 1913)				
HARMER, Alexander	*P*			$1,320
American (1856 - 1925)				
HARMON, Charles H.	*P*	$523	$919	$1,210
American (1859 - 1936)	*W*			$1,540
HARMON, Fred	*P*			$3,520
American (20th -)				
HARMS, Alfred	*P*			$825
American (19th - 20th)				
HARNDEN,	*P*			$220
(?)				
HARNETT, William M.	*P*	$38,500	$148,500	$264,000
American (1848 - 1892)				
HARNEY, Paul E.	*P*			$495
American (1850 - 1915)				
HARPER, Edward S.	*P*			$1,100
American (20th -)				

D=Drawing, P=Painting, S=Sculpture, W=Watercolor

		Low	Mean	High
			Current Price Range	
HARPER, William St. John American (1851 - 1910)	P			$16,500
HARPIGNIES, Henri J. French (1819 - 1916)	D	$1,485	$1,513	$1,540
	P	$1,210	$11,290	$33,000
	W	$385	$6,270	$24,200
HARPIGNIES, Henri J. (Attrib.) French (1819 - 1916)	P			$550
	W			$330
HARRIET, Fulchran J. French (1778 - 1805)	P			$15,400
HARRINGTON, George American (1833 - 1911)	P			$550
HARRINGTON, James American (20th -)	P	$110	$330	$550
HARRIS, B. American (19th - 20th)	P			$193
HARRIS, C. Gordon American (1891 -)	D	$220	$310	$468
	P	$413	$963	$1,430
	W	$138	$367	$770
HARRIS, Charles X. American (1856 -)	P			$1,320
HARRIS, Conley American (20th -)	W			$110
HARRIS, Edwin British (19th -)	P			$44,000
HARRIS, Harteric British (19th -)	P	$275	$289	$303
HARRIS, Henry British (1805 - 1865)	P			$1,760
	W			$187
HARRIS, Kenneth American (20th -)	W	$143	$197	$275
HARRIS, L. S. (19th -)	P			$440

D=Drawing, P=Painting, S=Sculpture, W=Watercolor

		Current Price Range		
		Low	Mean	High
HARRIS, Marion	*D*			$275
American (1904 -)				
HARRIS, Sam H.	*P*	$330	$2,340	$5,500
American (1889 - 1977)				
HARRISON,	*P*			$825
American (19th - 20th)				
HARRISON, Albert	*D*			$193
American (20th -)				
HARRISON, Alexander	*P*	$935	$2,379	$4,180
American (1853 - 1930)				
HARRISON, Birge	*D*	$3,410	$9,955	$16,500
American (1854 - 1929)	*P*	$2,750	$8,731	$19,800
HARRISON, C. P.	*P*			$1,540
American (19th -)				
HARRISON, F. H.	*P*			$2,200
British (19th -)				
HARRISON, Thomas A.	*P*	$550	$1,650	$3,300
American (1853 - 1930)				
HARROWING, Walter	*P*	$1,760	$2,255	$2,750
British (18th - 19th)				
HART,	*P*			$4,400
British (19th -)				
HART, Agnes	*W*			$187
(?)				
HART, Eleanor H.	*P*			$633
American (20th -)				
HART, George O."Pop"	*D*			$330
American (1868 - 1933)				
HART, James M.	*D*			$1,540
American (1828 - 1901)	*P*	$413	$9,173	$30,800
HART, James or William	*P*			$1,430
(19th -)				
HART, Mary E.	*P*			$468
American (? - 1899)				

D=Drawing, P=Painting, S=Sculpture, W=Watercolor

		Current Price Range		
		Low	Mean	High

		Low	Mean	High
HART, Mary T.	*P*	$330	$578	$825
American (1872 - 1921)				
HART, Salmon A.	*P*			$1,540
British (1806 - 1881)				
HART, Sydney G.	*W*			$330
British (19th -)				
HART, William M.	*D*			$275
American (1823 - 1894)	*P*	$660	$6,760	$39,600
	W			$385
HART, William M. (Attrib.)	*P*			$3,850
American (1823 - 1894)				
HARTIGAN, Grace	*D*			$2,310
American (1922 -)	*P*			$6,050
	S	$3,850	$4,675	$5,500
	W			$7,150
HARTING, Lloyd	*W*	$550	$798	$1,045
American (1901 - 1976)				
HARTINGER, Anton	*W*			$26,400
Austrian (1806 - 1890)				
HARTL, Leon	*W*			$110
American (20th -)				
HARTLAND, L.	*W*	$138	$248	$358
British (19th -)				
HARTLEY, J. W.	*D*			$165
British (19th -)				
HARTLEY, Jonathan S.	*S*	$193	$7,959	$18,700
American (1845 - 1912)				
HARTLEY, Marsden	*D*	$4,620	$10,874	$24,200
American (1877 - 1943)	*P*	$14,300	$86,154	$550,000
HARTLEY, Rachel	*P*	$275	$2,596	$8,250
American (1884 -)				
HARTLEY, Richard V.	*P*			$1,540
American (19th - 20th)				

D=Drawing, P=Painting, S=Sculpture, W=Watercolor

		Low	Mean	High
		Current Price Range		
HARTLY, Ernest (19th -)	W			$165
HARTMAN, Bertram American (1882 - 1960)	D			$138
	P			$4,015
	W	$110	$325	$578
HARTMAN, George (?)	P			$1,650
HARTMAN, Robert (20th -)	P			$715
HARTMAN, Sydney (1863 - 1929)	W			$138
HARTMANN, Johann J. Austrian (1753 - 1830)	W			$6,325
HARTRATH, Lucie American (?)	P			$8,800
HARTSHORNE, Howard M. American (19th - 20th)	P	$138	$1,527	$5,225
HARTSON, Walter C. German (1866 -)	P	$303	$812	$1,320
	W			$165
HARTUNG, Hans French (1904 -)	D	$7,150	$32,725	$44,000
	P	$880	$40,663	$93,500
HARTUNG, M. European (19th -)	P			$165
HARTWELL, Nina R. American (19th - 20th)	P			$19,800
HARTWICH, Herman American (1853 - 1926)	P	$3,080	$11,770	$24,200
HARTWICK, Gunther American (19th -)	P			$1,650
HARTWICK, Gunther (Attrib.) American (19th -)	P			$1,980
HARTWIG, Heinie American (1937 -)	P	$358	$663	$1,265

D=Drawing, P=Painting, S=Sculpture, W=Watercolor

		Current Price Range		
		Low	Mean	High
HARVEY,	P			$330
American (20th -)				
HARVEY, Alice	D			$250
(1894 -)				
HARVEY, Eli	S	$220	$1,330	$9,900
American (1860 - 1957)				
HARVEY, Eugene	P	$550	$550	$550
American (20th -)				
HARVEY, George	D			$385
American (1835 - 1920)	P	$2,420	$11,257	$26,950
	W	$110	$733	$1,980
HARVEY, George W.	D			$330
American (1800 - 1878)	P			$385
HARVEY, Gerald	P	$3,520	$15,275	$38,500
American (1933 -)	S	$3,850	$6,283	$8,000
HARVEY, Paul	P	$330	$688	$1,045
American (1878 - 1948)				
HARVEY, Robert	P			$440
(20th -)				
HARWOOD, James T.	P			$2,200
American (1860 - 1940)				
HASBROUCK, Dubois F.	P	$275	$1,201	$2,860
American (1860 - 1934)	W	$220	$568	$1,650
HASELTINE, Herbert	S			$35,200
American (1877 - 1962)				
HASELTINE, William S.	P	$495	$34,696	$110,000
American (1835 - 1900)				
HASILER, E.	P			$1,540
European (19th -)				
HASKELL, Ernest	D			$770
American (1876 - 1925)	W			$220
HASKELL, Ida C.	P			$330
American (1861 - 1932)				

D=Drawing, P=Painting, S=Sculpture, W=Watercolor

		Current Price Range		
		Low	Mean	High
HASKELL, William H. American (1875 - 1952)	P			$1,430
HASKINS, John British (20th -)	P			$1,430
HASLEHUST, E. W. Scottish (19th - 20th)	W	$176	$554	$935
HASS, J. H. L. de (Style) Dutch (1832 - 1908)	P			$275
HASSAM, Childe American (1859 - 1935)	D	$5,720	$59,224	$187,000
	P	$18,700	$394,188	$3.190M
	W	$14,300	$253,400	$990,000
HASSAM, Childe (Attrib.) American (1859 - 1935)	D			$2,970
	P			$1,100
HASSMAN, American (?)	W			$495
HASSON, (?)	W			$150
HATCH, Emily American (1871 - 1959)	P			$275
HATFIELD, Joseph H. American (1863 - 1928)	P			$2,530
HATHAWAY, Bruce British (20th -)	P	$1,100	$1,210	$1,320
HATHAWAY, George M. American (1852 - 1903)	P	$825	$1,034	$1,430
	W	$385	$926	$2,200
HATHAWAY, H. (Attrib.) (19th -)	P			$468
HATHAWAY, M. (?)	P			$1,210
HATTORI, Hiroshi (20th -)	P			$715
HAUBNER, (?)	S			$1,760

D=Drawing, P=Painting, S=Sculpture, W=Watercolor

		Current Price Range	
	Low	Mean	High

HAUBTMANN, Michael	*P*			$880
German (1843 - 1921)				
HAUENSTEIN, Oskar	*D*			$193
American (1883 -)	*P*	$138	$138	$138
HAULDIN, Naghel	*P*			$330
(?)				
HAUPT, Erik G.	*D*			$248
American (1891 -)				
HAUPTMANN, Karl	*P*			$770
German (19th - 20th)				
HAUSCH, Alexander F.	*P*			$6,050
Russian (1873 -)				
HAUSER, John	*P*			$27,500
American (1859 - 1913)	*W*	$220	$3,685	$7,150
HAUSER, John (Attrib.)	*P*			$138
American (1859 - 1913)				
HAUSHALTER, George M.	*P*	$440	$715	$990
American (1862 -)				
HAUSMANN, Raoul	*P*			$660
Austrian (1886 - 1971)				
HAUSRATH, M. E.	*P*			$220
American (19th - 20th)				
HAVANNES, John	*S*			$1,375
American (?)				
HAVARD, James	*P*	$4,950	$23,775	$82,500
American (1937 -)	*S*	$7,700	$25,850	$44,000
HAVELL, William	*P*			$7,700
British (19th -)				
HAVELL, JR., Robert	*P*			$2,750
American (1793 - 1878)				
HAVENS, James D.	*P*			$990
American (1900 - 1960)				
HAWES, Charles	*W*			$330
American (?)				

D=Drawing, P=Painting, S=Sculpture, W=Watercolor

		Low	Mean	High
		Current Price Range		
HAWGOOD, Belle	*P*	$110	$172	$220
American (20th -)				
HAWKINS, Cornelius H.	*P*			$550
American (1861 -)				
HAWKINS, Dennis	*W*			$550
(20th -)				
HAWKINS, Henry (Attrib.)	*P*			$935
British (19th -)				
HAWKINS, John F.	*P*	$110	$138	$165
American (20th -)				
HAWKINS, Rocky	*P*	$2,310	$2,803	$3,500
American (20th -)				
HAWKS, Edith B.	*P*			$248
American (20th -)				
HAWLEY, Hughson	*D*	$605	$743	$880
American (1850 - 1936)	*W*			$660
HAWLEY, Hughson (Et al.)	*D*			$550
American (19th - 20th)				
HAWLEY, Reginald A.	*P*			$248
American (20th -)				
HAWTHORNE, Charles W.	*D*	$4,180	$5,390	$6,600
American (1872 - 1930)	*P*	$495	$9,741	$44,000
	W			$990
HAWTHORNE, Charles W. (Att.)	*P*	$3,300	$3,438	$3,575
American (1872 - 1930)				
HAWTHORNE, Marion C.	*W*			$1,100
American (1870 - 1945)				
HAY, Bernard	*P*	$2,090	$2,558	$3,025
British (1864 -)				
HAY, George	*W*			$330
British (1831 - 1912)				
HAYDEN, Charles H.	*P*	$605	$1,448	$2,640
American (1856 - 1901)				
HAYDEN, Edward P.	*P*			$2,750
American (? - 1922)				

D=Drawing, P=Painting, S=Sculpture, W=Watercolor

		Current Price Range		
		Low	Mean	High
HAYDEN, Henri	*P*	$2,200	$2,750	$3,300
French (1883 - 1970)	*W*	$2,200	$2,200	$2,200
HAYE, Reinier de la	*P*			$35,200
Dutch (1640 - 1684)				
HAYEK, Hans Von	*P*	$550	$1,265	$1,980
Austrian (1869 -)				
HAYES, Charles	*P*			$2,090
British (19th -)				
HAYES, Edwin	*P*	$2,750	$5,775	$12,100
Irish (1819 - 1904)				
HAYES, Frederick W.	*P*			$880
British (1848 - 1918)				
HAYES, William J.	*P*			$990
American (19th -)				
HAYLLAR, Edith	*P*			$4,400
British (1860 - 1948)				
HAYLLAR, James	*P*			$1,210
British (1829 -)				
HAYLLAR, Jessica	*P*			$660
British (1858 - 1940)				
HAYMES, Charles	*P*			$468
(20th -)				
HAYMSON, John	*W*			$4,675
American (1902 - 1980)				
HAYNES, Elsie H.	*D*			$165
French (20th -)				
HAYNES, John W.	*P*			$1,430
British (1836 - 1908)				
HAYNES, Nancy	*P*			$3,850
(20th -)	*S*			$3,520
HAYNES, Perry	*P*			$193
American (1870 -)				
HAYNES-WILLIAMS, John	*P*	$220	$1,467	$2,200
British (19th -)				

D=Drawing, P=Painting, S=Sculpture, W=Watercolor

		Current Price Range		
		Low	Mean	High
HAYS, Barton S.	*P*	$1,320	$1,958	$2,640
American (1826 - 1914)				
HAYS, Bret	*P*			$1,650
British (1880 - 1940)				
HAYS, George A.	*P*	$605	$1,120	$3,300
American (1854 -)	*W*	$220	$358	$495
HAYS, William J.	*P*	$990	$2,585	$4,180
American (1830 - 1875)				
HAYTER, Stanley W.	*D*	$990	$1,650	$2,310
British (1901 - 1988)	*P*	$4,675	$6,669	$10,450
	W	$4,620	$5,060	$5,500
HAYWARD, Peter	*P*	$143	$209	$275
American (1905 -)				
HAZARD, Arthur M.	*P*	$110	$935	$1,760
American (1872 - 1930)	*W*			$385
HAZEL, C. van der	*P*	$495	$798	$1,100
Belgian (1876 - 1942)				
HAZELL, B.	*P*			$308
(?)				
HAZELTON, Mary B.	*D*			$330
American (19th - 20th)	*P*	$550	$1,320	$2,090
HAZEN, Bessie E.	*W*			$330
American (1862 - 1946)				
HEAD, Cecil	*P*	$2,860	$2,915	$2,970
American (1906 -)				
HEADE, Martin J.	*D*			$7,150
American (1819 - 1904)	*P*	$8,800	$214,371	$1.100M
HEADE, Martin J. (Attrib.)	*P*			$2,420
American (1819 - 1904)				
HEALEY, C. E. H. (Attrib.)	*P*			$440
British (19th -)				
HEALY, Francis D.	*P*			$209
American (? - 1948)				

D=Drawing, P=Painting, S=Sculpture, W=Watercolor

		Current Price Range		
		Low	Mean	High
HEALY, George P. A.	*D*			$468
American (1813 - 1894)	*P*	$550	$660	$770
HEALY, George P. A. (Attrib.)	*P*			$523
American (1813 - 1894)				
HEARD, Joseph	*P*	$4,400	$5,225	$6,050
British (1799 - 1859)				
HEARN, Jack	*W*			$770
American (?)				
HEARNE, Thomas	*W*	$248	$702	$1,155
British (1744 - 1817)				
HEATH, H. P.	*P*			$220
(?)				
HEATON, Augustus G.	*P*	$385	$2,310	$5,500
American (1844 - 1931)				
HEBER, Carl A.	*S*			$770
American (1875 - 1956)				
HEBERER, Charles	*P*	$825	$2,338	$3,850
American (19th -)				
HEBERT,	*P*			$303
American (20th -)				
HEBERT, Jules	*D*	$550	$578	$605
Swiss (1812 - 1897)				
HECKEL, Erich	*W*	$7,150	$10,918	$15,400
German (1883 - 1970)				
HECKER, Robert	*P*			$605
(?)				
HECKSCHER, E. H.	*P*			$242
American (20th -)				
HEDA, Gerrit W.	*P*	$33,000	$192,500	$352,000
Dutch (? - 1702)				
HEDA, Willem C.	*P*	$209,000	$330,000	$451,000
Dutch (1598 - 1680)				
HEEM, Cornelis de	*P*	$26,400	$100,100	$220,000
Dutch (1631 - 1695)				
HEEM, David D. de	*P*			$22,000
Dutch (17th -)				

D=Drawing, P=Painting, S=Sculpture, W=Watercolor

		Current Price Range		
		Low	Mean	High
HEEM, Jan D. de	*P*	$77,000	$495,000	$1.265M
Dutch (1606 - 1684)				
HEEM, Jan D. de (Manner)	*P*			$6,600
Dutch (1606 - 1684)				
HEEMSKERCK, Egbert van (Att.)	*P*			$1,210
Dutch (1634 - 1704)				
HEEMSKERK, Marten J. van	*D*			$50,600
Dutch (1498 - 1574)	*P*			$74,250
HEEREMANS, Thomas	*P*	$7,700	$24,200	$52,800
Dutch (1660 - 1697)				
HEESAKKER, Thomas	*P*	$550	$990	$1,430
Dutch (20th -)				
HEFFNER, Karl	*P*	$4,400	$14,025	$33,000
German (1849 - 1925)				
HEFFNER, R. (Attrib.)	*P*			$385
European (19th -)				
HEGG, Teresa	*W*			$770
Swiss (19th - 20th)				
HEGI, Johann S.	*W*			$4,950
German (1747 - 1799)				
HEICKE, Joseph	*P*			$2,420
Austrian (1811 - 1861)				
HEIDE, Johannes W. van der	*P*			$2,750
Dutch (1878 -)				
HEIKKA, Earle E.	*S*	$1,210	$4,818	$11,500
American (1910 - 1941)				
HEIL, Charles E.	*P*			$220
American (1870 -)				
HEIL, Daniel van	*P*			$2,860
Flemish (1604 - 1662)				
HEILBRUN, H.	*S*			$110
(20th -)				
HEILBUTH, Ferdinand	*D*			$16,500
German (1826 - 1889)	*P*			$22,000

D=Drawing, P=Painting, S=Sculpture, W=Watercolor

		Current Price Range		
		Low	Mean	High

HEILBUTH, Ferdinand	*W*			$495
German (1826 - 1889)				
HEILMANN, Ernst	*P*			$2,200
(?)				
HEIM, Francois J.	*D*			$1,100
French (1787 - 1865)				
HEIMHIZER, Marcellus	*W*			$2,200
American (20th -)				
HEIMICK, Howard	*P*			$1,100
American (1845 - 1907)				
HEIN,	*P*			$3,300
(19th -)				
HEINISCH, Karl A.	*P*			$8,250
German (1847 - 1923)				
HEINRICH, Johann (Attrib.)	*P*			$1,650
German (1722 - 1789)				
HEINSIUS, Johann E.	*P*			$3,850
German (1740 - 1812)				
HEINSIUS, Johann E. (Circle)	*P*			$11,000
German (1740 - 1812)				
HEINZ, Charles	*P*	$385	$605	$825
American (20th -)				
HEINZE, Adolph	*P*			$660
American (1887 -)	*W*			$495
HEINZMANN, Samilla J.	*P*			$193
American (1881 -)				
HEISCHMANN, Harry G.	*P*			$715
American (19th - 20th)				
HEISEN, Mat	*S*			$715
(?)				
HEISLER, W.O.	*P*			$715
(?)				
HEISS, J. S. C.	*W*			$468
American (19th -)				
HEITKAMP, Irving	*P*			$1,320
American (? - 1917)				

D=Drawing, P=Painting, S=Sculpture, W=Watercolor

		Current Price Range		
		Low	Mean	High
HEITLAND, Wilmat E.	*W*	$550	$1,012	$1,320
American (1893 -)				
HEIZER, Michael	*D*	$3,080	$5,253	$8,250
German (1944 -)	*P*			$7,150
	S	$5,500	$16,867	$30,800
	W			$6,600
HEKKING, J. Antonio	*P*	$990	$3,813	$6,600
American (19th -)				
HELBIG, A.	*P*			$880
German (19th -)				
HELBIG, Bud	*W*	$900	$1,050	$1,200
American (20th -)				
HELCK, Peter C.	*W*	$110	$983	$2,860
American (1893 -)				
HELD, Al	*D*	$3,850	$11,190	$27,500
American (1928 -)	*P*	$20,900	$142,340	$319,000
	W			$6,050
HELD, John	*D*	$220	$778	$1,700
American (1889 - 1958)				
HELDNER, Collette	*P*	$358	$1,326	$2,090
American (20th -)				
HELDNER, Knute	*P*	$220	$1,191	$4,620
American (1884 - 1952)				
HELFERT, P.	*P*			$385
European (20th -)				
HELFFERICH, Willem	*P*	$1,760	$2,017	$2,200
Dutch (20th -)				
HELIKER, John E.	*P*			$1,320
American (1909 -)	*W*			$330
HELLBUSCH, H.	*P*			$2,200
American (19th - 20th)				
HELLESEN, Thorvald	*P*			$3,850
(?)				

D=Drawing, P=Painting, S=Sculpture, W=Watercolor

		Current Price Range		
		Low	Mean	High
HELLEU, Paul C.	D	$1,760	$52,983	$220,000
French (1859 - 1927)	P			$110,000
HELLGREWE, R.	W			$550
German (1860 -)				
HELLWAG, Rudolf	P			$550
German (1867 - 1942)				
HELMBREKER, Theodor (Circle)	P			$17,600
Flemish (1633 - 1696)				
HELMICK, Howard	W			$880
American (1845 - 1907)				
HELMONT, Zager J. van	P			$7,700
Flemish (1683 - 1726)				
HELPS, Francis	P			$1,320
British (20th -)				
HELSBY, Alfredo	P	$550	$1,870	$2,860
Chilean (1862 - 1933)				
HELST, Bartholomeus (School)	P			$35,200
Dutch (1613 - 1670)				
HEMENWAY, Louis J.	P			$330
American (1893 -)				
HEMESSEN, Catherina van	P	$14,300	$14,300	$14,300
Flemish (1504 - 1566)				
HEMESSEN, Catherina van (Att.)	P			$26,400
Flemish (1504 - 1566)				
HEMESSEN, Jan van (Follower)	P			$9,900
Dutch (16th -)				
HEMESSEN, Jan van (Studio)	P			$44,000
Dutch (16th -)				
HEMMRICH, Georg	P			$1,320
German (?)				
HEMY, Charles N.	P	$1,045	$9,698	$26,400
British (1841 - 1917)				
HENDERSON, Charles C.	P	$7,700	$13,200	$18,700
British (1803 - 1877)	W			$495

D=Drawing, P=Painting, S=Sculpture, W=Watercolor

		Current Price Range		
		Low	Mean	High

		Low	Mean	High
HENDERSON, J. (?)	P			$523
HENDERSON, Jacob S. (?)	D			$1,760
HENDERSON, John British (1860 - 1924)	P			$2,090
HENDERSON, Joseph M. British (1863 -)	P			$3,850
HENDERSON, Luis American (20th -)	P	$138	$166	$193
HENDERSON, W. British (1836 - 1874)	P			$314
HENDERSON, William P. American (1877 - 1943)	D	$2,750	$4,015	$5,280
HENDON, Cham (20th -)	P	$880	$1,540	$2,200
HENDRICKS, Bessie American (1867 - 1929)	P			$495
HENDRIKS, Gerardus Dutch (19th -)	P	$1,210	$6,105	$11,000
HENDRIKS, Willem Dutch (1828 - 1891)	P	$1,760	$2,273	$2,860
HENFELD, Ernie (20th -)	P			$3,080
HENGST, Geradus J. Dutch (20th -)	P			$121
HENKE, Bernard A. American (1888 - 1949)	P	$138	$509	$880
HENLEY, Lionel C. British (1843 -)	P			$2,475
HENNAH, John E. British (1897 -)	P	$550	$633	$715
HENNECK, G. European (19th -)	P			$275
HENNECKE, F. American (20th -)	P			$187

D=Drawing, P=Painting, S=Sculpture, W=Watercolor

		Current Price Range		
		Low	Mean	High

		Low	Mean	High
HENNER, Jean J.	P	$880	$11,185	$28,600
French (1829 - 1905)				
HENNESSEY, Frank C.	D			$1,650
American (1894 - 1941)				
HENNESSY, Richard	P			$1,980
(20th -)				
HENNESSY, William J.	P	$880	$1,210	$1,540
British (1839 - 1917)				
HENNING, Albin	P			$770
American (? - 1943)				
HENNINGS, Ernest M.	P	$8,250	$18,013	$30,800
American (1886 - 1956)	W			$18,700
HENNINGSEN, Frants P. D.	P			$4,675
Danish (1850 - 1908)				
HENNINGSEN, Henning	P			$990
Danish (19th - 20th)				
HENOCH, S. Stella	W			$165
American (?)				
HENRI, Florence	D			$4,950
French (20th -)				
HENRI, Marjorie O.	D			$165
American (1851 - 1938)				
HENRI, Michel	P			$1,210
French (1928 -)				
HENRI, Robert	D	$110	$693	$6,050
American (1865 - 1929)	P	$2,376	$35,496	$165,000
	W	$385	$963	$1,540
HENRI, Robert (Attrib.)	D			$193
American (1865 - 1929)				
HENRICH, A. J.	P			$385
(19th -)				
HENRICKSEN, William	P			$110
Danish (20th -)				
HENRIQUE,	P			$440
European (19th -)				

D=Drawing, P=Painting, S=Sculpture, W=Watercolor

		Low	Mean	High
		Current Price Range		
HENRY, Edward L.	*P*	$9,900	$55,183	$192,500
American (1841 - 1919)	*W*			$4,510
HENRY, Edwin	*P*			$900
(?)				
HENRY, Harry R.	*P*			$6,600
American (1882 - 1974)				
HENRY, Michel	*P*	$660	$1,006	$1,760
French (20th -)				
HENRY, Paul	*P*			$8,800
Irish (1876 - 1958)				
HENSCHE, Henry	*P*			$330
American (1901 -)				
HENSEL, D.	*P*	$138	$282	$440
European (19th - 20th)				
HENSELER, Ernst	*P*			$19,800
German (1852 -)				
HENSHALL, John H.	*P*			$6,600
British (1856 -)	*W*			$7,700
HENSHAW, Frederick H.	*P*			$413
British (1807 - 1897)	*W*			$880
HENSHAW, Frederick H. (Attrib.)	*P*			$1,100
British (1807 - 1897)				
HENSHAW, Glenn	*D*	$248	$475	$715
American (1881 - 1946)	*P*	$1,210	$1,843	$2,475
HENSLER, Christy A.	*P*			$385
American (20th -)				
HENSON,	*P*	$440	$468	$495
American (20th -)	*W*			$110
HENSTENBURGH, Herman	*P*			$39,600
Dutch (1667 - 1726)	*W*	$3,300	$4,620	$6,600
HENTSCHEL,	*D*			$413
European (20th -)				

D=Drawing, P=Painting, S=Sculpture, W=Watercolor

		Low	Mean	High
		Current Price Range		

		Low	Mean	High
HENWOOD, Thomas	*P*			$19,800
British (19th -)				
HENZE,	*P*			$275
German (?)				
HEPLER, R. M.	*W*			$297
(?)				
HEPPLE, Wilson	*P*			$1,760
British (1854 - 1937)				
HEPWORTH, Barbara	*S*	$9,350	$51,023	$132,000
British (1903 -)	*W*			$44,000
HERAU, Jules	*P*			$5,060
Dutch (19th -)				
HERAUT, Henri	*P*			$440
French (1894 -)				
HERBERTE, Alfred	*W*			$880
British (? - 1861)				
HERBERTE, Edward B.	*P*	$4,180	$11,165	$18,150
British (1857 - 1893)				
HERBIN, Auguste	*P*	$14,300	$101,475	$319,000
French (1882 - 1960)	*W*	$8,250	$16,225	$24,200
HERBO, Fernand	*P*			$8,250
French (1905 -)				
HERBO, Leon	*P*	$1,980	$3,465	$4,950
Belgian (1850 - 1907)				
HERBST, Frank C.	*P*	$193	$193	$193
American (20th -)				
HERCKE, E. van (Attrib.)	*P*	$100	$100	$100
American (20th -)				
HERERA, G.	*P*			$1,210
European (20th -)				
HERGENRODER, Emile	*P*			$660
American (19th - 20th)				
HERING, Harry	*P*			$770
American (1887 - 1967)				

D=Drawing, P=Painting, S=Sculpture, W=Watercolor

		Current Price Range		
		Low	Mean	High
HERKOMER, Hubert	*P*			$248
British (1849 - 1914)				
HERLAND, Emma	*P*			$8,800
French (1856 - 1947)				
HERLEY, H. L.	*P*			$385
European (19th -)				
HERMANN, Emil	*P*	$550	$550	$550
German (19th - 20th)				
HERMANN, G.	*P*			$154
(?)				
HERMANN, Hans	*W*			$248
German (1813 - 1890)				
HERMANN, J.	*P*			$110
(19th -)				
HERMANN, Ludwig	*P*	$660	$11,880	$29,700
German (1812 - 1881)				
HERMANNSTORFER, Joseph	*P*			$2,640
German (1817 - 1901)				
HERMANS, T. O.	*W*			$660
European (19th -)				
HERMANSEN, Olaf A.	*P*			$3,300
Danish (1849 - 1897)				
HERNANDEZ, Caesar	*P*			$1,210
American (20th -)	*W*			$1,650
HERNANDEZ, J.	*P*			$1,540
(19th -)				
HERNANDEZ, Manuel	*P*			$4,400
Colombian (20th -)				
HERNDON, Charles	*S*			$1,100
American (20th -)				
HERON, Patrick	*W*			$660
British (1920 -)				
HERP, Willem van	*P*	$6,600	$12,421	$24,200
Flemish (1614 - 1676)				
HERP, Willem van (Attrib.)	*P*	$3,520	$6,710	$9,900
Flemish (1614 - 1676)				

D=Drawing, P=Painting, S=Sculpture, W=Watercolor

		Current Price Range		
		Low	Mean	High

		Low	Mean	High
HERPFER, Carl	P			$159,500
German (1836 - 1897)				
HERPIN, Leon-P.	P			$3,850
French (1841 - 1880)	W	$605	$963	$1,320
HERRERA, YOUNGER, Francisco	P			$396,000
Spanish (1622 - 1685)				
HERRICK, Henry W.	W	$110	$688	$1,320
American (1824 - 1906)				
HERRING, JR., John F.	P	$3,300	$22,042	$57,750
British (1815 - 1907)				
HERRING, JR., John F. (Attrib.)	P			$3,850
British (1815 - 1907)				
HERRING, JR., John F. (Follower)	P	$1,320	$5,665	$13,200
British (1815 - 1907)				
HERRING, JR., John F. (Manner)	P	$1,870	$3,410	$4,950
British (1815 - 1907)				
HERRING, JR., John F. (School)	P			$4,400
British (1815 - 1907)				
HERRING, JR., John F. (Studio)	P			$2,310
British (1815 - 1907)				
HERRING, SR., John F.	P	$1,430	$106,168	$495,000
British (1795 - 1865)				
HERRING, SR., John F. (Follower)	P			$6,050
British (1795 - 1865)				
HERRING, SR., John F. (Manner)	P			$3,025
British (1795 - 1865)				
HERRING, SR., John F. (Studio)	P			$2,750
British (1795 - 1865)				
HERRING,SR. & STUDIO, John F.	P			$25,300
British (1795 - 1865)				
HERRMANN, Hans	P			$10,450
German (1858 - 1942)				
HERRMANN, Leo	P			$1,100
French (1853 -)				
HERRMANNSTORFER, J.	P			$2,475
German (1817 - 1901)				

D=Drawing, P=Painting, S=Sculpture, W=Watercolor

		Current Price Range		
		Low	Mean	High

		Low	Mean	High
HERRON, Jason	*S*	$303	$365	$523
American (1900 -)				
HERSESHEIMER, Ella	*P*			$2,200
American (20th -)				
HERTEL, Paul	*P*			$468
American (?)				
HERTER, Adele	*P*	$935	$2,063	$3,190
American (1869 - 1946)				
HERTER, Albert	*P*	$33,000	$45,375	$57,750
American (1871 - 1950)	*W*			$4,400
HERVE, Jules-R.	*P*	$165	$4,111	$16,500
French (1887 - 1982)				
HERVIER, Louis A.	*P*			$1,650
French (19th -)				
HERWEGEN-MANINI, Veronica	*P*			$880
German (1851 -)				
HERZEL, Paul	*S*			$5,500
American (1876 -)				
HERZOG, Frans M.	*W*			$330
American (19th - 20th)				
HERZOG, Hermann	*D*			$110
American (1832 - 1932)	*P*	$110	$13,481	$49,500
HERZOG, Hermann (Attrib.)	*P*			$4,400
American (1832 - 1932)				
HERZOG, Lewis	*P*			$413
American (1868 -)				
HERZOG, Max	*P*			$110
American (19th -)				
HESS, A.	*P*			$330
(20th -)				
HESS, Sara	*P*	$550	$798	$1,045
American (1880 -)				
HESSE, Eve	*D*	$14,300	$40,150	$110,000
American (1936 - 1970)	*W*			$18,700

D=Drawing, P=Painting, S=Sculpture, W=Watercolor

		Current Price Range		
		Low	Mean	High
HESSE, Hans M. von	P			$2,310
German (20th -)				
HESSEL,	P			$550
(?)				
HESSELIUS, John	P	$4,400	$6,325	$8,250
American (1725 - 1778)				
HETZEL, George	P	$3,025	$3,850	$5,225
American (1826 - 1899)				
HETZEL, L.	P			$110
(20th -)				
HEULLANT, Felix A.	P			$7,480
French (1834 -)				
HEURLIN, Magnus R.	P			$33,000
American (19th - 20th)				
HEUSCH, Jacob de	P	$29,700	$39,600	$49,500
Dutch (1657 - 1701)				
HEUSTON, Frank Z.	P			$110
American (1880 -)				
HEVINSON, Estaer S.	P			$413
(?)				
HEWES, Horace G.	P	$121	$264	$578
American (19th -)				
HEWITT, Edward	P			$605
American (20th -)				
HEWITT, Enid	S			$1,210
American (20th -)				
HEWITT, Mabel	P			$385
American (1903 - 1987)				
HEYDEN, B. van der	P	$275	$440	$605
Dutch (20th -)				
HEYDEN, Gerard van der	P			$578
Belgian (19th -)				
HEYDEN, Jan van der	P	$16,500	$46,750	$77,000
Dutch (1637 - 1712)				
HEYDEN, Jan van der (After)	P			$770
Dutch (1637 - 1712)				

D=Drawing, P=Painting, S=Sculpture, W=Watercolor

		Current Price Range	
	Low	Mean	High

		Low	Mean	High
HEYDEN, Jan van der (Follower)	P			$3,300
Dutch (1637 - 1712)				
HEYDENDAHL, Friedrich J. N.	P	$1,870	$2,228	$2,750
German (1844 - 1906)				
HEYER, Arthur	P	$1,320	$3,652	$5,500
German (1872 - 1931)				
HEYERMANS, Jean A.	P			$3,740
Belgian (1837 -)				
HEYLIGERS, Hendrik	P			$4,950
Dutch (1877 - 1915)				
HEYN, August	P			$5,500
German (1837 -)				
HIBBARD, Aldro T.	D			$110
American (1886 - 1972)	P	$1,100	$4,640	$16,500
HIBBARD, Aldro T. (Attrib.)	P			$1,430
American (1886 - 1972)				
HIBBARD, Frederick C.	S			$1,540
American (1881 -)				
HIBBARD, Marsh	P			$2,475
American (20th -)				
HIBBARD, Mary	P			$880
(20th -)				
HIBEL, Edna	D			$275
American (1917 -)	P	$468	$537	$605
	W			$220
HICKEY, Thomas (Attrib.)	P			$3,300
British (1741 - 1824)				
HICKINS, Walter H.	S			$220
American (1936 - 1984)				
HICKS, D.	P			$165
American (?)				
HICKS, George E.	P	$10,450	$21,725	$33,000
British (1824 - 1914)				
HICKS, George H.	P	$1,265	$1,265	$1,265
American (19th - 20th)				

D=Drawing, P=Painting, S=Sculpture, W=Watercolor

		Current Price Range		
		Low	Mean	High
HICKS, Morley	P	$110	$261	$440
American (20th -)				
HICKS, Morley (Attrib.)	P			$200
American (20th -)				
HICKS, Richard C.	P			$193
American (20th -)				
HICKS, Thomas	P	$935	$4,868	$8,800
American (1823 - 1890)				
HICKS, Thomas (Attrib.)	P			$4,675
American (1823 - 1890)				
HIDALGO, Linares F.	P			$550
Spanish (1880 -)				
HIDER, Frank	P	$385	$803	$1,100
British (19th - 20th)				
HIER, A. Van	P			$1,650
Dutch (19th - 20th)				
HIGBY, Wayne	S	$2,200	$3,740	$5,280
(20th -)				
HIGGINS, Eugene	D	$110	$660	$1,210
American (1874 - 1958)	P	$385	$1,505	$6,600
	W	$248	$317	$385
HIGGINS, Fred	P			$138
British (19th -)				
HIGGINS, George	P	$385	$1,408	$3,080
American (19th -)				
HIGGINS, Michael	S			$110
American (20th -)				
HIGGINS, Tom	P			$132
(?)				
HIGGINS, Victor	W			$24,750
American (1884 - 1949)				
HIGGINSON, Dudley C.	P			$220
American (1908 -)				
HIGHMORE, Joseph	P			$10,450
British (1692 - 1780)				

D=Drawing, P=Painting, S=Sculpture, W=Watercolor

		Current Price Range		
		Low	Mean	High

HIGHMORE, Joseph (Follower)	P			$715
British (1692 - 1780)				
HIGHMORE, Joseph (Style)	P			$1,760
British (1692 - 1780)				
HIGHMORE, Thomas (School)	P			$935
British (18th -)				
HIGHSMITH, Robert	W			$110
(?)				
HIGHSTEIN, Jene	P			$2,420
(20th -)				
HIGUERO, Enrique M.	W			$1,100
(?)				
HILAIRE, Camille	D			$1,650
French (1916 -)	P	$4,675	$12,788	$20,900
HILBERT, C.	P			$303
German (19th - 20th)				
HILBERT, Robert	W			$165
American (?)				
HILDEBRANDT, Edouard	P			$2,750
German (1818 - 1869)	W			$715
HILDEBRANDT, Howard L.	P	$165	$1,073	$1,760
American (1872 - 1958)				
HILDERBRAND, Emile	P	$110	$193	$275
German (19th - 20th)				
HILDERBRANDT, Fritz	P			$6,050
German (1878 -)				
HILDITCH, George (Attrib.)	P			$4,400
British (1803 - 1857)				
HILER, Hilaire	P			$4,180
American (1898 -)				
HILGERS, Carl	P	$3,080	$4,428	$5,775
German (1818 - 1890)				
HILL, Albert D.	P	$1,210	$2,943	$4,675
American (19th -)				

D=Drawing, P=Painting, S=Sculpture, W=Watercolor

		Current Price Range		
		Low	Mean	High

		Low	Mean	High
HILL, Andrew P. American (1853 - 1922)	*P*			$220
HILL, Arthur British (19th -)	*P*			$2,530
HILL, C. W. American (20th -)	*P*			$110
HILL, Clara American (20th -)	*S*			$550
HILL, Derek British (1916 -)	*P*			$605
HILL, Edward American (1843 - 1923)	*P*	$330	$653	$935
HILL, Edward R. American (1852 - 1908)	*P*	$385	$1,166	$1,980
HILL, George S. American (19th -)	*P*			$825
HILL, Howard American (19th -)	*P*	$1,430	$3,121	$8,250
HILL, J. Henry American (1839 - 1922)	*D* *W*	$605	$2,959	$275 $5,720
HILL, James J. British (1811 - 1882)	*P*	$4,400	$9,900	$15,400
HILL, James S. British (1854 - 1921)	*P*			$1,100
HILL, John W. American (1812 - 1879)	*D* *W*	$7,150 $990	$7,425 $3,394	$7,700 $9,350
HILL, Julia American (1888 -)	*S*	$110	$128	$165
HILL, Margaret E. American (18th -)	*P*			$165
HILL, Mary B. American (?)	*W*			$165
HILL, Mason M. European (19th - 20th)	*P*			$1,980

D=Drawing, P=Painting, S=Sculpture, W=Watercolor

| | | Current Price Range | | |
		Low	Mean	High
HILL, Michael J. (?)	*P*			$198
HILL, Polly (?)	*W*			$600
HILL, Thomas American (1829 - 1908)	*P*	$132	$10,245	$41,250
HILL, Thomas (Attrib.) American (1829 - 1908)	*P*	$495	$1,668	$3,080
HILL, Thomas (Style) American (1829 - 1908)	*P*			$2,750
HILL, W. H. British (19th -)	*P*	$990	$1,045	$1,100
HILL, William E. American (1886 - 1962)	*D*			$605
HILL, JR., Thomas Virgil American (1871 - 1922)	*P*			$2,200
HILL, JR., Thomas Virgil (Attrib.) American (1871 - 1922)	*P*			$1,045
HILLAIRET, Anatole E. (Attrib.) French (1881 - 1928)	*P*			$303
HILLBOM, Henrik American (1863 - 1928)	*P*	$385	$427	$468
HILLEN, T. (?)	*P*			$550
HILLIARD, William H. American (1836 - 1905)	*P*	$303	$721	$1,320
HILLINGFORD, Robert A. British (1825 - 1904)	*P*	$1,650	$14,575	$27,500
HILLS, Anna A. American (1882 - 1930)	*P* *W*	$495	$1,657	$6,600 $935
HILLS, Laura C. American (1859 - 1952)	*D* *P*	$4,400 $2,310	$11,871 $5,830	$45,100 $9,350
HILLS, Robert (Attrib.) British (1769 - 1844)	*D*			$495

D=Drawing, P=Painting, S=Sculpture, W=Watercolor

		Current Price Range		
		Low	Mean	High

HILLSMITH, Fannie	*P*			$4,400
American (19th - 20th)				
HILLYARD, D. H.	*P*			$605
(19th - 20th)				
HILLYER, Catharine A.	*D*			$303
American (?)				
HILLYER, William	*P*			$1,430
British (19th -)				
HILTON, John W.	*D*			$413
American (1904 -)	*P*	$660	$803	$1,210
HILVERDINK, Johannes (Attrib.)	*P*			$1,600
Dutch (1813 - 1902)				
HINCKLEY, Thomas H.	*P*	$3,520	$4,840	$6,600
American (1813 - 1896)				
HINCKLEY, Thomas H. (Attrib.)	*P*			$2,200
American (1813 - 1896)				
HINE, Charles	*P*			$1,760
American (1821 - 1871)				
HINES, F. C.	*W*			$1,100
British (19th -)				
HINES, Fred M.	*P*	$193.	$207	$220
American (20th -)				
HINES, Jack	*W*			$1,600
American (20th -)				
HINGLER,	*P*			$110
American (20th -)				
HINKLE, Clarence K.	*D*			$935
American (1880 - 1960)	*P*	$413	$2,618	$7,700
	W	$605	$1,155	$2,475
HINLEY, Alfred	*W*			$369
British (1845 -)				
HINMAN, Charles	*P*	$2,640	$5,956	$9,900
American (1932 -)				
HINOJOSA, Armando	*W*			$400
American (20th -)				

D=Drawing, P=Painting, S=Sculpture, W=Watercolor

		Current Price Range		
		Low	Mean	High
HINTERMEISTER, Henry	*P*	$550	$4,219	$8,800
American (1897 -)				
HINTERREITER, Hans	*P*	$3,850	$5,363	$6,050
Swiss (1902 -)				
HIQUILY, Philippe	*S*			$35,200
French (20th -)				
HIRSCH, Alphonse	*P*			$55,000
French (1843 - 1884)				
HIRSCH, Joseph	*D*			$1,540
American (1920 - 1981)	*P*	$660	$8,863	$24,200
HIRSCH, Stefan	*P*	$330	$19,965	$39,600
American (1899 - 1964)				
HIRSCHBERG, Alice K. N.	*P*			$165
American (1856 -)				
HIRSCHBERG, Carl	*P*	$275	$1,045	$2,860
American (1854 - 1923)				
HIRSCHFELD, Al	*D*			$2,200
American (19th - 20th)				
HIRSCHMAN,	*D*			$468
German (19th -)				
HIRST, Claude R.	*P*	$13,200	$14,850	$16,500
American (1855 - 1942)	*W*			$4,620
HIRT, Heinrich	*P*			$38,500
German (19th -)				
HIRTZ, Albert	*P*			$220
European (20th -)				
HISPANO-FLEMISH SCHOOL,	*P*			$8,800
(16th -)				
HISPANUS, Johannes	*P*			$66,000
Spanish (15th - 16th)				
HITCHCOCK, George	*P*	$1,650	$16,178	$66,000
American (1850 - 1913)	*W*			$660
HITCHCOCK, Lucius W.	*P*			$3,520

D=Drawing, P=Painting, S=Sculpture, W=Watercolor

		Current Price Range		
		Low	Mean	High

		Low	Mean	High
HITCHCOCK, Lucius W. American (1868 - 1942)	W			$880
HITCHCOCK, M. R. (?)	P			$110
HITCHINGS, Henry American (? - 1903)	W			$193
HITTELL, Charles J. American (1861 - 1938)	P			$990
HITZ, Conrad Swiss (1798 - 1866)	P			$3,300
HOARE, William (Attrib.) British (1706 - 1799)	P			$1,980
HOBAN, Therese American (19th -)	P			$825
HOBART, Clark American (1868 - 1948)	P	$825	$6,032	$15,400
HOBBEMA, Meindert (After) Dutch (1638 - 1709)	P			$13,200
HOBBEMA, Meindert (Attrib.) Dutch (1638 - 1709)	P			$44,000
HOBBEMA, Meindert (M⸱⸱er) Dutch (1638 - 1709)	P	$2,200	$2,475	$2,750
HOBBEMA, Meindert (Style) Dutch (1638 - 1709)	P			$9,900
HOBBS, George T. American (1846 -)	P			$633
HOBBS, Louise A. American (?)	S			$1,430
HOBBS, Morris H. American (1892 - 1967)	D			$264
HOCH-LAND, John (20th -)	P			$165
HOCHE, Alyce American (19th - 20th)	W			$132
HOCKNEY, David	D	$12,100	$52,773	$209,000

D=Drawing, P=Painting, S=Sculpture, W=Watercolor

		Current Price Range		
		Low	Mean	High
HOCKNEY, David	*P*	$18,700	$678,563	$2.200M
British (1937 -)	*S*			$24,750
	W	$19,800	$121,825	$319,000
HODGDON, Sylvester	*P*	$220	$1,045	$2,200
American (1830 - 1906)				
HODGES, Charles H. (Attrib.)	*P*			$1,320
British (1764 - 1837)				
HODGIN, Marston D.	*P*			$475
American (1903 -)				
HODGKIN, Howard	*P*	$15,400	$262,680	$506,000
British (1932 -)				
HODGSON, John E.	*P*			$3,850
British (1836 - 1895)				
HODGSON, Phillip	*P*			$440
American (20th -)				
HODICKE, K. H.	*P*	$28,600	$30,800	$33,000
(20th -)				
HODL, C.	*P*			$550
Austrian (19th -)				
HOEBER, Arthur	*P*	$165	$2,079	$4,620
American (1854 - 1915)				
HOEDRIENG,	*P*			$660
European (19th -)				
HOEF, Abraham van der	*P*			$8,525
Dutch (17th -)				
HOEFFLER, Adolf	*P*	$3,850	$16,225	$28,600
German (1826 - 1898)				
HOERMANN, Theodor von	*P*	$41,800	$52,525	$63,250
Austrian (1840 - 1895)				
HOERNER, M. E.	*P*			$660
German (19th - 20th)				
HOESS, E. L.	*P*			$248
German (20th -)				
HOET, Gerard (Attrib.)	*P*			$5,500
Dutch (1648 - 1733)				

D=Drawing, P=Painting, S=Sculpture, W=Watercolor

		Current Price Range		
		Low	Mean	High

		Low	Mean	High
HOETGER, Bernhard	*S*			$3,300
German (1874 - 1949)				
HOFEL, Johann N.	*P*			$8,800
German (1786 - 1864)				
HOFER, Heinrich	*P*			$4,400
German (1825 - 1878)				
HOFER, Karl	*P*	$27,500	$55,000	$82,500
German (1878 - 1955)				
HOFER, M.	*P*			$1,210
German (19th -)				
HOFF, Guy	*D*	$600	$1,400	$2,200
American (1889 - 1962)				
HOFF, SR., Carl H.	*P*			$2,200
German (1838 - 1890)				
HOFFBAUER, Charles J.	*D*	$110	$1,506	$5,500
American (1875 - 1957)	*P*	$165	$1,189	$3,080
	W	$110	$270	$468
HOFFMAN, Adrian	*P*			$3,080
(?)				
HOFFMAN, Arnold	*P*			$1,430
American (1886 - 1966)	*W*			$110
HOFFMAN, Gustave A.	*P*	$248	$276	$303
American (1869 - 1945)	*W*			$1,018
HOFFMAN, Harry	*P*			$1,650
American (1874 - 1966)	*W*			$330
HOFFMAN, Irwin D.	*P*	$523	$757	$990
American (1901 -)				
HOFFMAN, Malvina	*S*	$1,320	$7,840	$24,200
American (1887 - 1966)				
HOFFMAN, Richard P.	*W*			$110
American (1911 -)				
HOFFMAN, Ronald	*P*			$110
American (20th -)				

D=Drawing, P=Painting, S=Sculpture, W=Watercolor

		Current Price Range		
		Low	Mean	High
HOFFMANN, Frank B.	*D*			$1,980
American (1888 - 1958)	*S*			$4,675
HOFLAND, K.	*P*			$633
Dutch (20th -)				
HOFLEHNER, Rudolph	*S*			$33,000
Austrian (1916 -)				
HOFLER, Max	*P*			$1,320
British (20th -)				
HOFMANN, A.	*P*			$3,850
German (19th -)				
HOFMANN, Ansen	*P*			$1,650
Scandinavn (19th -)				
HOFMANN, E. A.	*P*			$1,760
Austrian (19th - 20th)				
HOFMANN, E. F.	*P*			$1,430
American (20th -)				
HOFMANN, Earl	*P*	$880	$1,485	$2,090
American (20th -)				
HOFMANN, Hans	*D*	$715	$8,846	$41,800
American (1880 - 1966)	*P*	$12,100	$153,593	$682,000
	W	$3,575	$34,275	$66,000
HOFMANN, Heinrich	*P*	$770	$1,155	$1,540
German (19th -)				
HOFSTEN, H. von	*W*			$242
(?)				
HOGARTH, William (After)	*P*			$358
British (1697 - 1764)				
HOGARTH, William (Circle)	*P*			$2,750
British (1697 - 1764)				
HOGARTH, William (Manner)	*P*			$385
British (1697 - 1764)				
HOGARTH, William (Style)	*P*			$880
British (1697 - 1764)				
HOGG, George C.	*P*			$1,430
American (20th -)				

D=Drawing, P=Painting, S=Sculpture, W=Watercolor

		Current Price Range		
		Low	Mean	High

HOGG, W. (?)	P			$187
HOGGETT, William British (19th - 20th)	P			$495
HOGUET, Charles French (1821 - 1870)	P	$6,050	$6,050	$6,050
HOHENREIN, L.S. European (19th -)	P			$1,980
HOHLWEIN, L. German (1850 - 1920)	W			$1,650
HOHNSTEDT, Peter L. American (1872 - 1957)	P	$660	$880	$1,100
HOIN, Claude-Jean-Baptiste French (1750 - 1817)	P	$3,850	$9,075	$14,300
HOIT, William American (?)	P			$3,300
HOKE, M. H. (Et al.) American (19th - 20th)	D			$880
HOLBEIN, Hans (After) German (1497 - 1593)	P	$1,320	$5,060	$8,800
HOLBEIN, Hans (Manner) German (1497 - 1593)	P	$1,870	$2,365	$2,860
HOLBERG, Richard A. American (1889 - 1912)	P	$990	$1,045	$1,100
HOLBERTON, Walseman American (1839 - 1938)	P	$605	$1,183	$1,760
HOLBROOK, Hollis (1909 -)	P			$275
HOLDEN, Lephe American (1884 -)	W	$110	$110	$110
HOLDREDGE, Ransom G. American (1836 - 1899)	P	$550	$1,302	$2,750
HOLDREDGE, Ransom G. (Attrib.) American (1836 - 1899)	P			$523
HOLFFERICH, Wilhelm (19th -)	P			$2,200

D=Drawing, P=Painting, S=Sculpture, W=Watercolor

| | | Current Price Range | | |
		Low	Mean	High
HOLIDAY, Gilbert	*D*			$4,950
British (1879 - 1937)	*W*			$7,700
HOLL, Frank	*P*			$104,500
British (1845 - 1888)				
HOLL, Mildred	*P*			$440
British (19th -)				
HOLLAENDER, A.	*P*			$2,090
European (19th - 20th)				
HOLLAMS, Florence M.	*P*			$2,750
British (1877 - 1963)				
HOLLAND, James	*P*	$770	$853	$935
British (1799 - 1870)				
HOLLAND, Nathan	*P*			$165
(20th -)				
HOLLAND, Tom	*P*	$880	$4,758	$10,450
American (1936 -)	*S*	$1,100	$4,446	$13,200
HOLLANDER, Gino	*P*	$605	$770	$990
(20th -)				
HOLLEN, John	*P*			$2,475
American (19th -)				
HOLLERER, F.	*P*			$1,320
American (19th -)				
HOLLERN, Mike	*S*	$550	$800	$1,000
American (20th -)				
HOLLINGSWORTH, Thomas	*P*			$2,750
British (1857 - 1885)				
HOLLINS, J.	*P*			$143
American (19th -)				
HOLLIS, Samuel	*P*			$110
American (19th - 20th)				
HOLLISTER, Antoinette B.	*S*			$1,760
American (1873 -)				
HOLLOWAY,	*P*			$330
(?)				

D=Drawing, P=Painting, S=Sculpture, W=Watercolor

		Current Price Range		
		Low	Mean	High

HOLLOWAY, Charles	*P*			$990
American (1859 - 1941)				
HOLLOWAY, F.	*P*			$5,775
American (19th -)				
HOLLOWELL, Robert	*P*			$660
American (20th -)				
HOLLYER, Maud	*W*			$990
(?)				
HOLLYER, W. P.	*P*			$440
(?)				
HOLM, Carl O.	*P*			$1,430
American (1885 - 1918)				
HOLMAN, Louis A.	*P*			$275
American (1866 - 1939)				
HOLMBOE, Thorolf	*P*			$660
Norwegian (1866 - 1955)				
HOLMES, Ralph	*P*	$303	$911	$2,475
American (1876 - 1963)				
HOLMES, Rhoda	*P*			$1,980
British (19th -)				
HOLMES, S.	*P*			$303
(?)				
HOLMGREN, R. John	*W*			$1,210
American (1897 - 1963)				
HOLMSTEDT, J.	*P*			$440
Scandinavian (19th - 20th)				
HOLSOE, Carl V.	*P*	$17,600	$22,550	$27,500
Danish (1863 - 1935)				
HOLST, Johannes	*P*			$2,640
European (20th -)				
HOLST, Laurits B.	*P*			$1,540
American (19th -)				
HOLSTAYN, Josef	*P*			$4,950
German (20th -)				
HOLSTAYN, Josef (Attrib.)	*P*			$990
German (20th -)				

D=Drawing, P=Painting, S=Sculpture, W=Watercolor

| | | Current Price Range | | |
		Low	Mean	High
HOLT, Geoffrey	*P*			$715
American (1882 - 1977)				
HOLT, S.	*P*			$193
British (19th - 20th)				
HOLTY, Carl R.	*D*	$550	$1,147	$2,200
American (1900 - 1973)	*P*	$660	$2,534	$7,700
	S			$3,850
	W	$3,080	$3,603	$4,125
HOLUB, Georg	*P*	$990	$1,430	$1,870
Austrian (1861 - 1919)				
HOLYOKE, M. E.	*P*			$963
American (19th -)				
HOLZER, Jenny	*P*			$82,500
(20th -)	*S*	$3,740	$11,770	$19,800
HOLZER, Joseph	*P*			$8,800
Austrian (1824 - 1876)				
HOMAN, H. David	*W*			$385
American (20th -)				
HOMER, Winslow	*D*	$4,950	$37,331	$121,000
American (1836 - 1910)	*P*			$880,000
	W	$38,500	$260,250	$550,000
HOMER, Winslow (Attrib.)	*P*			$3,080
American (1836 - 1910)				
HOMEXT, H. M.	*W*			$1,210
Dutch (19th -)				
HOMITZKY, Peter	*P*	$1,100	$1,100	$1,100
(20th -)				
HONDECOETER, Melchior de	*P*	$18,700	$94,050	$165,000
Dutch (1636 - 1695)				
HONDECOETER, Melchior de (Sc)	*P*	$7,150	$8,250	$9,350
Dutch (1636 - 1695)				
HONDIUS, Abraham	*P*	$16,500	$24,750	$33,000
Dutch (1625 - 1693)				

D=Drawing, P=Painting, S=Sculpture, W=Watercolor

		Current Price Range		
		Low	Mean	High

		Low	Mean	High
HONDIUS, Gerrit	*D*			$220
American (1891 - 1970)	*P*	$600	$850	$1,100
	W	$225	$308	$425
HONE, Nathaniel	*P*			$3,850
Irish (1718 - 1784)				
HONGHAI, Pan	*P*	$330	$399	$440
Chinese (20th -)				
HONIGBERGER, E.	*P*			$605
European (20th -)				
HONIKE, A.	*W*			$165
American (?)				
HONNEGARD,	*P*			$220
American (19th -)				
HONTHORST, Gerrit van	*P*			$286,000
Dutch (1590 - 1656)				
HONTHORST, Gerrit van (Studio)	*P*			$7,700
Dutch (1590 - 1656)				
HONTHORST, Willem van	*P*			$16,500
Dutch (1594 - 1666)				
HOOCH, David de	*P*			$33,000
(17th -)				
HOOCH, Horatius de (Attrib.)	*P*			$6,600
Dutch (17th -)				
HOOCH, Horatius de (School)	*P*			$2,750
Dutch (17th -)				
HOOCH, Pieter de	*P*			$132,000
Dutch (1629 - 1684)				
HOOD, George W.	*P*			$385
American (1869 - 1949)				
HOOG, Bernard de	*D*			$110
French (1867 - 1943)	*P*	$1,980	$7,826	$23,100
HOOGSTRATEN, Samuel van	*P*	$33,000	$126,500	$220,000
Flemish (1627 - 1678)				
HOOKE, Richard	*W*			$600
British (1823 - 1887)				

D=Drawing, P=Painting, S=Sculpture, W=Watercolor

		Current Price Range		
		Low	Mean	High

HOOKS, Mitchell	*P*			$250
(1923 -)				
HOOPER, John H.	*P*	$935	$2,118	$3,300
British (19th -)				
HOOPER, William G.	*P*			$2,420
British (1870 - 1898)				
HOOVEN, Herbert N.	*P*	$908	$922	$935
American (1897 -)				
HOPE, C. A. W.	*P*			$2,860
(19th -)				
HOPE, C. H.	*P*			$1,650
American (19th -)				
HOPE, James	*P*	$2,695	$4,455	$6,600
American (1818 - 1892)				
HOPE, Thelma P.	*P*	$193	$289	$385
American (1898 -)				
HOPE, Thomas	*P*	$413	$981	$1,430
American (? - 1926)				
HOPKIN, Robert	*D*			$220
American (1832 - 1909)	*P*	$303	$928	$1,650
	W	$149	$286	$495
HOPKINS, Budd	*P*	$880	$1,100	$1,320
American (1931 -)	*S*	$1,100	$1,155	$1,210
HOPKINS, George E. (Attrib.)	*P*	$121	$121	$121
American (1855 -)				
HOPKINS, Peter	*P*			$5,500
American (?)				
HOPKINS, William H.	*P*			$550
British (19th - 20th)				
HOPKINS, William H. (Et al.)	*P*			$30,800
British (19th - 20th)				
HOPKINSON, Charles S.	*P*	$11,000	$11,550	$12,100
American (1869 - 1962)	*W*	$825	$1,018	$1,210

D=Drawing, P=Painting, S=Sculpture, W=Watercolor

		Current Price Range		
		Low	Mean	High
HOPKINSON, Glen	P	$770	$880	$990
American (20th -)	W			$450
HOPKINSON, Harold	P			$1,100
American (20th -)				
HOPPENBROUWERS, Johannes	P			$800
Dutch (1791 - 1866)	W			$770
HOPPER, Edward	D	$3,080	$7,576	$18,700
American (1882 - 1967)	P			$88,000
	W	$3,850	$61,820	$137,500
HOPPIN, Thomas F.	P			$1,870
American (1816 - 1872)				
HOPPNER, John	P	$3,850	$5,225	$7,150
British (1758 - 1810)				
HOPPNER, John (Circle)	P	$1,760	$2,668	$3,575
British (1758 - 1810)				
HOPPNER, John (Follower)	P			$2,200
British (1758 - 1810)				
HORACEK, Ferdinand	P			$495
(19th -)				
HORACIO,	P	$4,950	$7,538	$17,600
Mexican (1912 -)				
HOREMANS, ELDER, Jan J.	P			$23,100
Flemish (1682 - 1759)				
HOREMANS, ELDER, Jan J. (Att)	P			$4,400
Flemish (1682 - 1759)				
HOREMANS, YOUNGER, Jan J.	P			$1,980
Flemish (1714 - 1790)				
HORGER, D.	P			$248
(?)				
HORLOR, George W.	P	$1,760	$10,802	$35,750
British (19th -)				
HORLOR, Joseph	P			$880
British (19th -)				

D=Drawing, P=Painting, S=Sculpture, W=Watercolor

| | | Current Price Range | | |
		Low	Mean	High
HORN, H. G. American (19th -)	W			$176
HORN & NEY, C. & A. European (19th - 20th)	P			$523
HORNAK, Ian American (1944 -)	P			$935
HORNBARY, W. (?)	P	$660	$702	$743
HORNBY, Lester American (1882 - 1956)	D	$358	$404	$440
	P			$165
	W	$138	$226	$330
HORNE, C. L. American (19th -)	P			$358
HORRADEN, R. B. (Attrib.) (?)	P			$110
HORSCHELT, Theodore German (1829 - 1871)	P			$55,000
HORSLEY, John C. British (1817 - 1903)	P	$7,700	$14,850	$22,000
HORSTMEIER, Albert American (1869 - 1940)	P			$138
HORTER, Earle American (1881 - 1940)	D	$132	$796	$1,155
	P			$550
	W	$350	$3,209	$11,000
HORTIG, Hans (?)	P			$1,650
HORTON, American (20th -)	P			$440
HORTON, A. Gertrude American (20th -)	P			$165
HORTON, William S. American (1865 - 1936)	D	$303	$1,812	$4,400
	P	$660	$8,484	$24,200
	W	$330	$6,215	$12,100

D=Drawing, P=Painting, S=Sculpture, W=Watercolor

		Current Price Range		
		Low	Mean	High

		Low	Mean	High
HORVATH,	*P*			$413
Hungarian (19th - 20th)				
HORVATH, Bela	*P*			$198
American (20th -)				
HORWATER, Joseph E.	*P*			$935
European (1854 - 1925)				
HOSKINS, Gayle	*P*	$605	$1,993	$4,950
American (1877 -)	*W*			$1,375
HOTCHKISS, Edna B.	*W*			$358
American (20th -)				
HOTCHKISS, Thomas H.	*P*			$110
(19th -)				
HOTTOT, Louis	*S*			$550
French (1834 - 1905)				
HOUDON, Jean-A.	*S*			$880,000
French (1741 - 1828)				
HOUDON, Jean-A. (After)	*S*	$550	$5,353	$18,700
French (1741 - 1828)				
HOUGH, William	*W*			$825
British (19th -)				
HOUGUE, Jean de la	*P*			$1,870
French (1874 - 1959)				
HOUKE, Van Der	*P*			$1,073
Dutch (?)				
HOUSE, Van	*P*			$2,200
(?)				
HOUSSIN, Edouard C. M	*S*			$880
French (1847 - 1917)				
HOUSTON, Cody	*S*	$800	$2,050	$3,300
American (20th -)				
HOUSTON, John	*P*			$770
British (1812 - 1884)				
HOUSTON, N. Robert	*P*			$275
American (20th -)				
HOUTEN, Gerard van	*D*			$880
Dutch (18th -)				

D=Drawing, P=Painting, S=Sculpture, W=Watercolor

		Current Price Range		
		Low	Mean	High

HOUTMAN, M.	*W*			$9,350
(19th -)				
HOVE, Bartholomeus J. van	*W*			$1,320
Dutch (1798 - 1880)				
HOVE, Hubertus van	*P*	$132	$1,276	$2,420
Dutch (1814 - 1865)				
HOVENDEN, H. C.	*W*			$1,485
American (19th -)				
HOVENDEN, Thomas	*D*			$1,540
British (1840 - 1895)	*P*			$17,600
	W			$5,500
HOVENER, Jan	*P*			$825
Dutch (20th -)				
HOVSEPIAN, Leon	*W*			$231
American (1915 -)				
HOW, Jack B.	*S*			$330
(?)				
HOWARD, B. K.	*P*			$550
American (1872 -)				
HOWARD, Clara	*W*			$138
American (? - 1938)				
HOWARD, Hugh H.	*P*	$275	$674	$1,650
American (1860 - 1927)	*W*	$110	$169	$275
HOWARD, Hugh H. (Attrib.)	*P*			$358
American (1860 - 1927)				
HOWARD, Humbert	*P*			$330
American (1915 -)				
HOWARD, Joe	*P*			$800
American (20th -)				
HOWARD, John L.	*W*			$990
American (1902 -)				
HOWARD, Lucile	*P*			$176
American (1885 -)				
HOWARD, Marion	*P*			$880
American (1883 -)				

D=Drawing, P=Painting, S=Sculpture, W=Watercolor

		Current Price Range	
	Low	Mean	High

HOWARD, Nellie C.	*P*			$413
American (1855 - 1956)				
HOWE, (Of Edinburgh)	*P*			$5,500
British (19th -)				
HOWE, H. H.	*P*			$165
Canadian (20th -)				
HOWE, William H.	*P*	$1,100	$1,155	$1,210
American (1846 - 1929)				
HOWELL, Felice W.	*P*	$770	$8,250	$27,500
American (1897 - 1968)	*W*	$7,975	$12,008	$17,600
HOWELL, George	*W*			$303
American (19th -)				
HOWITT, John N.	*P*	$138	$319	$550
American (1885 - 1958)				
HOWITT, William S. (Attrib.)	*P*			$3,025
British (1765 - 1822)				
HOWLAND, Alfred C.	*P*	$715	$2,292	$4,950
American (1838 - 1909)				
HOYD, Thomas	*W*			$990
British (19th -)				
HOYLAND, John	*P*	$1,650	$5,622	$9,900
British (1934 -)				
HOYOS, Anna M.	*P*	$7,700	$17,757	$27,500
Colombian (1942 -)				
HOYT, Edith	*P*			$2,750
American (1894 -)				
HOYT, Vivian C.	*P*	$248	$303	$358
American (1880 -)				
HUBACEK, William	*P*			$14,300
American (1866 - 1958)				
HUBBARD, Charles	*D*			$220
American (1876 - 1951)	*P*			$660
HUBBARD, John E.	*P*			$198
(20th -)				

D=Drawing, P=Painting, S=Sculpture, W=Watercolor

		Current Price Range		
		Low	Mean	High
HUBBARD, Lydia M. B.	*P*			$1,980
American (1849 - 1911)				
HUBBARD, Richard W.	*P*	$3,300	$3,784	$4,510
American (1817 - 1888)				
HUBBARD, Whitney M.	*P*	$132	$387	$825
American (1875 -)				
HUBBELL, Charles H.	*P*			$715
American (?)				
HUBBELL, Henry S.	*P*	$468	$3,225	$6,600
American (1870 - 1949)				
HUBER, E.	*P*			$1,430
Dutch (19th -)				
HUBER, Helene G.	*P*			$138
American (20th -)				
HUBER, Josef I.	*P*			$1,320
(18th - 19th)				
HUBER, Leon Charles	*P*	$4,400	$10,313	$17,600
French (1858 - 1928)				
HUBERT, Laurent	*D*			$792
French (? - 1780)				
HUBERT, Leon	*P*			$1,650
French (1887 -)				
HUBNER, Carl W.	*P*	$4,950	$5,775	$6,600
German (1814 - 1879)				
HUBNER, Carl W. (After)	*P*			$1,650
German (1814 - 1879)				
HUCHTENBURGH, Jan van	*P*	$9,900	$13,750	$17,600
Dutch (1647 - 1733)				
HUCHTENBURGH, Jan van (Cir)	*D*			$825
Dutch (1647 - 1733)				
HUDSON, Charles B.	*D*			$193
American (1865 - 1938)	*P*	$550	$1,100	$1,650
HUDSON, Charles W.	*P*			$1,650
American (1871 - 1943)				
HUDSON, Grace C.	*P*	$550	$2,717	$4,125
American (1865 - 1937)				

D=Drawing, P=Painting, S=Sculpture, W=Watercolor

		Current Price Range		
		Low	Mean	High
HUDSON, John B.	W	$165	$327	$825
American (1832 - 1903)				
HUDSON, Kenneth	P	$248	$367	$523
American (1904 - 1988)				
HUDSON, Samuel A.	P			$3,520
American (1813 - 1894)				
HUDSON, Thomas	P	$9,900	$72,967	$198,000
British (1701 - 1779)				
HUDSON, Thomas (Attrib.)	P			$20,900
British (1701 - 1779)				
HUDSON, Thomas (Circle)	P			$4,180
British (1701 - 1779)				
HUDSON RIVER SCHOOL 19C,	P	$3,410	$3,905	$4,400
American (19th -)				
HUEFF, A.	P			$1,210
Dutch (20th -)				
HUERTAS, Segundo	P			$413
American (20th -)				
HUET, Christophe	P			$77,000
French (? - 1759)				
HUET, Ernestine	P			$880
American (?)				
HUET, Jean B.	D	$660	$2,778	$4,400
French (1745 - 1811)	P	$23,100	$28,600	$34,100
HUET, Jean B. (After)	D			$330
French (1745 - 1811)				
HUET, Jean B. (Attrib.)	D			$440
French (1745 - 1811)				
HUET, Jean B. (Circle)	D			$770
French (1745 - 1811)	P	$6,600	$12,100	$17,600
HUET, Jean B. (Follower)	P			$4,400
French (1745 - 1811)				
HUET, Jean B. (Studio)	W			$495
French (1745 - 1811)				

D=Drawing, P=Painting, S=Sculpture, W=Watercolor

		Current Price Range		
		Low	Mean	High

		Low	Mean	High
HUET, Jean B. (Style)	*P*			$1,045
French (1745 - 1811)				
HUFFINGTON, John C.	*P*			$660
American (1864 - 1929)				
HUGENHOLTZ, Arina	*P*			$880
Dutch (1848 - 1934)				
HUGENTOBLER, E. J.	*P*			$440
American (20th -)				
HUGGINS, M. W.	*P*			$220
(?)				
HUGH, W.	*P*			$3,300
British (19th -)				
HUGHES, Daisy M.	*P*			$6,600
American (1883 - 1968)				
HUGHES, Edwin	*P*			$770
British (19th -)				
HUGHES, George	*P*	$303	$2,627	$4,950
American (1907 -)	*W*			$138
HUGHES, J. A.	*P*			$275
American (19th -)				
HUGHES, J. J.	*P*	$220	$990	$1,760
British (19th -)				
HUGHES, Marilyn	*W*	$660	$825	$990
American (20th -)				
HUGHES, Stanley C.	*P*	$1,650	$1,675	$1,700
American (20th -)				
HUGHES, Talbot	*D*			$1,870
British (1869 - 1942)				
HUGHS, Marian B.	*P*			$440
American (1896 -)				
HUGHTO, Darryl	*P*			$5,500
American (1943 -)				
HUGNET, Georges	*W*			$2,420
(?)				
HUGO, Jean	*W*	$660	$917	$1,210
French (1894 - 1984)				

D=Drawing, P=Painting, S=Sculpture, W=Watercolor

		Current Price Range		
		Low	Mean	High
HUGO, Victor	*P*			$68,200
French (1802 - 1885)				
HUGUET, Victor P.	*P*			$9,350
French (1835 - 1902)				
HULDAH,	*P*	$550	$880	$1,320
American (20th -)				
HULETT, Ralph	*W*	$198	$710	$1,210
American (1915 - 1974)				
HULINGS, Clark	*D*			$605
American (1922 -)	*P*	$6,050	$43,607	$143,000
HULK, Abraham	*P*	$1,870	$3,713	$6,050
British (1813 - 1897)				
HULK, Johannes F.	*P*			$2,090
Dutch (1829 - 1911)				
HULK, John F.	*P*	$2,310	$7,405	$12,500
Dutch (1855 - 1913)				
HULK, William F.	*P*	$330	$1,815	$3,300
British (19th -)				
HULK, JR., Abraham	*P*	$660	$1,100	$1,540
British (1851 - 1922)				
HULL, John	*P*			$1,100
(20th -)				
HULL, Marie	*P*	$1,155	$1,348	$1,540
American (1890 - 1980)				
HULLENKREMER, Odon	*D*	$121	$149	$176
(?)				
HULME, Frederick W.	*P*			$2,200
British (1816 - 1884)				
HULTBERG, John	*D*			$825
American (1922 -)	*P*	$880	$963	$1,045
HUMANN, O. Victor	*P*	$165	$420	$660
American (19th - 20th)				
HUMBLOT, Robert	*P*	$495	$4,249	$9,350
French (1907 - 1962)				

D=Drawing, P=Painting, S=Sculpture, W=Watercolor

		Current Price Range		
		Low	Mean	High
HUMBORG, Adolf	*P*	$990	$3,245	$6,600
Austrian (1847 - 1913)				
HUMPHREY, Ralph	*P*	$660	$8,525	$24,200
American (1932 -)				
HUMPHREY, Walter B.	*D*	$110	$407	$935
American (1892 - 1966)	*P*	$550	$979	$1,540
HUMPHREYS, Malcolm	*P*			$1,100
American (1894 -)				
HUMPHRISS, Charles H.	*S*	$880	$8,259	$28,600
British (1867 - 1934)				
HUMPHRY, Ozias	*D*			$220
British (19th -)				
HUNAEUS, Andreas H.	*P*			$1,100
Danish (19th -)				
HUNLEY, Katherine J.	*P*			$660
American (1883 - 1964)				
HUNT, Bryan	*D*	$6,600	$13,200	$17,600
American (1947 -)	*P*	$4,950	$38,421	$126,500
	S	$11,000	$26,767	$77,000
	W	$9,350	$37,675	$66,000
HUNT, Charles	*P*			$4,675
British (1803 - 1877)				
HUNT, Charles D.	*P*	$660	$1,430	$2,200
American (1840 - 1914)	*W*	$220	$369	$495
HUNT, E. Aubrey	*P*	$4,400	$4,693	$5,280
British (1855 - 1922)	*W*	$330	$330	$330
HUNT, Edgar	*P*	$24,200	$25,300	$26,400
British (1876 - 1953)				
HUNT, Esther	*W*	$825	$1,173	$1,760
American (1875 - 1951)				
HUNT, Lynn B.	*D*			$2,200
American (1878 - 1960)	*P*	$1,045	$2,622	$5,500

D=Drawing, P=Painting, S=Sculpture, W=Watercolor

		Current Price Range		
		Low	Mean	High

		Low	Mean	High
HUNT, Lynn B. (Attrib.)	*P*			$330
American (1878 - 1960)				
HUNT, Richard	*S*	$2,090	$2,713	$3,850
American (1935 -)				
HUNT, Richard (Et al.)	*W*			$1,210
American (20th -)				
HUNT, Thomas L.	*P*	$330	$523	$715
American (1882 - 1938)				
HUNT, Walter	*P*			$14,300
British (1861 - 1941)				
HUNT, William E.	*D*			$2,200
British (1790 - 1864)				
HUNT, William E. (Style)	*P*			$385
British (1790 - 1864)				
HUNT, William H.	*S*	$8,800	$13,200	$17,600
British (1827 - 1910)	*W*			$688
HUNT, William M.	*D*	$1,045	$2,739	$6,050
American (1824 - 1879)	*P*	$1,650	$13,750	$24,200
HUNTEN, Emil	*W*			$3,575
German (1827 - 1902)				
HUNTER, Clementine	*P*	$253	$981	$2,530
American (19th - 20th)				
HUNTER, Colin (Attrib.)	*P*			$250
Russian (1842 -)				
HUNTER, Elizabeth	*W*			$138
British (19th -)				
HUNTER, Evangeline	*W*			$495
American (19th - 20th)				
HUNTER, F. Leo	*P*			$330
American (20th -)				
HUNTER, Frances T.	*D*			$165
American (1896 - 1957)	*P*			$550
	W			$1,210

D=Drawing, P=Painting, S=Sculpture, W=Watercolor

		Current Price Range		
		Low	Mean	High
HUNTER, Frederick L.	P			$1,540
American (1858 - 1945)				
HUNTER, G. Sherwood	P	$770	$1,485	$2,200
British (? - 1920)				
HUNTER, John Y.	P			$82,500
British (1874 - 1955)				
HUNTINGTON, Anna H.	S	$2,090	$6,985	$12,650
American (1876 - 1973)				
HUNTINGTON, Daniel	D			$880
American (1816 - 1906)	P	$1,045	$1,746	$2,420
HUNTINGTON, Dwight W.	W	$1,100	$1,760	$3,080
(19th -)				
HUNTINGTON, Elizabeth	D			$330
American (1878 - 1963)	W			$165
HUPIN, Jacques	W			$330
(?)				
HUPPE, Henri	S			$314
French (19th -)				
HUPPLER, Dudley	D			$110
(?)				
HURD, Clement	P			$110
American (20th -)				
HURD, Peter	D	$550	$15,400	$30,250
American (1904 - 1984)	P	$5,500	$13,273	$28,600
	W	$2,420	$5,280	$11,000
HURD, Peter (Attrib.)	P			$193
American (1904 - 1984)				
HURD, Richard	P			$220
American (20th -)				
HURST, Earl O.	W	$110	$124	$138
American (1895 - 1958)				
HURT, Louis B.	P	$12,100	$23,430	$35,750
British (1856 - 1929)				

D=Drawing, P=Painting, S=Sculpture, W=Watercolor

		Current Price Range		
		Low	Mean	High

HUS, Zultan	*P*			$660
(19th -)				
HUSSEY, K. L.	*W*			$110
(?)				
HUSTON, John K.	*P*			$1,265
(?)				
HUSTON, William	*W*			$110
(19th -)				
HUTCHENS, Arthur	*P*			$209
American (20th -)				
HUTCHENS, Frank T.	*D*			$1,200
American (1869 - 1937)	*P*	$138	$1,197	$3,960
HUTCHINS, Arthur	*P*			$440
American (20th -)				
HUTCHINS, Arthur (Attrib.)	*P*			$550
American (20th -)				
HUTCHINSON, D. C.	*P*	$375	$903	$1,430
American (1869 - 1954)				
HUTCHINSON, Ellen W.	*P*			$578
American (1868 -)				
HUTCHISON, Robert G.	*P*	$8,250	$8,800	$9,350
British (1855 - 1936)				
HUTTY, Alfred H.	*W*			$605
American (1877 - 1954)				
HUTTY, Alfred H. (Attrib.)	*W*			$138
American (1877 - 1954)				
HUVE, Jean J.	*D*			$3,300
French (1742 - 1808)				
HUYSMANS, Cornelis	*P*			$10,450
Flemish (1648 - 1727)				
HUYSMANS, Jacob	*P*	$1,870	$38,207	$110,000
Flemish (1633 - 1680)				
HUYSUM, Jan van	*D*	$2,475	$5,133	$10,450
Dutch (1682 - 1749)	*P*			$192,500

D=Drawing, P=Painting, S=Sculpture, W=Watercolor

		Current Price Range		
		Low	Mean	High

		Low	Mean	High
HUYSUM, Jan van (After)	P			$1,320
Dutch (1682 - 1749)				
HUYSUM, Jan van (Circle)	P	$6,600	$12,650	$18,700
Dutch (1682 - 1749)	W			$2,200
HUYSUM, Jan van (Manner)	D			$880
Dutch (1682 - 1749)	P			$4,125
HUYSUM, Jan van (School)	P			$2,200
Dutch (1682 - 1749)				
HUYSUM, Justus van	P			$66,000
Dutch (1659 - 1716)				
HYDE, George	P			$358
(?)				
HYDE, Leland	P			$248
American (20th -)				
HYDE, William H.	P	$220	$440	$660
American (1858 - 1943)				
HYETT, Will J.	P			$990
American (1876 -)				
HYND, Frederick	P			$1,100
American (20th -)				
HYNEMAN, Herman	P			$1,650
American (1859 - 1907)				
HYPOLITE, S.	P			$605
French (19th -)				
HYPPOLITE, Hector	P	$27,500	$32,633	$38,500
Haitian (1889 - 1948)				
HYRE, Laurent de la	D			$20,900
French (1606 - 1656)				
HYRE, Laurent de la (Circle)	D			$1,100
French (1606 - 1656)				
HYRE, Laurent de la (School)	P			$16,500
French (1606 - 1656)				
IACOVLEFF, Alexandre	D			$1,100
French (1887 -)	P	$880	$2,255	$3,520

D=Drawing, P=Painting, S=Sculpture, W=Watercolor

		Current Price Range	
	Low	Mean	High

		Low	Mean	High
IACOVLEFF, Alexandre	*W*			$385
French (1887 -)				
IANELLI, Alfonso	*P*	$1,100	$1,100	$1,100
Italian (?)				
IANELLI, Arcangelo	*P*	$4,675	$6,325	$8,800
Brazilian (1922 -)				
IANELLI, Thomaz	*P*			$3,575
Brazilian (1932 -)				
IBBETSON, Julius C.	*P*			$1,100
British (1759 - 1817)				
IBELS, Henri G.	*W*			$3,520
French (1867 - 1936)				
ICART, Louis	*D*	$525	$908	$1,320
French (1888 - 1950)	*P*			$7,150
	W	$468	$763	$935
ICAZA, Ernesto	*P*			$77,000
Mexican (1870 - 1926)				
IFOLD, Frederick	*P*			$2,640
British (19th -)				
IGNATIEV, Alex	*P*			$605
American (1913 -)	*W*			$550
IGOR,	*P*			$176
American (20th -)				
ILEGIUJAZ, A.	*W*			$187
European (19th - 20th)				
ILLES, Aladar E.	*P*			$550
Hungarian (1870 -)				
ILSEY, Frederick J.	*P*			$330
American (1855 - 1933)				
ILSTED, Peter V.	*P*	$24,200	$43,725	$63,250
Danish (1861 - 1933)				
IMBAULT, Leonce E.	*P*			$4,180
French (1845 - 1882)				
IMHOF, Joseph A.	*W*			$935
American (1871 - 1955)				

D=Drawing, P=Painting, S=Sculpture, W=Watercolor

		Current Price Range		
		Low	Mean	High
IMMENDORF, Jorg	P	$15,400	$29,700	$49,500
German (1945 -)				
IMMERMAN, David	P	$990	$990	$990
American (20th -)				
IMPERIALI, (Attributed)	P			$14,300
Italian (18th -)				
INDIANA, Robert	P			$104,500
American (1928 -)	S			$35,200
INDONI, Filippo	P	$1,760	$1,980	$2,200
Italian (19th -)	W	$358	$3,273	$12,100
INDUNO, Domenico	P			$253,000
Italian (1815 - 1878)				
INDUNO, Girolamo	D			$16,500
Italian (1827 - 1890)	P			$28,600
INFANTE-ARANA, Francesco	P			$35,200
Russian (1943 -)				
INGEN, Henry van	P			$3,300
American (1833 - 1899)				
INGERLE, Rudolph F.	P	$770	$1,210	$1,650
American (1879 -)				
INGHAM, Charles	P			$578
American (1796 - 1863)				
INGLIS, Antoinette	P			$286
American (1880 -)				
INGLIS, John J.	P			$770
American (1867 - 1946)				
INGRAM, W. Ayerst	P			$990
British (1855 - 1913)				
INGRES, Jean A. D.	D	$25,300	$30,250	$35,200
French (1780 - 1867)	P			$1.430M
INGRES, Jean A. D. (After)	D			$550
French (1780 - 1867)	P			$1,430

D=Drawing, P=Painting, S=Sculpture, W=Watercolor

		Current Price Range		
		Low	Mean	High

		Low	Mean	High
INJALBERT, Jean A. French (1845 - 1933)	S			$1,925
INMAN, Henry American (1801 - 1846)	P			$605
INMAN, Jerry American (20th -)	D			$1,100
INMAN, John O. American (1828 - 1896)	P	$550	$2,255	$7,700
INNERST, Mark (20th -)	P	$10,450	$23,100	$35,750
INNESS, George American (1825 - 1894)	P	$2,200	$83,490	$935,000
INNESS, George (After) American (1825 - 1894)	P	$193	$427	$660
INNESS, George (Attrib.) American (1825 - 1894)	P	$440	$2,237	$4,675
INNESS, George (Manner) American (1825 - 1894)	P	$171	$443	$715
INNESS, George (School) American (1825 - 1894)	P			$550
INNESS, George (Style) American (1825 - 1894)	P	$523	$2,070	$5,225
INNESS, JR., George American (1853 - 1926)	P	$1,650	$5,161	$12,100
INNESS, JR., George (Attrib.) American (1853 - 1926)	D			$400
INNOCENTI, Camilio Italian (1871 -)	D P	$2,200	$4,098	$1,320 $7,150
INNOCENTI, Guglielmo Italian (19th -)	P	$193	$3,474	$7,700
INO, Pierre Russian (1909 -)	P			$1,320
INSLEY, Albert B. American (1842 - 1937)	P W	$330	$1,760	$6,600 $220

D=Drawing, P=Painting, S=Sculpture, W=Watercolor

		Current Price Range		
		Low	Mean	High
INVELO, Roma	P			$187
(20th -)				
IPCAR, Dahlov	P			$2,200
American (1919 -)	W			$1,210
IPOUSTEGUY, Jean	S			$31,900
French (1920 -)				
IPPENS, W. H.	P			$220
American (20th -)				
IPRNSON,	P			$193
(?)				
IPSEN, Ernest L.	P	$330	$5,665	$11,000
American (1869 - 1934)				
IRARRAZABAL, Mario	S			$4,400
Chilean (1940 -)				
IRELAND, Leroy	P			$880
American (1889 - 1970)				
IRELAND, Taylor	W			$1,045
British (19th - 20th)				
IRIARTE,	P			$16,500
Colombian (1920 -)				
IRISH SCHOOL 19C,	D			$1,320
Irish (19th -)	P			$2,310
IRIZARRI, Carlos	P			$220
South American (20th -)				
IROLLI, Vincenzo	D	$3,300	$4,675	$6,050
Italian (1860 - 1942)	P	$6,325	$39,634	$88,000
	W	$5,500	$7,150	$8,800
IROLLI, Vincenzo (Attrib.)	P			$3,850
Italian (1860 - 1942)				
IRVINE, Wilson H.	P	$990	$13,041	$52,800
American (1869 - 1936)	W	$495	$1,210	$2,200
IRVINE, Wilson H. (Attrib.)	P			$1,870
American (1869 - 1936)				

D=Drawing, P=Painting, S=Sculpture, W=Watercolor

		Current Price Range		
		Low	Mean	High

		Low	Mean	High
IRVING, I.	*P*			$715
(19th -)				
IRVING, Jeannette B.	*P*			$825
(20th -)				
IRWIN, Robert	*P*			$198,000
American (20th -)	*S*			$93,500
IRWIN, William	*P*			$1,210
American (1903 -)				
ISAAKS,	*P*			$5,500
(18th -)				
ISABEY, Jean B.	*W*			$330
French (1767 - 1855)				
ISABEY, Louis G.	*P*	$1,100	$5,018	$10,450
French (1803 - 1886)				
ISABEY, Louis G. (Attrib.)	*P*			$1,650
French (1803 - 1886)				
ISEMBERT, Emile	*P*			$16,500
French (1846 - 1921)				
ISENBRANT, Adriaen (Circle)	*P*			$11,000
Flemish (1490 - 1551)				
ISENBURGER, Eric	*P*			$2,310
American (1902 -)				
ISENDYCK, Anton	*P*			$1,430
Belgian (1801 - 1875)				
ISHIKAWA, Kinichiro	*P*			$1,870
Japanese (19th -)	*W*	$193	$496	$798
ISHMAEL, Woodi	*P*			$1,650
American (1914 -)	*W*	$193	$523	$1,045
ISOLA, Giancarlo	*P*			$825
Italian (1927 -)				
ISOM, Graham	*P*			$440
American (20th -)				
ISQUIEL, Jose L.	*W*			$110
(?)				

D=Drawing, P=Painting, S=Sculpture, W=Watercolor

| | | Current Price Range | | |
		Low	Mean	High
ISRAEL, Daniel	P	$880	$4,840	$8,800
Austrian (1859 - 1901)				
ISRAEL, Marvin	D			$110
American (20th -)	P			$440
ISRAELS, Isaac	P	$2,200	$53,350	$104,500
Dutch (1865 - 1934)	W			$29,700
ISRAELS, Josef	P	$1,210	$14,870	$41,800
Dutch (1824 - 1911)	W			$1,870
ISRAELS, Josef (Attrib.)	P	$715	$715	$715
Dutch (1824 - 1911)				
ISSELSTEYN, Adrianus van	P			$9,900
Dutch (? - 1684)				
ISSUPOFF, Alessio	D			$385
Russian (1889 - 1957)	P	$1,100	$2,750	$4,400
ITALIAN SCHOOL,	P	$1,925	$2,819	$4,400
Italian (?)	S	$1,045	$3,282	$7,700
ITALIAN SCHOOL,	P	$1,210	$1,760	$2,420
Italian (17th - 18th)				
ITALIAN SCHOOL,	P	$1,650	$2,842	$4,125
Italian (18th - 19th)				
ITALIAN SCHOOL,	P			$1,045
Italian (19th - 20th)	W	$1,320	$1,351	$1,540
ITALIAN SCHOOL 15C,	P	$9,900	$11,000	$12,100
Italian (15th -)				
ITALIAN SCHOOL 16C,	D			$4,400
Italian (16th -)	P	$2,475	$4,308	$5,500
	W	$2,200	$3,483	$4,400
ITALIAN SCHOOL 17C,	D	$1,210	$1,980	$3,190
Italian (17th -)	P	$1,100	$13,383	$143,000
	W			$2,200

D=Drawing, P=Painting, S=Sculpture, W=Watercolor

		Current Price Range		
		Low	Mean	High

		Low	Mean	High
ITALIAN SCHOOL 18C,	*D*	$1,430	$1,782	$2,090
Italian (18th -)	*P*	$403	$4,713	$22,000
	W	$1,320	$1,760	$2,200
ITALIAN SCHOOL 19C,	*D*	$1,980	$2,420	$2,860
Italian (19th -)	*P*	$358	$5,535	$66,000
	S	$3,190	$5,170	$7,150
	W	$1,320	$2,387	$3,575
ITALIAN SCHOOL 20C,	*P*	$1,210	$1,320	$1,430
Italian (20th -)	*W*	$248	$1,096	$1,320
ITALO-FLEMISH SCHOOL 16C,	*D*	$2,475	$3,108	$3,740
(16th -)				
ITALO-FLEMISH SCHOOL 17C,	*W*			$9,900
(17th -)				
ITAYA, Foussa	*P*	$550	$660	$770
Japanese (1919 -)				
ITO, Miyoko	*W*			$1,045
American (1918 -)				
IVANOFF, Nicolai	*P*			$1,870
Russian (1853 -)				
IVANOVITCH, Paul	*P*			$8,800
Austrian (1859 -)				
IVANOWSKI, Sigismund de	*D*			$303
American (1875 - 1944)	*P*	$275	$1,145	$2,860
IVANYI-GRUNWALD, Bela	*P*	$2,750	$3,025	$3,300
Hungarian (19th - 20th)				
IVES, Chauncey B.	*S*	$13,200	$50,600	$88,000
American (1810 - 1894)				
IVES, Percy	*P*	$248	$887	$1,870
American (1864 - 1928)				
IVEY, James	*W*			$220
American (19th - 20th)				
IWILL, Joseph	*P*	$550	$1,687	$2,750
French (1850 - 1923)				

D=Drawing, P=Painting, S=Sculpture, W=Watercolor

		Low	Mean	High
		\multicolumn{3}{c}{Current Price Range}		

		Low	Mean	High
IZQUIERDO, Maria	P	$31,900	$56,320	$99,000
Mexican (1906 - 1950)	W	$11,000	$30,250	$55,000
JACKMAN, Oscar T.	P			$825
American (1878 - 1940)				
JACKMAN, Reva	P			$550
American (1892 -)				
JACKSON, Alexander Y.	P			$3,300
Canadian (1882 - 1974)				
JACKSON, Billy M.	P			$1,650
American (20th -)				
JACKSON, Clifford	P			$413
American (1923 -)				
JACKSON, E. M.	P			$2,300
American (1896 - 1962)				
JACKSON, Harry	P			$5,500
American (1924 -)	S	$1,210	$15,821	$154,000
JACKSON, John	D			$165
British (1778 - 1831)				
JACKSON, John W.	P			$550
American (1905 -)				
JACKSON, Lee	P	$330	$1,503	$3,520
American (1909 -)				
JACKSON, Martin	P	$248	$647	$1,045
American (1871 - 1955)				
JACKSON, Walter G.	P	$275	$319	$413
American (1890 -)				
JACKSON, William F.	P	$440	$440	$440
American (1850 - 1936)				
JACOB, Alexander	P			$990
French (1876 -)				
JACOB, Max	P			$8,250
French (1876 - 1944)	W			$2,530
JACOB, Ned	D			$3,080
(1938 -)				

D=Drawing, P=Painting, S=Sculpture, W=Watercolor

		Current Price Range		
		Low	Mean	High
JACOBI, M. M.	*P*			$605
European (19th -)				
JACOBS, Adolphe	*P*			$52,250
Belgian (19th - 20th)				
JACOBS, Franz	*P*			$1,650
Dutch (19th -)				
JACOBS, Harold	*P*			$220
(?)				
JACOBS, William	*W*			$198
American (1897 -)				
JACOBSEN, Amanda	*P*	$110	$264	$385
American (20th -)				
JACOBSEN, Antonio N. G.	*P*	$2,750	$9,102	$38,500
American (1850 - 1921)	*W*			$440
JACOBSEN, Antonio N. G. (Attrib.)	*P*			$4,950
American (1850 - 1921)				
JACOBSEN, Antonio N. G. (Style)	*P*			$1,980
American (1850 - 1921)				
JACOBSEN, Sophus	*P*	$2,310	$9,405	$16,500
Norwegian (1833 - 1912)				
JACOBSON, Albert	*W*	$605	$825	$1,045
Danish (1780 - 1836)				
JACOBSZ, Franz (Follower)	*P*			$2,750
Dutch (17th -)				
JACOBSZ, Jacobs L. (Follower)	*P*			$2,750
Dutch (17th -)				
JACOBUSZ,	*P*			$3,300
European (19th -)				
JACOPIN, Archille E.	*S*			$110
French (1874 -)				
JACOPS, A.	*P*			$715
(19th -)				
JACQUE, Charles E.	*D*	$1,760	$3,080	$4,400
French (1813 - 1894)	*P*	$616	$21,337	$68,200

D=Drawing, P=Painting, S=Sculpture, W=Watercolor

		Current Price Range		
		Low	Mean	High
JACQUE, Charles E. (Et al.)	*P*			$28,600
French (19th -)				
JACQUE, F.	*P*			$150
(20th -)				
JACQUEMART, Andre	*S*			$2,420
French (1841 - 1912)				
JACQUEMART, Henri A. M.	*S*			$5,225
French (1826 - 1896)				
JACQUEMON, Pierre	*P*			$1,100
French (1936 -)				
JACQUES, Rene	*P*			$248
French (19th - 20th)				
JACQUET, Alain	*P*			$6,050
French (20th -)				
JACQUET, Gustave J.	*D*			$3,850
French (1846 - 1909)	*P*	$1,870	$5,108	$8,250
JACQUET, Gustave J. (Attrib.)	*P*	$660	$3,455	$6,250
French (1846 - 1909)				
JACQUET, Henry-Leon	*W*	$138	$1,032	$1,925
French (1856 -)				
JACQUETTE, Yvonne	*D*	$990	$2,695	$4,400
American (1934 -)	*P*			$7,700
JACQUIN, F.	*P*			$990
French (19th -)				
JACQUIN, Victorine	*D*			$5,280
(19th -)				
JAEGER,	*S*			$825
German (1880 -)				
JAENISCH, Hans	*P*			$16,500
German (1907 -)				
JAFFE, Lee	*P*	$110	$286	$462
(20th -)				
JAHN, Louis	*P*			$1,210
German (1839 - 1911)				

D=Drawing, P=Painting, S=Sculpture, W=Watercolor

		Current Price Range		
		Low	Mean	High

		Low	Mean	High
JAKE & BLUE EAGLE, Albin	*W*			$440
(20th -)				
JAKOB, H.	*P*			$165
German (19th - 20th)				
JAKOBS, Paul E.	*P*			$88,000
German (1802 - 1866)				
JAMBOR, Louis	*P*	$495	$13,998	$27,500
American (1884 - 1955)				
JAMES, Alexander R.	*P*	$330	$798	$1,540
American (1890 - 1941)				
JAMES, David	*P*	$1,650	$5,500	$9,350
British (19th -)				
JAMES, E.	*P*			$200
(?)				
JAMES, Frederick	*P*			$5,775
American (1845 - 1907)	*W*			$1,430
JAMES, John W.	*P*	$220	$495	$770
American (1873 -)				
JAMES, Merle	*P*			$165
American (? - 1963)				
JAMES, Roy W.	*P*	$358	$1,554	$2,750
American (1897 -)				
JAMES, Will	*D*			$1,540
Canadian (1892 - 1942)				
JAMES, William	*P*	$715	$60,569	$110,000
British (18th -)				
JAMESON, Middleton	*P*			$19,800
British (? - 1919)				
JAMIESON, Bernice E.	*W*			$138
American (1898 -)				
JAMIESON, F. S.	*P*	$165	$605	$1,045
British (20th -)				
JAMIESON, Mitchell	*P*			$143
American (1915 -)				
JAMISON, Lee	*P*	$2,000	$2,343	$2,640
American (1957 -)				

D=Drawing, P=Painting, S=Sculpture, W=Watercolor

| | | Current Price Range | | |
		Low	Mean	High
JAMISON, Philip	*W*	$385	$1,969	$2,860
American (1929 -)				
JAN, Elvire	*P*			$1,870
Belgian (1904 -)				
JANCE, Paul C.	*P*	$220	$5,060	$9,900
French (1840 -)				
JANCK, Angelo	*P*	$825	$1,073	$1,320
German (1868 - 1956)				
JANCO, Marcel	*D*			$1,320
French (1895 -)	*P*	$5,280	$20,708	$39,600
JANEIRO, Molnez L.	*P*			$413
Czechoslovakian (19th - 20th)				
JANES, Margarite	*P*			$238
British (19th - 20th)				
JANESCH, Albert	*P*	$880	$3,080	$5,280
Austrian (1889 -)				
JANKOWSKI, Cheslas Bois de	*P*			$13,200
Polish (19th -)				
JANNECK, Franz C. (Attrib.)	*P*			$16,500
Austrian (1703 - 1761)				
JANNSON, Alfred	*P*			$2,750
Swedish (1863 - 1931)				
JANNY, Georg	*W*			$413
Austrian (20th -)				
JANOUSEK, Frantisek	*P*	$2,530	$2,860	$3,300
Czechoslovakian (1890 - 1943)				
JANOWITZ, Joel	*P*			$605
American (20th -)				
JANSEM, Jean	*D*	$990	$1,888	$2,640
French (1920 -)	*P*	$7,150	$29,416	$82,500
JANSEN, Joseph	*P*	$6,600	$8,938	$11,000
German (1829 - 1905)				
JANSEN, Willem G. F.	*P*	$605	$1,073	$1,540
Dutch (1871 - 1949)				

D=Drawing, P=Painting, S=Sculpture, W=Watercolor

		Current Price Range		
		Low	Mean	High

		Low	Mean	High
JANSSENS, Abraham (Circle)	*P*			$3,520
Flemish (1575 - 1632)				
JANSSENS, Hieronymus	*P*	$15,400	$22,000	$28,600
Flemish (1624 - 1693)				
JANSSENS, Hieronymus (Circle)	*P*			$2,090
Flemish (1624 - 1693)				
JANSSENS, Victor E.	*P*	$4,400	$4,620	$4,840
German (1807 - 1845)				
JANSSON, Alfred	*P*	$715	$1,964	$4,675
Swedish (1863 - 1931)				
JAPANESE SCHOOL 19C,	*S*			$2,200
Japanese (19th -)				
JAPY, Louis A.	*P*	$990	$5,143	$8,800
French (1840 - 1916)				
JAQUES, Francis L.	*P*			$5,280
American (1887 -)				
JARDINES, Jose M.	*P*	$1,870	$2,998	$4,290
Spanish (1862 -)				
JARGETH,	*P*			$660
French (20th -)				
JAROCKI, Wladyslav	*P*			$1,540
Polish (20th -)				
JARVIS, George	*P*			$3,025
British (19th - 20th)				
JARVIS, John W.	*D*			$880
American (1780 - 1840)	*W*	$528	$1,199	$1,870
JARVIS, John W. (Attrib.)	*P*	$660	$1,650	$2,640
American (1780 - 1840)				
JASMIN,	*P*			$303
British (20th -)				
JASZAY, Jozsef	*P*			$1,430
Hungarian (19th -)				
JAUDON, Valerie	*P*	$3,850	$23,772	$41,800
American (1945 -)	*W*			$2,420

D=Drawing, P=Painting, S=Sculpture, W=Watercolor

		Current Price Range		
		Low	Mean	High

JAUMANN, Rudolf A.	*P*			$248
German (1859 -)				
JAVIER, Maximino	*W*	$198	$1,199	$2,200
Mexican (20th -)				
JAWLENSKY, Alexej	*D*			$13,200
German (1864 - 1941)	*P*	$55,000	$253,000	$748,000
JEAN, Jean B.	*P*			$303
Haitian (20th -)				
JEAN, Marcel	*S*			$2,420
French (1900 -)				
JEANMOUGIN, Alfred P. J.	*P*			$6,600
French (19th -)				
JEANNIOT, Pierre G.	*P*			$1,870
French (1848 - 1934)				
JEANRON,	*P*			$770
French (19th -)				
JEAURAT, Etienne (Attrib.)	*D*			$4,950
French (1699 - 1789)				
JECT-KEY, D. Wu	*P*			$523
American (20th -)				
JEFFERSON, M.	*P*			$176
(?)				
JEFFERY, Dick	*P*			$1,980
(20th -)				
JELLICO, Nancy R.	*S*			$1,000
American (20th -)				
JENKINS,	*P*			$935
American (19th -)				
JENKINS, Burris	*D*			$358
American (1897 - 1966)				
JENKINS, F. Lynn	*S*			$1,045
American (1870 - 1929)				
JENKINS, G. H.	*W*			$330
British (19th - 20th)				
JENKINS, George	*P*			$880
British (20th -)				

D=Drawing, P=Painting, S=Sculpture, W=Watercolor

		Current Price Range		
		Low	Mean	High

		Low	Mean	High
JENKINS, Hannah T.	*P*			$550
American (1855 - 1927)				
JENKINS, Paul	*D*			$528
American (1923 -)	*P*	$1,430	$14,506	$55,000
	W	$880	$4,635	$9,350
JENKINS, Wilfred	*P*			$688
British (19th -)				
JENNEWEIN, Carl P.	*S*	$11,000	$11,000	$11,000
American (1890 -)				
JENNEY, Neil	*P*	$154,000	$206,800	$264,000
American (1945 -)	*S*			$4,180
JENNINGS-BROWN, H.W.	*P*			$22,000
British (19th -)				
JENSEN, Alfred	*D*			$22,000
American (1903 - 1981)	*P*	$3,520	$38,084	$77,000
	S			$35,200
JENSEN, Bill	*P*			$38,500
(20th -)				
JENSEN, C. Hornung	*P*			$220
Danish (20th -)				
JENSEN, Carl M.	*P*			$1,320
Danish (1855 -)				
JENSEN, George	*P*	$468	$807	$1,210
American (1878 -)				
JENSEN, Holger W.	*P*	$413	$441	$468
American (1880 -)				
JENSEN, Johann L.	*P*	$8,800	$27,712	$99,000
Danish (1800 - 1856)	*W*			$22,000
JENSEN, Johann L. (Manner)	*P*			$4,620
Danish (1800 - 1856)				
JENSEN, Laurits	*S*			$7,150
Danish (1859 -)				

D=Drawing, P=Painting, S=Sculpture, W=Watercolor

		Current Price Range		
		Low	Mean	High
JENSEN, Margaret	W			$110
American (20th -)				
JENSEN, Robert	W			$660
American (1922 -)				
JENSON, H.	D			$303
(20th -)				
JERICHAU, Holger H.	P			$1,320
Danish (1861 - 1900)				
JEROME, Pierre	P			$220
French (20th -)				
JERREMS, Lenore S.	P			$468
American (20th -)				
JERRLICZ, G.	P			$1,650
(?)				
JERVAS, Charles (Circle)	P			$1,650
British (1675 - 1739)				
JERZY, Richard	P			$176
(?)				
JESS,	S			$28,600
(20th -)				
JESSEN, T.Halver	P			$110
European (19th - 20th)				
JETTEL, Eugene	P	$6,600	$7,150	$7,700
Austrian (1845 - 1901)				
JEUNE, Eugene J. le	P	$2,090	$2,145	$2,200
French (1818 - 1897)				
JEWELL, Elizabeth G.	P	$110	$399	$880
American (1874 - 1956)				
JEWETT, Maude Sherwood	S	$2,200	$4,217	$8,250
American (1873 - 1953)				
JEX, Garnet W.	P			$385
American (1895 - 1979)				
JIMENEZ Y ARANDA, Jose	P	$8,250	$53,625	$99,000
Spanish (1837 - 1903)	W			$29,700
JIMENEZ Y MARTIN, Juan	P	$10,450	$13,475	$16,500
Spanish (1858 -)				

D=Drawing, P=Painting, S=Sculpture, W=Watercolor

		Current Price Range		
		Low	Mean	High

JOANOVITCH, Paul	*P*			$41,800
Austrian (1859 -)				
JOCELYN, Nathaniel	*P*			$3,850
(19th -)				
JOCHEMZ, P. F.	*P*			$330
Dutch (20th -)				
JOCHMUS, Harry	*P*			$7,150
German (1855 - 1915)				
JOHANES, Lens M.	*P*			$220
Dutch (1829 - 1897)				
JOHANSEN, Anders D.	*P*			$468
American (19th - 20th)				
JOHANSEN, John C.	*P*			$110
American (1876 - 1964)				
JOHN, Augustus (Attrib.)	*D*			$375
British (1878 - 1961)				
JOHNS, Jasper	*P*	$572,000	$5.621M	$17.050M
American (1930 -)	*S*	$385,000	$2.736M	$4.070M
	W			$990,000
JOHNS, Jeanette	*P*			$358
American (1877 - 1935)	*W*	$303	$317	$330
JOHNSON,	*P*			$110
American (20th -)				
JOHNSON, A. Hale	*P*			$1,320
(?)				
JOHNSON, Arthur	*P*			$165
American (1874 - 1954)				
JOHNSON, Arthur C.	*P*			$110
American (1897 -)				
JOHNSON, Avery	*W*	$330	$1,183	$1,980
American (1906 -)				
JOHNSON, Ben	*D*	$660	$660	$660
American (20th -)	*P*			$880

D=Drawing, P=Painting, S=Sculpture, W=Watercolor

		Current Price Range		
		Low	Mean	High

		Low	Mean	High
JOHNSON, Cecile (20th -)	*W*			$248
JOHNSON, Clarence American (1894 - 1981)	*P*	$13,200	$55,367	$121,000
JOHNSON, Clinton American (20th -)	*P*			$605
JOHNSON, David American (1827 - 1908)	*D*	$1,870	$3,960	$6,050
	P	$880	$14,245	$67,100
JOHNSON, David (Attrib.) American (1827 - 1908)	*P*			$1,100
JOHNSON, Eastman American (1824 - 1906)	*D*			$2,200
	P	$2,200	$15,202	$46,750
JOHNSON, Eastman (After) American (1824 - 1906)	*P*			$121
JOHNSON, Frank E. American (1873 - 1934)	*P*	$385	$440	$495
JOHNSON, Frank T. American (1874 - 1939)	*D*	$314	$1,577	$3,300
	P	$1,650	$29,150	$49,500
	W	$550	$2,017	$2,750
JOHNSON, G. American (20th -)	*P*			$248
JOHNSON, Horace (?)	*P*			$358
JOHNSON, J. William American (19th - 20th)	*P*			$5,500
JOHNSON, James American (1925 - 1963)	*P*			$330
JOHNSON, Jan American (20th -)	*W*			$605
JOHNSON, Joshua (Attrib.) American (18th -)	*W*			$1,760
JOHNSON, Lester American (1919 -)	*D*	$1,320	$4,400	$8,250
	P	$1,320	$17,270	$30,800

D=Drawing, P=Painting, S=Sculpture, W=Watercolor

		Current Price Range		
		Low	Mean	High

		Low	Mean	High
JOHNSON, Lester	*W*			$8,250
American (1919 -)				
JOHNSON, Marshall	*P*	$385	$2,992	$4,675
American (1850 - 1921)	*W*			$1,320
JOHNSON, Marshall (Attrib.)	*P*			$1,100
American (1850 - 1921)				
JOHNSON, Richard V.	*P*			$330
American (1905 -)	*W*			$248
JOHNSON, Robert W.	*P*			$209
American (1953 -)				
JOHNSON, Roy	*P*			$138
American (1890 - 1963)	*W*			$248
JOHNSON, Sidney Y.	*P*	$413	$598	$770
British (19th -)				
JOHNSON, William H.	*W*			$1,540
American (1901 - 1970)				
JOHNSTON, C. W.	*P*			$935
American (20th -)				
JOHNSTON, Frederic J.	*P*			$550
American (1890 -)				
JOHNSTON, John B.	*P*	$220	$289	$358
American (1847 - 1865)				
JOHNSTON, John H.	*P*	$1,700	$1,940	$2,420
American (1857 - 1941)				
JOHNSTON, John R.	*P*	$990	$1,320	$1,650
American (?)				
JOHNSTON, Reuben Le Grande	*P*	$413	$986	$1,870
American (1850 -)	*W*			$523
JOHNSTON, Robert E.	*P*	$2,420	$3,300	$4,180
American (1885 - 1933)				
JOHNSTON, Thomas M.	*P*			$825
American (19th - 20th)				
JOHNSTON, W. R.	*P*			$1,980
(19th -)				

D=Drawing, P=Painting, S=Sculpture, W=Watercolor

		Current Price Range		
		Low	Mean	High
JOINER, Harvey	*P*	$880	$1,397	$2,750
American (1852 - 1932)				
JOLI, Antonio	*P*	$17,600	$96,800	$176,000
Italian (1700 - 1777)				
JOLLY, C. E.	*P*			$633
European (18th - 19th)				
JOLLY, Emile	*W*			$330
French (19th -)				
JONAS, Leroy F.	*P*			$523
(1897 -)				
JONAS, Lucien H.	*D*			$550
French (1880 -)				
JONES, Albertus E.	*P*			$1,705
American (1882 - 1957)				
JONES, Allen	*P*	$22,000	$24,420	$28,600
British (1937 -)	*S*	$4,950	$5,775	$6,600
JONES, Andrew B.	*P*			$110
American (20th -)				
JONES, Charles	*P*	$3,520	$4,510	$5,500
British (1836 - 1892)				
JONES, Cora E.	*P*			$303
American (1875 - 1932)				
JONES, Daniel A. R.	*P*			$5,225
Belgian (1806 - 1874)				
JONES, Dennis	*S*	$385	$468	$550
American (20th -)				
JONES, Francis C.	*P*	$22,000	$34,650	$47,300
American (1857 - 1932)				
JONES, Grace C.	*P*			$110
American (20th -)				
JONES, Herbert H.	*P*	$1,760	$4,070	$6,380
British (19th - 20th)	*W*			$330
JONES, Hugh B.	*P*	$303	$7,237	$30,800
American (1848 - 1927)	*W*			$3,025

D=Drawing, P=Painting, S=Sculpture, W=Watercolor

		Current Price Range		
		Low	Mean	High
JONES, Jessie B.	*P*			$935
American (1865 - 1944)	*W*	$138	$674	$1,210
JONES, Joe	*P*	$110	$4,538	$14,300
American (1909 -)				
JONES, Leon F.	*P*			$385
American (1871 - 1940)				
JONES, Mary B.	*P*			$1,870
American (1868 - 1924)				
JONES, Mildred C.	*P*			$495
(?)				
JONES, Ott	*S*			$220
American (20th -)				
JONES, Paul	*P*	$2,090	$3,108	$4,125
British (19th -)				
JONES, Prescott M. M.	*W*			$220
American (1904 -)				
JONES, Robert	*W*			$110
American (1926 -)				
JONES, Samuel J. E.	*P*	$3,300	$13,200	$23,100
British (19th -)				
JONES, Seth	*W*			$193
American (1853 - 1930)				
JONES, Susan	*P*			$248
American (1897 -)				
JONES, T. Hampson	*W*			$165
(?)				
JONES, Timothy	*P*			$650
American (20th -)				
JONES, W.	*P*	$385	$385	$385
British (19th -)				
JONG, Jacobus S. de	*P*			$1,210
Dutch (1863 - 1901)				
JONGERE, Marius de	*P*	$1,540	$2,008	$2,475
Dutch (1912 -)				
JONGH, Oene R. de	*P*	$2,420	$4,235	$6,050
Dutch (1812 - 1896)				

D=Drawing, P=Painting, S=Sculpture, W=Watercolor

		Current Price Range		
		Low	Mean	High
JONGHE, Gustave L. de	*P*	$12,100	$33,000	$60,500
Belgian (1829 - 1893)				
JONGKIND, Johan B.	*D*			$1,760
Dutch (1819 - 1891)	*P*	$10,175	$56,696	$165,000
	W	$6,875	$19,938	$33,000
JONGKIND, Johan B. (Attrib.)	*P*			$3,575
Dutch (1819 - 1891)				
JONNEVOLD, Carl H.	*P*	$330	$916	$1,760
American (1856 - 1930)				
JONNIAUX, Alfred	*P*	$7,150	$12,925	$18,700
Belgian (1882 -)				
JONSON, Cornelis	*P*	$11,000	$77,000	$143,000
Dutch (1593 - 1664)				
JONSON, Cornelis (Circle)	*P*			$1,760
Dutch (1593 - 1664)				
JONSON, Raymond	*P*	$3,960	$37,620	$70,400
American (1891 - 1982)				
JOORS, Eugene	*P*			$3,300
Belgian (1850 -)				
JOOSTEN, Maria C.	*P*			$165
Dutch (20th -)				
JOOSTENS, Paul	*S*			$6,380
Belgian (20th -)				
JORDAENS, Hans	*P*			$13,200
Dutch (1595 - 1643)				
JORDAENS, Jacob (After)	*P*	$770	$3,135	$5,500
Flemish (1593 - 1678)				
JORDAENS, Jacob (Circle)	*P*			$1,320
Flemish (1593 - 1678)				
JORDAENS, Jacob (School)	*P*	$1,100	$2,200	$3,300
Flemish (1593 - 1678)				
JORDAENS & STUDIO, Jacob	*P*			$55,000
Flemish (1593 - 1678)				
JORDAN, Andrew	*W*			$550
American (20th -)				

D=Drawing, P=Painting, S=Sculpture, W=Watercolor

		Current Price Range		
		Low	Mean	High

JORDAN, Jerry	*P*	$7,700	$9,350	$11,000
American (1944 -)				
JORDAN, Norval	*P*			$193
German (19th -)				
JORDAN, R.	*P*			$935
European (19th -)				
JORDON, Eleanor	*P*			$165
American (20th -)				
JORGENSEN, Christian	*P*	$110	$220	$330
American (1860 - 1935)	*W*	$523	$1,256	$2,200
JORGENSON, Nels	*P*	$1,650	$1,815	$1,980
American (19th - 20th)				
JOSEPH, Julian	*D*			$330
American (20th -)	*P*	$605	$1,639	$3,025
JOSEPHI, Isaac	*P*			$385
American (19th - 20th)				
JOSLIN, Mary M.	*W*			$440
American (20th -)				
JOUBIOUX, Henry	*P*			$325
(?)				
JOULLIN, Amadee	*P*	$578	$1,712	$3,300
American (1862 - 1917)				
JOURDAIN, Roger	*P*			$2,420
French (1845 - 1918)				
JOURDAN, Adolphe	*P*	$2,970	$11,385	$19,800
French (1825 - 1889)				
JOURGUENEFF, P.	*S*			$770
(?)				
JOURGUENEFF, P. (After)	*S*			$154
(?)				
JOUVENET, Jean B.	*P*			$1,650
French (1644 - 1717)				
JOUVENET, Jean B. (Circle)	*D*			$2,200
French (1644 - 1717)	*P*			$3,300

D=Drawing, P=Painting, S=Sculpture, W=Watercolor

	Current Price Range		
	Low	Mean	High

		Low	Mean	High
JOUVENET, Jean B. (Follower) French (1644 - 1717)	P			$8,800
JOY, Robert American (1901 -)	P			$935
JOY, Thomas M. British (1812 - 1866)	P			$19,800
JOYCE, Marshall W. American (20th -)	P			$770
JOYNER, Jacob American (19th - 20th)	S			$1,650
JUAREZ, Jose Mexican (1939 -)	P			$16,500
JUAREZ, Roberto American (1952 -)	P			$7,150
JUDD, Donald American (1918 -)	D			$2,200
	P	$17,600	$81,400	$176,000
	S	$28,600	$97,405	$286,000
JUDSON, Alice American (? - 1948)	P	$220	$550	$880
JUDSON, William L. American (1842 - 1928)	P	$935	$2,159	$3,850
	W	$303	$574	$825
JUERGENS, Alfred American (1866 - 1934)	P	$248	$482	$715
JUETTE, G. (?)	P			$1,980
JULES, Mervin American (1912 -)	P	$385	$440	$495
JULIA, G. (?)	P			$495
JULIEN, (20th -)	P			$3,850
JULIEN, Joseph Belgian (19th -)	P			$6,820
JULIEN, Marvin American (1894 -)	P			$220

D=Drawing, P=Painting, S=Sculpture, W=Watercolor

		Current Price Range		
		Low	Mean	High
JUNG, (?)	P			$248
JUNG, Carl S. American (1880 -)	W			$110
JUNGWIRTH, Joseph Austrian (20th -)	P			$2,090
JUNQUET, (?)	P			$193
JUPP, G. H. European (19th - 20th)	P			$4,675
JURRES, Johannes H. Dutch (1875 - 1946)	D			$495
JUTSUM, Henry British (1816 - 1869)	P W	$908	$1,311	$1,320 $1,650
JUTZ, Carl German (1835 - 1916)	P	$15,950	$17,325	$18,700
JUVARRA, Filippo (Circle) Italian (1676 - 1736)	D			$1,760
KABAKOV, Iiya Russian (1933 -)	P			$154,000
KACERE, John American (1920 -)	P	$19,800	$26,400	$33,000
KACHADOORIAN, Zubel (?)	P	$132	$249	$523
KADAR, Bela Hungarian (1877 - 1955)	D W	$523 $385	$1,378 $5,414	$3,300 $26,400
KADISHMAN, Menashe (20th -)	P	$7,150	$9,075	$11,000
KADLACSIK, Laszlo Hungarian (1925 - 1989)	P			$12,100
KAELIN, Charles S. American (1858 - 1929)	D P	$550 $440	$1,619 $2,469	$3,630 $4,840
KAEMMERER, Frederik H.	D			$1,650

D=Drawing, P=Painting, S=Sculpture, W=Watercolor

		Current Price Range	
	Low	Mean	High
KAEMMERER, Frederik H.	P	$18,700	$360,800	$1.320M
Dutch (1839 - 1902)				
KAEP, Louis J.	W			$193
American (1903 -)				
KAERCHER, Amalie	P			$66,000
German (19th -)				
KAESELAU, Charles	W	$193	$264	$305
American (20th -)				
KAFRIARZKE, K. (Attrib.)	P			$115
American (20th -)				
KAGANOVE, J.	P			$715
European (20th -)				
KAHLER, Carl	P	$7,700	$11,367	$15,400
Austrian (1855 -)	W			$165
KAHLO, Frida	P	$99,000	$436,333	$1.430M
Mexican (1910 - 1954)	W	$30,800	$70,400	$110,000
KAHN, Gary	S			$1,980
(20th -)				
KAHN, Susan B.	P			$990
American (20th -)				
KAHN, Wolf	D	$825	$1,393	$2,310
American (1927 -)	P	$2,420	$7,599	$13,200
KAIHLANEN, Hilda	W	$165	$275	$385
(1919 -)				
KAISER, P. H.	P			$176
German (19th - 20th)				
KAISER, Richard	P			$1,760
German (1868 - 1941)				
KALBHENNS, A.	P			$165
European (19th -)				
KALCE, Alfredo	P			$1,650
Mexican (20th -)				
KALIN, Victor	P			$300
(?)				

D=Drawing, P=Painting, S=Sculpture, W=Watercolor

		Current Price Range		
		Low	Mean	High

		Low	Mean	High
KALINA, Richard (20th -)	P			$660
KALISH, Max American (1891 - 1945)	S			$9,900
KALLIS, Maurice (?)	P			$285
KALLOS, Paul French (1928 -)	P			$18,700
KALLSTENIUS, Gottfried Swedish (1861 - 1943)	P			$31,900
KALRAET, Abraham van Dutch (18th -)	P			$36,300
KAMP, Anton American (20th -)	P	$138	$556	$1,760
KAMP, Louise M. American (1867 - 1959)	P			$1,320
KAMPF, Arthur (After) German (1864 - 1950)	P			$605
KAMY, Bernard American (20th -)	P			$330
KANDINSKY, Wassily Russian (1866 - 1944)	D	$29,700	$172,608	$440,000
	P	$143,000	$3.085M	$20.900M
	W	$198,000	$329,313	$715,000
KANDINSKY, Wassily (After) Russian (1866 - 1944)	S			$15,400
KANE, John American (1860 - 1934)	P	$3,850	$7,150	$9,350
KANE, Morgan American (1916 -)	W	$110	$660	$1,210
KANEKO, Jun (20th -)	S			$990
KANIN, Michael American (20th -)	S			$3,080
KANNE, Benjamin American (1897 -)	P			$110

D=Drawing, P=Painting, S=Sculpture, W=Watercolor

| | | Current Price Range | | |
		Low	Mean	High
KANNEMANS, Christian C. Dutch (1812 - 1884)	P			$2,750
KANTOR, Frank American (20th -)	P			$110
KANZLER, Karl (?)	D			$220
KAPLAN, Edith J. American (20th -)	P			$275
KAPLAN, Joseph American (1900 -)	D W	$300	$325	$350 $700
KAPLINSKI, Buffalo (?)	W			$193
KAPOOR, Anish (20th -)	P			$41,250
KAPP, Gary American (1942 -)	P	$4,400	$4,950	$5,500
KAPPES, Alfred American (1850 - 1894)	P			$1,100
KAPPES, Karl American (1861 - 1943)	P W			$138 $330
KARASICK, Mary K. American (1888 -)	P			$550
KARASIN, Nicolai Russian (1842 - 1908)	P			$385
KARAWINA, Erica American (1904 -)	S W	$303	$344	$330 $385
KARAZIAN, Eduard Russian (1939 -)	P	$1,980	$3,300	$4,400
KARFIOL, Bernard American (1886 - 1952)	P	$633	$1,054	$1,650
KARFUNKLE, David American (1880 -)	P	$330	$358	$385
KARLBACH, F. A. von (?)	P			$935

D=Drawing, P=Painting, S=Sculpture, W=Watercolor

		Current Price Range		
		Low	Mean	High

		Low	Mean	High
KARLOVSZKY, Bertalan Hungarian (1858 - 1945)	P			$578
KARPATHY, Jeno Hungarian (1871 - 1950)	P			$2,860
KARRAS, Spiros J. American (1897 - 1941)	P	$248	$1,004	$1,760
KARSSEN, A. N. M. European (20th -)	P			$1,650
KARTH, Jean N. French (1795 - 1878)	W			$550
KARYIATH, E. Kenneth Belgian (19th - 20th)	P			$550
KASNYANSKY, Anatole Russian (20th -)	W			$550
KASSAY, K. (?)	P			$220
KATALING, E. Faqsa (20th -)	P			$413
KATWIJK, Arthur F. European (19th -)	W			$880
KATZ, Alex American (1927 -)	D	$1,210	$7,612	$14,300
	P	$5,720	$37,143	$121,000
	S	$4,070	$5,610	$7,150
	W			$1,320
KATZ, Raymond A. American (1895 - 1974)	P			$385
KATZEN, Lila (20th -)	S			$4,950
KAU, Georg German (1870 -)	P			$660
KAUBA, Carl American (1865 - 1922)	S	$495	$2,767	$14,300
KAUBA, Carl (After) American (1865 - 1922)	S	$468	$486	$523

D=Drawing, P=Painting, S=Sculpture, W=Watercolor

		Current Price Range		
		Low	Mean	High
KAUBA, Carl (Attrib.)	S			$2,860
American (1865 - 1922)				
KAUFFMAN, Angelica (Attrib.)	D			$1,210
Swiss (1740 - 1807)	P	$385	$3,773	$13,200
KAUFFMAN, Angelica (Circle)	P			$1,018
Swiss (1740 - 1807)				
KAUFFMAN, Angelica (Follower)	P			$1,210
Swiss (1740 - 1807)				
KAUFFMANN, Craig	S			$9,900
American (20th -)				
KAUFFMANN, Hermann	W			$1,045
German (1808 - 1889)				
KAUFFMANN, Hugo W.	P	$7,700	$37,400	$60,500
German (1844 - 1915)				
KAUFMAN,	P			$495
(?)				
KAUFMAN, John F.	P			$990
American (1870 -)				
KAUFMAN, Stuart	P			$275
(?)				
KAUFMANN, Adolf	P	$798	$2,578	$5,225
Austrian (1848 - 1916)				
KAUFMANN, Ferdinand	P	$935	$6,939	$12,100
American (1864 -)				
KAUFMANN, Karl	P	$660	$3,278	$9,900
Austrian (1843 - 1901)				
KAULA, Lee L.	P	$1,430	$7,077	$12,100
American (1865 - 1957)				
KAULA, William J.	P	$770	$1,623	$3,300
American (1871 - 1952)	W	$248	$1,286	$2,860
KAULBACH, Anton	P			$2,750
German (20th -)				
KAULBACH, Friedrich A. von	P			$8,800
German (1822 - 1903)				

D=Drawing, P=Painting, S=Sculpture, W=Watercolor

		Current Price Range		
		Low	Mean	High

		Low	Mean	High
KAULBACH, Hermann	P	$14,300	$15,950	$17,600
German (1846 - 1909)				
KAUS, Mas	P			$605
German (1891 -)				
KAUTZKY, Ted	P	$578	$1,220	$1,980
American (1896 - 1953)	W	$615	$1,078	$1,540
KAVANAGH, Joseph M.	P	$220	$1,210	$2,090
Irish (1856 - 1918)				
KAY, Bernard	P			$165
American (20th -)				
KAY, Gertrude	W			$220
American (20th -)				
KAYAMA, M.	P	$220	$248	$275
Japanese (20th -)				
KAYE, Otis	P	$28,600	$36,850	$45,100
American (1885 - 1974)				
KAYSER, Anne	P			$220
American (20th -)				
KAYSER, Bernita A.	P			$330
(20th -)				
KEANE,	P	$440	$440	$440
(?)				
KEANE, Frank	P			$275
American (1876 -)				
KEARNEY, John W.	P			$165
American (20th -)	S			$198
KEARNS, Jerry	P			$17,600
(20th -)				
KECK, Charles	S	$880	$1,994	$3,575
American (1875 - 1951)				
KECK, H.	S			$550
German (20th -)				
KEELHOFF, Frans	P	$660	$1,907	$2,530
Belgian (1820 - 1893)				

D=Drawing, P=Painting, S=Sculpture, W=Watercolor

		Current Price Range		
		Low	Mean	High
KEENAN, Ann E.	*P*	$385	$688	$990
American (1904 - 1982)				
KEEP, Virginia	*D*			$550
American (1878 -)				
KEEVER, Kim	*P*	$247	$330	$412
(?)				
KEFFER, Frances	*P*			$330
American (1881 - 1954)				
KEIFER, Anselm	*S*			$165,000
German (1945 -)				
KEILHAU, Bernhard (Follower)	*P*			$4,400
Danish (1624 - 1687)				
KEIRINCX, Alexander	*P*	$44,000	$52,250	$60,500
Flemish (1600 -)				
KEISERMAN, Franz	*D*			$13,200
Swiss (1765 - 1833)	*W*			$3,850
KEISTER, Roy	*P*			$1,430
American (1886 -)				
KEISTER, Steven	*P*	$308	$2,767	$5,225
(20th -)				
KEITH, Belle E.	*P*	$193	$221	$248
American (1865 -)				
KEITH, Castle	*P*	$110	$4,496	$15,510
American (19th - 20th)				
KEITH, Dora W.	*P*			$935
American (1857 - 1940)				
KEITH, William	*P*	$715	$3,746	$20,900
American (1839 - 1911)	*W*			$1,100
KEITH, William (Attrib.)	*P*			$2,475
American (1839 - 1911)				
KELDERMAN, Jan	*P*			$495
Dutch (1741 - 1820)				
KELLER, Adolphe	*P*			$13,200
Dutch (1880 - 1968)				

D=Drawing, P=Painting, S=Sculpture, W=Watercolor

		Current Price Range		
		Low	Mean	High
KELLER, Arthur	*D*			$440
American (1867 - 1924)	*W*	$275	$881	$1,900
KELLER, E.	*P*			$440
American (1822 - 1885)				
KELLER, Edgar M.	*P*			$5,225
American (1868 - 1932)				
KELLER, Ferdinand	*P*			$7,150
Brazilian (19th -)				
KELLER, Henry G.	*P*			$220
American (1870 - 1949)	*W*	$138	$344	$550
KELLER, Leonard	*P*			$220
(?)				
KELLER, R.	*P*			$1,045
Dutch (20th -)				
KELLER-KUHNE, Josef W.	*P*			$1,870
(?)				
KELLEY, Ramon	*D*			$1,800
American (20th -)	*P*	$3,100	$3,600	$4,100
KELLOG, E. J.	*P*			$358
(?)				
KELLOGG, C. B.	*W*			$330
American (20th -)				
KELLY, Alouicius O.	*P*			$523
American (?)				
KELLY, Ellsworth	*D*	$6,050	$18,543	$35,750
American (1923 -)	*P*	$154,000	$402,500	$715,000
	S	$38,500	$286,000	$577,500
KELLY, Grace V.	*W*	$110	$152	$193
American (1877 - 1950)				
KELLY, James E.	*S*			$3,575
American (1855 - 1933)				
KELLY, Leon	*D*	$165	$963	$1,760
American (1901 -)				

D=Drawing, P=Painting, S=Sculpture, W=Watercolor

		Current Price Range		
		Low	Mean	High

		Low	Mean	High
KELLY, Louise American (20th -)	P			$1,760
KELLY, Ramon American (20th -)	D			$1,870
KELLY, Sir Gerald British (1879 - 1972)	P	$6,050	$18,425	$30,800
KELMAN, Benjamin American (1887 -)	P			$1,100
KELPE, Paul American (1902 - 1985)	W	$9,350	$11,825	$14,300
KELSEY, Muriel C. American (20th -)	S			$248
KELSEY, Richard American (1905 -)	P			$220
KEMBLE, Edward W. American (1861 - 1933)	D	$650	$2,635	$4,620
KEMEYS, Edward American (1843 - 1907)	S			$550
KEMM, Robert British (19th -)	P			$3,850
KEMMER, Hans Dutch (15th -)	P			$242,000
KEMP, Oliver American (1887 - 1934)	P	$440	$482	$523
KEMPENER, Pieter de Spanish (1503 - 1580)	D			$7,150
KEMPENER, Pieter de (Circle) Spanish (1503 - 1580)	P			$2,640
KEMPSON, Julie H. American (1835 - 1913)	P			$121
KEMPTON, Elmira American (20th -)	P			$209
KEMPTON, Greta American (20th -)	P			$440
KENDALL, M. M. (?)	P			$110

D=Drawing, P=Painting, S=Sculpture, W=Watercolor

		Current Price Range		
		Low	Mean	High

		Low	Mean	High
KENDALL, Marie B.	*P*			$935
American (1885 - 1953)				
KENDALL, William S.	*D*			$4,500
American (1869 - 1938)	*P*			$220
KENDERTON, G.	*P*			$550
British (19th - 20th)				
KENDRICK, Albert H.	*P*			$2,750
British (19th -)				
KENDRICK, Mel	*P*	$8,800	$14,117	$20,350
(20th -)	*S*	$17,600	$20,533	$23,100
KENNARD,	*P*			$440
(?)				
KENNEDY, (Attributed)	*P*			$6,050
(?)				
KENNEDY, Cecil N.	*P*			$3,520
British (1852 - 1898)				
KENNEDY, Charles H.	*P*			$248
American (20th -)				
KENNEDY, E. Benson	*P*			$605
(?)				
KENNEDY, M. W.	*P*			$825
(?)				
KENNEDY, William	*P*			$2,970
American (1818 -)				
KENNEDY, William (Attrib.)	*P*			$3,190
American (1818 -)				
KENNEY, C.	*P*			$605
American (19th - 20th)				
KENNICOTT, Robert H.	*P*			$303
American (1892 - 1983)				
KENNINGTON, Thomas B.	*P*	$14,300	$21,450	$28,600
British (1856 - 1916)				
KENSETT, John F.	*D*			$5,775
American (1816 - 1872)	*P*	$2,420	$36,167	$308,000

D=Drawing, P=Painting, S=Sculpture, W=Watercolor

| | | Current Price Range | | |
		Low	Mean	High
KENSETT, John F. American (1816 - 1872)	*S*			$60,500
KENT, Douglas (?)	*P*			$138
KENT, Rockwell American (1882 - 1971)	*D*	$110	$569	$1,100
	P	$2,310	$22,022	$64,900
	S			$2,200
	W	$2,750	$4,565	$6,380
KENT, Walter W. American (20th -)	*P*			$220
KENT, William British (1684 - 1758)	*S*			$770
KENYON, Haidee American (? - 1944)	*P*			$440
KENYON, Henry American (1861 - 1926)	*P*	$413	$831	$1,430
KEOGH, Tom (20th -)	*D*			$330
KEPES, Gyorgy American (1906 -)	*P*	$1,100	$1,100	$1,100
KERBER, Franz German (1901 -)	*P*			$220
KERCHER, Bob American (20th -)	*W*	$550	$750	$1,100
KERFOOT, Margaret American (1901 -)	*W*	$385	$592	$798
KERKAM, Earl American (1890 - 1965)	*P*	$1,980	$2,200	$2,420
KERLOR, I. American (20th -)	*P*			$110
KERN, F. (?)	*P*			$110
KERN, Hermann Hungarian (1839 - 1912)	*P*	$1,430	$5,463	$15,400

D=Drawing, P=Painting, S=Sculpture, W=Watercolor

		Current Price Range	
	Low	Mean	High

KERNAN, Joseph F.	*P*			$6,200
American (1878 - 1958)				
KERR, Vernon	*P*	$385	$495	$605
American (1938 - 1982)				
KERRN, Hansine S. J.	*P*	$6,600	$7,700	$8,800
Danish (1826 - 1860)				
KERSEBOOM, Frederic	*P*			$2,860
British (1632 - 1690)				
KESSEL, Hieronymus	*P*			$3,850
Flemish (1578 - 1636)				
KESSEL, Jan van	*P*			$17,600
Flemish (1626 - 1679)				
KESSEL, Jan van (Attrib.)	*P*			$10,450
Flemish (1626 - 1679)				
KESSEL, Jan van (Et al.) (Att.)	*P*			$4,400
Flemish (1626 - 1679)				
KESSEL, Jan van (Manner)	*P*			$2,200
Flemish (1626 - 1679)				
KESSEL, Peter van	*P*			$22,000
Flemish (? - 1668)				
KESSEL, ELDER, Jan van (Foll.)	*P*			$8,250
Flemish (1626 - 1679)				
KESSLER, August	*P*			$990
German (1826 - 1906)				
KETCHUM, Edmund	*P*	$154	$160	$165
American (19th - 20th)				
KETCHUM, Hank	*D*			$275
American (20th -)				
KETTLE, Tilly	*P*	$440	$15,913	$37,400
British (1735 - 1786)				
KEULEYAN-LAFON, Jean	*P*			$1,210
French (1886 -)				
KEVER, Jacob S.	*P*	$1,430	$5,621	$15,400
Dutch (1854 - 1922)	*W*			$3,850
KEY, Adriaen T.	*P*			$18,700
Flemish (1544 - 1590)				

D=Drawing, P=Painting, S=Sculpture, W=Watercolor

		Current Price Range		
		Low	Mean	High
KEY, Adriaen T. (Attrib.)	P			$44,000
Flemish (1544 - 1590)				
KEY, Adriaen T. (Circle)	P			$3,300
Flemish (1544 - 1590)				
KEY, J. E.	W			$165
(20th -)				
KEY, John R.	D			$440
American (1837 - 1920)	P	$1,760	$8,672	$31,900
KEY, Mabel	W			$6,325
American (1874 - 1926)				
KEY, Willem	P	$7,700	$25,850	$44,000
Flemish (1520 - 1568)				
KEY, Willem (Attrib.)	P			$4,675
Flemish (1520 - 1568)				
KEYES, Bernard M.	P	$303	$1,238	$1,760
American (1898 - 1973)				
KEYSER, Ernest W.	S			$660
American (1875 - 1959)				
KEYSER, Nicaise de	P			$3,960
Flemish (1813 - 1887)				
KEYSER, Thomas de (Attrib.)	P			$5,500
Dutch (1596 - 1667)				
KEYSIL, William H.	P			$908
American (19th -)				
KIAERSKOU, Frederick	P			$9,350
Danish (1805 - 1891)				
KIECHLE, Edgar O.	P			$770
American (20th -)				
KIEFER, Anselm	P	$68,750	$144,375	$220,000
German (1945 -)	S			$16,500
	W			$77,000
KIENHOLZ, Edward	P	$2,200	$89,100	$176,000
American (1927 -)				
KIESEL, Conrad	D			$550

D=Drawing, P=Painting, S=Sculpture, W=Watercolor

| | | Current Price Range | | |
		Low	Mean	High
KIESEL, Conrad	*P*	$4,950	$33,550	$60,500
German (1846 - 1921)				
KIESLING, Ferdinand	*P*			$1,100
German (1810 - 1882)				
KIGGINS, Mary K.	*W*			$110
American (20th -)				
KIHN, William L.	*P*			$5,170
American (1898 - 1957)	*W*			$3,850
KIKOINE, Michel	*P*	$3,850	$14,263	$31,900
Russian (1892 - 1968)				
KILBERT, Robert	*P*			$253
American (20th -)				
KILBOURNE, Samuel A. (Attrib.)	*P*			$165
American (1836 - 1881)				
KILBURNE, George G.	*P*	$2,090	$2,970	$3,850
British (1839 - 1924)	*W*			$3,300
KILGORE, Charles	*P*	$248	$1,107	$2,090
American (20th -)				
KILPATRICK, Aaron E.	*P*			$2,750
American (1872 - 1953)				
KIMBALL, Alonzo M.	*P*			$413
American (1874 - 1923)	*W*			$330
KIMBALL, Charles F.	*P*			$2,200
American (1835 - 1907)				
KIMBEL, Richard M.	*P*			$3,080
American (1865 - 1942)				
KIMBELL, A. B.	*P*			$413
(?)				
KIMBERLY, Denison	*P*			$605
American (1814 - 1863)				
KINCAID, Bolton	*P*			$605
British (19th - 20th)				
KINDLEBERGER, David	*W*			$220
American (1834 - 1921)				

D=Drawing, P=Painting, S=Sculpture, W=Watercolor

| | | Current Price Range | | |
		Low	Mean	High
KINDLER, Alice L. R.	P			$880
American (1892 -)				
KING, Albert F.	P	$1,600	$6,796	$24,000
American (1854 - 1945)				
KING, Charles B.	P	$55,000	$220,000	$385,000
American (1785 - 1862)				
KING, E. Meade	W			$220
(?)				
KING, F. W.	P			$1,430
American (19th -)				
KING, George W.	P	$358	$1,586	$3,300
American (1836 - 1922)				
KING, Gordon	P			$1,045
British (20th -)				
KING, Hamilton	P			$275
American (1871 - 1952)				
KING, Henry J. Y.	P	$4,400	$6,050	$7,700
British (1855 - 1924)				
KING, J. W.	P			$10,450
American (19th - 20th)				
KING, John Y.	P	$330	$7,304	$16,500
British (1855 - 1924)				
KING, Paul	P	$303	$5,748	$13,200
American (1867 - 1947)	W			$1,430
KING, Tony	P			$2,530
(?)				
KING, William	S			$6,600
(20th -)				
KINGHAN, Charles	P			$700
(1895 -)				
KINGMAN, Dong	P			$495
American (1911 -)	W	$1,100	$5,524	$26,400
KINGMAN, Eduardo	D			$1,760
Ecuadoran (1913 -)	P	$110	$4,437	$7,700

D=Drawing, P=Painting, S=Sculpture, W=Watercolor

| | | Current Price Range | |
	Low	Mean	High
KINGMAN, W. F. *W*			$358
American (?)			
KINGSBURY, Edward *P*	$110	$298	$605
American (? - 1940)			
KINGSLEY, Elbridge *P*	$475	$623	$770
American (1841 - 1918)			
KINKADE, Thomas *P*			$4,400
American (20th -)			
KINKEAD, Charles E. *P*			$110
(20th -)			
KINLEY, Peter *P*	$550	$578	$605
British (20th -)			
KINNAIRD, Henry J. *P*	$3,080	$3,355	$3,630
British (19th -) *W*	$1,320	$2,512	$4,950
KINNAIRD, Wiggs *W*	$880	$935	$990
British (?)			
KINSBURGER, Sylvain *S*			$1,760
(?)			
KINSELLA, James *W*			$770
American (1857 - 1923)			
KINSEY, Alberta *P*	$275	$1,282	$5,170
American (1875 - 1955)			
KINTZ, W. C. *P*			$990
(19th - 20th)			
KINZEL, Josef *P*	$6,600	$8,800	$11,000
Austrian (1852 - 1925)			
KIPNISS, Robert *P*			$1,320
American (?)			
KIRCHNER, Ernst L. *D*	$1,100	$4,803	$7,700
German (1880 - 1938) *P*	$275,000	$1.155M	$1.650M
KIRCHNER, Ernst L. (Attrib.) *D*			$242
German (1880 - 1938)			
KIRCHNER, Otto *P*	$770	$1,403	$2,200
German (1887 -)			

D=Drawing, P=Painting, S=Sculpture, W=Watercolor

| | | Current Price Range | | |
		Low	Mean	High
KIRILI, Alain	S			$7,150
French (1946 -)				
KIRK, Thomas	P	$550	$633	$715
British (? - 1797)				
KIRKBY, Thomas	P			$1,760
British (? - 1847)				
KIRKEBY, Per	P	$26,400	$33,000	$39,600
Danish (1938 -)				
KIRKPATRICK,	P			$3,850
British (19th -)				
KIRKPATRICK, H.	P			$400
(?)				
KIRKPATRICK, J. L.	P			$330
European (20th -)				
KIRKPATRICK, Sheila	P			$6,900
American (20th -)				
KIRKPATRICK, W. A.	P			$715
(?)				
KIRKPATRICK, JR., Edward J.	P			$154
American (20th -)				
KIRMSE, Marguerite	D			$553
American (1885 - 1954)	S			$132
KIRSHNER, Otto	P			$880
(?)				
KIRSHTEN, A.	P			$413
American (19th -)				
KISELEWSKI, Joseph	S	$330	$8,562	$48,400
American (1901 - 1988)				
KISLING, Moise	P	$38,500	$165,922	$385,000
French (1891 - 1953)				
KISS, Radolphe	P	$605	$605	$605
American (19th - 20th)				
KISSACK, R. A.	P			$303
(?)				
KISSEL, C. M.	P			$605
American (20th -)				

D=Drawing, P=Painting, S=Sculpture, W=Watercolor

		Current Price Range		
		Low	Mean	High

KISSELEV, Lexandre A.	P			$6,710
Russian (1838 - 1911)				
KITCHELL, Hudson M.	P	$198	$590	$1,155
American (1862 - 1944)				
KITSON, Henry H.	S	$2,200	$5,225	$8,250
American (1863 - 1947)				
KITTELL, Nicholas B.	P			$220
(1822 - 1894)				
KJELDSEN, Lana	P			$165
American (19th - 20th)				
KLAER, T. van	P			$935
German (19th - 20th)				
KLAGES, Frank H.	P			$495
American (1892 -)				
KLAPPER, Siegfried	P			$2,420
(20th -)				
KLARWEIN, Mati	P			$550
German (1932 -)				
KLAUS, Joseph	P			$8,800
Belgian (19th -)				
KLEBE, Gene	P	$385	$399	$413
American (1907 -)	W			$165
KLEE, Paul	D	$20,900	$151,962	$1.210M
Swiss (1879 - 1940)	P	$330,000	$673,750	$1.017M
	S			$49,500
	W	$77,000	$339,326	$1.320M
KLEEHAAS, Theodor	P			$3,080
German (1854 - 1929)				
KLEEMAN, Ron	P	$880	$11,440	$22,000
American (1937 -)				
KLEIBER, Hans	P			$1,540
American (20th -)				
KLEIN, L.	P			$605
German (19th -)				

D=Drawing, P=Painting, S=Sculpture, W=Watercolor

		Current Price Range		
		Low	Mean	High

		Low	Mean	High
KLEINBARD, Alexa (20th -)	*P*	$220	$495	$770
KLEINERT, A.	*D*			$248
German (20th -)	*P*			$330
KLEINHOLZ, Frank American (1901 -)	*P*			$523
KLEINMEYER, B. (19th -)	*P*			$1,430
KLEINSCHMIDT, Paul German (1883 - 1949)	*P*			$19,800
KLEIST, R. (19th -)	*W*			$2,970
KLEITSCH, Joseph American (1885 - 1931)	*P*	$1,980	$18,398	$75,900
KLEMROTH, E. H. (19th -)	*D*			$193
KLENGEL, Johann C. (18th -)	*D*			$1,650
KLEVER, Julius S. von Russian (1850 - 1924)	*P*	$880	$11,440	$22,000
KLEY, George German (20th -)	*P*			$990
KLEY, Heinrich German (1863 - 1945)	*P*			$572
KLEY, Henri German (1908 -)	*P*	$880	$880	$880
KLEYN, Lodewyk J. Dutch (1817 - 1897)	*P*	$8,800	$14,392	$25,300
KLIMLEY, Stanley American (?)	*W*	$220	$310	$400
KLIMT, Gustav Austrian (1862 - 1918)	*D*	$5,280	$27,476	$41,800
KLIMT, Gustav (Attrib.) Austrian (1862 - 1918)	*D*			$3,000
KLINE, Edith American (1903 -)	*W*			$165

D=Drawing, P=Painting, S=Sculpture, W=Watercolor

		Low	Current Price Range Mean	High
KLINE, Franz	D	$880	$23,598	$154,000
American (1910 - 1962)	P	$425	$697,153	$2.860M
	W	$5,280	$28,875	$99,000
KLING, Wendall	W			$248
American (?)				
KLINGSBOYE, Rudolph	P			$385
Scandinavian (20th -)				
KLINKENBERG, Johannes C. K.	P			$2,475
Dutch (1852 - 1924)	W	$1,540	$6,270	$11,000
KLINKER, Orpha	P	$358	$523	$770
American (1891 - 1964)				
KLIROS, Theodore	P			$165
American (20th -)				
KLITGAARD, Georgina	P			$2,530
American (1893 -)				
KLITZ, Anthony	P			$165
British (1917 -)				
KLOHSS, Hans	P			$1,210
Austrian (1879 -)				
KLOK, Johannes	P			$550
(?)				
KLOMBBEK, Johann B.	P			$35,200
Dutch (19th -)				
KLOVSTAD, Eric	P			$770
European (19th - 20th)				
KLUGE, Constantine	P	$2,310	$5,715	$46,200
French (1912 -)				
KLUGE, Constantine (Attrib.)	P			$1,100
French (1912 -)				
KLUMPKE, Anna E.	P			$4,400
American (19th -)				
KMETTY,	P			$825
American (?)				
KNAPP, Charles W.	P	$770	$6,859	$26,400
American (1822 - 1900)				

D=Drawing, P=Painting, S=Sculpture, W=Watercolor

		Current Price Range		
		Low	Mean	High
KNATHS, Karl	*D*	$110	$322	$990
American (1891 - 1971)	*P*	$193	$5,528	$13,200
	W	$275	$506	$1,320
KNAUS, Ludwig	*P*	$6,050	$40,621	$99,000
German (1829 - 1910)				
KNAUS, Ludwig (Attrib.)	*P*			$1,760
German (1829 - 1910)				
KNEE, Gina	*W*			$3,300
American (1898 -)				
KNELL, William C.	*P*	$1,870	$3,410	$4,950
British (19th -)				
KNELL, William C. (Attrib.)	*P*			$935
British (19th -)				
KNELLER, Sir Godfrey	*P*	$4,675	$5,363	$6,050
British (1646 - 1723)				
KNELLER, Sir Godfrey (After)	*P*	$275	$1,788	$3,300
British (1646 - 1723)				
KNELLER, Sir Godfrey (Attrib.)	*P*			$1,210
British (1646 - 1723)				
KNELLER, Sir Godfrey (Follower)	*P*	$1,320	$1,485	$1,650
British (1646 - 1723)				
KNELLER, Sir Godfrey (Manner)	*P*	$880	$1,320	$1,760
British (1646 - 1723)				
KNELLER, Sir Godfrey (School)	*P*	$770	$2,723	$4,675
British (1646 - 1723)				
KNELLER, Sir Godfrey (Style)	*P*			$5,500
British (1646 - 1723)				
KNIGHT, A. Stuart	*P*			$110
American (20th -)				
KNIGHT, Charles R.	*P*	$1,210	$2,787	$3,850
American (1874 - 1953)				
KNIGHT, Dame Laura	*W*			$9,900
British (1877 - 1970)				
KNIGHT, Daniel R.	*P*	$3,575	$28,366	$66,000

D=Drawing, P=Painting, S=Sculpture, W=Watercolor

		Current Price Range	
		Low	Mean	High

		Low	Mean	High
KNIGHT, Daniel R.	*W*			$1,870
American (1839 - 1924)				
KNIGHT, Daniel R. (After)	*P*			$2,035
American (1839 - 1924)				
KNIGHT, F.	*P*	$715	$825	$935
British (19th -)				
KNIGHT, J. A.	*P*			$880
British (19th -)				
KNIGHT, Louis A.	*P*	$440	$9,125	$28,600
American (1873 - 1948)	*W*	$880	$1,760	$2,640
KNIGHT, M. W.	*P*			$110
American (20th -)				
KNIGHT, Mary	*W*			$413
American (19th -)				
KNIGHT, William H.	*P*			$13,200
British (1823 - 1863)				
KNIJF, Wouter	*P*	$11,000	$17,050	$23,100
(?)				
KNIKKER, Aris	*P*			$1,210
Dutch (19th -)				
KNIKKER, Jan	*P*	$715	$843	$1,100
Dutch (1911 -)				
KNIP, Joseph A. (Attrib.)	*W*			$605
Dutch (1777 - 1847)				
KNIP, William A.	*P*			$1,100
Dutch (1883 - 1967)				
KNOBLAUET, F. L.	*P*			$330
(19th -)				
KNOEBEL, Imi	*S*	$3,850	$6,050	$8,250
(20th -)				
KNOOP, Guitou	*S*			$550
French (20th -)				
KNOPF, Herman	*P*			$1,760
Austrian (1870 -)				
KNORR, Charles E.	*D*	$1,650	$1,650	$1,650
French (1890 -)				

D=Drawing, P=Painting, S=Sculpture, W=Watercolor

		Low	Mean	High
KNOTT, Arthur H.	*P*			$413
American (1883 - 1977)				
KNOWLES, Anna M.	*P*			$110
American (20th -)				
KNOWLES, C.B.	*P*			$4,675
British (19th -)				
KNOWLES, Elizabeth C.	*W*			$138
American (20th -)				
KNOWLES, F. McGillvray	*W*			$550
American (1860 - 1932)				
KNOWLES, Farquhar M. S.	*P*			$1,650
American (19th -)				
KNOWLES, George S.	*P*			$16,500
British (1863 - 1931)				
KNOWLTON, Helen M.	*D*			$154
American (1832 - 1913)				
KNOWLTON, Win	*S*			$22,000
(20th -)				
KNOX, James	*P*			$605
American (1866 -)				
KNOX, James (Attrib.)	*P*			$468
American (1866 -)				
KNOX, Susan R.	*P*	$138	$1,060	$5,390
American (1875 - 1959)	*W*	$165	$248	$330
KNOX, Susan R. (Attrib.)	*P*			$303
American (1875 - 1959)				
KNOX, Wilfred	*P*	$413	$1,066	$2,750
American (20th -)				
KNUDSEN, Peder	*P*			$330
American (20th -)				
KNUGER, Richard	*W*			$165
American (1880 -)				
KOBELL, Wilhelm von	*D*			$5,280
German (1766 - 1855)				
KOCH, Berthe C.	*P*			$165
American (1899 - 1975)				

Current Price Range

D=Drawing, P=Painting, S=Sculpture, W=Watercolor

		Current Price Range		
		Low	Mean	High

		Low	Mean	High
KOCH, Gail P. American (?)	*P*			$110
KOCH, Henry American (1846 - 1906)	*W*			$468
KOCH, John American (1909 -)	*P*	$1,210	$43,660	$363,000
KOCH, Ludwig Austrian (1866 - 1934)	*P*			$15,400
KOCH, Walther German (1875 - 1915)	*P*			$1,760
KOCHANOWSKI, Roman Polish (1856 - 1945)	*P*			$1,320
KOCHEISHVILI, Boris Russian (1940 -)	*D* *P*	$1,100	$1,155	$1,210 $6,050
KOCHER, Fritz American (1904 - 1973)	*P*	$303	$732	$1,100
KOEHLEN, P. R. (?)	*D*			$121
KOEHLER, Henry American (1927 -)	*P*			$19,800
KOEHLER, Henry (Et al.) American (20th -)	*P*			$1,320
KOEHLER, Paul R. American (1866 - 1909)	*D*	$330	$682	$1,760
KOEHLER, Robert American (1850 - 1917)	*P*			$220
KOEKKOEK, Barend C. Dutch (1803 - 1862)	*P*	$1,760	$9,570	$18,700
KOEKKOEK, Hendrick P. Dutch (1843 - 1890)	*P*	$7,700	$8,525	$9,350
KOEKKOEK, Hermanus Dutch (1867 - 1929)	*P*	$3,300	$19,690	$52,250
KOEKKOEK, Jan H. Dutch (1778 - 1851)	*P*	$2,860	$35,159	$126,500
KOEKKOEK, Johannes H. B. Dutch (1840 - 1912)	*P*	$6,600	$25,300	$41,800

D=Drawing, P=Painting, S=Sculpture, W=Watercolor

		Current Price Range		
		Low	Mean	High
KOEKKOEK, Marinus A.	P			$16,500
Dutch (1807 - 1870)				
KOEKKOEK, Willem	P	$68,200	$89,100	$110,000
Dutch (1839 - 1895)				
KOEKKOEK, Willem (Attrib.)	P			$550
Dutch (1839 - 1895)				
KOEKKOEK, JR., Hermanus	P	$2,860	$4,803	$6,050
Dutch (1836 - 1909)				
KOEKKOEK, SR., Hermanus	P			$7,150
Dutch (1815 - 1882)				
KOEMPOECZI, Balogh E.	P			$165
Hungarian (1911 -)				
KOENIGER, Walter	D			$121
American (1881 -)	P	$660	$5,587	$17,600
KOENIGSTEIN, George	P			$132
Austrian (19th -)				
KOENINGER, Walter	P			$2,090
American (1881 -)				
KOERNER, William H. D.	D			$1,100
American (1878 - 1938)	P			$15,400
KOERNER, William H.D.	P	$1,320	$4,329	$7,425
American (1878 - 1938)				
KOESSLER, W.	P	$440	$633	$825
German (19th - 20th)				
KOESTER, Alexander M.	P	$2,750	$127,050	$264,000
German (1864 - 1932)				
KOETS, Roelof	P	$33,000	$66,000	$99,000
Dutch (1592 - 1655)				
KOETS, Roelof (Attrib.)	P			$6,600
Dutch (1592 - 1655)				
KOFFERMANS, Marcellus	P			$18,700
Flemish (16th -)				
KOGAN, Nina	W	$16,500	$16,500	$16,500
Russian (1887 - 1942)				

D=Drawing, P=Painting, S=Sculpture, W=Watercolor

		Current Price Range		
		Low	Mean	High

KOGL, Benedict	*P*			$3,850
German (1892 - 1969)				
KOHL, Clemens	*D*			$1,650
Austrian (1754 - 1807)				
KOHLEN, Carl	*P*			$3,575
German (19th -)				
KOHLER, Gustav	*P*			$1,760
German (1859 -)				
KOHLHOFER, Christof	*P*			$1,650
(20th -)				
KOHLMEYER, Ida	*P*			$9,350
American (1912 -)				
KOHRL, Ludwig	*P*	$248	$839	$1,430
German (1858 -)				
KOKKEN, Henri	*P*			$7,425
Belgian (1860 -)				
KOKOSCHKA, Oskar	*D*	$3,630	$12,320	$33,000
Austrian (1886 - 1980)	*P*	$176,000	$876,857	$2.970M
	W			$2,860
KOLAR, Jiri	*S*	$275	$2,304	$4,950
Czech (1914 -)				
KOLBE, George	*S*	$2,200	$14,520	$26,400
German (1877 - 1947)				
KOLESNIKOFF, Sergei	*P*	$2,750	$3,190	$3,520
Russian (1889 -)				
KOLI,	*P*			$187
American (?)				
KOLLER, Wilhelm	*P*			$1,870
Austrian (1829 - 1884)				
KOLLOCK, M.	*P*			$413
American (19th -)				
KOLLWITZ, Kathe	*D*	$6,600	$9,625	$15,400
German (1867 - 1945)	*S*	$8,250	$12,925	$16,500
KOLOKOLCHIK,	*P*			$1,100
Russian (20th -)				

D=Drawing, P=Painting, S=Sculpture, W=Watercolor

		Current Price Range	
		Low	Mean	High

		Low	Mean	High
KOMAR & MELAMID, (20th -)	P			$48,400
KONCHALOVSKY, Piotr Russian (1876 - 1956)	P			$825
KONIG, P. (20th -)	P			$110
KONINCK, Philips Dutch (1619 - 1688)	D			$28,600
KONINGH, Leendert de Dutch (1810 - 1887)	P			$880
KONINGH, ELDER, Leendert de Dutch (1777 - 1849)	P			$1,760
KONO, Micao Japanese (20th -)	P	$6,600	$17,050	$27,500
KONRAD, Adolf American (?)	P	$935	$1,018	$1,100
KONTI, Isidore American (1862 - 1938)	S	$1,870	$3,053	$4,950
KONTULY, Bela Hungarian (20th -)	P			$330
KOOL, Willem G. Dutch (1608 - 1666)	P	$16,500	$24,750	$33,000
KOONING, Elaine de American (20th -)	P	$2,090	$6,298	$9,900
	W	$550	$715	$880
KOONING, Willem de American (1904 -)	D	$6,600	$97,539	$797,500
	P	$11,000	$1.131M	$20.680M
	S	$33,000	$266,063	$660,000
	W	$15,400	$26,950	$38,500
KOOPMAN, Augustus American (1869 - 1914)	P	$220	$880	$1,540
KOPEL, G. F. (?)	P			$1,265
KOPF, Maxim Austrian (20th -)	P			$440

D=Drawing, P=Painting, S=Sculpture, W=Watercolor

		Current Price Range		
		Low	Mean	High

		Low	Mean	High
KOPMAN, Benjamin	*D*			$220
American (1887 - 1965)	*P*	$523	$2,191	$5,280
KOPPENOL, Cornelis	*P*	$440	$2,190	$7,150
Dutch (1865 - 1946)				
KOPYSTIANSKY, Igor	*P*	$10,450	$16,363	$33,000
Russian (1954 -)				
KORBEL, Mario J.	*S*	$550	$1,716	$3,300
American (1882 - 1954)				
KORELL, Phil	*P*			$500
American (20th -)	*W*			$880
KORGA,	*P*			$303
Danish (20th -)				
KORNEMANN, Richard	*P*	$275	$358	$440
American (20th -)				
KOROVINE, Constantin A.	*P*	$1,100	$8,855	$26,400
Russian (1861 - 1939)	*W*			$990
KOROVINE, Constantin A. (Att.)	*P*			$7,700
Russian (1861 - 1939)				
KORTE, H. G. de	*P*			$4,400
European (19th - 20th)				
KOSA, Emil	*D*	$660	$1,568	$2,475
American (1903 - 1968)	*P*	$880	$4,840	$12,100
	W			$1,540
KOSA, SR, Emil	*P*			$1,100
American (1876 - 1955)				
KOSCIANSKI, Leonard	*S*			$990
American (20th -)				
KOSSAK, Wojciech	*P*	$2,640	$4,070	$5,500
Polish (1857 - 1942)				
KOST, Frederick W.	*P*			$770
American (1865 - 1923)				
KOSTABI, Mark	*D*	$220	$367	$660

D=Drawing, P=Painting, S=Sculpture, W=Watercolor

		Current Price Range		
		Low	Mean	High
KOSTABI, Mark	P	$220	$4,633	$12,100
(20th -)				
KOSUTH, Joseph	D	$2,860	$13,053	$33,000
American (1945 -)	P	$16,500	$44,000	$66,000
	S			$82,500
KOTASZ, Karoly	P			$385
Hungarian (1872 - 1941)				
KOTCH, George J.	W			$1,210
American (20th -)				
KOTSCHENREITER, G. Hugo	P			$1,485
German (1854 - 1908)				
KOTTLER, Howard	S			$4,400
(20th -)				
KOUGL, Judy	W			$275
American (20th -)				
KOUNELLIS, Jannis	P	$22,000	$84,700	$148,500
Greek (1936 -)				
KOUSNETSOFF, Constantine	P			$1,870
Russian (19th -)				
KOVACEVIC, S.	P			$132
Yugoslvian (19th - 20th)				
KOVACS, Vilmos T.	P			$220
Hungarian (1951 -)				
KOVESI, Dezso	P			$303
American (20th -)				
KOVICH, Loren	W	$300	$325	$350
American (20th -)				
KOVNER, Saul	P			$1,650
(?)				
KOWALCZEWSKI, Karl	S			$220
German (1876 -)				
KOWALCZEWSKI, P.	S			$138
European (19th - 20th)				
KOWALSKI,	P	$220	$330	$440
(?)				

D=Drawing, P=Painting, S=Sculpture, W=Watercolor

		Current Price Range		
		Low	Mean	High

		Low	Mean	High
KOWALSKI, A. Wierusz	*P*	$248	$2,324	$4,400
Polish (1849 - 1915)				
KOWALSKI, Ivan I.	*D*			$1,100
Russian (19th - 20th)				
KOWALSKI, Leopold F.	*P*	$77,000	$104,500	$132,000
French (1856 -)				
KOWALZEWSKI, P.	*S*			$605
Polish (1876 -)				
KOWLASKI,	*P*	$715	$715	$715
American (20th -)				
KOZLOW, Richard	*P*	$220	$633	$1,045
(?)				
KOZMON, George	*W*			$750
American (1960 -)				
KRABANSKY, Gustave	*P*			$10,450
French (19th -)				
KRABBE, Hendrik M.	*P*			$3,300
Dutch (1868 - 1931)				
KRAEMER, Peter	*P*	$5,720	$6,435	$7,150
German (1857 - 1941)	*W*	$1,320	$5,561	$11,000
KRAFFT, Carl R.	*P*	$1,430	$3,349	$6,490
American (1884 - 1938)				
KRAFFT, Gustav	*W*			$138
French (1861 -)				
KRAMER, James	*W*			$715
American (20th -)				
KRAMER, Simon	*P*			$330
French (20th -)				
KRAMO, A. B. C. de	*P*			$154
(20th -)				
KRASEMAN,	*P*			$193
European (20th -)				
KRASNER, Lee	*D*	$16,500	$18,700	$20,900
American (1911 -)	*P*	$6,050	$45,650	$85,250

D=Drawing, P=Painting, S=Sculpture, W=Watercolor

		Current Price Range		
		Low	Mean	High
KRASNER, Lee	S			$33,000
American (1911 -)	W	$16,500	$20,900	$25,300
KRASNOW, Peter (Attrib.)	P			$440
American (1886 - 1979)				
KRAUS, August	P			$2,640
German (19th -)				
KRAUS, Georg M.	P			$8,250
German (1737 - 1806)				
KRAUS, Jan	P			$4,125
Polish (1760 -)				
KRAUSE, Lina	P	$3,300	$5,757	$10,450
German (1857 -)				
KRAUSE, S.	P			$1,320
German (19th -)				
KRAUSKOPF, Bruno	W			$1,870
German (1892 -)				
KRAUSZ, W. V.	P			$550
American (20th -)				
KRAUTIK, All.	P			$2,200
European (19th -)				
KREMEGNE, Pinchus	P	$4,950	$7,123	$10,450
Russian (1890 - 1981)				
KRENN, Edmund	P			$11,000
Austrian (1846 - 1902)				
KRENZ, A.	P			$110
American (20th -)				
KRETSCHMER, W.	D			$242
(?)				
KRETZINGER, Clara J.	P			$7,975
American (1883 -)				
KREUTZER,	P	$495	$743	$990
(?)				
KREUZNACH, Konrad F. von	P			$82,500
German (1500 - 1553)				
KREYDER, Alexis J.	P	$15,400	$15,950	$16,500
French (1839 - 1912)				

D=Drawing, P=Painting, S=Sculpture, W=Watercolor

		Current Price Range		
		Low	Mean	High

		Low	Mean	High
KRICHELDORF, Carl	*P*			$5,500
German (1863 -)				
KRICKE, Norbert	*P*			$38,500
German (1922 -)				
KRIEGHOFF, Cornelius	*P*	$1,045	$17,861	$44,000
Canadian (1812 - 1872)				
KRIEHUBER, Josef	*W*	$2,640	$2,750	$2,860
Austrian (1800 - 1876)				
KRIPPENDORF, William H.	*P*	$110	$550	$880
Dutch (19th - 20th)				
KRISCHKE, Frank	*P*	$1,045	$1,183	$1,320
Austrian (19th - 20th)				
KROHG, Per	*P*			$935
Norwegian (1889 - 1949)				
KROHN, C.	*P*			$770
Norwegian (19th -)				
KROLL, Leon	*D*	$165	$618	$2,090
American (1884 - 1974)	*P*	$1,100	$18,619	$93,500
	W			$2,750
KRONBERG, Louis	*D*	$550	$1,493	$3,575
American (1872 - 1965)	*P*	$770	$2,695	$6,600
	W			$605
KRONBERGER, Carl	*P*	$6,050	$13,740	$17,600
Austrian (1841 - 1921)				
KRONENGOLD, Adolph	*P*			$550
American (20th -)				
KROTTER, R.	*P*			$358
Swiss (20th -)				
KROYER, Peder S.	*P*			$374,000
Danish (1851 - 1909)				
KRUGER, Barbara	*D*	$24,750	$35,829	$44,000
(20th -)	*P*			$17,600
KRUGER, Richard	*P*			$1,100
American (1880 -)				

D=Drawing, P=Painting, S=Sculpture, W=Watercolor

		Current Price Range		
		Low	Mean	High

		Low	Mean	High
KRULLAARS, William J. (1878 -)	P			$303
KRUMBACH, V. American (19th - 20th)	P			$1,320
KRUMEYER, American (20th -)	P			$413
KRUPKA, Dutch (20th -)	P			$495
KRUPP, Louis American (1888 -)	P			$303
KRUSE, Bruno F. E. German (1855 -)	S			$3,575
KRUSEMAN, F. V. (19th -)	P			$7,700
KRUSEMAN, Frederik M. Dutch (1816 - 1882)	P			$117,100
KRUSEMAN, Manner French (19th -)	P			$2,530
KRUSHENICK, Nicholas American (1929 -)	P	$3,080	$5,522	$13,200
KRUSOE, William American (20th -)	W			$385
KUEHNE, Max American (1880 - 1968)	P	$138	$5,074	$33,000
	W			$1,210
KUGLER, J. (?)	P			$248
KUHLMANN, Edward American (1882 - 1973)	P			$990
KUHN, Justus E. (After) American (18th -)	P			$3,410
KUHN, Walt American (1877 - 1949)	D	$250	$1,270	$5,280
	P	$4,400	$40,146	$192,500
	W	$247	$3,111	$8,800
KUHNE, August Austrian (1845 - 1895)	S			$990

D=Drawing, P=Painting, S=Sculpture, W=Watercolor

		Current Price Range		
		Low	Mean	High

		Low	Mean	High
KUITCA, Guillermo	P	$11,000	$12,833	$14,300
Argentine (1961 -)				
KUKA, King	P			$900
American (20th -)				
KULIK, Karl	P			$37,400
Austrian (1654 - 1713)				
KUMMER, Julius H.	P			$880
German (1817 -)				
KUNADISKO, T.	W			$660
(?)				
KUNC, Milan	P	$4,400	$6,325	$8,250
(20th -)				
KUNDERT, Balthasar	P	$275	$372	$468
American (20th -)				
KUNIYOSHI, Yasuo	D	$5,720	$17,105	$25,300
American (1893 - 1953)	P	$12,100	$107,525	$176,000
	W			$24,750
KUNO, Shin	P			$2,420
Japanese (20th -)				
KUNST, Pieter C.	D	$3,850	$4,125	$4,400
(1490 -)				
KUNSTLER, Mort	P			$1,870
American (1931 -)				
KUNTZ, Roger	P	$3,850	$4,125	$4,400
American (20th -)				
KUPETZKI, Johann	P	$1,100	$1,100	$1,100
Hungarian (1667 - 1740)				
KUPKA, Frank	D			$2,200
Czech. (1871 - 1957)	W			$4,950
KUR, Csaba	W			$105
American (20th -)				
KURILOFF, Edna	P	$110	$143	$176
American (1889 - 1979)				
KURTZ, Benjamin T.	S			$385
American (1899 -)				

D=Drawing, P=Painting, S=Sculpture, W=Watercolor

		Current Price Range		
		Low	Mean	High

		Low	Mean	High
KURTZ, Elaine	P			$440
American (20th -)				
KURZ, L.	P			$798
(?)				
KURZ, S.	P			$231
(?)				
KUSHNER, Robert	P			$15,400
American (1949 -)	S			$1,430
KUSS, Ferdinand	P			$19,800
Austrian (1800 - 1886)				
KUWASSEG, Charles E.	P	$1,100	$7,838	$17,600
French (1838 - 1904)				
KUYL, Gysbrecht van der	P			$115,500
Dutch (1604 - 1673)				
KUYPERS, Cornelis	P			$1,210
Dutch (1864 -)				
KVAPIL, Charles	P	$2,200	$6,600	$10,450
Belgian (1884 - 1957)				
KYLE, Georgina M.	P			$385
British (19th -)				
KYRL,	W			$303
American (19th - 20th)				
KYSER, H. L.	P			$1,155
American (19th -)				
L'ENGLE, Lucy	D			$660
American (20th -)	P	$275	$623	$1,100
	W			$1,100
L'ENGLE, William	P	$330	$625	$1,210
American (1884 - 1957)	W	$193	$523	$880
L'HEURLIN,	P			$165
American (20th -)				
L'ORDONNANCE, Isaac de	D			$4,400
(?)				

D=Drawing, P=Painting, S=Sculpture, W=Watercolor

		Low	Mean	High
			Current Price Range	

		Low	Mean	High
LA CAMBRA, (20th -)	*P*			$825
LA CAVE, Peter British (18th - 19th)	*W*			$880
LA COUR, Janus A. B. Danish (1837 - 1909)	*P*			$2,750
LA FARGE, John American (1835 - 1910)	*P* *W*	$4,400	$24,444	$110,000 $93,500
LA FARGE, John (Et al.) American (19th - 20th)	*D*			$3,300
LA FARGE, Mabel H. American (1875 - 1944)	*W*			$660
LA FARGUE, Paulus C. (Circle) Dutch (1732 - 2845)	*P*			$5,500
LA FONTAINE, Thomas S. British (1915 -)	*P*			$6,600
LA FOSSE, Charles A. C. de French (1829 - 1900)	*P*			$1,540
LA LYRE, Adolphe French (1850 -)	*P*			$143
LA NOR, European (?)	*D*			$138
LA PIRA, Italian (19th -)	*W*			$2,530
LA ROCHE, Charles de French (19th -)	*P*			$1,210
LA THANGUE, Henry H. British (1859 - 1929)	*P*			$220,000
LA TOUR, Maurice Q. de French (1704 - 1788)	*D*			$79,750
LA TOUR, Maurice Q. de (Attrib.) French (1704 - 1788)	*D*			$22,000
LAAN, Adolf van der Dutch (1684 - 1755)	*D*			$1,650
LAAR, Jan H. van de Dutch (1807 - 1874)	*P*			$4,950

D=Drawing, P=Painting, S=Sculpture, W=Watercolor

		Current Price Range		
		Low	Mean	High

		Low	Mean	High
LAAR, Jan H. van de (Attrib.) Dutch (1807 - 1874)	P			$880
LABAUDT, Lucien A. American (1880 - 1943)	P	$358	$784	$1,210
LABBE, Emile C. French (19th -)	W			$1,650
LABMEAUX, Joseph M. T. Belgian (1852 - 1908)	S			$880
LABOR, Charles French (1813 - 1900)	P			$15,400
LABROUCHE, Jean P. F. Belgian (1828 - 1911)	P			$578
LABROUCHE, Pierre French (19th - 20th)	P			$1,265
LABRUZZI, Carlo Italian (1786 - 1818)	D			$605
LACANO, Frank (?)	W			$400
LACAZE, Germaine French (?)	P			$3,300
LACEY, Charles J. de British (19th -)	P			$3,410
LACHAISE, Gaston American (1886 - 1935)	D	$1,320	$4,318	$8,250
	S	$14,080	$52,880	$165,000
LACHANCE, Georges American (1880 -)	P			$3,080
LACHMAN, Harry American (1886 - 1974)	P	$110	$3,153	$7,700
LACKTMAN, (20th -)	P			$176
LACOM, Wayne American (1922 -)	W			$330
LACOSTE, Emile-H. French (1838 - 1881)	P			$2,200
LACRETELLE, Jean E. French (1817 - 1900)	P			$13,200

D=Drawing, P=Painting, S=Sculpture, W=Watercolor

		Current Price Range		
		Low	Mean	High

		Low	Mean	High
LACROIX, Anton French (1848 - 1896)	*P*			$3,300
LACROIX, Charles F. de French (1720 - 1782)	*P*	$30,800	$38,225	$55,000
LACROIX, Paul American (19th -)	*P*			$3,850
LADBROOKE, H. British (19th -)	*P*			$2,200
LADBROOKE, John B. (Attrib.) British (1803 - 1879)	*P*			$880
LADD, Anna C. American (1878 - 1939)	*S*	$660	$5,940	$26,400
LADD, Laura D. Stroud American (1863 - 1943)	*P*			$1,375
LADDEY, Ernst German (19th -)	*P*			$880
LADELL, Edward British (1821 - 1886)	*P*	$4,510	$19,855	$35,200
LADERMAN, Gabriel (20th -)	*D*			$440
LADEUIL, Marcelle French (1895 -)	*P*			$150
LADOROJAY, Vasily S. Russian (20th -)	*P*			$605
LAER, Alexander T. van American (1857 - 1920)	*P*	$550	$1,430	$2,860
LAER, Pieter van (Circle) Dutch (17th -)	*P*			$2,200
LAESSIG, Robert American (20th -)	*P* *W*	$110	$495	$715 $715
LAESSLE, Albert American (1877 - 1945)	*S*			$330
LAFAGE, Raymond (Follower) French (1650 - 1684)	*D*			$605
LAFITTE, Louis French (1770 - 1828)	*D*	$2,860	$2,970	$3,080

D=Drawing, P=Painting, S=Sculpture, W=Watercolor

		Current Price Range		
		Low	Mean	High
LAFRAMBOISE, B. F.	*P*			$121
American (?)				
LAGATTA, John	*P*			$1,760
American (1894 - 1977)	*W*			$1,210
LAGLENNE, Jean F.	*P*			$715
French (1899 -)				
LAGNDT, H.	*P*			$3,300
(19th -)				
LAGNEAU,	*D*			$30,800
(16th - 17th)				
LAGOOR, Johannes	*P*			$14,300
Dutch (17th -)				
LAGORIO, Lev F.	*P*			$385
Russian (1827 - 1905)				
LAGRANDE, P.	*P*	$110	$220	$440
French (20th -)				
LAGRANGE, Jacques	*P*			$413
French (1917 -)				
LAGRENEE, Louis J. .	*P*	$44,000	$63,800	$88,000
French (1725 - 1805)				
LAHEE, Arnold W.	*P*	$550	$578	$605
American (1888 -)				
LAHNER, Emile	*P*	$660	$660	$660
French (1893 - 1980)				
LAIDLAY, William J.	*P*			$605
British (1846 - 1912)				
LAISSEMENT, Henri A.	*P*			$13,200
French (20th -)				
LAJOUE, Jacques de	*P*			$44,000
French (1687 - 1761)				
LALLEMAND, Jean-B.	*D*	$2,420	$2,640	$2,860
French (1710 - 1805)				
LAM, Jennett	*P*			$193
American (20th -)				
LAM, Wifredo	*D*	$2,860	$31,361	$71,500

D=Drawing, P=Painting, S=Sculpture, W=Watercolor

		Current Price Range		
		Low	Mean	High
LAM, Wifredo	*P*	$11,000	$103,950	$605,000
Cuban (1902 - 1982)	*S*	$2,860	$6,580	$19,800
	W	$11,550	$29,838	$77,000
LAMASURE, Edwin	*W*	$275	$447	$660
American (1886 - 1916)				
LAMB, Ella C.	*P*			$138
American (1862 - 1936)				
LAMB, F. Mortimer	*D*	$495	$568	$660
American (1861 - 1936)	*P*	$275	$1,639	$7,000
	W	$110	$321	$633
LAMB, Frederick S.	*P*			$990
American (1863 - 1928)				
LAMBDIN, George C.	*P*	$2,640	$11,416	$22,000
American (1830 - 1896)				
LAMBDIN, James R.	*P*			$1,155
American (1807 - 1889)				
LAMBDIN, Robert	*D*	$110	$248	$385
American (1886 - 1981)	*W*	$275	$344	$413
LAMBDIN, Victor R.	*D*			$220
American (?)				
LAMBECHSTS, Jan B.	*P*			$4,290
(1680 - 1731)				
LAMBERT, Bradford	*P*			$220
American (19th - 20th)				
LAMBERT, Camille N.	*P*			$1,210
Belgian (1876 -)				
LAMBERT, George	*P*	$385	$715	$1,045
American (20th -)				
LAMBERT, Jack L.	*P*			$248
American (1892 -)	*S*	$330	$330	$330
LAMBERT, Ted R.	*P*			$4,400
American (1905 - 1960)				

D=Drawing, P=Painting, S=Sculpture, W=Watercolor

		Current Price Range		
		Low	Mean	High

		Low	Mean	High
LAMBERTI, Italian (19th -)	W			$4,620
LAMBINET, Emile C. French (1815 - 1877)	P	$4,400	$5,500	$6,600
LAMBRECHTS, Jan B. Flemish (1680 - 1731)	P	$3,850	$4,400	$4,950
LAMBRECHTS, Jan B. (Manner) Flemish (1680 - 1731)	P			$3,575
LAMME, Arie J. Dutch (1812 - 1900)	P			$5,500
LAMME, Biago P. D. (Circle) (?)	D			$1,100
LAMOND, W. B. British (20th -)	P			$990
LAMONT, Louis American (20th -)	D			$138
LAMOTTE, Bernard French (1903 -)	D			$660
	P	$220	$4,351	$22,000
LAMOTTE, William A. De British (1775 - 1863)	W			$330
LAMPE, L. Belgian (19th -)	P			$1,650
LAMPI, Giovanni B. Italian (1751 - 1830)	P	$8,250	$25,575	$42,900
LAMPLOUGH, Augustus (Attrib.) British (1877 - 9930)	W			$600
LAMY, Pierre D. E. F. French (1855 - 1919)	P	$8,800	$8,800	$8,800
LANAZIN, European (19th -)	P			$44,000
LANCASTER, Sarah American (20th -)	P			$138
LANCE, Orville American (19th - 20th)	P			$2,090
LANCERAY, Eugene A. Russian (1848 - 1886)	S	$935	$3,641	$13,200

D=Drawing, P=Painting, S=Sculpture, W=Watercolor

		Current Price Range		
		Low	Mean	High

		Low	Mean	High
LANCERAY, Eugene A. (After) Russian (1848 - 1886)	S			$440
LANCEROTTO, Egisto Italian (1848 - 1916)	P	$8,800	$15,400	$22,000
LANCKEN, Frank Von De American (1872 - 1950)	P			$715
LANCKOW, Ludwig German (19th -)	P			$1,595
LANCON, Auguste A. French (1836 - 1887)	P			$2,420
LANCRET, Nicolas French (1690 - 1743)	D	$17,600	$55,550	$93,500
	P	$22,000	$27,500	$33,000
LANCRET, Nicolas (Attrib.) French (1690 - 1743)	P			$1,045
LANCRET, Nicolas (Follower) French (1690 - 1743)	P			$7,700
LANCRET, Nicolas (School) French (1690 - 1743)	P			$1,210
LANDELLE, Charles Z. French (1812 - 1908)	P			$27,500
LANDELLS, Robert T. British (1833 - 1877)	D			$165
LANDFIELD, Ronnie (20th -)	P	$1,045	$1,238	$1,430
LANDI, Ricardo V. Italian (19th - 20th)	P			$8,800
LANDRE, L. French (19th -)	P			$990
LANDRIANI, Paolo Italian (1755 - 1839)	D			$605
LANDRY, John American (20th -)	P			$193
LANDRY, Paul American (20th -)	W			$440
LANDSEER, Sir Edwin	D			$193

D=Drawing, P=Painting, S=Sculpture, W=Watercolor

		Current Price Range		
		Low	Mean	High

		Low	Mean	High
LANDSEER, Sir Edwin British (1802 - 1873)	*P*	$6,600	$227,700	$577,500
LANDSEER, Sir Edwin (After) British (1802 - 1873)	*D* *P*	$523	$2,324	$165 $4,125
LANDSEER, Sir Edwin (Attrib.) British (1802 - 1873)	*D*			$990
LANDSEER, Sir Edwin (Style) British (1802 - 1873)	*P*			$1,320
LANE, Fitz Hugh American (1804 - 1865)	*P*	$33,000	$542,667	$825,000
LANE, Francis American (20th -)	*P*			$440
LANE, Harry American (1891 -)	*P*			$2,420
LANE, Leonard Canadian (20th -)	*P*			$1,650
LANE, Lois (20th -)	*S*			$770
LANE, Martella American (1875 - 1964)	*P*	$110	$156	$247
LANE, Susan M. American (1832 - 1893)	*D*			$330
LANFAIR, Harold E. American (1898 -)	*W*	$220	$437	$935
LANFRANCO, Giovanni Italian (1582 - 1647)	*D*	$2,200	$3,850	$5,500
LANFRANCO, Giovanni (After) Italian (1582 - 1647)	*P*			$3,520
LANG, Albert German (1847 -)	*P*	$990	$1,155	$1,320
LANG, Charles M. American (1860 - 1934)	*P*			$176
LANG, Louis German (1814 - 1893)	*P*	$1,045	$1,870	$3,850
LANGE, (?)	*P*			$330

D=Drawing, P=Painting, S=Sculpture, W=Watercolor

		Current Price Range		
		Low	Mean	High

LANGENBACH, Clara	*P*			$1,540
American (1871 -)				
LANGENDIJK, Dirk	*D*	$1,650	$4,290	$14,300
Dutch (1748 - 1805)				
LANGENDIJK, Dirk (Attrib.)	*D*			$14,300
Dutch (1748 - 1805)				
LANGER,	*P*			$165
American (20th -)				
LANGEVIN, Claude	*P*	$495	$811	$1,045
Canadian (1946 -)				
LANGLAIS, T.	*P*			$750
(?)				
LANGLEY, Edith M.	*P*			$2,750
American (19th - 20th)				
LANGLEY, Edith M. (Attrib.)	*P*			$2,200
American (19th - 20th)				
LANGLEY, Edward	*P*	$165	$317	$468
American (1870 -)				
LANGLEY, Jane P.	*P*			$605
(20th -)				
LANGLEY, William	*P*	$715	$853	$990
British (19th - 20th)				
LANGLIN, Victoriano	*P*			$16,500
Spanish (1844 - 1911)				
LANGLOIS,	*P*			$2,200
(?)				
LANGLOIS, Jerome M.	*P*			$440,000
French (1779 - 1838)				
LANGLOIS, Mark W.	*P*			$1,870
British (19th -)				
LANGNETIN, Paul F. B.	*W*			$198
(?)				
LANGWORTHY, William H.	*P*	$165	$303	$440
American (19th -)				
LANMAN, Charles	*D*			$110

D=Drawing, P=Painting, S=Sculpture, W=Watercolor

		Current Price Range		
		Low	Mean	High
LANMAN, Charles	P			$1,155
American (1819 - 1895)				
LANNING, Mary	P			$110
(?)				
LANNY,	P			$138
European (19th - 20th)				
LANOUE, Terence	P	$220	$3,135	$6,050
American (1941 -)				
LANSER, Fay	D			$121
(?)				
LANSIL, Walter F.	P	$110	$1,071	$3,410
American (1846 - 1925)				
LANSIL, Walter F. (Attrib.)	P			$1,210
American (1846 - 1925)				
LANSKOY, Andre	P	$14,300	$68,200	$126,500
Russian (1902 - 1976)	W	$6,600	$6,875	$7,150
LANTING, B.	P			$440
Dutch (17th -)				
LANTZ, Paul	P			$275
American (1908 -)				
LANZA,	P			$165
American (20th -)				
LANZONI, P.	P			$413
Italian (19th -)				
LAOUST, Andre L. A.	S			$4,400
French (1843 -)				
LAPELLE, Roger	P			$110
American (20th -)				
LAPICQUE, Charles	P			$28,600
French (1898 -)				
LAPIDOTH, M. C.	P			$440
Dutch (1868 -)				
LAPIERRE, Louis E.	P			$2,860
French (1817 - 1886)				
LAPINI, Cesare (Studio)	S			$19,800
Italian (1848 -)				

D=Drawing, P=Painting, S=Sculpture, W=Watercolor

		Current Price Range		
		Low	Mean	High

		Low	Mean	High
LAPIRA,	*W*	$660	$3,355	$6,050
Italian (19th -)				
LAPORTE, Emile	*S*			$1,210
French (1841 - 1919)				
LAPORTE, George H.	*P*	$4,950	$4,950	$4,950
German (1799 - 1873)				
LAPOSTOLET, Charles	*P*			$17,600
French (1824 - 1890)				
LARA, Ernest	*P*			$715
British (1870 -)				
LARA, Georgina	*P*	$1,650	$3,850	$8,250
British (19th -)				
LARCHE, Raoul (After)	*S*			$220
French (1860 - 1912)				
LARENNE, Roger	*P*			$715
American (20th -)				
LARGILLIERE, Nicolas de	*P*			$74,250
French (1656 - 1746)				
LARGILLIERE, Nicolas de (Att.)	*P*	$330	$440	$550
French (1656 - 1746)				
LARGILLIERE, Nicolas de (Sc.)	*P*	$3,300	$7,040	$13,200
French (1656 - 1746)				
LARIMER, Ruth	*P*			$192
American (19th - 20th)				
LARIONOV, Mikhail	*D*			$1,210
Russian (1881 - 1964)	*P*	$16,500	$68,750	$121,000
LARKIN, William (Attrib.)	*P*			$13,200
British (17th -)				
LARMON, Kevin	*S*			$4,400
(20th -)				
LARONZE, Jean	*P*			$4,400
French (1852 - 1937)				
LAROON, Marcellus	*D*			$605
British (1679 - 1772)				
LARRAZ, Julio	*D*			$4,675

D=Drawing, P=Painting, S=Sculpture, W=Watercolor

		Current Price Range		
		Low	Mean	High
LARRAZ, Julio	P	$11,000	$24,750	$46,200
Cuban (1944 -)				
LARREGIEU, Fulbert	S			$660
French (19th -)				
LARRINAGA, Mario	P			$440
American (1895 - 1979)				
LARRUE, Guillaume	P			$7,150
French (1851 -)				
LARSEN, Knud	P	$1,265	$10,533	$19,800
Danish (1865 - 1922)				
LARSEN, M. F.	P			$286
American (19th - 20th)				
LARSEN, Ole	P			$330
American (20th -)				
LARSON, Edward	S			$825
American (20th -)				
LARSON, W.	P			$633
(?)				
LARSSON, Carl	D			$330,000
Swedish (1853 - 1919)	P			$550
LASAR, Charles A.	P			$880
French (19th - 20th)				
LASCANO, Juan	P	$10,450	$17,050	$25,300
Argentine (1947 -)				
LASCARI, Salvatore	P			$138
French (1884 - 1967)				
LASCAUX, Elie	P	$578	$1,806	$2,860
French (20th -)				
LASH, Lee	P	$5,225	$35,613	$66,000
American (1864 - 1935)				
LASKE, Oskar	W	$523	$674	$825
Austrian (1874 - 1911)				
LASKER, Jonathan	P	$1,760	$11,303	$16,500
(20th -)				
LASKY, Bessie M.	P			$1,210
American (1890 - 1972)				

D=Drawing, P=Painting, S=Sculpture, W=Watercolor

		Current Price Range		
		Low	Mean	High

		Low	Mean	High
LASSALLE, Camille L. C.	*P*			$3,300
French (19th -)				
LASSALLE, M.	*P*			$440
(20th -)				
LASSAW, Ibram	*S*	$880	$7,205	$23,100
American (1913 -)				
LASSEN, Hans A.	*P*	$1,100	$2,695	$4,290
German (1847 -)				
LASSO, Salvador V. y	*P*			$4,400
Spanish (1862 - 1915)				
LASSONDE, Omer T.	*P*	$413	$567	$715
American (1903 - 1980)				
LASTMAN, Pieter	*P*			$57,750
Dutch (1583 - 1633)				
LASZLO, Aldor	*P*			$990
(?)				
LASZLO DE LOMBOS, Philip A.	*P*	$468	$5,839	$12,100
British (1869 - 1937)				
LATACH, W.	*P*			$440
American (20th -)				
LATHAM, James (Attrib.)	*P*			$66,000
British (1696 - 1747)				
LATHROP, Dorothy P.	*P*	$385	$578	$770
(1891 -)				
LATHROP, Francis	*P*			$825
American (1849 - 1909)				
LATHROP, Ida P.	*P*			$440
American (1859 - 1937)				
LATHROP, William L.	*P*	$1,045	$4,828	$18,700
American (1859 - 1938)	*W*			$743
LATHROP, William L. (Et al.)	*D*	$770	$853	$935
American (19th - 20th)				
LATIMER, Lorenzo P.	*P*			$1,100
American (1857 - 1941)	*W*			$1,320

D=Drawing, P=Painting, S=Sculpture, W=Watercolor

		Current Price Range		
		Low	Mean	High
LATORTUE, Ph. (?)	P			$1,980
LATOUCHE, Gaston de French (1854 - 1913)	P	$13,200	$29,333	$55,000
LATOUCHE, L. French (19th -)	P			$880
LATOUR, Adrian French (20th -)	P			$605
LATOUR, D'Assier de French (19th -)	P			$220
LATOUR, Maurice Q. de (School) French (1704 - 1788)	D	$330	$715	$1,100
LAUDA, Richard Czech (1873 - 1929)	P			$605
LAUDER, Charles J. British (? - 1920)	P W			$6,600 $2,750
LAUDY, Jean Belgian (20th -)	P			$8,800
LAUFFER, Erwin American (20th -)	P			$165
LAUFMAN, Sidney American (1891 -)	P	$413	$1,274	$2,420
LAUGE, Achille French (1861 - 1944)	P			$17,600
LAUGEE, George French (1853 -)	P	$1,540	$5,019	$9,075
LAUGHLIN, American (20th -)	P			$880
LAUGHLIN, E. Ernest American (19th - 20th)	P			$303
LAUGHLIN, T. (?)	P			$303
LAUR, Marie Y. French (1879 -)	P	$5,500	$9,350	$13,200
LAURANT, Robert American (1890 - 1970)	D			$935

D=Drawing, P=Painting, S=Sculpture, W=Watercolor

		Low	Mean	High
		\multicolumn{3}{c}{Current Price Range}		

		Low	Mean	High
LAURENCE, Sydney	P	$1,210	$17,109	$187,000
American (1865 - 1940)	W	$440	$3,092	$6,050
LAURENCIN, Marie	D	$1,650	$13,544	$38,500
French (1883 - 1956)	P	$2,310	$310,372	$1.430M
	W	$1,540	$63,533	$187,000
LAURENCIN, Marie (After)	P			$330
French (1883 - 1956)				
LAURENCIN, Marie (Attrib.)	D			$1,100
French (1883 - 1956)				
LAURENS, Henri	S	$99,000	$250,556	$687,500
French (1885 - 1954)				
LAURENS, Jean P.	P	$3,850	$4,538	$5,225
French (1838 - 1921)				
LAURENS, Paul A.	P			$3,850
French (1870 - 1934)				
LAURENSON, Edward L.	P	$303	$385	$550
British (1868 -)				
LAURENT, Ernest	P	$8,800	$13,933	$17,600
French (1859 - 1929)	S			$564
LAURENT, Ernest (After)	S			$990
French (1859 - 1929)				
LAURENT, Eugene	S			$1,210
French (1832 - 1898)				
LAURENT, Jean	P			$605
French (20th -)				
LAURENT, John	P			$550
American (20th -)				
LAURENT, V.	P			$880
French (19th -)				
LAURENTY, S.	P			$550
(?)				
LAURENTZ,	P			$2,090
European (19th -)				

D=Drawing, P=Painting, S=Sculpture, W=Watercolor

| | | Current Price Range | |
	Low	Mean	High
LAURET, F. *P*			$2,200
(19th -)			
LAURITZ, Jack *P*			$715
American (20th -)			
LAURITZ, Paul *P*	$550	$2,037	$8,250
American (1889 - 1975) *W*	$468	$633	$715
LAURON, Albert F. *P*			$4,400
French (1841 -)			
LAUTER, Flora *P*			$330
American (1874 -)			
LAUVERNAY, Jeanne (Et al.) *P*	$825	$1,623	$2,420
French (1875 -)			
LAUX, August *P*	$650	$3,963	$11,000
American (1847 - 1921)			
LAUZERO, Albert *P*			$1,100
French (1909 -)			
LAVALLE, John *P*	$468	$1,004	$1,540
American (1896 - 1971) *W*	$193	$268	$440
LAVALLEY, Jonas J. *P*	$660	$1,474	$2,090
American (1858 - 1930) *W*			$138
LAVALLEY, William *P*			$330
(19th - 20th)			
LAVARENNE, Pierre *P*	$220	$289	$358
(?)			
LAVENANT, A. *D*			$193
European (19th -)			
LAVER, Alexa *S*			$385
(?)			
LAVERGNE, Adolphe J. *S*			$1,540
French (?)			
LAVERTY, Elizabeth S. *W*			$138
American (1899 -)			
LAVERY, John *P*	$10,725	$24,131	$60,500
British (1856 - 1941)			

D=Drawing, P=Painting, S=Sculpture, W=Watercolor

		Current Price Range		
		Low	Mean	High

		Low	Mean	High
LAVES, G.	*D*			$132
(19th -)				
LAVILLE, Joy	*D*	$2,750	$3,575	$4,400
British (1923 -)	*P*	$7,150	$9,790	$11,000
LAVREINCE, Nicolas	*P*			$39,600
Swedish (1737 - 1807)				
LAWES, Harold	*P*			$605
British (19th -)	*W*			$385
LAWLESS, Carl	*P*	$935	$2,063	$3,190
American (1896 - 1934)				
LAWLEY, J. Douglas	*P*			$385
Canadian (20th -)				
LAWLOR, George W.	*P*			$770
American (1878 -)				
LAWLOR, John	*S*			$2,860
(19th -)				
LAWRENCE, Betty	*P*			$110
American (20th -)				
LAWRENCE, C. M.	*W*			$110
(?)				
LAWRENCE, Charles A.	*P*			$578
American (1865 -)				
LAWRENCE, Edna N.	*D*	$220	$312	$385
American (1898 -)	*P*	$550	$825	$1,100
	W			$220
LAWRENCE, Henry	*P*			$275
American (20th -)				
LAWRENCE, Jacob	*D*			$7,700
American (1917 -)	*P*	$26,400	$27,500	$28,600
	W	$36,300	$40,700	$44,000
LAWRENCE, Rod	*W*			$990
American (20th -)				

D=Drawing, P=Painting, S=Sculpture, W=Watercolor

		Current Price Range		
		Low	Mean	High

		Low	Mean	High
LAWRENCE, Sir Thomas British (1769 - 1830)	*P*	$4,400	$50,380	$110,000
LAWRENCE, Sir Thomas (After) British (1769 - 1830)	*P*	$880	$4,015	$7,150
LAWRENCE, Sir Thomas (Attrib.) British (1769 - 1830)	*D*			$2,200
	P	$660	$2,516	$5,225
LAWRENCE, Sir Thomas (Circle) British (1769 - 1830)	*P*	$1,100	$1,595	$2,090
LAWRENCE, Sir Thomas (Foll.) British (1769 - 1830)	*P*	$1,650	$1,650	$1,650
LAWRENCE, Sir Thomas (Mann.) British (1769 - 1830)	*P*	$1,870	$2,585	$3,300
LAWRENCE, Sir Thomas (Studio) British (1769 - 1830)	*P*	$12,100	$47,300	$82,500
LAWRENCE, William G. (?)	*P*			$9,350
LAWRENCE, William H. American (1866 - 1938)	*P*			$440
LAWRIE, Alexander S. American (1828 - 1917)	*P*	$935	$1,430	$1,925
LAWS, Arthur J. American (1894 - 1960)	*P*	$110	$485	$1,430
LAWS, Robin American (20th -)	*S*			$385
LAWSHE, Hank American (20th -)	*W*			$825
LAWSON, Alexander British (19th - 20th)	*P*			$715
LAWSON, Ernest American (1873 - 1939)	*P*	$1,100	$63,096	$528,000
LAWSON, Ernest (Attrib.) American (1873 - 1939)	*P*			$495
LAWTON, Florian American (20th -)	*W*			$440
LAYTON, (?)	*P*			$385

D=Drawing, P=Painting, S=Sculpture, W=Watercolor

		Current Price Range		
		Low	Mean	High

		Low	Mean	High
LAZARUS, Jacob H.	*P*			$550
American (19th -)				
LAZARUS, Mattie	*W*			$578
American (19th - 20th)				
LAZERGES, Jean-B. P.	*P*	$660	$5,005	$9,350
French (1845 - 1902)				
LAZZARI, Pietro	*D*			$248
Italian (1898 - 1979)				
LAZZELL, Blanche	*P*	$1,500	$13,083	$26,400
American (1878 - 1956)	*W*	$495	$1,991	$4,950
LE BEY, Barbara	*P*			$5,775
(1939 -)				
LE BOEUFF, Pierre	*W*			$440
French (19th -)				
LE BROCQUY, Louis	*P*			$16,500
Irish (1916 -)				
LE CLERCQ, A.	*P*			$770
(19th -)				
LE DOUX, Charles P.	*P*			$440
French (1881 - 1959)				
LE GUAY, Charles E.	*D*			$1,650
French (1762 - 1840)				
LE PERSAN, Raffy	*P*	$1,430	$1,430	$1,430
(?)				
LE ROUX, Jacques	*P*			$495
French (20th -)				
LE ROUX, Jacques (Et al.)	*P*			$825
French (20th -)				
LE VA, Barry	*D*	$16,500	$17,050	$17,600
American (1941 -)				
LEA,	*W*			$330
(20th -)				
LEACH, Alice F.	*P*	$193	$647	$1,100
American (1857 - 1943)				
LEADER, Benjamin W.	*P*	$110	$12,602	$52,800
British (1831 - 1923)				

D=Drawing, P=Painting, S=Sculpture, W=Watercolor

		Current Price Range		
		Low	Mean	High
LEADER, Benjamin W. (Attrib.)	P	$1,650	$2,475	$3,300
British (1831 - 1923)				
LEADER, Charles	P	$495	$578	$660
British (19th - 20th)				
LEADER, Mrs. Benjamin	P	$193	$193	$193
British (19th -)				
LEAH, K. C.	P			$242
American (19th -)				
LEAHY, Eda V.	P			$165
American (?)				
LEAKE, Gerald	P	$495	$688	$880
American (1885 - 1975)				
LEAL, Juan de V.	P	$26,400	$53,075	$79,750
Spanish (1622 - 1690)				
LEAL, Juan de V. (Circle)	P			$1,320
Spanish (1622 - 1690)				
LEAR, Edward	D			$19,800
British (1812 - 1888)	W	$6,050	$6,050	$6,050
LEAR, John	D			$330
American (20th -)	P	$193	$207	$220
	W			$523
LEATHERS, Estelle	P			$358
American (20th -)				
LEAVER, Noel H.	W	$1,100	$1,496	$1,760
British (1889 - 1951)				
LEAVERS, Lucy A.	P			$13,200
British (19th -)				
LEAVITT, Edward C.	P	$523	$2,561	$8,250
American (1842 - 1904)				
LEBADANG,	P			$138
(20th -)				
LEBARBIER, Jean Jacques F.	P			$31,900
French (1738 - 1826)				
LEBAS, Jacques-P.	D			$2,750
French (1708 - 1783)				

D=Drawing, P=Painting, S=Sculpture, W=Watercolor

		Low	Mean	High
		Current Price Range		

		Low	Mean	High
LEBASQUE, Henri	*D*			$990
French (1865 - 1937)	*P*	$4,400	$124,779	$440,000
	W	$605	$9,176	$27,500
LEBDUSKA, Lawrence H.	*P*	$550	$1,352	$2,750
American (1894 - 1974)				
LEBEDJEV, Vladimir	*W*	$935	$1,903	$4,400
Russian (1891 - 1967)				
LEBEY, Barbara	*P*			$1,430
(1939 -)				
LEBLANC, Lee	*P*			$248
(1920 - 1988)				
LEBOT, V.	*P*			$605
French (20th -)				
LEBOURG, Albert C.	*P*	$9,900	$38,068	$82,500
French (1849 - 1928)				
LEBRECHT, Alma	*P*			$231
(?)				
LEBRET, Paul	*W*			$2,090
French (19th - 20th)				
LEBRUN, Charles (Circle)	*D*			$2,640
French (1619 - 1690)				
LEBRUN, Charles (School)	*P*			$7,150
French (1619 - 1690)				
LEBRUN, Christopher	*P*	$20,900	$26,950	$33,000
(20th -)				
LEBRUN, Eric	*P*			$2,750
French (20th -)				
LEBRUN, G.	*P*			$330
(20th -)				
LEBRUN, Rico	*W*	$660	$1,343	$2,600
American (1900 - 1964)				
LECAMUS, Jules A. D.	*P*			$9,350
French (1814 - 1878)				
LECHERE,	*P*			$550
French (?)				

D=Drawing, P=Painting, S=Sculpture, W=Watercolor

		Current Price Range		
		Low	Mean	High

		Low	Mean	High
LECHESNE, August	S			$3,080
French (1815 - 1888)				
LECLAIRE, Victor	P			$33,000
French (1830 - 1885)				
LECLEAR, Thomas	P	$330	$990	$1,650
American (1818 - 1882)				
LECOMTE, Hippolyte	P			$1,760
French (1781 - 1857)				
LECOMTE, Paul E.	P	$770	$5,033	$9,900
French (1877 - 1950)	W	$770	$908	$1,045
LECOMTE, Philippe P.	P			$1,870
French (19th -)				
LECOMTE-VERNET, Charles	P			$57,750
French (1821 - 1900)				
LECOQUE, Alois	P	$1,100	$2,231	$6,050
American (1891 - 1981)	W			$1,100
LECOURNEY, Nicholas	S			$1,210
French (19th - 20th)				
LECOURTIER, Prosper	S	$495	$1,118	$1,760
French (1855 - 1924)				
LECOURTIER, Prosper (After)	S	$715	$2,008	$3,300
French (1855 - 1924)				
LEDELI, Moritz	W			$1,320
Czechoslovakian (19th - 20th)				
LEDERER, Lucy	P			$200
American (20th -)				
LEDESMA, Gabriel F.	P			$33,000
Mexican (1900 - 1983)				
LEDFORD, Freda W.	P			$248
American (20th -)				
LEDOUX, Jean P.	D			$7,150
French (1767 - 1840)				
LEDOUX, Jean P. (Attrib.)	P			$4,620
French (1767 - 1840)				

D=Drawing, P=Painting, S=Sculpture, W=Watercolor

		Low	Mean	High
		Current Price Range		
LEDUC, Arthur	S			$4,180
French (1848 - 1918)				
LEDUC, Paul	P			$4,400
Belgian (1876 - 1943)				
LEE, Arthur	S			$18,700
American (1881 -)				
LEE, Bertha S.	P	$385	$1,139	$4,125
American (1873 - 1937)				
LEE, Colin	P			$1,650
(20th -)				
LEE, Doris	P	$3,300	$14,850	$33,000
American (1905 - 1983)	W			$1,980
LEE, Frank	P			$468
American (20th -)				
LEE, Frederick R.	P	$358	$1,183	$2,200
British (1798 - 1879)				
LEE, Jake	W			$550
American (1915 -)				
LEE, Robert E.	P			$6,600
American (1899 -)				
LEE, Roland	P			$231
(?)				
LEE, Ruth H.	W			$138
American (1885 -)				
LEEKE, Ferdinand	P			$1,650
German (1859 -)				
LEEMANS, Antonius	P	$9,350	$27,775	$46,200
Dutch (1631 - 1673)				
LEEMPOELS, Jef.	P			$38,500
Belgian (1867 - 1935)				
LEEMPUTTEN, C. van (Et al.)	P			$4,400
Belgian (19th -)				
LEEMPUTTEN, Cornelis van	P	$1,320	$2,451	$3,410
Belgian (1841 - 1902)				
LEEMPUTTEN, Jef L. van	P	$880	$2,493	$4,400
Belgian (1850 - 1914)				

D=Drawing, P=Painting, S=Sculpture, W=Watercolor

| | | Current Price Range | | |
		Low	Mean	High
LEEUW, Alexis de	*P*	$4,180	$4,428	$4,675
Belgian (19th -)				
LEFEBVRE, Augustin F.	*P*			$3,575
French (19th -)				
LEFEBVRE, Claude (Circle)	*P*			$770
French (1632 - 1675)				
LEFEBVRE, Jules J.	*P*	$8,800	$20,350	$35,200
French (1836 - 1911)				
LEFEUVRE, Jean	*P*			$13,200
French (1882 -)				
LEFEVRE, Robert	*P*			$33,000
French (1756 - 1830)				
LEFLER, Franz	*P*	$16,500	$16,500	$16,500
Czech (1831 - 1898)				
LEFORT, Jean L.	*P*	$440	$10,120	$19,800
French (1875 -)				
LEGANGER, Nicolay T.	*P*	$248	$399	$550
American (1832 - 1894)				
LEGAT, Leon	*P*			$20,900
French (20th -)				
LEGEAY, Jean L.	*D*			$6,600
French (18th -)				
LEGER, Fernand	*D*	$17,600	$43,381	$165,000
French (1881 - 1955)	*P*	$4,400	$1.026M	$8.525M
	S	$3,520	$8,177	$12,100
	W	$11,000	$111,228	$770,000
LEGER, Fernand (After)	*S*	$2,090	$5,720	$9,350
French (1881 - 1955)				
LEGER, Fernand (Attrib.)	*D*			$110
French (1881 - 1955)				
LEGER, H.	*P*			$1,100
(?)				
LEGERE, Jon S.	*P*			$1,100
American (20th -)				

D=Drawing, P=Painting, S=Sculpture, W=Watercolor

		Current Price Range		
		Low	Mean	High

		Low	Mean	High
LEGGETT, Alexander	P	$660	$715	$770
British (19th -)				
LEGLER, Wilhelm	P			$193
(?)				
LEGOUT-GERARD, Fernand M.	D			$2,860
French (1856 - 1924)	P	$11,000	$11,000	$11,000
LEGRAND, Jenny	P			$39,600
French (19th -)				
LEGRAND, Pierre-Nicolas	D			$3,850
French (18th -)				
LEHMAN,	P			$440
(19th -)				
LEHMANN, Ad	W			$220
European (19th - 20th)				
LEHMANN, Henri	D			$715
French (19th -)				
LEHMANN, Wilhelm	P			$1,100
German (1819 - 1905)				
LEHMBRUCK, Wilhelm	S			$143,000
German (1881 - 1919)				
LEHR, Adam	P	$440	$1,029	$2,860
American (1853 - 1910)				
LEIBL, Wilhelm M. H.	P			$198,000
German (1844 - 1900)	W			$17,600
LEICKERT, Charles H. J.	P	$9,350	$20,350	$41,250
Belgian (1818 - 1907)				
LEIENDECKER, Jon	P			$700
(1860 -)				
LEIGH, Dora B.	P			$633
British (20th -)				
LEIGH, William R.	P	$165	$52,502	$187,000
American (1866 - 1955)				
LEIGHTON, Frederick Lord	P	$440	$40,788	$154,000
British (1830 - 1896)	S			$17,600

D=Drawing, P=Painting, S=Sculpture, W=Watercolor

		Current Price Range		
		Low	Mean	High

LEIGHTON, Kathryn W.	*P*	$660	$1,364	$3,080
American (1876 - 1952)				
LEIGHTON, Scott	*P*	$660	$1,930	$3,850
American (1849 - 1898)				
LEIGHTON, Scott (Attrib.)	*P*			$715
American (1849 - 1898)				
LEIRIS, Jeanne W. de	*D*			$385
American (20th -)				
LEISSER, Martin B.	*P*	$660	$1,137	$1,650
American (1846 - 1940)				
LEISTEN, Jacobus	*P*			$3,080
German (1844 - 1918)				
LEITCH, William L.	*D*			$110
British (1804 - 1883)	*W*			$660
LEITH-ROSS, Harry	*P*	$275	$1,351	$3,190
American (1886 - 1973)	*W*	$550	$1,709	$2,750
LEITZ, Robert	*D*			$880
American (20th -)				
LEJEUNE, A. A.	*D*			$7,700
French (18th -)				
LEJEUNE, Henry	*P*	$3,960	$8,580	$13,200
British (1819 - 1904)				
LELAND, A. Maxwell	*P*			$715
(19th - 20th)				
LELAND, Henry	*P*			$935
American (19th -)				
LELAND, Joel	*P*			$1,980
American (19th -)				
LELEU, Alexandre F.	*P*			$3,850
French (1871 -)				
LELIENBERGH, Cornelis	*P*			$10,450
Dutch (1626 - 1676)				
LELOIR, Alexandre L.	*P*	$6,875	$15,125	$19,800
French (1843 - 1884)	*W*			$5,720

D=Drawing, P=Painting, S=Sculpture, W=Watercolor

		Current Price Range		
		Low	Mean	High

		Low	Mean	High
LELOIR, Jean-B. A. French (1809 - 1892)	P			$66,000
LELOIR, Louis (19th -)	P			$578
LELOIR, Maurice French (1853 - 1940)	P			$6,380
LELONG, P. French (20th -)	P			$880
LELONG, Rene French (19th -)	P	$9,900	$19,433	$34,100
LELY, Sir Peter British (1618 - 1680)	P			$17,600
LELY, Sir Peter (After) British (1618 - 1680)	P	$3,850	$6,600	$9,350
LELY, Sir Peter (Attrib.) British (1618 - 1680)	P			$2,200
LELY, Sir Peter (Circle) British (1618 - 1680)	P	$990	$2,695	$4,400
LELY, Sir Peter (Follower) British (1618 - 1680)	P	$2,200	$3,300	$4,400
LELY, Sir Peter (School) British (1618 - 1680)	P	$1,320	$2,567	$4,400
LELY, Sir Peter (Studio) British (1618 - 1680)	P	$3,300	$11,000	$18,700
LELY, Sir Peter (Style) British (1618 - 1680)	P			$3,025
LEMAIRE, J. French (19th -)	P			$660
LEMAIRE, Madeleine French (1845 - 1928)	P W	$4,675 $1,100	$12,833 $2,486	$28,600 $4,950
LEMAIRE, R. European (19th - 20th)	D			$2,750
LEMAITRE, French (19th -)	S			$660
LEMBECK, Jack American (20th -)	P	$6,600	$8,938	$15,400

D=Drawing, P=Painting, S=Sculpture, W=Watercolor

		Current Price Range		
		Low	Mean	High
LEMBERGER, Georg (Attrib.)	*P*			$55,000
German (15th - 16th)				
LEMBERT, P.	*P*			$3,520
European (19th - 20th)				
LEMEUNIER, Alfred L.	*W*			$770
European (19th -)				
LEMEUNIER, Basile	*P*			$10,450
French (1852 -)				
LEMLY, Bessie C.	*W*			$880
American (1871 -)				
LEMMEN, Georges	*D*	$2,420	$4,510	$6,600
Belgian (1865 - 1916)	*P*	$15,400	$52,433	$121,000
LEMMENS, Theophile V. E.	*P*			$2,475
French (1821 - 1867)				
LEMOINE, Elizabeth (Attrib.)	*P*	$9,900	$13,567	$16,500
French (1754 - 1820)				
LEMOINE, Francois (Attrib.)	*P*			$16,500
French (1688 - 1737)				
LEMOINE, Francois (Circle)	*D*			$5,775
French (1688 - 1737)				
LEMON, F. H.	*P*			$275
American (19th -)				
LEMONIER, Leven	*D*			$495
(?)				
LEMOS, Pedro J.	*P*			$990
American (1882 - 1954)				
LEMOYNE, Jean B.	*S*			$3,575
French (18th -)				
LEMPICKA, L.	*P*	$3,025	$3,025	$3,025
European (19th -)				
LEMPICKA, Tamara de	*D*			$3,080
Polish (1898 -)	*P*	$2,860	$96,985	$1.320M
LENBACH, Franz von	*P*	$4,950	$7,700	$12,100
German (1836 - 1904)				

D=Drawing,   P=Painting,   S=Sculpture,   W=Watercolor

		Current Price Range		
		Low	Mean	High

		Low	Mean	High
LENDT, Adrian van	P			$715
Dutch (1901 - 1984)				
LENGO Y MARTINEZ, Horacio	P			$8,800
Spanish (1890 -)				
LENK, Kaspar T.	P			$220
(20th -)				
LENKEY, J.	P			$2,750
French (19th -)				
LENNON, John	D			$1,760
(?)				
LENOIR, Charles A.	P			$88,000
French (1861 -)				
LENORDEZ, Pierre (Et al.)	S	$3,025	$4,538	$6,050
French (19th -)				
LENS, YOUNGER, Bernhard	P			$17,600
British (1682 - 1740)				
LENTELLI, Leo	S			$550
American (1879 - 1962)				
LENTINE,	S			$176
(?)				
LENZ, Alfred D.	S			$1,760
American (1872 - 1926)				
LENZ, Maximilien	D			$880
Austrian (1860 - 1948)				
LEOCAT,	P			$990
(20th -)				
LEON, Noe	P			$7,700
Colombian (1907 -)				
LEON Y ESCOSURA, Ignacio de	P	$6,600	$18,700	$30,800
Spanish (1834 - 1901)				
LEONARD, George H.	P			$880
American (1869 -)				
LEONARD, John H.	P			$3,520
(19th -)				
LEONARDO DA VINCI, (After)	P	$5,500	$6,875	$8,250
Italian (1452 - 1519)				

D=Drawing, P=Painting, S=Sculpture, W=Watercolor

		Current Price Range		
		Low	Mean	High
LEONE, John	P	$2,310	$4,368	$7,150
American (1929 -)				
LEONE, M.	W			$110
(?)				
LEONEL,	P			$2,860
European (19th -)				
LEONHARDT, J.	P			$358
American (20th -)				
LEONI, Ottavio M.	D			$39,600
Italian (1587 - 1630)				
LEONODS,	P			$2,750
(19th -)				
LEPEINTRE, Charles	P	$2,475	$2,778	$3,080
French (1735 - 1803)				
LEPERE, Alfred (Et al.)	D			$275
French (19th - 20th)				
LEPICIE, Nicolas B.	P			$16,500
French (1735 - 1784)				
LEPICIE, Nicolas B. (Circle)	P			$5,225
French (1735 - 1784)				
LEPINAY, Paul C. E. G.	P	$6,600	$7,425	$8,250
French (1842 - 1885)				
LEPINE, Stanislas V. E.	P	$5,500	$28,256	$77,000
French (1835 - 1892)				
LEPOITTEVIN, E. M. E.	P			$1,100
French (1806 - 1870)				
LEPOITTEVIN, Louis	P			$2,860
French (1847 - 1909)				
LEPRIN, Marcel	P	$2,090	$7,728	$12,100
French (1891 - 1933)				
LEPRINCE, August-Xavier	P			$10,450
French (1799 - 1826)				
LEPRINCE, Jean Baptiste	D			$550
French (1734 - 1781)				
LEPRINCE, Jean Baptiste (Attrib.)	P			$15,400
French (1734 - 1781)				

D=Drawing, P=Painting, S=Sculpture, W=Watercolor

	Current Price Range		
	Low	Mean	High

		Low	Mean	High
LEQUESNE, Eugene L. French (1815 - 1887)	*P*			$1,650
LERAY, Prudent L. French (1820 - 1879)	*P*	$1,980	$3,190	$4,400
LERBERGHE, O. van Belgian (1755 - 1810)	*P*			$440
LERIN, Giralt (?)	*P*			$193
LERMONTE, P. European (19th -)	*P*			$4,950
LERNER, Leslie American (1949 -)	*P*			$1,760
LEROLLE, Henry French (1848 - 1929)	*P*	$1,100	$1,595	$2,090
LEROUX, Georges French (20th -)	*P*			$220
LEROY, French (20th -)	*P*			$275
LEROY, Jules French (19th - 20th)	*P*	$4,180	$5,977	$7,150
LEROY, Paul A. A. French (1860 - 1942)	*P*	$440	$62,480	$115,500
LEROY, S. European (19th -)	*P*			$1,430
LERSY, Roger French (1920 -)	*P*	$330	$587	$1,100
LESIEUR, Pierre (20th -)	*P*	$3,300	$5,390	$7,975
LESLIE, Alfred American (1927 -)	*D*			$4,125
	P	$13,200	$28,600	$44,000
	S			$1,870
LESLIE, Charles British (1840 -)	*P*	$303	$674	$1,045
LESLIE, Charles R. British (1794 - 1859)	*P*	$688	$4,930	$11,000

D=Drawing, P=Painting, S=Sculpture, W=Watercolor

		Current Price Range		
		Low	Mean	High
LESLIE, Charles R. (Attrib.)	*D*			$330
British (1794 - 1859)	*P*			$1,540
LESLIE, Charles R. (Et al.)	*W*			$385
British (18th - 19th)				
LESLIE, Charles R. (Style)	*P*			$3,575
British (1794 - 1859)				
LESLIE, George D.	*P*			$1,650
British (1835 - 1921)				
LESLIE, George D. (Attrib.)	*P*			$825
British (1835 - 1921)				
LESNE, Camille	*P*			$4,180
(?)				
LESREL, Adolphe A.	*P*	$5,720	$15,840	$28,600
French (1839 - 1890)				
LESSER, Ron	*W*			$138
American (?)				
LESSI, Giovanni	*D*			$825
(?)				
LESSING, Carl F.	*D*			$7,425
German (1808 - 1880)				
LESSING, F.	*P*			$468
German (19th -)				
LESSORE, Jules	*W*			$1,870
French (? - 1892)				
LESUR, Henri V.	*P*			$8,800
French (1863 -)				
LETHIERE, Guillaume	*D*			$275
French (1760 - 1832)				
LETOUX, Julian	*W*			$770
(?)				
LETTELIER, Pearl	*P*			$358
American (20th -)				
LEU, August W.	*P*			$9,075
German (1819 - 1897)				
LEU, Oscar	*P*			$1,760
German (1864 -)				

D=Drawing, P=Painting, S=Sculpture, W=Watercolor

		Current Price Range		
		Low	Mean	High

		Low	Mean	High
LEUTZE, Emanuel	P	$7,700	$7,975	$8,250
American (1816 - 1868)				
LEUTZE, Emanuel (Et al.)	D			$1,430
American (19th -)				
LEUUS, Jesus M.	P	$1,650	$3,864	$7,150
Mexican (20th -)				
LEVASSEUR, Henri	S	$2,530	$5,665	$8,800
French (1853 -)				
LEVE, Frederic L.	P			$13,200
French (1877 -)				
LEVEBRE, Jules J. (Attrib.)	P			$2,750
(?)				
LEVENE, Sherrie	S			$52,250
(20th -)				
LEVEQUE, Gabriel	P			$715
Haitian (1923 -)				
LEVER, Richard Hayley	D	$220	$536	$880
American (1876 - 1958)	P	$248	$5,912	$30,800
	W	$275	$1,428	$4,400
LEVER, Richard Hayley (Att.)	P			$413
American (1876 - 1958)				
LEVI, Julian C.	W			$440
American (1874 -)				
LEVI, Julian E.	W			$1,760
American (1900 -)				
LEVICK, Milnes	P	$412	$426	$440
American (1887 -)				
LEVIER, Charles	P	$220	$1,432	$5,500
American (1920 -)	W			$385
LEVIKOVA, Bela	P			$14,300
Russian (1939 -)				
LEVINE, David	D	$110	$862	$1,980
American (1910 -)	W			$1,760

D=Drawing, P=Painting, S=Sculpture, W=Watercolor

		Current Price Range		
		Low	Mean	High
LEVINE, Jack	*D*	$110	$2,426	$7,700
American (1915 -)	*P*	$6,600	$25,025	$52,800
	W			$935
LEVINE, Les	*P*			$3,300
Irish (20th -)				
LEVINE, Marilyn	*S*			$8,800
(20th -)				
LEVINE, Sherrie	*D*			$7,700
(20th -)	*P*			$7,700
LEVINSON, Mon	*P*			$660
(20th -)				
LEVIS, Maurice	*P*	$4,400	$6,325	$9,350
French (1860 - 1902)				
LEVOLGER, A. J. P.	*P*			$6,325
Dutch (1853 - 1952)				
LEVRAC-TOURNIERES, R.	*P*			$7,700
French (1667 - 1752)				
LEVRAC-TOURNIERES, R. (Att.)	*P*			$6,600
French (1667 - 1752)				
LEVRAC-TOURNIERES, R. (Cir.)	*P*			$2,200
French (1667 - 1752)				
LEVRAC-TOURNIERES, R. (Sc.)	*P*			$1,980
French (1667 - 1752)				
LEVY, Alexander O.	*P*	$110	$963	$1,430
American (1881 - 1947)				
LEVY, Beatrice S.	*P*			$440
American (1892 - 1974)				
LEVY, Diane	*P*			$1,210
American (1948 -)				
LEVY, G.	*S*			$935
European (19th -)				
LEVY, Gidi	*D*	$303	$303	$303
Israeli (20th -)	*P*			$248

D=Drawing, P=Painting, S=Sculpture, W=Watercolor

		Current Price Range	
	Low	Mean	High

		Low	Mean	High
LEVY, Henri L.	*P*			$3,850
French (1840 - 1904)				
LEVY, Henry	*P*	$110	$477	$770
American (1868 -)				
LEVY, Herbert	*P*			$1,320
American (19th -)				
LEVY, J.	*P*			$2,750
European (19th -)				
LEVY, Nat	*W*	$303	$1,396	$2,475
American (1896 - 1984)				
LEVY, William A.	*P*	$110	$237	$358
American (1889 -)				
LEVY-DHURMER, Lucien	*D*	$2,200	$16,133	$33,000
French (1865 - 1953)	*P*			$264,000
LEWANDOWSKI, Edmund D.	*P*			$4,675
American (1914 -)				
LEWEN, Van	*P*			$209
Dutch (20th -)				
LEWIS,	*W*			$248
(19th -)				
LEWIS, Charles J.	*P*			$770
British (1830 - 1892)				
LEWIS, Edmund D.	*P*	$250	$3,356	$13,200
American (1835 - 1910)	*W*	$193	$877	$6,600
LEWIS, Edmund D. (Manner)	*P*			$1,155
American (1835 - 1910)				
LEWIS, Emerson	*P*	$468	$1,313	$2,090
American (1892 - 1958)				
LEWIS, F.	*W*	$110	$138	$165
British (19th - 20th)				
LEWIS, Frederick C.	*W*			$3,080
British (1779 - 1856)				
LEWIS, Geoffrey	*P*	$715	$743	$770
American (20th -)				

D=Drawing, P=Painting, S=Sculpture, W=Watercolor

		Current Price Range		
		Low	Mean	High
LEWIS, Harry E.	P	$660	$963	$1,650
American (1892 - 1958)	W	$385	$482	$660
LEWIS, John F.	P	$440	$367,253	$1.100M
British (1805 - 1876)	W			$14,300
LEWIS, Martin	W			$2,310
American (1881 - 1962)				
LEWIS, Ruth	P			$660
(?)				
LEWIS, Stanley M.	P			$248
American (20th -)				
LEWIS, Thomas L.	P			$880
American (1907 - 1978)				
LEWISOHN, Rafael	P			$413
German (1863 - 1923)				
LEWITT, Sol	D	$495	$21,191	$88,000
American (1928 -)	P			$66,000
	S	$7,150	$61,550	$165,000
	W	$5,500	$22,733	$57,200
LEWY, James	P			$825
American (19th - 20th)				
LEYENDECKER, Frank X.	P			$3,575
American (1877 - 1924)				
LEYENDECKER, Joseph C.	P	$650	$9,421	$28,600
American (1874 - 1951)				
LEYENDECKER, Paul	P			$4,675
French (1842 -)				
LEYS, Henri J.	P	$1,980	$5,665	$9,350
Belgian (1815 - 1869)				
LEYSTER, Judith	P	$143,000	$335,500	$528,000
Dutch (1600 - 1660)				
LHERMITTE, Leon A.	D	$4,180	$33,515	$82,500
French (1844 - 1925)	P	$6,050	$101,970	$363,000

D=Drawing, P=Painting, S=Sculpture, W=Watercolor

		Current Price Range		
		Low	Mean	High

LHOTE, Andre	D	$1,540	$5,060	$9,350
French (1885 - 1962)	P	$7,150	$38,403	$165,000
	W	$1,430	$7,954	$19,800
LIBBY, Francis O.	P	$165	$193	$220
American (1883 -)	W			$110
LIBERDANG,	P			$350
(20th -)				
LIBERI, Marco	P			$2,750
Italian (1640 - 1725)				
LIBERI, Pietro	P			$33,000
Italian (1614 - 1687)				
LIBERI, Pietro (Attrib.)	P			$11,000
Italian (1614 - 1687)				
LIBERI, Pietro (Circle)	P			$1,870
Italian (1614 - 1687)				
LIBERICH, Nicolai (After)	S			$550
Russian (1828 - 1883)				
LIBERMAN, Alexander	P	$4,620	$4,785	$4,950
(20th -)	S	$1,210	$5,280	$9,350
	W			$2,640
LIBERT, George E.	P			$425
Danish (1820 - 1908)				
LIBRONET, (After)	S			$495
(?)				
LICENSE, R. J.	W			$578
American (20th -)				
LICHENSTEIN, Manes	P			$1,100
American (1923 -)				
LICHTENSTEIN, Roy	D	$33,000	$133,375	$231,000
American (1923 -)	P	$3,080	$747,484	$6.050M
	S	$3,850	$89,002	$1.100M
LICHTENSTEIN, Roy (After)	S	$5,500	$19,433	$28,600
American (1923 -)				

D=Drawing, P=Painting, S=Sculpture, W=Watercolor

		Current Price Range		
		Low	Mean	High
LIDDERDALE, Charles S.	P	$1,650	$4,950	$8,250
British (1831 - 1895)				
LIDOV, Arthur	P			$935
American (1917 -)				
LIE, Jonas	P	$935	$18,549	$30,800
American (1880 - 1940)				
LIEBENWEIN, Maximilien	D			$2,420
Austrian (1869 - 1926)				
LIEBER, Tom	P	$4,400	$5,225	$6,050
(20th -)				
LIEBERICH, Nicolai I.	S			$1,870
Russian (1828 - 1893)				
LIEBERICH, Nicolai I. (After)	S			$1,540
Russian (1828 - 1893)				
LIEBERMANN, Max	D	$275	$11,846	$44,000
German (1847 - 1935)	P	$743	$27,961	$88,000
LIEGEOIS, Paul (Attrib.)	P			$39,600
French (17th -)				
LIENDER, Paulus van	D			$1,650
Dutch (1731 - 1797)				
LIER, J. van	P			$1,540
Belgian (20th -)				
LIESTE, Cornelis	P			$3,410
Dutch (19th -)				
LIETZMAN, Hans	P			$440
(1872 -)				
LIEVENS, Jan	P	$28,600	$129,800	$231,000
Dutch (1607 - 1674)				
LIEVIN, Jacques	P			$1,650
French (1850 -)				
LIGHT, Leonard R.	W			$715
(?)				
LIGNIER, J.	W	$770	$917	$1,210
French (19th - 20th)				
LIGNON, Bernard	P			$1,100
French (1928 -)				

D=Drawing, P=Painting, S=Sculpture, W=Watercolor

		Current Price Range		
		Low	Mean	High

		Low	Mean	High
LIGORIO, Pirro Italian (1513 - 1583)	*D*			$15,400
LIGORIO, Pirro (Attrib.) Italian (1513 - 1583)	*D*			$7,150
LIGORIO, Pirro (Circle) Italian (1513 - 1583)	*D*			$660
LIGOZZI, Jacopo Italian (1543 - 1627)	*P*			$396,000
LIGOZZI, Jacopo (Attrib.) Italian (1543 - 1627)	*W*			$49,500
LILJEFORS, Bruno A. Swedish (1860 - 1939)	*P*	$2,860	$42,680	$82,500
LILJESTROM, Gustave American (1882 -)	*P*			$495
LILLIE, Ella F. American (1887 -)	*P*			$330
LILLIE, John American (1867 -)	*P*			$110
LILLO, L. de European (20th -)	*P*			$1,045
LIMOT, Baron (19th -)	*W*			$132
LIMOUSE, Roger French (1894 -)	*P*	$3,300	$17,967	$31,900
LINCK, Louis American (20th -)	*S*	$330	$495	$825
LIND, F. C. (?)	*P*			$100
LINDABURY, H. American (?)	*P*			$220
LINDBERG, Arthur H. American (1895 -)	*D*	$1,650	$1,650	$1,650
LINDE, Ossip L. American (19th - 20th)	*P*			$3,740
LINDEMUTH, Arlington N. American (20th -)	*P*			$175

D=Drawing, P=Painting, S=Sculpture, W=Watercolor

		Current Price Range		
		Low	Mean	High
LINDEN, Carl	P	$110	$715	$1,320
American (1869 - 1942)				
LINDENFELD, E.	P	$165	$262	$358
(?)				
LINDENMUTH, Arlington N.	P			$880
American (1867 -)				
LINDENMUTH, Tod	P	$660	$1,650	$2,640
American (1885 - 1976)				
LINDER, Harry	D			$880
American (1886 - 1931)				
LINDER, Henry	P			$1,320
American (1854 - 1910)	S			$770
LINDER, J.	P			$2,420
German (19th - 20th)				
LINDERGREEN, Harold F.	W	$248	$248	$248
American (1902 -)				
LINDERMEIR, G	P			$220
(?)				
LINDERUM, Richard	P	$1,018	$2,759	$5,500
German (1851 -)				
LINDIN, Carl O.	P			$3,300
American (1869 -)				
LINDLAR, Johann W.	P			$5,000
German (1816 - 1896)				
LINDNER, Anna	W	$385	$413	$440
(?)				
LINDNER, Richard	D	$3,520	$23,059	$66,000
American (1901 - 1978)	P	$220,000	$319,000	$418,000
	S			$31,900
	W	$8,800	$34,729	$71,500
LINDNEUX, Robert	P	$935	$990	$1,045
American (1887 -)				
LINDSAY, Frank	P			$1,100
British (19th -)				

D=Drawing, P=Painting, S=Sculpture, W=Watercolor

		Current Price Range		
		Low	Mean	High
LINDSAY, Ruth	P			$165
American (1888 -)				
LINDSAY, Sir Daryl E.	W			$440
Australian (1889 -)				
LINDSAY, Thomas C.	P	$440	$1,331	$3,300
American (19th -)				
LINDSELL, Violet	W			$935
British (19th -)				
LINDSFORS,	P			$2,860
(19th -)				
LINFORD, Charles	P	$165	$523	$880
American (1846 - 1897)				
LINGELBACH, Johannes	P			$38,500
Dutch (1622 - 1674)				
LINGELBACH, Johannes (Circle)	P			$26,400
Dutch (1622 - 1674)				
LINGEN, A. V.	P			$825
Dutch (19th - 20th)				
LINK, B. Lillian	S			$715
American (1880 -)				
LINNBORG, Sven	P			$110
(19th -)				
LINNELL, John	P	$1,265	$16,005	$44,000
British (1792 - 1882)				
LINNELL, John (Attrib.)	P	$1,870	$2,035	$2,200
British (1792 - 1882)				
LINNIG, Egide	P			$4,125
Belgian (1821 - 1860)				
LINS, Adolf	P			$6,600
German (1856 - 1927)				
LINSLY, Wilford	P			$275
American (? - 1898)				
LINSON, Corwin K.	P	$110	$4,098	$17,600
American (1864 - 1959)				
LINT, Hendrik F. van	P			$38,500
Flemish (1684 - 1763)				

D=Drawing, P=Painting, S=Sculpture, W=Watercolor

		Current Price Range		
		Low	Mean	High

		Low	Mean	High
LINT, Hendrik F. van (Circle)	P			$25,300
Flemish (1684 - 1763)				
LINT, Hendrik F. van (Studio)	P			$115,500
Flemish (1684 - 1763)				
LINT, Pieter van	P			$8,250
Flemish (? - 1690)				
LINT, Pieter van (Attrib.)	P			$11,000
Flemish (? - 1690)				
LINTON, William	P			$17,600
British (1791 - 1876)				
LINTON, William E.	W			$660
British (1878 -)				
LINTOTT, Edward B.	D			$138
American (1875 - 1951)	P	$220	$605	$1,650
	W	$138	$729	$1,320
LION, Flora	P			$825
British (19th - 20th)				
LIONARD, A.	P			$275
French (20th -)				
LIONE, Andrea di	P			$99,000
Italian (1610 - 1685)				
LIPCHITZ, Jacques	D	$1,760	$13,530	$38,500
American (1891 - 1973)	P			$9,900
	S	$5,225	$170,241	$1.540M
	W	$2,860	$4,455	$6,050
LIPCHYTZ, L.	S			$880
(?)				
LIPPE, P.	W			$275
French (19th - 20th)				
LIPPERT, Leon	P			$4,950
American (? - 1950)				
LIPPI, Fillipino (After)	P			$440
Italian (1457 - 1504)				

D=Drawing, P=Painting, S=Sculpture, W=Watercolor

		Current Price Range		
		Low	Mean	High

LIPPINCOTT, M.	*W*			$275
American (19th -)				
LIPPINCOTT, William H.	*P*	$2,090	$7,948	$18,700
American (1849 - 1920)				
LIPPMANN, Alphonse	*S*			$990
French (19th -)				
LIPSKI, Donald	*P*	$2,475	$3,025	$3,300
(20th -)	*S*	$3,300	$3,713	$4,125
LIPTON, Seymour	*S*	$1,210	$8,525	$24,200
American (1903 -)				
LIRA, Benjamin	*P*			$3,300
Chilean (1950 -)				
LISANI,	*P*			$275
European (20th -)				
LISIO, Arnaldo De	*P*			$2,200
Italian (1869 -)				
LISSE, Dirck van (Attrib.)	*P*			$6,600
Dutch (1669 -)				
LISSER, Onrico	*P*			$8,800
European (19th -)				
LISSITSKY, El	*D*			$57,750
Russian (1890 - 1941)	*S*			$605,000
LISTERE, A. de	*P*			$2,420
French (18th -)				
LITTLE, Joseph W.	*P*			$523
American (?)	*W*	$358	$372	$385
LITTLE, Nat	*W*			$286
American (1893 -)				
LITTLE, Philip	*P*	$550	$1,628	$2,750
American (1857 - 1942)	*W*			$770
LITTLE, Richard	*D*			$330
(?)				
LITTLEFIELD, William H.	*D*			$100

D=Drawing, P=Painting, S=Sculpture, W=Watercolor

		Current Price Range		
		Low	Mean	High
LITTLEFIELD, William H.	P			$275
American (1902 - 1969)	W			$165
LITZINGER, Dorothea M.	P	$1,210	$2,713	$5,830
American (1889 - 1925)	W			$440
LIVERMORE, F. D.	W			$165
American (20th -)				
LIVERS, Ernestine	P			$176
American (20th -)				
LIVESAY, Richard	P			$605
British (? - 1823)				
LIZ, Domingo	P	$3,300	$4,767	$5,500
Dom. Rep. (1931 -)				
LIZEN, Marcel	P			$138
French (20th -)				
LJUBA,	P	$7,150	$8,663	$10,450
(20th -)				
LLOYD, C.	P			$1,265
(?)				
LLOYD, Edward	P			$3,850
British (? - 1891)				
LLOYD, Frank E.	P			$605
American (? - 1945)				
LLOYD, Norman	P			$149
(?)				
LLOYD, Stuart	W	$220	$1,210	$2,090
British (1875 - 1929)				
LO SCARPETTA,	P			$77,000
Italian (? - 1750)				
LOAN, Dorothy van	P	$220	$504	$935
American (1904 -)				
LOBE, F.	P			$385
European (19th -)				
LOBER, Georg J.	S			$880
American (19th -)				

D=Drawing, P=Painting, S=Sculpture, W=Watercolor

		Current Price Range		
		Low	Mean	High
LOBINGIER, Elizabeth M.	*P*			$550
American (1889 -)				
LOBOS, Alfredo	*P*	$248	$262	$275
Chilean (1890 - 1917)				
LOBRICHON, Timoleon M.	*P*	$1,430	$2,640	$3,850
French (1831 - 1914)				
LOCATELLI, Andrea	*P*			$88,000
Italian (1693 - 1741)				
LOCATELLI, Andrea (Attrib.)	*P*			$5,775
Italian (1693 - 1741)				
LOCKE, A. S.	*P*			$330
American (1860 -)				
LOCKHART, William E.	*P*			$330
British (1846 - 1900)				
LOCKRIDGE,	*P*			$275
American (?)				
LOCKWOOD, Wilton	*P*			$220
American (1862 - 1914)				
LODDER, Captain C. A.	*W*			$165
British (19th -)				
LODENKAMP,	*P*			$4,400
(20th -)				
LODER, James	*P*	$5,280	$9,460	$14,300
British (19th -)				
LODGE, George E.	*W*			$3,300
British (1860 - 1954)				
LODONE, Eusebio	*P*			$3,630
Italian (19th -)				
LOEB, Dorothy	*P*	$3,850	$3,988	$4,125
American (1887 -)				
LOEB, Louis	*P*	$220	$6,710	$13,200
American (1866 - 1909)				
LOECHEL, William	*W*			$248
(?)				
LOEDINGH, Harmen	*P*			$154,000
(1637 - 1673)				

D=Drawing, P=Painting, S=Sculpture, W=Watercolor

		Current Price Range	
	Low	Mean	High

		Low	Mean	High
LOEDINGH, Harmen (Attrib.) (1637 - 1673)	*P*			$28,600
LOEMANS, Alexander F. American (19th -)	*P*	$523	$2,261	$6,050
LOFFLER, Auguste German (1822 - 1866)	*D*			$352
LOFTHUS, Arne W. Norwegian (1881 -)	*P*			$550
LOGAN, American (?)	*P*	$110	$440	$770
LOGAN, Maurice American (1886 - 1977)	*W*	$660	$853	$1,045
LOGAN, Robert F. American (1899 -)	*P*			$5,500
LOGAN, Robert H. American (1874 - 1942)	*P*	$330	$532	$770
LOGSDAIL, William British (1859 -)	*P*			$5,280
LOGUE, John J. American (19th -)	*P*			$4,620
LOHR, August German (1843 - 1919)	*P* *W*	$7,150 $220	$28,325 $4,033	$49,500 $8,800
LOHR, Hugo (20th -)	*P*			$1,430
LOIR, Luigi French (1845 - 1916)	*P* *W*	$16,500	$32,175	$55,000 $15,400
LOIR, Nicolas French (1624 - 1679)	*P*			$17,600
LOISEAU, Gustave French (1865 - 1935)	*P*	$44,000	$130,900	$308,000
LOJACONO, Francesco Italian (1841 - 1915)	*P*			$2,640
LOMBARD SCHOOL, Italian (?)	*D*			$8,800

D=Drawing, P=Painting, S=Sculpture, W=Watercolor

		Current Price Range		
		Low	Mean	High

		Low	Mean	High
LOMBARD SCHOOL 16C, Italian (16th -)	*D*	$1,320	$3,135	$4,950
LOMBARD SCHOOL 17C, Italian (17th -)	*W*			$1,650
LOMBAS, Arthur (?)	*P*			$550
LOMI, Aurelio Italian (1556 - 1622)	*P*			$28,600
LOMMEN, Wilhelm German (1838 - 1895)	*P*			$7,700
LONDONER, Amy American (1878 -)	*W*			$385
LONE WOLF, American (20th -)	*P*			$7,700
LONG, Betty American (20th -)	*P*			$110
LONG, Christopher (20th -)	*P*			$18,700
LONG, Edwin British (1829 - 1891)	*P*			$5,225
LONG, Richard British (1945 -)	*S*	$46,750	$114,583	$209,000
LONG, Stanley M. American (1892 - 1972)	*W*			$440
LONGENECKER, Paul American (20th -)	*P*			$220
LONGFELLOW, Ernest W. American (1845 - 1921)	*P*			$1,045
LONGFELLOW, Mary American (19th - 20th)	*W*	$110	$578	$1,045
LONGHI, Alessandro (Attrib.) Italian (1733 - 1813)	*P*			$5,500
LONGHI, Alessandro (Circle) Italian (1733 - 1813)	*P*			$4,620
LONGHI, Pietro (Attrib.) Italian (1702 - 1785)	*P*			$880

D=Drawing, P=Painting, S=Sculpture, W=Watercolor

		Current Price Range		
		Low	Mean	High

		Low	Mean	High
LONGHI, Pietro (Style)	*P*			$660
Italian (1702 - 1785)				
LONGMAN, Evelyn B.	*S*			$19,800
American (1874 -)				
LONGO, Robert	*D*	$6,600	$48,950	$154,000
American (1953 -)	*P*	$11,000	$53,808	$154,000
	S	$4,950	$17,050	$23,100
LONGOBARDI, Nino	*D*	$1,320	$2,310	$3,300
Italian (20th -)	*P*			$2,640
LONGONI, Emilio	*P*			$935
Italian (1859 - 1933)				
LONGPRE, Paul De	*D*	$2,200	$2,200	$2,200
French (1855 - 1911)	*P*			$523
	W	$1,430	$3,913	$11,550
LONGPRE, Paul De (Attrib.)	*W*			$110
French (1855 - 1911)				
LONGPRE, Raoul M. De	*D*	$2,200	$3,025	$3,850
American (19th - 20th)	*P*			$11,000
	W	$2,200	$4,785	$8,800
LONGSTAFFE, Edgar	*P*			$1,100
British (1849 - 1912)				
LONZA, Antonia	*P*			$3,520
Italian (1864 -)				
LOO, Carle van	*D*	$4,180	$6,215	$8,250
French (1705 - 1765)				
LOO, Carle van (Attrib.)	*D*			$11,000
French (1705 - 1765)	*P*			$44,000
LOO, Carle van (Circle)	*D*			$440
French (1705 - 1765)	*P*	$2,640	$24,420	$46,200
LOO, Carle van (School)	*P*			$2,640
French (1705 - 1765)				

D=Drawing, P=Painting, S=Sculpture, W=Watercolor

		Current Price Range	
	Low	Mean	High

		Low	Mean	High
LOO, Jacob van (School)	*P*			$2,420
Dutch (1614 - 1670)				
LOO, Jean B. van (Attrib.)	*D*			$20,900
French (1684 - 1745)	*P*			$7,700
LOO, Jean B. van (Studio)	*P*			$6,600
French (1684 -.1745)				
LOO, Louis M. van	*P*			$231,000
French (1707 - 1771)				
LOO, Van (Circle)	*P*			$2,200
French (1719 - 1795)				
LOODGE, William	*P*			$605
French (19th - 20th)				
LOOKING ELK, Albert	*P*			$605
American (20th -)				
LOOMIS, Andrew	*D*			$275
American (1892 - 1959)	*P*	$770	$2,489	$4,800
LOOMIS, Charles R.	*P*	$1,210	$1,980	$2,750
American (1857 - 1936)	*W*	$138	$334	$550
LOOMIS, Charles R. (Et al.)	*W*			$385
American (19th - 20th)				
LOOMIS, Chester	*P*	$660	$715	$770
American (1852 - 1924)	*W*			$385
LOOMIS, L. A.	*P*			$495
American (19th -)				
LOOP, Henry A.	*P*			$1,980
American (1831 - 1895)				
LOOP, Henry A. (Et al.)	*P*			$110
American (19th -)				
LOOTEN, Jan (Attrib.)	*P*			$4,400
Dutch (1618 - 1681)				
LOPER, Edward	*P*	$220	$611	$1,870
American (20th -)	*W*			$165

D=Drawing, P=Painting, S=Sculpture, W=Watercolor

		Current Price Range		
		Low	Mean	High

LOPEZ, Carlos	*P*			$1,430
American (20th -)				
LOPEZ, Gasparo	*P*			$22,000
Italian (1650 - 1732)				
LOPEZ, Gasparo (Attrib.)	*P*			$9,350
Italian (1650 - 1732)				
LOPEZ, Gasparo (Circle)	*P*	$2,750	$4,675	$6,600
Italian (1650 - 1732)				
LOPEZ, Gasparo (Manner)	*P*			$6,050
Italian (1650 - 1732)				
LOPEZ, Gustavo A.	*P*			$3,850
Argentina (1949 -)				
LOPEZ Y PORTANA, Vincente	*P*	$880	$11,440	$22,000
Spanish (1772 - 1850)				
LOPP, Harry L.	*P*			$605
American (1888 -)				
LORD, Andrew	*S*			$9,350
(20th -)				
LORD, Caroline	*P*			$440
American (1860 -)				
LORENSE, S. F.	*P*			$220
American (20th -)				
LORENTZ, Alcide J.	*P*			$660
French (1813 -)				
LORENTZEN, Christian A.	*P*			$4,400
Danish (1749 - 1828)				
LORENZ,	*P*	$385	$587	$825
(20th -)				
LORENZ, Richard	*D*			$250
German (1858 - 1915)	*P*	$770	$1,343	$2,950
LORENZ, Willi	*P*			$605
German (19th -)				
LORENZINI, Gianantonio	*D*			$4,125
Italian (1665 - 1740)				
LORIA, Vincenzo	*W*	$110	$395	$605
Italian (1850 -)				

D=Drawing, P=Painting, S=Sculpture, W=Watercolor

		Current Price Range		
		Low	Mean	High

		Low	Mean	High
LORIAN, Dolia (20th -)	*P*	$770	$1,870	$2,970
LORING, George B. (?)	*P*			$2,200
LORJOU, Bernard French (1908 -)	*P*	$3,025	$12,977	$46,200
	W	$1,210	$1,320	$1,430
LORME, Anthonie de (Circle) French (1653 - 1723)	*P*			$24,200
LORRAIN, Claude French (1600 - 1682)	*D*	$8,250	$23,283	$35,200
	P	$7,150	$278,575	$550,000
LORRAIN, Claude (After) French (1600 - 1682)	*P*	$1,045	$1,903	$3,300
LORRAIN, Claude (Follower) French (1600 - 1682)	*D*			$880
LORRAIN, Claude (Manner) French (1600 - 1682)	*P*	$1,760	$4,455	$7,150
LORRAIN, Claude (School) French (1600 - 1682)	*D*			$3,850
LOS, H. de (18th -)	*P*			$2,090
LOS, Waldemar Polish (1849 - 1888)	*P*			$2,200
LOSCANOS, Pedro American (20th -)	*P*			$578
LOSIK, Thomas Polish (1849 - 1896)	*P*			$1,760
LOSTUTTER, Robert American (20th -)	*W*			$1,210
LOTERLET, J. B. (19th -)	*P*			$220
LOTH, Johann C. German (1632 - 1698)	*D*			$1,650
	P	$8,800	$14,850	$20,900
LOTH, Johann C. (Follower) German (1632 - 1698)	*P*			$1,210

D=Drawing, P=Painting, S=Sculpture, W=Watercolor

		Current Price Range		
		Low	Mean	High
LOTHAR, Ernst	P			$143
European (20th -)				
LOTTO, Lorenzo	P			$110,000
Italian (1480 - 1556)				
LOTTO, Lorenzo (School)	P	$4,675	$10,038	$15,400
Italian (1480 - 1556)				
LOTZ, Matilda	P			$9,900
American (1858 - 1923)				
LOUARDIRI, Ahmed	P			$248
Moroccan (20th -)				
LOUBON, Emile C. J.	P			$3,850
French (1809 - 1863)				
LOUDEN, Norman P.	P			$550
American (1895 -)				
LOUDERBACK, Walt S.	P	$110	$953	$2,090
American (1887 - 1941)				
LOUGHEED, Robert E.	P	$990	$4,202	$9,350
American (1910 -)				
LOUIS, Morris	P	$66,000	$376,477	$1.045M
American (1912 - 1962)				
LOUIS, S.	P			$528
(?)				
LOUNSBERY, Richard M.	S			$1,045
American (?)				
LOUTHERBOURG, Philippe	D			$1,980
French (1740 - 1812)	P	$11,000	$66,000	$121,000
LOUTHERBOURG, Philippe (Att.)	P			$99,000
French (1740 - 1812)	W			$110
LOUTHERBOURG, Philippe (Cir.)	P			$1,870
French (1740 - 1812)				
LOUYOT, Edmond	P			$4,400
German (19th -)				
LOVATTI, Matteo	P			$4,840
Italian (1861 -)				

D=Drawing, P=Painting, S=Sculpture, W=Watercolor

| | | Current Price Range | | |
| --- | --- | Low | Mean | High |

		Low	Mean	High
LOVEJOY, Rupert S.	*P*	$275	$1,687	$2,585
American (1885 - 1975)				
LOVELL, Tom	*D*	$660	$3,703	$7,700
American (1909 -)	*P*	$605	$2,251	$4,400
	W			$220
LOVEN, Frank W.	*P*	$440	$1,004	$2,310
American (1868 - 1941)				
LOVERIDGE, Clinton	*P*	$495	$1,874	$6,050
British (1824 - 1902)	*W*			$550
LOVET-LORSKI, Boris	*S*	$19,800	$24,420	$29,700
American (1894 - 1973)				
LOVING, James	*P*			$1,100
American (1826 -)				
LOVMAND, Christine	*P*	$9,900	$20,533	$29,700
Danish (1803 - 1872)				
LOW, Mary F.	*P*	$275	$536	$770
American (1858 - 1946)				
LOW, Will H.	*P*	$3,740	$9,680	$18,700
American (1853 - 1932)	*W*			$385
LOWELL, Milton H.	*P*	$165	$878	$1,870
American (1848 - 1927)				
LOWELL, Milton H. (Attrib.)	*P*			$400
American (1848 - 1927)				
LOWELL, Orson B.	*D*	$220	$1,027	$2,090
American (1871 - 1956)	*P*			$2,200
LOWELL, W. W.	*W*			$495
American (?)				
LOWERY, Ronald	*S*			$660
American (20th -)				
LOWITH, Wilhelm	*P*			$200
Austrian (1861 -)				
LOYALFIELD,	*P*			$1,210
American (?)				

D=Drawing, P=Painting, S=Sculpture, W=Watercolor

		Current Price Range	
	Low	Mean	High

LOYSEN, A. P.	*P*			$248
American (19th - 20th)				
LOYSEN, Arthur	*P*	$165	$252	$385
American (20th -)				
LOZANO, Manuel R.	*P*	$16,500	$18,150	$19,800
Mexican (20th -)				
LOZANO, Margarita	*P*			$7,150
Lat. Amer. (20th -)				
LOZOWICK, Louis	*P*			$2,860
American (1892 - 1973)				
LUBBERS, Holger	*P*			$8,800
Danish (1850 - 1928)				
LUBIENIECKI, Christoffel	*P*			$14,300
Polish (1660 - 1728)				
LUBIN, Arieh	*P*			$1,650
Israeli (20th -)				
LUCAS, Albert P.	*P*	$990	$1,485	$1,980
American (1862 - 1945)				
LUCAS, Eugenio (Circle)	*P*			$3,300
(19th -)				
LUCAS, John S.	*D*			$193
European (1849 - 1923)	*P*	$1,760	$5,005	$8,250
LUCAS, M. C.	*P*			$385
(?)				
LUCAS Y PADILLA, Eugenio	*P*	$17,600	$40,425	$63,250
Spanish (1824 - 1870)				
LUCAS Y VILLAMIL, Eugenio	*P*	$9,900	$11,550	$13,200
Spanish (1858 - 1918)				
LUCAS-ROBIQUET, Marie A. E.	*P*	$4,675	$13,925	$44,000
French (1864 -)				
LUCCHESI, Bruno	*S*	$275	$1,503	$3,300
American (1926 -)				
LUCE, Maximilien	*D*	$165	$5,071	$13,200
French (1858 - 1941)	*P*	$4,400	$48,488	$550,000

D=Drawing, P=Painting, S=Sculpture, W=Watercolor

		Current Price Range		
		Low	Mean	High

LUCE, Maximilien French (1858 - 1941)	*W*			$1,320
LUCE, Maximilien (Attrib.) French (1858 - 1941)	*D*			$220
LUCE, Molly American (1896 - 1986)	*P*			$440
LUCE, Percival de American (1847 - 1914)	*P* *W*	$165	$963	$1,760 $5,500
LUCEBERT, Jean Dutch (1924 -)	*P* *S*	$15,400	$16,500	$17,600 $7,700
LUCERO, Michael (20th -)	*P*			$20,900
LUCIEN, (?)	*P*			$990
LUCIEN-GILBERT, Darpy French (1875 -)	*P*			$770
LUCIONI, Luigi American (1900 - 1988)	*P*	$2,475	$18,518	$77,000
LUCKENBACH, Reuben D. American (?)	*P*			$4,400
LUCO, F. S. de (?)	*S*			$6,050
LUDBY, Max (Attrib.) British (1858 - 1943)	*P*			$935
LUDENS, Eugene American (20th -)	*P*			$440
LUDLOW, Mike American (1921 -)	*W*			$110
LUDU, J. P. (19th - 20th)	*W*			$275
LUDWIG, C. German (20th -)	*P*			$193
LUGERTH, Ferdinand (19th -)	*S*			$1,650

D=Drawing, P=Painting, S=Sculpture, W=Watercolor

		Current Price Range		
		Low	Mean	High

		Low	Mean	High
LUIGINI, Ferdinand J.	*P*			$1,100
French (1870 - 1943)				
LUIGINI, Ferdinand J. (Attrib.)	*P*			$660
French (1870 - 1943)				
LUINI, Bernadino	*P*			$44,000
Italian (1475 - 1532)				
LUINI, Bernadino (Follower)	*P*			$60,500
Italian (1475 - 1532)				
LUKER, William	*P*			$4,510
British (19th -)				
LUKIN, S.	*D*			$198
(20th -)				
LUKITS, Theodore N.	*W*			$385
American (1897 -)				
LUKS, George B.	*D*	$550	$2,838	$15,400
American (1867 - 1933)	*P*	$3,575	$70,104	$660,000
	W	$3,300	$14,850	$19,800
LUKS, George B. (Attrib.)	*P*			$13,200
American (1867 - 1933)				
LUM, Bertha B.	*W*			$550
American (1879 - 1954)				
LUMIS, E. D.	*P*			$605
(19th -)				
LUMIS, Harriet R.	*P*	$2,860	$7,920	$16,500
American (1870 - 1953)				
LUMLEY, Augustus S.	*P*			$1,760
British (19th -)				
LUNAMARK,	*P*			$220
American (20th -)				
LUND, Carl O. J.	*P*			$8,250
Danish (1857 - 1936)				
LUND, Harold M.	*P*	$440	$820	$1,200
American (1904 -)				
LUNDBERG, August	*P*	$385	$541	$825
American (1878 - 1928)				

D=Drawing, P=Painting, S=Sculpture, W=Watercolor

		Current Price Range		
		Low	Mean	High

LUNDEEN, James L.	*P*			$495
American (1895 - 1961)				
LUNDMARK, Leon	*P*	$193	$647	$1,100
American (1879 -)				
LUNENFELD, Ethel	*P*			$275
American (1918 -)				
LUNGREN, Fernand H.	*P*	$4,400	$5,408	$6,050
American (1857 - 1932)				
LUNGREN, Fernand H. (Attrib.)	*P*			$880
American (1857 - 1932)				
LUNY, Thomas	*P*	$5,500	$14,850	$24,200
British (1759 - 1837)				
LUNY, Thomas (Circle)	*P*			$880
British (1759 - 1837)				
LUNY, Thomas (Style)	*P*			$138
British (1759 - 1837)				
LUQUIENS, Elizabeth K.	*P*			$375
American (1878 -)				
LURCAT, Jean	*D*			$935
French (1892 - 1966)	*P*	$2,090	$5,438	$10,450
	S			$1,650
	W	$2,200	$2,805	$3,575
LURCAT, Jean (After)	*S*	$3,850	$5,500	$7,150
French (1892 - 1966)				
LUSTY, Otto	*P*			$550
Danish (19th - 20th)				
LUTERO, Giovanni	*P*			$4.070M
(?)				
LUTI, Benedetto	*D*			$17,600
Italian (1666 - 1724)	*P*			$88,000
LUTI, Benedetto (Attrib.)	*D*			$1,320
Italian (1666 - 1724)				
LUTI, Benedetto (Circle)	*D*			$2,750
Italian (1666 - 1724)				

D=Drawing, P=Painting, S=Sculpture, W=Watercolor

		Current Price Range		
		Low	Mean	High

LUTI, Benedetto (Studio)	*D*			$1,540
Italian (1666 - 1724)				
LUTZ, A. A.	*P*			$165
American (20th -)				
LUTZ, Dan	*P*	$248	$926	$1,320
American (1906 - 1978)	*W*			$440
LUYKEN, Jan	*D*	$660	$880	$1,100
Dutch (1649 - 1712)				
LUZAK, Dennis	*W*			$275
American (?)				
LUZZATI, Emmanuele	*D*			$660
(?)				
LYFORD, Philip	*W*			$125
American (1887 - 1950)				
LYLE, Byron	*P*			$5,500
British (19th -)				
LYMAN, Harry	*P*			$1,760
British (19th - 20th)				
LYMAN, William	*P*			$143
(?)				
LYNCH, Albert	*D*			$440
Peruvian (1851 -)	*P*	$3,300	$13,017	$28,600
LYNCH, David	*P*			$110
American (20th -)				
LYNCH, Robert	*P*			$385
American (20th -)				
LYND,	*P*			$1,815
British (20th -)				
LYNDE, R.	*P*			$2,750
(?)				
LYNE, Michael	*P*	$4,950	$8,543	$15,400
British (1912 -)	*S*	$440	$532	$605
	W	$660	$3,053	$4,400

D=Drawing, P=Painting, S=Sculpture, W=Watercolor

		Current Price Range		
		Low	Mean	High

LYNER, T. R.	*P*			$2,090
European (19th -)				
LYNN, Louise	*W*			$154
American (20th -)				
LYNTON, Henry S.	*P*			$825
British (19th - 20th)				
LYON, Corneille de	*P*			$35,200
Flemish (16th -)				
LYON, Dustin	*W*			$450
American (20th -)				
LYON, Jeannette	*P*			$330
American (1862 -)				
LYON, Richard	*P*			$908
American (20th -)				
MAAS, Dirk	*P*			$44,000
Italian (1659 - 1717)	*W*			$1,210
MAAS, Ray	*P*			$688
American (20th -)				
MAASDIJK, Alexander H. van	*P*			$825
Dutch (1856 - 1931)				
MAASS, David	*P*			$3,960
American (20th -)				
MABE, Manabu	*P*	$5,500	$9,900	$18,700
Japanese (1924 -)				
MABERRY, Philip	*S*			$1,100
(20th -)				
MACALLUM, John T. H.	*W*			$440
British (1841 - 1896)				
MACALPINE, William (Attrib.)	*W*			$495
British (19th -)				
MACAULIFFE, James J.	*P*			$2,860
American (1848 - 1921)				
MACCALLUM, Hamilton	*P*	$550	$798	$1,045
British (19th -)				
MACCARTAN, Edward	*S*	$660	$7,480	$14,300
American (1878 -)				

D=Drawing, P=Painting, S=Sculpture, W=Watercolor

		Current Price Range		
		Low	Mean	High
MACCIO, Romulo	P	$1,320	$13,860	$26,400
Argentine (1931 -)				
MACCONNEL, Kim	P			$11,000
American (1946 -)	W			$1,980
MACDONALD, Chris	S			$9,900
(20th -)				
MACDONALD, Grant	P	$330	$6,464	$9,790
American (1944 -)				
MACDONALD, James W.	S			$2,200
American (1824 - 1908)				
MACDONALD, Stanton	P			$484,000
American (1890 - 1974)	W			$6,600
MACDONALD, W. Alister	W			$715
British (20th -)				
MACDONALL, Angus P.	W	$330	$990	$1,650
American (1876 - 1927)				
MACENTYRE, Eduardo	P			$5,500
(20th -)				
MACFADDEN, James	P	$127	$174	$220
American (?)				
MACFARLANE, J. R.	D			$1,320
Scottish (19th -)				
MACGEORGE, William S.	P			$2,750
British (1861 - 1931)	W			$880
MACGILVARY, Norwood H.	P	$2,805	$2,988	$3,300
American (1874 - 1950)				
MACGINNIS, Henry R.	P	$165	$193	$220
American (1875 - 1962)				
MACGREGOR, Jessie	P			$330
American (20th -)				
MACGREGOR, Robert	W			$1,760
Scottish (1848 - 1922)				
MACHEN, William H.	P	$149	$226	$303
American (1832 - 1911)				

D=Drawing, P=Painting, S=Sculpture, W=Watercolor

		Current Price Range		
		Low	Mean	High

MACHEREN, Philip van (Attrib.)	P			$3,850
Dutch (17th -)				
MACHETANZ, Fred	P	$6,050	$9,488	$17,600
American (1908 -)				
MACINTOSH, Marian T.	P	$825	$1,678	$2,530
American (1871 - 1936)				
MACKAY, Edwin M.	P	$330	$440	$605
American (1869 - 1926)				
MACKAY, Thomas	W			$385
American (19th -)				
MACKE, August	D			$3,300
French (1887 - 1914)				
MACKENZIE, Alexander	P			$770
British (1848 -)				
MACKENZIE, Frank	P			$935
American (1867 - 1939)				
MACKENZIE, Kenneth	P			$3,080
Scottish (19th -)				
MACKENZIE, Warren	S			$528
(20th -)				
MACKEY, Edward	P			$605
British (19th -)				
MACKEY, H.	P			$315
(?)				
MACKLIN, Nada	P			$220
(20th -)				
MACKNIGHT, Dodge	W	$660	$3,421	$9,350
American (1860 - 1950)				
MACKY, Eric S.	P			$1,870
American (1880 - 1958)	W			$385
MACLAUGHLIN, Charles J.	P			$1,210
American (20th -)				
MACLELLAN, Charles	P			$1,760
American (1887 -)				
MACLENNAN, Eunice C.	P			$550
American (1886 - 1966)				

D=Drawing, P=Painting, S=Sculpture, W=Watercolor

		Current Price Range		
		Low	Mean	High

		Low	Mean	High
MACLET, Elisee	*D*			$4,950
French (1881 - 1962)	*P*	$990	$16,081	$37,400
	W	$495	$2,541	$4,950
MACLISE, Daniel	*P*			$1,650
British (1806 - 1870)				
MACMONNIES, Frederick W.	*S*	$2,460	$18,322	$104,500
American (1863 - 1937)				
MACNEAL, Frederic A.	*W*			$165
American (20th -)				
MACNEE, Sir Daniel	*P*			$1,100
Scottish (1806 - 1882)				
MACNEIL, Carol Brooks	*S*			$385
American (1871 - 1944)				
MACOMBER, Mary L.	*P*	$165	$3,761	$11,000
American (1861 - 1916)				
MACRAE, Elmer L.	*D*	$352	$530	$880
American (1875 - 1953)	*P*	$660	$14,346	$46,200
	W			$330
MACRAE, Emma F.	*P*	$1,760	$5,537	$8,800
American (1887 - 1974)				
MACWIRTER, John	*P*	$1,100	$2,750	$4,400
British (1839 - 1911)				
MACY, Wendell	*P*	$413	$537	$660
American (1845 - 1913)				
MACY, William S.	*P*	$1,760	$2,493	$3,850
American (1853 - 1916)	*W*			$137
MADDEN, Jan	*P*	$880	$1,430	$1,980
American (20th -)				
MADDERSTEEG, Michiel	*P*			$28,600
Dutch (1659 - 1709)				
MADDI, P.	*W*	$193	$207	$220
(?)				
MADELAIN, Gustave	*P*	$16,500	$20,350	$24,200
French (1867 - 1944)				

D=Drawing, P=Painting, S=Sculpture, W=Watercolor

		Current Price Range	
		Low	Mean	High
MADELINE, Paul	*P*			$5,500
French (1863 - 1920)				
MADIONO, Luis	*P*			$935
Spanish (19th -)				
MADJEN, Oho	*P*			$110
American (?)				
MADLENER, A.Joseph	*P*			$2,475
German (1881 -)				
MADRASSI, L.	*S*			$550
(19th -)				
MADRAZO, Mariano F. y de	*P*			$5,500
Spanish (1949 -)				
MADRAZO Y GARRETA, Raim.	*P*	$27,500	$90,750	$154,000
Spanish (1841 - 1920)				
MADSEN, Otto	*P*			$275
American (1882 -)				
MAENTEL, Jacob (Attrib.)	*W*	$3,080	$4,400	$5,720
American (19th -)				
MAES, Eugene R.	*P*	$2,750	$5,665	$9,350
Belgian (1849 - 1931)				
MAES, Nicholaes	*P*	$22,000	$71,500	$165,000
Dutch (1632 - 1693)				
MAES, Nicholaes (Attrib.)	*P*			$7,700
Dutch (1632 - 1693)				
MAES & COL, Eugene R. & Jan D.	*P*			$13,200
Belgian (19th - 20th)				
MAESTOSI, F.	*P*	$1,100	$4,675	$8,250
Italian (19th -)				
MAESTRI, Michelangelo	*P*	$4,620	$4,620	$4,620
Italian (? - 1812)				
MAGANZA, Alessandro (Attrib.)	*D*			$3,575
Italian (1556 - 1630)				
MAGAVENA, C.	*P*			$150
(?)				
MAGENIS, H.	*W*	$165	$179	$193
French (19th -)				

D=Drawing, P=Painting, S=Sculpture, W=Watercolor

		Current Price Range		
		Low	Mean	High

		Low	Mean	High
MAGGI, Cesare	P			$8,250
Italian (1881 - 1961)				
MAGGIOTTO, Domenico (attrib.)	P			$16,500
Italian (1713 - 1794)				
MAGGS, John C.	P	$2,750	$7,150	$14,300
British (1819 - 1896)				
MAGIDEY, W.	P			$550
European (19th - 20th)				
MAGIE, Gertrude	P			$1,980
American (1862 -)				
MAGNASCO, Alessandro	P			$35,200
Italian (1667 - 1749)				
MAGNASCO, Alessandro (Circle)	P			$19,800
Italian (1667 - 1749)				
MAGNASCO, Alessandro (Foll.)	P	$3,300	$3,300	$3,300
Italian (1667 - 1749)				
MAGNASCO, Alessandro (School)	P	$1,540	$9,460	$24,750
Italian (1667 - 1749)				
MAGNASCO, Alessandro (Style)	P			$2,475
Italian (1667 - 1749)				
MAGNE, Desire A.	P			$4,950
French (1855 -)				
MAGNI, Giuseppe	P	$5,775	$25,644	$47,300
Italian (1869 -)				
MAGNUS, Camille	P	$330	$6,188	$16,500
French (1850 -)				
MAGNUS, T.	P			$468
European (19th -)				
MAGRATH, Georges A. de	W			$2,530
French (19th -)				
MAGRITTE, Rene	D	$4,125	$37,015	$88,000
Belgian (1898 - 1967)	P	$24,200	$611,270	$1.650M
	S	$93,500	$101,750	$110,000
	W	$41,250	$187,165	$352,000

D=Drawing, P=Painting, S=Sculpture, W=Watercolor

		Current Price Range	
	Low	Mean	High

		Low	Mean	High
MAGRUM, George H. (?)	*P*			$517
MAGUIRE, Jeanne American (20th -)	*P*			$2,750
MAGY, Louis de American (19th - 20th)	*P*			$468
MAHAFFEY, Noel American (1944 -)	*P*	$4,675	$13,338	$22,000
MAHLAY, (19th -)	*P*			$165
MAHLKNECHT, Edmund Austrian (1820 - 1903)	*P*			$9,075
MAIDMENT, Henry British (19th - 20th)	*P*	$990	$1,018	$1,045
MAIER, Claus German (19th - 20th)	*P*			$880
MAIER, Emil German (1845 -)	*P*			$1,650
MAIER-KREIG, Eugene American (1897 -)	*P*			$523
MAIGNAN, Albert French (1845 - 1908)	*P*			$3,080
MAIK, Henri (?)	*P*			$440
MAILLART, Diogene French (1840 - 1926)	*D*			$165
MAILLAUD, Fernand French (1863 - 1948)	*P*	$3,410	$8,103	$14,300
MAILLOL, Aristide French (1861 - 1944)	*D* *S*	$4,950 $16,500	$18,100 $148,500	$40,700 $1.100M
MAINELLA, Raffaele Italian (1858 -)	*W*	$303	$372	$440
MAIROVICH, Zvi Israeli (20th -)	*P*			$1,540
MAISON, Mary E. American (1886 - 1954)	*P*	$330	$501	$880

D=Drawing, P=Painting, S=Sculpture, W=Watercolor

		Current Price Range		
		Low	Mean	High
MAJEWICZ, G.	P	$330	$385	$440
German (1894 -)				
MAJO, Paolo de	P			$2,200
(?)				
MAJOR, B.	P	$303	$349	$413
American (19th - 20th)				
MAJOR, Ernest L.	P	$330	$372	$413
American (1864 - 1950)				
MAJORELLE, Jacques	W			$825
French (19th - 20th)				
MAJORS, Robert J.	W	$303	$509	$715
American (1913 -)				
MAKART, Hans	P			$4,400
Austrian (1840 - 1884)				
MAKIELSKI, Leon A.	P	$165	$358	$550
American (1885 -)				
MAKOVSKY, Alexander	P			$12,100
(20th -)				
MAKOVSKY, Vladimir Y.	P			$8,250
Russian (1846 - 1920)				
MAKOWSKY, Constantin J.	P	$3,575	$11,138	$18,700
Russian (1839 - 1915)				
MALBET, Aurelie L.	P			$7,150
French (19th -)				
MALBRANCHE, Louis-Claude	P			$1,540
French (1790 - 1838)				
MALDARELLI, Federico	P			$8,800
Italian (1826 - 1893)				
MALDONADO, Estrardo	S			$523
Ecuadorian (20th -)				
MALER, Hans (Manner)	P			$1,540
Austrian (16th -)				
MALET, Albert	P			$2,970
French (19th - 20th)				
MALEVICH, Kasimir	D			$19,800
Russian (1878 - 1935)				

D=Drawing, P=Painting, S=Sculpture, W=Watercolor

		Current Price Range		
		Low	Mean	High

		Low	Mean	High
MALFROY, Charles	*P*			$3,080
French (1862 -)				
MALFROY, Henry	*P*	$1,100	$2,475	$3,850
French (1895 -)				
MALHAUPT, Frederick J.	*P*	$1,760	$3,630	$5,500
(1871 - 1938)				
MALHERBE, William	*P*	$825	$2,379	$4,180
French (19th - 20th)				
MALI, Christian F.	*P*	$30,800	$38,775	$46,750
German (1832 - 1906)				
MALIAVINE, Philippe	*P*			$13,200
Russian (1869 - 1939)				
MALICOAT, Philip C.	*P*	$2,200	$2,613	$3,025
American (1908 -)				
MALLET, Gabrielle	*P*			$303
American (19th -)				
MALLO, Maruja	*P*			$8,800
Spanish (1910 -)				
MALLORY, Ronald	*S*			$440
American (20th -)				
MALLOUEL, Jean (Follower)	*P*			$3,300
(?)				
MALMQUIST, Olaf C.	*P*			$495
American (1894 - 1975)				
MALMSTROM, August	*P*			$99,000
Swedish (1829 - 1901)				
MALONEY, Dave	*D*	$1,100	$1,550	$2,000
American (20th -)				
MALTESE, Francesco F. (Circle)	*P*			$11,000
Italian (17th -)				
MAMANI, C.	*S*			$1,430
Italian (19th -)				
MAMMEN, Jeanne	*D*			$2,090
French (20th -)				
MAN-RAY,	*D*	$1,870	$13,182	$31,900

D=Drawing, P=Painting, S=Sculpture, W=Watercolor

		Current Price Range		
		Low	Mean	High
MAN-RAY,	P	$4,400	$12,825	$46,750
American (1890 - 1976)	S	$2,200	$3,988	$4,675
	W	$9,900	$10,450	$11,000
MANASTERSKI, Tadeusz	P			$209
(?)				
MANCINELLI, Guiseppi	P			$13,200
Italian (1817 - 1875)				
MANCINI, Antonio	P	$880	$13,127	$19,800
Italian (1852 - 1930)				
MANCINI, Antonio (Attrib.)	P			$2,200
Italian (1852 - 1930)				
MANCINI, Francesco (Manner)	P			$5,500
Italian (1694 - 1758)				
MANCINI, Francesco L.	P	$330	$385	$440
Italian (1880 -)				
MANCINI, M.	W			$275
Italian (19th -)				
MANCUSO, F.	P	$100	$270	$440
American (20th -)				
MANDEL, John	D			$1,210
(20th -)				
MANDER, William H.	P	$1,980	$2,457	$2,860
British (1880 - 1922)				
MANDYN, Jan (Circle)	P			$13,200
Dutch (1500 - 1560)				
MANE-KATZ,	D	$770	$2,736	$4,400
French (1894 - 1962)	P	$3,025	$12,840	$38,500
	S	$1,870	$4,593	$12,100
	W	$605	$4,336	$14,300
MANES, Descollines	P			$121
Haitian (20th -)				
MANESSIER, Alfred	P	$17,600	$26,400	$35,200
French (1911 -)				

D=Drawing, P=Painting, S=Sculpture, W=Watercolor

		Current Price Range		
		Low	Mean	High

		Low	Mean	High
MANET, Edouard	D			$1,980
French (1832 - 1883)	P	$374,000	$11.739M	$26.400M
MANFREDI, Circle	P			$8,800
Italian (?)				
MANGER, L.	P			$605
(19th -)				
MANGIONE, Pat	P			$550
American (20th -)				
MANGOLD, Robert	D	$4,950	$14,575	$24,200
American (1937 -)	P	$2,860	$71,594	$154,000
MANGOLD, Sylvia	D			$1,760
American (1938 -)	P			$1,870
MANGRAVITE, Pepino	P			$825
American (1896 -)				
MANGUIN, Henri	D			$2,750
French (1874 - 1943)	P	$14,300	$32,450	$55,000
	W			$14,300
MANHU,	P	$825	$853	$880
(20th -)				
MANIATTY, Stephen G.	P	$358	$940	$1,650
American (1910 -)				
MANIGAULT, Edward M.	P	$6,050	$6,875	$7,700
American (1887 - 1922)				
MANLEY, Thomas R.	P	$660	$1,173	$1,650
American (1853 - 1938)				
MANLIN, R.	P			$2,750
French (19th - 20th)				
MANN, David	P	$2,310	$6,872	$14,850
American (1948 -)				
MANN, Joshua H.	W			$110
British (? - 1886)				
MANN, Parker	P			$468
American (1852 - 1918)				

D=Drawing, P=Painting, S=Sculpture, W=Watercolor

		Current Price Range		
		Low	Mean	High

		Low	Mean	High
MANN-GROTZING, (20th -)	P			$138
MANNHEIM, Jean American (1863 - 1945)	P	$1,210	$5,242	$33,000
MANNING, W. W. American (?)	P			$2,640
MANOIR, Georges (?)	P			$248
MANS, Martha American (20th -)	W	$700	$790	$880
MANSER, Percy L. American (1886 -)	P			$330
MANSFIELD, Louise B. American (1876 -)	W			$138
MANSHIP, Paul American (1885 - 1966)	S	$935	$53,959	$297,000
MANSUROFF, Pavel Russian (1896 - 1984)	D			$2,200
MANTELET-MARTEL, Andre French (1876 -)	P			$7,425
MANUEL, Dave American (20th -)	S			$990
MANUEL, Victor Cuban (1867 - 1969)	P	$6,600	$8,525	$10,450
MANWARING, Lewis H. American (1825 - 1855)	P			$1,430
MANZONI, P. Italian (1933 - 1963)	P			$2,860
MANZU, Giacomo Italian (1908 -)	S	$27,500	$79,860	$176,000
MANZUOLI, Tomasso D. Italian (1536 - 1571)	D			$3,850
MANZUR, David Colombian (1929 -)	D			$15,400
	P	$2,200	$3,300	$4,400
	W			$5,500

D=Drawing, P=Painting, S=Sculpture, W=Watercolor

		Current Price Range		
		Low	Mean	High

MAR, David de la	*P*			$605
French (19th - 20th)				
MARAIS, V.	*P*			$110
(?)				
MARAIS-MILTON, Victor	*P*	$4,400	$7,590	$9,900
French (1872 -)				
MARANTONIO,	*P*			$165
Italian (19th - 20th)				
MARANTZ, Irving	*D*			$220
American (20th -)				
MARASCO, Antonio	*P*			$15,400
Italian (1886 -)				
MARATTA, Carlo	*D*	$770	$7,068	$16,500
Italian (1625 - 1713)				
MARATTA, Carlo (After)	*P*			$550
Italian (1625 - 1713)				
MARATTA, Carlo (Circle)	*D*	$462	$2,977	$7,700
Italian (1625 - 1713)	*P*			$77,000
MARATTA, Carlo (Follower)	*D*			$990
Italian (1625 - 1713)				
MARBLE, J. N. (Et al.)	*D*			$770
American (19th - 20th)				
MARC, Franz	*P*			$1.595M
German (1880 - 1916)	*W*			$66,000
MARC, Wilhelm	*P*			$6,050
German (1839 - 1907)				
MARCA-RELLI, Conrad	*P*	$46,750	$67,375	$88,000
American (1913 -)	*S*	$4,675	$12,336	$38,500
MARCEL, Lawrence	*S*			$1,925
American (20th -)				
MARCEL-BERONNEAU, Pierre A.	*P*			$990
French (1869 - 1937)				
MARCEL-CLEMENT, Amedee J.	*P*			$9,075
French (1873 -)				

D=Drawing, P=Painting, S=Sculpture, W=Watercolor

		Current Price Range		
		Low	Mean	High
MARCH Y MARCO, Vincente	*P*			$49,500
Spanish (1859 - 1914)				
MARCHAND, Andre	*P*	$425	$1,734	$4,400
French (1907 -)				
MARCHAND, Jean H.	*P*			$2,200
French (1883 - 1940)				
MARCHAND, John N.	*D*			$358
American (?)	*W*			$1,100
MARCHAND, Phillipe	*P*	$2,200	$3,300	$4,400
French (20th -)				
MARCHANT, Edward Dalton	*P*	$550	$1,100	$1,650
American (1806 - 1887)				
MARCHE, Nathalie de la	*D*			$4,620
(19th -)				
MARCHETTI, Louis	*P*			$500
(?)				
MARCHETTI, Ludovico	*P*	$3,300	$5,225	$7,150
Italian (1853 - 1909)				
MARCHETTI, Ludovico (After)	*S*			$1,760
Italian (1853 - 1909)				
MARCHI, Vincenzo	*P*			$9,350
Italian (1818 - 1894)				
MARCHIONI, Elisabetta (Manner)	*P*			$3,850
Italian (17th - 18th)				
MARCKE, Emil van	*P*			$1,155
Belgian (1797 - 1839)				
MARCKE DE LUMMEN, Emile v.	*P*	$1,045	$6,288	$13,200
French (1827 - 1890)				
MARCKS, Gerhard	*S*	$4,620	$27,060	$49,500
German (1889 -)				
MARCO DEL PINO, (Attributed)	*P*			$935
Italian (1525 - 1588)				
MARCOLA, Giovanni B. (Circle)	*D*			$1,540
Italian (1711 - 1780)				
MARCOLA, Marco	*D*			$880
Italian (1740 - 1793)				

D=Drawing, P=Painting, S=Sculpture, W=Watercolor

		Current Price Range		
		Low	Mean	High

		Low	Mean	High
MARCON, Charles French (1920 -)	*P*	$11,000	$11,000	$11,000
MARCONI, Rocco (Attrib.) Italian (? - 1529)	*P*			$14,300
MARCOUSSIS, Louis French (1883 - 1941)	*P*			$99,000
MARCUS, Peter American (1889 - 1934)	*P*			$605
MARD, Paul French (20th -)	*P*			$523
MARDEN, Brice American (1938 -)	*D*	$3,850	$49,940	$220,000
	P	$110,000	$553,667	$1.100M
	W			$165,000
MAREC, Victor French (1862 - 1920)	*P*			$660
MARESCA, M. Italian (1865 -)	*P*	$303	$413	$523
MARESCA, T. (?)	*P*			$198
MARET, Belgian (20th -)	*P*			$165
MARGO, Boris American (1902 -)	*D*	$880	$2,640	$3,520
MARGOULIES, Berta American (1907 -)	*S*			$715
MARGRITTE, Rene Belgian (1898 -)	*D*			$4,070
MARGULIES, Joseph American (1896 -)	*P*	$660	$1,141	$1,980
	W	$193	$853	$3,080
MARIA, Walter de (1935 -)	*D*			$4,400
	S			$110,000
MARIAI, Francesco de Italian (1845 - 1908)	*W*			$2,200

D=Drawing, P=Painting, S=Sculpture, W=Watercolor

		Current Price Range		
		Low	Mean	High
MARIANI, Carlo M.	D			$5,500
Italian (1931 -)	P	$9,900	$12,100	$14,300
	W			$5,500
MARIANI, Pompeo	D			$12,100
Italian (1857 - 1927)				
MARIANI, Vincent	P			$385
American (20th -)				
MARIATTI, A.	D			$138
(?)				
MARIE, Jacques	P			$3,575
French (19th - 20th)				
MARIESCHI, Jacopo (Attrib.)	P	$33,000	$42,625	$52,250
Italian (1711 - 1791)				
MARIESCHI, Jacopo (Circle)	P			$3,300
Italian (1711 - 1791)				
MARIESCHI, Michele	P	$121,000	$170,500	$220,000
Italian (1696 - 1743)				
MARIESCHI, Michele (Circle)	P			$14,300
Italian (1696 - 1743)				
MARIESCHI, Michele (Follower)	P			$5,500
Italian (1696 - 1743)				
MARIESCHI, Michele (School)	P	$2,860	$6,930	$11,000
Italian (1696 - 1743)				
MARIESCHI, Michele (Studio)	P			$36,300
Italian (1696 - 1743)				
MARIESCHI, Michele (Style)	P			$2,090
Italian (1696 - 1743)				
MARIN, John	D	$3,850	$9,717	$19,800
American (1870 - 1953)	W	$7,700	$39,859	$165,000
MARIN, Joseph C	D			$19,800
French (1759 - 1834)				
MARINELLI, Vincenzo	P			$4,180
Italian (1820 - 1892)				
MARINI, Leonardo	D	$1,430	$4,807	$16,500
Italian (1730 - 1797)				

D=Drawing, P=Painting, S=Sculpture, W=Watercolor

		Current Price Range		
		Low	Mean	High
MARINI, Marino	*D*	$1,320	$8,140	$12,100
Italian (1901 -)	*P*	$110	$95,480	$308,000
	S	$17,600	$494,935	$2.200M
	W	$18,700	$36,190	$57,200
MARINKO, George	*D*	$880	$1,595	$2,310
American (1908 - 1989)	*P*	$330	$1,063	$1,760
MARIOTON, Eugene	*S*	$880	$908	$935
French (1854 - 1925)				
MARIS, Jacob	*P*	$2,640	$31,423	$88,000
Dutch (1837 - 1899)				
MARIS, Willem	*P*	$495	$5,775	$15,400
Dutch (1844 - 1910)	*W*			$1,320
MARISOL,	*D*	$2,860	$3,520	$4,180
American (1930 -)				
MARIZON, Armand	*P*			$1,320
American (?)				
MARK, Brenda	*P*			$2,200
Scottish (19th - 20th)				
MARKART, Hans	*P*			$2,420
(1840 - 1883)				
MARKE, Emile von	*P*			$165
(?)				
MARKHAM, Charles C.	*P*			$9,900
American (1837 - 1907)				
MARKHAM, Kyra	*P*	$275	$1,311	$2,310
American (1891 -)				
MARKO, Karl	*P*	$3,575	$5,088	$6,600
Hungarian (1822 - 1891)				
MARKOV, Helena	*D*			$550
(?)				
MARKS, Graham	*S*	$3,300	$3,740	$4,180
(20th -)				
MARKS, Henry S.	*P*			$2,640
British (1829 - 1898)				

D=Drawing, P=Painting, S=Sculpture, W=Watercolor

		Current Price Range		
		Low	Mean	High

		Low	Mean	High
MARKS, Henry S. (Style) British (1829 - 1898)	*P*			$1,650
MARKS, W. P. (?)	*P*			$385
MARLOTTI, E. Italian (20th -)	*P*			$330
MARLOW, William British (1740 - 1813)	*D*			$3,960
MARLOW, William (Circle) British (1740 - 1813)	*P*			$1,320
MARNY, Paul British (1829 - 1914)	*W*	$440	$706	$1,210
MARONIEZ, George P. French (1865 -)	*P*	$1,100	$1,100	$1,100
MARPLE, William L. American (1827 - 1910)	*P*	$468	$853	$1,540
MARQUES, Francisco D. y Spanish (1842 - 1920)	*P*			$8,800
MARQUET, Albert French (1875 - 1947)	*D*	$715	$1,494	$3,190
	P	$30,800	$271,446	$506,000
	W	$1,430	$12,107	$22,000
MARR, Carl von (Attrib.) German (? - 1936)	*D*			$200
MARREL, Jacob (Attrib.) Dutch (1614 - 1681)	*P*			$12,100
MARSANS, Luis (20th -)	*P*			$16,500
MARSCHALL, Nicola American (1829 - 1917)	*P*			$1,320
MARSDEN, David American (19th - 20th)	*P*	$825	$1,183	$1,540
MARSH, Pearl American (20th -)	*W*	$165	$220	$275
MARSH, Reginald	*D*	$330	$3,639	$19,800

D=Drawing, P=Painting, S=Sculpture, W=Watercolor

		Current Price Range		
		Low	Mean	High

MARSH, Reginald	*P*	$990	$37,921	$363,000
American (1889 - 1954)	*W*	$330	$6,138	$15,400
MARSHALL, Albert S.	*P*			$303
American (20th -)				
MARSHALL, Ben	*P*	$3,575	$21,588	$39,600
German (1768 - 1834)				
MARSHALL, Ben (Follower)	*P*			$13,200
German (1768 - 1834)				
MARSHALL, Ben (Manner)	*P*			$2,200
German (1768 - 1834)				
MARSHALL, Clark S.	*P*			$250
American (?)				
MARSHALL, Frank W.	*P*	$248	$399	$550
American (1866 - 1930)				
MARSHALL, L. J.	*P*			$1,430
American (20th -)				
MARSHALL, Roberto A. K.	*W*	$1,430	$1,705	$1,980
British (1849 - 1902)				
MARSHALL, Thomas F.	*P*			$6,600
British (1818 - 1878)				
MARSTON, Richard	*P*			$138
American (1842 - 1917)				
MARTAIS, Philippe	*W*			$385
French (20th -)				
MARTEL, Paul J.	*P*			$715
American (1879 - 1942)				
MARTELLY, John de	*P*			$1,760
American (1903 -)				
MARTENS, Ernst E.	*P*			$2,750
French (19th - 20th)				
MARTENS, W.	*P*			$18,700
(17th -)				
MARTENS, W. T.	*P*			$385
French (19th -)				
MARTENS, Willem J.	*P*			$7,700
Dutch (1838 - 1895)				

D=Drawing, P=Painting, S=Sculpture, W=Watercolor

		Current Price Range		
		Low	Mean	High
MARTENS, Willy Dutch (1856 - 1927)	P			$1,760
MARTIN, Agnes American (1912 -)	D	$17,600	$32,560	$44,000
	P	$24,200	$155,711	$352,000
	S	$264,000	$315,333	$385,000
	W			$26,400
MARTIN, Benito Q. Argentine (1890 - 1977)	P	$5,500	$11,660	$19,800
MARTIN, C. F. American (19th - 20th)	P			$165
MARTIN, David British (1737 - 1798)	P	$14,300	$29,333	$49,500
MARTIN, E. American (19th -)	P			$154
MARTIN, E. Spanish (19th -)	P			$2,860
MARTIN, Etienne French (1858 - 1945)	S			$17,600
MARTIN, Fletcher American (1904 - 1979)	D			$1,705
	P	$220	$18,625	$60,500
MARTIN, Fritz German (1859 -)	P			$2,200
MARTIN, H. British (19th -)	W			$303
MARTIN, Harry H. (Attrib.) American (19th -)	P			$850
MARTIN, Henri French (1860 - 1943)	P	$6,600	$155,472	$632,500
MARTIN, Homer D. American (1836 - 1897)	D			$248
	P	$1,210	$4,895	$14,300
MARTIN, J. American (20th -)	P			$1,650
MARTIN, J. British (18th - 19th)	W			$523

D=Drawing, P=Painting, S=Sculpture, W=Watercolor

		Current Price Range		
		Low	Mean	High

		Low	Mean	High
MARTIN, J. Edward B.	*P*			$3,300
American (20th -)				
MARTIN, J. H.	*P*			$330
American (19th -)				
MARTIN, J. R.	*P*			$45,100
British (19th -)				
MARTIN, Knox	*P*			$1,870
American (1923 -)	*S*			$440
	W			$462
MARTIN, Maurice	*P*			$1,870
French (1894 - 1978)				
MARTIN, Nancy	*W*			$330
American (1906 -)				
MARTIN, Scott	*P*			$2,970
(20th -)				
MARTIN, Sylvester	*P*	$2,750	$6,325	$9,900
British (1856 - 1906)				
MARTIN, Thomas M.	*P*	$330	$770	$1,210
Canadian (1838 - 1934)				
MARTIN, William	*P*	$770	$935	$1,100
British (19th -)	*W*			$1,430
MARTIN-DELESTRE, Adolphe A.	*P*			$3,025
French (1823 - 1858)				
MARTIN-FERRIERES, Jac	*P*	$3,300	$10,880	$33,000
French (1893 - 1974)				
MARTIN-KAVEL, Francois	*P*	$550	$5,060	$7,700
French (19th -)				
MARTINDALE, G. Thomas	*P*			$7,700
British (19th -)				
MARTINDALE, Percy H.	*P*			$2,640
British (1869 -)				
MARTINELLI, Giovanni	*P*	$2,860	$5,005	$7,150
Italian (1610 - 1659)				
MARTINETTI, Maria	*P*			$19,800

D=Drawing, P=Painting, S=Sculpture, W=Watercolor

		Current Price Range		
		Low	Mean	High

		Low	Mean	High
MARTINETTI, Maria	W			$3,300
Italian (1864 -)				
MARTINEZ,	P			$303
(?)				
MARTINEZ, Alfredo R.	D			$5,500
Mexican (1872 - 1946)	P	$28,600	$39,875	$46,200
	W			$4,400
MARTINEZ, F. E.	P			$1,320
Spanish (19th - 20th)	W			$1,320
MARTINEZ, J.	P			$1,540
European (19th -)				
MARTINEZ, John Paul	P			$550
(?)				
MARTINEZ, Jose I.	P			$7,700
Spanish (1879 -)				
MARTINEZ, Pedro-Luis	P			$4,675
Cuban (?)				
MARTINEZ, Ricardo	P	$4,400	$17,200	$35,200
Mexican (1918 -)				
MARTINEZ, Xavier	D			$413
American (1869 - 1943)	P	$2,750	$5,225	$7,700
	W	$825	$880	$935
MARTINI, J. D.	P			$231
(?)				
MARTINI, M.	W			$220
American (?)				
MARTINIERE, Constance	P			$132,000
French (1755 - 1821)				
MARTINO, Antonio P.	P	$770	$2,732	$5,600
American (1902 - 1988)				
MARTINO, Babette	P	$400	$513	$625
(?)				
MARTINO, Eduardo di	P			$193
Italian (1838 - 1912)				

D=Drawing, P=Painting, S=Sculpture, W=Watercolor

		Current Price Range		
		Low	Mean	High

		Low	Mean	High
MARTINO, Eva M. American (20th -)	P	$150	$282	$413
MARTINO, Giovanni American (1908 -)	P	$275	$1,118	$2,860
MARTINO, Nina F. (?)	P			$335
MARTINS, Maria Brazilian (1900 -)	S			$11,550
MARTINUS, Elsa (20th -)	S	$4,400	$5,225	$6,050
MARTOSS, Ivan (Attrib.) Russian (1754 -)	D			$4,400
MARTSZEN, Jan Dutch (17th -)	P			$9,350
MARUCCI, Lucio (?)	W			$2,200
MARUSSIG, Anton Austrian (1868 - 1925)	P			$1,100
MARX, Alphonse French (19th -)	P			$9,900
MARX, Johann German (1866 -)	P			$220
MARX, Lucy American (20th -)	P			$220
MARYAN, Burstein P. French (1927 -)	D P	 $4,950	 $6,875	$10,450 $8,800
MARYINSSEN, European (?)	P			$638
MARZELLE, Jean French (1916 -)	P			$1,760
MARZI, Ergio Italian (19th -)	P			$2,200
MARZOLO, Leo A. American (1887 -)	P			$990
MASCART, Gustave French (19th -)	P	$8,250	$8,525	$8,800

D=Drawing, P=Painting, S=Sculpture, W=Watercolor

		Current Price Range		
		Low	Mean	High
MASEREEL, Frans	D			$990
Belgian (1889 - 1971)				
MASO DA SAN FRIANO,	D			$16,500
Italian (1536 - 1571)				
MASON, Frank H. (Attrib.)	P			$660
British (1876 - 1965)				
MASON, Frank R.	W			$770
(20th -)				
MASON, George F.	W			$880
British (1850 - 1915)				
MASON, J. Vincent	P			$193
American (20th -)				
MASON, Lowell	P			$1,100
American (20th -)				
MASON, Maud M.	P	$605	$1,980	$3,025
American (20th -)				
MASON, Roy M.	P	$330	$1,210	$2,090
American (1886 - 1972)				
MASON, William S.	P	$1,210	$1,705	$2,200
American (1824 - 1864)				
MASONI, Fausto	P			$440
(?)				
MASSANI, Pompeo	P	$468	$6,353	$13,200
Italian (1850 - 1920)				
MASSARI, Lucio	D			$6,050
Italian (1569 - 1633)				
MASSARI, Lucio (Circle)	P			$4,400
Italian (1569 - 1633)				
MASSON,	P			$3,520
French (19th -)				
MASSON, Andre	D	$14,850	$50,463	$88,000
French (1896 -)	P	$46,200	$266,640	$605,000
	S			$14,300
	W	$99,000	$110,000	$121,000

D=Drawing, P=Painting, S=Sculpture, W=Watercolor

		Low	Current Price Range Mean	High
MASSON, Andre (After)	*P*			$16,500
French (1896 -)	*S*			$2,200
MASSON, Clovis E.	*S*	$990	$1,320	$1,650
French (1838 - 1913)				
MASSON, Emil	*W*			$121
American (19th -)				
MASSON, Jules E.	*S*			$1,650
French (1871 -)				
MASSYS, Quentin (Circle)	*P*	$3,850	$4,125	$4,400
Flemish (1466 - 1530)				
MAST, Gerald	*W*			$160
American (1908 - 1971)				
MASTENBROEK, Johann H. van	*D*			$1,320
Dutch (1875 -)	*P*	$880	$3,557	$8,800
	W			$1,210
MASTER, Of 1518 (Circle)	*P*			$4,180
(16th -)				
MASTER, Of A. (Attrib.)	*D*			$2,420
Spanish (16th -)				
MASTER, Of Annunciation (Att.)	*P*			$6,600
(17th - 18th)				
MASTER, Of B. B.	*P*			$82,500
(17th -)				
MASTER, Of Fem. Half Lengths	*P*	$8,800	$31,900	$55,000
Flemish (16th -)				
MASTER, Of Frankfort	*P*			$46,750
(15th - 16th)				
MASTER, Of Ghislieri Apse	*W*			$23,100
(16th -)				
MASTER, Of Greenville Tondo	*P*			$71,500
(16th -)				
MASTER, Of Hermitage	*D*	$14,300	$16,500	$18,700
(?)				
MASTER, Of Johnson Tabernacle	*P*			$20,900
(15th -)				

D=Drawing, P=Painting, S=Sculpture, W=Watercolor

		Current Price Range		
		Low	Mean	High

		Low	Mean	High
MASTER, Of Judgement of Sol. (17th -)	*P*			$38,500
MASTER, Of Langezenn (15th -)	*P*			$22,000
MASTER, Of Leonardesque Fem. (16th -)	*P*			$385,000
MASTER, Of Mag. Legend Dutch (?)	*P*			$220,000
MASTER, Of Mansi Magdalene (?)	*P*			$12,000
MASTER, Of Naumberg Madonna (15th -)	*P*	$25,300	$40,150	$55,000
MASTER, Of Panzano Triptych Italian (?)	*P*			$176,000
MASTER, Of Saint Giles (Circle) (?)	*P*			$3,850
MASTER, Of Saint-Sang (Circle) (16th -)	*P*			$41,250
MASTER, Of The Parrot Flemish (16th -)	*P*			$16,500
MASTER OF MILLER TONDO, Italian (15th -)	*P*			$275,000
MASTER OF NATIVITY, (15th -)	*P*			$52,250
MASTON, Robert T. American (20th -)	*P*			$468
MASUROUSKY, Gregory French (1929 -)	*D*			$825
MATANIA, Fortunino Italian (1881 -)	*D*	$250	$675	$1,100
MATHEWS, Arthur American (1860 - 1945)	*W*	$110	$8,855	$17,600
MATHEWS, John C. British (1884 - 1912)	*P*			$5,220
MATHEWS, S. E. (19th - 20th)	*P*			$303

D=Drawing, P=Painting, S=Sculpture, W=Watercolor

		Current Price Range		
		Low	Mean	High

		Low	Mean	High
MATHEWSON, Frank C.	*P*	$193	$776	$2,750
American (1862 - 1941)				
MATHIEU, Georges	*D*	$7,700	$7,700	$7,700
French (1921 -)	*P*	$770	$63,184	$132,000
	W			$11,000
MATHONAT, Alexis (Attrib.)	*P*			$550
French (1832 -)				
MATILLA, Segundo	*P*			$5,500
Spanish (19th -)				
MATISSE, Auguste	*P*			$550
French (1866 - 1931)				
MATISSE, Henri	*D*	$9,900	$197,770	$990,000
French (1869 - 1954)	*P*	$319,000	$2.675M	$12.375M
	S	$3,850	$805,261	$4.180M
	W	$34,100	$620,033	$1.650M
MATISSE, Henri (After)	*S*	$4,950	$5,317	$5,775
French (1869 - 1954)				
MATSON, Victor	*P*	$220	$321	$523
American (20th -)				
MATTA,	*D*	$3,575	$23,973	$187,000
Chilean (1911 -)	*P*	$12,100	$134,383	$1.155M
	W	$6,050	$6,600	$7,150
MATTEI, Antonio	*P*	$176	$193	$209
American (20th -)				
MATTEIS, Paolo de	*P*			$35,200
Italian (1662 - 1728)				
MATTHEWS, Anna L. (Attrib.)	*W*	$100	$163	$225
American (1882 -)				
MATTHEWS, Ferdinand	*P*			$358
American (1854 - 1938)				
MATTHEWS, George	*P*			$275
American (20th -)				

D=Drawing, P=Painting, S=Sculpture, W=Watercolor

		Current Price Range		
		Low	Mean	High
MATTHEWS, Michael	*P*	$138	$179	$220
British (1933 -)				
MATTHEWS, Paul	*P*			$143
American (20th -)				
MATTHEWS, William F.	*P*	$330	$2,393	$5,830
American (1878 -)				
MATTHIASDOTTIR, Louisa	*D*			$990
(20th -)				
MATTOIN, Henri	*P*			$275
French (19th - 20th)				
MATTSON, Henry	*P*			$935
American (1877 - 1971)				
MATULKA, Jan	*D*			$1,100
American (1890 - 1972)	*P*	$2,200	$8,818	$46,750
MATZ, E. D.	*P*			$275
American (20th -)				
MAU,	*S*			$248
(?)				
MAUBERT, James (Attrib.)	*P*			$11,000
British (? - 1746)				
MAUER, Sascha	*W*			$110
American (1897 - 1961)				
MAUFRA, Maxime	*D*			$770
French (1861 - 1918)	*P*	$2,750	$41,305	$82,500
MAURER, Alfred H.	*P*	$7,700	$44,990	$154,000
American (1868 - 1932)	*W*	$462	$9,332	$19,800
MAURER, H.	*P*			$143
German (20th -)				
MAURER, Louis	*P*			$3,520
American (1852 - 1932)	*W*			$2,310
MAURER, M.	*W*			$138
American (20th -)				
MAURIER, Georges L. M. B. du	*D*			$880
French (1834 - 1896)				

D=Drawing, P=Painting, S=Sculpture, W=Watercolor

		Current Price Range	
		Low	Mean	High
---	---	---	---	---

		Low	Mean	High
MAURY, Francois	*P*			$1,540
French (1861 - 1933)				
MAUVE, Anton	*D*			$165
Dutch (1838 - 1888)	*P*	$770	$6,288	$16,500
MAUZEY, Merritt	*P*			$2,860
American (1898 - 1975)				
MAX, Peter	*D*			$220
American (1937 -)	*P*			$4,180
MAXENCE, Edgard	*D*			$7,150
French (1871 - 1954)				
MAXFIELD, Clara	*W*	$440	$495	$550
American (1879 - 1959)				
MAXFIELD, James E.	*P*	$605	$1,403	$2,200
American (1848 -)				
MAY, Philip W.	*D*	$330	$385	$440
British (1864 - 1903)				
MAYAN, Earl	*P*			$248
American (?)	*W*			$450
MAYBRIDGE, Everett	*P*			$303
(?)				
MAYBURY, F.	*P*			$340
(?)				
MAYER, Constant	*P*			$110
American (1829 - 1911)				
MAYER, Frank B.	*P*	$1,760	$6,930	$12,100
American (1827 - 1899)				
MAYER, Peter Bela	*P*	$770	$2,294	$6,600
American (1888 -)				
MAYER, William C.	*P*			$7,700
American (20th -)				
MAYERNIK, Ken	*S*	$770	$1,235	$1,700
American (20th -)				
MAYGER, Chris	*W*			$550
(20th -)				

D=Drawing, P=Painting, S=Sculpture, W=Watercolor

		Current Price Range		
		Low	Mean	High

MAYHEW, Nell Brooker	*P*	$413	$702	$990
American (1876 - 1940)				
MAYHEW, Pat	*P*			$110
(?)				
MAYNARD, E.	*P*			$176
(?)				
MAYNARD, George W.	*D*			$1,650
American (1843 - 1923)	*P*	$165	$1,632	$4,180
MAYNARD, Richard F.	*P*			$880
American (1875 -)				
MAYNE, A.	*P*			$110
American (19th - 20th)				
MAYOKOK,	*P*			$468
American (?)				
MAYR, K. V.	*P*			$1,430
European (19th - 20th)				
MAZE, Paul	*D*			$880
French (1887 - 1979)	*W*			$715
MAZEROLLE, Alexis J.	*P*			$3,300
French (1826 - 1889)				
MAZETTI,	*P*			$110
Italian (20th -)				
MAZOT, Angeline	*W*			$10,450
French (19th -)				
MAZOTTI, R.	*P*			$2,200
(?)				
MAZUHI, D.	*P*			$138
European (20th -)				
MAZZANOVICH, Lawrence	*P*	$1,650	$5,771	$11,000
American (1872 - 1946)				
MAZZANTI, Lodovico	*P*	$4,950	$6,050	$7,150
Italian (1679 - 1775)				
MAZZOLA, Filippo	*P*			$44,000
Italian (1460 - 1505)				

D=Drawing, P=Painting, S=Sculpture, W=Watercolor

		Current Price Range		
		Low	Mean	High
MAZZOLA, Filippo (Attrib.)	P			$22,000
Italian (1460 - 1505)				
MAZZOLA, Francesco M.	D			$6,600
Italian (1503 - 1540)				
MAZZOLA, Francesco M. (After)	P	$6,600	$17,600	$28,600
Italian (1503 - 1540)				
MAZZOLA-BEDOLI, Giro. (Cir.)	P			$3,025
Italian (?)				
MAZZOLINI, G.	P	$3,080	$7,480	$13,750
Italian (19th -)				
MAZZOLINI, Guiseppe	P	$3,080	$3,465	$3,850
Italian (1748 - 1838)				
MAZZOTTA, Federico	P			$6,600
Italian (19th -)				
McADAM, J. W.	P			$385
American (20th -)				
McAFEE, Ila	P			$660
American (1900 -)				
McARTHUR, C.	W			$187
British (19th -)				
McATEER,	P			$330
European (19th -)				
McAULIFFE, James J.	P	$715	$4,534	$12,650
American (1848 - 1921)				
McBEY, James	D			$495
British (1883 - 1959)	W	$385	$675	$1,375
McCALLION, Peter	P			$688
American (19th -)				
McCALLION, Peter (Attrib.)	P			$550
American (19th -)				
McCANN, C. Barton	P			$110
American (?)				
McCANN, Gerald P.	P			$2,200
American (1916 -)				
McCANN, Henry (Attrib.)	P			$1,650
(19th -)				

D=Drawing, P=Painting, S=Sculpture, W=Watercolor

		Current Price Range		
		Low	Mean	High
McCARTAN, Edward	*S*	$2,200	$17,600	$44,000
American (1879 -)				
McCARTER, Henry	*P*	$3,300	$5,500	$8,250
American (1866 - 1942)	*W*	$143	$306	$468
McCARTHY, Francis	*D*			$138
American (20th -)	*P*			$16,500
	W	$110	$220	$468
McCARTHY, Frank	*P*	$8,250	$25,465	$55,000
American (1924 -)				
McCARTHY, Jack	*S*			$825
American (20th -)				
McCARTHY, Ralph	*P*			$275
American (20th -)				
McCARTNEY, Jack	*P*			$715
American (1893 - 1976)				
McCAW, Dan	*P*	$3,080	$3,740	$4,950
American (1942 -)				
McCHESNEY, Clara T.	*P*			$165
American (1860 - 1928)				
McCLARD, Michael	*P*			$660
(20th -)				
McCLEAN, Blanche	*P*			$440
American (19th - 20th)				
McCLEARY, D.	*P*			$413
American (20th -)				
McCLINTOCK, Lucy	*P*			$2,420
American (20th -)				
McCLOSKEY, James B.	*P*	$468	$894	$1,320
American (1925 -)				
McCLOUD,	*P*			$1,045
American (20th -)				
McCLURE, Lousile H.	*P*			$193
American (20th -)				
McCLUSKY, John	*P*			$413
American (20th -)				

D=Drawing, P=Painting, S=Sculpture, W=Watercolor

| | | Current Price Range | | |
		Low	Mean	High
McCLYMONT, John	*P*			$770
American (1858 - 1934)				
McCOLLUM, Elizabeth G.	*P*			$385
American (20th -)				
McCOLVIN, John	*P*	$248	$317	$385
British (19th -)				
McCOMAS, Eugenia F. B.	*P*			$358
American (1886 - 1982)				
McCOMAS, Francis J.	*D*			$16,500
American (1875 - 1938)	*W*	$2,200	$2,750	$3,300
McCONKEY, William	*P*			$4,675
(19th -)				
McCONNELL, Emlen	*P*			$880
American (1872 - 1947)	*W*			$1,400
McCONNELL, George	*P*	$110	$501	$2,200
American (1852 - 1929)				
McCORD, Charles H.	*P*			$319
American (?)				
McCORD, George H.	*P*	$440	$2,086	$5,500
American (1848 - 1909)	*W*	$275	$275	$275
McCORD, Mary	*W*			$605
American (?)				
McCORMICK, Arthur D.	*P*			$3,575
British (1860 - 1943)				
McCORMICK, Howard	*P*			$220
American (1875 - 1943)				
McCOY, John W.	*W*			$220
American (1910 -)				
McCOY, Pat D.	*P*			$248
American (20th -)				
McCOY, Wilton	*P*	$523	$592	$660
American (20th -)				
McCRACKEN, John	*P*	$4,620	$11,660	$18,700
American (1934 -)				

D=Drawing, P=Painting, S=Sculpture, W=Watercolor

		Current Price Range		
		Low	Mean	High
McCRADY, John	P			$3,300
American (1911 - 1968)				
McCREA, S. Harkness	P	$220	$688	$1,100
American (1867 -)				
McCULLENN, Mark	S			$110
(20th -)				
McCULLOCH, Horatio	P	$1,100	$3,575	$6,050
Scottish (1805 - 1867)				
McCULVIN, T.	P			$715
(?)				
McDERMITT, William T.	P			$880
American (1884 - 1961)	W	$358	$454	$550
McDERMOTT, David (Et al.)	P	$5,280	$14,696	$24,200
(20th -)	S			$8,800
McDOUGALL, Walter H.	W			$275
American (19th - 20th)				
McDUFF, Frederick	P			$3,300
American (19th - 20th)				
McENTEE, Jervis	D	$138	$506	$1,650
American (1828 - 1891)	P	$935	$8,265	$35,200
McENTEE, Jervis (Attrib.)	P			$16,500
American (1828 - 1891)				
McEWAN, Tom	P	$1,980	$2,750	$3,520
British (1846 - 1949)				
McEWAN, William	P			$3,300
American (19th - 20th)				
McEWEN,	P			$440
American (?)				
McEWEN, Walter (Attrib.)	P			$770
American (1860 -)				
McFEE, Henry L.	P			$22,000
American (1886 - 1953)				
McFEE, Henry L. (Studio)	P			$110
American (1886 - 1953)				

D=Drawing, P=Painting, S=Sculpture, W=Watercolor

		Current Price Range		
		Low	Mean	High

McGAW, Blanche E.	*P*			$248
American (1874 -)				
McGHIE, John	*P*	$358	$2,929	$5,500
British (1867 - 1941)				
McGINLEY, James	*P*	$275	$275	$275
(?)				
McGINLEY, Louise	*S*			$3,300
American (19th - 20th)				
McGINNIS, Robert	*W*			$1,100
(1926 -)				
McGLYNN, Thomas A.	*P*	$4,950	$8,617	$13,200
American (1878 - 1966)				
McGONIGLE,	*P*			$825
(?)				
McGRATH, Clarence	*P*			$5,225
American (20th -)				
McGREGOR, Robert	*P*			$3,080
British (1848 - 1922)				
McGREW, Ralph B.	*P*			$6,050
American (20th -)				
McILHENNEY, Charles	*P*	$825	$1,128	$1,430
American (1858 - 1908)				
McINTOSH, Amanda	*P*			$1,210
American (1865 - 1941)				
McINTOSH, Pleasant R.	*P*	$935	$1,558	$2,200
American (1897 -)	*W*			$495
McINTYRE, May	*W*			$110
American (?)				
McKAY, Edwin	*P*	$660	$770	$825
American (19th -)				
McKAY, F. H.	*P*			$193
American (20th -)				
McKECHNIE, Alexander B.	*W*			$660
Scottish (1860 - 1930)				
McKENNA, Stephen	*P*	$990	$1,265	$1,540
(20th -)				

D=Drawing, P=Painting, S=Sculpture, W=Watercolor

		Current Price Range		
		Low	Mean	High
McKENZIE, Robert T.	S	$1,650	$8,388	$24,200
American (1867 -)				
McKERSON, V. D.	D			$1,100
American (19th -)				
McKEY, Edward M.	P			$2,200
American (? - 1918)				
McKICKARD, James P.	P			$352
American (?)				
McKIE, Todd	W			$550
(20th -)				
McKILLOP, William	P			$1,320
American (20th -)				
McKINLEY, James	P			$302
American (20th -)				
McKNIGHT, Dodge	W			$2,090
American (1860 - 1950)				
McLAUGHLIN, C. J.	P			$275
(?)				
McLAUGHLIN, John	P	$18,700	$41,861	$60,500
(20th -)				
McLAUGHLIN, Nancy	D			$660
American (20th -)				
McLEARY, Bonnie	S			$7,150
American (1890 -)				
McLELLAN, Ralph	P			$12,100
American (?)				
McMAHN, William F.	P			$2,310
(?)				
McMAHON, Franklin	D	$154	$176	$198
American (20th -)				
McMAHON, Mike	D			$220
(?)				
McMANUS, James G.	P	$523	$1,091	$1,870
American (1882 - 1958)				
McMANUS, James G. (Attrib.)	P			$110
American (1882 - 1958)				

D=Drawing, P=Painting, S=Sculpture, W=Watercolor

		Current Price Range		
		Low	Mean	High

McMANUS, Louis M.	W			$495
American (1898 - 1968)				
McMEIN, Neysa	D			$605
American (1890 - 1949)				
McMULLIN, Jeanette W.	D			$660
American (19th - 20th)				
McNAIR, Duncan	P			$275
(?)				
McNEIL, George	P			$1,760
American (1908 -)				
McNUTT, Bryan	P			$468
American (20th -)	S	$275	$344	$413
McPHEE, Olive	P			$138
American (20th -)				
McPHERSON, Henry	P			$605
(20th -)				
McPHERSON, John	W			$1,100
British (?)				
McQUAID, Lois	P			$121
American (20th -)				
McRICKARD, James P.	P	$225	$225	$225
American (1872 -)				
McVEY, William	S			$523
American (1905 -)				
McVICKAR, Harry W.	D			$385
(19th -)				
MEACCHI, Ricciardo	W			$990
Italian (1856 -)				
MEADE-KING, E.	W			$1,320
(?)				
MEADOR, Joshua	P	$193	$417	$825
American (1911 -)				
MEADOWS, Arthur J.	P	$880	$13,214	$24,200
British (1843 - 1907)				
MEADOWS, Gordon A.	P			$660
British (1868 -)				

D=Drawing, P=Painting, S=Sculpture, W=Watercolor

		Current Price Range		
		Low	Mean	High
MEADOWS, H.	W			$165
British (19th - 20th)				
MEADOWS, J. E. (Attrib.)	P			$3,300
British (1790 - 1874)				
MEADOWS, James E.	P	$3,080	$3,575	$4,400
British (1828 - 1888)	W			$495
MEADOWS, W. G.	P			$3,850
British (19th - 20th)				
MEADOWS, William	P	$1,870	$3,988	$6,600
British (19th - 20th)				
MEAKIN, Lewis H.	P	$880	$2,759	$6,050
American (1850 - 1917)				
MEARS, Henrietta D.	P	$358	$702	$1,045
American (1877 -)	W			$715
MEAUX, J.	P			$330
European (18th - 19th)				
MEDCALF, William	P	$990	$1,595	$2,200
American (20th -)				
MEDINA, John (Attrib.)	P			$1,210
British (1721 - 1796)				
MEDINA-CAMPENY, Xavier	S			$17,600
(20th -)				
MEEGREEN, H. van	D			$385
(?)				
MEEKER, Edwin (Et al.)	D	$770	$911	$1,100
American (19th - 20th)				
MEEKER, Edwin J.	D	$154	$781	$3,520
American (19th -)				
MEEKER, Joseph R.	P	$990	$8,344	$38,500
American (1827 - 1889)				
MEEKER, Joseph R. (Attrib.)	P			$275
American (1827 - 1889)				
MEER, Barend van der	P	$11,000	$39,875	$68,750
Dutch (1659 - 1702)				

D=Drawing, P=Painting, S=Sculpture, W=Watercolor

		Current Price Range		
		Low	Mean	High

		Low	Mean	High
MEER, ELDER, Jan van der	*P*			$11,000
Dutch (1628 - 1691)				
MEERTS, Frans	*P*	$523	$5,108	$16,500
German (1836 - 1896)				
MEESER, Lillian B.	*P*	$880	$1,320	$1,760
American (1864 -)	*W*			$110
MEESON, Dora	*P*			$440
Australian (? - 1955)				
MEGARGEE, Edwin	*P*			$193
American (?)				
MEGARGEE, Lon	*P*	$880	$1,485	$2,090
American (1883 - 1960)				
MEGE, Lydia M.	*W*			$1,320
French (19th -)				
MEHUS, Livio	*P*	$13,200	$16,500	$19,800
Flemish (1630 - 1691)				
MEI, Paolo	*P*			$880
Italian (19th -)				
MEIERRHANS, Joseph	*P*			$1,155
American (1890 -)				
MEIERS, Alan	*W*	$193	$240	$286
(20th -)				
MEIERSDORF, Leo	*P*			$880
American (20th -)	*W*			$275
MEIFREN Y ROIG, Eliseo	*P*			$18,700
Spanish (1859 - 1940)				
MEINDL, Albert	*P*	$248	$784	$1,320
Austrian (1891 - 1967)				
MEIRA, Monica	*P*			$2,750
Colombian (1949 -)				
MEISELS, Marvin	*P*			$468
American (20th -)				
MEISSEN,	*S*			$1,100
(?)				

D=Drawing, P=Painting, S=Sculpture, W=Watercolor

		Current Price Range		
		Low	Mean	High
MEISSNER, Adolf E.	P	$1,650	$14,025	$26,400
German (1837 - 1902)				
MEISSONIER, Jean C.	P			$55,000
French (1848 - 1917)	W			$2,090
MEISSONIER, Jean L. E.	D			$1,320
French (1815 - 1891)	P	$3,300	$8,140	$12,100
	S			$11,000
MEISSONIER, Jean L. E. (After)	P			$165
French (1815 - 1891)				
MEISSONIER, Jean L. E. (Attrib.)	P	$1,650	$2,347	$3,300
French (1815 - 1891)				
MEISSONIER, Jean L. E. (Circle)	D			$3,520
French (1815 - 1891)				
MEISTER, John	P			$660
(19th - 20th)				
MEKELIN,	P			$4,400
(19th -)				
MELBYE, Fritz S. G.	P			$1,760
Danish (1826 - 1896)				
MELCARTH, Edward	P			$1,100
American (20th -)				
MELCHER, George	P			$3,850
American (1881 - 1975)				
MELCHERS, Julius Gari	P	$15,400	$15,950	$16,500
American (1860 - 1932)				
MELDOLLA, Andrea Schiavone	P			$55,000
Italian (1522 - 1563)				
MELEZET,	P			$550,000
(17th -)				
MELLAN, Claude (Circle)	D			$3,850
French (1598 - 1688)				
MELLON, Eleanor M.	S	$330	$523	$1,100
American (1894 - 1979)				
MELLOR, William	P	$1,650	$2,666	$3,980
British (1851 - 1931)				

D=Drawing, P=Painting, S=Sculpture, W=Watercolor

		Current Price Range		
		Low	Mean	High

MELOHS, Charle	*P*			$165
American (20th -)				
MELROSE, Andrew	*P*	$990	$4,983	$13,200
American (1836 - 1901)				
MELTSNER, Paul R.	*P*	$1,650	$1,980	$2,310
American (1905 -)				
MELTZER, Anna E.	*P*			$3,575
American (1896 -)				
MELTZER, Arthur	*P*	$550	$3,025	$4,950
American (1893 -)				
MELVILLE, R.	*P*			$1,100
British (19th -)				
MELVIN, Terry	*W*	$650	$920	$1,210
American (20th -)				
MEMLING, Hans	*P*			$71,500
Flemish (15th -)				
MEMLING, Hans (School)	*P*			$2,640
Flemish (15th -)				
MEMMI, Lippo (Manner)	*P*			$28,600
Italian (14th -)				
MENAGEOT, Francois G.	*P*			$13,200
French (1744 - 1816)				
MENARD, Marie A.	*P*	$1,210	$7,205	$13,200
French (1862 - 1930)				
MENARY, H.	*P*			$440
European (20th -)				
MENASCO, Milton	*P*	$495	$908	$1,320
American (20th -)				
MENASSE, L.	*P*			$2,530
French (18th - 19th)				
MENCHETTI, R.	*P*	$220	$385	$550
(?)				
MENDELSON, George	*P*			$1,980
(19th -)				
MENDENHALL, Jack	*P*			$17,600
American (1937 -)				

D=Drawing, P=Painting, S=Sculpture, W=Watercolor

		Current Price Range	
		Low	Mean	High

		Low	Mean	High
MENDES, Carlos	*P*			$220
Portuguese (19th -)				
MENDIETA, Anna	*P*			$5,500
Cuban (1948 - 1985)				
MENDJISKY, Serge	*P*			$1,870
French (1919 -)				
MENDT, G. P.	*W*			$248
(?)				
MENE, Pierre J.	*S*	$220	$3,413	$17,600
French (1810 - 1879)				
MENE, Pierre J. (After)	*S*	$297	$809	$1,430
French (1810 - 1879)				
MENEGAZZI, Carlo	*W*	$550	$798	$1,045
Italian (19th -)				
MENGER, Edward	*P*			$110
American (19th -)				
MENGS, Anton R. (Circle)	*P*	$3,300	$3,850	$4,400
German (1728 - 1779)				
MENGS, Anton R. (Studio)	*P*			$7,700
German (1728 - 1779)				
MENKES, Sigmund	*P*	$1,320	$4,280	$9,350
Polish (1896 -)				
MENNIE, Florence	*P*			$660
American (20th -)				
MENS, I. van	*P*			$1,980
Dutch (1923 -)				
MENTE, Charles	*W*			$550
American (19th - 20th)				
MENTOR, Will	*P*	$6,600	$7,700	$8,800
(20th -)				
MENZE, J.	*P*			$550
American (19th -)				
MENZEL, Adolf von	*D*	$8,800	$26,583	$60,500
German (1815 - 1905)				
MENZINGER, Hans	*P*			$303
Hungarian (1943 -)				

D=Drawing, P=Painting, S=Sculpture, W=Watercolor

		Current Price Range		
		Low	Mean	High

		Low	Mean	High
MENZLER-PEYTON, Bertha	P			$2,860
American (1871 - 1950)				
MERCIE, Marius J. A.	S	$4,675	$7,786	$10,450
French (1845 - 1916)				
MERCIER, Philippe	P			$16,500
French (1689 - 1760)				
MERCIER, Philippe (Attrib.)	P	$9,900	$14,300	$18,700
French (1689 - 1760)				
MERCIER, Philippe (Manner)	P			$6,600
French (1689 - 1760)				
MERCIER, Victor	P			$330
French (1833 -)				
MERCKAERT, Jules	P			$3,575
Belgian (1872 - 1924)				
MERIDA, Carlos	D	$4,400	$4,950	$5,500
Guatemalan (1891 - 1984)	P	$4,400	$20,350	$82,500
	S			$9,900
	W	$6,050	$13,970	$38,500
MERIDITH, Isaac	P			$1,650
American (1878 - 1954)				
MERIMEE, Prosper	W			$1,980
French (1803 - 1870)				
MERK, Eduard	P	$825	$1,100	$1,650
German (1816 - 1888)				
MERLE, Gilbert	P			$413
(?)				
MERLE, Hughes	P	$16,500	$21,633	$27,500
French (1823 - 1881)				
MERLIN, Daniel	P	$165	$4,708	$8,525
French (1861 - 1933)				
MERLIN, James	P			$165
(?)				
MERRIAM, James A.	D			$605
American (1880 - 1951)	P	$220	$571	$1,045

D=Drawing, P=Painting, S=Sculpture, W=Watercolor

		Current Price Range		
		Low	Mean	High
MERRILL, Robert S.	*P*	$138	$509	$880
American (1842 - 1924)				
MERRITT, Anna L.	*P*	$550	$953	$1,320
American (1844 - 1930)				
MERRITT, Warren C.	*W*			$303
American (1897 - 1968)				
MERSFELDER, Jules R.	*P*	$275	$509	$660
American (1865 - 1937)	*W*			$330
MERSON, Luc O.	*P*			$12,100
French (1846 - 1920)				
MERVINE,	*S*			$1,760
(?)				
MERWE, Lvd	*P*			$248
(?)				
MERWIN, Antoinette deForest	*P*			$1,210
American (1861 -)				
MERZ, Mario	*P*			$88,000
Italian (1925 -)				
MESDAG, Hendrick W.	*P*	$1,210	$6,398	$17,600
Dutch (1831 - 1915)				
MESDAG, Hendrick W. (Attrib.)	*P*	$440	$825	$1,210
Dutch (1831 - 1915)	*W*			$220
MESLE, Joseph P.	*P*			$1,100
French (1855 - 1929)				
MESMER, G.	*P*			$990
Swiss (19th -)				
MESPLES, Paul-E.	*P*			$7,150
French (1849 -)				
MESROS,	*P*			$303
American (19th -)				
MESSENGER, Ivan	*P*			$303
American (1895 - 1983)	*W*			$330
MESSIER, Gregory	*W*			$660
(20th -)				

D=Drawing, P=Painting, S=Sculpture, W=Watercolor

		Current Price Range		
		Low	Mean	High
METCALF, W. J.	*P*			$8,800
British (19th -)				
METCALF, Willard L.	*P*	$2,310	$111,858	$308,000
American (1858 - 1925)	*W*			$1,430
METCALF, Willard L. (Attrib.)	*P*	$1,210	$1,265	$1,320
American (1858 - 1925)				
METCALF, Willard L. (Manner)	*P*			$200
American (1858 - 1925)				
METSU, Gabriel (After)	*P*	$275	$1,742	$3,080
Dutch (1629 - 1667)				
METSU, Gabriel (Circle)	*P*			$10,450
Dutch (1629 - 1667)				
METZ, Francois L. L. de	*P*	$2,420	$2,787	$3,300
French (1814 - 1892)				
METZ, Johann M.	*P*			$41,250
German (1717 - 1790)				
METZ, K.	*P*			$440
(20th -)				
METZER, A.	*P*			$578
American (20th -)				
METZINGER, Jean	*D*	$2,750	$8,938	$17,600
French (1883 - 1956)	*P*	$13,200	$120,707	$632,500
MEUCCI, Michelangelo	*P*	$468	$1,316	$4,400
Italian (19th -)				
MEULEN, Adam van der	*D*	$2,640	$4,070	$5,500
Flemish (1632 - 1690)				
MEULEN, Adam van der (After)	*P*			$2,200
Flemish (1632 - 1690)				
MEULEN, Adam van der (Attrib.)	*P*			$2,475
Flemish (1632 - 1690)				
MEULEN, Adam van der (Circle)	*P*			$3,850
Flemish (1632 - 1690)				
MEULEN, Adam van der (Foll.)	*D*			$715
Flemish (1632 - 1690)				

D=Drawing, P=Painting, S=Sculpture, W=Watercolor

		Current Price Range		
		Low	Mean	High
MEULEN, Franz P. Ter	*P*	$825	$2,626	$4,840
Dutch (1843 - 1927)				
MEUNIER, Constantin	*P*			$440
Belgian (1831 - 1905)	*S*			$2,860
MEUNIER, Georgette	*P*			$770
Belgian (1859 - 1951)				
MEURER, Charles A.	*P*	$385	$4,523	$16,000
American (1865 - 1955)				
MEXICAN SCHOOL 19C,	*P*	$4,125	$23,581	$77,000
Mexican (19th -)				
MEXINER, Ludwig	*P*			$1,870
Bavarian (1828 - 1855)				
MEYER,	*P*			$154
(?)				
MEYER, Adolph C.	*W*			$633
British (1866 - 1919)				
MEYER, Alvin	*S*			$1,650
American (?)				
MEYER, Claus	*P*	$495	$1,458	$2,420
German (1856 - 1919)				
MEYER, Emile	*P*			$16,500
French (19th -)				
MEYER, Ernest	*P*	$165	$337	$550
American (1863 - 1961)				
MEYER, Felicia	*P*	$248	$372	$495
American (1913 -)				
MEYER, Georges	*P*			$1,980
French (19th -)				
MEYER, Herbert	*W*			$330
American (1882 - 1960)				
MEYER, J.	*D*			$1,210
American (19th -)				
MEYER, Louis	*P*			$9,020
Dutch (1809 - 1866)				
MEYER, Louise	*P*			$28,600
German (1789 - 1861)				

D=Drawing, P=Painting, S=Sculpture, W=Watercolor

		Current Price Range		
		Low	Mean	High

MEYER, ELDER, Hendrick (Att.) Dutch (1600 - 1690)	*P*	$1,870	$1,925	$1,980
MEYER, YOUNGER, Hendrick Dutch (1737 - 1793)	*P*			$16,500
MEYER-PYRITZ, Martin A. R. German (1870 -)	*S*			$880
MEYERHEIM, Friedrich E. German (1808 - 1879)	*P*			$3,850
MEYERHEIM, Friedrich E. (Att.) German (1808 - 1879)	*P*			$4,400
MEYERHEIM, Hermann German (1840 - 1880)	*P*			$16,500
MEYERHEIM, Paul German (1842 - 1915)	*P*			$2,200
MEYERHEIM, Wilhelm A. German (1815 - 1882)	*P*			$12,100
MEYERHEIM, Wilhelm A. (Att.) German (1815 - 1882)	*P*			$6,050
MEYEROWITZ, William American (1887 - 1921)	*P*	$550	$1,271	$1,760
MEYERS, Frank H. American (?)	*P*			$990
MEYERS, Jerome American (1867 - 1940)	*P*			$5,500
MEZA, Guillermo Mexican (1921 -)	*P* *W*	$3,300 $1,210	$3,300 $2,761	$3,300 $5,500
MEZZERA, Rosa Italian (1791 - 1826)	*P*			$14,300
MIARTANI, P. British (19th -)	*P*			$2,750
MICALI, G. Italian (20th -)	*W*			$193
MICAS, Jeanne S. N. French (19th -)	*P*			$3,080
MICHAEL, H. (?)	*P*			$990

D=Drawing, P=Painting, S=Sculpture, W=Watercolor

		Current Price Range		
		Low	Mean	High

		Low	Mean	High
MICHAEL, Judy	W			$450
American (20th -)				
MICHAELIS, Arthur	P			$1,045
German (1864 -)				
MICHAELS, Glen	P			$440
(?)				
MICHAELS, S.	P			$495
(?)				
MICHALLON, Achille E. (Attrib.)	P			$3,025
French (1796 - 1822)				
MICHAU, Theobald	P	$2,860	$9,020	$15,400
Flemish (1676 - 1765)				
MICHAU, Theobald (Circle)	P	$5,280	$5,390	$5,500
Flemish (1676 - 1765)				
MICHAUD, Leonie	P			$7,700
French (1873 -)				
MICHAUX, Michael	P			$248
French (20th -)				
MICHEL, Charles	D			$2,420
French (1874 - 1940)	P	$440	$688	$935
MICHEL, Emile	P			$1,100
French (1818 - 1909)				
MICHEL, Georges	P	$1,870	$14,234	$33,000
French (1763 - 1843)				
MICHEL, Robert	S			$10,450
(20th -)				
MICHELANGELO, (After)	D			$22,000
Italian (1475 - 1564)	P			$3,960
MICHELANGELO, (Follower)	D			$25,300
Italian (1475 - 1564)				
MICHIELI, Andrea dei	P			$13,200
Italian (1539 - 1614)				
MICHIELS, Giull	P			$110
Belgian (20th -)				

D=Drawing, P=Painting, S=Sculpture, W=Watercolor

		Current Price Range		
		Low	Mean	High

		Low	Mean	High
MICO, (?)	*P*			$605
MIDDAUGH, Robert B. American (1935 -)	*P*	$440	$523	$605
MIDDENDORF, Helmut German (20th -)	*P* *W*	$2,200	$12,558	$22,000 $2,750
MIDDLETON, C. W. American (19th -)	*P*			$248
MIDDLETON, H. (?)	*P*			$715
MIDDLETON, Stanley G. American (1852 -)	*P*	$193	$564	$935
MIEL, Jan Flemish (1559 - 1663)	*P*	$2,200	$17,600	$33,000
MIEL, Jan (Attrib.) Flemish (1559 - 1663)	*P*			$10,450
MIELICH, Leopold Austrian (1863 - 1929)	*P*			$5,500
MIEREN, (?)	*P*			$303
MIEREVELT, Michiel van Dutch (1567 - 1641)	*P*	$3,300	$7,315	$11,000
MIERIS, Frans van Dutch (1635 - 1681)	*P*	$55,000	$396,000	$726,000
MIERIS, Frans van (Manner) Dutch (1635 - 1681)	*P*			$1,650
MIERIS, Willem van Dutch (1662 - 1747)	*D* *P*	$2,200	$42,350	$7,150 $82,500
MIFFLIN, Lloyd American (1846 - 1921)	*P*			$550
MIGLIARA, Giovanni (Circle) Italian (1785 - 1837)	*P*			$18,700
MIGLIARO, Vincenzo Italian (1858 - 1938)	*P*			$63,250

D=Drawing, P=Painting, S=Sculpture, W=Watercolor

		Current Price Range		
		Low	Mean	High
MIGNARD, Pierre	*P*			$77,000
French (1612 - 1695)				
MIGNARD, Pierre (Attrib.)	*P*	$4,125	$5,958	$7,700
French (1612 - 1695)				
MIGNARD, Pierre (Circle)	*P*	$6,050	$7,425	$8,800
French (1612 - 1695)				
MIGNARD, Pierre (Follower)	*P*	$2,200	$5,317	$11,000
French (1612 - 1695)				
MIGNARD, Pierre (School)	*P*			$2,860
French (1612 - 1695)				
MIGNARD, Pierre (Studio)	*P*			$4,950
French (1612 - 1695)				
MIGNERY, Herb	*S*			$8,000
American (1937 -)				
MIGNON, Abraham	*P*	$11,770	$267,923	$451,000
German (1640 - 1679)				
MIGNON, Abraham (After)	*P*			$3,300
German (1640 - 1679)				
MIGNONE, Leon	*S*			$3,575
Belgian (1847 - 1898)				
MIGNOT, Louis R.	*P*	$385	$16,940	$56,100
American (1831 - 1870)				
MIHAILESEN, D.	*P*			$110
Rumanian (?)				
MIHALY, Livia	*P*			$1,100
Hungarian (20th -)				
MIKKER, Jean C. (Attrib.)	*P*			$1,100
Dutch (1600 - 1664)				
MILANESE SCHOOL 17C,	*D*	$660	$3,355	$6,050
Italian (17th -)	*P*			$19,800
MILANESE SCHOOL 18C,	*D*			$7,150
Italian (18th -)				
MILBOURNE, Henri	*P*	$1,018	$1,032	$1,045
French (1781 - 1826)				
MILDER, Jay	*P*	$1,650	$2,888	$4,125
American (1934 -)				

		Current Price Range		
		Low	Mean	High

MILEHAM, Benjamin	*P*			$330
American (20th -)				
MILES, Courtney L.	*P*			$330
American (20th -)				
MILES, Eugene	*P*	$165	$213	$330
American (20th -)				
MILES, J. C.	*W*			$176
(?)				
MILES, Samuel S.	*P*			$385
American (19th -)				
MILES, Thomas R.	*P*	$880	$1,815	$3,025
British (19th -)				
MILESI, Alessandro	*P*			$3,630
Italian (1856 - 1945)				
MILLAIS, H. Raoul	*P*			$2,750
British (1901 -)				
MILLAIS, Sir John E.	*D*			$1,650
British (1829 - 1896)	*P*	$25,300	$151,360	$407,000
MILLAR, Addison T.	*P*	$523	$8,278	$33,000
American (1860 - 1913)	*W*	$165	$473	$990
MILLAR, H. B.	*P*			$1,430
British (19th - 20th)				
MILLAR, T. H. C.	*P*	$385	$413	$440
American (19th -)				
MILLARD, Charles S.	*W*			$385
American (20th -)				
MILLARES, Manolo	*D*	$22,000	$39,600	$55,000
Spanish (1926 - 1972)	*W*	$60,500	$82,500	$104,500
MILLE, Mark (Attrib.)	*P*	$500	$713	$950
American (20th -)				
MILLER, Alec	*S*			$303
British (20th -)				
MILLER, Alfred J.	*D*			$2,640

D=Drawing, P=Painting, S=Sculpture, W=Watercolor

		Current Price Range		
		Low	Mean	High
MILLER, Alfred J.	*P*	$2,090	$30,116	$137,500
American (1810 - 1874)	*W*			$45,100
MILLER, Alfred J. (Manner)	*P*			$1,760
American (1810 - 1874)				
MILLER, Barse	*P*	$2,475	$2,888	$3,300
American (1904 - 1973)	*W*			$880
MILLER, Blanche E.	*P*			$193
American (20th -)				
MILLER, C. W.	*P*			$3,300
American (20th -)				
MILLER, Carol	*S*			$8,250
American (1933 -)				
MILLER, Charles H.	*P*	$550	$1,014	$1,650
American (1842 - 1922)				
MILLER, Charles K.	*P*			$5,720
(?)				
MILLER, Edith M.	*P*	$165	$207	$248
American (20th -)	*W*			$385
MILLER, Evylena N.	*P*	$110	$1,288	$4,950
American (1888 - 1966)				
MILLER, Francis	*P*			$1,650
American (1885 - 1930)				
MILLER, Henry	*W*			$1,210
American (20th -)				
MILLER, J. A.	*P*			$825
(20th -)				
MILLER, Jacob	*D*			$275
American (1810 - 1874)				
MILLER, John	*P*			$1,430
American (19th -)				
MILLER, Joseph	*P*			$8,525
German (19th -)				
MILLER, Kate R.	*P*			$1,650
American (1874 - 1929)				

D=Drawing, P=Painting, S=Sculpture, W=Watercolor

		Current Price Range		
		Low	Mean	High

MILLER, Keith	*W*			$1,540
(20th -)				
MILLER, Kenneth H.	*P*	$935	$5,046	$7,700
American (1876 - 1952)				
MILLER, Lester W.	*P*			$132
American (1848 - 1931)				
MILLER, Melvin	*P*			$880
American (1937 -)				
MILLER, Mildred B.	*P*	$265	$633	$1,000
American (1892 -)				
MILLER, R. A.	*P*			$330
American (20th -)				
MILLER, Ralph D.	*P*	$165	$770	$1,980
American (1858 - 1945)				
MILLER, Richard E.	*P*	$330	$151,016	$638,000
American (1875 - 1943)				
MILLER, William R.	*D*	$660	$1,100	$1,540
American (1818 - 1893)	*P*	$550	$2,234	$4,950
	W			$358
MILLER, William R. (Attrib.)	*P*			$550
American (1818 - 1893)				
MILLES, Carl	*S*	$2,200	$35,200	$110,000
Swedish (1875 - 1955)				
MILLESON, Royal H.	*P*	$303	$541	$880
American (1849 -)	*W*			$330
MILLET, Aguste	*P*			$2,640
European (19th - 20th)				
MILLET, Clarence	*P*	$385	$2,017	$3,850
American (1897 - 1959)				
MILLET, Fanny F.	*W*			$248
French (1926 -)				
MILLET, Francis D.	*D*			$880
American (1846 - 1912)	*P*	$2,860	$4,169	$6,325

D=Drawing, P=Painting, S=Sculpture, W=Watercolor

		Current Price Range		
		Low	Mean	High
MILLET, Jean-Francois	D	$990	$18,282	$77,000
French (1814 - 1875)	P	$19,800	$322,300	$797,500
MILLET, Jean-Francois (Attrib.)	D			$1,430
French (1814 - 1875)				
MILLET, Jean-Francois (School)	P			$935
French (1814 - 1875)				
MILLET, Jean-Francois (Style)	P			$7,150
French (1814 - 1875)				
MILLETT, G. Van	P			$275
American (1864 -)				
MILLIER, Arthur H.	W	$303	$592	$880
American (1893 - 1975)				
MILLIERE, Maurice	P			$2,750
French (1871 -)				
MILLMAN, Edward	P			$495
American (1907 - 1964)				
MILLNER, Karl	P			$11,000
German (1825 - 1894)				
MILLNER, Karl (After)	P			$1,100
German (1825 - 1894)				
MILLS, Clark	S			$22,000
American (1810 - 1883)				
MILLS, Kevin	P			$138
(?)				
MILNE, A. (Et al.)	P			$275
American (19th -)	W	$110	$220	$330
MILNER, D.	P			$550
British (19th -)				
MILONE, Giuseppi	P	$440	$660	$880
Italian (19th -)				
MILTLES, Ruth	S			$440
(?)				
MILTON, John	P			$104,500
British (18th -)				

D=Drawing, P=Painting, S=Sculpture, W=Watercolor

		Current Price Range		
		Low	Mean	High

		Low	Mean	High
MILTSNER, Paul	*P*			$660
American (1905 -)				
MIMNAUGH, Terry	*D*	$2,310	$2,505	$2,700
American (20th -)	*P*	$1,210	$3,905	$6,600
MINAUX, Andre	*P*			$713
French (1923 -)				
MINGERS, C.	*P*			$5,060
(?)				
MINGUZZI, Luciano	*S*	$14,300	$28,050	$41,800
Italian (1911 -)				
MINIER, Suzanne	*P*			$5,500
French (1884 -)				
MINNE, Georges	*S*			$3,080
Belgian (1866 - 1941)				
MINOR, Anne R.	*P*	$330	$427	$523
American (1864 -)				
MINOR, Robert C.	*P*	$550	$2,021	$6,600
American (1839 - 1904)				
MINTCHINE, Andre	*P*			$715
Russian (20th -)				
MINTZ, Harry	*P*			$578
American (1907 -)				
MINUJIN, Marta	*S*	$7,700	$8,250	$8,800
Argentine (1943 -)				
MINUMBOC, Rodolfo	*S*			$6,600
Venezuelan (1933 -)				
MIOLA, Camillo	*P*			$3,300
Italian (1840 -)				
MIRA, Alfred S.	*P*	$275	$1,568	$2,860
(20th -)				
MIRALLES, Jose D.	*W*			$3,300
Spanish (1850 - 1900)				
MIRALLES Y GALUP, Francisco	*P*	$14,300	$106,006	$242,000
Spanish (1848 - 1901)				
MIRANDA, Juan C. de (Circle)	*P*			$16,500
(1614 - 1685)				

D=Drawing, P=Painting, S=Sculpture, W=Watercolor

| | | Current Price Range | | |
| --- | --- | Low | Mean | High |

		Low	Mean	High
MIRANDA, R.	*P*			$605
Spanish (19th -)				
MIRKO (BASALDELLA),	*D*			$1,100
Italian (1910 - 1969)	*S*	$825	$1,403	$1,980
MIRO, Joachim	*P*	$1,540	$8,338	$17,600
Spanish (19th - 20th)	*W*	$33,000	$148,500	$264,000
MIRO, Joan	*D*	$3,520	$97,680	$550,000
Spanish (1893 - 1983)	*P*	$2,640	$1.224M	$9.350M
	S	$4,950	$203,546	$550,000
	W	$35,200	$296,195	$2.695M
MIRO, Joan (After)	*S*	$4,400	$9,167	$12,100
Spanish (1893 - 1983)				
MIROU, Anton	*P*			$10,450
Flemish (1586 - 1661)				
MIRRI, Sabina	*W*			$1,320
(20th -)				
MISSIRUIS, S.	*P*			$440
(20th -)				
MITCHELL,	*P*			$770
American (20th -)				
MITCHELL, Alfred R.	*P*	$1,045	$2,743	$4,400
American (1888 - 1972)				
MITCHELL, C. T.	*P*			$110
(19th - 20th)				
MITCHELL, Charles D.	*D*	$385	$413	$440
American (1887 - 1940)				
MITCHELL, Colin S.	*P*			$440
American (?)				
MITCHELL, George B.	*P*	$193	$284	$440
American (1872 - 1966)	*W*			$1,045
MITCHELL, Glen	*P*			$3,300
American (1894 - 1972)				

D=Drawing, P=Painting, S=Sculpture, W=Watercolor

		Current Price Range	
	Low	Mean	High

		Low	Mean	High
MITCHELL, Harry C.	*P*			$605
American (19th -)				
MITCHELL, James A.	*P*	$330	$19,261	$93,500
American (20th -)	*W*	$275	$550	$825
MITCHELL, Joan	*D*			$20,900
American (1926 -)	*P*	$19,800	$184,294	$506,000
	W	$8,800	$14,300	$19,800
MITCHELL, John C.	*P*			$4,180
Scottish (1862 - 1922)				
MITCHELL, Neil	*W*			$385
American (1858 - 1934)				
MITCHELL, Thomas	*P*			$1,760
American (1875 - 1940)				
MITCHELL, William	*P*	$187	$237	$286
British (19th -)				
MIYAKE, K.	*W*			$138
Japanese (19th - 20th)				
MIZEN, Frederick	*P*	$2,800	$3,000	$3,200
American (1888 - 1964)				
MOATTI, C.	*D*			$220
(?)				
MODERSOHN, Otto	*P*			$13,200
German (1865 - 1943)				
MODIGLIANI, Amedeo	*D*	$6,600	$55,393	$357,500
Italian (1884 - 1920)	*P*	$1.430M	$5.236M	$11.550M
	W	$57,750	$83,875	$110,000
MODIUS, K.	*S*			$413
(?)				
MOELLER, Gustave	*P*	$250	$338	$425
American (1881 - 1931)				
MOELLER, Gustave (Attrib.)	*P*	$200	$225	$250
American (1881 - 1931)				
MOELLER, H.	*W*			$110
American (20th -)				

D=Drawing, P=Painting, S=Sculpture, W=Watercolor

		Low	Current Price Range Mean	High
MOELLER, Louis C. American (1855 - 1930)	P	$880	$10,032	$27,500
MOELLER, Louis C. (Attrib.) American (1855 - 1930)	P			$220
MOESSNER, T. F. (Et al.) American (19th -)	D			$770
MOFFAT, Curtis American (1887 - 1949)	P			$1,100
MOFFETT, Ross E. American (1888 - 1971)	P	$440	$848	$1,650
	W	$250	$288	$325
MOHALY, Yolanda Hungarian (1909 - 1978)	P			$3,410
MOHOLY-NAGY, Laszlo Hungarian (1895 - 1946)	D			$4,400
	P	$23,100	$23,650	$24,200
	S	$30,800	$45,650	$60,500
	W			$11,000
MOHREN, Jean German (1876 -)	P	$110	$2,521	$7,150
MOIGNIEZ, Jules French (1835 - 1894)	S	$303	$2,292	$11,000
MOIGNIEZ, Jules (After) French (1835 - 1894)	S	$110	$699	$1,540
MOLA, Pier F. Italian (1612 - 1666)	D			$7,150
	P			$26,400
MOLA, Pier F. (Attrib.) Italian (1612 - 1666)	D			$1,760
	P			$7,700
MOLA, Pier F. (Circle) Italian (1612 - 1666)	P			$20,900
MOLARSKY, Abram American (1883 -)	D			$2,090
	P			$330
MOLARSKY, Maurice American (1885 - 1950)	P	$1,320	$2,823	$4,400

D=Drawing, P=Painting, S=Sculpture, W=Watercolor

		Current Price Range		
		Low	Mean	High

		Low	Mean	High
MOLAS, N. de (?)	*W*			$660
MOLENAER, Claes Flemish (1540 - 1589)	*P*	$14,300	$36,025	$57,750
MOLENAER, Jan M. Dutch (1610 - 1668)	*P*	$3,300	$16,569	$39,600
MOLENAER, Klaes Dutch (1630 - 1676)	*P*			$4,400
MOLES, E. European (19th -)	*P*			$4,400
MOLET, Salvador Spanish (1773 - 1836)	*P*			$99,000
MOLIJN, Pieter Dutch (1595 - 1661)	*P*			$7,700
MOLINARI, Antonio Italian (1665 - 1727)	*P*	$33,000	$35,200	$37,400
MOLINARI, Antonio (Circle) Italian (1665 - 1727)	*D*			$770
MOLINARY, Andres American (1847 - 1915)	*P*			$1,870
MOLINE, A. de French (19th -)	*P*			$27,500
MOLL, A. (?)	*P*			$402
MOLL, Evert Dutch (1878 - 1955)	*P*	$990	$6,545	$12,100
MOLLBACK, Christian Danish (1853 - 1921)	*P*			$358
MOLLER, F. German (19th -)	*P*			$1,760
MOLLER, Olaf American (1903 -)	*P*			$660
MOLLET, Ernest French (1831 - 1902)	*P*			$275
MOLLICK, A. European (19th - 20th)	*P*			$3,850

D=Drawing, P=Painting, S=Sculpture, W=Watercolor

		Current Price Range		
		Low	Mean	High
MOLNAR, R. (?)	P	$330	$440	$550
MOLS, Robert Belgian (1848 - 1903)	P			$2,860
MOLTMAN, E. T. European (19th - 20th)	P			$330
MOLYN, Pieter Dutch (1637 - 1701)	P			$28,600
MOLYNEUX, Edward European (20th -)	P	$1,100	$1,430	$1,980
MOMENT, Barbara American (20th -)	P			$1,210
MOMPER, Joos de Flemish (1564 - 1635)	P	$55,000	$102,667	$176,000
MOMPER, Joos de (Circle) Flemish (1564 - 1635)	P			$8,800
MOMPER I, Philips de Flemish (17th -)	P			$26,400
MONALDI, Paolo Italian (18th -)	P	$13,750	$15,675	$17,600
MONALDI, Paolo (Circle) Italian (18th -)	P			$5,500
MONAMY, Peter British (1689 - 1749)	P			$2,090
MONARD, Louis de French (19th -)	S			$3,520
MONCALVO, Guglielmo G. Italian (1568 - 1625)	D	$2,090	$4,913	$7,150
MONCAYO, E. Latin American (19th - 20th)	P			$110
MONCHABLON, Jean F. French (1855 - 1904)	P	$9,900	$16,115	$30,800
MONDRIAN, Piet Dutch (1872 - 1944)	D	$12,100	$46,642	$159,500
	P	$35,750	$3.211M	$9.625M
	W	$27,500	$94,417	$220,000

D=Drawing, P=Painting, S=Sculpture, W=Watercolor

		Current Price Range		
		Low	Mean	High
MONE, W. le	*D*			$165
French (19th -)				
MONET, Claude	*D*	$297,000	$313,500	$330,000
French (1840 - 1926)	*P*	$605,000	$4.947M	$14.300M
MONFALLET, Adolphe F.	*P*	$2,750	$19,525	$36,300
French (1816 - 1900)				
MONFREID, Georges D. de	*P*			$9,900
French (1856 - 1929)				
MONGE, Luis	*P*			$18,700
Lat. Amer. (20th -)				
MONGIN, Antoine P.	*W*			$12,100
French (1761 - 1827)				
MONGINOT, Charles	*P*	$2,200	$28,417	$63,250
French (1825 - 1900)				
MONI, Louis de	*P*			$11,000
Dutch (1698 - 1771)				
MONKS, John A.	*P*	$550	$1,210	$1,870
American (1850 - 1917)				
MONLEON, Raphael	*P*			$633
Spanish (1847 - 1900)				
MONNICK, Heinz	*P*			$198
(?)				
MONNICKENDAM, J.	*P*			$990
Dutch (19th -)				
MONNICKENDAM, Martin	*P*			$550
Dutch (1874 - 1943)				
MONNICKENDAM, Martin (Att.)	*P*			$330
Dutch (1874 - 1943)				
MONNIER, Henry	*D*			$1,650
French (1805 - 1877)				
MONNOYER, Antoine (Circle)	*P*			$14,300
French (1670 - 1747)				
MONNOYER, Jean-B.	*P*	$33,000	$94,600	$154,000
French (1636 - 1699)				
MONNOYER, Jean-B. (Attrib.)	*P*	$5,500	$11,733	$24,200
French (1636 - 1699)				

D=Drawing, P=Painting, S=Sculpture, W=Watercolor

		Current Price Range	
	Low	Mean	High

		Low	Mean	High
MONNOYER, Jean-B. (Circle) French (1636 - 1699)	P			$6,600
MONNOYER, Jean-B. (Manner) French (1636 - 1699)	P			$3,300
MONOGRAMMIST, GVD Flemish (?)	P			$3,575
MONREAL, Andres (20th -)	P			$2,200
MONSTED, Peder M. Danish (1859 - 1941)	P	$14,300	$34,589	$154,000
MONTAGNA, Bartolommeo (Cir.) Italian (15th - 16th)	P			$71,500
MONTAGUE, A. V. American (20th -)	W			$110
MONTALLIER, Pierre French (1643 - 1697)	P			$8,800
MONTELATICI, Francesco Italian (1600 - 1661)	P			$33,000
MONTEMEZZANO, Francesco Italian (16th - 17th)	P			$6,050
MONTENEGRO, Jose Spanish (19th - 20th)	P	$550	$1,650	$2,750
MONTENEGRO, Roberto Mexican (1881 - 1968)	P	$9,900	$16,500	$22,000
MONTES, R. Spanish (20th -)	P			$358
MONTESI, Carlo Italian (1920 -)	P	$100	$380	$660
MONTESINOS, A. (?)	P			$143
MONTEZIN, Pierre E. French (1874 - 1946)	P	$10,450	$24,907	$60,500
MONTFALLET, Adolphe French (1816 - 1900)	P			$1,760
MONTFORT, Antoine A. French (1802 - 1884)	P			$8,800

D=Drawing, P=Painting, S=Sculpture, W=Watercolor

		Current Price Range		
		Low	Mean	High

		Low	Mean	High
MONTFORT, Octavius (Attrib.) (?)	*W*			$20,900
MONTGOMERY, Alfred American (1857 - 1922)	*P*			$6,050
MONTGOMERY, Hugh J. American (20th -)	*P*			$275
MONTI, A. European (19th -)	*P*			$468
MONTI, Francesco Italian (1646 - 1712)	*P*			$3,300
MONTICELLI, Adolphe French (1824 - 1886)	*P*	$330	$22,227	$74,250
MONTICELLI, Adolphe (After) French (1824 - 1886)	*P*			$440
MONTICELLI, Adolphe (Circle) French (1824 - 1886)	*P*			$5,500
MONTINI, Giovanni Italian (19th -)	*D*			$2,750
MONTOVA, J. American (20th -)	*P*			$715
MONTOYA, Gustavo Mexican (1905 -)	*P*	$3,520	$5,095	$7,150
MONTPEZAT, Henri D. C. de French (1817 - 1859)	*P*			$2,090
MONTULLO, European (19th -)	*P*	$660	$1,430	$2,200
MONTZAIGLE, Edgar de S.P. de French (1867 -)	*W*			$8,800
MONVOISIN, Raymond A. Q. French (1794 - 1870)	*P*			$55,000
MOOERS, Jacob B. (19th -)	*P*			$2,530
MOON, Carl American (1879 - 1948)	*P*			$2,750
MOONELIS, Judy (20th -)	*S*			$2,090

D=Drawing, P=Painting, S=Sculpture, W=Watercolor

		Current Price Range		
		Low	Mean	High
MOOR, Carel de	P			$6,600
Dutch (1656 - 1738)				
MOORE, Albert J.	D			$22,000
British (1841 - 1893)	P	$154,000	$192,500	$231,000
MOORE, B. Robert	P			$1,100
British (20th -)				
MOORE, Benson B.	P	$468	$963	$1,540
American (1882 - 1974)	W			$330
MOORE, Brett F.	P	$358	$1,614	$4,125
American (20th -)				
MOORE, Ernest	P			$110
American (20th -)				
MOORE, Frank M.	P	$2,090	$2,273	$2,530
American (1877 - 1967)				
MOORE, Harry H.	D			$20,900
American (1844 - 1926)				
MOORE, Henry	D	$4,400	$27,060	$77,000
British (1898 - 1986)	P			$29,700
	S	$6,600	$397,550	$4.070M
	W	$7,700	$66,650	$165,000
MOORE, Henry (After)	S			$22,000
British (1898 - 1986)				
MOORE, Henry R.	P			$1,320
British (1831 - 1895)				
MOORE, Henry W.	D			$46,200
American (1879 -)	S			$28,600
	W			$825
MOORE, John	P			$4,400
American (1941 -)	W			$825
MOORE, Josephine	P			$358
American (20th -)				

D=Drawing, P=Painting, S=Sculpture, W=Watercolor

		Current Price Range	
	Low	Mean	High

		Low	Mean	High
MOORE, K. Aubrey	*W*			$110
(?)				
MOORE, Martha	*P*			$495
American (20th -)				
MOORE, Nelson Agustus	*P*	$880	$3,946	$11,000
American (1824 - 1902)				
MOORE, Rebecca S.	*W*			$200
(19th -)				
MOORE, Robert	*P*			$220
American (20th -)	*W*			$231
MOORE, Terry	*P*			$358
American (20th -)				
MOR, Antonis (Circle)	*P*			$16,500
Dutch (1519 - 1575)				
MORA, F. Luis	*D*	$110	$425	$2,475
American (1874 - 1940)	*P*	$495	$2,601	$5,500
	W	$385	$1,139	$2,310
MORA, Joseph J.	*P*			$1,430
American (1876 -)				
MORAGAS Y TORRES, Tomas	*W*			$8,800
Spanish (1837 - 1906)				
MORAHAN, Eugene	*S*			$1,925
American (1869 -)				
MORALES, Armando	*D*	$13,200	$23,320	$35,200
Nicaraguan (1927 -)	*P*	$1,650	$23,163	$66,000
	W	$1,980	$1,980	$1,980
MORALES, Dario	*D*			$33,000
Colombian (1944 -)	*P*			$24,750
	S	$15,400	$23,833	$38,500
MORALES, Luis de	*P*			$15,400
Spanish (1509 - 1586)				
MORALES, Rodolfo	*P*			$33,000
Mexican (1952 -)				

D=Drawing, P=Painting, S=Sculpture, W=Watercolor

		Current Price Range		
		Low	Mean	High
MORAN, E. Percy	P	$1,210	$3,019	$7,700
American (1862 - 1935)	W	$330	$543	$935
MORAN, Edward	P	$660	$11,214	$34,100
American (1829 - 1901)	W			$193
MORAN, H. Marcus	P			$5,500
American (20th -)				
MORAN, Leon	P			$1,540
American (1864 - 1941)	W	$1,485	$1,843	$2,200
MORAN, Mary	P			$138
American (19th - 20th)				
MORAN, Peter	D	$440	$2,310	$4,180
American (1841 - 1914)	P	$110	$1,210	$1,980
	W			$4,400
MORAN, Thomas	D	$2,200	$2,750	$3,300
American (1837 - 1926)	P	$3,575	$89,903	$341,000
	W	$1,925	$20,121	$38,500
MORAN, Thomas (After)	P			$550
American (1837 - 1926)				
MORAN, Thomas (School)	P			$825
American (1837 - 1926)				
MORAN, Thomas Sidney	D			$165
American (19th - 20th)				
MORANDI, Giorgio	D	$3,300	$9,075	$12,100
Italian (1890 - 1964)	P	$495,000	$715,917	$1.485M
MORAS, W. Walter	P			$2,860
German (1856 - 1925)				
MORAZZONE, Pier F. M. (Circle)	D			$1,760
Italian (1571 - 1626)				
MORDT, Gustave A.	P			$5,500
Norwegian (1826 - 1856)				
MORE, Hermon	P			$440
American (1887 - 1968)				

D=Drawing, P=Painting, S=Sculpture, W=Watercolor

		Current Price Range		
		Low	Mean	High
MOREAU, Adrien	P	$1,320	$11,000	$28,600
French (1843 - 1906)				
MOREAU, Auguste	S	$248	$1,733	$3,850
French (1861 -)				
MOREAU, Auguste (After)	S	$495.	$898	$1,320
French (1861 -)				
MOREAU, Charles	P			$4,400
French (1830 -)				
MOREAU, Chocarne	P			$9,350
French (19th -)				
MOREAU, Gustave	P	$726,000	$1.738M	$2.750M
French (1826 - 1898)				
MOREAU, Hippolyte	S			$2,750
French (1832 - 1917)				
MOREAU, Hippolyte (After)	S			$660
French (1832 - 1917)				
MOREAU, Louis A. (After)	S			$550
French (1855 - 1919)				
MOREAU, Louis G.	W	$6,050	$26,125	$46,200
French (1740 - 1806)				
MOREAU, Louis G. (Attri	W	$3,850	$5,867	$9,350
French (1740 - 1806)				
MOREAU, Mathurin	S			$3,850
French (1822 - 1912)				
MOREAU, Mathurin (After)	S	$1,430	$8,415	$15,400
French (1822 - 1912)				
MOREAU, Paul C.	P			$605
French (19th -)				
MOREAU L'AINE, Louis G. (Foll)	W			$3,300
(18th -)				
MOREAU-VAUTHIER, Paul	S	$1,100	$2,613	$4,125
French (1831 - 1893)				
MOREELSE, Paulius	P			$1,540
Dutch (1571 - 1638)				
MOREELSE, Paulius (Attrib.)	P			$29,700
Dutch (1571 - 1638)				

D=Drawing, P=Painting, S=Sculpture, W=Watercolor

		Current Price Range		
		Low	Mean	High

		Low	Mean	High
MOREL, Charles (Attrib.)	*P*			$600
French (1861 - 1908)				
MOREL, Jan E.	*P*	$935	$1,471	$2,640
Dutch (1835 - 1905)				
MORELAND, Marylee	*W*	$770	$785	$800
American (20th -)				
MORELLI, Eugene (Et al.)	*S*			$2,420
American (20th -)				
MORENO, L. Marin	*P*	$1,650	$1,788	$1,925
French (19th -)				
MORET, Henry	*P*	$44,000	$84,573	$165,000
French (1856 - 1913)				
MORETTI, R.	*W*			$1,100
Italian (19th -)				
MORETTO DA BRESCIA, Aless.	*P*			$66,000
Italian (1498 - 1554)				
MORGAN,	*P*	$220	$234	$248
(?)				
MORGAN, C.	*P*			$220
(?)				
MORGAN, Frederick	*P*	$6,600	$30,067	$55,000
British (1856 - 1927)				
MORGAN, Howard	*P*			$165
American (20th -)				
MORGAN, Mary D.	*D*	$220	$532	$770
American (1868 - 1948)	*P*	$990	$3,104	$9,350
	W	$385	$1,392	$3,575
MORGAN, Robert F.	*P*	$1,400	$1,653	$1,800
American (20th -)				
MORGAN, Sister G.	*D*	$495	$633	$770
(?)				
MORGAN, Theodore J.	*P*	$1,045	$1,155	$1,265
American (1872 - 1947)				
MORGAN, Wallace	*D*	$100	$143	$220
American (1873 - 1948)				

D=Drawing, P=Painting, S=Sculpture, W=Watercolor

		Current Price Range		
		Low	Mean	High

		Low	Mean	High
MORGAN, William	P	$1,485	$2,393	$3,300
American (1826 - 1900)				
MORGENSTJERNE-MUNTHE, G.	P			$440
Dutch (1875 -)				
MORGER, Brian	P			$950
American (20th -)				
MORGHEN, L.	P			$935
Italian (19th -)				
MORIANI, A.	W			$358
Italian (19th -)				
MORICE,	S			$28,600
French (19th -)				
MORIER, David	P			$15,400
Swiss (1705 -)				
MORIN, Adolphe	P			$2,860
French (1841 -)				
MORIN, L.	P			$5,500
(19th -)				
MORIN, Louis	D			$935
French (19th -)				
MORIS, J.	P			$2,063
(?)				
MORIS, Louis M.	S			$2,310
(19th -)				
MORISE,	S			$6,600
(19th -)				
MORISE, Marie L.	S			$5,500
French (1818 -)				
MORISOT, Berthe	D	$3,025	$149,639	$440,000
French (1841 - 1895)	P	$605,000	$880,000	$1.045M
MORLAND, George	P	$220	$6,096	$22,000
British (1763 - 1804)				
MORLAND, George (After)	P	$440	$642	$770
British (1763 - 1804)				
MORLAND, George (Attrib.)	P	$330	$1,228	$2,200
British (1763 - 1804)				

D=Drawing, P=Painting, S=Sculpture, W=Watercolor

| | | Current Price Range | | |
		Low	Mean	High
MORLAND, George (Follower) British (1763 - 1804)	P	$660	$688	$715
MORLAND, George (Manner) British (1763 - 1804)	P			$330
MORLAND, George (School) British (1763 - 1804)	P			$1,320
MORLEY, Malcolm American (1931 -)	D	$935	$3,487	$7,700
	P	$4,125	$109,395	$506,000
	W	$3,575	$11,675	$27,500
MORLEY, T. W. British (1859 - 1925)	W			$770
MORMILE, Andre Haitian (20th -)	P			$990
MORMILE, Gaetano Italian (1839 - 1890)	P	$1,045	$2,878	$4,180
MORO, Paolo American (20th -)	P			$330
MORONI, J. European (18th -)	P			$1,320
MOROSINI, George Italian (? - 1882)	D			$413
MORPHEY, Garret (Attrib.) British (? - 1715)	P			$3,300
MORREAU, Mathurin French (1822 - 1912)	S			$880
MORREL, Owen (20th -)	D			$935
MORRELL, Wayne American (1923 -)	P	$110	$348	$660
MORRICE, James W. Canadian (1865 - 1924)	P	$18,700	$37,033	$48,400
MORRIEN, Johannes H. Dutch (1819 - 1878)	P			$303
MORRIS, American (20th -)	P			$358

D=Drawing, P=Painting, S=Sculpture, W=Watercolor

		Current Price Range		
		Low	Mean	High
MORRIS, Charles	*P*	$248	$541	$1,100
British (19th -)				
MORRIS, Charles (Attrib.)	*P*			$3,520
British (19th -)				
MORRIS, F. E.	*P*			$935
(?)				
MORRIS, George F.	*D*			$2,090
American (1873 -)	*P*			$495
MORRIS, George L. K.	*D*	$1,650	$3,135	$4,620
American (1905 - 1975)	*P*	$440	$14,740	$39,600
	S			$9,900
MORRIS, John F.	*D*	$132	$235	$352
American (20th -)	*P*			$8,800
	W	$550	$1,031	$1,430
MORRIS, Kyle	*P*	$880	$4,153	$7,425
American (1918 - 1979)				
MORRIS, Louise	*W*			$121
American (20th -)				
MORRIS, Philip R.	*P*	$1,430	$5,793	$12,100
British (1833 - 1902)				
MORRIS, Robert	*D*	$3,300	$12,650	$19,800
American (1931 -)	*P*	$9,900	$10,450	$11,000
	S	$165	$36,333	$63,250
MORRIS, T.	*W*			$248
American (20th -)				
MORRIS, William	*P*			$4,950
British (1834 - 1896)				
MORRIS, JR., John B.	*W*			$110
American (20th -)				
MORRISON, K. M.	*P*			$770
British (20th -)				
MORRISON, Van	*P*			$2,640
European (19th - 20th)				

D=Drawing, P=Painting, S=Sculpture, W=Watercolor

		Current Price Range		
		Low	Mean	High
MORRISON, Zaidee L.	*P*			$1,210
American (1872 -)				
MORROW, Julie	*P*			$110
American (20th -)				
MORSE, George R.	*P*			$1,045
(19th -)				
MORSE, Henry D.	*P*			$385
American (1826 - 1888)				
MORSE, Ruth	*P*	$110	$413	$715
American (1887 -)				
MORSE, Samuel F. B.	*P*	$1,155	$29,178	$57,200
American (1791 - 1872)	*W*			$14,300
MORSE, Vernon Jay	*P*	$1,760	$2,420	$3,025
American (1898 - 1965)				
MORTEL, Jan van (Attrib.)	*P*			$11,000
Dutch (1650 - 1719)				
MORTELMANS, Franz	*P*	$3,520	$8,928	$14,300
Belgian (1865 - 1936)				
MORTIMORE, Mary	*P*	$935	$2,118	$3,300
British (19th -)				
MORTON, Andrew	*P*			$385
British (1802 - 1845)				
MORTON, Christina	*P*			$770
American (19th - 20th)				
MORTON, Edward	*D*			$385
(20th -)				
MORTON, J.	*P*	$248	$248	$248
American (20th -)				
MORTON, William	*P*			$1,760
American (20th -)				
MORVILLER, Joseph	*P*	$1,045	$4,923	$8,800
American (19th -)				
MOSAR, Michelle	*P*			$330
(?)				
MOSEDALE, A. W. T. (Et al.)	*W*			$220
British (19th -)				

D=Drawing, P=Painting, S=Sculpture, W=Watercolor

		Current Price Range		
		Low	Mean	High

MOSEER, G. H. (?)	P			$660
MOSELSIO, Simon American (1890 - 1963)	S			$248
MOSENGEL, Adolph German (1837 - 1885)	W			$275
MOSER, Frank American (1886 - 1964)	P	$110	$678	$990
MOSER, H. (?)	P			$149
MOSER, Kolo Austrian (1868 - 1918)	W			$1,210
MOSES, A. M. R. "Grandma" American (1860 - 1961)	P	$1,650	$39,183	$77,000
MOSES, Ed American (1926 - 1974)	D P S			$880 $14,300 $27,500
MOSES, Forrest K. American (1893 - 1974)	P			$2,420
MOSES, Thomas G. American (1856 - 1934)	W			$495
MOSES, Walter F. American (1874 -)	P	$275	$660	$1,430
MOSKOWITZ, Ira American (1912 -)	P W	$633	$1,032	$1,430 $193
MOSKOWITZ, Robert American (1935 -)	P S	$47,300 $20,900	$166,650 $21,450	$286,000 $22,000
MOSLER, Gustave H. American (1875 - 1906)	P			$248
MOSLER, Henry American (1841 - 1920)	P	$440	$5,500	$22,000
MOSMAN, Gulliver German (18th -)	P			$2,090

D=Drawing, P=Painting, S=Sculpture, W=Watercolor

| | | Current Price Range | | |
		Low	Mean	High
MOSS, Charles E. American (1860 - 1901)	P			$605
MOSS, Kevin American (20th -)	P			$4,400
MOSS, Tom American (1935 -)	S	$1,540	$3,368	$5,720
MOSSA, Gustave A. French (1883 - 1971)	W			$715
MOTE, George W. British (1883 - 1909)	P			$6,600
MOTE, George W. (Attrib.) British (1883 - 1909)	P			$468
MOTHERWELL, Robert American (1915 -)	D	$2,310	$45,232	$121,000
	P	$4,950	$192,867	$1.100M
	S	$24,200	$71,000	$148,500
	W	$6,050	$27,913	$44,000
MOTINSKY, A. Russian (19th - 20th)	P			$385
MOTLEY, Robert American (20th -)	P			$1,045
MOTSCHALL, Robert R. (?)	W			$116
MOTT-SMITH, May American (1879 - 1952)	P			$660
MOTTA, Raffaellino Italian (1550 - 1578)	W	$33,000	$48,125	$63,250
MOTTET, Yvonne French (1906 - 1968)	P			$770
MOTTETT, Jeanie American (1934 -)	P			$1,320
MOTTEZ, Victor (Attrib.) French (1809 - 1987)	P			$275
MOTTRAM, Charles S. British (1876 - 1903)	P			$138

D=Drawing, P=Painting, S=Sculpture, W=Watercolor

		Current Price Range		
		Low	Mean	High

MOUCHERON, Frederik de	P			$2,200
Dutch (1633 - 1686)				
MOUCHERON, Issac de	D	$4,950	$13,017	$20,900
Dutch (1667 - 1744)	P			$24,200
MOUCHERON, Issac de (Follower)	P			$4,675
Dutch (1667 - 1744)				
MOUCHOT, Ludvic	P			$550
French (19th -)				
MOUCK, A.	P			$2,530
Dutch (19th - 20th)				
MOULY, Marcel	P			$715
(20th -)				
MOUNSBACH,	P			$193
(?)				
MOUNT, Shepard A.	P	$2,420	$4,098	$4,950
American (1804 - 1868)				
MOUNT, William S.	D	$385	$4,318	$8,250
American (1807 - 1869)	P	$11,000	$93,940	$286,000
MOUSSET, Pierre	P			$3,025
French (? - 1894)				
MOUTON, Georges	W			$149
French (?)				
MOWBRAY, Henry S.	P	$2,200	$39,600	$77,000
American (1858 - 1928)				
MOWER, Martin	P			$3,575
American (1870 -)				
MOYAERT, Claes	P			$35,200
Dutch (17th -)				
MOYE, Paul	S			$330
German (1877 - 1926)				
MOYERS, William	S			$2,750
American (1916 -)	W			$770
MOYES, Frederick	P			$605
European (19th -)				

D=Drawing, P=Painting, S=Sculpture, W=Watercolor

		Current Price Range		
		Low	Mean	High
MOZART, Anton (Circle)	P			$2,200
German (1573 - 1625)				
MOZART, Anton (Manner)	P			$248
German (1573 - 1625)				
MOZERT, Zoe	D	$3,300	$3,850	$4,400
American (?)				
MOZZI,	P			$385
Italian (19th -)				
MRAZ, Franjo	P			$358
Hungarian (1910 -)				
MUCCINI, Marcello	P			$330
Italian (1926 -)				
MUCCIOLI, Anna	W			$220
(?)				
MUCHA, Alphonse M.	P	$44,000	$78,833	$115,500
Czechoslovakian (1860 - 1939)				
MUCKE, Carl E.	P			$1,540
German (1847 - 1923)				
MUCKLEY, William J.	W	$2,860	$3,905	$4,950
British (1837 - 1905)				
MUDGE, Alfred	P			$440
British (19th -)				
MUELLER, Ned	D			$990
American (20th -)	P			$650
MUELLER, Otto	D			$7,150
German (1874 - 1930)				
MUELLER, Stephen	P	$605	$3,053	$5,500
(20th -)				
MUENIER, Jules A.	P			$7,700
French (1863 - 1942)				
MUGHAL SCHOOL 18C,	P			$1,320
(18th -)				
MUHL, Roger	P	$138	$3,733	$7,150
French (1929 -)				
MUHLER, B.	P			$385
American (?)				

D=Drawing, P=Painting, S=Sculpture, W=Watercolor

		Current Price Range	
	Low	Mean	High

		Low	Mean	High
MUHLIG, Albert E.	*P*			$220
German (1862 -)				
MUHLIG, Bernard	*P*			$6,050
German (1829 - 1910)				
MUHRMAN, Henry	*D*			$1,760
American (1854 -)				
MUIRHEAD, John	*P*			$770
British (1867 - 1930)				
MULATO, O.	*P*			$275
American (20th -)				
MULDER, Anna	*P*	$170	$223	$275
Dutch (1935 -)				
MULDER, Johan C. A. W. (Attrib.)	*P*			$550
Dutch (1895 -)				
MULER, Eugene	*P*			$6,380
European (19th - 20th)				
MULERTT, Carl E.	*P*	$880	$1,210	$1,540
American (1869 - 1915)	*W*			$935
MULHAUPT, Frederick J.	*P*	$1,705	$10,823	$26,400
American (1871 - 1938)				
MULHOLLAND, Samuel A.	*P*	$440	$4,070	$7,700
British (19th -)	*W*	$220	$367	$605
MULHOLLAND, Sydney	*W*	$165	$440	$715
British (19th -)				
MULIER, Pieter	*P*			$27,500
Dutch (1615 - 1670)				
MULIER, Pieter (Circle)	*P*			$4,950
Dutch (1615 - 1670)				
MULL, Evert	*P*			$660
Dutch (19th - 20th)				
MULLER, Ans	*P*			$715
Austrian (1873 -)	*S*			$825
MULLER, C.	*P*	$990	$1,797	$3,300
German (19th -)				

D=Drawing, P=Painting, S=Sculpture, W=Watercolor

		Current Price Range	
	Low	Mean	High

		Low	Mean	High
MULLER, Carl	*P*			$10,450
German (1839 - 1904)				
MULLER, Charles L. L.	*D*			$165
French (1815 - 1892)				
MULLER, E.	*P*			$715
(?)				
MULLER, Fritz	*P*	$440	$633	$825
German (1913 -)				
MULLER, George F.	*P*			$440
American (1866 - 1934)				
MULLER, Jan	*D*	$4,400	$5,775	$7,150
American (20th -)	*P*			$19,800
	S			$4,400
	W			$935
MULLER, Moritz	*P*	$900	$3,005	$8,800
German (1841 - 1899)				
MULLER, Richard	*P*			$660
Austrian (1874 - 1930)	*W*			$1,100
MULLER, William J.	*P*			$1,540
British (1812 - 1845)				
MULLER-GRANTZOW, Ad.	*P*			$2,750
German (19th - 20th)				
MULLER-LINGKE, Albert	*P*			$3,300
German (1844 -)				
MULLER-SCHWOLERN,	*P*			$132
Austrian (19th - 20th)				
MULLER-URY, Adolph	*P*	$220	$1,302	$3,410
American (1868 - 1947)				
MULLEY, Oskar	*P*			$11,000
Austrian (1891 -)				
MULLHOLLAND, John	*W*			$413
European (19th -)				
MULLICAN, Matt	*P*	$23,100	$28,050	$33,000

D=Drawing, P=Painting, S=Sculpture, W=Watercolor

		Current Price Range		
		Low	Mean	High

		Low	Mean	High
MULLICAN, Matt	*S*			$2,640
(20th -)	*W*	$9,900	$20,075	$30,250
MULVAD, Emma	*P*			$2,750
Danish (1838 -)				
MUNAKATA, Shiko	*D*			$57,750
Japanese (1903 - 1975)				
MUNARI, Cristoforo	*P*	$22,000	$103,400	$231,000
Italian (1667 - 1720)				
MUNCH, Edvard	*P*	$704,000	$2.324M	$3.300M
Norwegian (1863 - 1944)				
MUNCHAUSEN, A. von	*D*	$1,045	$1,678	$2,310
German (19th - 20th)				
MUNDELL, J. G.	*P*			$1,320
British (1818 - 1875)				
MUNDHENK, August	*W*			$660
American (1848 - 1922)				
MUNDY, Ethel F.	*S*			$330
American (? - 20th)				
MUNGER, Gilbert D.	*P*	$770	$1,998	$3,575
American (1837 - 1903)				
MUNIER, Emile	*P*	$27,500	$60,500	$93,500
French (1810 -)				
MUNK, Loren	*P*			$2,750
(20th -)				
MUNKACSY, Mihaly	*D*			$1,100
Hungarian (1844 - 1900)	*P*	$5,775	$30,305	$96,250
MUNKINS, Cornelius	*P*			$1,430
(?)				
MUNNINGS, Sir Alfred J.	*D*	$2,420	$2,998	$3,575
British (1878 - 1959)	*P*	$6,050	$144,608	$825,000
MUNNINGS, Sir Alfred J. (Attrib.)	*P*			$1,320
British (1878 - 1959)				
MUNOZ, M.	*P*			$1,650
Spanish (19th -)				

D=Drawing, P=Painting, S=Sculpture, W=Watercolor

		Current Price Range	
		Low	Mean	High
---	---	---	---	---

		Low	Mean	High
MUNOZ, Oscar	*D*	$2,310	$2,805	$3,300
Colombian (1951 -)				
MUNOZ Y CUESTRA, Domingo	*P*			$9,350
Spanish (1850 - 1912)				
MUNOZ Y LUCENA, Tomas	*P*			$11,000
Spanish (1860 - 1942)				
MUNOZ-VERA, Guillermo	*D*			$2,750
Chilean (1949 -)	*P*	$9,900	$11,000	$13,200
MUNRO, Janet	*P*	$110	$481	$880
American (20th -)				
MUNSELL, C. H.	*P*	$198	$263	$319
(?)				
MUNSON, Lucius	*W*			$138
American (1796 - 1823)				
MUNSTEKOG, Beich	*P*			$715
German (19th - 20th)				
MUNSTER, D.	*W*			$110
(?)				
MUNTER, Gabriele	*P*	$11,000	$35,200	$77,000
German (1877 - 1962)				
MUNTHE, Ludvig	*P*	$3,300	$8,067	$13,200
Norwegian (1841 - 1896)				
MURA, Francesco de	*P*			$24,200
Italian (1698 - 1782)				
MURA, Francesco de (Attrib.)	*P*			$5,500
Italian (1698 - 1782)				
MURA, Francesco de (Circle)	*P*	$1,760	$8,727	$20,900
Italian (1698 - 1782)				
MURA, Francesco de (Fol.)	*P*			$2,200
Italian (1698 - 1782)				
MURA, Francesco de (School)	*P*			$2,200
Italian (1698 - 1782)				
MURATON, Euphemie	*P*			$3,025
French (1840 -)				
MURATON, Louis	*P*			$2,860
French (19th - 20th)				

D=Drawing, P=Painting, S=Sculpture, W=Watercolor

		Current Price Range		
		Low	Mean	High

		Low	Mean	High
MURCH, Walter T.	*P*	$18,700	$36,667	$52,800
American (1907 - 1967)	*W*	$880	$1,907	$2,970
MURDOCH, M. Burn	*P*			$2,420
British (19th -)				
MURILLO, Bartolome E.	*P*			$14,300
Spanish (1618 - 1682)				
MURILLO, Bartolome E. (After)	*P*	$341	$1,003	$1,650
Spanish (1618 - 1682)				
MURILLO, Bartolome E. (Attrib)	*P*	$4,400	$26,400	$60,500
Spanish (1618 - 1682)				
MURILLO, Bartolome E. (Circle)	*P*			$8,250
Spanish (1618 - 1682)				
MURILLO, Bartolome E. (School)	*P*	$1,650	$2,255	$2,860
Spanish (1618 - 1682)				
MURPHY, Catherine	*P*	$275	$15,125	$27,500
American (20th -)				
MURPHY, Herman D.	*D*			$1,540
American (1867 - 1945)	*P*	$770	$5,541	$18,000
	W			$1,650
MURPHY, J. Francis	*D*			$220
American (1853 - 1921)	*P*	$1,320	$5,399	$13,200
	W	$1,430	$2,684	$4,950
MURPHY, Lucille D.	*W*			$220
American (? - 1956)				
MURPHY, P. W.	*P*			$275
American (20th -)				
MURPHY, Terry	*S*	$1,000	$3,125	$5,775
American (20th -)				
MURRAY, Eben H.	*P*			$8,800
British (19th -)				
MURRAY, Elizabeth	*D*	$13,200	$19,983	$24,750
British (20th -)	*P*	$7,150	$10,450	$16,500

D=Drawing, P=Painting, S=Sculpture, W=Watercolor

		Current Price Range		
		Low	Mean	High
MURRAY, Elizabeth	W			$2,850
British (20th -)				
MURRAY, F. Richardson	W	$3,850	$5,060	$6,270
American (20th -)				
MURRAY, H.	W	$935	$2,742	$5,280
British (19th -)				
MURRAY, Jim	D			$1,100
(20th -)				
MURRAY, John	W	$4,400	$4,950	$5,500
(20th -)				
MUSCHAMP, F. Sydney	P	$880	$14,025	$33,000
British (? - 1929)				
MUSGRAVE, William (Attrib.)	W			$425
British (17th - 18th)				
MUSIC, Zoran A.	D	$1,100	$9,350	$14,300
Italian (1909 - 1952)	P	$45,100	$104,867	$209,000
	W	$12,650	$20,625	$28,600
MUSIN, Auguste H.	P	$5,500	$6,050	$6,600
Belgian (1852 - 1920)				
MUSIN, Francois E.	P	$17,600	$23,100	$27,500
Belgian (1820 - 1888)				
MUSMEEI, G.	W			$154
Italian (20th -)				
MUSS-ARNOLDT, Gustav	P			$5,500
American (1858 - 1927)				
MUSSCHER, Michiel van	D			$1,540
Dutch (1645 - 1705)	P			$2,750
MUSSELMAN, Darwin B.	P			$1,210
American (1916 -)				
MUSSELMAN, M.	D			$165
American (20th -)				
MUTH, A.	P			$1,320
American (19th -)				
MUTTONI, Pietro (Circle)	P			$3,960
Italian (1605 - 1678)				

D=Drawing, P=Painting, S=Sculpture, W=Watercolor

		Current Price Range		
		Low	Mean	High
MY, Hieronymus van der	*P*			$2,200
Dutch (1687 - 1761)				
MYERS, Bob	*P*			$3,300
American (20th -)				
MYERS, Ethel H. K.	*D*			$990
American (1881 - 1960)				
MYERS, Frank H.	*P*	$286	$677	$1,045
American (1899 - 1956)				
MYERS, Jerome	*D*	$715	$2,567	$6,600
American (1867 - 1940)				
MYERS, Mary	*W*			$440
American (1878 -)				
MYERS, Paul	*P*			$1,650
(?)				
MYGATT, Robertson K.	*P*	$1,155	$1,238	$1,320
American (? - 1919)				
MYLES, J.	*P*			$6,050
British (19th -)				
MYLNE, W.	*W*			$193
American (20th -)				
MYN, Frances van der (Attrib.)	*P*			$2,530
Dutch (1719 - 1783)				
MYRBACH-RHEINFELD, Baron	*W*	$1,650	$2,365	$3,080
German (1853 -)				
MYRICK, H. B.	*P*			$220
American (20th -)				
MYTENS, Jan (Attrib.)	*P*			$330,000
Dutch (1614 - 1670)				
MYTENS, Jan (Circle)	*P*			$15,400
Dutch (1614 - 1670)				
MYTENS, ELDER, Daniel	*P*			$12,100
Dutch (1590 - 1648)				
MYTENS, II, Martin van (Attrib.)	*P*			$77,000
Swedish (1695 - 1770)				
NABERT, Wilhelm J. A.	*P*			$4,950
German (1830 - 1904)				

D=Drawing, P=Painting, S=Sculpture, W=Watercolor

		Current Price Range		
		Low	Mean	High
NADELMAN, Elie	*D*	$1,650	$3,366	$6,050
American (1882 - 1946)	*S*	$3,850	$29,394	$74,250
NAGANO, Shozo	*P*	$2,200	$2,310	$2,420
(20th -)				
NAGEL, Hans	*P*	$143	$237	$330
American (20th -)				
NAGI, G.	*W*			$248
Italian (19th -)				
NAGLE, Ron	*S*	$1,540	$1,760	$1,980
American (20th -)				
NAGLER, Edith	*P*			$468
American (1892 - 1975)	*W*	$110	$124	$138
NAGLEY, SR., Lester C.	*W*			$248
(?)				
NAGY, Ernest de	*P*	$220	$473	$825
American (1906 - 1944)				
NAGY, Ygan de	*P*			$300
(?)				
NAHAPETIAN, Y.	*W*			$330
Iranian (20th -)				
NAHL, Perham	*P*			$15,400
American (?)				
NAIN, Mathieu Le (Circle)	*P*			$3,080
French (1607 - 1648)				
NAIN, Mathieu Le (School)	*P*			$14,300
French (1607 - 1648)				
NAISH, John G.	*P*			$88,000
British (1824 - 1905)				
NAIVEU, Matthys (Attrib.)	*P*			$8,800
Dutch (1647 - 1721)				
NAIWINCX, Herman	*D*			$13,200
Flemish (17th -)				
NAKAGAWA, Hachiro	*P*			$3,850
Japanese (1877 - 1922)	*W*			$1,650

D=Drawing, P=Painting, S=Sculpture, W=Watercolor

		Current Price Range		
		Low	Mean	High

		Low	Mean	High
NAKIAN, Reuben	S	$1,760	$3,144	$3,575
American (1897 -)	W	$1,210	$1,320	$1,430
NALDINI, Giovanni B.	D			$12,100
Italian (1537 - 1591)				
NANKIVELL, Frank A.	P	$330	$633	$935
American (1869 - 1959)				
NANKIVELL, Fred	P	$110	$1,342	$3,575
American (1876 - 1950)				
NANTEUIL, Celestin F. L.	W			$330
French (1813 - 1873)				
NANTEUIL, Pierre (Attrib.)	P			$27,500
French (1623 - 1678)				
NANTEUIL, Pierre (Circle)	P			$1,210
French (1623 - 1678)				
NAOUMOVA, Larissa	P	$4,950	$10,725	$16,500
Russian (1945 -)				
NARAZZI, F.	W			$165
(?)				
NARCISSE, Pierre (Attrib.)	P	$5,500	$11,550	$17,600
French (1774 - 1833)				
NARDI, E.	W			$7,700
Italian (19th -)				
NARIMANBEKOV, Togrul	P	$6,600	$9,900	$14,300
Russian (1930 -)				
NARVAEZ, Francisco	S			$26,400
Venezuelan (1905 - 1982)				
NASAGI, J.	W			$1,100
European (19th - 20th)				
NASH, E. R.	P			$330
American (20th -)				
NASH, Frederick (Attrib.)	W			$523
British (1782 - 1856)				
NASH, Joseph	W	$715	$1,403	$2,090
British (1808 - 1878)				
NASH, Manley K.	P			$2,640
American (?)				

D=Drawing, P=Painting, S=Sculpture, W=Watercolor

		Current Price Range		
		Low	Mean	High

		Low	Mean	High
NASH, Willard	P	$30,250	$31,625	$33,000
American (1898 - 1943)				
NASI, G.	W			$935
Italian (19th -)				
NASINI, Giuseppe N. (Attrib.)	D			$2,200
Italian (1657 - 1736)				
NASMYTH, Alexander (School)	P			$275
British (1758 - 1804)				
NASMYTH, Charlotte	P			$2,200
British (1804 -)				
NASMYTH, Patrick	P	$1,100	$1,155	$1,210
British (1787 - 1831)				
NASMYTH, Patrick (Attrib.)	P			$1,320
British (1787 - 1831)				
NASON, Gertrude	P	$220	$770	$1,100
American (1890 - 1969)				
NASON, Thomas	W			$523
American (1889 - 1971)				
NAST, Thomas	D	$468	$6,497	$20,900
American (1840 - 1902)				
NATALE, G.	P			$248
American (20th -)				
NATIORE, Charles	D			$1,650
French (1700 - 1777)				
NATKIN, Robert	P	$770	$5,987	$16,500
American (1930 -)	W	$2,420	$3,410	$4,400
NATOIRE, Charles-J.	D	$29,700	$33,550	$37,400
French (1700 - 1777)				
NATOIRE, Charles-J. (Follower)	D			$1,320
French (1770 - 1777)				
NATTIER, Jean-Marc	P	$39,600	$47,667	$52,800
French (1685 - 1766)				
NATTIER, Jean-Marc (After)	P	$275	$1,375	$2,475
French (1685 - 1766)				
NATTIER, Jean-Marc (Circle)	D	$1,870	$1,925	$1,980

D=Drawing, P=Painting, S=Sculpture, W=Watercolor

		Current Price Range		
		Low	Mean	High

		Low	Mean	High
NATTIER, Jean-Marc (Circle)	*P*			$7,700
French (1685 - 1766)				
NATTIER, Jean-Marc (Follower)	*P*	$2,200	$9,900	$17,600
French (1685 - 1766)				
NATTIER, Jean-Marc (Manner)	*P*			$2,750
French (1685 - 1766)				
NATTIER, Jean-Marc (School)	*P*			$1,760
French (1685 - 1766)				
NATTIER, Jean-Marc (Studio)	*P*			$44,000
French (1685 - 1766)				
NAUDIN, Charles	*P*			$275
French (19th -)				
NAUER, Albert	*P*			$2,475
German (1873 -)				
NAUEZ, Joseph F.	*P*			$1,650
Belgian (1787 - 1869)				
NAUMAN, Bruce	*D*	$27,500	$240,625	$407,000
American (1941 -)	*P*	$148,500	$288,750	$429,000
	S	$63,250	$67,375	$71,500
	W			$143,000
NAUMANN, Carl G.	*P*			$6,325
German (1827 - 1902)				
NAUMER, Helmuth	*D*	$303	$867	$1,430
American (1907 -)				
NAVARRA, Pietro	*P*			$24,200
Italian (17th - 18th)				
NAVARRO, Enrique	*P*			$358
Spanish (20th -)				
NAVARRO Y LLORENS, Jose	*P*			$4,400
Spanish (1867 - 1923)				
NAVEZ, Francois J.	*P*			$11,000
Belgian (1787 - 1869)				
NAVEZ, Francois J. (Attrib.)	*P*			$1,100
Belgian (1787 - 1869)				

D=Drawing, P=Painting, S=Sculpture, W=Watercolor

		Current Price Range		
		Low	Mean	High

		Low	Mean	High
NAVONE, Edoardo	W	$330	$403	$475
Italian (19th -)				
NAVRATIL, Joseph	W			$440
Czech. (1798 - 1865)				
NAVROS, David	P	$2,200	$9,717	$24,750
(20th -)				
NAZZARI, Bartolomeo	D			$1,100
Italian (1699 - 1758)				
NEALE, Maud H.	P			$2,860
British (19th - 20th)				
NEAPOLITAN SCHOOL 17C,	P	$1,100	$10,175	$30,800
Italian (17th -)				
NEAPOLITAN SCHOOL 18C,	P	$1,650	$17,666	$55,000
Italian (18th -)				
NEAPOLITAN SCHOOL 19C,	W	$1,045	$3,997	$7,700
Italian (19th -)				
NEARY,	P			$550
(?)				
NEBBIA, Cesare	D			$4,400
Italian (1536 - 1614)				
NEBEL, Otto	W	$2,420	$3,135	$3,850
German (1892 -)				
NECK, Jan van	P	$2,750	$3,575	$4,400
Dutch (1635 - 1714)				
NEEBE, Louis A.	P			$1,430
American (1873 -)				
NEEBE, Minnie H.	P	$330	$880	$1,430
American (1873 - 1946)				
NEEDHAM,	P			$275
(?)				
NEEFFS, ELDER, Pieter	P	$30,800	$48,400	$66,000
Flemish (1578 - 1658)				
NEEFFS, ELDER, Pieter (Circle)	P			$4,675
Flemish (1578 - 1658)				
NEER, Aert van	P			$16,500
Dutch (1603 - 1677)				

D=Drawing, P=Painting, S=Sculpture, W=Watercolor

		Current Price Range		
		Low	Mean	High

NEER, Aert van (Attrib.)	*P*			$18,700
Dutch (1603 - 1677)				
NEER, Eglon H. van der	*P*			$8,800
Dutch (1634 - 1703)				
NEERGAARD, Hermania S.	*P*			$7,700
Danish (1799 - 1875)				
NEGRET, Edgar	*P*			$3,520
Colombian (1920 -)	*S*	$5,500	$7,755	$12,100
NEGRI, Mario	*S*			$35,750
Italian (1916 -)				
NEGULESCO, Jean	*P*			$825
Hungarian (19th - 20th)				
NEHER, Caspar	*W*			$605
German (20th -)				
NEILL, Francis I.	*P*			$633
American (20th -)				
NEILSON, Raymond	*P*			$1,760
American (1881 - 1964)				
NEIMAN, Leroy	*P*			$1,760
American (1926 -)				
NEL-DUMOUCHEL, Jules	*P*			$1,870
French (19th -)				
NELAN, Charles	*D*			$220
(1854 - 1904)				
NELLI, Ottaviano (Circle)	*P*			$15,400
Italian (14th - 15th)				
NELLY, Hollo	*P*			$330
(?)				
NELSON, Andy	*P*	$440	$440	$440
American (1928 -)				
NELSON, Edward H.	*W*			$138
British (1871 -)				
NELSON, Ernest B.	*P*			$2,750
American (1888 - 1952)				
NELSON, Ernest O.	*P*			$4,675
American (19th -)				

D=Drawing, P=Painting, S=Sculpture, W=Watercolor

		Current Price Range		
		Low	Mean	High
NELSON, George L.	*D*			$330
American (1887 - 1978)	*P*	$138	$1,082	$8,910
	W	$110	$605	$1,100
NELSON, Joan	*D*			$3,850
(20th -)	*P*	$7,700	$13,383	$19,800
NELSON, M. D. P.	*S*			$110
American (20th -)				
NELSON, O.	*P*			$3,300
(19th -)				
NELSON, Roger L.	*P*			$6,050
(20th -)				
NEME, Clarel	*P*	$5,500	$7,040	$8,250
Uruguayan (1926 -)				
NEMETH, Gyorgy	*P*	$248	$312	$358
Hungarian (19th - 20th)				
NEMETHY, Albert	*P*	$825	$1,788	$2,750
American (20th -)				
NEOGRADY, Antal	*P*			$825
Hungarian (1861 - 1942)				
NEOGRADY, Laszlo	*P*	$220	$1,601	$6,050
Hungarian (1900 -)	*W*			$715
NEPOTE, Alexander	*W*			$1,540
American (1913 -)				
NERI, Manuel	*P*			$3,025
American (20th -)				
NERLY, Frederick	*P*			$18,700
Austrian (1807 - 1878)				
NERLY, JR., Frederick	*P*			$1,210
Austrian (19th - 20th)				
NERMANN, Robert von	*P*			$303
American (?)				
NESBITT, Lowell	*P*	$935	$3,232	$7,700
American (1933 -)				

D=Drawing, P=Painting, S=Sculpture, W=Watercolor

		Current Price Range		
		Low	Mean	High

NESDAG, Hendrik (Attrib.)	*P*			$1,650
Dutch (1831 - 1915)				
NESMITH, Bessie F.	*P*			$138
American (20th -)				
NESTEROV, Mikhail V.	*P*			$19,800
Russian (1862 - 1942)				
NESTEROVA, Natalia	*P*	$4,400	$8,708	$13,200
Russian (1944 -)				
NETER, Laurentius de	*P*			$6,600
German (1600 -)				
NETHERLANDISH SCHOOL 16C,	*P*	$6,600	$25,300	$44,000
(16th -)	*W*			$198,000
NETHERLANDISH SCHOOL 17C,	*D*			$2,200
(17th -)				
NETHERWOOD, Arthur	*W*			$143
British (19th - 20th)				
NETSCHER, Caspar	*P*			$8,250
Dutch (1639 - 1684)				
NETSCHER, Caspar (Attrib.)	*D*	$550	$798	$1,045
Dutch (1639 - 1684)	*P*			$24,200
NETSCHER, Constantyn	*P*			$4,400
Dutch (1668 - 1723)				
NETSCHER, Constantyn (Circle)	*P*	$1,540	$1,760	$1,980
Dutch (1668 - 1723)				
NETSCHER, Constantyn (School)	*P*			$4,950
Dutch (1668 - 1723)				
NETTIN, W. J.	*W*			$248
(19th -)				
NETTLETON, Walter	*P*			$2,750
American (1861 - 1936)				
NEUBERT, Ludwig	*P*			$2,860
German (1846 - 1892)				
NEUENDAM, V.	*P*			$5,500
Scandinavian (19th - 20th)				

D=Drawing, P=Painting, S=Sculpture, W=Watercolor

		Current Price Range		
		Low	Mean	High

		Low	Mean	High
NEUHAUS, Karl E.	P			$1,100
American (1879 - 1963)				
NEUHUYS, Albert	P			$4,400
Dutch (1844 - 1914)	S			$248
NEUHUYS, Joseph H.	P			$3,080
Dutch (1841 - 1890)				
NEUMANN, Arnold	P			$1,650
German (1836 - 1920)				
NEUMANN, B.	P			$660
American (20th -)				
NEUMANN, Johan J.	P	$165	$2,008	$3,850
Danish (1860 - 1940)				
NEUMANN, Robert von	P	$440	$1,320	$2,200
American (1888 - 1976)				
NEUMANN, Robert von (Attrib.)	P	$375	$1,050	$1,725
American (1888 - 1976)	W			$450
NEUMANS, JR., H.	P			$1,870
Dutch (19th -)				
NEUQUELMAN, Lucien	P	$3,300	$5,225	$8,800
French (1909 -)				
NEUSER, Louis A. W.	P	$165	$317	$660
American (1856 - 1902)				
NEUSTATTER, Ludwig	P			$7,150
German (1829 - 1899)				
NEUVILLE, Alfred A. B. de	P	$1,155	$5,676	$24,200
French (1879 - 1907)				
NEUVILLE, Alfred A. B. de (Att.)	P	$715	$1,293	$1,870
French (1879 - 1907)				
NEUVILLE, Alphonse M. de	D			$275
French (1835 - 1885)	P	$1,760	$7,062	$13,200
	W			$770
NEVELSON, Louise	D	$935	$1,971	$5,500
American (1900 -)	P	$3,300	$48,070	$121,000

D=Drawing, P=Painting, S=Sculpture, W=Watercolor

		Current Price Range		
		Low	Mean	High

		Low	Mean	High
NEVELSON, Louise	S	$3,850	$51,333	$253,000
American (1900 -)	W	$1,650	$6,875	$12,100
NEVILL, Eunice M.	W			$1,100
British (19th - 20th)				
NEWANN, Robert von	S			$468
(?)				
NEWCASTLE, Lene	W			$165
American (20th -)				
NEWELL, Ada	P			$468
(20th -)				
NEWELL, George G.	P	$440	$1,210	$1,980
American (1870 - 1947)				
NEWELL, Hugh	D	$165	$2,255	$3,520
Irish (1830 - 1915)	P	$193	$9,231	$26,400
NEWELL, Peter S.	P			$1,650
American (1862 - 1924)	W			$770
NEWELL, R.	W			$330
(20th -)				
NEWGASS, Bettie	P			$165
(?)				
NEWHOUSE, Charles B.	W	$165	$289	$413
British (19th -)				
NEWMAN, Allen G.	S			$6,600
American (1875 - 1940)				
NEWMAN, Barnett	D	$203,500	$266,750	$330,000
American (1905 - 1970)	P	$418,000	$885,500	$1.650M
NEWMAN, Benjamin T.	P			$248
American (1859 -)	W			$220
NEWMAN, Donald	P	$418	$1,305	$3,080
American (20th -)				
NEWMAN, George A.	P	$300	$618	$935
American (20th -)				

D=Drawing, P=Painting, S=Sculpture, W=Watercolor

		Current Price Range		
		Low	Mean	High
NEWMAN, George A. (Attrib.)	*P*			$138
American (20th -)				
NEWMAN, H. R.	*W*			$660
(19th -)				
NEWMAN, Henry R.	*D*			$6,600
American (1833 - 1917)	*W*			$71,500
NEWMAN, Howard	*S*	$550	$3,410	$9,350
(20th -)				
NEWMAN, Malcolm	*D*			$138
American (?)				
NEWMAN, Robert L.	*P*	$935	$3,149	$5,720
American (1827 - 1912)				
NEWTON, Elizabeth Peck	*P*	$231	$240	$248
American (20th -)				
NEWTON, Gilbert S.	*P*	$248	$454	$660
British (1794 - 1835)				
NEWTON, Gordon	*D*			$3,520
(20th -)				
NEWTON, Herbert H.	*P*			$770
British (1881 -)				
NEWTON, Parker A.	*P*			$275
American (20th -)				
NEWTON, JR., Richard	*P*			$990
American (20th -)				
NEYLAND, Harry	*P*	$3,520	$3,548	$3,575
American (1877 - 1958)				
NEYMARK, Gustave M.	*P*			$880
French (1850 -)				
NEYN, Pieter de	*P*			$66,000
Dutch (1597.- 1639)				
NEYRAC, Guye de	*D*			$165
French (19th - 20th)	*W*	$165	$165	$165
NIBBS, Richard H.	*P*			$1,045
British (1816 - 1893)				

D=Drawing, P=Painting, S=Sculpture, W=Watercolor

		Current Price Range		
		Low	Mean	High
NIBLETT, Gary	P	$2,640	$4,345	$7,150
American (1943 -)	W			$1,430
NICCOLO, Lorenzo di	P			$93,500
(?)				
NICE, Don	D			$2,475
American (1932 -)	P			$8,800
	W			$6,050
NICHOLAS, David	P			$110
American (20th -)				
NICHOLAS, Lori	P			$700
American (20th -)				
NICHOLAS, Thomas	W	$220	$262	$303
American (1934 -)				
NICHOLL, Charles W.	P			$3,850
Irish (1831 - 1903)				
NICHOLL, T. J.	P			$770
American (19th -)				
NICHOLLS, Bertram	P			$3,410
British (1883 -)				
NICHOLLS, Burr H.	P	$495	$2,255	$5,500
American (1848 - 1915)				
NICHOLLS, George F.	W	$770	$1,063	$1,430
British (1885 - 1937)				
NICHOLLS, Rhoda H.	W			$2,750
American (1854 - 1938)				
NICHOLS, Abel	P			$1,100
American (19th -)				
NICHOLS, C. M.	W			$150
(?)				
NICHOLS, Dale W.	P	$2,420	$9,649	$24,200
American (1904 -)	W			$1,870
NICHOLS, Henry H.	P	$1,210	$3,749	$11,000
American (1869 - 1962)				

D=Drawing, P=Painting, S=Sculpture, W=Watercolor

		Current Price Range		
		Low	Mean	High
NICHOLS, William	*P*			$22,000
(20th -)				
NICHOLSON, Ben	*D*	$17,600	$26,767	$44,000
British (1894 - 1982)	*P*	$46,750	$175,389	$451,000
	W	$8,250	$30,250	$93,500
NICHOLSON, Ben (After)	*S*	$4,400	$6,967	$9,900
British (1894 - 1982)				
NICHOLSON, Charles W.	*P*	$138	$207	$275
American (1886 - 1965)				
NICHOLSON, Edward H.	*W*	$138	$284	$440
American (1901 - 1966)				
NICHOLSON, Ethel	*P*			$110
British (19th -)				
NICHOLSON, George W.	*P*	$193	$2,565	$8,250
American (1832 - 1912)	*W*	$143	$379	$715
NICKELE, Isaac van	*P*			$11,000
Dutch (18th -)				
NICKELSEN, Ralf E.	*P*			$385
American (1903 -)				
NICKLE, Robert	*W*			$125
(?)				
NICOL, Erskine	*P*	$143	$983	$2,200
British (1825 - 1904)				
NICOLE, George	*P*			$330
European (20th -)				
NICOLET, Gabriel E. E.	*D*			$330
Swiss (1856 - 1921)				
NICOLI, Charles	*S*			$2,970
(?)				
NICOLL, James C.	*P*	$165	$248	$330
American (1847 - 1918)				
NICOLL, John W.	*P*			$138
American (1865 - 1943)				
NICOLLE, Victor-J.	*D*			$2,475

D=Drawing, P=Painting, S=Sculpture, W=Watercolor

		Current Price Range	
	Low	Mean	High

		Low	Mean	High
NICOLLE, Victor-J.	*W*			$1,430
French (1754 - 1826)				
NICOLS, Audley D.	*P*			$1,210
American (20th -)				
NICOLSON, Charles W.	*P*			$220
American (1886 - 1965)				
NICZKY, Eduard	*P*	$3,410	$5,445	$8,800
German (1850 - 1919)				
NIELSON, Harry A.	*P*			$468
American (1881 -)				
NIELSON, Peter	*P*			$15,400
American (20th -)				
NIEMANN, Edmund J.	*P*	$770	$5,296	$16,500
British (1813 - 1876)				
NIEMANN, Edmund J. (Attrib.)	*P*	$1,870	$2,860	$3,850
British (1813 - 1876)				
NIEMANN, Edward H.	*P*	$605	$2,365	$4,125
British (19th -)				
NIEMEYER, John H.	*P*			$6,050
American (1839 - 1932)	*W*			$220
NIEPOLD, Frank	*P*	$825	$1,128	$1,430
American (1890 -)				
NIERMAN, Leonardo	*P*	$330	$1,173	$2,860
Mexican (1932 -)				
NIETO, Rudolfo	*P*	$3,520	$7,348	$14,300
Mexican (1936 - 1988)	*W*	$4,950	$5,775	$6,600
NIEULANDT, Willem (Attrib.)	*P*			$6,050
Flemish (1584 - 1636)				
NIJLAND, Gesina	*P*			$660
Dutch (1937 -)				
NIKICH, Anatol	*P*	$1,320	$1,375	$1,430
Russian (1918 -)				
NIKIFOR,	*D*			$523
Polish (1893 - 1968)				

D=Drawing, P=Painting, S=Sculpture, W=Watercolor

		Current Price Range		
		Low	Mean	High

		Low	Mean	High
NILES, George E. American (1837 - 1898)	*P*			$1,100
NILES, George E. (Attrib.) American (1837 - 1898)	*P*			$303
NILES, H. J. American (20th -)	*P*			$440
NINO, European (20th -)	*P*			$248
NINO, Carmelo Venezuelan (?)	*P*	$4,400	$5,500	$6,600
NISBET, Pollok Sinclair British (1848 - 1922)	*W*			$2,750
NISBET, Robert H. American (1879 - 1961)	*P* *W*	$165 $110	$3,044 $183	$22,000 $220
NISSL, Rudolf Austrian (1870 - 1955)	*P*	$3,850	$4,400	$4,950
NITTIS, Giuseppe de Italian (1846 - 1884)	*D* *P*	$24,200	$261,067	$4,400 $440,000
NITTIS, Giuseppe de (Attrib.) Italian (1846 - 1884)	*P*			$82,500
NIVERT, Georgette French (20th -)	*P*			$440
NIXON, W. R. British (19th -)	*P*			$1,320
NOBLE, John American (1874 - 1935)	*P*			$330
NOBLE, Matthew British (19th -)	*S*			$1,100
NOBLE, Robert British (19th -)	*P*			$3,850
NOBLE, Thomas S. American (1835 - 1907)	*P*			$1,100
NOBLE, William C. American (1858 -)	*S*			$550

D=Drawing, P=Painting, S=Sculpture, W=Watercolor

		Current Price Range	
	Low	Mean	High

		Low	Mean	High
NOCK, F.	*S*			$2,750
American (19th - 20th)				
NODO, Keiko	*P*			$495
Japanese (20th -)				
NOE, E.	*P*			$220
American (20th -)				
NOEL, Alexandre J.	*P*			$1,980
French (1752 - 1834)	*W*	$2,750	$3,988	$5,225
NOEL, John B.	*P*			$743
British (19th -)				
NOEL, Jules A.	*P*	$1,980	$14,263	$24,200
French (1813 - 1881)				
NOELSMITH, Thomas	*W*	$468	$894	$1,320
British (19th -)				
NOGUCHI, Isamu	*P*	$121,000	$203,500	$286,000
American (1904 - 1988)	*S*	$1,100	$107,665	$632,500
NOHA, Franz J.	*P*			$330
(?)				
NOLAN, Daniel	*D*			$165
American (1862 - 1920)	*P*			$330
NOLAND, Kenneth	*D*			$18,700
American (1924 -)	*P*	$17,600	$156,501	$2.035M
	S			$7,700
NOLDE, Emil	*P*	$825,000	$880,000	$935,000
German (1867 - 1956)	*W*	$38,500	$79,406	$170,500
NOLPE, Pieter	*P*			$27,500
Dutch (17th -)				
NOME, Francois de (Circle)	*P*			$23,100
French (16th - 17th)				
NONNENBRUCH, Max	*P*			$14,300
German (1857 - 1922)				
NONNOTTE, Donat	*P*			$27,500
French (1708 - 1785)				

D=Drawing, P=Painting, S=Sculpture, W=Watercolor

		Current Price Range	
	Low	Mean	High

		Low	Mean	High
NOOMS, Reinier	P			$13,200
Dutch (1623 - 1667)				
NOORDT, Jan van	P			$41,800
Dutch (1587 -)				
NOORDT, Joannes van	P			$16,500
Dutch (1620 - 1676)				
NOORT, Adrianus C. van	P	$770	$2,145	$4,950
Dutch (1914 -)				
NORBERT, A. B.	W			$121
(?)				
NORDALM, Federico	P	$4,950	$8,761	$17,600
Nicaraguan (1949 -)				
NORDELL, Carl J.	P	$303	$2,044	$3,960
American (1885 -)				
NORDELL, Emma (Polly)	W	$248	$385	$468
American (1876 - 1956)				
NORDEN, Gerald	P			$660
British (20th -)				
NORDENBERG, Bengt	P			$17,600
Swedish (1822 - 1902)				
NORDFELDT, Bror J. O.	D	$275	$1,412	$2,090
American (1878 - 1955)	P	$2,200	$13,933	$33,000
	W	$715	$798	$880
NORDHAUSEN, A. Henry	P			$2,860
American (1901 -)				
NORDSTROM, Carl H.	D	$138	$193	$248
American (1876 - 1934)	P	$330	$1,161	$2,310
	W	$165	$234	$303
NORIE, O.	W			$220
(?)				
NORMANN, Adelsteen	P	$1,100	$5,500	$9,900
Norwegian (1848 - 1918)				
NORRIS, Walter S.	P			$1,320
American (1868 -)				

D=Drawing, P=Painting, S=Sculpture, W=Watercolor

		Current Price Range		
		Low	Mean	High

		Low	Mean	High
NORTH, A. (?)	*P*			$303
NORTH ITALIAN SCHOOL 15C, Italian (15th -)	*P*			$16,500
NORTH ITALIAN SCHOOL 16C, Italian (16th -)	*D* *P*			$11,000 $3,300
NORTH ITALIAN SCHOOL 17C, Italian (17th -)	*P*	$1,650	$5,844	$23,100
NORTH ITALIAN SCHOOL 18C, Italian (18th -)	*P*	$1,100	$7,040	$28,600
NORTH ITALIAN SCHOOL 19C, Italian (19th -)	*P*			$1,430
NORTHCOTE, James British (1746 - 1831)	*P*	$715	$4,414	$14,300
NORTHEN, Adolf German (1828 - 1876)	*P*			$4,675
NORTHLEACH, J. Miles of British (19th -)	*P*			$9,900
NORTON, Benjamin C. British (1835 - 1900)	*P*			$2,860
NORTON, Elizabeth American (1887 -)	*S*			$2,970
NORTON, William E. American (1843 - 1916)	*P* *W*	$660 $550	$1,855 $1,558	$4,675 $3,025
NORWELL, Graham Canadian (1901 - 1967)	*W*			$385
NOSIDA, J. R. (19th -)	*P*			$154
NOSSAL, J. Dutch (19th - 20th)	*P*			$1,320
NOTER, David Belgian (1818 - 1892)	*P*	$10,450	$12,650	$15,400
NOTER, David (Et al.) Belgian (19th -)	*P*	$18,700	$23,100	$27,500

D=Drawing, P=Painting, S=Sculpture, W=Watercolor

		Current Price Range		
		Low	Mean	High
NOTER, Louis de	*P*			$1,320
Flemish (19th -)				
NOTERMAN, Zacharias	*P*	$3,520	$5,624	$8,525
Belgian (1820 - 1890)				
NOTT, Raymond	*D*	$220	$704	$1,760
American (1888 - 1948)	*P*	$248	$509	$770
NOURSE, Elizabeth	*D*	$10,450	$19,525	$28,600
American (1859 - 1938)	*P*	$3,520	$35,805	$82,500
	W	$7,150	$12,558	$22,000
NOVAK, Louis	*W*	$193	$234	$275
American (1903 -)				
NOVAK, V.	*P*			$110
Czechoslovakian (19th - 20th)				
NOVATI, Marco	*P*	$3,575	$3,575	$3,575
(?)				
NOVELLI, Gastone	*D*			$7,150
Italian (1925 - 1968)				
NOVELLI, Pietro (Attrib.)	*P*			$4,400
Italian (1603 - 1647)				
NOVELLI, Pietro (Manner)	*P*			$85,800
Italian (1603 - 1647)				
NOVELLI, Pietro A.	*D*			$1,980
Italian (1729 - 1804)	*P*			$3,300
NOVO, Stefano	*P*	$7,150	$29,700	$52,250
Italian (1862 -)				
NOVOTNY, E. L.	*P*	$220	$4,521	$9,900
American (1909 -)				
NOVROS, David	*P*	$6,600	$15,950	$25,300
(20th -)				
NOWAK, Ernst	*P*	$550	$2,338	$4,125
Austrian (1853 - 1919)				
NOWAK, Franz	*P*	$908	$922	$935
Austrian (20th -)				

D=Drawing, P=Painting, S=Sculpture, W=Watercolor

		Current Price Range	
	Low	Mean	High

		Low	Mean	High
NOWAK, Herman	P			$550
Hungarian (19th - 20th)				
NOWEY, Adolf D.	P	$193	$262	$330
British (20th -)				
NOYER, Denis P.	P			$413
French (1940 -)				
NOYER, Philippe	D			$4,125
French (1917 -)	P	$1,100	$3,296	$8,250
	W			$715
NOYES, George L.	D			$770
American (1864 - 1951)	P	$550	$4,615	$27,500
	W	$275	$585	$1,100
NUDERSCHER, Frank B.	D			$413
American (1880 - 1959)	P	$715	$2,454	$8,800
	W	$440	$550	$660
NUDERSCHER, Frank B. (Attrib.)	P	$935	$2,393	$3,850
American (1880 - 1959)				
NUGENT, A.	P			$193
French (20th -)				
NUMAN, Hermanus	D			$3,300
Dutch (1744 - 1820)				
NUNAMAKER, Kenneth	P			$38,500
American (1890 - 1957)				
NUNEZ, Armando G.	D			$2,860
Mexican (20th -)	P	$550	$4,675	$8,800
NUNEZ DEL PRADO, Marina	S			$2,750
(20th -)				
NUNN, Frederick	P	$176	$212	$248
American (1879 - 1959)				
NUNNS, J. W.	P			$770
(?)				
NURICK, Irving	W	$110	$156	$193
American (1894 - 1963)				

D=Drawing, P=Painting, S=Sculpture, W=Watercolor

		Current Price Range		
		Low	Mean	High
NUTT, Jim	D	$1,980	$2,228	$2,475
American (20th -)	P	$7,700	$20,020	$38,500
NUTTING, Wallace	P			$440
American (1861 -)				
NUVOLONE, Carlo F.	D			$2,200
Italian (1608 - 1665)	P	$12,100	$19,800	$27,500
NUYSSEN, Abraham J. (Attrib.)	P			$28,600
Flemish (1575 - 1632)				
NYE, Edgar	P	$110	$1,069	$2,310
American (1879 - 1943)	W	$110	$152	$193
NYHOLM, Arvid F.	P			$16,500
American (1866 - 1927)				
NYLAND, Gerard	P	$468	$509	$550
Dutch (20th -)				
NYROP, Borge	P	$880	$990	$1,100
Danish (1881 - 1948)				
NYS, Carl	P			$4,950
Belgian (1858 -)				
O'BOURKE, Terina	P			$825
American (20th -)				
O'BRIEN, Lucius R.	W			$523
Canadian (1832 - 1899)				
O'BRIEN, Smith	P			$660
American (1868 - 1952)				
O'CONNELL, M. J.	P			$825
British (19th - 20th)				
O'CONNER, Sean	P			$110
(?)				
O'CONNOR, James A.	P			$22,000
Irish (1792 - 1841)				
O'DONNELL, Hugh	P	$5,170	$9,735	$14,300
(20th -)	S	$3,080	$3,465	$3,850
	W	$5,500	$9,900	$14,300

D=Drawing, P=Painting, S=Sculpture, W=Watercolor

		Current Price Range		
		Low	Mean	High
O'DONOVAN, William R.	D			$303
American (1844 - 1920)				
O'GORMAN, Juan	D	$2,090	$10,098	$16,500
Mexican (1905 - 1982)	P	$44,000	$216,700	$550,000
O'HARA, Eliot	W			$495
American (1890 - 1969)				
O'HIGGINS, Pablo	P	$4,400	$8,067	$12,100
Lat. Amer. (20th -)				
O'KEEFFE, Georgia	D			$605,000
American (1887 - 1986)	P	$203,500	$776,722	$1.650M
O'KELLEY, Mattie L.	P	$375	$1,885	$4,400
American (20th -)				
O'MALLEY, A.	W			$165
American (20th -)				
O'NEIL, Henry N.	P	$55,000	$55,000	$55,000
British (1817 - 1880)				
O'NEILL, George B.	P			$16,500
British (1828 - 1917)				
O'NEILL, Rose	D			$900
American (1875 - 1944)				
O'SHEA, John	P			$1,210
American (1876 - 1956)				
O'SICKEY, Joseph B.	P			$440
American (20th -)				
O'SULLIVAN, M. L.	P			$248
American (20th -)				
O'TOOLE, Larry	P			$110
American (20th -)				
OAKES, Ann T.	P			$880
(19th -)				
OAKES, Wilbur L.	P	$303	$1,210	$2,970
American (1876 - 1934)				
OAKLEY, Octavius	W			$990
British (1800 - 1867)				

D=Drawing, P=Painting, S=Sculpture, W=Watercolor

		Current Price Range		
		Low	Mean	High
OAKLEY, Thorton	P			$9,900
American (1881 - 1953)	W			$550
OAKLEY, Violet	D	$220	$660	$1,100
American (1874 - 1960)	P			$1,870
OAKMAN, Arthur	P			$440
American (1910 -)				
OBATA, Chiura	W			$495
Japanese (20th -)				
OBEDIAS, Luiz	P			$121
Brazilian (20th -)				
OBERHAUSER, Emanuel	P			$12,100
Austrian (19th -)				
OBERMULLER, F.	P			$4,125
(?)				
OBERSTEINER, Ludwig	P	$880	$2,915	$4,950
Austrian (1857 -)				
OBERTEUFFER, George	P	$3,300	$13,750	$24,200
American (1878 -)				
OBICAN, Jovan	S			$143
(?)				
OBIN, Philome	P	$7,700	$18,792	$46,200
Haitian (1892 -)				
OBIN, Seneque	P	$2,750	$5,592	$9,900
Haitian (20th -)				
OBIT, L.	P			$770
European (19th -)				
OBREGON, Alejandro	P	$2,750	$28,233	$60,500
Spanish (1920 -)	S			$16,500
	W			$5,225
OCHI, Tasseki	P			$248
Japanese (20th -)				
OCHTERVELT, Jacob	P			$93,500
Dutch (17th - 18th)				

D=Drawing, P=Painting, S=Sculpture, W=Watercolor

		Current Price Range	
	Low	Mean	High

		Low	Mean	High
OCHTERVELT, Jacob (School)	P			$1,210
Dutch (17th - 18th)				
OCHTMAN, Dorothy	P	$275	$413	$550
American (1892 - 1971)				
OCHTMAN, Leonard	P	$1,870	$4,147	$11,000
American (1854 - 1934)	W			$110
OCHTMAN, Leonard (Attrib.)	P			$935
American (1854 - 1934)				
OCHTMAN, Mina F.	P			$880
American (1862 - 1924)				
OCTPAYZAHS, U.	P			$275
European (19th - 20th)				
ODDIE, Walter M.	P			$1,650
American (1808 - 1865)				
ODIERNA, Guido	P	$165	$358	$550
Italian (20th -)				
ODIO, Pucho	S			$220
Cuban (20th -)				
ODON, Mel	P			$1,650
(20th -)				
OEDER, George	P	$3,300	$3,410	$3,520
German (1846 - 1931)				
OEHME, Ernst E.	P			$3,575
German (1831 - 1907)				
OELSCHIG, Augusta	D			$110
American (20th -)				
OERTEL, Johannes A. S.	P			$30,800
American (1823 - 1909)				
OERTEL, Wilhelm	P			$825
German (1870 -)				
OETS, Pieter	D			$3,850
Dutch (1720 - 1790)				
OFFER, F. Rawlings	P			$1,045
British (19th -)				
OFFERMANSS, Tony L. G.	P			$2,090
Dutch (1854 - 1911)				

D=Drawing, P=Painting, S=Sculpture, W=Watercolor

		Current Price Range		
		Low	Mean	High
OGDEN, Frederick D.	P			$275
American (19th - 20th)				
OGDEN, Henry A.	D			$605
American (1856 - 1936)				
OGILVIE, J. Clinton	P	$660	$1,155	$1,650
American (1838 - 1900)				
OGLE, Mark	P	$900	$945	$990
American (20th -)	W			$800
OGUISS, Takanari	P	$52,800	$362,267	$572,000
Japanese (20th -)				
OHTAKE, Tomie	P			$7,700
(?)				
OIESTAD, H. Steven	D			$1,430
American (20th -)	W			$1,100
OKADA, Kenzo	P	$46,200	$53,900	$66,000
Japanese (1902 -)	S			$28,600
	W			$4,400
OKADA, Koen	P			$1,870
Japanese (1919 -)				
OKAMURA, Arthur	P	$330	$523	$770
American (1932 -)				
OKIMOTO,	P			$2,420
(?)				
OKOTO, J.	W			$110
Japanese (20th -)				
OKULICK, John	D	$605	$743	$880
(20th -)				
OLBRICH, W.	P	$220	$523	$825
American (19th -)				
OLDENBURG, Claes	D	$13,200	$39,008	$71,500
American (1929 -)	P	$16,500	$116,404	$308,000
	S	$11,000	$157,009	$495,000

D=Drawing, P=Painting, S=Sculpture, W=Watercolor

		Current Price Range		
		Low	Mean	High

OLDENBURG, Claes	*W*	$9,900	$30,800	$71,500
American (1929 -)				
OLDFIELD, Fred	*P*			$3,400
American (20th -)				
OLDFIELD, Otis	*P*			$22,000
American (1890 - 1969)				
OLDS, Gary L.	*S*			$2,100
American (20th -)				
OLINSKY, Ivan	*D*			$275
American (1878 - 1962)	*P*	$550	$1,664	$2,860
OLINSKY, Tosca	*P*	$187	$578	$1,430
American (1909 -)				
OLITSKI, Jules	*D*			$8,800
American (1922 -)	*P*	$1,650	$72,628	$352,000
OLIVA, F.	*P*			$825
Spanish (?)				
OLIVA, Lela	*P*			$495
(?)				
OLIVE, Jacinto	*P*			$7,700
Spanish (1896 - 1967)				
OLIVEIRA, Nathan	*D*			$19,800
American (1928 -)	*W*			$1,430
OLIVER, Cecily	*P*			$495
(19th -)				
OLIVER, Elizabeth P.	*P*			$110
American (1894 -)				
OLIVER, Frederick W.	*P*	$220	$990	$1,760
American (1876 - 1963)				
OLIVER, J.	*P*			$2,090
British (19th -)				
OLIVER, Sandi	*P*	$2,310	$3,758	$4,730
American (1941 -)				
OLIVER, William	*P*	$1,320	$3,007	$4,400
British (1805 - 1853)				

D=Drawing, P=Painting, S=Sculpture, W=Watercolor

| | | Current Price Range | | |
		Low	Mean	High
OLIVERIA, Oswald (19th -)	P			$248
OLIVETTI, Luigi Italian (19th - 20th)	W	$660	$1,155	$2,475
OLIVIER, Emile E. French (1800 - 1864)	P			$1,650
OLIVIER, Emma L. French (1887 -)	P			$523
OLIVIER, J. French (20th -)	P			$1,980
OLLER, Francisco Puerto Rican (1833 - 1917)	P	$23,100	$28,050	$33,000
OLNEY, Helen (Attrib.) American (20th -)	P			$180
OLSEN, Chr Benjamin Danish (1818 - 1878)	P			$1,870
OLSEN, Christina B. Danish (1873 - 1935)	P			$3,410
OLSEN, George W. American (1876 - 1938)	P			$1,870
OLSEN, Herb American (20th -)	W	$110	$253	$358
OLSON, Carl G. T. American (1875 -)	P	$138	$230	$330
OLSON, Joseph O. American (1894 - 1979)	W	$220	$376	$715
OLSON, Olaf American (1894 - 1979)	P			$358
OLYPHANT, Donald American (20th -)	P			$385
OMAN, Edwin American (1905 -)	W			$248
OMWAKE, William (19th - 20th)	P			$110
ONDERDONCK, Julian American (1892 - 1922)	P	$990	$4,770	$22,000

D=Drawing, P=Painting, S=Sculpture, W=Watercolor

		Current Price Range		
		Low	Mean	High

		Low	Mean	High
ONDERDONCK, Robert J.	P			$2,750
American (1853 - 1917)				
ONGANIA, U.	W			$550
Italian (19th - 20th)				
ONGLY, W.	P			$660
American (?)				
ONSAGER, Soren	P			$5,225
Norwegian (19th - 20th)				
ONTHANK, Nahum B.	P			$1,980
American (1823 - 1888)				
OOST, Jacob van	P			$18,700
Belgian (1601 - 1671)				
OOSTEN, Izaack van	P	$13,200	$22,550	$31,900
Flemish (1613 - 1661)				
OPDENHOFF, George W.	P			$2,750
Dutch (1807 - 1873)				
OPDENHOFF, George W. (Attrib.)	P			$770
Dutch (1807 - 1873)				
OPERTI, Albert	W	$248	$303	$358
American (1852 - 1927)				
OPIE, John	P			$4,400
British (1761 - 1807)				
OPIE, Julian	P	$8,800	$10,083	$11,550
(20th -)				
OPPENHEIM, Dennis	D	$2,200	$4,400	$7,700
American (1938 -)	P	$3,300	$4,758	$7,150
	W	$4,400	$5,427	$6,050
ORANGE, Maurice	P	$1,320	$2,173	$3,025
French (1868 - 1916)	W	$880	$1,265	$1,650
ORD, Joseph B.	P			$13,750
American (?)				
ORDONEZ, Sylvia	P	$1,650	$2,613	$3,575
Mexican (1957 -)				
ORDWAY, Alfred T.	P	$275	$625	$1,210
American (1819 - 1897)				

D=Drawing, P=Painting, S=Sculpture, W=Watercolor

		Current Price Range		
		Low	Mean	High
ORGAN, Marjorie	*D*	$110	$174	$220
American (1886 - 1930)				
ORKIN, Tilden	*P*			$275
American (19th -)				
ORLEY, Barend van	*P*	$77,000	$77,000	$77,000
Flemish (1492 - 1542)				
ORLEY, Barend van (Follower)	*P*			$68,750
Flemish (1492 - 1542)				
ORLEY, Richard van (Attrib.)	*D*			$880
Flemish (1663 - 1732)				
ORLOFF, Chana	*S*			$42,900
French (1888 - 1968)				
ORLOV, Igor	*P*			$1,100
Russian (1935 -)	*W*			$275
ORMISTON, Macgregor	*D*			$385
(1899 - 1956)	*P*	$605	$825	$1,045
ORMO, B.	*P*			$413
American (20th -)				
OROZCO, Jose C.	*D*	$1,760	$8,272	$26,400
Mexican (1883 - 1949)	*P*	$1,980	$43,419	$93,500
	W	$4,400	$14,300	$22,000
OROZCO, Jose C. (Circle)	*W*			$468
Mexican (1883 - 1949)				
ORPEN, Sir William N. M.	*P*	$5,720	$55,110	$104,500
Irish (1878 - 1931)				
ORR, C. S.	*W*			$1,100
American (19th -)				
ORR, Eric	*P*			$7,150
(20th -)				
ORR, Forest	*W*			$110
American (1895 -)				
ORR, Francis W.	*P*			$605
American (19th -)				

D=Drawing, P=Painting, S=Sculpture, W=Watercolor

	Current Price Range		
	Low	Mean	High

		Low	Mean	High
ORRENTE, Pedro (Attrib.)	P			$5,500
Spanish (1570 - 1644)				
ORSELLI, Arturo	W			$4,950
Italian (19th -)				
ORTADE,	P			$935
German (18th -)				
ORTEGA, Martin R.	P	$413	$66,928	$165,000
Spanish (1833 - 1908)	W	$4,400	$9,900	$15,400
ORTIZ, Emilio	P			$1,650
Mexican (1936 - 1988)				
ORTKENS, Aert	D			$38,500
Flemish (16th -)				
ORTLIEB, Friedrich	P	$4,400	$7,883	$12,100
German (1839 - 1909)				
ORTLIP, Aileen	P			$165
American (20th -)				
ORTLIP, Aimee E.	P			$385
American (1888 -)				
ORTLIP, H. Willard	P	$165	$330	$495
American (1886 -)				
ORTMAN, George	P			$1,540
American (1926 -)				
OS, Georgius J. van	P			$7,700
Dutch (1782 - 1861)				
OS, Georgius J. van (Manner)	P			$138
Dutch (1782 - 1861)				
OS, Jan van	P	$38,500	$60,500	$82,500
Dutch (1744 - 1808)				
OS, Jan van (Circle)	P	$4,950	$10,725	$16,500
Dutch (1744 - 1808)				
OS, Pieter F.van	P			$2,200
Dutch (1776 - 1839)				
OS-DELHEZ, Henri van	P	$1,430	$1,485	$1,540
Dutch (1880 - 1976)				
OSBORNE, C.	P			$440
European (19th - 20th)				

D=Drawing, P=Painting, S=Sculpture, W=Watercolor

		Current Price Range		
		Low	Mean	High

		Low	Mean	High
OSBY, Larissa American (?)	P			$358
OSEN, Erwin D. (20th -)	W			$8,800
OSGOOD, Phillips E. (?)	P			$1,100
OSGOOD, Ruth American (? - 1977)	P	$248	$798	$1,650
OSGOOD, Samuel T. American (19th -)	P			$1,320
OSINAGHI, J. European (19th -)	P			$1,045
OSLEAT, W. A. European (20th -)	P			$165
OSNIS, Benedict A. American (1872 -)	P			$220
OSSO, A. German (20th -)	W			$358
OSSORIO, Alfonso American (1916 -)	P			$26,400
OSTADE, Adriaen van Dutch (1610 - 1685)	P	$165	$53,941	$110,000
OSTADE, Adriaen van (Attrib.) Dutch (1610 - 1685)	P			$33,000
OSTADE, Adriaen van (Circle) Dutch (1610 - 1685)	D P			$550 $5,500
OSTADE, Isaak van Dutch (1621 - 1649)	P			$60,500
OSTADE, Isaak van (After) Dutch (1621 - 1649)	P			$3,080
OSTADE, Isaak van (Attrib.) Dutch (1621 - 1649)	P			$19,800
OSTADE, Isaak van (Circle) Dutch (1621 - 1649)	P			$8,800
OSTADE, Isaak van (Et al.) Dutch (17th -)	D			$4,180

D=Drawing, P=Painting, S=Sculpture, W=Watercolor

| | | Current Price Range | | |
		Low	Mean	High
OSTERLIND, Allan	P			$3,080
Swedish (1855 - 1938)				
OSTERLIND, Anders	P	$825	$1,485	$2,200
French (1887 - 1960)				
OSTERMAN, Karl E.	P			$1,980
Swedish (1870 -)				
OSTERSETZER, Carl	P	$2,860	$3,355	$3,850
German (19th - 20th)				
OSTHAUS, Edmund H.	P	$19,800	$28,188	$39,600
American (1858 - 1928)	W	$770	$5,737	$17,600
OSTHAUS, Edmund H. (Attrib.)	P			$523
American (1858 - 1928)				
OSTROWSKY, Sam	P	$275	$578	$880
American (1886 -)				
OSWALD, C. J.	P			$825
British (19th -)				
OSWALD, John H.	P			$220
British (19th -)				
OSWALDO, Carlos	P			$1,650
Italian (1882 - 1971)				
OTIS, Bass (Attrib.)	P	$660	$1,430	$2,200
American (1784 - 1861)				
OTIS, George D.	P	$1,650	$10,284	$30,250
American (1879 - 1962)				
OTIS, Samuel D.	D			$1,000
American (1889 - 1961)	P			$110
OTT, Jerry	P			$1,100
(20th -)				
OTT, Peter P.	S			$132
American (20th -)				
OTT, Sabina	P			$413
American (20th -)				
OTTE, William L.	D			$660
American (1871 - 1957)	P			$1,045

D=Drawing, P=Painting, S=Sculpture, W=Watercolor

		Current Price Range		
		Low	Mean	High
OTTER, Thomas P.	P	$275	$605	$935
American (1870 -)				
OTTERNESS, Tom	S			$1,870
(20th -)				
OTTERSON, Joel	P			$14,300
(20th -)				
OTTESEN, Otto D.	P	$2,200	$17,077	$68,500
Danish (1816 - 1892)				
OTTINGER, Kenneth	S	$1,100	$2,387	$3,850
American (1945 -)				
OTTMANN, Henri	P			$2,860
French (1877 - 1927)				
OTTO, Carl	P			$1,540
German (1830 - 1902)				
OUBORG, Piet	P			$1,430
Dutch (1893 -)				
OUDINOT, Achille F.	P			$605
French (1820 - 1891)				
OUDOT, Roland	P	$1,320	$3,135	$6,600
French (1897 -)				
OUDRY, Jacques-Charles	P			$55,000
French (1720 - 1778)				
OUDRY, Jacques-Charles (Circle)	P			$6,600
French (1720 - 1778)				
OUDRY, Jean-B.	D	$3,300	$9,433	$28,600
French (1686 - 1755)	P	$3,300	$64,625	$110,000
OUDRY, Jean-B. (Circle)	P	$4,125	$4,263	$4,400
French (1686 - 1755)				
OUDRY, Jean-B. (School)	P			$5,500
French (1686 - 1755)				
OUDSHOORM, Albert J.	W			$413
Dutch (1877 - 1930)				
OUREN, Karl	P	$935	$963	$990
American (1882 - 1934)				
OVCHINNIKOV, Nikolai	P	$8,250	$20,790	$48,400
Russian (1958 -)				

D=Drawing, P=Painting, S=Sculpture, W=Watercolor

| | | Current Price Range | | |
		Low	Mean	High
OVENS, Jurgen	*P*			$66,000
German (1623 - 1678)				
OVERSTREET, Anne A.	*W*			$600
American (20th -)				
OVIC, Alex B.	*P*	$275	$330	$385
(?)				
OVIEDO, Ramon	*P*	$5,225	$8,754	$13,200
Dom. Rep. (1927 -)				
OWEN,	*P*			$440
(?)				
OWEN, Esther S. D.	*D*			$248
American (1843 - 1927)				
OWEN, Frank	*P*			$550
(20th -)				
OWEN, Joel D.	*D*			$385
American (19th -)	*P*			$605
OWEN, Robert E.	*P*	$413	$1,683	$4,950
American (1878 - 1957)				
OWEN, V. H.	*P*			$1,870
American (20th -)				
OWEN, William	*P*			$5,500
British (1769 - 1825)				
OWENS, Edward (Attrib.)	*P*	$125	$250	$375
American (20th -)				
OXLEY, W. H.	*P*			$110
American (20th -)				
OZENFANT, Amedee	*P*			$220,000
French (20th -)				
OZONOFF, Ida (Attrib.)	*S*			$150
American (20th -)				
PAALEN, Wolfgang	*P*			$52,250
Austrian (1905 - 1959)				
PAAR, James	*W*			$1,540
American (20th -)				
PACCHIAROTTI, Giacomo	*P*			$66,000
Italian (1474 - 1540)				

D=Drawing, P=Painting, S=Sculpture, W=Watercolor

		Current Price Range		
		Low	Mean	High
PACETTI, M.	P			$990
(?)				
PACHECO, Maria L.	P			$1,925
Bolivian (1919 -)				
PACHECO ALT AMIRANO, Art.	P			$4,950
Chilean (1903 -)				
PADDOCK, Ethel L.	D	$260	$508	$935
American (1887 -)				
PADDOCK, Josephine	P			$303
American (1885 -)				
PADILLA, Eugenio L. (Attrib.)	P			$3,300
(?)				
PADUAN SCHOOL 17C,	P			$1,320
Italian (17th -)				
PADWICK, Philip H.	P			$275
British (1876 - 1936)				
PAEFF, Bashka	S			$275
American (1893 -)				
PAEZ, Jose de	P			$8,800
American (18th -)				
PAEZ, Jose de (Attrib.)	P			$12,100
American (18th -)				
PAEZ, Joseph de	P	$6,600	$19,800	$33,000
Mexican (17th -)				
PAFSET, B.	P			$9,900
French (19th - 20th)				
PAGANI, Gregorio	P			$3,850
Italian (1558 - 1605)				
PAGE, Edward A.	P	$440	$1,412	$2,640
American (1850 - 1928)	W			$220
PAGE, J.	P			$220
British (19th -)				
PAGE, Walter G.	P	$330	$935	$2,640
American (1862 - 1934)				
PAGE, William	P			$358
American (19th - 20th)				

D=Drawing, P=Painting, S=Sculpture, W=Watercolor

| | | Current Price Range | | |
		Low	Mean	High
PAGES, Irene	*P*	$110	$715	$1,210
French (1934 -)				
PAGES, Jules	*P*			$4,400
American (1867 - 1946)				
PAGLIACCI, Aldo	*P*	$110	$605	$990
Italian (20th -)				
PAGNONI, B.	*P*			$264
(?)				
PAGON, Katherine D.	*P*			$413
American (20th -)				
PAICE, George	*P*	$1,320	$1,485	$1,650
British (1854 - 1925)				
PAICE, George (Attrib.)	*P*			$550
British (1854 - 1925)				
PAIK, Nam June	*P*	$93,500	$101,750	$110,000
(20th -)				
PAIL, Edouard	*P*	$2,420	$4,510	$6,600
French (1851 -)				
PAILES, Isaac	*P*			$2,750
French (1895 -)				
PAILLER, Henri	*P*	$1,210	$3,135	$5,060
French (20th -)				
PAILLET, Charles	*S*			$6,875
French (1871 -)				
PAINE, Dorothy P.	*D*			$1,100
American (19th - 20th)				
PAINE, L. Gerard	*W*			$154
(?)				
PAINE, Susan	*P*			$9,020
(1792 - 1862)				
PAJETTA, Pietro	*P*			$1,650
Italian (1845 - 1911)				
PALACI, Fran	*P*	$880	$963	$1,045
(?)				
PALACIOS, Alirio	*P*	$9,350	$12,430	$16,500

D=Drawing, P=Painting, S=Sculpture, W=Watercolor

		Current Price Range		
		Low	Mean	High

		Low	Mean	High
PALACIOS, Alirio	S			$11,000
Venezuelan (1944 -)				
PALADINO, Mimmo	D			$41,800
Italian (1948 -)	P	$4,950	$67,980	$181,500
	S	$6,600	$94,600	$247,500
	W			$9,900
PALAMEDES, Anthonie	P	$3,300	$6,692	$13,200
Dutch (1601 - 1673)				
PALAMEDES, Anthonie (School)	P			$3,850
Dutch (1601 - 1673)				
PALAMEDESZ, Palamedes	P			$4,950
Dutch (1607 - 1638)				
PALERMO, Blinky	S			$38,500
(20th -)				
PALIN, William M.	P			$4,950
British (1862 - 1947)				
PALING, Johannes J.	P			$3,025
(19th -)				
PALIZZI, Filippo	P			$28,600
Italian (1818 - 1899)				
PALIZZI, Nicola (Attrib.)	P			$4,400
Italian (1820 - 1870)				
PALKO, Franz X.	P			$24,200
Austrian (1724 - 1767)				
PALLARES ALLUSTANTE, Joa.	P	$2,310	$2,915	$3,520
Spanish (19th -)				
PALLISER, Robert	P			$1,100
American (19th - 20th)				
PALLOCK, David	P			$110
American (20th -)				
PALLOCK, James A.	P			$110
American (20th -)				
PALLYA, Carolus	P			$385
Hungarian (1875 -)				

D=Drawing, P=Painting, S=Sculpture, W=Watercolor

		Current Price Range	
		Low	Mean	High

		Low	Mean	High
PALLYA, Celesztin	P			$358
Hungarian (1864 - 1948)				
PALMA, ELDER, Jacopo (Attrib.)	P			$2,310
Italian (1480 - 1528)				
PALMA, ELDER, Jacopo (Foll.)	P			$6,050
Italian (1480 - 1528)				
PALMA, YOUNGER, Jacopo	D	$2,860	$8,373	$20,900
Italian (1544 - 1628)				
PALMA, YOUNGER, Jacopo (Att.)	D			$3,025
Italian (1544 - 1628)				
PALMAROLI, Vincente	P	$15,400	$25,850	$36,300
Spanish (1834 - 1896)				
PALMAROLI, Vincente (Attrib.)	W			$990
Spanish (1834 - 1896)				
PALMER, Adelaide	P	$330	$880	$1,430
American (19th - 20th)				
PALMER, Erastus D.	S			$3,300
American (1817 - 1904)				
PALMER, Fanny F.	W			$440
American (1812 - 1876)				
PALMER, Fanny F. (Attrib.)	P			$3,025
American (1812 - 1876)				
PALMER, Harry S.	D			$330
British (1854 - 1933)	W	$165	$578	$990
PALMER, J. S.	P			$193
American (19th -)	W			$2,090
PALMER, Lynwood	P			$22,000
British (1868 - 1941)				
PALMER, Maude	W			$193
British (20th -)				
PALMER, Pauline	P	$385	$2,358	$4,950
American (1867 - 1938)				
PALMER, Walter L.	P	$2,200	$26,325	$143,000
American (1854 - 1932)	W	$3,520	$5,830	$9,350

D=Drawing, P=Painting, S=Sculpture, W=Watercolor

		Current Price Range		
		Low	Mean	High
PALMER, William American (1906 -)	P	$1,210	$3,905	$6,600
PALMEZZANO, Marco Italian (1458 - 1539)	P			$29,700
PALOTA, Hungarian (19th - 20th)	P			$132
PALTRONIERI, Pietro Italian (1673 - 1741)	W			$104,500
PALUMBO, Alphonso American (1890 -)	P	$935	$1,852	$2,420
PANCOAST, Morris American (1877 - 1963)	P	$385	$1,968	$3,860
PANCORBO, Alberto Colombian (1956 -)	P	$11,000	$12,100	$13,200
PANESCH, Hermine Austrian (19th - 20th)	P			$1,430
PANFILI, Pio Italian (1723 - 1812)	D			$1,650
PANINI, Giovanni Italian (1691 - 1765)	P	$82,500	$104,500	$126,500
PANINI, Giovanni (After) Italian (1691 - 1765)	P			$2,750
PANINI, Giovanni (Circle) Italian (1691 - 1765)	P			$66,000
PANINI, Giovanni (Follower) Italian (1691 - 1765)	P			$11,000
PANINI, Giovanni (Manner) Italian (1691 - 1765)	P			$4,675
PANINI, Giovanni (School) Italian (1691 - 1765)	P	$35,750	$37,125	$38,500
PANINI, Giovanni (Studio) Italian (1691 - 1765)	P	$19,800	$23,100	$25,300
PANINI & STUDIO, Giovanni Italian (17th - 18th)	P			$44,000
PANK, Arthur A. (?)	P			$1,100

D=Drawing, P=Painting, S=Sculpture, W=Watercolor

		Current Price Range		
		Low	Mean	High

PANORIOS, K.	*P*			$3,520
Greek (19th - 20th)				
PANSING, Fred	*P*			$38,500
American (1854 - 1912)	*W*			$1,870
PANTON, Alexander	*P*			$1,045
British (19th -)				
PANUNZI, Sebastiano	*W*	$138	$152	$165
Italian (1845 -)				
PANZA, Giovanni	*P*			$2,750
Italian (19th -)				
PAOLETTI, Antonio E.	*P*	$7,150	$7,975	$8,800
Italian (1834 - 1912)				
PAOLETTI, Paolo (Attrib.)	*P*	$16,500	$22,550	$28,600
Italian (? - 1735)				
PAOLINI, Giulio	*S*			$35,750
Italian (1949 -)				
PAOLINI, Pietro	*P*			$46,200
Italian (1603 - 1682)				
PAOLINI, Pietro (Circle)	*P*			$3,300
Italian (1603 - 1682)				
PAOLOZZI, Edouardo	*S*	$770	$14,218	$44,000
British (1924 -)				
PAPALUCA, L.	*P*	$275	$396	$468
Italian (1842 - 1912)				
PAPART, Max	*P*	$4,125	$4,492	$4,675
French (1911 -)				
PAPE, Eric	*D*	$4,070	$4,785	$5,500
American (1870 - 1938)	*P*	$1,760	$4,767	$9,900
PAPE, Friedrich E.	*P*			$6,600
German (1817 - 1905)				
PAPPAS, John L.	*P*			$605
Greek (1898 -)				
PAPPERITZ, Fritz G.	*P*			$3,520
German (1846 - 1918)				

D=Drawing, P=Painting, S=Sculpture, W=Watercolor

		Current Price Range		
		Low	Mean	High
PAPSDORF, Frederick	P	$110	$110	$110
American (20th -)				
PAQUIN, Milton	W			$303
American (20th -)				
PARADES, Vincent de	P	$7,150	$11,825	$16,500
Spanish (19th -)	W	$358	$729	$1,100
PARADISE, John	P			$495
American (1783 - 1833)				
PARENT, Edgar	P			$138
(?)				
PARENT, Leon	P			$1,485
French (1869 -)				
PARET Y ALCAZAR, Luis (Cir.)	P			$6,050
Spanish (1746 - 1799)				
PARINI,	W			$385
Italian (19th - 20th)				
PARIS, George De	W			$2,750
French (1829 - 1911)				
PARIS, Harold	S			$1,320
American (20th -)				
PARIS, Pierre A.	D			$770
French (1745 - 1819)				
PARIS, Rene	S			$6,600
French (19th -)				
PARIS, Walter	W	$220	$1,293	$6,600
American (1842 - 1906)				
PARIS, Walter (Attrib.)	W			$413
American (1842 - 1906)				
PARISH, Betty W.	W			$110
American (1910 -)				
PARIZEAU, Phillipe L.	D	$4,950	$4,950	$4,950
French (1740 - 1801)				
PARK, David	D			$9,350
American (1960 -)	P			$88,000

D=Drawing, P=Painting, S=Sculpture, W=Watercolor

		Current Price Range		
		Low	Mean	High

		Low	Mean	High
PARK, David	*W*			$4,180
American (1960 -)				
PARK, Henry (Attrib.)	*P*			$1,100
British (1816 - 1871)				
PARK, J. A.	*P*			$1,100
British (20th -)				
PARK, N. K.	*P*			$275
American (20th -)				
PARK, Patric	*S*			$3,080
Scottish (1811 - 1855)				
PARK, Richard H.	*S*			$1,210
American (1832 -)				
PARKE, I. N.	*P*			$578
American (19th -)				
PARKER, Alfred	*W*			$165
American (1906 -)				
PARKER, Bill	*P*			$3,300
American (1922 -)				
PARKER, E. A.	*P*			$248
American (1876 -)				
PARKER, Greg	*P*			$700
American (20th -)				
PARKER, H. E.	*P*			$935
British (19th -)				
PARKER, Henry H.	*P*	$4,620	$6,032	$8,525
British (1858 - 1930)				
PARKER, J. C. H.	*P*			$385
American (19th - 20th)				
PARKER, John A.	*P*			$2,750
American (1827 -)				
PARKER, Lawton S.	*D*			$1,320
American (1868 - 1954)	*P*	$1,210	$23,393	$79,750
PARKER, Paul	*P*			$413
American (1905 -)				
PARKER, Ray	*P*	$2,860	$4,389	$6,600
American (1922 -)				

D=Drawing, P=Painting, S=Sculpture, W=Watercolor

| | | Current Price Range | | |
		Low	Mean	High
PARKHURST, (19th -)	*P*			$770
PARKHURST, Clifford E. American (1885 -)	*D*			$825
PARKHURST, H. (20th -)	*P*			$950
PARKHURST, Thomas American (1853 - 1923)	*P*			$1,320
PARKINGTON, R. L. American (20th -)	*P*			$138
PARKS, American (20th -)	*P*			$138
PARKS, Bob American (1916 -)	*S*			$1,100
PARKS, Madeleine American (20th -)	*S*			$2,860
PARRA, Carmen Mexican (1944 -)	*P*			$15,400
PARRA, Jose F. Spanish (19th -)	*P*			$4,400
PARRIS, Edmund T. British (1793 - 1853)	*P*			$770
PARRISH, David American (1939 -)	*P*			$14,300
PARRISH, Maxfield American (1870 - 1966)	*D*	$550	$2,108	$4,950
	P	$2,200	$79,750	$198,000
PARRISH, Maxfield (Attrib.) American (1870 - 1966)	*P*			$770
	W			$220
PARRISH, Stephen American (1846 - 1938)	*D*			$220
	P	$1,100	$3,758	$5,500
PARROCEL, Charles French (1688 - 1752)	*P*			$9,900
PARROCEL, Joseph F. (Attrib.) French (1704 - 1791)	*D*			$1,760

D=Drawing, P=Painting, S=Sculpture, W=Watercolor

		Current Price Range		
		Low	Mean	High
PARROTT, William S.	*P*	$688	$2,778	$3,300
American (1844 - 1915)				
PARSHALL, Dewitt	*P*			$330
American (1864 - 1956)	*W*			$770
PARSHALL, Douglas E.	*P*	$468	$633	$715
American (1899 -)	*W*	$468	$482	$495
PARSON, Alfred W.	*D*			$138
British (1847 - 1920)				
PARSON, Del	*D*			$715
American (20th -)				
PARSONS, Alfred	*D*			$110
British (1847 - 1920)	*W*	$605	$1,293	$1,980
PARSONS, Arthur W.	*W*			$1,760
British (1854 - 1931)				
PARSONS, Betty	*P*	$1,045	$1,623	$2,200
American (20th -)	*W*			$165
PARSONS, Charles	*W*			$165
American (1821 - 1910)				
PARSONS, Edith B.	*S*	$660	$2,921	$9,900
American (1878 - 1956)				
PARSONS, Marion	*P*	$1,980	$2,503	$3,025
American (1880 - 1953)				
PARSONS, Orrin S.	*P*			$30,250
American (1866 - 1943)				
PARSONS, Phillip B.	*P*	$110	$165	$220
American (1896 - 1977)	*W*	$110	$219	$303
PARTON, Arthur B.	*P*	$825	$2,442	$8,800
American (1842 - 1914)				
PARTON, Ernest	*P*	$2,750	$4,318	$6,050
American (1845 - 1933)				
PARTON, Henry W.	*P*			$605
American (1858 - 1933)				

D=Drawing, P=Painting, S=Sculpture, W=Watercolor

		Current Price Range		
		Low	Mean	High

		Low	Mean	High
PARTON, Professor B.	*P*			$2,750
British (19th - 20th)				
PARTRIDGE, William H.	*P*	$110	$578	$1,155
American (1858 -)				
PARTRIDGE, William O.	*S*			$1,100
American (1861 - 1930)				
PARYS, A.	*D*			$7,150
French (19th -)				
PASCAL, Jean	*P*			$605
French (1837 - 1920)				
PASCAL, Paul	*D*			$578
French (1867 -)	*W*	$385	$763	$1,760
PASCALIS, Louise	*P*			$1,100
French (1893 - 1934)				
PASCHKE, Ed	*P*	$11,000	$19,800	$26,400
American (1939 -)				
PASCIN, Jules	*D*	$330	$7,658	$137,500
French (1885 - 1930)	*P*	$2,255	$149,237	$451,000
	W	$715	$3,753	$8,250
PASCOE, William	*P*	$715	$853	$990
British (19th -)				
PASCUAL, Placido	*P*			$8,250
Spanish (1840 -)				
PASCUTTI, Antonio	*P*			$1,650
Austrian (19th -)				
PASINELLI, Lorenzo (Circle)	*P*			$11,000
Italian (1629 - 1700)				
PASINI, Alberto	*P*	$3,300	$34,100	$198,000
Italian (1826 - 1899)				
PASINI, Emilio	*P*			$248
Italian (1899 - 1924)				
PASINI, Lazzaro	*P*			$220
Italian (1861 - 1946)				
PASKELL, William F.	*P*	$330	$619	$908

D=Drawing, P=Painting, S=Sculpture, W=Watercolor

		Current Price Range		
		Low	Mean	High

PASKELL, William F.	*W*	$138	$348	$990
American (1866 - 1951)				
PASMORE, Daniel	*P*			$440
British (19th -)				
PASQUELL, R. B.	*P*	$440	$440	$440
French (19th -)				
PASSAROTTI, Bartolomeo	*D*	$5,500	$9,350	$13,200
Italian (1529 - 1592)				
PASSAROTTI, Bartolomeo (Circle)	*P*	$5,500	$5,500	$5,500
Italian (1529 - 1592)				
PASSAROTTI, Tiburzio	*W*			$29,700
Italian (1555 - 1612)				
PASSE, Crispin de (Attrib.)	*D*			$1,320
Dutch (1564 - 1637)				
PASSERI, Giuseppe	*D*			$1,650
Italian (1654 - 1714)				
PASSET, Gerard	*P*			$1,540
French (1936 -)				
PASSINI, Ludwig	*W*	$2,200	$10,450	$20,900
Austrian (1832 - 1903)				
PASTEGA, Luigi	*P*	$4,675	$5,885	$7,700
Italian (1858 - 1927)				
PASTINA, Giuseppe	*P*			$2,475
Italian (1863 -)				
PATA, Cherubin	*P*			$8,800
French (19th -)				
PATEL, Pierre (Circle)	*P*			$2,640
French (1605 - 1676)				
PATEL, Pierre (Manner)	*P*			$4,400
French (1605 - 1676)				
PATEL, YOUNGER, Pierre	*P*			$24,200
French (1648 - 1707)				
PATEL, YOUNGER, Pierre (Att.)	*P*			$18,700
French (1648 - 1707)				
PATEL, YOUNGER, Pierre (Sch.)	*P*			$1,430
French (1648 - 1707)				

D=Drawing, P=Painting, S=Sculpture, W=Watercolor

		Current Price Range	
	Low	Mean	High
PATELLIERE, Amedee de la *P*			$8,800
French (1890 - 1932)			
PATER, Jean B. (Manner) *P*			$13,750
French (1695 - 1736)			
PATERSON, George M. *P*			$990
British (1873 -)			
PATERSON, Mary V. *P*			$2,530
American (1899 - 1982)			
PATKIN, Itzar *P*			$24,200
(20th -)			
PATMAGRION, *P*			$100
(?)			
PATON, Frank *P*			$1,980
American (1856 - 1909)			
PATON, Sir Joseph N. *P*			$2,750
British (1821 - 1900) *S*			$176
PATON, Waller H. *W*			$550
British (1828 - 1895)			
PATRICK, James M. *W*			$1,320
British (1907 -)			
PATTEIN, Cesar *P*	$7,150	$10,908	$16,500
French (19th - 20th)			
PATTEN, George *P*			$8,800
British (1801 - 1865)			
PATTEN, Leonard *P*	$440	$468	$495
European (20th -)			
PATTERSON, Charles R. *P*	$550	$660	$770
American (1878 - 1958)			
PATTERSON, Margaret J. *D*			$1,100
American (1867 - 1950) *P*	$220	$990	$1,760
W	$330	$750	$1,540
PATTERSON, Marion L. *P*			$121
American (1909 -)			
PATTERSON, Robert *W*			$200
American (1898 - 1981)			

D=Drawing, P=Painting, S=Sculpture, W=Watercolor

		Current Price Range		
		Low	Mean	High

		Low	Mean	High
PATTERSON, Russell American (1896 - 1977)	D			$600
PATTISON, Abbott American (1916 -)	S			$523
PATTON, A. F. American (20th -)	P			$358
PATTY, William A. American (1889 - 1961)	P			$176
PAUL, Bruno German (1861 -)	P			$495
PAUL, J. (18th - 19th)	P			$2,750
PAUL, Jeremiah (Attrib.) American (19th -)	P			$2,860
PAUL, John British (19th -)	P			$15,400
PAULI, Richard American (1855 - 1892)	P	$605	$688	$770
PAULIS, (20th -)	P			$110
PAULSEN, N. Chr. Danish (19th -)	P			$2,750
PAULSON, E. American (?)	P			$132
PAULUS, Francis P. American (1862 - 1933)	P			$770
PAULY, Erik B. Hungarian (1869 -)	P			$825
PAUS, Herbert American (1880 - 1946)	D W			$193 $935
PAUSINGER, Clemens von German (1855 - 1936)	D			$1,980
PAUTROT, Ferdinand French (19th -)	S	$550	$1,547	$4,125
PAUWELS, H. J. Belgian (20th -)	P			$935

D=Drawing, P=Painting, S=Sculpture, W=Watercolor

		Current Price Range		
		Low	Mean	High

		Low	Mean	High
PAVESI, Pietro	*W*	$1,430	$1,815	$2,200
Italian (19th -)				
PAVESI, Pietro (Attrib.)	*W*			$550
Italian (19th -)				
PAVIA, Philip	*W*			$605
(20th -)				
PAVIL, Elie Anatole	*P*			$2,310
French (1873 - 1948)				
PAVY, Eugene	*P*	$770	$4,785	$8,800
French (19th -)				
PAVY, Philippe	*P*			$3,080
French (19th -)				
PAWLIKOWSKI, Andre	*P*	$550	$688	$825
Polish (1940 -)				
PAXSON, Edgar S.	*P*	$8,250	$11,825	$15,400
American (1852 - 1915)	*W*	$1,320	$2,695	$3,520
PAXSON, Ethel	*D*			$275
American (1885 - 1982)	*P*	$110	$598	$2,860
PAXTON,	*P*			$110
American (20th -)				
PAXTON, Elizabeth V. O.	*P*	$303	$4,277	$8,250
American (1877 - 1971)				
PAXTON, William M.	*D*	$523	$11,255	$38,500
American (1869 - 1941)	*P*	$990	$36,093	$126,500
PAYNE, Charlie J.	*W*			$27,500
British (1884 - 1967)				
PAYNE, David	*P*			$4,125
British (19th -)				
PAYNE, Edgar A.	*D*			$605
American (1882 - 1947)	*P*	$550	$10,311	$49,500
	W	$330	$1,815	$3,300
PAYNE, George F.	*W*			$495
American (20th -)				

D=Drawing, P=Painting, S=Sculpture, W=Watercolor

| | | Current Price Range | | |
		Low	Mean	High
PAYNE, George S.	*W*	$193	$427	$660
American (1860 - 1938)				
PAYNE, Ken	*S*			$1,650
American (20th -)				
PAYNE, William	*W*			$550
British (1760 - 1830)				
PAYZANT, Charles	*W*	$495	$836	$1,430
American (1898 - 1980)				
PAYZANT, Claude L.	*P*	$110	$440	$770
American (20th -)				
PEAK, Robert	*P*			$248
American (1928 -)				
PEALE, Anna C.	*P*			$8,250
American (?)				
PEALE, Charles W.	*P*			$12,100
American (1741 - 1827)				
PEALE, James	*P*	$28,600	$115,775	$181,500
American (1749 - 1831)				
PEALE, James (Attrib.)	*P*			$4,180
American (1749 - 1831)				
PEALE, Margaretta	*P*			$5,225
American (1795 - 1882)				
PEALE, Margaretta (Attrib.)	*P*			$605
American (1795 - 1882)				
PEALE, Mary Jane	*P*	$5,775	$7,288	$8,800
American (1827 - 1902)				
PEALE, R.	*P*	$935	$935	$935
(?)				
PEALE, Raphaelle	*P*			$20,900
American (1774 - 1825)				
PEALE, Rembrandt	*P*	$4,125	$41,525	$115,500
American (1778 - 1860)				
PEALE, Sarah M.	*P*			$42,900
American (1800 - 1885)				
PEALE, Titian Ramsey	*W*			$33,000
American (1799 - 1885)				

D=Drawing, P=Painting, S=Sculpture, W=Watercolor

		Current Price Range		
		Low	Mean	High
PEALLZOR, Estelle	P	$248	$248	$248
American (20th -)				
PEAN, Rene	P	$2,310	$3,098	$4,675
French (1875 -)				
PEARCE, Charles S.	P			$16,500
American (1851 - 1914)				
PEARCE, Edger L.	P			$550
American (1885 -)				
PEARCE, W. H. S.	P	$385	$399	$413
American (19th - 20th)				
PEARL, Moses P.	W			$743
American (20th -)				
PEARLMUTTER, Stella	P	$385	$691	$1,100
American (?)				
PEARLSTEIN, Philip	D	$1,650	$3,457	$5,500
American (1924 -)	P	$9,900	$37,194	$57,750
	W	$1,210	$9,937	$19,800
PEARSON, Albert	W			$330
American (1911 -)				
PEARSON, Dennis	W			$440
American (20th -)				
PEARSON, M. A.	W			$248
American (19th - 20th)				
PEARSON, Marguerite S.	P	$275	$4,439	$17,600
American (1898 - 1978)	W			$330
PEASLEE, Marguerite E.	P			$303
American (20th -)	W			$138
PEBBLES, Francis M.	P			$440
American (1839 - 1928)				
PECHAUBES, Eugene	P	$385	$3,817	$12,100
French (1890 - 1967)	W			$330
PECHE, Dale	P			$990
American (20th -)				

D=Drawing, P=Painting, S=Sculpture, W=Watercolor

		Current Price Range		
		Low	Mean	High

		Low	Mean	High
PECHEUR, Emile	*P*			$15,400
French (19th -)				
PECHSTEIN, Max H.	*D*	$880	$6,893	$11,000
German (1881 - 1955)	*P*	$82,500	$237,875	$440,000
	W	$9,900	$28,993	$57,750
PECHSTEIN, Max H. (Attrib.)	*W*			$660
German (1881 - 1955)				
PECHY, K.	*P*			$143
(?)				
PECK,	*W*			$150
(20th -)				
PECK, Charles E.	*P*	$770	$845	$919
American (1827 - 1900)				
PECK, E. M.	*P*			$193
American (20th -)				
PECK, Henry J.	*D*			$660
American (1880 - 1934)				
PECK, Orrin M.	*P*			$2,750
American (1860 - 1921)				
PECK, Roy	*P*			$1,980
(?)				
PECZELY, Antal	*P*	$550	$633	$715
Hungarian (1891 -)				
PEDERSEN, Finn	*P*	$990	$1,992	$6,380
Danish (20th -)				
PEDERSEN, Hugo V.	*P*			$3,575
Danish (1870 -)				
PEDERSEN, Sharon	*W*			$550
American (20th -)				
PEDERSEN, Viggo C. F. W.	*P*			$5,500
Danish (1854 - 1926)				
PEDERSEN-MOLS, Neils	*P*			$17,600
Danish (1859 -)				
PEDRINI, Domenico	*D*			$1,760
Italian (1728 - 1800)				

D=Drawing, P=Painting, S=Sculpture, W=Watercolor

| | | Current Price Range | | |
		Low	Mean	High
PEDULLI, F.	*W*			$1,210
Italian (19th -)				
PEEL, James	*P*	$330	$2,145	$3,850
British (1811 - 1906)				
PEETERS, Jacob	*P*			$17,600
Flemish (17th - 18th)				
PEIFFER, Auguste J.	*S*			$1,320
German (1830 - 1896)				
PEIRCE, H. Winthrop	*P*	$1,540	$1,595	$1,650
American (1850 - 1936)	*W*	$165	$853	$1,540
PEIRCE, Waldo	*D*			$468
American (1884 - 1970)	*P*	$2,200	$3,699	$7,150
	W	$495	$970	$1,760
PEIXOTTO, Ernest C.	*P*	$1,430	$4,510	$8,800
American (1869 - 1940)				
PELAEZ, Amelia	*P*	$7,700	$15,033	$22,000
Mexican (1897 - 1968)	*W*	$2,200	$9,900	$15,400
PELHAM, J.	*P*			$2,860
(19th -)				
PELHAM, Thomas K.	*P*	$715	$2,768	$6,820
British (19th -)				
PELIKAN,	*S*			$880
(?)				
PELIKAN, A. G.	*P*	$200	$250	$300
American (20th -)				
PELIKAN, Alfred S. (Attrib.)	*P*			$120
American (1893 -)				
PELL, Harvey	*W*			$138
American (20th -)				
PELL, Jacob	*P*			$1,430
American (1900 -)				
PELLAGALE, W. E.	*P*	$330	$385	$440
American (19th -)				

D=Drawing, P=Painting, S=Sculpture, W=Watercolor

		Current Price Range		
		Low	Mean	High
PELLEGRINI, Giovanni (Attrib.)	*D*			$3,025
Italian (1675 - 1741)				
PELLEGRINI, Giovanni (Circle)	*P*			$2,750
Italian (1675 - 1741)				
PELLEGRINI, Giovanni (Manner)	*D*			$2,310
Italian (1675 - 1741)	*P*			$2,090
PELLEGRINO, J.	*P*			$605
Italian (19th -)				
PELLON, Jo-Alice	*P*	$358	$386	$413
(20th -)				
PELOUSE, Leon G.	*P*	$1,100	$6,644	$12,100
French (1838 - 1891)				
PELS, Albert	*P*	$220	$1,503	$3,080
American (1910 -)				
PELTON, Agnes	*D*			$1,210
American (1881 - 1961)	*P*	$2,090	$3,630	$6,600
	W	$3,740	$4,070	$4,400
PELUSO, Francesco	*P*	$2,860	$4,565	$7,700
Italian (1836 -)				
PEN, Rudolph	*P*			$935
American (1918 -)				
PENA, Angel	*P*	$4,400	$9,900	$15,400
S. American (20th -)				
PENA, Narcisse	*P*			$550
French (1807 - 1876)				
PENALBA, Alicia	*S*	$2,750	$8,617	$15,400
Argentina (1918 -)				
PENALOSA Y SANDOVAL, J.	*P*			$13,200
Spanish (? - 17th)				
PENCA, T. E.	*P*			$550
European (20th -)				
PENCK, A. R.	*D*	$7,425	$18,608	$26,400
German (1939 -)	*P*	$17,600	$75,350	$242,000

D=Drawing, P=Painting, S=Sculpture, W=Watercolor

		Current Price Range		
		Low	Mean	High
PENCK, A. R.	W	$7,700	$10,560	$13,200
German (1939 -)				
PENCK, T. C.	P			$358
(?)				
PENE DU BOIS, Guy	D	$660	$898	$1,045
American (1884 - 1958)	P	$3,850	$20,934	$52,250
	W	$303	$997	$2,420
PENFIELD, Edward	P			$825
American (1866 - 1925)	W			$3,575
PENGLAOU, Michel	P			$275
French (1925 -)				
PENLEY, Aaron E.	W			$5,280
British (1807 - 1870)				
PENNE, Charles O. de	P	$550	$15,059	$66,000
French (1831 - 1897)	W			$2,750
PENNELL, Eugene H.	P			$1,870
British (19th -)				
PENNELL, Joseph	D	$330	$1,506	$6,600
American (1860 - 1926)	W	$550	$2,105	$3,850
PENNELL, Nolan	P			$110
American (1894 - 1972)				
PENNEY, Frederick	P			$1,540
American (1900 - 1988)	W	$248	$688	$1,100
PENNOYER, Albert S.	P	$550	$1,155	$2,200
American (1888 - 1957)	W			$660
PENNY, Edward	P			$44,000
British (1714 - 1791)				
PENNY, James	P			$3,300
(?)				
PENNY, William D.	P			$2,970
British (1834 - 1924)				

D=Drawing, P=Painting, S=Sculpture, W=Watercolor

		Current Price Range		
		Low	Mean	High

		Low	Mean	High
PENOT, Albert J.	P			$3,300
French (19th -)	W			$330
PENOT, Jean V.	P			$88,000
French (1710 - 1777)				
PEOPLES, Agusta H.	W			$220
American (20th -)				
PEPPER, Beverly	S	$2,200	$9,558	$25,300
American (1924 -)				
PERAIRE, Paul E.	P			$20,900
French (1829 - 1893)				
PERBANDT, Carl von	P	$1,650	$3,300	$5,225
American (1832 - 1911)				
PERBOYRE, Paul E. L.	P	$3,575	$4,813	$6,050
French (19th -)				
PERCEVAL, Don	W			$6,050
American (1908 - 1979)				
PERCRUS, Charles	P			$2,640
French (1826 - 1907)				
PERCY, F.	P			$220
(?)				
PERCY, Sidney R.	P	$6,600	$22,458	$52,800
British (1821 - 1886)				
PERDRIAT, Helene M. M.	P			$1,430
French (1894 -)				
PEREDA, Antonio de (Attrib.)	P			$35,200
Spanish (1599 - 1669)				
PEREDA, Antonio de (Circle)	P			$19,800
Spanish (1599 - 1669)				
PEREDA, Antonio de (School)	P			$7,150
Spanish (1599 - 1669)				
PEREIRA, Irene R.	P	$2,750	$6,380	$10,450
American (1907 - 1971)	S	$4,125	$6,738	$9,350
	W	$605	$792	$1,430
PERELLE, Adam (Attrib.)	D			$4,950
French (1638 - 1695)				

D=Drawing, P=Painting, S=Sculpture, W=Watercolor

		Current Price Range		
		Low	Mean	High

PERETTI, Achille	P			$2,200
American (? - 1923)				
PEREZ, Alonso	P	$2,750	$12,095	$46,750
Spanish (1893 - 1914)	W			$2,145
PEREZ, Alonso (Style)	P			$2,475
Spanish (1893 - 1914)				
PEREZ, Cayetano	P			$825
(?)				
PEREZ, Enrique C.	P			$7,700
Spanish (19th -)				
PERICONI, Domingo F.	P	$660	$1,375	$2,090
American (?)				
PERIGAL, Arthur	P	$3,025	$3,163	$3,300
British (1784 - 1847)				
PERIGNON, Alex-Noel (Circle)	D			$1,760
French (1726 - 1782)				
PERIGNON, Alexis J.	P			$15,400
French (1806 - 1882)				
PERILLO, Gregory	P	$1,320	$1,980	$2,420
American (1929 -)	S			$1,540
PERINI, Sandro	P			$440
(?)				
PERKINS, A.	P			$660
American (19th -)				
PERKINS, Granville	D			$825
American (1830 - 1895)	P	$660	$4,950	$14,300
	W	$220	$650	$1,760
PERKINS, Harley	P			$110
American (1883 -)				
PERKINS, M. S.	P			$963
American (19th - 20th)				
PERKINS, Parker S.	P	$248	$680	$1,540
American (1862 -)				

D=Drawing, P=Painting, S=Sculpture, W=Watercolor

		Low	Mean	High
		\multicolumn{3}{c}{Current Price Range}		

		Low	Mean	High
PERKINS, Phillip (20th -)	D			$850
PERKINS, R. N. (?)	P			$650
PERKINS, W. Thompson American (20th -)	P	$110	$147	$220
PERLBERG, Friedrich German (1848 - 1921)	W	$4,125	$4,263	$4,400
PERLIN, Bernard American (1918 -)	P	$880	$5,940	$11,000
PERLMAN, Joel (20th -)	S	$935	$3,108	$5,280
PERMEKE, Constant Belgian (1886 - 1951)	D			$2,530
PEROT, Anna L. American (1854 -)	P			$165
PERRACHON, Andre French (1827 - 1909)	P			$3,080
PERRACHON, Andre (Attrib.) French (1827 - 1909)	W			$3,080
PERRAULT, Leon J. B. French (1832 - 1908)	P	$1,980	$24,298	$55,000
PERRAULT, Marie American (?)	W			$1,210
PERREIRA, Joan American (20th -)	P			$242
PERRET, Aime French (1847 - 1927)	P			$13,200
PERRET, Aime (Attrib.) French (1847 - 1927)	P			$2,200
PERRIE, Bertha American (? - 1921)	P W			$3,080 $358
PERRIER, Francois (Attrib.) French (1590 - 1650)	P			$49,500
PERRINE, Robert American (20th -)	P			$550

D=Drawing, P=Painting, S=Sculpture, W=Watercolor

		Current Price Range		
		Low	Mean	High
PERRINE, Van Dearing	*P*			$2,200
American (1868 -)				
PERRON, Charles C. F.	*P*	$2,310	$4,917	$6,875
French (1893 - 1958)				
PERRONEAU, Jean B.	*P*	$2,420	$4,510	$6,600
French (1715 - 1783)				
PERRONEAU, Jean B. (Sch.)	*P*			$4,180
French (1715 - 1783)				
PERROT, F. J. Beth	*S*			$688
(?)				
PERRY, Clara G.	*D*			$358
American (1871 -)	*P*	$1,320	$2,613	$3,905
PERRY, Enoch W.	*P*	$880	$6,362	$30,800
American (1831 - 1915)				
PERRY, J.	*W*			$1,210
Lat. Amer. (19th -)				
PERRY, Lilla C.	*P*	$440	$7,316	$31,900
American (1848 - 1933)				
PERRY, O. H.	*W*			$110
American (19th - 20th)				
PERRY, Roland H.	*P*			$1,320
American (1870 - 1941)	*S*			$5,060
PERTAK, Diana L.	*D*			$715
(?)				
PERTGEN, Karl M.	*P*			$88,000
German (1881 -)				
PERUVIAN SCHOOL,	*P*	$2,200	$4,675	$7,150
Peruvian (?)				
PERUZZI, Baldassare	*D*			$17,600
Italian (1481 - 1536)				
PERZL, L.	*P*			$1,320
German (19th -)				
PESCI, Ottilio	*S*	$528	$704	$880
American (1877 -)				

D=Drawing, P=Painting, S=Sculpture, W=Watercolor

		Current Price Range		
		Low	Mean	High

PESKE, Jean	*P*			$2,420
French (1880 - 1949)				
PESNE, Antoine	*P*			$33,000
French (1683 - 1757)				
PESNE, Antoine (Attrib.)	*P*	$1,210	$2,897	$4,620
French (1683 - 1757)				
PESNE, Antoine (Circle)	*P*			$2,200
French (1683 - 1757)				
PETE, W.	*P*			$138
German (19th - 20th)				
PETER,	*P*			$19,800
(?)				
PETER, Emanuel	*P*			$1,320
Austrian (1799 - 1873)	*W*			$1,760
PETER, George	*P*			$220
American (?)				
PETERS, Anna	*P*			$3,520
German (1843 - 1926)				
PETERS, Bernard E.	*P*			$660
American (1893 -)				
PETERS, Carl W.	*P*	$385	$2,029	$4,950
American (1898 - 1980)				
PETERS, Carl W. (Attrib.)	*P*			$100
American (1898 - 1980)				
PETERS, Charles R.	*P*	$495	$3,960	$17,600
American (1862 - 1928)				
PETERS, Charles R. (Attrib.)	*P*			$275
American (1862 - 1928)				
PETERS, Constance	*P*			$1,430
American (1878 - 1935)				
PETERS, Les	*P*	$880	$880	$880
American (20th -)				
PETERS, Matthew W.	*P*			$26,400
British (1742 - 1814)				
PETERS, Matthew W. (Attrib.)	*P*			$3,850
British (1742 - 1814)				

D=Drawing, P=Painting, S=Sculpture, W=Watercolor

		Current Price Range		
		Low	Mean	High
PETERSEN, Edvard F.	P			$13,200
Davish (1841 - 1911)				
PETERSEN, Hans R. von	P			$2,200
German (1850 - 1914)				
PETERSEN, Johann E. C.	P	$2,970	$4,785	$6,600
American (1839 - 1874)				
PETERSEN, K. Gunnor	P	$110	$154	$193
American (1905 - 1985)	W	$138	$175	$248
PETERSEN-FLENSBURG, Hein.	P			$770
German (1861 - 1908)				
PETERSON, H.	P	$220	$248	$275
American (20th -)				
PETERSON, Jane	D	$165	$495	$825
American (1876 - 1965)	P	$550	$8,374	$126,500
	W	$330	$3,658	$17,600
PETERSON, Jane (Attrib.)	W			$4,125
American (1876 - 1965)				
PETHER, Abraham	P	$1,650	$2,255	$2,860
British (1756 - 1812)				
PETHER, Henry	P			$11,000
British (19th -)				
PETHER, Sebastian	P			$3,300
British (1790 - 1844)				
PETICOLAS, Philip A.	W			$495
American (1760 - 1843)				
PETIT, Charles	P			$3,850
French (19th -)				
PETIT, Eugene	P	$660	$1,045	$1,430
French (1839 - 1886)				
PETIT-GERARD, Pierre	P			$8,800
French (1852 -)				
PETITJEAN, Edmond M.	P	$5,775	$10,588	$16,500
French (1844 - 1925)				
PETITJEAN, Hippolyte	P	$3,300	$62,453	$143,000

D=Drawing, P=Painting, S=Sculpture, W=Watercolor

		Current Price Range		
		Low	Mean	High
PETITJEAN, Hippolyte	W	$1,210	$15,070	$24,200
French (1854 - 1929)				
PETITT, Edwin A.	P			$440
American (1840 - 1912)				
PETO, John F.	P	$16,500	$101,200	$418,000
American (1854 - 1907)				
PETRASSI, L.	P			$660
(19th -)				
PETRI, P.	P			$132
(20th -)				
PETROCELLI, Arturo	P	$176	$865	$2,200
Italian (1856 -)				
PETRONI, Andrea	P			$1,320
Italian (1863 -)	W			$330
PETROSIAN, Rafael	S			$1,100
(20th -)				
PETROV, Arkadi	P			$7,700
Russian (1940 -)				
PETRUK, Yuri	P			$2,200
Russian (1950 -)				
PETRUOLA, Salvatore	P			$6,050
Italian (1857 - 1946)				
PETRY, Victor	P			$880
American (1903 -)				
PETTENKOFEN, August von	P			$4,950
Austrian (1822 - 1889)				
PETTENKOFEN, August von (Att.)	P			$2,200
Austrian (1822 - 1889)				
PETTER, Franz X.	P	$28,600	$38,500	$48,400
Austrian (1791 - 1866)				
PETTIBONE, Richard	P			$3,520
(20th -)				
PETTITT, Charles	P			$11,000
British (19th -)	W	$132	$286	$440

D=Drawing, P=Painting, S=Sculpture, W=Watercolor

| | | Current Price Range | | |
		Low	Mean	High
PETTITT, Joseph P.	*P*			$1,210
British (? - 1882)				
PETTORUTI, Emilio	*D*	$4,400	$4,510	$4,620
Argentina (1892 - 1971)	*P*	$3,300	$71,585	$132,000
	W			$4,400
PETUA, Leon J.	*P*			$24,200
French (1846 - 1921)				
PEVSNER, Antoine	*P*			$77,000
French (1884 - 1962)				
PEYRAT, Louis	*P*	$165	$426	$550
French (20th -)				
PEYRAUD, Frank C.	*P*	$413	$1,521	$4,180
American (1858 - 1928)				
PEYROL-BONHEUR, Juliette	*P*			$2,860
French (1830 - 1891)				
PEYTON, Bertha M.	*P*	$2,310	$2,355	$2,400
American (1871 - 1950)				
PFAFF, Judy	*P*			$49,500
(20th -)	*S*			$30,250
PFAHL, Charles	*P*			$4,125
American (1946 -)				
PFEIFER, Wilhelm	*P*	$3,850	$4,235	$4,620
German (1822 - 1891)				
PFEIFFER, Fritz	*P*			$660
American (1889 - 1960)	*W*			$743
PFEIFFER, G. P.	*P*			$495
Canadian (19th - 20th)				
PFEIFFER, Heinrich	*P*	$248	$379	$468
American (1874 - 1960)				
PFEIFFER, Herman	*D*			$300
American (1879 - 1931)				
PFLEIDERER, F. Emile	*P*			$605
(?)				

D=Drawing, P=Painting, S=Sculpture, W=Watercolor

		Low	Mean	High
		Current Price Range		

		Current Price Range		
		Low	Mean	High
PFLUG, Johanes B.	*P*			$143,000
German (1785 - 1866)				
PHELAN, Charles T.	*P*	$138	$344	$550
American (1840 -)				
PHELAN, Charles T. (Attrib.)	*P*			$165
American (1840 -)				
PHELAN, Ellen	*D*			$2,640
(20th -)	*P*			$6,600
PHELPS,	*P*			$138
American (?)				
PHELPS, Edith C.	*P*	$798	$1,114	$1,430
American (1875 - 1961)				
PHELPS, Helen W.	*P*	$110	$155	$200
American (1864 - 1944)				
PHELPS, William P.	*P*	$440	$1,045	$2,090
American (1848 - 1923)				
PHIEFFER, Richard	*P*			$385
German (1878 -)				
PHILBRICK, A. P.	*W*			$110
American (19th -)				
PHILBRICK, Allen E.	*P*			$385
American (1879 - 1964)				
PHILIPP, Robert	*D*	$1,045	$1,441	$1,650
American (1895 - 1981)	*P*	$330	$2,408	$6,875
	W			$3,190
PHILIPP, Robert (Attrib.)	*P*			$1,100
American (1895 - 1981)				
PHILIPPEAU, Karel F.	*P*			$4,400
Dutch (1825 - 1897)				
PHILIPS, Marjorie	*P*			$413
American (1895 -)				
PHILLIP, John	*P*	$2,750	$3,850	$4,950
British (1817 - 1867)				
PHILLIP, John (Attrib.)	*P*			$1,100
British (1817 - 1867)				

D=Drawing, P=Painting, S=Sculpture, W=Watercolor

		Current Price Range		
		Low	Mean	High
PHILLIPP, Werner	*P*			$550
American (1897 - 1982)				
PHILLIPPS, Carlotta V.	*P*	$248	$262	$275
American (20th -)				
PHILLIPS, Ammi	*P*	$7,700	$17,600	$27,500
American (1787 - 1865)				
PHILLIPS, Ammi (Attrib.)	*P*	$7,150	$18,700	$30,250
American (1787 - 1865)				
PHILLIPS, Bert G.	*P*	$5,500	$16,500	$41,250
American (1868 - 1956)				
PHILLIPS, Charles	*P*			$3,300
British (1737 - 1783)				
PHILLIPS, Dorothy S.	*W*			$825
American (20th -)				
PHILLIPS, G. Whitehead	*P*			$165
American (20th -)				
PHILLIPS, Gordon	*P*			$6,050
American (1927 -)	*S*			$2,860
PHILLIPS, J. Campbell	*P*	$225	$507	$715
American (1873 - 1949)				
PHILLIPS, James M.	*W*	$303	$399	$495
American (1913 -)				
PHILLIPS, Margaret M.	*P*	$495	$1,045	$1,595
American (1910 - 1978)				
PHILLIPS, Michael	*D*			$138
(20th -)				
PHILLIPS, Paul B.	*P*			$330
American (20th -)				
PHILLIPS, Peter	*S*			$1,045
(20th -)				
PHILLIPS, S. George	*P*	$660	$4,136	$9,350
American (20th -)				
PHILLIPS, T. N.	*P*			$165
American (19th -)				
PHILLIPSEN, N.	*P*			$275
American (19th - 20th)				

D=Drawing, P=Painting, S=Sculpture, W=Watercolor

| | | Current Price Range | | |
		Low	Mean	High
PHILOPPOUTH,	*P*			$550
French (20th -)				
PHIPPEN, George	*P*	$3,300	$6,967	$9,900
American (1916 - 1966)	*W*			$3,960
PHIPPS, George	*S*			$275
American (20th -)				
PHIPPS, George G.	*W*			$121
American (19th -)				
PHIZ,	*W*			$825
American (19th - 20th)				
PHO, Le	*P*	$550	$1,137	$1,540
French (1907 -)				
PHYSIOC, Lewis	*P*			$248
American (20th -)				
PHYSNE, Joseph A.	*P*			$220
(?)				
PIANG, J. F.	*P*			$1,980
French (19th - 20th)				
PIAZZETTA, Giovanni B.	*D*			$1,100
Italian (1682 - 1754)	*P*			$605,000
PIAZZETTA, Giovanni B. (Att.)	*D*			$2,860
Italian (1682 - 1754)				
PIAZZETTA, Giovanni B. (School)	*P*			$8,800
Italian (1682 - 1754)				
PIAZZONI, Gottardo	*P*	$1,100	$1,357	$1,870
American (1872 - 1945)				
PICABIA, Francis	*D*	$12,100	$160,325	$495,000
French (1879 - 1953)	*P*	$4,400	$82,207	$528,000
	W	$1,870	$22,092	$82,500
PICART, O.	*P*			$2,310
European (20th -)				
PICASSO, Pablo	*D*	$1,265	$240,234	$4.840M
Spanish (1881 - 1974)	*P*	$2,860	$3.866M	$47.850M

D=Drawing, P=Painting, S=Sculpture, W=Watercolor

| | | Current Price Range | | |
		Low	Mean	High
PICASSO, Pablo	S	$880	$208,974	$15.400M
Spanish (1881 - 1974)	W	$6,600	$323,881	$1.980M
PICASSO, Pablo (After)	S	$4,125	$6,435	$10,450
Spanish (1881 - 1974)				
PICAULT, Emile L.	S	$187	$3,928	$12,100
French (1839 -)				
PICCINI, Gaetano	D			$825
Italian (17th -)				
PICCIRILLI, Attilio	S			$2,200
American (1860 -)				
PICCOLI, Juanita P.	P	$110	$165	$220
American (1915 -)				
PICHE, Henri le	P			$1,650
French (19th -)				
PICHETTE, James	P			$9,350
French (1920 -)				
PICHLER, Adolf	P			$8,250
Hungarian (1835 - 1905)				
PICHLER, Rudolf	P			$935
German (1863 -)				
PICHOT, Emile J.	D			$880
French (19th -)				
PICHOT, Ramon	P	$330	$605	$880
Spanish (1872 - 1925)				
PICINICH, C. E.	P			$935
American (20th -)				
PICK, Anton	P	$413	$922	$1,430
Austrian (19th -)				
PICKENS, George	P			$578
American (20th -)				
PICKERING, Henry	P			$4,400
British (18th -)				
PICKETT, Joseph	P			$2,200
American (1848 - 1918)				
PICKFORD, JR., Rollin	W			$468
American (1912 -)				

D=Drawing, P=Painting, S=Sculpture, W=Watercolor

| | | Current Price Range | |
	Low	Mean	High
PICKHARDT, JR., Carl E.	*D*			$880
American (1908 -)				
PICKLES, H.	*P*			$253
(?)				
PICKNELL, George W.	*P*	$385	$825	$1,650
American (1864 - 1943)				
PICKNELL, William L.	*D*			$220
American (1854 - 1897)	*P*	$6,600	$26,308	$49,500
PICKTHORN, A. Nadine	*P*			$1,650
American (20th -)	*S*			$1,800
PICOT, Andre	*P*	$110	$405	$700
(?)				
PICOT, Francois E.	*P*			$154,000
French (1786 - 1868)				
PICOT, Jean	*P*			$440
French (20th -)				
PICOU, Henri P.	*P*	$5,500	$6,875	$8,250
French (1824 - 1895)				
PIEDMONTESE SCHOOL 16C,	*P*			$52,800
Italian (16th -)				
PIELER, Franz X.	*P*	$3,850	$11,825	$20,900
Austrian (1879 - 1952)				
PIENEMAN, Nikolaas	*P*			$4,950
Dutch (1809 - 1860)				
PIEPENBURG, Allen R.	*P*			$150
American (20th -)				
PIER FRANCESCO, Pseudo	*P*			$165,000
Italian (15th -)				
PIERCE, Charles F.	*D*			$303
American (1844 - 1920)	*P*	$358	$1,146	$1,650
	W	$165	$385	$633
PIERCE, Dorothy R.	*S*			$1,100
(?)				

D=Drawing, P=Painting, S=Sculpture, W=Watercolor

		Current Price Range		
		Low	Mean	High
PIERCE, Edgar L. (?)	P			$688
PIERCE, J. M. (?)	P			$110
PIERCE, M. W. American (?)	D			$3,520
PIERCE, R. E. American (20th -)	P	$770	$1,243	$1,700
PIERCE, William American (1858 - 1940)	P	$330	$440	$550
PIERRE, Fernand Haitian (1922 -)	P			$248
PIERRE, Jean B. M. French (1713 - 1789)	D			$11,000
PIERRE DE CORTONE, Pietro Italian (1596 - 1669)	P			$15,400
PIETA, A. Italian (19th -)	P			$770
PIETERS, Evert Dutch (1856 - 1932)	P	$550	$11,451	$46,200
PIETRI, Pietro A. de Italian (1663 - 1716)	D			$16,500
PIETRI, Pietro A. de (Attrib.) Italian (1663 - 1716)	D			$2,200
PIETRO, Cartaino di S. American (1886 - 1918)	S			$2,860
PIETRONI, Antonio Italian (20th -)	P	$303	$777	$1,100
PIETTE, Ludovic French (1826 - 1877)	P			$27,500
PIFFARD, Harold British (19th -)	P	$3,960	$16,830	$33,000
PIGALLE, French (?)	S			$990
PIGMA, A. Italian (19th -)	P			$8,250

D=Drawing, P=Painting, S=Sculpture, W=Watercolor

		Current Price Range		
		Low	Mean	High

		Low	Mean	High
PIGNON, Edouard	*P*	$1,760	$11,921	$30,800
French (1905 -)	*W*			$7,150
PIGNONI, Simone (Circle)	*P*			$1,870
Italian (1614 - 1698)				
PIKE, C. N.	*S*			$357
American (19th -)				
PIKE, John	*W*			$2,640
American (1911 -)				
PIKE, William	*P*			$880
British (1846 - 1908)				
PIKELNY, Robert	*P*			$1,100
Polish (1904 -)				
PILAR, J.	*S*			$253
(?)				
PILETTI, Arturo	*P*	$220	$351	$440
Italian (20th -)				
PILLEMENT, Jean-B.	*D*	$990	$9,295	$17,600
French (1728 - 1808)	*P*	$14,300	$18,700	$24,200
	W			$18,700
PILLEMENT, Jean-B. (Circle)	*D*			$990
French (1728 - 1808)				
PILNY, Otto	*P*			$26,400
Swiss (1866 -)				
PILOT, Robert W.	*P*			$13,200
Canadian (1898 - 1968)				
PILOTY, Carl T. von	*D*			$660
German (1826 - 1886)				
PILTZ, Otto	*P*			$14,300
German (1846 - 1910)				
PIMENTEL, Rodrigo	*P*	$4,620	$8,910	$13,200
Mexican (1945 -)				
PINAL, Ferdinand	*P*			$3,520
French (1881 -)				
PINCHON, Robert	*P*	$40,700	$42,350	$44,000
French (1886 - 1943)				

D=Drawing, P=Painting, S=Sculpture, W=Watercolor

		Current Price Range		
		Low	Mean	High

PINE, Geri	*P*			$935
American (1914 -)				
PINE, Theodore E.	*P*			$1,210
American (1828 - 1905)				
PINEDO, Emile (After)	*S*			$1,430
French (19th -)				
PINEL, Gustave N.	*P*			$11,000
French (1842 - 1896)				
PINELLI, A. de	*P*			$1,650
(19th -)				
PINELLI, Bartolomeo (Attrib.)	*D*			$1,980
Italian (1781 - 1835)				
PINETTI, Mario	*P*			$715
French (20th -)				
PINGRET, Edouard	*P*			$3,200
French (1788 - 1875)				
PINNEY, Eunice (Attrib.)	*W*			$770
American (1770 - 1849)				
PINNGERA, H.	*P*			$605
European (19th - 20th)				
PINTO, Biagio	*P*			$2,200
American (20th -)				
PINTO, Jody	*W*			$1,210
(20th -)				
PINTO, Lorraine	*S*			$660
(?)				
PINWELL, George J.	*W*			$303
British (1882 - 1975)				
PINZARRONE, Paul	*S*			$303
American (20th -)				
PIOLA, Domenico	*D*			$1,650
Italian (17th - 18th)				
PIOLA, Domenico (Circle)	*P*			$1,980
Italian (17th - 18th)				
PIOMBO, Sebastiano (Circle)	*P*			$44,000
Italian (1485 - 1547)				

D=Drawing, P=Painting, S=Sculpture, W=Watercolor

		Current Price Range		
		Low	Mean	High

		Low	Mean	High
PIOT, Adolph French (1850 - 1910)	P	$4,400	$14,713	$30,800
PIOT, Antoine French (1869 - 1934)	P			$1,100
PIOTROWSKI, Antoni Polish (1853 - 1924)	P			$6,325
PIPER, John British (1903 -)	P			$5,500
	W	$5,720	$10,157	$15,400
PIPO, Manolo (20th -)	P	$770	$1,210	$1,650
PIPPEL, Otto German (1878 - 1960)	P			$605
PIPPI, Giulio Italian (1499 - 1546)	D			$4,950
PIPPIN, Horace American (1888 - 1946)	P	$19,800	$98,267	$165,000
PIQUET, P. French (19th -)	P			$1,705
PIRA, Gioacchino la Italian (19th -)	W	$825	$1,073	$1,320
PIRANDELLO, Fousto Italian (1899 -)	P	$14,300	$14,300	$14,300
PIRANESI, Giovanni B. Italian (1720 - 1778)	D			$10,450
PISAN SCHOOL 14C, Italian (14th -)	P	$14,300	$133,650	$253,000
PISCHON, Marie German (1856 - 1898)	P			$248
PISIS, Filippo de Italian (1896 - 1956)	P	$3,850	$20,717	$41,800
PISSARRO, Camille French (1830 - 1903)	D	$715	$20,405	$99,000
	P	$4,620	$1.195M	$2.420M
	W	$2,750	$38,579	$104,500
PISSARRO, Claude French (20th -)	P	$6,600	$11,668	$22,000

D=Drawing, P=Painting, S=Sculpture, W=Watercolor

		Low	Current Price Range Mean	High
PISSARRO, Lucien French (1863 - 1944)	P	$27,500	$40,333	$55,000
PISSARRO, Ludovic Rodo French (1878 - 1952)	W			$770
PISSARRO, Paulemile French (1884 - 1972)	D	$825	$1,133	$1,650
	P	$550	$2,331	$7,700
	W	$528	$751	$1,430
PISTOLETTO, Michelangelo Italian (1933 -)	S	$27,500	$31,625	$35,750
PITALL, Rhoda H. American (?)	W			$715
PITMAN, J. American (20th -)	P			$357
PITT, William British (19th -)	P			$2,860
PITTMAN, Hobson American (1899 - 1972)	P			$2,860
	W	$358	$598	$880
PITTONI, Francesco Italian (20th -)	P			$193
PITTONI, Giambattista (Attrib.) Italian (1687 - 1767)	D			$2,200
PITZNER, Max J. German (1855 - 1912)	P			$6,050
PIVOT, Louis (?)	P			$1,650
PIZZIZANI, E. Italian (20th -)	P			$330
PIZZUTI, Michele Italian (1882 -)	D			$1,430
PLA Y RUBIO, Alberto Spanish (1867 -)	P	$11,000	$11,550	$12,100
PLACZEK, Matthew American (20th -)	S			$1,540
PLANQUETTE, Felix French (1873 -)	P			$1,760

D=Drawing, P=Painting, S=Sculpture, W=Watercolor

		Current Price Range		
		Low	Mean	High

		Low	Mean	High
PLANSON, Andre	*P*			$1,540
French (1898 -)				
PLAS, Lourentius	*P*			$605
Dutch (1828 - 1888)				
PLAS, Pieter van	*P*			$8,800
Dutch (1810 - 1853)				
PLASSAN, Antoine E.	*P*	$2,420	$4,767	$8,250
French (1817 - 1903)				
PLATHNER, Hermann	*P*			$2,860
German (1831 - 1902)				
PLATT, Laurence	*P*			$248
Canadian (20th -)				
PLATT, Martha	*P*	$660	$770	$880
American (19th - 20th)				
PLAYZER, Joseph	*W*			$550
Austrian (1752 - 1806)				
PLAZZOTTA, Enzo	*S*	$1,100	$2,310	$3,520
Italian (20th -)				
PLEASONTON, Ruth C.	*W*			$140
(?)				
PLEISSNER, Ogden M.	*P*	$1,650	$14,135	$41,250
American (1905 - 1983)	*W*	$4,400	$24,006	$52,250
PLEISSNER, Ogden M. (Attrib.)	*W*			$495
American (1905 - 1983)				
PLEPP, Hans J.	*D*			$7,150
Swiss (1560 - 1595)				
PLESNER, R.	*P*			$1,705
French (20th -)				
PLIMPTON, William E.	*P*	$880	$963	$1,045
American (19th - 20th)				
PLOQUIN, Gaston	*P*	$3,300	$4,400	$5,500
French (?)				
PLUMB, N. F.	*W*			$605
British (19th - 20th)				
PLUMMER, William H.	*P*			$9,350
American (19th - 20th)				

D=Drawing, P=Painting, S=Sculpture, W=Watercolor

		Current Price Range		
		Low	Mean	High

PLUYM, Carel van der (Fol.) Dutch (1625 - 1677)	*P*			$7,150
PO, Giacomo del Italian (1652 - 1726)	*P*			$154,000
PO, Giacomo del (School) Italian (1652 - 1726)	*P*			$1,650
POCCETTI, Bernardino Italian (1548 - 1612)	*D*			$880
PODCHERNIKOFF, Alexis M. American (1886 - 1933)	*P*	$495	$3,575	$6,600
PODOLAK, American (19th - 20th)	*S*			$1,430
POEL, A. D. Dutch (17th -)	*P*			$3,080
POEL, Egbert van der Dutch (1621 - 1664)	*P*			$3,300
POEL, Theo van der Dutch (20th -)	*P*			$330
POELENBURGH, Cornelis Dutch (1586 - 1667)	*P*	$14,300	$77,367	$176,000
POELENBURGH, Cornelis (Cir.) Dutch (1586 - 1667)	*P*			$1,100
POELENBURGH, Cornelis (Mann) Dutch (1586 - 1667)	*P*			$2,860
POERSON, Charles French (1653 - 1725)	*P*			$28,600
POERTZEL, Otto German (1876 -)	*S*			$715
POGEDAIEFF, George Russian (1897 -)	*W*			$1,210
POGZEBA, Wolfgang American (1936 - 1982)	*D*			$2,500
POHL, Ernest H. American (1874 - 1956)	*P*			$248
POINCY, Paul American (1833 - 1909)	*P*			$1,320

D=Drawing, P=Painting, S=Sculpture, W=Watercolor

		Current Price Range		
		Low	Mean	High

POIRIER, Anne & Patrick	*S*			$9,900
French (20th -)				
POISSON, Louverature	*P*	$2,200	$4,400	$6,600
Haitian (1914 - 1985)				
POISSON, Louverature (After)	*S*			$1,540
Haitian (1914 - 1985)				
POITEVIN, Auguste F.	*P*			$15,400
French (19th -)				
POKITONOV, Ivan	*P*			$6,820
Russian (1851 - 1924)				
POL, Christian van	*P*			$187,000
Dutch (1752 - 1813)				
POL, Louis van der	*P*	$165	$678	$1,320
Dutch (1896 - 1982)				
POLASEK, Albin	*S*	$440	$1,705	$4,125
Czech (1879 -)				
POLEO, Hector	*P*	$11,000	$52,983	$110,000
Venezuelan (1918 -)	*S*			$8,800
POLESELLO, Rogelio	*P*			$5,500
Argentina (1939 -)				
POLICASTRA, E.	*D*			$110
Spanish (20th -)				
POLIDORI, C.	*P*			$3,960
Italian (19th - 20th)				
POLIDORO DA, Caravaggio (Aft.)	*D*	$550	$1,045	$1,540
Italian (1492 - 1543)	*W*			$2,475
POLIDORO DA, Caravaggio (Foll.)	*D*			$385
Italian (1492 - 1543)				
POLISH SCHOOL,	*P*			$1,540
Polish (19th - 20th)				
POLKE, Sigmar	*D*	$13,200	$28,600	$39,600
German (1941 -)	*P*	$15,400	$113,080	$253,000
	W	$19,800	$31,900	$38,500

D=Drawing, P=Painting, S=Sculpture, W=Watercolor

		Current Price Range		
		Low	Mean	High
POLLACK, Mark (?)	P			$550
POLLAK, Theresa American (1899 -)	P			$660
POLLARD, James British (1797 - 1859)	P	$3,850	$8,525	$13,200
POLLARD, James (After) British (1797 - 1859)	P			$3,190
POLLARD, James (Attrib.) British (1797 - 1859)	P			$7,150
POLLARD, James (Manner) British (1797 - 1859)	P			$2,200
POLLARD, Robert (Attrib.) British (19th -)	P			$2,750
POLLENTINE, Alfred British (19th -)	P	$1,760	$4,877	$9,350
POLLET, Jean French (1929 -)	P	$303	$981	$1,320
POLLET, Joseph American (1897 - 1979)	P			$880
POLLI, F. Italian (19th -)	W			$248
POLLNEK, Mark American (20th -)	P			$121
POLLOCK, Jackson American (1912 - 1956)	D	$25,300	$167,200	$451,000
	P	$209,000	$3.430M	$11.550M
	W	$220,000	$751,667	$1.155M
POLLOG, Robert K. German (1882 -)	P			$1,980
POLOWETSKI, Charles American (1884 -)	P			$198
POMERENKE, Heinrich European (19th -)	P			$2,640
POMODORO, Arnaldo Italian (1926 -)	S	$605	$19,397	$55,000

D=Drawing, P=Painting, S=Sculpture, W=Watercolor

		Current Price Range		
		Low	Mean	High

		Low	Mean	High
POMODORO, Gio	S	$1,760	$3,080	$4,400
Italian (1930 -)				
PONCE DE LEON, Fidelio	D			$4,180
Cuban (1896 - 1957)	P	$4,400	$6,600	$8,800
POND, Clayton	P			$1,210
(?)				
POND, Dana	P	$220	$495	$770
American (1880 - 1962)				
PONDEL, Friederich	P			$1,650
German (1830 -)				
PONGIALIS, Constantine	P			$700
American (1894 -)				
PONSEN, Tunis	P	$248	$889	$1,650
American (1891 - 1978)				
PONSON, Aime E.	P			$1,760
French (1850 - 1924)				
PONTE, Francesco da (Follower)	P			$2,200
Italian (1549 - 1592)				
PONTE, Gerolamo da (Follower)	P			$6,600
Flemish (1566 - 1621)				
PONTE, Jacopo da	P			$2,475
Italian (1510 - 1592)				
PONTE, Jacopo da (Manner)	P			$33,000
Italian (1510 - 1592)				
PONTE, Leandro da (Attrib.)	P			$7,700
Italian (1557 - 1622)				
PONTORMO, Jacopo	P	$385,000	$17.792M	$35.200M
Italian (1494 - 1556)				
POOLE, Earl L.	P			$180
American (1891 -)				
POOLE, James	P			$1,100
British (1804 - 1886)				
POOLE, Paul F.	P			$1,760
British (1807 - 1879)				
POONS, Larry	P	$3,025	$28,309	$176,000
American (1937 -)				

D=Drawing, P=Painting, S=Sculpture, W=Watercolor

		Current Price Range		
		Low	Mean	High

POOR, Anne	*P*			$550
(?)				
POOR, Henry V.	*D*	$450	$720	$990
American (1888 - 1970)	*P*	$770	$1,497	$3,300
POORE, Henry R.	*P*	$1,870	$4,689	$7,425
American (1859 - 1940)				
POORTER, Willem de	*P*			$15,400
Dutch (1608 - 1648)				
POORTER, Willem de (After)	*P*			$1,760
Dutch (1608 - 1648)				
POORTERE, C. D.	*P*			$350
(19th -)				
POPE, Alexander	*D*			$660
American (1849 - 1924)	*P*	$1,760	$6,600	$19,800
	S			$165
POPE, G.	*P*			$550
(19th - 20th)				
POPE, H. A.	*P*			$1,210
American (?)				
POPE, Henry M.	*W*			$303
British (1843 - 1908)				
POPELIN, Gustave L.	*P*			$9,900
French (1859 -)				
POPLASKI,	*P*	$413	$482	$550
(?)				
POPLOWSKI,	*P*			$413
(?)				
POPOVA, Liubov	*P*			$1.760M
Russian (1889 - 1924)				
POPP,	*P*	$303	$303	$303
American (19th - 20th)				
POPPENGA, C. S.	*D*			$660
American (20th -)				
POPPLEIN,	*P*			$550
French (19th -)				

D=Drawing, P=Painting, S=Sculpture, W=Watercolor

		Current Price Range		
		Low	Mean	High

		Low	Mean	High
PORAY, Stanislaus P.	P	$523	$1,093	$1,430
American (1888 - 1948)				
PORCELLIS, Jan	P			$13,200
Dutch (16th - 17th)				
PORCELLIS, Jan (Circle)	P			$1,540
Dutch (16th - 17th)				
PORCELLIS, Julius	P			$16,500
Dutch (1610 - 1645)				
PORCIA, Francesco A. di	P			$49,500
Italian (16th -)				
PORPORA, Paolo	P			$55,000
Italian (? - 1673)				
PORPORA, Paolo (Circle)	P			$3,850
Italian (? - 1673)				
PORTA, Baccio della (Studio)	P			$8,250
Italian (1472 - 1517)				
PORTA, Giuseppe (School)	P			$13,200
Italian (18th -)				
PORTANA, Vencente L.	P			$22,000
(1772 - 1850)				
PORTANEL, Jose Armet	P			$27,500
Spanish (19th -)				
PORTER, Charles E.	P	$2,200	$6,716	$15,100
American (1847 - 1923)				
PORTER, Fairfield	D			$1,650
American (1907 - 1976)	P	$9,900	$63,470	$247,500
	W	$2,860	$3,795	$4,400
PORTER, Katherine	P	$3,300	$14,536	$33,000
American (20th -)				
PORTER, Norman	W			$193
American (20th -)				
PORTER, R. T.	P			$2,420
British (19th -)				
PORTER, S. C.	P			$550
(19th - 20th)				

D=Drawing, P=Painting, S=Sculpture, W=Watercolor

		Current Price Range		
		Low	Mean	High

		Low	Mean	High
PORTER, Vivian F.	*P*	$110	$587	$990
American (1888 - 1982)				
PORTIELJE, Edward	*D*			$2,200
Belgian (1861 - 1949)	*P*	$6,600	$8,195	$9,350
PORTIELJE, Gerard	*P*			$16,500
Belgian (1856 - 1929)				
PORTIELJE, Jan F.	*P*	$11,000	$14,667	$19,800
Belgian (1829 - 1895)				
PORTINARI, Candido	*D*	$1,430	$3,117	$6,050
Brazilian (1903 - 1962)	*P*	$35,000	$119,025	$275,000
PORTOCARRERO, Rene	*D*			$3,300
Cuban (1912 -)	*P*	$3,740	$6,506	$9,350
	W	$4,180	$8,910	$17,600
PORTOGHESE, Alvaro di Piero	*P*			$85,000
(?)				
PORUBSZKY, Istvan	*P*			$440
Hungarian (20th -)				
POSCHEWSKY, H.	*W*			$220
(?)				
POSEN, Leonid V.	*S*			$4,400
Russian (1849 -)				
POSEN, Stephen	*P*	$3,850	$22,550	$41,250
American (20th -)				
POSITANO,	*D*			$220
Italian (20th -)				
POSSIN, Rudolf	*P*			$1,540
German (1861 -)				
POSSNER, Hugo A.	*P*			$413
American (19th - 20th)				
POST, Anne B.	*S*			$303
American (20th -)				
POST, George B.	*W*	$440	$591	$770
American (1906 -)				

D=Drawing, P=Painting, S=Sculpture, W=Watercolor

		Current Price Range		
		Low	Mean	High

		Low	Mean	High
POST, William M.	*P*	$275	$2,080	$4,675
American (1856 - 1935)	*W*	$358	$647	$935
POST, William M. (Attrib.)	*P*	$330	$399	$468
American (1856 - 1935)				
POSTIGLIONE, Salvatore	*P*			$22,000
Italian (1861 - 1906)				
POTERLET, Pierre Saint-Ange	*P*			$1,100
French (1804 - 1881)				
POTHAST, Bernard	*D*			$990
Dutch (1882 - 1966)	*P*	$12,100	$17,325	$27,500
POTT, Laslett J.	*P*			$60,500
British (1837 - 1898)				
POTTENGER, Mary L.	*P*			$385
American (20th -)				
POTTER, H. O.	*P*			$495
(?)				
POTTER, Louis	*S*	$770	$1,338	$2,420
American (1873 - 1912)				
POTTER, Paul (School)	*P*			$3,300
Dutch (1625 - 1654)				
POTTER, William J.	*P*	$1,018	$1,169	$1,320
American (1883 - 1964)				
POTTHAST, Edward H.	*P*	$3,300	$65,980	$253,000
American (1857 - 1927)	*W*	$1,925	$10,725	$22,000
POUCETTE,	*P*			$110
French (1935 -)				
POUGNY, Jean	*P*			$3,960
French (1894 - 1956)				
POURBUS, Franz	*P*			$9,350
Flemish (1570 - 1622)				
POURBUS, Franz (Manner)	*P*			$605
Flemish (1570 - 1622)				
POURBUS, Franz (Style)	*P*			$770
Flemish (1570 - 1622)				

D=Drawing, P=Painting, S=Sculpture, W=Watercolor

| | | Current Price Range | | |
		Low	Mean	High
POURBUS, Peeter J. (Attrib.) Flemish (1523 - 1584)	P	$22,000	$55,000	$88,000
POURBUS, ELDER, Franz (School) Flemish (1545 - 1581)	P	$2,200	$2,933	$3,300
POUSETTE-DART, Richard	P	$7,700	$39,738	$99,000
American (1916 -)	W	$2,200	$14,850	$27,500
POUSSIN, Nicholas French (1593 - 1665)	D			$90,750
POUSSIN, Nicholas (After)	D			$358
French (1593 - 1665)	P	$660	$1,467	$2,200
POUSSIN, Nicholas (Attrib.) French (1593 - 1665)	W			$523
POUSSIN, Nicholas (Circle) French (1593 - 1665)	D			$3,300
POUSSIN, Nicholas (Manner) French (1593 - 1665)	P			$880
POUSSIN, Nicholas (School)	D			$1,540
French (1593 - 1665)	P			$2,860
POVEDA, Carlos Costa Rican (1940 -)	P	$3,300	$4,263	$5,225
POWELL, Ace	D			$1,800
American (1912 - 1978)	P	$1,100	$2,381	$5,500
	S	$900	$1,367	$2,200
POWELL, Arthur American (1864 - 1956)	P	$385	$825	$1,540
POWELL, Charles M. British (? - 1824)	P			$13,200
POWELL, Jim American (20th -)	W			$660
POWELL, Lucien W.	P	$770	$1,854	$5,500
American (1846 - 1930)	W	$330	$759	$1,210
POWELL, William E. British (19th -)	W	$440	$1,430	$2,200

D=Drawing, P=Painting, S=Sculpture, W=Watercolor

		Current Price Range		
		Low	Mean	High

		Low	Mean	High
POWER-O'MALLEY, Michael	*P*			$495
American (1878 - 1946)				
POWERS, Asahel L.	*P*			$5,500
(?)				
POWERS, Hiram	*S*	$28,600	$31,900	$35,200
American (1805 - 1873)				
POWERS, Marilyn	*P*			$1,430
(1925 - 1976)				
POWERS, Marion	*D*			$220
American (20th -)	*P*			$165
POWERS, Richard G.	*P*			$220
American (20th -)				
POWIS, Paul	*P*			$1,320
American (19th -)				
POWLES, Reuben	*P*			$495
(?)				
POWNALL, J. A.	*P*			$605
British (19th -)				
POYNTER, Sir Edward	*D*			$385
British (1836 - 1919)	*P*			$37,400
POYNTER, Sir Edward (Attrib.)	*P*			$4,070
British (1836 - 1919)				
POZZI, Francesco	*S*			$88,000
Italian (1779 - 1844)				
POZZO, Stefano	*D*			$880
Italian (1707 - 1768)				
PRADES, Alfred de	*P*	$3,520	$26,510	$49,500
British (19th -)				
PRADIER, Jean Jacques	*S*	$3,300	$6,600	$11,000
French (19th -)				
PRADILLA Y ORTIZ, Francisco	*W*	$5,225	$6,738	$8,250
Spanish (1848 - 1921)				
PRAMPOLINI, Enrico	*S*	$110,000	$154,000	$220,000
Italian (1894 - 1956)	*W*			$6,050

D=Drawing, P=Painting, S=Sculpture, W=Watercolor

		Current Price Range		
		Low	Mean	High

		Low	Mean	High
PRASSINOS, Mario Turkish (1916 - 1985)	*P*	$6,600	$7,150	$7,700
PRAT, Arthur Portuguese (1861 -)	*P*	$193	$220	$275
PRATCHENKO, Paul American (20th -)	*P*			$1,540
PRATELLA, Attilio Italian (1856 - 1949)	*P* *W*	$1,650	$16,854	$38,500 $1,980
PRATELLA, Attilio (Attrib.) Italian (1856 - 1949)	*P*	$1,320	$10,010	$18,700
PRATELLA, Fausto Italian (1888 - 1964)	*P*			$1,980
PRATT, Baldwin American (1903 -)	*P*	$330	$440	$660
PRATT, Bela L. American (1867 - 1917)	*S*	$3,575	$4,400	$5,225
PRATT, D. Dewey (?)	*P*			$523
PRATT, Emmett A. (20th -)	*P*			$880
PRATT, H. C. American (19th -)	*P*			$1,650
PRATT, Jonathon British (19th -)	*P*			$1,430
PRATT, Sam American (1903 -)	*P*	$275	$294	$303
PRATT, William British (1855 -)	*P*	$220	$660	$1,100
PRECKO, J. J. American (19th - 20th)	*P*			$198
PREHN, A. European (19th - 20th)	*P*			$880
PREISS, Johann P. F. German (?)	*S*	$2,200	$4,950	$7,700
PRELL, Hermann German (1854 - 1922)	*P*			$15,400

D=Drawing, P=Painting, S=Sculpture, W=Watercolor

		Current Price Range		
		Low	Mean	High
PRELL, Walter	*P*			$5,500
German (1857 -)				
PRELLWITZ, Henry	*P*			$880
American (1865 - 1940)				
PRENDERGAST, Charles	*S*			$550
American (1868 - 1948)				
PRENDERGAST, J.	*D*	$9,900	$9,900	$9,900
(20th -)				
PRENDERGAST, Maurice B.	*D*	$1,320	$43,093	$165,000
American (1859 - 1924)	*P*	$49,500	$432,506	$1.815M
	S	$2,750	$3,575	$4,400
	W	$10,450	$236,714	$1.870M
PRENDERGAST, Maurice B. (Att)	*P*	$2,200	$2,200	$2,200
American (1859 - 1924)				
PRENTICE, Levi Wells	*P*	$2,475	$16,894	$40,700
American (1851 - 1935)				
PRENTISS, Thomas	*P*			$990
American (20th -)				
PRESCOTT, C. B.	*P*			$1,430
American (19th -)				
PRESSER, Josef	*D*	$110	$204	$341
American (1907 -)	*P*	$330	$372	$413
	W	$165	$440	$605
PRESSMANE, Joseph	*P*			$7,150
French (1904 - 1967)				
PRESTON, Alice B.	*W*			$825
American (1889 - 1958)				
PRESTON, Bruce M.	*P*			$385
American (20th -)				
PRESTON, Edward	*D*			$770
British (19th -)				
PRESTON, Jesse G.	*P*	$385	$385	$385
American (1880 -)				

D=Drawing, P=Painting, S=Sculpture, W=Watercolor

		Current Price Range		
		Low	Mean	High
PRESTON, May W.	*D*	$193	$486	$660
American (1873 - 1949)	*P*			$605
	W	$110	$738	$2,200
PRESTON, William	*P*			$220
American (20th -)				
PRESTOPINO, Gregario	*D*			$770
American (1907 -)	*P*	$1,650	$3,575	$5,500
PRETI, Mattia	*P*	$46,750	$600,875	$1.155M
Italian (1613 - 1699)				
PRETI, Mattia (Circle)	*P*			$3,740
Italian (1613 - 1699)				
PREUSSER, Robert O.	*S*			$7,700
American (1919 -)				
PREVAL, Christiane de	*P*			$1,100
French (1876 -)				
PREVOST, Amdec	*P*			$1,540
French (19th -)	*W*			$121
PREY, Joan de	*D*			$165
Mexican (20th -)				
PREYER, Emilie	*P*	$13,200	$24,750	$36,300
German (1849 - 1930)				
PREYER, Johann W.	*P*			$110,000
German (1803 - 1889)				
PRICE, Alan	*P*	$193	$1,234	$1,980
American (20th -)				
PRICE, Cheryl	*W*	$275	$413	$550
American (20th -)				
PRICE, Chester B.	*D*			$1,760
American (1885 - 1962)				
PRICE, Elizabeth F.	*P*	$135	$180	$225
(20th -)	*W*			$275
PRICE, Ken	*P*			$8,250

D=Drawing, P=Painting, S=Sculpture, W=Watercolor

		Current Price Range		
		Low	Mean	High

PRICE, Ken	*S*	$20,900	$30,983	$52,250
American (1935 -)				
PRICE, Mary E.	*P*			$550
American (1875 - 1960)				
PRICE, Norman M.	*D*			$220
American (1877 - 1951)	*W*	$220	$790	$1,600
PRICE, Raymon	*P*			$303
(?)				
PRICE, Robert	*P*			$1,100
(20th -)				
PRICE, William H.	*P*			$1,540
American (1864 - 1940)				
PRIEBE, Karl	*P*	$220	$234	$248
American (20th -)				
PRIEBE, Karl (Attrib.)	*D*			$100
American (20th -)	*P*	$125	$279	$500
	W			$175
PRIECHENFRIED, Alois	*P*			$4,125
French (1867 - 1953)				
PRIESTLEY, E.	*P*	$770	$798	$825
British (19th -)				
PRIESTMAN, Bertram W.	*P*			$220
American (1868 -)				
PRIEUR, Barthelemy	*S*			$110,000
French (? - 1611)				
PRIKING, Frantz	*P*	$1,430	$12,862	$63,800
German (1927 - 1979)				
PRINCE, P.	*P*			$275
American (19th - 20th)				
PRINCE, William M.	*P*			$1,770
American (1893 - 1951)				
PRINCETEAU, Rene	*P*			$33,000
French (1844 - 1914)				
PRINDLE,	*P*			$1,650
American (20th -)				

D=Drawing, P=Painting, S=Sculpture, W=Watercolor

| | | Current Price Range | | |
	Low	Mean	High
PRINQUET, H.	*P*			$358
British (19th - 20th)				
PRINS, Benjamin	*P*			$2,090
Dutch (1860 -)				
PRINS, Pierre E.	*P*			$17,600
French (1838 - 1913)				
PRIOR, M. Elizabeth	*P*			$770
American (20th -)				
PRIOR, Scott	*P*			$1,100
(20th -)				
PRIOR, William M.	*P*	$1,870	$4,738	$8,500
American (1806 - 1873)				
PRIOR, William M. (Attrib.)	*P*	$3,080	$10,340	$17,600
American (1806 - 1873)				
PRIOR-HAMBLIN, (School)	*P*	$3,630	$7,315	$11,000
American (19th -)				
PRITCHARD,	*P*			$110
(20th -)				
PRITCHARD, Edward	*P*	$550	$1,045	$1,540
British (1809 - 1905)				
PRITCHARD, George T.	*P*	$413	$1,652	$3,850
American (1878 - 1962)	*W*			$358
PRITCHARD, H.	*P*			$550
American (19th -)				
PRITCHARD, J. Ambrose	*P*	$550	$752	$990
American (1858 - 1905)	*W*			$385
PRITCHARD, J. Thompson	*P*			$1,100
British (19th -)				
PRITCHETT, Edward	*P*			$18,700
British (19th -)				
PRITCHETT, Robert T.	*W*			$440
British (1823 - 1907)				
PROBST, Carl	*P*			$1,100
Austrian (1854 - 1924)				

D=Drawing, P=Painting, S=Sculpture, W=Watercolor

		Current Price Range		
		Low	Mean	High

		Low	Mean	High
PROBST, Thorwald	*P*	$825	$1,045	$1,320
American (1886 - 1948)				
PROCACCINI, Camillo	*D*			$880
Italian (1546 - 1629)				
PROCACCINI, Ercole	*D*			$4,675
Italian (1596 - 1676)	*P*			$22,000
PROCACCINI, Ercole (Attrib.)	*P*			$3,575
Italian (1596 - 1676)				
PROCACCINI, Giulio C.	*D*			$8,250
Italian (1570 - 1625)				
PROCACCINI, Giulio C. (Attrib.)	*D*			$7,150
Italian (1570 - 1625)				
PROCHAZKA, Karl	*D*			$7,150
Austrian (1862 -)				
PROCTOR, Alexander P.	*D*	$440	$605	$770
American (1862 - 1950)	*S*	$2,750	$11,642	$38,500
PROCTOR, Burt	*P*	$2,200	$3,273	$4,180
American (1901 - 1980)				
PROCTOR, Howard	*W*			$165
American (?)				
PROCTOR, J. S.	*P*			$440
American (19th - 20th)				
PRODING, Austin	*S*			$330
American (20th -)				
PROHASKA, Ray	*D*			$193
American (1901 - 1981)				
PROL, Rick	*P*			$550
(20th -)				
PROLSS, Friedrich A. O.	*P*	$6,380	$19,690	$33,000
German (1855 -)				
PRON, Louis H.	*P*			$29,700
French (1817 - 1902)				
PRONK, Cornelis	*P*			$41,800
Dutch (1691 - 1759)				

D=Drawing, P=Painting, S=Sculpture, W=Watercolor

| | | Current Price Range | | |
		Low	Mean	High
PROOM, Al	P			$3,025
American (1933 -)				
PROSDOCINI, Alberto	W	$275	$1,054	$1,870
Italian (1852 -)				
PROTAIS, Paul A.	P			$495
French (1826 - 1890)				
PROTTI, Alfredo	P			$715
Italian (1882 - 1949)				
PROUST, E.	S			$358
(?)				
PROUT, Margaret F.	P			$825
British (1875 - 1963)				
PROUT, Samuel	P			$935
British (1783 - 1852)	W	$358	$6,646	$17,600
PROUT, Samuel (Attrib.)	P			$330
British (1783 - 1852)				
PROVAGGI, A.	W			$193
Italian (19th -)				
PROVINCIAL SCHOOL 19C,	P	$1,760	$4,290	$9,075
British (19th -)				
PROVISOR, Janis	P	$110	$165	$220
(20th -)				
PROVOST, Jan	P			$418,000
Flemish (15th - 16th)				
PROVOST, Jan (Circle)	P			$8,800
Flemish (15th - 16th)				
PROW, Hallie P.	P			$385
American (1868 - 1945)				
PROWELER,	P			$176
American (20th -)				
PRUDHON, Pierre P.	D			$15,400
French (1758 - 1823)	P			$30,800
PRUDHON, Pierre P. (Attrib.)	P			$2,200
French (1758 - 1823)				

D=Drawing, P=Painting, S=Sculpture, W=Watercolor

		Current Price Range		
		Low	Mean	High

		Low	Mean	High
PRUDHON, Pierre P. (Follower) French (1758 - 1823)	P			$9,900
PRUDHON, Pierre P. (Style) French (1758 - 1823)	P			$1,650
PRUNA, Pedro Spanish (1904 -)	P			$7,700
PUCCI, Silvio Italian (1899 -)	P	$165	$193	$220
PUCCINELLI, Raimondo (?)	S			$220
PUDDEFOOT, W. G. (19th -)	W			$143
PUEBLA SCHOOL, (?)	P			$15,400
PUGI, F. (?)	S			$1,100
PUHLMANN, Alexis German (20th -)	P			$1,100
PUIG-RODA, G. Italian (19th - 20th)	W			$7,700
PUIGAUDEAU, Fernand du French (1866 - 1930)	P			$77,000
PULIGO, Domenico Italian (1492 - 1527)	P			$110,000
PULIGO, Domenico (Attrib.) Italian (1492 - 1527)	P	$7,700	$13,750	$19,800
PULIGO, Domenico (Follower) Italian (1492 - 1527)	P			$4,400
PULIGO, Domenico (School) Italian (1492 - 1527)	P			$3,300
PULLIN, Edgar British (19th - 20th)	P			$440
PULLINGER, Herbert American (1878 -)	P			$1,050
PULZONE, Scipione Italian (1550 - 1598)	P			$286,000

D=Drawing, P=Painting, S=Sculpture, W=Watercolor

		Current Price Range		
		Low	Mean	High
PULZONE, Scipione (Circle)	P			$4,400
Italian (1550 - 1598)				
PULZONE, Scipione (School)	P			$2,200
Italian (1550 - 1598)				
PUMMIL, Robert	P	$3,575	$5,841	$9,900
American (1936 -)				
PUPINI, Biagio	D	$5,500	$5,500	$5,500
Italian (16th -)	W			$6,050
PURDY, Donald	P	$121	$143	$165
American (20th -)				
PURGAU, Siegmund von	P			$10,450
Austrian (1677 - 1754)				
PURVES, Austin	P			$385
American (1900 -)				
PURYEAR, Martin	S			$44,000
American (1941 -)				
PUSH-E-NE-QUA,	W			$358
(20th -)				
PUSHMAN, Hovsep	P	$9,350	$17,600	$28,600
American (1877 - 1966)	W			$220
PUTEANI, Friedrich von	P			$3,850
German (1849 - 1917)				
PUTHUFF, Hanson	D			$2,200
American (1875 - 1972)	P	$715	$7,763	$17,600
PUTNAM, Arthur	S	$880	$2,228	$3,575
American (1873 - 1930)				
PUVIS DE CHAVANNES, Pierre	D			$1,100
French (1824 - 1898)				
PUY, Jean	P	$14,300	$18,150	$22,000
French (1876 - 1959)				
PUYET, Jose	P			$1,100
Spanish (1922 -)				
PUYL, Louis F. G. van der	P			$1,870
Dutch (1750 - 1824)				

D=Drawing, P=Painting, S=Sculpture, W=Watercolor

		Current Price Range		
		Low	Mean	High

		Low	Mean	High
PUYROCHE-WAGNER, Elise	*P*			$9,900
German (1828 - 1895)				
PUYT, A.	*S*			$220
(?)				
PYE, Fred	*W*			$258
(?)				
PYLE, Howard	*P*			$12,500
American (1853 - 1911)				
PYNE, James B.	*P*	$1,650	$2,530	$3,850
British (1800 - 1870)	*W*	$413	$1,527	$2,640
PYNE, Robert L.	*P*			$1,045
American (20th -)				
QUAEDVLIEG, Carl M.	*P*			$1,650
Dutch (1823 - 1874)				
QUARTERLY, Charles	*P*			$1,650
American (19th -)				
QUARTLEY, Arthur	*P*	$1,320	$1,760	$2,200
American (1839 - 1886)	*W*			$330
QUAST, Pieter (Attrib.)	*P*			$11,000
Dutch (1606 - 1647)				
QUAYTMAN, Harvey	*P*	$3,520	$3,520	$3,520
(20th -)				
QUEFURT, August	*P*			$14,300
German (1696 - 1761)				
QUELLINUS, Eramus II	*P*	$12,100	$29,425	$46,750
Flemish (1607 - 1678)				
QUELLINUS, Jan E.	*D*			$1,320
Flemish (1634 - 1715)				
QUELLINUS, ELDER, Artus	*S*			$308,000
Flemish (1609 - 1668)				
QUENCE, Raymond	*P*			$770
French (?)				
QUENTEL, Holt	*P*			$16,500
(20th -)				

D=Drawing, P=Painting, S=Sculpture, W=Watercolor

		Current Price Range		
		Low	Mean	High
QUERENA, Luigi	P			$3,520
Italian (1860 - 1890)				
QUICK, Israel	P			$248
American (19th - 20th)				
QUIER, Jerry	P			$330
American (20th -)				
QUIGNON, Fernand J.	P			$8,800
French (1854 -)				
QUILES, Manuel	S			$220
Mexican (20th -)				
QUINLAN, Will J.	P	$165	$262	$358
American (1877 -)				
QUINN, James P.	P			$385
Austrian (1870 - 1951)				
QUINQUELA MARTIN, Benito	P			$15,400
Argentina (1890 - 1977)				
QUINSA, Giovanni	P			$35,200
Spanish (17th -)				
QUINTERO, Daniel	P			$1,540
(20th -)				
QUINTON, James	P	$1,210	$2,273	$2,860
British (19th -)				
QUIRT, Walter	P			$2,750
American (1902 -)				
QUISTGAARD, Johan V.	P			$550
Danish (1877 -)				
QUIZET, Alphonse	P	$1,870	$10,872	$17,600
French (1885 - 1955)				
RAAB, Ada	W	$193	$193	$193
American (? - 1950)				
RAAB, George (Attrib.)	P			$145
American (1866 - 1943)				
RAAPHORST, Cornelis	P	$3,520	$4,235	$4,950
Dutch (1875 - 1954)				
RABES, Max	P	$550	$2,888	$5,225
German (1868 - 1944)				

D=Drawing,   P=Painting,   S=Sculpture,   W=Watercolor

		Current Price Range		
		Low	Mean	High

		Low	Mean	High
RABIN, Ethel	*P*			$165
(?)				
RABIN, Michael	*S*			$1,100
(20th -)				
RABUT, Paul	*P*			$220
American (1914 - 1983)	*W*			$250
RACHMIEL, A.	*P*			$1,210
French (19th - 20th)				
RACKHAM, Arthur	*D*	$8,800	$23,467	$39,600
British (1867 - 1939)	*W*	$11,000	$12,100	$13,200
RACOFF, Rotislaw	*P*	$2,200	$2,640	$3,300
Russian (20th -)				
RADCLIFE, Paul	*P*			$1,980
(?)				
RADEMAKER, Abraham	*W*			$7,150
Dutch (1675 - 1735)				
RADENKOVITCH, Yovan	*P*			$193
American (1903 -)				
RADULOVICH, Savo	*P*			$330
American (20th -)				
RAEBURN, Sir Henry	*P*	$1,540	$21,824	$110,000
Scottish (1756 - 1823)				
RAEBURN, Sir Henry (After)	*P*			$275
Scottish (1756 - 1823)				
RAEBURN, Sir Henry (Attrib.)	*P*	$990	$1,247	$1,650
Scottish (1756 - 1823)				
RAEBURN, Sir Henry (Manner)	*P*			$440
Scottish (1756 - 1823)				
RAFFAEL, Joseph	*P*			$6,600
American (1933 -)	*S*			$1,210
	W			$1,980
RAFFAELLI, Jean-F.	*P*	$6,600	$27,913	$57,750
French (1850 - 1924)				

D=Drawing, P=Painting, S=Sculpture, W=Watercolor

		Current Price Range		
		Low	Mean	High
RAFFET, Auguste	*D*	$550	$825	$1,100
French (1804 - 1860)				
RAGAN, Leslie D.	*W*			$2,200
American (1897 -)				
RAGGI, E.	*W*	$825	$1,086	$1,650
Italian (19th -)				
RAGGIO, Giuseppe	*P*	$880	$2,200	$3,520
Italian (1823 - 1916)				
RAGIONE, Raffaele	*P*			$6,050
Italian (1851 - 1925)				
RAGOT, Jules F.	*P*	$990	$1,870	$2,750
French (19th -)				
RAHMING, Norris	*W*			$303
American (1886 -)				
RAIANO, G.	*S*			$1,320
Italian (19th - 20th)				
RAIMONDI, Aldo	*W*			$440
Italian (19th - 20th)				
RAIN, Charles	*P*	$550	$1,723	$2,860
American (20th -)				
RAINER, Arnulf	*P*			$2,750
Austrian (1929 -)				
RAINER, Paul	*P*			$275
British (20th -)				
RAISBECK, D.	*P*			$303
American (20th -)				
RAKUSA, E.	*P*			$165
(?)				
RALEIGH, Charles S.	*P*	$14,300	$14,575	$14,850
American (1831 - 1925)				
RALEIGH, Henry P.	*D*	$275	$303	$330
American (1880 - 1944)	*W*	$165	$408	$750
RALLI, Theodore J.	*P*			$44,000
Greek (1852 - 1909)				
RALLY, Peter	*P*			$110
American (20th -)				

D=Drawing, P=Painting, S=Sculpture, W=Watercolor

		Current Price Range		
		Low	Mean	High
RALSTON, James K.	P	$110	$380	$700
American (1896 -)	S	$605	$605	$605
RAM,	D			$275
European (20th -)				
RAMAS, Michael	W			$303
American (?)				
RAMBERT, Rene	P	$1,045	$1,623	$2,200
French (19th - 20th)				
RAMEL, Pierre	P			$1,870
French (1927 -)				
RAMM, John H.	P	$303	$674	$1,045
American (1879 - 1948)				
RAMOS, Carlos J.	P			$1,210
(?)				
RAMOS, Domingo	P	$7,700	$11,550	$15,400
Cuban (1894 -)				
RAMOS, Mel	D	$7,700	$12,650	$18,700
American (1935 -)	P	$20,900	$104,072	$187,000
	W			$28,600
RAMSAY, Allan	P			$17,600
British (1713 - 1784)				
RAMSAY, Allan (Manner)	P			$715
British (1713 - 1784)				
RAMSAY, H.	P			$770
American (1920 -)				
RAMSAY, Martha D.	W			$1,540
American (19th - 20th)				
RAMSAY, Milne	P	$1,210	$3,520	$7,150
American (1847 - 1915)	W	$935	$963	$990
RAMSDELL, Frederick W.	P	$880	$1,210	$1,540
American (1865 - 1915)				
RAMSDELL, M. Lee	P	$385	$550	$715
American (1883 - 1970)				

D=Drawing, P=Painting, S=Sculpture, W=Watercolor

		Current Price Range		
		Low	Mean	High

RANC, Jean	*P*			$40,700
French (1674 - 1735)				
RANCOULET, Ernest	*S*			$3,300
French (19th -)				
RAND, Ellen G. E.	*P*			$165
American (1876 - 1941)				
RAND, Henry A.	*P*			$605
American (1886 -)				
RANDALL, Bill	*W*			$330
American (?)				
RANDALL, Ruth H.	*W*			$248
American (1896 -)				
RANE, Bill	*P*			$935
American (20th -)				
RANFT, Richard	*P*			$2,750
Swiss (1862 - 1931)				
RANGEL, Mario	*W*			$2,200
Mexican (1938 -)				
RANGER, Henry W.	*P*	$660	$2,429	$6,710
American (1858 - 1916)	*W*	$138	$784	$1,430
RANKIN, George	*D*			$495
(?)				
RANN, Vollian B.	*P*			$1,000
American (1897 - 1956)	*W*			$500
RANNEY, William T.	*W*			$8,800
American (1813 - 1857)				
RANSOM, Fletcher C.	*P*			$7,150
American (19th -)				
RANSON, Paul	*P*			$30,800
French (1864 - 1909)				
RANSWYK, J.	*P*			$880
Dutch (19th - 20th)				
RANZONI, ELDER, Hans	*P*			$1,320
Austrian (1868 -)				

D=Drawing, P=Painting, S=Sculpture, W=Watercolor

		Current Price Range		
		Low	Mean	High

RAOUX, Jean (Attrib.)	*P*			$4,400
French (1677 - 1743)				
RAOUX, Jean (Circle)	*P*			$4,675
French (1677 - 1743)				
RAPHAEL, Joseph	*D*	$770	$1,155	$1,540
American (1869 - 1950)	*P*	$110	$3,988	$9,350
RAPHAEL, Sanzio (After)	*D*			$1,210
Italian (1483 - 1520)	*P*	$110	$1,528	$3,575
RAPPAPORT, Maurice	*P*			$275
Russian (1899 -)				
RASCH, Gustav	*P*			$1,760
American (1836 - 1906)				
RASCHEN, Henry	*P*	$715	$6,853	$11,000
American (1854 - 1937)				
RASKIN, Joseph	*P*	$1,320	$3,089	$6,050
American (1897 - 1981)				
RASKIN, Saul	*P*			$275
American (20th -)	*W*			$550
RASMUSSEN, Daniel	*W*	$138	$147	$165
(?)				
RASMUSSEN, Georg A.	*P*			$2,750
Norwegian (1842 - 1914)				
RASMUSSEN, Martin	*P*			$440
European (20th -)				
RATHBONE, Harold S.	*P*			$935
British (1850 - 1920)				
RATLIFF, Blanche C.	*P*			$198
American (1896 -)				
RATON, C.	*P*			$330
American (19th - 20th)				
RATTNER, Abraham	*P*	$1,210	$4,778	$12,100
American (1895 - 1978)				
RATZ, A.	*P*			$605
Hungarian (20th -)				

D=Drawing, P=Painting, S=Sculpture, W=Watercolor

		Current Price Range		
		Low	Mean	High

		Low	Mean	High
RAU, Emil	P	$8,800	$11,825	$14,300
German (1858 - 1940)				
RAUCH, Johann	P			$1,980
Austrian (19th -)				
RAUFER, Aloys	P			$3,190
German (1794 - 1856)				
RAUGHT, John W.	P			$385
American (1857 - 1931)				
RAUPP, Karl	P			$15,400
German (1837 - 1871)				
RAUPP, O.	P			$149
(?)				
RAUSCHENBERG, Robert	D	$26,400	$138,967	$275,000
American (1925 -)	P	$6,050	$560,027	$3.740M
	S	$8,800	$358,467	$6.325M
	W			$41,250
RAUX, Louis M. des	P	$132	$594	$1,045
(?)				
RAV, F.	P			$1,045
German (19th -)				
RAVENSTEYN, H.	P			$2,200
(?)				
RAVESTEYN, Dirck de Quade van	P			$17,600
Dutch (16th - 17th)				
RAVESTEYN, Jan van	P	$13,200	$14,300	$15,400
Dutch (1570 - 1657)				
RAVESTEYN, Jan van (Follower)	P			$165
Dutch (1570 - 1657)				
RAVESTEYN, Jan van (Studio)	P			$15,400
Dutch (1570 - 1657)				
RAWSON, Carl W.	P	$330	$715	$1,045
American (1884 - 1970)				
RAY, Jay	P			$187
(?)				

D=Drawing, P=Painting, S=Sculpture, W=Watercolor

		Current Price Range		
		Low	Mean	High
RAYMOND, H.	*D*			$187
(?)				
RAYNAUD, Louis F.	*P*			$330
American (1905 -)				
RAYNER, Ada	*P*	$200	$309	$485
American (20th -)				
RAYNER, Louise	*W*			$3,740
British (1829 - 1924)				
RAYNES, Sidney	*P*			$220
American (1907 -)				
RAYO, Omar	*P*	$3,300	$6,050	$8,800
Colombian (1928 -)				
READ, Thomas	*P*			$4,400
British (19th -)				
READ, Thomas B.	*P*			$220
American (1822 - 1872)				
REALFONSO, Tommaso (Masillo)	*P*			$23,100
Italian (18th -)				
REAM, Carducius P.	*P*	$1,430	$4,011	$11,000
American (1837 - 1917)				
REAM, Ethel	*P*	$210	$330	$450
American (20th -)				
REAM, Morston C.	*P*	$3,520	$3,630	$3,850
American (1840 - 1898)				
REARICK, Nola	*P*			$121
American (20th -)				
REASER, Wilbur A.	*P*			$1,870
American (1860 - 1942)				
REASONER, Gladys T.	*D*			$660
American (1886 -)				
REBAY, Hilla	*D*			$1,430
American (1890 -)	*P*	$2,200	$5,408	$14,300
	W	$990	$2,079	$3,575
REBEYROLLE, Paul	*P*			$14,300
French (1926 -)				

D=Drawing, P=Painting, S=Sculpture, W=Watercolor

		Current Price Range		
		Low	Mean	High

RECCHI, Giovanni P. (Attrib.)	*P*			$22,000
Italian (17th -)				
RECKHARD, Gardner A.	*P*			$1,100
American (1858 - 1908)				
RECKNAGEL, Theodore	*P*			$660
German (19th -)				
REDDIE, Mac Ivor	*P*	$990	$1,045	$1,100
American (20th -)	*W*			$1,320
REDEIN, Alexander	*P*			$770
American (20th -)				
REDEN, Dorothy J.	*P*			$193
American (20th -)				
REDER, Bernard	*S*	$2,420	$2,823	$3,575
American (1897 - 1963)				
REDER, Christian (Attrib.)	*P*			$6,600
German (1656 - 1729)				
REDFERN, Helen L.	*P*			$110
American (20th -)				
REDFIELD, Edward W.	*P*	$715	$47,349	$137,500
American (1869 - 1965)				
REDGATE, Arthur W.	*P*			$633
(?)				
REDGRAVE, Richard (Manner)	*W*			$110
(20th -)				
REDIN, Paul	*P*			$8,250
American (20th -)				
REDMAN, J. J.	*D*			$193
(?)				
REDMAN, T. H.	*P*			$495
European (19th -)				
REDMOND, Al	*P*	$165	$211	$303
American (?)				
REDMOND, Granville	*P*	$2,475	$22,481	$132,000
American (1871 - 1935)				
REDMORE, Henry	*P*	$2,200	$3,025	$3,850
British (1820 - 1887)				

D=Drawing, P=Painting, S=Sculpture, W=Watercolor

| | | Current Price Range | | |
		Low	Mean	High
REDON, Odilon	*D*	$12,100	$649,733	$2.310M
French (1840 - 1916)	*P*	$99,000	$826,375	$1.650M
	W			$57,200
REDOUTE, Pierre-J.	*D*	$6,050	$17,188	$28,600
French (1759 - 1840)	*W*	$132	$14,711	$24,200
REDOUTE, Pierre-J. (After)	*W*			$198
French (1759 - 1840)				
REDWOOD, Allen C.	*D*			$825
American (1844 - 1922)	*P*			$7,150
	W	$385	$2,118	$3,850
REECE, Maynard	*P*			$523
American (20th -)				
REED, Frederick	*W*			$330
American (20th -)				
REED, Marjorie	*P*	$413	$672	$1,400
American (1915 -)				
REED, Paul	*P*			$1,760
(20th -)				
REED, Scott	*P*			$1,100
American (20th -)				
REED, W. T.	*P*			$1,650
(19th -)				
REEDY, Leonard H.	*P*			$2,475
American (1899 - 1956)	*W*	$358	$609	$990
REEP, Edward A.	*W*			$495
American (1918 -)				
REESE, William	*P*			$1,100
American (20th -)				
REEVS, George	*W*			$715
American (1864 - 1930)				
REGGIANINI, Vittorio	*P*	$14,300	$28,160	$55,000
Italian (1858 -)				

D=Drawing, P=Painting, S=Sculpture, W=Watercolor

		Current Price Range		
		Low	Mean	High

		Low	Mean	High
REGGIANINI, Vittorio (Attrib.)	P			$16,500
Italian (1858 -)				
REGHT, Bruno	P			$110
(?)				
REGINATO, Peter	S			$6,600
(20th -)				
REGNAULT, Henri A. G.	D			$2,200
French (1843 - 1871)	P			$2,310
REGNAULT, Jean B.	D			$605
French (1754 - 1829)	P			$825,000
REGNIER, Nicolas	P	$14,300	$59,400	$104,500
Flemish (1590 - 1667)				
REHDER, Julius C.	P	$138	$451	$1,100
German (1861 - 1955)				
REHDER, Julius C. (Attrib.)	P			$300
German (1861 - 1955)				
REHN, Frank K. M.	P	$165	$1,596	$7,425
American (1848 - 1914)	W	$248	$509	$935
REHN, Frank K. M. (Attrib.)	P			$605
American (1848 - 1914)				
REICHERT, Carl	P	$4,125	$7,425	$10,450
Austrian (1836 - 1918)				
REICHMAN, Josephine	P			$1,650
American (1864 - 1939)				
REICHMANN, Franz	W			$1,760
Austrian (1868 -)				
REID, Flora M.	P	$7,150	$24,475	$41,800
British (19th -)				
REID, J. B.	W	$193	$289	$385
American (20th -)				
REID, Jean A.	W	$176	$226	$275
American (1882 -)				
REID, John R.	P			$15,400

D=Drawing, P=Painting, S=Sculpture, W=Watercolor

		Current Price Range		
		Low	Mean	High

		Low	Mean	High
REID, John R. British (1851 - 1926)	*W*			$770
REID, Patty American (20th -)	*D*	$550	$903	$1,210
REID, Robert American (1862 - 1929)	*D*	$1,595	$2,860	$4,125
	P	$1,210	$56,062	$341,000
	W	$165	$351	$825
REID, Stephen British (1873 -)	*P*	$1,650	$2,063	$2,475
REIFFEL, Charles American (1862 - 1942)	*P*	$1,100	$11,000	$30,800
REIMAUN, A. German (19th - 20th)	*S*			$413
REIMERS, Johannes American (19th - 20th)	*D*	$220	$413	$605
REIN, Surica American (20th -)	*P*			$990
REINAGLE, Philipp (Manner) British (1749 - 1833)	*P*			$1,100
REINAGLE, Philipp (School) British (1749 - 1833)	*P*			$2,090
REINAGLE, Ramsay R. British (1775 - 1862)	*P*			$6,600
REINBERG, Conrad German (19th -)	*P*			$2,640
REINDEL, William G. American (1871 - 1948)	*P*			$468
REINER, Wenzel L. German (1689 - 1743)	*D*			$3,300
REINERT, Frederick (?)	*P*			$110
REINHARDT, Ad American (1913 - 1967)	*P*	$34,100	$346,150	$2.530M
REINHARDT, Ludwig German (1870 -)	*P*	$550	$2,750	$4,950

D=Drawing, P=Painting, S=Sculpture, W=Watercolor

| | | Current Price Range | | |
		Low	Mean	High
REINHARDT, Wilhelm	P	$1,100	$1,430	$1,760
German (1815 - 1881)				
REINHART, Benjamin	P			$1,650
American (1829 - 1885)				
REINHART, Charles S.	D			$330
American (1844 - 1896)				
REINHART, Johann C.	D			$935
German (1761 - 1847)				
REINHOLD, Heinrich (Attrib.)	W			$495
Austrian (1788 - 1825)				
REINHOLD, YOUNGER, Friedrich	P			$5,225
Austrian (1814 - 1881)				
REINIGER, Otto	P			$1,045
German (1863 - 1909)				
REINMUTH, Kim	D			$300
American (20th -)				
REINPRECHT, K.	P			$248
Polish (1904 -)				
REISENEGGER, Bernhard	P			$2,200
German (1868 -)				
REISER, Carl	P			$330
German (1877 -)				
REISS, Jacob	P			$165
American (20th -)				
REISS, Lionel	P			$1,980
(?)				
REISS, Winold	D			$550
American (1886 - 1953)				
REISZ, Frank	P			$880
American (?)				
REITZ, Don	S			$440
(20th -)				
REITZEL, Marques E.	P			$1,430
American (1869 -)				
REKOWSKY, F.	P			$880
European (19th - 20th)				

D=Drawing, P=Painting, S=Sculpture, W=Watercolor

		Current Price Range		
		Low	Mean	High

RELYEA, Charles	*P*			$440
American (1863 - 1932)				
REMBRANDT, H. van Rijn	*D*			$610,000
Dutch (1606 - 1669)				
REMBRANDT, H. van Rijn (Att.)	*D*			$9,350
Dutch (1606 - 1669)	*P*			$41,800
REMBRANDT, H. van Rijn (Cir.)	*P*	$3,740	$16,170	$28,600
Dutch (1606 - 1669)				
REMBRANDT, H. van Rijn (Foll)	*P*	$3,300	$4,400	$5,500
Dutch (1606 - 1669)				
REMBRANDT, H. van Rijn (Mann)	*P*			$605
Dutch (1606 - 1669)				
REMBRANDT, H. van Rijn (Sc.)	*P*	$578	$18,159	$49,500
Dutch (1606 - 1669)				
REME, F.	*P*			$110
(?)				
REMENICK, Seymour	*P*	$330	$532	$660
American (20th -)	*W*			$220
REMINGTON, Frederic S.	*D*	$1,100	$19,800	$49,500
American (1861 - 1909)	*P*	$60,500	$583,982	$4.730M
	S	$2,200	$327,925	$4.400M
	W	$6,600	$23,807	$66,000
REMINGTON, Frederic S. (After)	*S*	$220	$8,208	$50,600
American (1861 - 1909)				
REMINGTON, Frederic S. (Attrib.)	*P*			$1,265
American (1861 - 1909)				
REMISOFF, Nicolai	*W*	$935	$963	$990
Russian (1894 - 1975)				
REN, Chuck	*P*	$6,050	$7,260	$8,470
American (1941 -)				
RENARD, Emile	*P*	$330	$1,155	$1,980
French (1850 - 1930)				
RENARD, Jean A.	*D*			$4,620
French (1744 - 1807)				

D=Drawing, P=Painting, S=Sculpture, W=Watercolor

		Current Price Range		
		Low	Mean	High
RENARD, Paul	*P*			$880
French (1871 - 1920)	*W*	$3,025	$3,850	$4,675
RENAUDIN, Alfred	*P*	$1,100	$8,800	$18,700
French (1866 -)				
RENAULT, Charles E.	*P*			$330
French (1829 - 1905)				
RENCK, Ernest E. (Attrib.)	*P*			$121
German (1842 - 1912)				
RENDEUSE, Renier	*D*			$1,870
(1684 - 1754)				
RENDON, Manuel	*P*			$2,750
French (1894 -)				
RENE, Jean J.	*P*			$1,980
French (20th -)	*S*			$121
RENEE, E.	*P*			$3,300
French (19th -)				
RENESSE, Constantine (Circle)	*P*			$5,225
Dutch (1626 - 1680)				
RENGNAULT,	*P*			$110
(?)				
RENI, Guido	*D*			$17,600
Italian (1575 - 1642)				
RENI, Guido (After)	*D*			$770
Italian (1575 - 1642)	*P*	$715	$1,934	$3,025
	W			$385
RENI, Guido (Follower)	*P*			$2,200
Italian (1575 - 1642)				
RENI, Guido (Studio)	*D*			$1,760
Italian (1575 - 1642)				
RENIER, Joseph E.	*S*			$3,575
American (1887 - 1966)				
RENNER, O.	*W*	$550	$633	$715
(19th -)				

D=Drawing, P=Painting, S=Sculpture, W=Watercolor

		Current Price Range	
		Low	Mean	High

		Low	Mean	High
RENNIE, Geo Melvin	*P*			$550
(?)				
RENOIR, Pierre-Auguste	*D*	$26,400	$704,220	$2.860M
French (1841 - 1919)	*P*	$17,600	$2.766M	$78.100M
	S			$5,225
	W	$17,600	$104,867	$242,000
RENOIR, Pierre-Auguste (Et al.)	*S*	$66,000	$119,167	$198,000
French (19th - 20th)				
RENOUARD, George	*P*	$495	$935	$1,210
American (1885 -)				
RENOUF, Edda	*D*			$550
American (1943 -)	*P*	$1,650	$2,475	$3,300
RENOUF, Emile	*P*			$137,500
French (1845 - 1894)				
RENOUX, Charles C.	*P*			$7,700
French (1795 - 1846)				
REPIN, Ilia	*P*	$8,800	$554,400	$1.100M
Russian (1844 - 1930)				
REPIN, Ilia (Attrib.)	*W*			$358
Russian (1844 - 1930)				
RESCHI, Pandolfo	*P*			$25,300
Italian (1643 - 1699)				
RESEDER, F. M. T.	*P*			$1,980
American (19th -)				
RESIKA, Paul	*D*			$700
American (1928 -)	*P*			$935
RESNICK, Milton	*P*	$2,200	$25,453	$132,000
American (1917 -)				
RESS, Paul	*P*			$110
(?)				
RESSLER, I.	*P*	$176	$253	$330
American (20th -)				
RESTOUT, Jean	*P*			$9,900
French (1692 - 1768)				

D=Drawing, P=Painting, S=Sculpture, W=Watercolor

		Current Price Range		
		Low	Mean	High
RESTOUT, Jean (Circle)	*P*			$18,700
French (1692 - 1768)				
RET, Etienne	*P*			$110
(?)	*W*			$193
RETBERG, Ralf L. von	*D*			$220
German (1812 - 1885)				
RETH, Alfred	*D*			$4,400
French (1884 - 1966)				
RETH, Caspar von	*P*			$16,500
German (1858 - 1913)				
RETHEL, Alfred	*P*			$22,000
German (1816 - 1859)				
RETTIG, John	*P*	$110	$990	$2,310
American (1860 - 1932)	*W*			$242
RETTIG, Martin	*P*	$220	$513	$770
American (20th -)				
REUBEN, Rowley (Attrib.)	*P*			$11,000
(?)				
REUILLARD, Roger	*W*			$110
(?)				
REUSSWIG, William	*W*			$248
American (1902 - 1978)				
REUTERDAHL, Henry	*D*			$385
American (1871 - 1925)	*W*	$248	$1,026	$1,430
REUTHER, Gertrude E. (Attrib.)	*P*			$825
German (1788 - 1845)				
REUTLINGEN, Paul	*P*			$3,300
German (1854 - 1920)				
REVEL, Gabriel	*P*			$4,620
French (1642 - 1712)				
REVERON, Armando	*P*	$26,400	$116,050	$308,000
Venezuelan (1890 -)	*W*			$26,400
REYERSON, L. L.	*P*			$550
American (19th - 20th)				

D=Drawing,   P=Painting,   S=Sculpture,   W=Watercolor

		Current Price Range		
		Low	Mean	High

REYES, Jesus	*P*			$660
Mexican (20th -)				
REYMANN, J.	*P*			$1,650
(19th -)				
REYMERSWAEL, Marinus (Cir.)	*P*	$2,200	$10,450	$18,700
Dutch (15th - 16th)				
REYMOND, Carlos	*P*			$2,420
French (1884 - 1970)				
REYNA, Antonio	*P*	$8,250	$23,045	$48,400
Spanish (1862 - 1937)				
REYNARD, Grant	*D*			$700
American (1887 - 1967)				
REYNAUD, Marius	*P*			$880
French (19th -)				
REYNOLD, Jan	*P*	$440	$523	$605
(?)				
REYNOLDS, Alan	*W*			$1,760
(20th -)				
REYNOLDS, Charles H.	*P*	$165	$165	$165
American (20th -)	*W*	$220	$220	$220
REYNOLDS, James E.	*P*	$1,980	$19,745	$33,000
American (1926 -)				
REYNOLDS, Sharon T.	*P*			$850
American (20th -)				
REYNOLDS, Sir Joshua	*P*	$2,860	$49,926	$220,000
British (1723 - 1792)				
REYNOLDS, Sir Joshua (After)	*P*	$440	$74,327	$363,000
British (1723 - 1792)				
REYNOLDS, Sir Joshua (Attrib.)	*P*			$1,210
British (1723 - 1792)				
REYNOLDS, Sir Joshua (Circle)	*P*	$3,300	$4,056	$5,225
British (1723 - 1792)				
REYNOLDS, Sir Joshua (Follower)	*P*			$990
British (1723 - 1792)				
REYNOLDS, Sir Joshua (School)	*P*	$1,320	$4,235	$7,150
British (1723 - 1792)				

D=Drawing, P=Painting, S=Sculpture, W=Watercolor

		Current Price Range		
		Low	Mean	High
REYNOLDS, Wellington J.	*P*	$165	$633	$1,100
American (1866 -)				
REYNTJENS, Henrich E.	*P*	$550	$2,145	$3,850
Dutch (1817 - 1900)				
REZIA, Felice A.	*P*			$825
French (19th - 20th)				
REZNIKOFF, Misha	*P*	$495	$660	$825
American (20th -)				
RHOMBERG, Hanno	*P*			$1,980
German (1820 - 1869)				
RHYS, Oliver	*P*	$7,700	$9,900	$12,100
American (19th -)				
RIBA-ROVIRA, Francois	*P*			$4,950
Spanish (1913 -)				
RIBAK, Louis	*P*	$770	$1,320	$1,650
American (1902 - 1979)				
RIBALTA, (After)	*P*			$1,980
(?)				
RIBAS,	*P*			$110
American (?)				
RIBCOWSKY, Dey de	*P*	$110	$1,408	$4,400
American (1880 - 1936)				
RIBERA, Jusepe de (Circle)	*D*			$550
French (1588 - 1656)	*P*	$3,300	$44,000	$93,500
RIBERA, Jusepe de (Follower)	*P*			$38,500
French (1588 - 1656)				
RIBERA, Jusepe de (Manner)	*P*	$220	$1,705	$3,190
French (1588 - 1656)				
RIBERA, Jusepe de (School)	*P*	$4,400	$8,250	$12,100
French (1588 - 1656)				
RIBERA, Pierre	*P*			$121,000
French (1867 - 1932)				
RIBLOWSKY, D.	*P*			$1,540
(?)				
RIBOT, Germaine T.	*P*	$6,875	$50,875	$121,000
French (1830 - 1893)				

D=Drawing, P=Painting, S=Sculpture, W=Watercolor

		Current Price Range		
		Low	Mean	High
RIBOT, Theodule A.	P	$3,300	$27,550	$90,200
French (1823 - 1891)				
RICARDI, G.	P			$825
Italian (20th -)				
RICCARDI, A.	D			$160
(20th -)				
RICCI, Arturo	P	$275	$1,378	$2,480
Italian (1854 -)				
RICCI, Danti	W			$248
Italian (1879 -)				
RICCI, Jerri	W			$165
American (20th -)				
RICCI, Marco (Circle)	D			$352
Italian (1676 - 1729)	P			$5,500
RICCI, Marco (Manner)	P	$4,125	$4,813	$5,500
Italian (1676 - 1729)				
RICCI, Marco (School)	P	$1,320	$1,980	$2,860
Italian (1676 - 1729)				
RICCI, Pio (Attrib.)	P			$2,860
Italian (? - 1919)				
RICCI, Sebastiano	P	$46,200	$127,600	$209,000
Italian (1659 - 1734)				
RICCI, Sebastiano (Attrib.)	P			$5,500
Italian (1659 - 1734)				
RICCI, Sebastiano (Circle)	D			$2,860
Italian (1659 - 1734)				
RICCI, Sebastiano (School)	P			$6,050
Italian (1659 - 1734)				
RICCI, Sebastiano (Style)	P			$3,300
Italian (1659 - 1734)				
RICCI, Ulysses A.	P			$110
American (1888 - 1960)				
RICCIARDI,	P			$990
(?)				
RICCIARDI, Cesare A.	D	$165	$245	$325

D=Drawing, P=Painting, S=Sculpture, W=Watercolor

		Current Price Range		
		Low	Mean	High
RICCIARDI, Cesare A.	*P*	$100	$298	$880
American (1892 -)				
RICCIARDI, Cesare A. (Attrib.)	*P*			$330
American (1892 -)				
RICCIARDI, Oscar	*P*	$150	$1,723	$4,675
Italian (1864 - 1935)				
RICCIO,	*P*			$165
(?)				
RICCIO, Bartolomeo N. Il (Circle)	*P*			$16,500
Italian (15th -)				
RICCO, A.	*P*			$660
(?)				
RICE, Henry W.	*D*			$275
American (1853 - 1934)	*W*	$220	$454	$825
RICE, M.	*P*			$880
(?)				
RICE, William M. J.	*P*			$523
American (1854 - 1922)				
RICH, John H.	*P*			$660
American (1876 - 1954)	*W*			$275
RICHARD,	*S*			$1,100
(?)				
RICHARD, George M.	*P*			$550
American (1880 -)				
RICHARD, J. H. J.	*D*			$220
American (20th -)				
RICHARD, Jacob	*P*			$154
American (1883 -)				
RICHARD-PUTZ, Michel	*P*			$17,600
French (1868 -)				
RICHARDS, Anna M.	*P*			$523
American (1870 -)				
RICHARDS, Ella	*P*	$220	$1,100	$1,980
American (19th - 20th)				

D=Drawing, P=Painting, S=Sculpture, W=Watercolor

		Current Price Range		
		Low	Mean	High

RICHARDS, Frederick de Bourg	*P*	$220	$7,157	$23,100
American (1822 - 1903)	*W*	$175	$280	$385
RICHARDS, J. W.	*W*			$440
American (19th -)				
RICHARDS, Thomas A.	*P*	$550	$1,334	$2,805
American (1820 - 1900)				
RICHARDS, W.	*P*	$550	$798	$1,045
British (19th -)				
RICHARDS, Walter	*W*			$495
American (1907 -)				
RICHARDS, William Trost	*D*	$825	$2,108	$3,300
American (1833 - 1905)	*P*	$550	$21,882	$275,000
	W	$660	$10,498	$41,800
RICHARDS, William Trost (After)	*P*			$1,320
American (1833 - 1905)				
RICHARDSON, Agnes	*W*			$300
(?)				
RICHARDSON, Francis H.	*P*	$358	$459	$523
American (1859 - 1934)				
RICHARDSON, G. M.	*P*	$468	$633	$798
American (19th - 20th)				
RICHARDSON, J.	*W*			$165
(?)				
RICHARDSON, Jonathan	*P*			$2,860
British (1665 - 1745)				
RICHARDSON, Louis H.	*P*	$138	$1,348	$4,180
American (1853 - 1923)				
RICHARDSON, Margaret F.	*P*			$138
American (1881 -)				
RICHARDSON, Mary C.	*P*	$660	$770	$880
American (1848 - 1931)				
RICHARDSON, Sam	*P*			$1,100
American (20th -)				
RICHARDSON, Theodore J.	*D*			$650

D=Drawing, P=Painting, S=Sculpture, W=Watercolor

		Current Price Range		
		Low	Mean	High
RICHARDSON, Theodore J.	*W*	$193	$867	$1,540
American (1855 - 1914)				
RICHARDSON, Thomas	*W*			$1,980
British (1813 - 1890)				
RICHARDSON, Thomas (Mann.)	*W*			$385
British (1813 - 1890)				
RICHARDSON, Volnay A.	*P*	$1,540	$2,090	$2,640
American (1880 -)				
RICHARDSON, W.	*P*			$1,320
European (19th -)				
RICHARDT, Ferdinand	*D*			$880
American (1819 - 1895)	*P*	$8,250	$9,213	$11,000
RICHENBURG, Robert	*P*			$4,400
(20th -)	*W*			$165
RICHERT, Carl	*P*			$440
(?)				
RICHERT, Charles H.	*D*			$110
American (1880 - 1974)	*P*	$138	$386	$885
	W	$131	$338	$770
RICHET, Leon	*P*	$1,320	$8,195	$16,500
French (1847 - 1907)				
RICHET, Leon (Attrib.)	*P*			$385
French (1847 - 1907)				
RICHEY, Rik	*P*			$330
American (20th -)				
RICHIER, Germaine	*S*	$13,200	$135,850	$550,000
French (1904 - 1959)				
RICHMOND, Agnes M.	*P*	$2,640	$10,047	$14,300
American (1870 - 1964)				
RICHMOND, Leonard	*P*	$220	$523	$825
British (? - 1965)				
RICHTER, A.	*D*			$715
German (19th -)	*P*			$495

D=Drawing, P=Painting, S=Sculpture, W=Watercolor

		Current Price Range		
		Low	Mean	High
RICHTER, Edouard F. W.	*P*	$12,100	$22,550	$33,000
French (1844 - 1913)				
RICHTER, Gerhard	*D*	$2,640	$2,860	$3,080
German (1932 -)	*P*	$11,000	$126,759	$616,000
	W			$7,150
RICHTER, Guido P.	*P*			$121,000
German (1859 - 1941)				
RICHTER, H. Davis	*P*	$1,045	$1,568	$2,090
British (1874 - 1955)				
RICHTER, H. P.	*P*			$303
(?)				
RICHTER, Hans T.	*P*			$330
German (1902 - 1969)				
RICHTER, Henry	*P*	$303	$592	$880
American (1870 - 1960)	*W*			$413
RICHTER, Johann	*P*			$429,000
Swedish (1665 - 1745)				
RICHTER, Johann (Attrib.)	*P*			$16,500
Swedish (1665 - 1745)				
RICHTER, Leopoldo	*P*			$4,400
German (1896 -)	*W*			$2,200
RICHTER, Wilmer S.	*W*			$200
American (1891 -)				
RICHTER-REICH, F. M.	*P*			$550
German (1896 -)				
RICK, Mary Ann	*D*			$1,000
American (20th -)				
RICKEY, George	*P*	$15,400	$18,700	$22,000
American (1907 -)	*S*	$880	$19,440	$71,500
RICKMAN, Phillip	*W*			$1,980
British (1891 -)				
RICKS, Don	*P*			$770
American (20th -)				

D=Drawing, P=Painting, S=Sculpture, W=Watercolor

		Current Price Range		
		Low	Mean	High

		Low	Mean	High
RICKS, Douglas	P	$4,620	$5,160	$5,700
American (1954 -)				
RICO Y ORTEGA, Martin	P	$27,500	$39,600	$55,000
Spanish (1833 - 1908)				
RICO Y ORTEGA, Martin (Att.)	P			$1,320
Spanish (1833 - 1908)				
RICOIS, Frances E.	P			$3,190
French (1795 - 1881)				
RIDEOUT, Phillip H.	P	$633	$1,128	$1,760
British (20th -)				
RIDEOUT, Phillip H. (Attrib.)	P			$1,925
British (20th -)				
RIDER, Arthur	P	$825	$3,245	$7,150
American (1886 - 1975)	W	$330	$504	$660
RIDER, Arthur (Attrib.)	P			$2,400
American (1886 - 1975)				
RIDER, Henry O.	P	$605	$605	$605
American (1860 -)				
RIDGELY, M.	W			$193
American (20th -)				
RIDGEWOOD, Lester	P			$578
American (19th - 20th)				
RIDINGER, Johann Elias	D	$2,090	$5,445	$8,800
German (1698 - 1767)				
RIDINGER, Johann Elias (Attrib.)	P			$3,850
German (1698 - 1767)				
RIECK, Ernst	P			$2,750
German (19th -)				
RIEDER, D.	S			$715
European (19th - 20th)				
RIEDMAYER, Francesco M.	P			$3,300
(18th -)				
RIEGEN, Nicholas	P			$2,475
Dutch (1827 - 1889)				
RIEGER, Albert	P			$1,760
Austrian (1834 - 1905)				

D=Drawing, P=Painting, S=Sculpture, W=Watercolor

		Current Price Range		
		Low	Mean	High

		Low	Mean	High
RIESENBERG, Sidney	*P*	$248	$262	$275
American (1885 -)				
RIESTER, Garey	*P*	$413	$614	$880
(20th -)				
RIETVELD, Antonie	*P*	$6,050	$12,100	$17,600
European (19th -)				
RIFKA, Judy	*P*	$3,300	$4,583	$5,500
American (20th -)	*S*			$6,820
RIGARDO, L.	*P*	$468	$537	$605
(19th - 20th)				
RIGAUD, Gaspard	*P*			$7,150
French (1661 - 1705)				
RIGAUD, Hyacinthe	*P*			$110,000
French (1659 - 1743)				
RIGAUD, Hyacinthe (Follower)	*P*			$990
French (1659 - 1743)				
RIGAUD, John F.	*P*			$34,100
British (1742 - 1810)				
RIGAUD, Pierre G.	*P*			$1,980
French (1874 -)				
RIGAUT, B.	*P*			$605
(?)				
RIGDEN, Cynthia	*S*			$710
American (1943 -)				
RIGGS, Robert	*P*	$2,420	$5,023	$8,250
American (1896 - 1970)				
RIGNANO, Vittorio	*P*	$2,420	$2,640	$2,860
Italian (1860 - 1916)				
RIGOLOT, Albert G.	*P*	$8,800	$21,633	$39,600
French (1862 - 1932)				
RIGOTARD, Alexandre	*P*			$880
French (19th -)				
RIJSWIJK, Johanna van	*P*			$1,045
Dutch (1893 - 1956)				
RIJSWIJK, Joseph V.	*P*			$330
Dutch (20th -)				

D=Drawing, P=Painting, S=Sculpture, W=Watercolor

		Current Price Range		
		Low	Mean	High

		Low	Mean	High
RIKELME, Claudio	P	$4,620	$6,490	$9,350
Argentine (1933 -)				
RIKNER, H.	W			$715
European (19th -)				
RILEY, Bridget	P	$26,400	$59,950	$93,500
British (1931 - 1984)	S			$5,720
	W			$5,500
RILEY, John	P			$3,575
British (1646 - 1691)				
RILEY, Ken	P	$700	$18,538	$41,000
American (1919 -)				
RILEY, W. Edward	W			$605
(?)				
RIMA,	P			$715
American (20th -)				
RIMBOECK, Max	P			$1,650
(20th -)				
RIMMER, William	S			$29,700
American (1816 - 1879)				
RINALDI, F.	P			$2,200
Italian (19th -)				
RINCON, Agapito	D			$3,080
Lat. Amer. (20th -)				
RINEHARDT, Siegfried	P			$1,650
American (1925 - 1984)				
RINEHART, William H.	S			$8,800
American (1825 - 1874)				
RINES, Frank M.	P			$385
American (1892 -)				
RING, Pieter de	P			$49,500
Dutch (1615 - 1660)				
RINOVIANA,	P			$825
(?)				
RIODET,	P			$176
(?)				

D=Drawing, P=Painting, S=Sculpture, W=Watercolor

| | | Current Price Range | | |
		Low	Mean	High
RION, Hanna	P			$715
American (1875 - 1924)				
RIOPELLE, Jean-P.	D			$30,800
Canadian (1922 -)	P	$6,875	$291,775	$1.540M
	S			$33,000
	W			$23,100
RIOS, Celso Z.	P			$248
Mexican (1947 -)				
RIP, Willem C.	W			$495
Dutch (1856 - 1922)				
RIPARI, Virgilio	P			$2,200
Italian (1846 -)				
RIPATRANSONE, Francesco M.	D			$4,620
Italian (?)				
RIPLEY, Aiden Lassell	D	$110	$368	$1,210
American (1896 - 1969)	P	$303	$10,928	$58,300
	W	$110	$2,205	$18,150
RIPLEY, Robert	D			$110
American (? - 1950)				
RIPPER, Chuck	W			$121
American (20th -)				
RIPPS, Rodney	P			$5,500
American (1950 -)				
RISCHELL, Claude	P			$908
American (20th -)				
RISING,	P	$253	$539	$825
(?)				
RITCHIE, Duncan S.	P			$2,530
British (19th -)				
RITMAN, Louis	P	$715	$108,833	$451,000
American (1889 - 1963)				
RITSCHEL, William	P	$330	$17,828	$66,000
American (1864 - 1949)	W	$825	$1,925	$2,750

D=Drawing, P=Painting, S=Sculpture, W=Watercolor

		Current Price Range		
		Low	Mean	High
RITTENBERG, Henry R. American (1879 - 1969)	*P*	$1,045	$2,723	$4,400
RITTER, Caspar German (1861 - 1923)	*P*	$1,650	$2,475	$3,300
RITTER, Edward (?)	*P*			$1,760
RITTER, Paul American (1829 - 1907)	*P*	$1,210	$1,595	$1,980
RITTWEGER, J. G. German (19th -)	*P*			$4,950
RIVAS, Antonio Italian (19th - 20th)	*P*	$1,320	$4,318	$6,050
RIVAS, E. M. (?)	*W*			$688
RIVAS, J. M. Spanish (19th - 20th)	*P*			$1,430
RIVERA, (Attributed) (?)	*D*			$220
RIVERA, Diego Mexican (1886 - 1957)	*D*	$1,100	$11,870	$30,250
	P	$17,600	$260,893	$605,000
	W	$6,050	$35,175	$181,500
RIVERA, Diego (Circle) Mexican (1886 - 1957)	*W*			$825
RIVERA, Diego (School) Mexican (1886 - 1957)	*D*			$440
RIVERA, Jose de American (1904 -)	*S*	$8,800	$18,386	$25,300
RIVEROS, Jorge Colombian (1934 -)	*P*			$4,400
RIVERS, Larry American (1923 -)	*D*	$3,850	$44,000	$88,000
	P	$5,500	$116,219	$467,500
	S	$1,540	$36,196	$132,000
RIVERS, Leopold British (1852 - 1905)	*P*			$660

D=Drawing, P=Painting, S=Sculpture, W=Watercolor

		Current Price Range		
		Low	Mean	High

RIVES, Frances E. American (1890 - 1968)	*P*			$4,675
RIVEST, Roland (?)	*P*			$220
RIVET, Adolphe French (19th -)	*D*			$248
RIVIERE, Briton British (1840 - 1920)	*P*	$3,300	$5,225	$7,150
RIVOIRE, Francois French (1842 - 1919)	*W*	$3,080	$7,040	$11,000
RIVOIRE, Raymond L. French (1884 - 1966)	*S*			$495
RIX, Julian W. American (1850 - 1903)	*P* *W*	$358 $468	$3,369 $674	$10,450 $880
RIZOS, Jacques Greek (19th -)	*P*			$7,150
ROBB, Elizabeth B. American (20th -)	*P*			$5,225
ROBB, J. E. American (19th - 20th)	*P*			$14,300
ROBBE, Henri Belgian (1807 - 1899)	*P*			$55,000
ROBBE, Louis Belgian (1806 - 1887)	*P*	$2,200	$2,420	$2,640
ROBBINS, Bruce American (20th -)	*D* *P*	$154	$6,127	$3,300 $12,100
ROBBINS, Ellen American (1828 - 1905)	*P* *W*	$330 $303	$385 $1,733	$440 $4,125
ROBBINS, Ellen (Attrib.) American (1828 - 1905)	*P*			$413
ROBBINS, John W. American (1856 - 1939)	*P*			$330
ROBBINS, R. F. American (1912 -)	*W*			$275

D=Drawing, P=Painting, S=Sculpture, W=Watercolor

		Current Price Range		
		Low	Mean	High

		Low	Mean	High
ROBERSON, Charles	*P*			$165
British (19th -)				
ROBERT, Hubert	*D*	$495	$20,799	$25,300
French (1733 - 1808)	*P*	$44,000	$209,000	$484,000
ROBERT, Hubert (Attrib.)	*D*	$935	$7,352	$18,700
French (1733 - 1808)	*P*	$7,700	$64,625	$132,000
ROBERT, Hubert (Circle)	*D*			$3,850
French (1733 - 1808)				
ROBERT, Hubert (School)	*P*			$2,860
French (1733 - 1808)				
ROBERT, Hubert (Studio)	*P*			$26,400
French (1733 - 1808)				
ROBERT, Marius	*P*			$330
French (20th -)	*W*	$193	$262	$330
ROBERT-FLEURY, Joseph N.	*D*			$880
French (1797 - 1890)				
ROBERTO, Luigi	*W*			$440
(19th -)				
ROBERTS, Betty R.	*P*			$220
American (1905 -)				
ROBERTS, Bruce E.	*P*	$1,320	$1,485	$1,650
American (20th -)				
ROBERTS, David	*P*	$605	$21,203	$41,800
British (1796 - 1864)	*W*			$1,760
ROBERTS, David (Manner)	*P*			$1,760
British (1796 - 1864)				
ROBERTS, Edith H.	*W*			$165
American (19th - 20th)				
ROBERTS, Edwin	*P*	$2,200	$8,869	$26,400
British (1840 - 1917)				
ROBERTS, Elizabeth	*D*	$660	$770	$880
American (1871 - 1927)	*P*			$1,980

D=Drawing, P=Painting, S=Sculpture, W=Watercolor

		Current Price Range		
		Low	Mean	High

		Low	Mean	High
ROBERTS, Ellen J. American (19th - 20th)	P			$1,100
ROBERTS, G. (?)	W			$908
ROBERTS, Goodridge American (1904 - 1974)	P			$14,300
ROBERTS, Henry B. British (1831 - 1915)	P			$1,760
ROBERTS, Joseph L. American (19th -)	P			$3,300
ROBERTS, Lewis European (20th -)	P			$2,750
ROBERTS, Priscilla American (1918 -)	P	$550	$715	$880
ROBERTSON, Charles British (1844 - 1891)	W			$7,700
ROBERTSON, J. D. (?)	P			$165
ROBIE, Jean-B. Belgian (1821 - 1910)	P	$1,650	$6,270	$14,300
ROBILLARD, Marcel French (19th -)	P			$2,420
ROBIN, Jean B. C. French (1734 - 1818)	P			$115,500
ROBINS, Thomas S. British (1814 - 1880)	P W			$990 $4,400
ROBINSON, (19th - 20th)	P			$413
ROBINSON, Alexander American (1867 -)	W	$220	$678	$990
ROBINSON, Boardman American (1876 - 1952)	D	$138	$194	$250
ROBINSON, C. British (19th - 20th)	P			$248
ROBINSON, Carrie B American (20th -)	W			$275

D=Drawing, P=Painting, S=Sculpture, W=Watercolor

		Current Price Range		
		Low	Mean	High
ROBINSON, Charles D.	D			$468
American (1847 - 1933)	P	$440	$2,107	$5,225
ROBINSON, David	W			$220
American (20th -)				
ROBINSON, Florence V.	W	$220	$367	$715
American (1874 - 1937)				
ROBINSON, Gladys L.	P	$440	$578	$715
American (20th -)				
ROBINSON, Hal	P	$358	$1,028	$1,650
American (1875 - 1933)				
ROBINSON, Irene B.	P			$605
American (1891 - 1973)	W			$523
ROBINSON, J. M.	P	$248	$276	$303
American (19th - 20th)				
ROBINSON, Jim	P	$2,530	$2,640	$2,750
American (20th -)				
ROBINSON, Margaret F.	P			$248
American (1908 -)				
ROBINSON, Mattias	P			$3,025
British (19th -)				
ROBINSON, Robert	P			$165
American (?)				
ROBINSON, Theodore	D			$71,500
American (1852 - 1896)	P	$9,900	$110,629	$330,000
ROBINSON, Theodore (Circle)	P			$4,400
American (1852 - 1896)				
ROBINSON, Thomas	P			$770
American (1835 - 1888)				
ROBINSON, William H.	D			$605
British (1872 - 1944)				
ROBINSON, William S.	P	$440	$1,642	$6,050
American (1861 - 1945)	W	$303	$559	$770
ROBINSON, William S. (Attrib.)	P			$715
American (1861 - 1945)				

D=Drawing, P=Painting, S=Sculpture, W=Watercolor

		Current Price Range		
		Low	Mean	High

		Low	Mean	High
ROBINSON, William T.	*P*	$165	$358	$495
American (1852 -)				
ROBUS, Hugo	*D*			$2,090
American (1885 - 1964)	*S*	$6,600	$11,000	$18,700
ROBUSTI, Domenico	*P*	$19,800	$27,500	$35,200
Italian (1560 - 1635)				
ROBUSTI, Jacopo (Attrib.)	*P*			$30,800
Italian (1518 - 1594)				
ROBUSTI, Jacopo (Circle)	*P*			$15,400
Italian (1518 - 1594)				
ROCCA, Giovanni Della	*P*			$1,320
Italian (1788 - 1858)				
ROCCHI, Giuseppe	*W*			$220
Italian (19th -)				
ROCHAS, M.	*P*			$275
(?)				
ROCHE, M. Paul	*W*			$165
(?)				
ROCHET, Louis	*S*			$2,860
French (1813 - 1878)				
ROCHUSSEN, Charles	*W*			$660
Dutch (1824 - 1894)				
ROCKBURNE, Dorothea	*P*	$10,450	$15,675	$20,900
American (20th -)				
ROCKENSCHAUB, Gerwald	*P*	$1,650	$2,475	$3,300
(20th -)				
ROCKMORE, Noel	*D*	$165	$303	$468
American (1928 -)	*P*	$358	$1,309	$2,310
	W			$110
ROCKWELL, Augustus	*P*			$1,210
American (1822 - 1882)				
ROCKWELL, Cleveland	*P*			$1,320
American (1837 - 1907)	*W*			$3,025

D=Drawing, P=Painting, S=Sculpture, W=Watercolor

		Current Price Range		
		Low	Mean	High
ROCKWELL, Norman	D	$3,300	$8,250	$17,600
American (1894 - 1978)	P	$7,700	$68,544	$264,000
	S			$20,900
	W	$16,500	$31,350	$46,200
ROCKWELL, Norman (Attrib.)	D			$193
American (1894 - 1978)				
RODDE,	P			$385
(?)				
RODDE, Michel	P	$385	$2,393	$4,400
French (1913 -)				
RODER, E. A. C.	P			$3,190
Belgian (20th -)				
RODGERS, Isabel F.	P			$200
American (1890 -)				
RODGERS, Ruth Eastman	W	$110	$656	$1,540
American (20th -)				
RODIN, Auguste	D	$2,200	$11,880	$24,200
French (1840 - 1917)	S	$4,675	$196,577	$4.290M
	W	$2,420	$12,155	$22,000
RODIN, Auguste (After)	S			$242
French (1840 - 1917)				
RODIN, Auguste (Attrib.)	W			$2,860
French (1840 - 1917)				
RODON, Francisco	P	$93,500	$99,000	$104,500
Puerto Rican (1934 -)				
RODRIGUE, George	P	$330	$990	$1,650
American (20th -)				
RODRIGUEZ, A.	P			$880
Spanish (19th - 20th)				
RODRIGUEZ, Alirio	P			$1,650
Venezuelan (1934 -)	W			$2,750
RODRIGUEZ, Francisco	P	$12,100	$12,100	$12,100
Spanish (1861 - 1956)				

D=Drawing, P=Painting, S=Sculpture, W=Watercolor

		Current Price Range		
		Low	Mean	High

		Low	Mean	High
RODRIGUEZ, Manuel G.	*P*	$8,800	$8,983	$9,350
Spanish (1863 - 1925)				
RODRIGUEZ, Mariano	*P*			$15,400
Cuban (1912 -)	*W*			$9,900
RODRIGUEZ, Miguel	*P*			$3,575
Spanish (19th -)				
RODRIGUEZ LOZANO, Manuel	*P*			$19,800
Mexican (1895 - 1971)				
ROE, Clarence	*P*	$523	$842	$1,210
British (? - 1909)				
ROE, Colin G.	*P*			$1,320
British (19th - 20th)				
ROE, Frederick R.	*P*			$165
American (20th -)				
ROE, Robert H.	*P*			$990
British (1739 - 1880)				
ROECKER, Henry L.	*P*			$495
American (1860 -)				
ROEHN, Jean A.	*P*			$7,150
French (1799 - 1864)				
ROEHNER, William	*P*			$1,705
Austrian (19th -)				
ROELOFS, Willem	*P*	$7,150	$21,010	$33,000
Dutch (1822 - 1897)	*W*	$220	$5,372	$9,075
ROERICH, Nikolai K.	*W*			$1,870
Russian (1874 - 1947)				
ROESEN, Severin	*P*	$1,980	$36,007	$104,500
American (19th -)				
ROESEN, Severin (Attrib.)	*P*	$4,125	$5,363	$6,600
American (19th -)				
ROESLER, Ettore F.	*W*	$3,520	$8,360	$13,200
Italian (1845 - 1907)				
ROESSLER, Walter	*P*	$165	$660	$880
German (19th - 20th)				

D=Drawing, P=Painting, S=Sculpture, W=Watercolor

		Current Price Range		
		Low	Mean	High

ROESTRATEN, Pieter G. van	*P*			$28,600
Dutch (17th - 18th)				
ROFFIAEN, Jean F. X.	*P*	$3,190	$3,245	$3,300
Belgian (1820 - 1898)				
ROGER,	*D*			$1,045
American (19th -)				
ROGER, Augustin	*P*			$358
French (19th -)				
ROGER, Guillaume	*P*			$275
Dutch (1867 - 1943)				
ROGER, Suzanne	*P*			$3,740
French (1899 -)				
ROGERS, Bart	*P*			$248
American (?)				
ROGERS, D.	*P*			$3,575
(19th -)				
ROGERS, G.	*P*			$495
(?)				
ROGERS, Howard	*P*			$3,000
American (20th -)	*S*			$2,100
ROGERS, John	*S*			$2,200
American (1829 - 1904)				
ROGERS, Mary	*P*			$209
American (1882 - 1920)				
ROGERS, Randolph	*S*	$1,045	$6,023	$11,000
American (1825 - 1892)				
ROGERS, Steve	*P*			$1,210
(?)				
ROGERS, T.	*P*			$2,200
American (20th -)				
ROGERS, Wendell	*P*			$275
(?)				
ROGERS, William	*P*			$3,190
British (19th -)				
ROGHMAN, Roeland (Attrib.)	*D*			$2,090
Dutch (1597 - 1686)				

D=Drawing, P=Painting, S=Sculpture, W=Watercolor

| | | Current Price Range | | |
		Low	Mean	High
ROGHT, E. T.	*P*			$220
European (19th - 20th)				
ROHDE, H.	*P*			$121
(?)				
ROHL, Peter K.	*W*			$3,520
German (1890 - 1975)				
ROHLFS, Christian	*P*			$71,500
German (1849 - 1938)				
ROHN, Ray	*W*	$138	$152	$165
American (1888 - 1935)				
ROHNER, George	*P*			$5,280
French (1913 -)				
ROHR, Fred	*P*			$3,850
Swiss (?)				
ROHRBECK, Franz	*P*			$935
German (19th -)				
ROHRHIRSCH, K.	*P*			$407
(?)				
ROIG, Jose	*P*	$1,650	$1,870	$2,090
Spanish (19th - 20th)				
ROINA,	*P*			$880
European (?)				
ROINE, Jean	*P*			$330
French (20th -)				
ROJAS, Elmar	*P*			$19,800
Guatemalan (1938 -)				
ROLANDS, J.	*P*			$248
(?)				
ROLDAN, Enrique	*P*	$1,540	$2,145	$2,750
Spanish (19th -)				
ROLF, R.	*P*			$330
(?)				
ROLFE, Edmund (Attrib.)	*P*			$578
American (1877 - 1917)				
ROLFE, Henry L.	*P*			$9,900
British (19th -)				

D=Drawing, P=Painting, S=Sculpture, W=Watercolor

		Current Price Range	
	Low	Mean	High

		Low	Mean	High
ROLLAND, Olga	*P*			$138
French (1937 -)				
ROLLE, August H. O.	*P*	$1,870	$2,860	$4,510
American (1875 - 1941)	*W*			$825
ROLLIN, J.	*P*			$523
(?)				
ROLLINS,	*D*			$220
American (20th -)				
ROLLINS, Warren E.	*P*	$330	$4,974	$27,500
American (1862 - 1962)				
ROLLINS & K.O.S., Tim	*S*			$6,600
(20th -)				
ROLSHOVEN, Julius	*D*			$660
American (1858 - 1930)	*P*	$550	$1,416	$2,860
ROLT, Charles	*P*			$209
Italian (19th -)				
ROMA, Ferranti	*P*			$1,650
Italian (20th -)	*W*			$330
ROMAGNONI, Bepi	*P*			$1,650
Italian (1930 - 1964)				
ROMAIN, Filippo	*D*			$4,400
European (19th -)				
ROMAN SCHOOL 16C,	*D*	$3,850	$11,917	$19,800
Italian (16th -)				
ROMAN SCHOOL 17C,	*D*	$1,100	$3,392	$6,600
Italian (17th -)	*P*	$2,750	$34,705	$110,000
ROMAN SCHOOL 18C,	*D*			$1,100
Italian (18th -)	*P*	$2,750	$12,925	$23,100
ROMANACH, Leopoldo	*P*			$1,980
Cuban (1862 - 1951)				
ROMANELLI, B.	*P*			$358
(?)				

D=Drawing, P=Painting, S=Sculpture, W=Watercolor

		Current Price Range		
		Low	Mean	High

		Low	Mean	High
ROMANELLI, Giovanni F. Italian (1610 - 1662)	*P*			$165,000
ROMANELLI, Giovanni F. (Sc.) Italian (1610 - 1662)	*P*			$1,210
ROMANELLI, Pasquale Italian (1812 - 1887)	*S*			$3,300
ROMANELLI, Raffaello Italian (1856 - 1928)	*S*			$3,300
ROMANELLI, T. (?)	*S*			$143
ROMANI, Juana Italian (1869 - 1924)	*P*			$2,420
ROMANNE, Valentine French (19th -)	*P*			$2,200
ROMANO, Antoniazzo (Studio) Italian (1461 - 1508)	*P*			$57,750
ROMANO, Giulio (Attrib.) Italian (1499 - 1546)	*D*			$1,430
ROMANO, Giulio (Follower) Italian (1499 - 1546)	*D*			$495
ROMANO, Giulio (Manner) Italian (1499 - 1546)	*P*			$1,925
ROMANO, Roberto Italian (20th -)	*P*	$385	$440	$495
ROMANO, Umberto American (1905 -)	*D*			$468
ROMANOVSKY, Dimitri American (20th -)	*P*	$1,430	$1,953	$2,475
ROMBOUTS, Gillis (School) Dutch (1630 - 1678)	*P*			$16,500
ROMBOUTS, Salomon Dutch (17th -)	*P*			$14,300
ROMBOUTS, Theodor (Manner) Flemish (1597 - 1637)	*P*			$3,960
ROMEK, Arpad Hungarian (1883 -)	*P*	$550	$743	$935

D=Drawing, P=Painting, S=Sculpture, W=Watercolor

		Current Price Range		
		Low	Mean	High

ROMER, William	*P*			$110
British (19th -)				
ROMERO, Carlos O.	*P*	$6,600	$8,800	$13,200
Latin American (20th -)	*W*			$6,050
ROMIER, P.	*P*			$385
European (20th -)				
ROMIN, G.	*W*			$303
American (19th - 20th)				
ROMITI, Sergio	*P*			$3,300
Italian (1928 -)				
ROMNEY, George	*D*			$1,650
British (1734 - 1802)	*P*	$3,520	$100,202	$660,000
ROMNEY, George (After)	*P*			$248
British (1734 - 1802)				
ROMNEY, George (Attrib.)	*P*			$825
British (1734 - 1802)				
ROMULO, Teodulo	*P*	$3,300	$4,583	$5,500
Mexican (1943 -)				
RONAI, Jozef R.	*P*			$3,080
Hungarian (1861 - 1930)				
RONALD, William	*P*			$880
Canadian (1926 -)				
RONAY, Erno (Attrib.)	*W*			$185
Hungarian (1899 -)				
RONDEL, Frederick	*D*			$1,650
American (1826 - 1892)	*P*	$880	$3,722	$9,075
RONDEL, Henri	*P*	$4,400	$7,333	$12,100
French (1857 - 1919)				
RONEY, Harold A.	*P*			$880
American (1899 -)				
RONMY, Guillaume F.	*P*			$7,700
French (1786 - 1854)				
RONNEBECK, Arnold	*S*			$3,520
American (1885 - 1947)				

D=Drawing, P=Painting, S=Sculpture, W=Watercolor

		Current Price Range		
		Low	Mean	High

		Low	Mean	High
RONNER, Madame	*P*			$605
French (19th -)				
RONNER-KNIP, Henriette	*P*	$495	$4,826	$11,000
Dutch (1821 - 1909)	*W*	$1,430	$3,465	$5,500
RONTINI, Ferruccio	*P*			$1,980
Italian (20th -)				
ROODENBURG, Hendrikus E.	*P*			$2,200
Dutch (1895 - 1983)				
ROOK, Edward F.	*P*			$1,540
(?)				
ROOKE, Henri	*P*			$1,100
French (19th -)				
ROOS, Johann H.	*P*			$16,500
German (1631 - 1685)				
ROOS, Joseph	*P*			$9,900
Austrian (1726 - 1805)				
ROOS, Peter	*P*			$2,860
American (1850 -)				
ROOS, Philipp P.	*P*	$3,300	$17,600	$38,500
German (1656 - 1706)				
ROOS, Phillip P. (Circle)	*P*			$4,400
German (1656 - 1706)				
ROOSENBOOM, Albert	*P*	$4,125	$5,431	$8,800
Belgian (1845 - 1875)				
ROOSENBOOM, Margarete	*P*			$23,100
Dutch (1843 - 1896)				
ROOSENBOOM, Nicolaas J.	*P*			$2,640
Dutch (1808 - 1880)				
ROOSEVELT, Samuel M.	*P*			$193
American (1863 - 1929)				
ROOSKENS, Anton	*W*			$3,740
Dutch (1906 - 1976)				
ROOTIUS, Jan A. (Circle)	*P*			$38,500
Dutch (1615 - 1674)				
ROSA, Pacecco di	*P*			$60,500
Italian (1600 - 1654)				

D=Drawing, P=Painting, S=Sculpture, W=Watercolor

		Current Price Range		
		Low	Mean	High

		Low	Mean	High
ROSA, Salvator	D	$8,250	$14,369	$23,100
Italian (1615 - 1673)	P	$71,500	$82,500	$93,500
ROSA, Salvator (After)	P			$8,800
Italian (1615 - 1673)				
ROSA, Salvator (Attrib.)	D			$3,300
Italian (1615 - 1673)	P	$198	$30,349	$60,500
ROSA, Salvator (Circle)	P			$9,900
Italian (1615 - 1673)				
ROSA, Salvator (Manner)	D			$468
Italian (1615 - 1673)	P			$275
ROSA, Salvator (School)	P	$3,080	$4,840	$6,600
Italian (1615 - 1673)				
ROSAI, Ottone	P	$3,300	$3,960	$4,620
Italian (1895 - 1957)	W			$1,760
ROSAIRE, Arthur D.	P			$1,485
Canadian (1879 - 1922)				
ROSAM, Walter A.	P			$17,600
German (1883 - 1916)				
ROSATI, Giulio	P	$13,200	$16,500	$22,000
Italian (1858 - 1917)	W			$5,500
ROSATI, James	S			$6,050
American (1912 -)				
ROSE, Guy	P	$110,000	$118,250	$126,500
American (1867 - 1925)				
ROSE, Herman	P	$193	$2,276	$4,950
American (1909 -)				
ROSE, Iver	P	$440	$1,100	$2,310
American (1899 - 1972)	W			$880
ROSE, Julius	P	$605	$1,678	$3,025
German (1828 - 1911)				
ROSE, Martin	P			$330
American (20th -)				

D=Drawing, P=Painting, S=Sculpture, W=Watercolor

		Current Price Range		
		Low	Mean	High
ROSE, Samuel	*P*	$1,210	$1,797	$2,970
American (1941 -)				
ROSE, William	*P*			$605
American (19th -)	*W*			$110
ROSEBEE,	*P*	$275	$422	$550
American (20th -)				
ROSELAND, Harry H.	*P*	$550	$8,687	$31,900
American (1866 - 1950)				
ROSELAND, Harry H. (Attrib.)	*D*			$165
American (1866 - 1950)				
ROSELL, Juan	*P*			$523
(?)				
ROSEN, Charles	*P*	$880	$10,626	$35,200
American (1878 - 1950)				
ROSEN, Charles (Attrib.)	*P*			$5,500
American (1878 - 1950)				
ROSEN, G. van	*P*			$303
Scandinavian (19th -)				
ROSEN, Jan	*D*			$880
Polish (1854 - 1936)	*P*			$7,810
ROSEN, K.	*P*			$3,850
Dutch (20th -)				
ROSENBERG, Charles G.	*P*			$660
American (1857 - 1866)				
ROSENBERG, Henry M.	*P*			$660
American (1858 -)				
ROSENBERG, James N.	*P*			$1,100
American (1874 - 1970)				
ROSENBERG, L.	*P*			$248
(?)				
ROSENBERG, Samuel	*P*	$1,100	$2,733	$5,000
American (1896 - 1972)				
ROSENBORG, Ralph	*W*			$330
American (1910 -)				

D=Drawing, P=Painting, S=Sculpture, W=Watercolor

		Current Price Range		
		Low	Mean	High

		Low	Mean	High
ROSENFELD, Edward	P			$187
American (20th -)				
ROSENFELD, Eugen	P			$2,640
(?)				
ROSENKRANTZ, Clarence C.	P	$220	$266	$330
American (19th - 20th)				
ROSENMEYER, Bernard J.	P		.	$660
American (1870 -)				
ROSENQUIST, James	P	$6,050	$128,021	$418,000
American (1933 -)	S	$24,750	$37,070	$60,500
ROSENSON, Olga	W			$110
American (20th -)				
ROSENTHAL, Albert	P	$385	$413	$440
American (1863 -)				
ROSENTHAL, Bernard	S			$990
(20th -)				
ROSENTHAL, Doris	P			$141
American (1895 - 1971)				
ROSENTHAL, Lillian	P	$110	$509	$908
American (20th -)				
ROSENTHAL, Louis	S			$165
American (19th - 20th)				
ROSENTHAL, Max	P	$385	$385	$385
Polish (1833 - 1918)				
ROSENTHAL, Tony	S			$1,430
American (1914 -)				
ROSENWEY, Paul	P	$110	$247	$358
American (20th -)	W			$220
ROSIN, Harry	W			$165
American (1897 - 1973)				
ROSLIN, Alexandre	P			$82,500
Swedish (1718 - 1793)				
ROSLIN, Alexandre (Manner)	P			$2,200
Swedish (1718 - 1793)				

D=Drawing, P=Painting, S=Sculpture, W=Watercolor

		Current Price Range		
		Low	Mean	High

ROSNER, Charles	*W*			$143
American (?)				
ROSS, Alex	*W*	$165	$233	$300
American (1909 -)				
ROSS, Gordon	*P*			$110
American (1873 - 1946)				
ROSS, Louise	*S*	$110	$660	$1,210
American (20th -)				
ROSS, M.	*P*			$275
(?)				
ROSS, R. F.	*W*			$248
Canadian (20th -)				
ROSS, T.	*P*			$6,600
(?)				
ROSSEAU, Percival L.	*P*	$385	$17,969	$44,000
American (1859 - 1937)				
ROSSELLI, Cosimo	*P*			$44,000
Italian (1439 - 1507)				
ROSSELLI, Cosimo (Manner)	*P*			$2,200
Italian (1439 - 1507)				
ROSSELLI, Matteo (Attrib.)	*P*			$15,950
Italian (1578 - 1650)				
ROSSER, C.	*P*			$358
American (20th -)				
ROSSERT, Paul	*P*			$7,150
French (1851 - 1918)				
ROSSETTI, A.	*P*			$1,320
Italian (1819 -)				
ROSSETTI, Dante G.	*D*	$143,000	$154,000	$165,000
British (1828 - 1882)				
ROSSETTO,	*S*			$13,200
Italian (19th -)				
ROSSI,	*P*			$220
(?)				
ROSSI, A.	*P*			$468
(19th -)				

D=Drawing, P=Painting, S=Sculpture, W=Watercolor

		Current Price Range		
		Low	Mean	High
ROSSI, Alexander M.	P			$14,300
British (19th -)				
ROSSI, Francesco del	D			$49,500
Italian (1510 - 1563)				
ROSSI, Francesco del (Attrib.)	P			$15,400
Italian (1510 - 1563)				
ROSSI, Joseph	P			$770
French (1892 - 1930)				
ROSSI, Lucio	P	$31,900	$33,825	$35,750
Italian (1846 - 1913)	W			$4,180
ROSSI, Luigi	P			$60,500
Italian (1853 - 1923)				
ROSSLER, Rudolf	P	$303	$5,143	$7,975
Austrian (1864 -)				
ROSSO, Medardo	S	$137,500	$199,833	$242,000
Italian (1858 - 1928)				
ROSZAK, Theodore	D			$2,200
American (1907 -)				
ROTARI, Pietro	P			$77,000
Italian (1707 - 1762)				
ROTARI, Pietro (Circle)	P			$15,400
Italian (1707 - 1762)				
ROTH, Andrew	P	$385	$468	$550
American (20th -)				
ROTH, Ernest	D			$330
American (1879 - 1964)	P	$358	$674	$1,210
ROTH, Frederick G. R.	S	$715	$1,348	$1,980
American (1872 - 1944)				
ROTHAUG, Alexander	P	$22,000	$30,800	$39,600
Austrian (1870 -)				
ROTHAUG, Leopold	W			$1,045
Austrian (1868 - 1959)				
ROTHBORT, Laurence	P			$1,100
American (20th -)				

D=Drawing, P=Painting, S=Sculpture, W=Watercolor

| | | Current Price Range | | |
		Low	Mean	High
ROTHBORT, Samuel	P	$1,650	$3,768	$7,150
American (1882 - 1959)				
ROTHENBERG, Susan	D	$25,300	$31,900	$38,500
American (20th -)	P	$38,500	$159,814	$550,000
ROTHENSTEIN,	P			$138
American (20th -)				
ROTHENSTEIN, Sir William	P			$66,000
British (1872 - 1945)				
ROTHERMEL, Peter F.	P			$350
American (1817 - 1895)				
ROTHKO, Mark	P	$16,500	$1.468M	$3.630M
American (1903 - 1970)	W	$3,025	$61,142	$176,000
ROTHWELL, Elizabeth L.	P			$330
(?)				
ROTIG, Georges F.	P	$2,200	$3,988	$5,775
French (1873 - 1961)				
ROTTENHAMMER, Hans (Foll)	P			$2,200
German (? - 1668)				
ROTTENHAMMER, Johann	D			$104,500
German (1564 - 1625)				
ROTTENHAMMER, Johann (Cir)	D			$3,080
German (1564 - 1625)				
ROTTMANN, Mozart	P	$3,300	$4,675	$6,050
Hungarian (1874 -)				
ROTTONARA, Franz A.	W			$1,100
Austrian (1848 -)				
ROUAULT, Georges	P	$93,500	$517,090	$1.210M
French (1871 - 1958)	S			$110,000
	W	$12,100	$78,577	$187,000
ROUBAUD, Franz	P	$3,850	$4,538	$5,225
German (1856 - 1928)				
ROUBY, Alfred	P			$5,500
French (1949 -)				

D=Drawing, P=Painting, S=Sculpture, W=Watercolor

| | | Current Price Range | | |
		Low	Mean	High
ROUERE, Pietro L. de la	*P*			$6,325
Italian (19th - 20th)				
ROULAND, Orlando	*P*	$550	$2,860	$7,260
American (1871 - 1945)				
ROUMEGOUS, Auguste F.	*P*			$1,980
French (19th -)				
ROUSE, A. F.	*P*			$1,320
British (19th -)				
ROUSSE, F.	*W*			$198
(?)				
ROUSSEAU,	*S*			$1,980
(?)				
ROUSSEAU, Helen	*P*	$1,650	$2,383	$3,300
American (1898 -)				
ROUSSEAU, Henri	*P*			$495,000
French (1844 - 1910)				
ROUSSEAU, Henri E.	*P*			$18,700
French (1875 - 1933)				
ROUSSEAU, Jacques de (Manner)	*P*			$1,320
French (1861 - 1911)				
ROUSSEAU, Margarite	*P*	$4,125	$6,650	$9,350
Belgian (1888 - 1948)				
ROUSSEAU, Philippe	*P*	$4,400	$6,325	$8,250
French (1816 - 1887)				
ROUSSEAU, Theodore	*P*	$3,575	$69,450	$418,000
French (1812 - 1867)				
ROUSSEL, Ker-Xavier	*D*	$1,430	$2,365	$3,300
French (1867 - 1944)				
ROUSSEL, Pierre	*P*	$3,960	$7,737	$10,725
French (20th -)	*W*			$3,300
ROUX, Mathieu A. (Attrib.)	*P*			$330
French (1799 - 1872)				
ROVELLO, G.	*P*			$550
Italian (19th -)				
ROVERE, Giovanni M. delle	*D*	$990	$1,357	$1,760
Italian (1575 - 1640)				

D=Drawing, P=Painting, S=Sculpture, W=Watercolor

| | | Current Price Range | | |
		Low	Mean	High
ROWBOTHAM, Charles	*W*	$550	$660	$770
British (1877 -)				
ROWBOTHAM, T. L.	*W*			$220
American (19th -)				
ROWE, Charles	*P*			$440
American (20th -)				
ROWE, Guy	*P*			$110
American (1894 - 1969)				
ROWE, Sydney G.	*W*			$990
British (19th - 20th)				
ROWELL, Louis	*P*	$176	$212	$248
American (1873 - 1928)				
ROWLANDSON, George D.	*P*	$2,200	$3,190	$4,180
British (19th -)				
ROWLANDSON, Thomas	*D*	$1,980	$5,491	$16,500
British (1756 - 1827)	*W*	$825	$2,522	$3,850
ROWLANDSON, Thomas (Attrib.)	*W*			$1,100
British (1756 - 1827)				
ROWSE, Samuel W.	*D*			$660
American (1822 - 1901)				
ROXSONOWICH,	*W*			$220
Russian (19th - 20th)				
ROY, J.	*W*			$1,870
(?)				
ROY, Lynn Aus	*D*			$440
American (20th -)				
ROY, Pierre	*P*	$44,000	$71,500	$93,500
French (1880 - 1950)				
ROYBET, Ferdinand	*P*	$1,100	$4,125	$7,150
French (1840 - 1920)				
ROYLE, Herbert	*P*			$9,680
British (1870 - 1958)				
ROZEL,	*S*			$440
European (19th -)				
ROZIER, Jules	*P*			$1,320
French (1821 - 1882)				

D=Drawing, P=Painting, S=Sculpture, W=Watercolor

		Current Price Range		
		Low	Mean	High

		Low	Mean	High
RUBEN, Franz L.	*P*			$25,300
Austrian (1842 - 1920)				
RUBENS, Jos	*P*			$1,540
German (18th - 19th)				
RUBENS, Sir Peter P.	*P*	$77,000	$355,667	$528,000
Flemish (1577 - 1640)				
RUBENS, Sir Peter P. (After)	*P*	$770	$3,642	$7,150
Flemish (1577 - 1640)				
RUBENS, Sir Peter P. (Attrib)	*P*			$33,000
Flemish (1577 - 1640)				
RUBENS, Sir Peter P. (Circle)	*P*	$1,650	$18,229	$63,250
Flemish (1577 - 1640)				
RUBENS, Sir Peter P. (Fol.)	*P*	$4,400	$7,425	$10,450
Flemish (1577 - 1640)				
RUBENS, Sir Peter P. (Manner)	*P*	$1,100	$3,053	$5,500
Flemish (1577 - 1640)				
RUBENS, Sir Peter P. (School)	*P*	$1,100	$6,270	$13,200
Flemish (1577 - 1640)				
RUBENS, Sir Peter P. (Studio)	*P*	$7,150	$17,783	$24,200
Flemish (1577 - 1640)				
RUBERSTEIN, Barnet	*D*			$2,090
(20th -)				
RUBIN, Reuven	*D*	$1,540	$3,913	$6,600
Israeli (1893 - 1974)	*P*	$13,750	$29,272	$44,000
	W	$4,950	$4,950	$4,950
RUCKER, Robert	*P*	$715	$1,115	$1,514
American (20th -)				
RUCKMAN, Grace M.	*P*			$550
American (1873 -)				
RUCKREIM, Ulrich	*S*			$19,800
German (1938 -)				
RUDD, N.	*P*			$2,750
American (19th -)				
RUDDICK, Dorothy	*D*			$220
(?)				

D=Drawing, P=Painting, S=Sculpture, W=Watercolor

		Current Price Range		
		Low	Mean	High

RUDE, Francois	*S*			$26,400
French (1784 - 1855)				
RUDE, Olaf	*P*			$6,600
Danish (1886 - 1957)				
RUDE, Sophie	*P*	$2,090	$69,795	$137,500
French (1797 - 1867)				
RUDISUHLI, Hermann	*P*			$3,080
Swiss (1864 - 1945)				
RUDOLPH, Harold	*P*	$495	$743	$990
American (1850 - 1884)				
RUELAS, Julio	*P*			$57,750
Mexican (1870 - 1907)				
RUELLAN, Andree	*P*			$3,520
American (1905 -)				
RUEPING, K.	*D*			$1,430
American (20th -)				
RUETER, Georg	*P*			$1,210
Dutch (1875 -)				
RUFF, Andor	*S*			$605
Hungarian (1885 -)				
RUFFOLO, Gasper J.	*P*			$358
American (1908 -)				
RUGENDAS, George P. (After)	*P*			$1,100
German (1666 - 1742)				
RUGENDAS, Johann M.	*D*			$5,500
German (1802 - 1858)	*P*	$41,250	$64,625	$88,000
	W			$15,400
RUGENDAS, Johann M. (Circle)	*P*			$770
German (1802 - 1858)				
RUGER, H. Otto	*P*			$2,200
German (19th -)				
RUGGERIO,	*P*			$330
(?)				
RUGGLERS, Dr.	*P*			$275
(?)				

D=Drawing, P=Painting, S=Sculpture, W=Watercolor

		Current Price Range		
		Low	Mean	High
RUIS, Joanes P. (16th -)	*P*			$3,080
RUISDAEL, Jacob van Dutch (1630 - 1682)	*P*	$35,200	$215,600	$440,000
RUISDAEL, Jacob van (Circle) Dutch (1630 - 1682)	*P*	$5,500	$9,900	$14,300
RUISDAEL, Jacob van (Follower) Dutch (1630 - 1682)	*P*			$12,100
RUISDAEL, Jacob van (Manner) Dutch (1630 - 1682)	*P*	$4,400	$4,950	$5,500
RUISDAEL, Jacob van (School) Dutch (1630 - 1682)	*P*			$20,900
RUISDAEL, Jacob van (Style) Dutch (1630 - 1682)	*P*			$1,650
RUIZ, Juan P. M. (Attrib.) Spanish (18th -)	*P*			$6,600
RUIZ PIPO, Manolo Spanish (1929 -)	*P*	$1,045	$1,302	$1,650
RULE, Gallagher American (1930 -)	*S*			$495
RULLE, R. French (19th -)	*S*			$468
RUMMELL, Richard American (1848 - 1924)	*P*			$2,750
RUMMLER, Alex J. American (1867 - 1959)	*P*			$303
RUNDELL, Helen American (20th -)	*P*			$300
RUNGALDIER, Ignaz Austrian (1799 - 1876)	*W*			$1,980
RUNGE, J. F. American (?)	*D* *W*			$176 $935
RUNGIUS, Carl American (1869 - 1959)	*P* *S*	$248	$16,535	$63,250 $60,500

D=Drawing, P=Painting, S=Sculpture, W=Watercolor

		Current Price Range		
		Low	Mean	High
RUNYON, Grace A.	*P*	$220	$394	$495
American (20th -)				
RUOPPOLO, Giovanni B. (Circle)	*P*			$77,000
Italian (1629 - 1693)				
RUOPPOLO, Giuseppe (Manner)	*P*			$31,900
Italian (17th - 18th)				
RUSCH, B. W.	*D*			$3,575
European (19th -)				
RUSCHA, Ed	*D*	$23,100	$36,300	$49,500
American (1937 -)	*P*	$27,500	$90,429	$297,000
	S	$20,900	$34,100	$55,000
	W	$35,200	$52,250	$68,750
RUSH, Olive	*P*			$1,430
American (1873 - 1966)				
RUSH, William (After)	*S*			$1,980
American (1756 - 1833)				
RUSINOL, Santiago	*P*			$352,000
Spanish (1861 - 1931)				
RUSS, C. B.	*P*	$330	$568	$715
American (20th -)	*W*			$248
RUSS, Robert	*P*			$68,750
Austrian (1847 - 1922)				
RUSSELL, Charles	*P*			$1,210
British (1852 - 1910)				
RUSSELL, Charles M.	*D*	$1,430	$10,846	$17,600
American (1864 - 1926)	*P*	$330,000	$607,750	$1.100M
	S	$330	$5,913	$39,600
	W	$4,620	$74,438	$209,000
RUSSELL, Charles M. (After)	*S*	$550	$1,446	$2,200
American (1864 - 1926)				
RUSSELL, Charles M. (Attrib.)	*D*			$220
American (1864 - 1926)				

D=Drawing, P=Painting, S=Sculpture, W=Watercolor

		Current Price Range		
		Low	Mean	High

RUSSELL, Donn	*P*			$550
(20th -)				
RUSSELL, Gyrth	*P*			$385
Canadian (1892 -)				
RUSSELL, John	*D*			$10,450
British (1745 - 1806)	*P*	$880	$8,543	$17,600
RUSSELL, M. B. (Attrib.)	*S*			$660
(19th -)				
RUSSELL, Morgan	*P*	$2,200	$60,133	$176,000
American (1886 - 1953)				
RUSSELL, W. S.	*P*			$330
American (20th -)				
RUSSELL, William	*P*			$495
British (1780 - 1870)				
RUSSIAN SCHOOL,	*S*			$2,310
Russian (?)				
RUSSIAN SCHOOL,	*P*			$1,650
Russian (19th - 20th)				
RUSSIAN SCHOOL 19C,	*P*	$1,760	$2,695	$3,300
Russian (19th -)	*S*			$6,600
RUSSIAN SCHOOL 20C,	*P*	$1,210	$1,430	$1,650
Russian (20th -)				
RUSSLAND, R. Wolff	*P*			$193
Russian (19th - 20th)				
RUSSO, E	*P*			$385
(?)				
RUSSOLO, Luigi	*P*			$462,000
Italian (1885 - 1947)				
RUST, Johan A.	*P*			$990
Dutch (1828 - 1915)				
RUTH, Jan de	*P*			$138
(?)				
RUTHVEN, Jerry	*P*			$4,400
American (20th -)				

D=Drawing, P=Painting, S=Sculpture, W=Watercolor

		Current Price Range		
		Low	Mean	High

RUTLEDGE, June	P			$220
American (20th -)				
RUTTEN, V.	W			$1,760
French (19th -)				
RUTTER, Frank	P			$660
British (19th - 20th)				
RUTTER, W. B.	P			$770
American (19th -)				
RUYSCH, Anna E. (Attrib.)	P			$8,250
Dutch (18th -)				
RUYSCH, Rachel	P			$165,000
Dutch (1664 - 1750)				
RUYSCH, Rachel (After)	P	$5,775	$7,288	$8,800
Dutch (1664 - 1750)				
RUYSCH, Rachel (Manner)	P			$7,700
Dutch (1664 - 1750)				
RUYSDAEL, Salomon van	P	$1,760	$176,293	$517,000
Dutch (1600 - 1670)				
RUYTENBACH, E.	P			$11,000
Dutch (17th -)				
RUYTINX, Alfred	P			$9,075
Belgian (1871 -)				
RUZICKA-LAUTENSCHLAGER,	P			$110
(?)				
RYAN, Anne	P			$358
American (1889 - 1954)				
RYAN, L. S.	P			$688
American (19th -)				
RYAN, Patrick	P			$5,280
European (19th - 20th)				
RYAN, Tom	D			$5,500
American (1922 -)	P			$5,500
RYCKAERT, Marten (Follower)	P			$11,000
Flemish (1587 - 1631)				
RYCKAERT, III, David (Attrib.)	P			$1,650
Flemish (17th -)				

D=Drawing, P=Painting, S=Sculpture, W=Watercolor

		Current Price Range		
		Low	Mean	High
RYDER,	*P*			$1,650
American (20th -)				
RYDER, Albert P.	*P*			$1,540
American (1847 - 1917)				
RYDER, Albert P. (Attrib.)	*P*			$1,540
American (1847 - 1917)				
RYDER, Chauncey F.	*D*			$358
American (1868 - 1949)	*P*	$440	$6,322	$31,900
	W	$1,595	$3,703	$6,875
RYDER, Chauncey F. (Attrib.)	*P*			$330
American (1868 - 1949)				
RYDER, J. S.	*P*			$660
American (?)				
RYDER, Jack van	*P*			$1,045
American (1898 - 1968)				
RYDER, Platt P.	*P*			$1,760
American (1821 - 1896)				
RYERSON, Margery	*P*			$7,150
American (1886 -)				
RYLAND, Robert K.	*P*	$193	$1,142	$2,090
American (1873 - 1951)				
RYMAN, Robert	*D*	$41,250	$61,875	$82,500
American (1930 -)	*P*	$121,000	$977,900	$2.310M
	S	$143,000	$148,500	$154,000
RYSBRACK, John M.	*D*			$1,430
Flemish (1693 - 1770)				
RYSEWYK, Jan van	*P*			$350
Belgian (20th -)				
RYSEWYK, Johanna B. van	*P*			$495
Dutch (1873 - 1956)				
RYSSELBERGHE, Theo van	*D*			$1,430
Belgian (1862 - 1926)	*P*	$11,000	$223,438	$770,000
	W	$1,760	$14,630	$27,500

D=Drawing, P=Painting, S=Sculpture, W=Watercolor

		Current Price Range		
		Low	Mean	High

		Low	Mean	High
S. AMERICAN SCHOOL, (?)	*P*	$1,430	$1,430	$1,430
SAAR, Betye American (20th -)	*S*			$330
SAATY, Wallace American (20th -)	*P*	$165	$193	$220
SABATINI, Andrea Italian (1487 - 1530)	*P*			$52,250
SABATINI, I. Italian (19th -)	*P*			$39,600
SABOURAUD, Emile French (1900 -)	*P*	$1,210	$1,375	$1,540
SACCARO, John American (1913 - 1981)	*P* *W*			$4,675 $7,700
SACCO, Luca American (1858 - 1912)	*P*	$990	$1,870	$2,750
SACKS, Joseph American (1887 -)	*P*	$1,073	$1,578	$2,640
SACKS, Walter T. American (1895 -)	*P* *W*			$605 $220
SADEE, Philippe L. Dutch (1837 - 1904)	*P*	$16,500	$21,450	$26,400
SADLER, Walter D. British (1854 - 1923)	*P*	$1,320	$8,507	$13,200
SAETTI, Bruno Italian (1902 - 1984)	*W*	$5,500	$5,500	$5,500
SAFTLEVEN, Cornelis Dutch (1607 - 1681)	*D*	$3,575	$5,363	$7,150
SAFTLEVEN, Cornelis (Circle) Dutch (1607 - 1681)	*P*	$6,600	$8,250	$9,900
SAFTLEVEN, Herman Dutch (1609 - 1685)	*D* *P*	$7,700	$22,733	$39,600 $15,400
SAFTLEVEN, Herman (Attrib.) Dutch (1609 - 1685)	*D*	$220	$733	$990

D=Drawing, P=Painting, S=Sculpture, W=Watercolor

		Current Price Range		
		Low	Mean	High
SAGE, Kay	*D*			$1,760
American (1898 - 1961)				
SAIN, Paul J. M.	*P*			$660
French (1853 - 1908)				
SAINSBURY, Grace E.	*W*			$1,870
British (19th - 20th)				
SAINT MEMIN, Charles B. F. de	*D*			$4,400
American (1770 - 1852)				
SAINT PHALLE, Niki de	*P*	$2,750	$41,350	$104,500
American (1930 -)	*S*	$7,700	$51,150	$110,000
	W	$13,200	$14,300	$15,400
SAINT-ANDRE, Simon R. De	*P*			$187,000
French (1613 - 1677)				
SAINT-EVRE, Gillot	*P*			$1,100
French (1791 - 1858)	*W*			$660
SAINT-GAUDENS, Augustus	*S*	$176	$49,906	$242,000
American (1848 - 1907)				
SAINT-GAUDENS, Augustus (Aft)	*S*			$3,850
American (1848 - 1907)				
SAINT-MARCEAUX, Charles R.	*S*			$2,860
French (1845 - 1915)				
SAINT-OURS, Jean P. P.	*D*			$660
French (1752 - 1809)				
SAINTIN, Jules E.	*D*	$1,760	$2,420	$3,080
French (1829 - 1894)				
SAITER, Johann G.	*D*			$880
German (1717 - 1800)				
SAKAI, Kazuya	*P*			$3,300
Lat. Amer. (20th -)				
SALA, Paolo	*P*	$5,500	$5,775	$6,050
Italian (1859 - 1929)	*W*	$798	$2,049	$3,300
SALA Y FRANCES, Emilio	*P*	$2,310	$17,655	$33,000
Spanish (1850 - 1910)				

D=Drawing, P=Painting, S=Sculpture, W=Watercolor

		Current Price Range	
	Low	Mean	High

SALABET, Jean	P			$193
French (20th -)				
SALADINI, A.	P			$660
(?)				
SALANSON, Eugenie M.	P			$20,900
French (19th -)				
SALAS, Tito	P			$3,300
South American (1887 -)				
SALAZAR, Carlos	P	$4,400	$4,538	$4,675
Lat. Amer. (20th -)				
SALAZAR, Ignacio	P			$5,500
Mexican (1947 -)				
SALAZAR, Jose	D			$154
American (18th - 19th)				
SALAZAR Y MENDOZA, Jose	P			$68,200
Mexican (18th - 19th)				
SALEH, Raden	P			$1,100
Dutch (1816 - 1880)				
SALEMME, Attilio	D	$1,650	$2,145	$2,640
American (1911 - 1955)	P	$3,300	$4,469	$6,050
	W	$2,200	$2,842	$3,575
SALESION, L.	S			$770
Italian (19th - 20th)				
SALICETI, Jeanne	P			$660
French (1873 - 1950)				
SALIMBENI, Lorenzo	P			$9,350
Italian (1374 - 1420)				
SALINAS, Pablo	P	$11,000	$26,767	$44,000
Spanish (1871 - 1946)				
SALING, Paul	P	$105	$580	$1,210
American (1876 - 1936)				
SALING, Paul (Attrib.)	P			$660
American (1876 - 1936)				
SALISBURY, J. Elmer	P			$330
American (20th -)				

D=Drawing, P=Painting, S=Sculpture, W=Watercolor

		Current Price Range		
		Low	Mean	High
SALLAI,	*P*			$2,200
European (19th -)				
SALLE, David	*D*			$7,700
American (1952 -)	*P*	$14,300	$59,479	$143,000
	S	$66,000	$231,000	$550,000
	W	$13,200	$17,600	$28,600
SALMON, John C.	*P*	$550	$880	$1,210
British (1844 - 1917)				
SALMON, Robert	*P*	$31,900	$78,980	$126,500
American (1775 - 1842)				
SALMON, Robert (Attrib.)	*W*			$440
American (1775 - 1842)				
SALMSON, Hugo F.	*P*	$4,400	$11,000	$17,600
Swedish (1844 - 1894)				
SALOME,	*P*	$8,800	$12,283	$15,400
(20th -)				
SALOMON, Gabriel	*P*			$2,200
(?)				
SALSA, Philip van	*W*			$1,100
(?)				
SALT, James	*P*			$1,100
British (19th -)				
SALT, John	*P*			$46,750
American (1937 -)				
SALTFLEET, Frank	*W*			$165
British (? - 1937)				
SALTINI, Pietro	*P*			$16,500
Italian (1839 - 1908)				
SALTOFT, Edvard	*D*			$1,320
Danish (1883 -)				
SALTONSTALL, Elizabeth	*D*			$220
American (1900 -)				
SALVATI,	*P*			$633
(?)				

D=Drawing, P=Painting, S=Sculpture, W=Watercolor

| | | Current Price Range | |
	Low	Mean	High
SALVATO, J.	*P*			$440
(?)				
SALVI, Giovanni B. (After)	*P*			$1,100
Italian (1605 - 1685)				
SALVI, Giovanni B. (School)	*P*			$3,080
Italian (1605 - 1685)				
SALVIATI, Francesco (Follower)	*D*			$1,320
Italian (1510 - 1563)				
SALVO,	*P*	$3,575	$4,098	$4,620
Italian (20th -)				
SAM, Joe	*P*			$1,760
American (20th -)				
SAMACCHINI, Orazio	*D*			$11,000
Italian (1532 - 1577)	*W*			$17,600
SAMARAS, Lucas	*D*	$3,300	$4,125	$4,675
American (1936 -)	*P*	$3,080	$38,048	$132,000
	S	$2,090	$39,298	$110,000
	W			$5,500
SAMBROOK, Russell	*P*			$715
American (20th -)				
SAMMANN, Detlef	*P*			$1,045
American (19th - 20th)				
SAMMONS, Carl	*D*			$633
American (1886 - 1968)	*P*	$880	$1,399	$2,090
	W			$990
SAMPLE, Paul S.	*P*	$688	$6,302	$19,800
American (1896 - 1974)	*W*	$1,045	$1,939	$2,750
SAMPSON, A.	*P*			$132
American (19th - 20th)				
SAN ANGELO, Mary	*P*	$110	$312	$660
American (1915 -)				
SAN FRIANO, Maso da (Circle)	*P*			$15,400
(?)				

D=Drawing, P=Painting, S=Sculpture, W=Watercolor

		Current Price Range	
		Low	Mean	High

		Low	Mean	High
SANBORN, Percy	*P*			$660
American (1849 - 1929)				
SANCHEZ, Adolfo	*P*			$1,760
(20th -)				
SANCHEZ, Edgar	*P*	$440	$5,335	$8,800
Venezuelan (1940 -)				
SANCHEZ, Emilio	*P*			$6,600
Cuban (1921 -)	*W*			$2,200
SANCHEZ, Enrique	*P*			$7,150
Mexican (1940 -)				
SANCHEZ, Harriet de	*P*			$220
American (20th -)				
SANCHEZ, Mario	*P*			$770
(?)				
SANCHEZ-PERRIER, Emilio	*P*	$15,400	$22,393	$28,600
Spanish (1855 - 1907)				
SAND, Alice L.	*P*			$198
American (20th -)				
SANDBACK, Fred	*S*	$35,200	$36,850	$38,500
(20th -)				
SANDBY, Paul	*W*	$3,850	$4,125	$4,400
British (1725 - 1809)				
SANDE BAKHUYZEN, Julius	*P*			$8,800
Dutch (1835 - 1925)	*W*			$1,100
SANDECKI, Albert	*P*			$105
(?)				
SANDER, Ludwig	*P*			$2,640
American (1906 -)				
SANDER, Sherry	*S*	$1,000	$1,542	$2,090
American (1941 -)				
SANDER, Tom	*P*	$2,100	$2,680	$3,410
American (20th -)	*S*	$880	$1,100	$1,320
	W	$600	$1,025	$1,760

D=Drawing, P=Painting, S=Sculpture, W=Watercolor

		Current Price Range		
		Low	Mean	High

		Low	Mean	High
SANDERS, (?)	*D*			$2,090
SANDERS, Carrie (?)	*P*			$209
SANDERS, J. (19th -)	*P*			$275
SANDERS, Phillip British (20th -)	*P*			$770
SANDERS, Walter G. British (?)	*P*			$3,025
SANDERSON, John British (19th -)	*P*			$495
SANDERSON-WELLS, J. S. (?)	*P*	$5,500	$5,500	$5,500
SANDHAM, Henry American (1842 - 1912)	*W*	$110	$281	$605
SANDOR, Mathias American (1857 - 1920)	*P*			$495
SANDORFI, Istvan (20th -)	*P*			$16,500
SANDORHAZE, W. B. Hungarian (20th -)	*D* *P*			$193 $1,870
SANDRART, Joachim von (Attrib.) German (17th -)	*P*			$5,775
SANDRART, Joachim von (Circle) German (17th -)	*P*			$3,850
SANDRUCCI, Giovanni Italian (19th -)	*P*	$3,575	$6,751	$15,400
SANDS, J. American (19th - 20th)	*P*			$330
SANDWEG, Rosemarie American (20th -)	*P*			$275
SANDZEN, Birger American (1871 - 1954)	*P*	$220	$4,015	$6,600
SANESI, Niccolo Italian (1818 - 1889)	*P*			$2,200

D=Drawing, P=Painting, S=Sculpture, W=Watercolor

		Current Price Range		
		Low	Mean	High

SANFORD, W. G.	*P*			$1,980
American (20th -)				
SANG, Frederick J.	*P*	$330	$413	$495
French (19th -)				
SANGER, H. L.	*P*	$275	$358	$440
American (19th -)				
SANGER, William	*P*			$303
American (1875 -)	*W*			$358
SANGSTER, J. L.	*P*	$143	$237	$330
American (19th - 20th)				
SANI, Alessandro	*P*	$1,210	$4,554	$7,700
Italian (19th - 20th)				
SANI, David	*P*	$1,650	$3,850	$6,050
Italian (19th - 20th)				
SANIN, Fanny	*P*			$16,500
Colombian (1938 -)				
SANO, A.	*W*			$165
(19th -)				
SANO DI PIETRO,	*P*			$77,000
Italian (1406 - 1481)				
SANOJA, Miguel	*S*			$3,520
(20th -)				
SANQUIRICO, Alessandro (Attrib.)	*D*			$1,320
Italian (1777 - 1849)	*W*			$1,650
SANSHALL, G. J.	*P*			$330
British (19th -)				
SANT, James	*P*	$880	$16,940	$33,000
British (1820 - 1916)				
SANTA CROCE, Francesco	*P*			$38,500
Italian (1443 - 1508)				
SANTACROCE, Girolamo	*P*			$17,600
Italian (16th -)				
SANTACROCE, Girolamo (School)	*P*	$2,860	$10,780	$18,700
Italian (16th -)				

D=Drawing, P=Painting, S=Sculpture, W=Watercolor

		Current Price Range		
		Low	Mean	High

		Low	Mean	High
SANTERRE, Jean B. French (1651 - 1717)	*P*	$18,700	$23,100	$27,500
SANTERRE, Jean B. (Attrib.) French (1651 - 1717)	*P*			$4,950
SANTERRE, Jean B. (Circle) French (1651 - 1717)	*P*			$4,400
SANTERRE, Jean B. (Manner) French (1651 - 1717)	*P*			$2,200
SANTINI, Giuseppe (?)	*D*	$715	$798	$880
SANTO, H. E. (?)	*P*			$880
SANTOLINO, A. American (?)	*P*			$132
SANTOMASSO, Giuseppe Italian (1907 -)	*P*			$16,500
SANTORO, Joseph L American (20th -)	*W*			$550
SANTORO, Rubens Italian (1859 - 1942)	*P*	$4,400	$20,075	$35,200
SANTOS, S. L. Gonzales Spanish (19th - 20th)	*P*			$2,420
SANTOSH & CHAND, (20th -)	*W*			$220
SANTRY, Daniel American (1867 - 1951)	*P*	$385	$646	$880
SANTVOORT, Dirk Dutch (1610 - 1680)	*P*			$20,900
SANTVOORT, Dirk (Attrib.) Dutch (1610 - 1680)	*P*			$10,450
SANZ, A. American (20th -)	*P*	$440	$468	$495
SANZEL, Felix French (1829 - 1883)	*S*			$990
SAPORETTI, Adolpho (?)	*P*			$522

D=Drawing, P=Painting, S=Sculpture, W=Watercolor

		Current Price Range		
		Low	Mean	High

		Low	Mean	High
SARASSIN, Jean-Philippe	*P*			$1,650
(17th -)				
SARDI, Istvan	*P*	$1,155	$1,155	$1,155
Hungarian (1846 - 1901)				
SARET, Alan	*D*	$2,860	$3,080	$3,300
American (1944 -)	*S*	$4,400	$9,350	$14,300
	W			$2,200
SARGEANT, Geneve R.	*D*			$495
American (1868 - 1957)	*P*	$275	$781	$1,430
SARGENT, F. T.	*P*			$165
(?)				
SARGENT, G. Henry	*P*			$2,200
American (?)				
SARGENT, John S.	*D*	$1,100	$10,450	$20,900
American (1856 - 1925)	*P*	$2,750	$112,357	$264,000
	S			$4,675
	W	$23,100	$65,136	$203,500
SARGENT, John S. (After)	*P*			$110
American (1856 - 1925)				
SARGENT, John S. (Attrib.)	*P*			$1,045
American (1856 - 1925)				
SARGENT, John S. (Manner)	*D*			$523
American (1856 - 1925)				
SARGENT, Paul T.	*P*	$715	$880	$1,045
American (1880 -)				
SARGENT, Richard	*W*			$7,000
American (1911 - 1978)				
SARGENT, Sidney F.	*P*			$165
American (20th -)				
SARGENT, Walter	*P*			$220
American (1868 - 1927)				
SARISAWA,	*P*			$2,640
American (19th -)				

D=Drawing, P=Painting, S=Sculpture, W=Watercolor

		Current Price Range		
		Low	Mean	High

		Low	Mean	High
SARKISIAN, Paul American (1928 -)	*P*			$19,800
SARKISIAN, Sarkis American (1909 - 1977)	*P*	$550	$913	$1,100
SARNOFF, Arthur American (1912 -)	*P* *W*	$138 $110	$922 $482	$1,705 $853
SARTAIN, Emily American (? - 1927)	*P*			$2,200
SARTAIN, William S. American (1843 - 1924)	*P*	$578	$702	$825
SARTELLE, H. American (20th -)	*P*			$138
SARTO, Andrea del (After) Italian (1487 - 1531)	*P*	$2,200	$2,338	$2,475
SARTO, Andrea del (Circle) Italian (1487 - 1537)	*D*			$15,400
SARTORIO, Guilio A. Itlaian (1861 - 1932)	*P*	$3,520	$6,857	$9,350
SARTORIS, Italian (20th -)	*P*			$138
SARTORIUS, Francis (Attrib.) British (1734 - 1804)	*P*			$2,475
SARTORIUS, Francis (Style) British (1734 - 1804)	*P*	$6,600	$6,875	$7,150
SARTORIUS, John N. British (1759 - 1828)	*P*	$3,300	$20,923	$60,500
SARTORIUS, John N. (Follower) British (1759 - 1828)	*P*			$6,875
SARTORIUS, Virginie de Belgian (1828 -)	*P*	$11,000	$26,950	$42,900
SASPORTAS, Ch. L. European (19th - 20th)	*P*			$110
SASSOFERRATO, Giovanni Italian (1605 - 1685)	*P*	$11,000	$24,200	$37,400
SASSOFERRATO, Giovanni (Aft) Italian (1605 - 1685)	*P*			$770

D=Drawing, P=Painting, S=Sculpture, W=Watercolor

		Current Price Range		
		Low	Mean	High

SATLOFT, Edward A.	D			$3,300
Danish (20th -)				
SATO, Key	P			$5,775
Japanese (1906 -)				
SATTERLEE, Walter	P			$1,650
American (1844 - 1908)				
SATURNIN, Felix	P			$440
French (1818 - 1892)				
SAUBERT, Tom	D			$350
American (20th -)	W			$1,200
SAUL, Peter	D	$1,320	$6,490	$9,900
American (20th -)	P	$8,250	$14,850	$24,200
SAUNDERS, F. Wenderoth	P	$248	$317	$385
American (20th -)				
SAUNDERS, Norman	P	$1,100	$1,450	$1,800
(?)				
SAUNDERS, Raymond	P			$330
American (1934 -)				
SAUNIER, Charlotte	W			$138
French (19th -)				
SAUNIER, Noel	P			$29,700
French (1847 - 1890)				
SAURA, Antonio	D	$17,600	$18,700	$19,800
Spanish (1930 -)	P			$96,250
SAURET, M.	P			$715
(?)				
SAURFELT, Leonard	P	$825	$3,988	$7,150
French (19th -)				
SAUVAGE, Piet J.	P			$12,100
Flemish (1744 - 1818)				
SAUZAY, Adrien J.	P			$6,600
French (1841 - 1928)				
SAVARY, Caroline	P			$193
American (20th -)				

D=Drawing, P=Painting, S=Sculpture, W=Watercolor

		Current Price Range		
		Low	Mean	High

		Low	Mean	High
SAVERY, Jacob	W			$24,200
Dutch (16th - 17th)				
SAVERY, Roelant	P			$49,500
Dutch (1576 - 1639)				
SAVERY, Roelant (Circle)	P			$5,500
Dutch (1576 - 1639)				
SAVIN, Maurice	P	$3,960	$15,312	$25,300
French (1894 - 1973)				
SAVINI, A.	W			$550
Italian (19th - 20th)				
SAVINIO, Alberto	D			$7,700
Italian (1891 - 1952)				
SAWADA, Tetsuro	D			$550
Japanese (20th -)				
SAWYER, Helen A.	P	$330	$743	$1,210
American (1900 -)				
SAWYER, Warren F.	P	$770	$2,090	$3,410
(20th -)	W			$3,520
SAWYERS, Martha	D	$303	$937	$4,950
American (1902 - 1987)	P	$300	$836	$1,760
SAWYIER, Paul	W	$2,200	$12,650	$23,100
American (19th - 20th)				
SAXILD, Karl	P	$110	$997	$3,300
American (19th - 20th)				
SAYRE, Fred G.	P	$1,760	$3,982	$5,500
American (1879 - 1939)	W	$440	$990	$1,540
SCACCIATI, Andrea (Attrib.)	P			$6,600
Italian (1642 - 1710)				
SCAEFERS, Karen	S			$468
(?)				
SCAFFAI, Luigi	P			$3,850
Italian (1837 -)				
SCAGLIONE, Carlos	P			$2,860
Argentine (1942 -)				

D=Drawing, P=Painting, S=Sculpture, W=Watercolor

		Current Price Range		
		Low	Mean	High
SCALBERT, Jules	P	$7,700	$8,800	$9,900
French (1851 -)	W			$550
SCALINI, F.	P			$7,425
Italian (19th - 20th)				
SCALLARO,	P			$220
Italian (19th -)				
SCAMPERLE, Livio	P	$3,300	$3,410	$3,520
(20th -)				
SCANDINAVIAN SCHOOL 19C,	P			$4,400
European (19th -)				
SCANGA, Italo	D			$1,760
American (1932 -)	P	$4,400	$11,660	$17,600
	S			$11,000
SCARISBRICK, W. R.	W			$330
(?)				
SCARLETT, Rolph	P	$2,750	$11,000	$19,800
American (20th -)	W			$6,600
SCARPITTA, G. Salvatore C.	S			$880
American (1887 - 1948)				
SCARSELLA, Ippolito (Circle)	P			$3,300
Italian (1551 - 1620)				
SCARVELLI,	W	$385	$660	$935
Italian (19th - 20th)				
SCHACHNER, Friederich	D			$154
(20th -)				
SCHAD-ROSSA, Paul	P			$1,210
German (1862 - 1916)				
SCHAEFELS, Hendrik F.	P			$2,500
Belgian (1827 - 1904)				
SCHAEFELS, Lucas	P			$33,000
Belgian (1824 - 1885)				
SCHAEFER, Henry T.	P	$1,540	$4,345	$7,150
British (19th - 20th)				

D=Drawing, P=Painting, S=Sculpture, W=Watercolor

		Current Price Range		
		Low	Mean	High

		Low	Mean	High
SCHAEFER, Herman (19th -)	*P*			$715
SCHAEFERS, Karin American (1942 -)	*S*	$303	$413	$523
SCHAEFFER, August Austrian (1833 - 1916)	*P*			$41,250
SCHAEFFER, Henri French (1924 -)	*P*	$770	$2,163	$2,860
SCHAEFFER, John S. American (19th -)	*P*			$1,980
SCHAEFFER, Mead American (1898 - 1980)	*P*	$605	$3,403	$6,200
SCHAENEWORK, (After) (19th -)	*S*			$770
SCHAEP, Henri A. Dutch (1826 - 1870)	*P*			$2,420
SCHAEP, Henri A. (Attrib.) Dutch (1826 - 1870)	*P*			$825
SCHAFER, Dirch Dutch (1864 - 1941)	*P*			$1,870
SCHAFER, Frederick F. American (1839 - 1927)	*P*	$220	$1,305	$2,750
SCHAFER, Henry T. British (1854 -)	*P*	$2,475	$3,208	$3,850
	W	$303	$1,139	$1,540
SCHAFER, Henry Thomas British (1873 - 1915)	*P*			$1,320
	W	$193	$1,307	$2,420
SCHAFER, Herman German (1880 -)	*P*			$770
SCHAFFERT, W. (20th -)	*S*			$440
SCHAGEN, Gerbrand F. van Dutch (1880 - 1968)	*P*			$1,210
SCHAIK, (?)	*P*			$150

D=Drawing, P=Painting, S=Sculpture, W=Watercolor

		Current Price Range	
	Low	Mean	High

		Low	Mean	High
SCHALCKEN, Godfried	P			$16,500
Dutch (1643 - 1706)				
SCHALCKEN, Godfried (Follower)	P			$1,100
Dutch (1643 - 1706)				
SCHALDACH, William J.	W			$193
American (1896 -)				
SCHALL, Jean-Frederic	P	$9,350	$78,283	$148,500
French (1752 - 1825)				
SCHALL, Jean-Frederic (Attrib.)	P			$9,900
French (1752 - 1825)				
SCHAMBERG, Morton L.	D	$2,750	$4,648	$8,800
American (1881 - 1918)	P	$33,000	$135,667	$308,000
SCHANKER, Louis	P	$8,250	$10,725	$13,200
American (1903 -)	W			$440
SCHAPHERDERS, Jaak	P			$935
Dutch (19th - 20th)				
SCHAPLEIGH, Frank H.	P			$110
American (1842 - 1906)				
SCHARF, Kenny	D			$990
American (1958 -)	P	$1,870	$33,736	$93,500
	W	$6,050	$6,600	$7,150
SCHARFF, William	P			$248
Danish (1886 - 1959)				
SCHARY, Saul	D			$165
American (1904 - 1978)	P	$154	$278	$495
SCHATTENSTEIN, Nicol	P			$3,850
American (1877 - 1954)				
SCHATZ,	P			$275
(?)				
SCHAUDOLPH, Johann	P			$605
German (19th -)				
SCHAUERMANN, Judy W.	P	$495	$509	$523
(20th -)				

D=Drawing, P=Painting, S=Sculpture, W=Watercolor

		Current Price Range		
		Low	Mean	High

SCHEDONE, Circle	*P*			$8,800
Italian (1570 - 1615)				
SCHEDONI, Bartholomeo (After)	*P*			$2,200
Italian (1578 - 1615)				
SCHEERES, Hendricus J.	*P*			$1,100
Dutch (1829 - 1864)				
SCHEFFEL, Hans	*P*			$187
(?)				
SCHEFFER, Ary	*P*	$2,200	$14,300	$26,400
French (1795 - 1858)				
SCHEFFLER, Rudolph	*D*			$1,320
American (1884 -)	*P*			$31,900
	W			$1,430
SCHEIBER, Hugo	*D*	$495	$1,224	$2,420
Hungarian (1873 - 1950)	*P*	$3,300	$3,713	$4,125
	W	$935	$2,610	$5,500
SCHEIDEL, Franz Anton von	*W*	$770	$2,066	$3,300
Austrian (1731 - 1801)				
SCHEIDEL, Franz Anton von (Att)	*W*			$440
Austrian (1731 - 1801)				
SCHELFHOUT, Andreas	*P*	$6,600	$10,450	$14,300
Dutch (1787 - 1870)				
SCHELL, Frank	*D*	$770	$825	$880
American (1834 - 1909)				
SCHELL, Frank (Et al.)	*D*	$660	$1,221	$1,760
American (19th - 20th)				
SCHELLBACH, Karl H.	*P*			$990
German (1850 - 1921)				
SCHELLINI,	*P*			$110
Italian (20th -)				
SCHENAU, Johann E.	*D*	$385	$633	$880
German (1737 - 1806)				
SCHENCK, August F.	*P*			$3,520
Danish (1828 - 1901)				

D=Drawing, P=Painting, S=Sculpture, W=Watercolor

		Current Price Range	
	Low	Mean	High

		Low	Mean	High
SCHENCK, Edwin (19th -)	P			$523
SCHENCKS, Penelope J. American (1883 -)	P			$880
	W			$1,430
SCHENDEL, Petrus van Belgian (1806 - 1870)	P	$2,200	$20,831	$60,500
SCHENK, J. (?)	P			$132
SCHERMAN, Tony (20th -)	P			$3,850
SCHERREWITZ, Johan Dutch (1868 - 1951)	P	$770	$3,813	$7,700
SCHEUERER, Julius German (1859 - 1913)	P	$1,100	$4,895	$12,100
SCHEUERLE, Joseph American (19th - 20th)	D			$358
	W	$418	$622	$825
SCHIAVONE, Andrea M. (Attrib.) Italian (1522 - 1563)	P			$2,750
SCHIDONE, Bartolomeo (School) Italian (1570 - 1615)	P	$1,760	$1,760	$1,760
SCHIELE, Egon Austrian (1890 - 1918)	D	$18,700	$94,270	$209,000
	P	$82,500	$2.410M	$5.940M
	W	$88,000	$336,600	$880,000
SCHIELE, Egon (Attrib.) Austrian (1890 - 1918)	W			$110
SCHIERL, Josef German (19th -)	P			$3,300
SCHIFANO, Mario Italian (1934 -)	P			$13,200
SCHIFFER, Ethel B. American (1879 -)	P			$220
SCHIFFNER, Barbara British (20th -)	P			$935
	S			$550

D=Drawing, P=Painting, S=Sculpture, W=Watercolor

		Current Price Range		
		Low	Mean	High

		Low	Mean	High
SCHILDER, Andrei N. Russian (1861 -)	P			$6,050
SCHILDT, Gary American (20th -)	P	$660	$1,205	$1,800
	S	$660	$910	$1,300
SCHILLE, Alice American (? - 1955)	W	$908	$3,479	$6,050
SCHILLING, Carl German (19th -)	P			$605
SCHIMMELPHFENNIG, Oswalt German (19th -)	S			$1,650
SCHINDLER, Edwin P. American (20th -)	P	$330	$565	$800
SCHINDLER, Emil J. Austrian (1842 - 1892)	P			$29,700
	W			$4,400
SCHINDLER, Thomas German (20th -)	P	$2,750	$4,675	$6,600
SCHIODTE, Harald V. I. Danish (1852 - 1924)	P			$7,700
SCHIPPER, L. (?)	P			$330
SCHIRM, Carl C. German (1852 - 1928)	P			$523
SCHIRMER, Johann W. German (1807 - 1863)	W			$2,420
SCHISSLER, Janeen American (20th -)	W	$1,100	$1,300	$1,500
SCHIVERT, Victor Rumanian (1863 -)	P			$1,540
SCHJELDERUP, Leis Norwegian (19th - 20th)	P			$12,650
SCHLEICH, Robert German (1854 - 1934)	P			$3,850
SCHLEICH, JR, Eduard German (1853 - 1893)	P			$7,150

D=Drawing, P=Painting, S=Sculpture, W=Watercolor

		Current Price Range		
		Low	Mean	High
SCHLEICH, JR, Eduard (Follower)	*P*	$880	$1,155	$1,430
German (1853 - 1893)				
SCHLEICHER, C.	*P*			$825
German (19th -)				
SCHLEISCH, Anton	*D*			$154
German (1809 - 1851)				
SCHLESINGER, Carl	*P*			$1,650
Swiss (1825 - 1893)				
SCHLESINGER, Henry	*P*			$12,100
French (1814 - 1893)	*W*			$1,650
SCHLESINGER, Mark	*P*			$2,750
(20th -)	*W*			$880
SCHLESSINGER, Felix	*P*	$17,050	$21,725	$26,400
German (1833 - 1910)				
SCHLETTER,	*P*			$990
(?)				
SCHLICHTING, Walter	*P*			$770
American (20th -)				
SCHLUTER, Richard	*P*			$385
American (?)				
SCHMEDTGEN, William H.	*P*			$220
American (1862 - 1936)				
SCHMID, Richard	*P*			$8,800
(1934 -)				
SCHMIDT, Adolf	*P*			$8,250
German (1804 -)				
SCHMIDT, Albert H.	*P*			$7,700
Swiss (1883 - 1957)				
SCHMIDT, Alfred	*P*			$1,760
German (1867 -)				
SCHMIDT, Bruno	*P*			$770
(20th -)				
SCHMIDT, C. W.	*P*			$138
American (20th -)				

D=Drawing, P=Painting, S=Sculpture, W=Watercolor

		Current Price Range		
		Low	Mean	High

SCHMIDT, Carl	*D*			$330
American (1885 - 1969)	*P*	$385	$770	$1,320
SCHMIDT, Eduard	*P*			$7,150
German (1806 - 1862)				
SCHMIDT, Franz	*W*	$550	$825	$1,100
German (20th -)				
SCHMIDT, Harold von	*P*	$1,000	$12,871	$33,000
American (1893 - 1982)	*W*	$800	$1,293	$2,200
SCHMIDT, Jay	*P*			$1,540
American (20th -)				
SCHMIDT, Karl	*P*	$330	$2,292	$4,675
American (1890 - 1962)	*W*	$880	$1,274	$1,980
SCHMIDT, Martin J.	*D*			$5,280
German (1718 - 1801)				
SCHMIDT, Martin J. (Circle)	*P*			$3,300
German (1718 - 1801)				
SCHMIDT, Nandor	*P*			$248
European (20th -)				
SCHMIDT, Rudolf	*W*			$1,760
Austrian (1873 -)				
SCHMIDT-ROTTLUFF, Karl	*D*			$330
German (1884 - 1976)	*P*	$115,500	$255,750	$396,000
	W			$49,500
SCHMITT, D.	*P*			$4,950
(?)				
SCHMITT, Georg P.	*P*			$1,210
German (1808 - 1873)				
SCHMITT, Paul A.	*P*			$275
American (1893 - 1983)				
SCHMITT, Paul L. F.	*P*			$2,750
French (1856 - 1902)				
SCHMITT, Phil	*P*			$358
German (19th - 20th)				

D=Drawing, P=Painting, S=Sculpture, W=Watercolor

		Current Price Range		
		Low	Mean	High

		Low	Mean	High
SCHMUZER, Jakob M.	D	$220	$2,408	$6,050
Austrian (1733 - 1811)				
SCHMUZER, Leopold	P	$9,900	$12,650	$15,400
Austrian (1864 - 1941)				
SCHNABEL, Julian	D	$16,500	$18,700	$20,900
American (1951 -)	P	$11,000	$142,560	$242,000
	S			$30,800
	W	$20,900	$26,950	$33,000
SCHNAKENBERG, Henry E.	W			$110
American (1892 - 1970)				
SCHNEIDAU, Christian von	P	$440	$1,506	$4,125
American (1893 - 1976)				
SCHNEIDER, George	P	$880	$7,443	$19,800
German (19th -)				
SCHNEIDER, Jose	P			$3,300
Spanish (1848 - 1893)				
SCHNEIDER, Ken	W			$160
(?)				
SCHNEIDER, Otto H.	P			$22,000
American (?)				
SCHNEIDER, William G.	W			$1,183
American (1863 -)				
SCHNELLE, William	P	$220	$231	$242
American (1897 -)				
SCHOBER, Peter J.	P			$4,400
German (1897 -)				
SCHODL, Max	P	$1,650	$2,475	$3,300
Austrian (1834 - 1921)				
SCHOENBERG, Violeta	P			$143
American (20th -)				
SCHOENFELD,	P			$385
(?)				
SCHOENFELD, Flora	P			$1,870
American (20th -)				

D=Drawing, P=Painting, S=Sculpture, W=Watercolor

		Current Price Range	
	Low	Mean	High

		Low	Mean	High
SCHOENFELD, Johann H. (Circle)	P			$4,400
German (1809 - 1845)				
SCHOENHERR, John	P			$450
(?)				
SCHOFIELD, J. W.	P			$715
American (20th -)				
SCHOFIELD, John W.	P			$523
British (19th - 20th)				
SCHOFIELD, Walter E.	D			$303
American (1867 - 1944)	P	$2,530	$11,328	$33,000
SCHOFIELD, Walter E. (Attrib.)	P			$385
American (1867 - 1944)				
SCHOLDER, Fritz	D			$110
American (1937 -)	P			$5,500
SCHOLZ, Max	P			$3,850
German (1855 -)				
SCHOMBURG, Alex	P			$1,760
American (?)				
SCHONFELD, Johann H. (Attrib.)	P			$5,775
German (1609 - 1682)				
SCHONIAN, Alfred	P			$3,520
German (1856 -)				
SCHONIAN, Alfred (Attrib.)	P			$250
German (1856 -)				
SCHONLEBER, Gustav	P	$4,950	$5,225	$5,500
German (1851 - 1917)				
SCHOONLINGEN, J. H.	P			$990
Dutch (20th -)				
SCHOONOVER, Frank E.	P	$880	$5,170	$15,400
American (1877 - 1972)				
SCHOOTEN, Floris G.	P			$33,000
Dutch (16th - 17th)				
SCHOPIN, Frederic H.	P	$66,000	$96,250	$126,500
French (1804 - 1880)				

D=Drawing, P=Painting, S=Sculpture, W=Watercolor

		Current Price Range		
		Low	Mean	High
SCHOR, Giovanni P. (Attrib.)	D			$3,575
German (1615 - 1674)				
SCHOTEL, E.C.	P			$1,045
Dutch (20th -)				
SCHOTT, Fred	P	$358	$427	$495
American (20th -)				
SCHOUMAN, Aert	D	$6,050	$8,525	$11,000
Dutch (1710 - 1792)	P			$77,000
	W	$2,750	$4,538	$6,325
SCHOUMAN, Aert (Circle)	P			$27,500
Dutch (1710 - 1792)				
SCHOUMANN, Martinus	P			$11,000
Dutch (1770 - 1848)				
SCHOUTEN, Henri	P	$4,400	$4,950	$5,500
Belgian (1864 - 1927)				
SCHOUTEN, Henry	P			$1,870
Dutch (1791 - 1835)				
SCHOYERER, Josef	P			$1,100
German (1844 - 1923)				
SCHRADER, Julius F. A.	P			$46,750
German (1815 - 1900)				
SCHRADER, Theodore	P			$7,700
European (19th -)				
SCHRAEGLE, Gustave	P			$880
German (19th -)				
SCHRAM, Abraham J.	P			$440
American (1891 -)				
SCHRAM, Alois H.	P	$4,675	$4,813	$4,950
Austrian (1864 - 1919)				
SCHRANZ, Anton	P			$8,800
German (1769 - 1839)				
SCHRECKENGOST, Viktor	W			$495
American (1906 -)				
SCHREIBER, Charles B.	P			$8,800
French (? - 1903)				

D=Drawing, P=Painting, S=Sculpture, W=Watercolor

		Current Price Range		
		Low	Mean	High

		Low	Mean	High
SCHREIBER, George L.	*D*			$2,200
American (1904 - 1977)	*P*	$2,420	$4,510	$6,600
	W	$550	$2,017	$2,860
SCHREUDER, F. J.	*P*			$715
Dutch (19th - 20th)				
SCHREYER, Adolf	*P*	$4,290	$48,526	$148,500
German (1828 - 1899)				
SCHREYER, Adolf (After)	*P*	$303	$349	$385
German (1828 - 1899)				
SCHREYER, Adolf (Attrib.)	*P*	$2,090	$6,197	$12,100
German (1828 - 1899)				
SCHREYVOGEL, Charles	*P*	$352	$69,784	$198,000
American (1861 - 1912)	*S*			$19,800
SCHRIECK, Otto M. van	*P*			$104,500
Dutch (1619 - 1678)				
SCHRIJVER, A.	*P*			$605
Dutch (20th -)				
SCHRIMPF,	*S*			$193
German (20th -)				
SCHRODER, Albert F.	*P*			$3,080
German (1854 -)				
SCHRODER, Albert H.	*P*	$259	$364	$468
American (1929 -)				
SCHRODER, Paul	*P*			$2,860
European (19th -)				
SCHRODER, Povl	*P*			$770
Danish (1894 - 1957)				
SCHROEDER,	*S*			$495
American (20th -)				
SCHROEDER, Heinrich J.	*P*			$715
German (1866 - 1935)				
SCHROEDTER, Howard (Attrib.)	*P*	$150	$150	$150
American (20th -)				
SCHROFF, Alfred	*W*			$165
American (1863 - 1939)				

D=Drawing, P=Painting, S=Sculpture, W=Watercolor

		Current Price Range		
		Low	Mean	High
SCHROTER, G.	P			$550
European (20th -)				
SCHRYVER, Louis M. de	P	$4,400	$89,100	$209,000
French (1862 - 1942)				
SCHUBERT, Orlando V.	P			$264
American (1844 - 1928)	W	$121	$169	$193
SCHUCKER, James	P	$193	$259	$325
American (1903 -)				
SCHUELTER, Jesse	P			$330
American (20th -)				
SCHUFFENECKER, Claude E.	D	$4,180	$8,756	$13,200
French (1851 - 1934)	P	$30,800	$81,400	$132,000
SCHULLE, Alice	P			$248
(20th -)				
SCHULMAN, David	P			$1,540
Dutch (1881 - 1966)				
SCHULTZ, George F.	D	$660	$1,082	$1,925
American (1869 -)	P	$110	$979	$2,420
SCHULTZE, Bernard	P			$8,250
German (1915 -)	S			$15,400
	W			$6,820
SCHULTZE, Carl	P			$4,400
German (1856 -)				
SCHULTZE, Louis	P	$121	$391	$660
German (19th -)				
SCHULTZE, Robert	P			$6,600
German (1828 -)				
SCHULZ, Charles	D	$165	$207	$248
American (20th -)				
SCHURR, Claude	P			$990
French (1921 -)				
SCHURZ, Karl	P			$120
(19th -)				

D=Drawing, P=Painting, S=Sculpture, W=Watercolor

		Current Price Range		
		Low	Mean	High

SCHUSTER, Donna	*P*	$1,540	$2,943	$6,050
American (1883 - 1953)	*W*	$413	$1,002	$2,200
SCHUSTER, Joseph	*P*			$1,760
Austrian (19th - 20th)				
SCHUSTER, Karl M.	*P*			$8,800
Austrian (1871 - 1953)				
SCHUT, Cornelis	*P*			$4,180
Flemish (1597 - 1655)				
SCHUTHEIS,	*S*			$165
American (20th -)				
SCHUTZ, Christian G.	*P*	$2,475	$5,133	$9,350
German (1718 - 1791)				
SCHUTZE, August	*P*			$12,100
German (1805 - 1847)				
SCHUYFF, Peter	*P*	$2,750	$12,826	$33,000
(20th -)	*W*			$1,760
SCHVETEIN, Julius W.	*P*			$330
German (?)				
SCHWAB, Edith F.	*D*			$220
American (1862 - 1924)				
SCHWACHA, George	*P*	$880	$963	$1,045
American (1908 -)				
SCHWANKOVSKY, Frederick J.	*P*	$330	$523	$715
American (1885 - 1974)				
SCHWAR, Wilhelm	*P*			$2,750
German (19th - 20th)				
SCHWARTZ, Albert G.	*P*			$6,875
German (1833 -)				
SCHWARTZ, Andrew T.	*P*	$220	$3,400	$22,000
American (1867 - 1942)				
SCHWARTZ, Carl	*P*			$110
American (20th -)				
SCHWARTZ, Chaija	*P*			$220
Israeli (20th -)				

D=Drawing, P=Painting, S=Sculpture, W=Watercolor

		Current Price Range		
		Low	Mean	High
SCHWARTZ, Davis F.	P			$358
American (1879 - 1969)	W	$165	$403	$660
SCHWARTZ, William S.	P	$935	$5,459	$8,250
American (1896 - 1977)	W			$2,310
SCHWARTZE, Albert G.	P			$5,500
German (1833 -)				
SCHWARTZWILDER, Rich. (Att)	P			$138
(?)				
SCHWARZ, Christoph (Attrib.)	P			$8,800
German (16th -)				
SCHWARZSCHILD, Alfred	P			$3,850
German (1874 -)				
SCHWEDLER, William	D	$110	$139	$176
(20th -)	P	$550	$660	$770
	S	$110	$220	$330
SCHWEICKHARDT, Hendrick W.	P	$2,090	$3,190	$4,290
German (1746 - 1797)				
SCHWEINITZ, H. von	P			$330
European (?)				
SCHWEIRING, Conrad	P	$275	$1,073	$1,870
American (20th -)				
SCHWEIZER, J. Otto	S			$660
Swiss (1863 -)				
SCHWENINGER, Carl	P	$7,700	$15,950	$30,250
Austrian (1818 - 1887)				
SCHWENINGER, Rosa	P			$17,600
Austrian (1849 -)				
SCHWITTERS, Kurt	P			$115,500
German (1887 - 1948)	S	$38,500	$89,925	$148,500
SCHWURLES, Theodore	P			$605
Dutch (19th - 20th)				
SCIALOJA, Toti	P			$4,125
Italian (1914 -)				

D=Drawing, P=Painting, S=Sculpture, W=Watercolor

		Current Price Range		
		Low	Mean	High

SCIVER, Pearl A. van	*P*			$880
(1896 -)				
SCOGNAMIGLIO,	*P*			$2,310
Italian (18th - 19th)				
SCOPETTA, Pietro	*P*			$3,520
Italian (1863 - 1920)				
SCOPPA, R.	*P*			$110
(?)				
SCOREL, Jan van (Attrib.)	*P*			$33,000
Dutch (1495 - 1562)				
SCOREL, Jan van (Circle)	*P*	$14,300	$17,050	$19,800
Dutch (1495 - 1562)				
SCOTT,	*W*			$187
American (19th -)				
SCOTT, A. P.	*P*			$495
(?)				
SCOTT, Alexander	*P*			$1,210
British (19th - 20th)				
SCOTT, Campbell	*P*	$193	$344	$495
British (20th -)				
SCOTT, Edith	*P*			$990
American (19th - 20th)				
SCOTT, Edwin	*P*	$440	$674	$908
(19th - 20th)				
SCOTT, F. B.	*P*			$450
American (20th -)				
SCOTT, Frank E.	*P*	$743	$1,698	$3,850
American (1862 - 1929)				
SCOTT, James P.	*P*			$825
American (1909 -)				
SCOTT, John W. A.	*P*	$523	$2,581	$4,510
American (1815 - 1907)	*W*			$275
SCOTT, John W. A. (Attrib.)	*P*			$1,210
American (1815 - 1907)				
SCOTT, Julian	*P*	$3,300	$3,850	$4,400
American (1846 - 1901)				

D=Drawing, P=Painting, S=Sculpture, W=Watercolor

		Current Price Range		
		Low	Mean	High
SCOTT, Louise	*P*			$1,320
American (20th -)				
SCOTT, Margaret	*W*			$253
American (20th -)				
SCOTT, Peter	*P*	$385	$2,063	$3,740
(20th -)				
SCOTT, R. Bagge	*P*			$880
British (19th -)				
SCOTT, Ralph (Attrib.)	*P*			$1,540
American (1896 -)				
SCOTT, Samuel	*P*			$26,400
British (1703 - 1772)				
SCOTT, Tom	*W*			$770
British (1859 - 1927)				
SCOTT, W. J.	*P*			$825
British (19th -)				
SCOTT, William	*P*	$18,150	$18,150	$18,150
American (1822 - 1905)				
SCOTT, William B.	*P*			$44,000
British (1811 - 1890)	*W*			$3,850
SCRIVER, Bob	*S*	$1,200	$2,479	$6,600
American (20th -)				
SCROTS, William (Follower)	*P*			$10,450
(16th -)				
SCUDDER, Janet	*S*	$14,300	$21,267	$27,500
American (1875 - 1940)				
SCULLY, Sean	*D*	$4,400	$12,650	$28,600
British (1946 -)	*P*	$9,900	$92,675	$341,000
SCULLY, Sean (Et al.)	*D*			$880
British (20th -)				
SCUTENAIRE, Jean	*S*			$2,200
(?)				
SEAGER, Edward	*D*	$110	$247	$880
American (1809 - 1886)	*W*	$110	$370	$1,100

D=Drawing, P=Painting, S=Sculpture, W=Watercolor

		Current Price Range		
		Low	Mean	High

		Low	Mean	High
SEAGO, Edward	P	$880	$12,540	$24,200
British (1910 - 1974)	W			$5,500
SEALE, Ronald	D			$495
(?)				
SEALEY, E. Leone	P			$360
(20th -)				
SEALY, Allen C.	P			$2,640
American (?)				
SEARS, Benjamin	P	$303	$1,038	$1,650
American (1846 - 1905)				
SEARS, Francis	P			$4,675
British (19th - 20th)				
SEAVER, Hugh	W			$110
American (20th -)				
SEAVEY, E. W.	P	$248	$427	$605
(19th -)				
SEAVEY, George W.	P	$468	$656	$880
American (1841 - 1916)				
SEBEN, Henry van	P			$3,300
Belgian (1825 - 1913)				
SEBES, Pieter W.	P			$8,800
Dutch (1830 - 1906)				
SEBILLE, A.	P			$330
French (19th -)				
SEBIRE, Gaston	P	$715	$2,928	$6,600
French (1920 -)				
SEBIRE, Gaston (Attrib.)	P			$110
French (1920 -)				
SEBOTH, Josef	P			$34,100
Austrian (1814 - 1883)				
SECOLA, A.	P			$6,050
Italian (19th -)				
SEDGLEY, Peter	P			$2,200
British (1930 -)				
SEDGWICK, Francis M.	S			$330
American (1904 -)				

D=Drawing, P=Painting, S=Sculpture, W=Watercolor

		Current Price Range		
		Low	Mean	High
SEDGWICK, G. V.	*P*			$3,850
(19th -)				
SEDLACEK, Stephan	*P*	$1,210	$4,455	$7,700
Czechoslovakian (19th -)				
SEDLICKY, J.	*P*			$1,210
American (19th -)				
SEEGER, Hermann	*P*	$8,250	$18,975	$29,700
German (1857 -)				
SEEL, Adolf	*P*			$16,500
German (1829 - 1907)				
SEELEY, George H.	*P*			$330
American (19th - 20th)				
SEERY, John	*P*	$2,640	$2,750	$2,860
American (1914 -)				
SEEVAGEN, Lucien	*P*			$550
French (1887 - 1959)				
SEFARBI, Harry	*P*			$358
American (1917 -)				
SEGAL, George	*D*	$880	$8,439	$44,000
American (1924 -)	*P*	$11,550	$277,888	$528,000
	S	$14,300	$84,260	$187,000
SEGALL, Lasar	*D*			$2,860
French (1889 - 1957)				
SEGAR, Sir William	*P*			$38,500
British (16th -)				
SEGHERS, Gerard (After)	*P*			$3,575
Flemish (1591 - 1651)				
SEGHERS, Hendrik	*W*			$286
Flemish (19th -)				
SEGOROV, A.	*W*			$495
Scandinavian (20th -)				
SEGOVIA, Andres	*P*	$550	$1,485	$2,420
Spanish (1929 -)				
SEGUI, Antonio	*P*	$143	$4,224	$19,800

D=Drawing, P=Painting, S=Sculpture, W=Watercolor

		Current Price Range	
	Low	Mean	High

SEGUI, Antonio	*S*			$495
Argentina (1934 -)	*W*	$715	$853	$990
SEGUIN, Felix (Attrib.)	*P*			$358
French (19th - 20th)				
SEHRING, Adolf	*P*	$8,800	$9,350	$9,900
Russian (1930 -)				
SEHSPMAN, Raphael	*W*			$110
American (?)				
SEIBERT, Edward S.	*P*			$358
American (1856 - 1938)				
SEIDEL, Emory P.	*P*			$138
American (20th -)	*S*	$275	$317	$358
SEIDENECK, George J.	*P*			$770
American (1885 - 1972)				
SEIFERT, Alfred	*P*	$990	$9,845	$18,700
Czech. (1850 - 1901)				
SEIFEST, V.	*S*			$495
(?)				
SEIGNAC, Guillaume	*P*	$3,300	$45,320	$99,000
French (19th - 20th)				
SEIGNAC, Paul	*P*	$4,950	$12,925	$20,900
French (1826 - 1904)				
SEILER, Carl W. A.	*P*			$2,200
German (1846 - 1921)				
SEILGER, Charles	*D*			$1,045
American (20th -)				
SEITZ, Alexander M.	*P*			$5,500
German (1811 - 1888)				
SEITZ, Anton	*P*			$9,900
German (1829 - 1900)				
SEITZ, Georg	*P*			$8,800
German (1810 - 1870)				
SEKINE, Yoshio	*P*			$2,420
Japanese (1922 -)				

D=Drawing, P=Painting, S=Sculpture, W=Watercolor

		Current Price Range		
		Low	Mean	High
SEKOTO, Gerard	*P*	$990	$1,027	$1,100
South African (1913 -)				
SELDEN, Dixie	*P*			$825
American (1871 - 1936)				
SELDEN, Henry Bill	*W*			$495
American (1886 - 1934)				
SELDRON, Alisabeth	*P*			$5,225
Dutch (18th - 19th)				
SELIGMANN, Kurt	*D*	$2,310	$2,943	$3,575
American (1900 - 1961)	*P*			$12,100
SELIKMAN, A. E.	*W*			$605
American (20th -)				
SELINGER, Emily H.	*P*	$495	$1,073	$1,650
American (19th - 20th)				
SELINGER, Jean P.	*P*	$385	$688	$990
American (1850 - 1909)				
SELK, Madeline	*P*	$413	$468	$495
British (20th -)				
SELL, Christian	*P*	$605	$1,888	$4,400
German (1831 - 1883)				
SELLAER, Vincent (School)	*P*			$11,000
Flemish (16th -)				
SELLAR, Jenny	*P*			$495
Scottish (19th -)				
SELLENT, E.	*P*			$110
German (19th -)				
SELLIN, H.	*P*			$143
British (20th -)				
SELMYHR, Conrad	*P*			$550
European (20th -)				
SELOUS, Henry C.	*P*			$23,100
British (1811 - 1890)				
SELTZER, Olaf C.	*P*	$495	$43,170	$88,000
American (1877 - 1957)	*W*	$468	$7,773	$27,500

D=Drawing, P=Painting, S=Sculpture, W=Watercolor

		Current Price Range		
		Low	Mean	High

SELTZER, W. Steve	*P*	$1,870	$3,520	$5,900
American (20th -)	*W*			$4,400
SELZER, Frank	*P*			$303
(?)				
SEMENOWSKY, Eisman	*P*	$1,760	$8,910	$24,200
French (19th -)				
SEMINO, Andrea (Attrib.)	*D*			$3,025
Italian (1525 - 1595)				
SEMINO, Ottavio	*D*			$5,280
Italian (1520 - 1604)				
SEMON, John	*P*			$110
American (1852 - 1917)				
SENAT, Prosper L.	*P*	$1,045	$2,768	$7,150
American (1852 - 1925)	*W*			$330
SENCE, J.	*P*			$605
(?)				
SENDAK, Maurice	*D*	$165	$248	$330
American (1938 -)				
SENET, Rafael	*W*			$1,980
Spanish (1856 -)				
SENEZCOURT, Charlotte de	*P*			$3,850
French (19th -)				
SENNHAUSER, John	*W*			$660
American (19th -)				
SENQUIST, Raphael	*P*			$700
(20th -)				
SENSEMAN, Raphael	*W*			$110
American (1870 - 1965)				
SEPESHY, Zolton L.	*D*			$2,530
Hungarian (1898 -)	*P*	$220	$2,341	$9,350
	S			$330
	W			$605
SERENI, G.	*W*			$1,980
(19th -)				

D=Drawing, P=Painting, S=Sculpture, W=Watercolor

		Current Price Range		
		Low	Mean	High

		Low	Mean	High
SERGEANT, Edgar	*P*			$1,100
American (1877 -)				
SERIN, H.	*P*			$1,100
Dutch (18th -)				
SERLIN, Beatrice	*P*			$165
(?)				
SERNA, Ismael de la	*P*	$17,600	$20,350	$23,100
Spanish (1887 -)	*S*			$12,100
SERPAN, Jaroslav	*P*			$3,520
Czechoslovakian (1922 -)				
SERRA, Richard	*D*			$25,300
American (1943 -)	*P*	$20,900	$32,780	$46,750
	S	$23,100	$46,200	$66,000
SERRA Y AUQUE, Enrique	*P*			$20,900
Spanish (1859 - 1918)				
SERRANO, Manuel G.	*P*	$5,500	$6,710	$9,350
Lat. Amer. (1917 - 1948)				
SERRANO, Pablo	*S*	$357	$426	$495
Spanish (1910 -)				
SERRAS, John T.	*P*			$5,500
British (1759 - 1825)				
SERRES, Anthony	*P*			$935
French (1828 - 1898)				
SERRES, Dominic	*P*	$1,430	$19,965	$38,500
British (1722 - 1793)				
SERRET, Alan	*D*			$1,210
(?)				
SERRI, Alfredo	*P*	$550	$550	$550
Italian (1897 - 1972)				
SERRIER, Jean P.	*P*	$110	$849	$3,080
French (1934 - 1989)				
SERRURE, Auguste	*P*			$16,500
Flemish (1825 - 1903)				
SERUSIER, Paul	*D*	$1,100	$2,888	$4,675

D=Drawing, P=Painting, S=Sculpture, W=Watercolor

| | | Current Price Range | |
	Low	Mean	High
SERUSIER, Paul	*P*	$9,350	$182,783	$440,000
French (1863 - 1927)	*W*			$5,280
SERVALID, P.	*P*			$110
Mexican (19th -)				
SERVEAU, Clement	*P*	$2,200	$3,300	$4,400
French (1886 - 1972)				
SERVER, John W.	*P*			$121
American (1862 -)				
SERVIER, M.	*P*			$358
(?)				
SESSIONS, James	*W*	$825	$2,448	$4,675
American (1882 - 1962)				
SETHER, Gulbrand	*P*	$110	$605	$1,100
Norwegian (19th - 20th)	*W*			$963
SETHER, Gunther	*P*			$440
American (20th -)				
SETON, John T. (Attrib.)	*P*			$20,900
British (18th -)				
SETTLE, William F.	*W*			$1,045
British (1821 - 1897)				
SEURAT, Georges	*D*	$19,800	$277,933	$407,000
French (1859 - 1891)				
SEVERDONCK, Franz van	*P*	$1,210	$2,377	$3,300
Belgian (1809 - 1889)				
SEVERE, J. E. Claude	*P*			$330
Haitian (20th -)				
SEVERINI, Gino	*D*	$4,125	$196,396	$550,000
Italian (1883 - 1966)	*P*	$37,400	$948,200	$3.630M
	S	$77,000	$291,500	$506,000
	W	$4,180	$174,827	$506,000
SEVILLE SCHOOL 17C,	*P*			$19,800
Spanish (17th -)				
SEWELL, Amos	*D*	$110	$480	$850

D=Drawing, P=Painting, S=Sculpture, W=Watercolor

| | | Current Price Range | | |
		Low	Mean	High
SEWELL, Amos	*P*			$1,100
American (1901 - 1983)	*W*			$660
SEWELL, Robert	*P*	$660	$2,750	$4,840
American (1860 - 1924)				
SEXTON, B. (Attrib.)	*P*			$3,740
(?)				
SEXTON, Emily Stryker	*P*	$170	$205	$280
American (1880 -)				
SEXTON, Frederick L.	*P*			$523
American (1889 -)	*W*			$550
SEYBOLD, Louis	*P*			$770
American (19th - 20th)				
SEYLER, Julius	*P*	$4,125	$5,913	$7,700
German (1873 - 1958)	*W*	$880	$1,375	$1,870
SEYMORE, JR., Thomas	*P*			$110
(?)				
SEYMOUR, George	*P*			$2,640
British (19th -)				
SEYMOUR, James	*P*			$18,700
British (1702 - 1752)				
SEYMOUR, James (After)	*P*			$9,900
British (1702 - 1752)				
SEYMOUR, James (Circle)	*P*	$10,450	$18,425	$26,400
British (1702 - 1752)				
SEYMOUR, M.	*W*			$193
American (19th - 20th)				
SEYMOUR, Tom	*P*			$825
British (19th -)				
SEYSSAUD, Rene	*P*			$20,900
French (1867 - 1952)				
SEYSSES, Auguste	*S*			$1,265
French (1862 -)				
SHADDIX, Bill	*P*	$660	$1,180	$1,700
American (1931 -)				

D=Drawing, P=Painting, S=Sculpture, W=Watercolor

		Current Price Range	
		Low	Mean	High
---	---	---	---	---
SHAFER, L. E. Gus	S			$715
American (20th -)				
SHAFER, Minnie	W			$385
(19th -)				
SHAFER, S. P.	P			$440
American (?)				
SHAFFER, Win	P			$110
American (20th -)				
SHAHN, Ben	D	$1,100	$5,561	$25,300
American (1898 - 1969)	P	$9,350	$36,630	$66,000
	W	$1,650	$16,958	$57,750
SHALDERS, George	P	$3,080	$3,777	$4,950
British (1826 - 1873)				
SHALER, Frederick	D			$385
American (1880 - 1916)				
SHAMPANG, Wayne H.	P	$220	$220	$220
(?)				
SHANKER, Louis	P			$495
American (20th -)				
SHANNON, Sir James J.	P	$13,200	$161,260	$687,500
British (1862 - 1923)				
SHAPI,	W			$110
American (20th -)				
SHAPIRO, Babe	P			$550
American (20th -)				
SHAPIRO, Betty D.	P			$308
American (?)				
SHAPIRO, Joel	D	$6,600	$47,300	$88,000
American (1941 -)	P	$7,700	$17,600	$27,500
	S	$15,400	$151,800	$242,000
SHAPLEIGH, Frank H.	P	$385	$2,210	$7,150
American (1842 - 1906)	W	$275	$367	$495
SHARE, H. Pruett	W			$550
American (1853 - 1905)				

D=Drawing, P=Painting, S=Sculpture, W=Watercolor

		Current Price Range		
		Low	Mean	High

SHARMAN, John	*P*	$990	$1,045	$1,100
American (20th -)				
SHARON, Mary B	*P*			$193
(1878 - 1961)				
SHARP, David	*P*			$1,045
(?)				
SHARP, John	*P*			$300
British (18th -)				
SHARP, Joseph H.	*P*	$440	$20,533	$68,750
American (1859 - 1953)				
SHARP, Joseph H. (Attrib.)	*P*			$1,430
American (1859 - 1953)				
SHARP, Louis H.	*P*	$990	$1,357	$1,650
American (1875 - 1946)				
SHARP, William A.	*D*			$2,475
American (1864 - 1944)	*W*	$248	$275	$303
SHARPE, Jim	*P*			$550
(1936 -)				
SHARPLES, John (Attrib.)	*D*			$605
(1792 - 1811)				
SHARPS, R.	*P*			$193
American (20th -)				
SHATTENSTEIN, Nikol	*P*			$880
American (19th - 20th)				
SHATTUCK, Aaron D.	*D*	$220	$1,128	$2,860
American (1832 - 1928)	*P*	$1,100	$2,713	$4,125
SHATTUCK, Aaron D. (Attrib.)	*P*			$440
American (1832 - 1928)				
SHATTUCK, William R.	*P*			$468
American (1895 - 1962)				
SHAVER, L. D.	*P*			$143
(?)				
SHAVER, L. P.	*P*			$1,650
American (19th -)				

D=Drawing, P=Painting, S=Sculpture, W=Watercolor

		Low	Mean	High
		\multicolumn{3}{Current Price Range}		

			Current Price Range	
		Low	Mean	High
SHAW, Alan W.	W			$825
American (1894 -)				
SHAW, Charles G.	P	$275	$10,495	$24,200
American (1892 - 1974)	W			$330
SHAW, Charles P.	P			$633
British (19th -)				
SHAW, E. J.	P			$891
(?)				
SHAW, John B. L.	P	$1,650	$9,075	$16,500
British (1872 - 1919)				
SHAW, Katherine H.	P			$770
(?)				
SHAW, Sydney	P			$1,100
American (1879 -)				
SHAYER, Charles	P			$5,060
British (19th -)				
SHAYER, William	P	$1,980	$17,663	$55,000
British (1788 - 1879)				
SHAYER, William (Attrib.)	P	$990	$1,958	$2,970
British (1788 - 1879)				
SHAYER, William (Et al.)	P			$37,400
British (18th - 19th)				
SHAYER, William (Manner)	P	$1,760	$4,455	$7,150
British (1788 - 1879)				
SHAYER, JR., William	P	$2,860	$11,016	$28,600
British (1811 - 1885)				
SHEA, Don	D			$231
American (20th -)				
SHEA, Frank	P			$220
American (20th -)				
SHEAN, Charles M.	W			$880
American (? - 1925)				
SHEARER, Christopher H.	P	$250	$1,520	$5,170
American (1840 - 1926)				
SHEARER, Victor	P	$110	$196	$350
(20th -)				

D=Drawing, P=Painting, S=Sculpture, W=Watercolor

| | | Current Price Range | | |
		Low	Mean	High
SHEE, Sir Martin A.	*P*	$2,750	$10,083	$22,000
British (1769 - 1850)				
SHEE, Sir Martin A. (Attrib)	*P*	$16,500	$17,600	$18,700
British (1769 - 1850)				
SHEE, Sir Martin A. (Circle)	*P*	$2,475	$5,500	$8,525
British (1769 - 1850)				
SHEELER, Charles	*D*	$39,600	$47,300	$55,000
American (1883 - 1965)	*P*	$44,000	$220,000	$396,000
	W			$38,500
SHEETS, Millard	*D*			$303
American (1907 - 1989)	*P*	$6,050	$11,275	$16,500
	W	$1,650	$8,643	$27,500
SHEETS, Nan	*P*	$385	$935	$2,640
American (1889 - 1976)				
SHEFFER, Glen C.	*P*	$358	$1,348	$2,750
American (1881 - 1948)				
SHEFFIELD, Isaac	*P*	$2,090	$13,970	$25,850
American (1798 - 1845)				
SHEIRE, Mary	*P*			$1,045
European (19th -)				
SHELBY, J.	*P*			$110
(20th -)	*W*			$880
SHELDON, Charles	*D*	$110	$110	$110
American (1894 - 1961)	*P*			$605
	W			$303
SHELTON, Alphonse J.	*P*			$468
American (1905 - 1972)				
SHELTON, William H.	*D*	$330	$550	$770
American (1840 - 1932)	*W*			$660
SHELTON, William H. (Et al.)	*D*			$1,650
American (19th - 20th)				

D=Drawing, P=Painting, S=Sculpture, W=Watercolor

		Current Price Range		
		Low	Mean	High

		Low	Mean	High
SHENK, G.	*P*	$248	$266	$275
American (20th -)				
SHEPARD, B. S.	*P*			$413
American (20th -)				
SHEPARD, Ernest	*D*	$3,575	$7,150	$14,300
British (1879 - 1976)				
SHEPHERD, George S.	*W*			$660
British (? - 1858)				
SHEPHERD, J. Clinton	*P*	$358	$1,164	$2,475
American (1888 - 1975)				
SHEPHERD, Warren	*P*			$3,300
American (1858 - 1937)				
SHEPLER, Dwight	*W*			$165
(20th -)				
SHEPPARD, Joseph	*P*	$138	$1,016	$2,200
American (1930 -)				
SHEPPARD, Richard	*P*			$825
(?)				
SHEPPARD, Warren J.	*P*	$330	$2,217	$6,820
American (1882 -)	*W*			$2,200
SHEPPARD, Warren W.	*P*	$385	$4,057	$7,700
American (1858 - 1937)	*W*	$110	$495	$880
SHEPPARD, William L.	*D*	$880	$1,650	$2,420
American (1833 - 1912)	*W*			$495
SHERIDAN, Claire	*S*			$1,650
American (19th - 20th)				
SHERINYAN, Elizabeth	*P*			$358
American (1877 - 1947)				
SHERMAN,	*S*			$303
(?)				
SHERMAN, Cindy	*D*	$6,600	$11,550	$19,800
(20th -)				
SHERMAN, Eloise L.	*W*			$193
(?)				

D=Drawing, P=Painting, S=Sculpture, W=Watercolor

		Current Price Range		
		Low	Mean	High

		Low	Mean	High
SHERMAN, G. (20th -)	P	$413	$944	$1,870
SHERMAN, John W. American (20th -)	P			$825
SHERRIN, Daniel British (20th -)	P	$330	$1,597	$2,750
	W			$880
SHERRIN, John British (1819 - 1896)	W			$1,045
SHERRY, William G. (?)	W			$330
SHERWOOD, Rosina American (1854 -)	W			$3,300
SHERWOOD, Vladimir O. Russian (1832 - 1897)	P			$6,600
SHERWOOD, W. S. American (20th -)	P			$385
SHERWOOD, William A. American (1875 - 1951)	P	$1,375	$1,823	$2,860
SHIEL, D. Cordon American (20th -)	P			$110
SHIELDS, Alan American (1944 -)	P	$1,540	$2,434	$3,300
	W			$308
SHIELDS, Bonnie American (20th -)	D			$1,100
SHIELDS, Emma J. (19th - 20th)	P			$165
SHIELDS, Thomas W. American (1849 -)	P	$990	$1,320	$1,650
SHILLING, Alexander American (1860 -)	P	$770	$880	$990
SHIMIZU, Y. Japanese (20th -)	P			$523
SHINN, Everett American (1876 - 1953)	D	$248	$7,435	$55,000
	P	$2,860	$21,309	$52,800

D=Drawing, P=Painting, S=Sculpture, W=Watercolor

		Current Price Range		
		Low	Mean	High

		Low	Mean	High
SHINN, Everett	W	$990	$8,723	$26,400
American (1876 - 1953)				
SHINN, Everett (Attrib.)	P			$220
American (1876 - 1953)	W			$1,045
SHIRLAW, Walter	D	$248	$454	$660
American (1838 - 1909)	P			$2,200
	W	$220	$475	$880
SHLEPPY, Rose	P			$1,760
American (20th -)				
SHOEMAKER, Vaughn	D	$110	$385	$660
American (1902 -)				
SHOGREN,	W			$248
American (20th -)				
SHOKLER, Harry	P			$2,090
(1896 -)				
SHOOK, Euclid	W			$358
American (?)				
SHOPE, Irvin	P			$5,000
American (1900 - 1978)				
SHORE, Robert	P			$175
(1924 -)				
SHORES, J. W.	P			$660
British (19th -)				
SHORT, Frederick G.	P	$495	$983	$2,310
British (19th -)				
SHORT, George A.	W	$248	$248	$248
British (1856 - 1945)				
SHORT, Sir Frank	P			$990
British (1857 - 1945)				
SHOTWELL, Helen	P	$413	$592	$770
American (1908 -)				
SHOTWELL, Margaret (Attrrib.)	P			$660
American (1873 - 1965)				
SHOULBERG, Harry	P			$980
American (1903 -)				

D=Drawing, P=Painting, S=Sculpture, W=Watercolor

		Current Price Range		
		Low	Mean	High
SHOUP, Charles	*D*			$495
American (20th -)	*P*	$3,850	$4,950	$6,050
SHOWELL, Ken	*P*	$330	$578	$825
American (20th -)				
SHRADER, E. Roscoe	*P*			$440
American (1879 - 1960)				
SHRADY, Henry M.	*S*	$550	$4,744	$15,400
American (1871 - 1922)				
SHRAPNEL, Edward S.	*P*			$440
American (19th - 20th)				
SHREVE, Carl J.	*P*			$220
(?)				
SHRINER, H.	*P*			$523
American (19th - 20th)				
SHUCK, C. F.	*W*			$110
(?)				
SHULGOLD, William	*P*	$495	$1,705	$2,915
American (20th -)				
SHULHUFF, William (Attrib.)	*P*			$275
American (20th -)				
SHULTTE, Arthur	*P*			$110
American (20th -)				
SHULTZ, James W.	*P*			$1,980
American (19th - 20th)				
SHULZ, Adolph R.	*P*	$138	$1,162	$2,420
American (1869 - 1963)				
SHURTLEFF, Roswell M.	*P*	$715	$963	$1,265
American (1838 - 1915)	*W*	$550	$688	$825
SHUSEN,	*W*			$358
(20th -)				
SHUTE, R. W. & S. A.	*P*			$2,640
(?)				
SHUTE, Ruth W. (Et al.)	*P*	$3,630	$4,840	$6,050
(?)				

D=Drawing, P=Painting, S=Sculpture, W=Watercolor

		Current Price Range	
	Low	Mean	High

		Low	Mean	High
SHUTTLEWORTH, Claire	*P*			$2,200
American (1930 -)				
SIBERECHTS, Jan	*P*	$19,800	$56,100	$110,000
Flemish (1627 - 1703)				
SIBLEY, Mary Elizabeth	*D*			$165
American (19th - 20th)				
SICARD, Francois L.	*S*			$880
French (1862 - 1934)				
SICHEL, Harold M.	*P*	$176	$1,507	$4,125
American (1881 -)				
SICILIA, Jose M.	*P*	$19,800	$49,450	$71,500
Spanish (1954 -)				
SICKERT, Walter R.	*D*			$1,430
British (1860 - 1942)	*P*			$3,300
SICKLE, Jan van	*W*			$440
(20th -)				
SICKLES, Noel D.	*W*			$300
American (1910 -)				
SIDANER, Henri le	*D*			$49,500
French (1862 - 1939)	*P*	$11,000	$179,748	$495,000
SIDERIS, Alexander	*P*			$248
(?)				
SIEBERT, Edward S.	*P*	$358	$5,377	$19,800
American (1856 - 1944)				
SIEFFERT, Paul	*P*			$3,080
French (1874 -)				
SIEGERT, August	*P*	$770	$2,732	$4,400
German (1786 - 1869)				
SIEGFRIED, Edwin C.	*D*	$413	$564	$715
American (1889 - 1955)				
SIEGRIEST, Louis B.	*P*	$935	$2,668	$4,400
American (1899 -)				
SIEMER, Christian	*P*	$2,090	$6,270	$10,450
American (1874 - 1940)				

D=Drawing, P=Painting, S=Sculpture, W=Watercolor

		Current Price Range	
	Low	Mean	High

		Low	Mean	High
SIENESE SCHOOL 15C,	P			$7,700
Italian (15th -)				
SIENESE SCHOOL 16C,	W			$2,200
Italian (16th -)				
SIENESE SCHOOL 17C,	D			$2,200
Italian (17th -)				
SIEVERS, Gregory	P			$1,210
American (20th -)				
SIGAFOOS, Richard D.	P			$413
American (20th -)				
SIGARD, Enzio	P			$275
Italian (20th -)				
SIGLER, Hollis	P			$7,700
(20th -)				
SIGMUND, Benjamin D.	W			$3,080
British (? - 1904)				
SIGNAC, Paul	D			$35,200
French (1863 - 1935)	P	$121,000	$1.054M	$2.750M
	W	$5,225	$23,711	$52,800
SIGNAC, Paul (Attrib.)	P			$2,860
French (1863 - 1935)				
SIGNORELLI, Luca	D			$66,000
Italian (1441 - 1523)				
SIGNORELLI & STUDIO, Luca	P			$93,500
Italian (1441 - 1523)				
SIGNORET, Charles L. E.	P			$17,600
French (1867 - 1932)				
SIGNORI, Sergio	S			$2,860
Italian (1906 -)				
SIGNORI, Sergio (Et al.)	S			$4,400
Italian (20th -)				
SIGNORINI, Giovanni	P			$7,150
Italian (19th -)				
SIGNORINI, Giuseppe	P			$5,500

D=Drawing, P=Painting, S=Sculpture, W=Watercolor

		Current Price Range		
		Low	Mean	High

SIGNORINI, Giuseppe	*W*	$1,430	$2,365	$4,675
Italian (1857 - 1933)				
SIGNORINI, Telemaco (Et al.)	*P*			$18,700
Italian (19th - 20th)				
SIGRIST, Franz (Attrib.)	*D*			$1,870
Austrian (1727 - 1803)				
SIGRISTE, Guido	*P*			$6,600
Swiss (1864 - 1915)				
SIGWORTH, Martha P.	*P*	$110	$124	$138
American (20th -)				
SIJAN, Marc	*P*	$2,200	$2,310	$2,420
American (20th -)				
SIKIERS, A. Von	*P*			$990
European (19th -)				
SILAS, L.	*P*			$605
(?)				
SILBERT, Ben	*W*			$330
American (20th -)				
SILBERT, Max	*P*	$3,850	$7,975	$12,100
French (1871 -)				
SILLARS, R.	*P*			$468
European (19th -)				
SILLETT, James	*P*			$12,100
British (1764 - 1840)				
SILSBEE, Martha	*D*			$110
American (20th -)				
SILSBY, Clifford	*D*			$550
American (1896 -)				
SILSBY, Wilson E.	*P*			$468
American (1883 - 1952)				
SILVA, Benjamin	*P*	$715	$2,998	$5,280
Cuban (20th -)				
SILVA, Francis A.	*P*	$4,840	$24,764	$60,500
American (1835 - 1886)	*W*			$77,000
SILVA, Maria E. V. da	*W*			$60,500
French (1908 - 1956)				

D=Drawing, P=Painting, S=Sculpture, W=Watercolor

		Current Price Range		
		Low	Mean	High
SILVA, William P.	*P*	$330	$1,560	$4,675
American (1859 - 1948)				
SILVERMAN, Burt	*P*			$412
American (20th -)	*W*			$660
SILVERMAN, Martin	*S*	$1,100	$3,344	$6,600
(20th -)				
SILVERT, Max	*P*			$2,200
French (1871 -)				
SILVESTRE, Israel (Circle)	*D*			$990
French (1621 - 1691)				
SILVESTRE, Louis de (School)	*P*			$4,180
French (1675 - 1760)				
SIMBARI, Nicola	*P*	$660	$5,904	$14,300
Italian (1927 -)				
SIME, Sidney H.	*W*	$1,100	$2,090	$3,520
British (1867 - 1941)				
SIMMONDS, A.	*P*			$330
American (19th - 29th)				
SIMMONDS, Charles	*S*			$11,000
(20th -)				
SIMMONS,	*P*			$110
(?)				
SIMMONS, Edward E.	*P*	$1,320	$24,874	$66,000
American (1852 - 1931)	*W*	$1,650	$4,583	$7,150
SIMMONS, Franklin W.	*P*			$330
American (1839 - 1913)				
SIMMONS, H. Leonard	*P*			$330
(20th -)				
SIMON, Emile	*P*			$605
French (20th -)				
SIMON, Hermann G.	*P*	$193	$1,284	$3,300
American (19th -)				
SIMON, J.	*P*			$660
French (19th - 20th)				

D=Drawing, P=Painting, S=Sculpture, W=Watercolor

		Current Price Range		
		Low	Mean	High

		Low	Mean	High
SIMON, Lucien	*P*			$110
French (1861 - 1945)				
SIMON, Yohanan	*P*			$550
Israeli (20th -)				
SIMONE, Tommasso de	*P*			$8,250
Italian (19th -)	*W*	$1,650	$2,072	$2,475
SIMONETTI, A.	*W*			$825
Italian (19th -)				
SIMONETTI, Amedeo M.	*W*			$578
Italian (1874 - 1925)				
SIMONETTI, Attilio	*P*			$2,475
Italian (1843 - 1925)				
SIMONETTI, C. G.	*W*			$770
Italian (19th -)				
SIMONETTI, Ettore	*P*	$880	$3,190	$5,500
Italian (19th -)	*W*	$1,155	$13,778	$26,400
SIMONETTI, R.	*P*			$1,980
Italian (19th - 20th)				
SIMONI, Alfredo de	*P*			$6,050
Italian (19th -)				
SIMONI, Gustavo	*P*			$16,500
Italian (1846 -)	*W*	$1,210	$3,410	$5,610
SIMONI, Mary Bell E.	*P*	$2,200	$3,062	$3,850
American (1897 - 1986)				
SIMONINI, Francesco	*P*	$2,750	$7,563	$12,100
Italian (1686 - 1753)				
SIMONINI, Francesco (Attrib.)	*P*			$7,150
Italian (1686 - 1753)				
SIMONINI, Francesco (Circle)	*P*			$4,180
Italian (1686 - 1753)				
SIMONS, Michiel	*P*			$63,250
Dutch (? - 1673)				
SIMONSEN, Niels	*P*	$12,100	$19,433	$28,600
Danish (1807 - 1885)				

D=Drawing, P=Painting, S=Sculpture, W=Watercolor

		Current Price Range		
		Low	Mean	High

		Low	Mean	High
SIMONSEN, Simon L. Danish (1841 - 1928)	*P*			$6,600
SIMONSON, David German (1831 - 1896)	*P*			$11,000
SIMONSON, J. T. American (19th - 20th)	*P*			$770
SIMPLOT, Alexander (1837 - 1914)	*D*	$165	$468	$770
SIMPSON, Charles W. British (1885 - 1971)	*P*	$1,705	$7,453	$13,200
SIMPSON, Henry British (1853 - 1921)	*P* *W*			$1,100 $275
SIMPSON, Michael S. (?)	*P*			$110
SIMS, Charles British (1873 - 1926)	*D* *P*			$3,080 $4,180
SINCLAIR, Gerrit American (1890 - 1955)	*P*			$310
SINCLAIR, Irving American (1895 - 1969)	*P*	$385	$385	$385
SINCLAIR, Olga Panamanian (1957 -)	*P*			$6,600
SINGELY, T. American (20th -)	*P*			$220
SINGER, Burr American (1912 -)	*P*	$330	$3,307	$8,250
SINGER, Clyde American (1908 -)	*P* *W*	$165 $220	$1,737 $289	$9,900 $358
SINGER, William H. American (1868 - 1943)	*P* *W*	$3,300	$3,575	$3,850 $770
SINGIER, Gustave French (1909 - 1984)	*P*			$23,100
SINIBALDI, Jean P. French (1857 - 1909)	*P*			$20,900

D=Drawing, P=Painting, S=Sculpture, W=Watercolor

		Current Price Range		
		Low	Mean	High
SINIBALDI, Nino	P			$1,100
European (19th - 20th)				
SINTENIS, Renee	D			$6,050
German (1888 - 1965)	S	$3,850	$5,885	$7,700
SINZ, Walter	S			$550
American (1881 -)				
SIPLE, Jessie	D			$138
(20th -)				
SIQUEIROS, David A.	D			$11,000
Mexican (1896 - 1974)	P	$5,225	$55,481	$363,000
	S			$25,300
	W			$4,950
SIRANI, Elisabetta (Attrib.)	D			$1,320
Italian (1638 - 1665)	P			$3,300
SIRONI, Mario	D			$187,000
Italian (1885 - 1961)	P			$3,025
	S			$121,000
	W	$4,400	$75,779	$330,000
SISLEY, Alfred	D	$29,700	$111,100	$192,500
French (1839 - 1899)	P	$660,000	$1.486M	$3.410M
SISLEY, Alfred (School)	P			$770
French (1839 - 1899)				
SISSON, Laurence	D			$330
American (1928 -)	P	$1,650	$2,658	$4,675
	W	$935	$1,348	$1,760
SISTERE, A. De	P			$1,210
French (19th -)				
SITNIKOV, Alexander	P			$44,000
Russian (1945 -)				
SITWAK, Israel	P			$825
(20th -)				

D=Drawing, P=Painting, S=Sculpture, W=Watercolor

		Current Price Range		
		Low	Mean	High

SITZMAN, Edward R.	*D*			$935
American (1874 -)	*W*	$248	$289	$330
SJAMAAR, Pieter G.	*P*			$1,430
Dutch (1819 - 1876)				
SJOSTRAND, Carl J.	*P*			$7,150
Swedish (19th -)				
SKAAR, Jane	*W*			$440
American (20th -)				
SKALA, H.	*P*			$715
Czech (19th - 20th)				
SKEAPING, John	*W*			$3,300
British (1901 - 1980)				
SKEELE, Hannah B.	*P*			$523
American (1829 - 1901)				
SKELTON, Red	*P*	$1,650	$1,723	$1,760
American (20th -)				
SKEMP, Robert O.	*P*			$8,250
American (1910 - 1984)				
SKINNER, Charlotte B.	*P*			$495
American (1879 -)				
SKINNER, Jessie R.	*P*			$250
American (1863 - 1946)				
SKIPWORTH, Frank M.	*P*			$88,000
British (1854 - 1929)				
SKLAR, Dorothy	*W*	$385	$440	$495
American (20th -)				
SKOR, Walter	*W*			$248
American (1918 -)				
SKOU, Sigurd	*P*	$880	$2,475	$7,150
American (1878 - 1929)	*W*			$330
SKOV, Christian	*P*			$330
American (1856 - 1942)				
SKUDE, Charles M. (Attrib.)	*P*			$125
American (20th -)				

D=Drawing, P=Painting, S=Sculpture, W=Watercolor

		Current Price Range		
		Low	Mean	High
SKY EAGLE,	*P*			$209
American (20th -)				
SLADE, Caleb A.	*P*	$165	$472	$1,210
American (1882 - 1961)	*W*			$578
SLATER, John F.	*P*	$275	$1,632	$3,300
British (1857 - 1937)				
SLATER, P.	*P*			$259
(?)				
SLEPYSHEV, Anatoli	*P*	$6,600	$19,800	$44,000
Russian (1932 -)				
SLOAN, Jeanette P.	*P*			$220
American (1946 -)				
SLOAN, John	*D*	$550	$2,079	$5,280
American (1871 - 1951)	*P*	$2,420	$37,977	$209,000
	W			$7,700
SLOAN, Junius R.	*P*			$2,475
American (1827 - 1900)	*W*	$440	$715	$990
SLOAN, Richard	*P*			$1,320
American (20th -)				
SLOANE, Eric	*D*	$495	$523	$550
American (1910 - 1985)	*P*	$413	$6,174	$14,960
	W			$825
SLOANE, Marion P.	*P*	$605	$1,251	$2,310
American (1875 - 1955)				
SLOBE, Ura	*S*			$385
(?)				
SLOCOMBE, Frederick A.	*P*			$12,100
British (1847 -)				
SLOMAN, Joseph	*P*	$110	$162	$220
American (20th -)				
SLOUN, Frank van	*D*	$660	$697	$770
American (1879 - 1938)	*P*	$330	$651	$1,210

D=Drawing, P=Painting, S=Sculpture, W=Watercolor

		Current Price Range		
		Low	Mean	High
SLOUN, Frank van	W	$385	$1,128	$1,870
American (1879 - 1938)				
SLUYS, Theodor van	P	$1,540	$2,623	$3,800
Belgian (1849 - 1931)				
SMALL, Frank O.	P			$330
American (1860 -)				
SMALL, H.	P			$2,200
(19th -)				
SMART, J.	P			$715
Scottish (19th -)				
SMEAD, H. G.	W			$193
(?)				
SMEDLEY, W. L.	W			$220
American (19th -)				
SMEDLEY, William T.	D			$935
American (1858 - 1921)				
SMEE, Esther	D			$523
American (20th -)				
SMEERS, Frans	P			$2,420
Belgian (1873 -)				
SMET, F.	P			$3,520
Belgian (19th -)				
SMET, Gustave de	P			$9,350
Belgian (1877 - 1943)				
SMET, Leon de	P			$8,800
Belgian (1881 -)				
SMETS, Louis	P			$8,250
Dutch (1918 -)				
SMILLIE, George H.	D			$165
American (1840 - 1921)	P	$880	$4,446	$9,900
	W			$2,640
SMILLIE, George H. (Attrib.)	P			$440
American (1840 - 1921)				
SMILLIE, James D.	P	$770	$1,760	$2,750
American (1833 - 1909)				

D=Drawing, P=Painting, S=Sculpture, W=Watercolor

		Current Price Range		
		Low	Mean	High
SMIRKE, Robert (Attrib.)	P			$110
British (1752 - 1845)				
SMIRNOV, Nikolai	P	$14,300	$30,067	$38,500
Russian (1938 -)				
SMITH,	P			$413
American (20th -)				
SMITH, Al	D			$330
American (20th -)				
SMITH, Alfred H.	P			$1,210
French (1953 -)				
SMITH, Andre	W			$440
French (20th -)				
SMITH, Archibald C.	P	$798	$3,383	$6,050
American (1837 - 1911)				
SMITH, C.	P			$248
(?)				
SMITH, Carolyn F.	P			$550
American (20th -)				
SMITH, Charles L.	P			$1,650
British (1751 - 1835)				
SMITH, Charles L. A.	P	$1,045	$1,412	$1,760
American (1871 - 1937)	W	$605	$752	$880
SMITH, D.	P			$110
(?)				
SMITH, David	D	$5,500	$11,183	$13,200
American (1906 - 1965)	P			$11,000
	S	$8,800	$121,489	$352,000
	W			$11,000
SMITH, DeCost	W			$880
American (1864 - 1939)				
SMITH, Denzil	P	$990	$1,430	$1,870
British (20th -)				
SMITH, E.	P			$275
British (19th - 20th)				

D=Drawing, P=Painting, S=Sculpture, W=Watercolor

		Current Price Range		
		Low	Mean	High
SMITH, Elmer B.	P			$2,860
American (1860 - 1943)	W			$660
SMITH, Ernest B.	P	$440	$1,705	$6,600
American (1866 - 1951)				
SMITH, F. Carl	P	$220	$358	$495
American (1868 - 1955)	W			$385
SMITH, F. Rollin	P			$935
American (19th -)				
SMITH, Francis	P			$2,750
British (1881 - 1961)				
SMITH, Francis H.	D	$385	$4,272	$9,350
American (1838 - 1915)	P			$9,350
	W	$880	$9,830	$46,200
SMITH, Frank V.	D			$990
American (1879 - 1967)	P	$358	$2,478	$5,500
	W			$440
SMITH, Frederick C.	P	$193	$372	$550
American (1868 - 1955)	W			$770
SMITH, Frederick W.	P			$1,430
American (1885 -)				
SMITH, Gary	P			$440
American (20th -)				
SMITH, Gean	P	$165	$708	$1,870
American (1851 - 1928)				
SMITH, Geoffrey	S			$1,320
American (20th -)				
SMITH, George	P			$1,100
British (1829 - 1901)				
SMITH, Graham	W			$385
(19th -)				
SMITH, H.	P	$440	$673	$1,100
American (1885 -)				

D=Drawing, P=Painting, S=Sculpture, W=Watercolor

		Current Price Range		
		Low	Mean	High

		Low	Mean	High
SMITH, H.	P			$495
British (19th -)				
SMITH, Harriet F.	W			$154
American (1873 - 1935)				
SMITH, Harry C.	P	$110	$341	$495
American (20th -)				
SMITH, Hassel	P			$12,100
American (1915 -)				
SMITH, Helen	P			$385
American (19th -)	W			$220
SMITH, Hely	W	$330	$550	$770
British (1862 - 1941)				
SMITH, Henry P.	P	$550	$4,086	$7,150
American (1854 - 1907)	W	$193	$1,527	$2,860
SMITH, Henry P. (Attrib.)	P			$429
American (1854 - 1907)				
SMITH, Hobbe	P			$770
Dutch (1862 - 1942)				
SMITH, Howard E.	P	$660	$3,190	$8,250
American (1885 - 1970)				
SMITH, J.	P			$209
(?)				
SMITH, J. Christopher	P	$275	$1,228	$3,025
American (1891 - 1943)				
SMITH, J. Henry	P			$715
American (19th -)				
SMITH, Jack W.	P	$1,320	$2,420	$4,290
American (1873 - 1949)				
SMITH, James B.	P			$6,325
American (19th -)				
SMITH, James M.	P			$220
American (20th -)				
SMITH, James R.	P			$550
American (1900 -)				

D=Drawing, P=Painting, S=Sculpture, W=Watercolor

| | | Current Price Range | | |
		Low	Mean	High
SMITH, Jessie W.	*D*	$605	$2,938	$7,000
American (1863 - 1935)	*P*	$14,300	$20,900	$27,500
	W			$10,010
SMITH, Joelle	*W*	$1,800	$2,367	$3,100
American (20th -)				
SMITH, John Brandon	*P*	$2,090	$7,498	$14,300
British (1848 - 1884)	*W*			$413
SMITH, John H. (Attrib.)	*P*			$2,200
British (19th -)				
SMITH, Joseph L.	*P*	$330	$1,169	$2,475
American (1863 - 1950)	*W*	$880	$3,328	$5,775
SMITH, Joseph M.	*D*	$1,100	$1,100	$1,100
American (1854 - 1923)	*W*			$5,500
SMITH, Langdon	*P*			$468
American (1870 - 1959)				
SMITH, Lawrence B.	*P*			$3,850
American (20th -)				
SMITH, Leon Polk	*P*	$13,200	$33,733	$44,000
American (20th -)				
SMITH, Letta	*D*			$16,500
American (?)				
SMITH, Lowell E.	*W*	$3,000	$3,205	$3,410
American (1924 -)				
SMITH, M. T.	*P*			$1,540
American (19th - 20th)				
SMITH, Martin	*S*			$770
(20th -)				
SMITH, Mary	*P*	$330	$4,048	$8,250
American (1842 - 1878)				
SMITH, Mary P.	*P*			$303
American (19th -)				
SMITH, Miriam T.	*P*			$495
American (20th -)				

D=Drawing, P=Painting, S=Sculpture, W=Watercolor

		Current Price Range		
		Low	Mean	High

		Low	Mean	High
SMITH, Nataline H. American (1908 - 1985)	*W*	$110	$131	$138
SMITH, Nathaniel American (1866 - 1943)	*P*			$358
SMITH, Patty (20th -)	*D*	$770	$825	$880
SMITH, Richard British (1931 -)	*D*			$770
	P			$165
	S			$550
SMITH, Rosamond L. American (20th -)	*P*			$28,600
SMITH, Russell American (1812 - 1896)	*P*	$220	$1,929	$8,800
	W	$110	$161	$225
SMITH, Russell (Attrib.) American (1812 - 1896)	*P*			$825
	W			$935
SMITH, Sidney G. American (20th -)	*P*			$248
SMITH, Sidney L. (Et al.) American (19th - 20th)	*D*			$352
SMITH, Steve (?)	*P*			$555
SMITH, T. A. American (19th -)	*P*			$770
SMITH, T. Henry American (19th -)	*P*			$660
SMITH, Thomas H. American (19th -)	*P*			$1,375
SMITH, Thomas L. American (1835 - 1884)	*P*			$3,080
SMITH, Tony American (1912 -)	*P*	$2,310	$8,837	$16,500
	S	$44,000	$104,500	$165,000
SMITH, Virginia American (20th -)	*P*			$2,640

D=Drawing, P=Painting, S=Sculpture, W=Watercolor

| | | Current Price Range | | |
---	---	Low	Mean	High
SMITH, W. British (19th - 20th)	*P*			$198
SMITH, W. B. (?)	*D*			$400
SMITH, Walter G. American (1870 - 1938)	*D*	$400	$640	$880
	P	$880	$2,900	$6,050
	W	$495	$2,310	$5,225
SMITH, William British (?)	*P*			$3,850
SMITH, William A. American (1918 - 1989)	*P*			$450
SMITH, William C. British (1815 - 1887)	*W*			$715
SMITH, William H. British (1848 - 1922)	*P*	$2,090	$2,970	$3,850
SMITH, William T. American (19th -)	*P*			$3,850
SMITH, William T. R. American (1812 - 1896)	*P*			$4,290
SMITH, Xanthus American (1838 - 1929)	*P*	$100	$771	$2,750
	W	$523	$2,191	$5,280
SMITH OF CHICHESTER, Will. British (1707 - 1764)	*P*			$5,500
SMITH, ELDER, Stephen C. British (1806 - 1872)	*P*			$27,500
SMITHSON, Robert American (20th -)	*D*	$3,300	$13,998	$25,300
	S	$28,600	$101,200	$165,000
SMOL, Bernard French (20th -)	*P*			$523
SMYTHE, Edward R. British (1810 - 1899)	*P*	$3,575	$5,088	$6,600
SMYTHE, Eugene L. American (1857 - 1932)	*P*	$165	$440	$715

D=Drawing, P=Painting, S=Sculpture, W=Watercolor

		Current Price Range		
		Low	Mean	High

		Low	Mean	High
SMYTHE, F.	*P*			$880
American (19th -)				
SMYTHE, Thomas	*P*	$4,620	$9,460	$14,300
British (1825 - 1906)				
SNAFFLES,	*W*			$440
British (20th -)				
SNELL, Henry B.	*P*	$770	$2,756	$6,600
American (1858 - 1943)				
SNELL, Henry B. (Attrib.)	*P*			$700
American (1858 - 1943)				
SNELSON, Kenneth	*S*	$5,225	$12,336	$46,200
American (1927 -)				
SNIDER, Dan L.	*S*			$770
American (20th -)				
SNODGRASS, J. L.	*S*			$1,900
American (20th -)				
SNOECK, Jacques	*P*	$1,870	$1,925	$1,980
Dutch (1881 - 1921)				
SNOW,	*P*			$330
American (19th -)				
SNOW, Charles H.	*P*			$330
American (19th - 20th)				
SNOW, Eben H.	*P*			$193
American (1870 - 1945)				
SNOW, G. H.	*W*			$248
American (19th - 20th)				
SNOW, Nicholas	*P*			$275
(20th -)				
SNOW, R. W.	*P*			$193
American (19th - 20th)				
SNOW, W. F.	*P*	$264	$270	$275
(?)				
SNYDER, Clarence W.	*P*	$200	$238	$275
American (1883 -)	*W*			$330
SNYDER, Joan	*P*	$3,850	$12,788	$18,700

D=Drawing, P=Painting, S=Sculpture, W=Watercolor

		Current Price Range		
		Low	Mean	High
SNYDER, Joan American (20th -)	S			$24,200
SNYDER, W. Mek. Danish (19th -)	P			$1,650
SNYDER, W. P. (?)	W			$1,100
SNYDER, William American (20th -)	P			$1,540
SNYDER, William H. American (1829 - 1910)	P			$935
SNYDERS, Frans Flemish (1579 - 1657)	P			$3,080
SNYDERS, Frans (Attrib.) Flemish (1579 - 1657)	P			$19,800
SNYDERS, Frans (Circle) Flemish (1579 - 1657)	P	$8,800	$16,500	$24,200
SNYDERS, Frans (Follower) Flemish (1579 - 1657)	P			$33,000
SNYERS, Pieter Flemish (1681 - 1752)	P			$132,000
SOARES, Pablo (20th -)	P			$3,300
SOBEL, Ida (20th -)	P			$715
SOCHOR, Richard European (19th -)	W	$825	$1,128	$1,430
SOCHOR, Richard (Attrib.) European (19th -)	W			$990
SODERBERG, Yngve (1896 -)	W			$138
SODERSTON, Herman (1862 - 1926)	P			$825
SOESTOR, S. Dutch (19th -)	P			$523
SOHIER, Alice R. American (1880 -)	P			$9,900

D=Drawing, P=Painting, S=Sculpture, W=Watercolor

		Current Price Range		
		Low	Mean	High

		Low	Mean	High
SOHN, E.	*P*			$413
American (20th -)				
SOKOLOFF, Anatolio	*P*			$1,650
Russian (1891 - 1971)				
SOKOLOFF, Stanley N.	*P*			$110
American (20th -)				
SOLANA, Jose G.	*P*			$101,750
Spanish (1885 - 1945)				
SOLANA, Nicolas (Attrib.)	*P*			$6,050
Spanish (15th -)				
SOLAR, Alejandro X.	*S*			$28,600
Argentina (1887 - 1963)	*W*	$20,900	$22,367	$24,200
SOLARI, Achille	*P*			$413
Italian (1835 -)				
SOLDI, Andrea	*P*			$49,500
Italian (1703 - 1771)				
SOLDNER, Paul	*S*	$1,650	$1,815	$1,980
(20th -)				
SOLDWEDEL, Frederic	*W*	$258	$679	$1,100
American (1886 -)				
SOLER Y LLOPIS, Eduardo	*P*			$3,300
Spanish (1829 - 1928)				
SOLIMENA, Francesco	*P*	$42,900	$43,450	$44,000
Italian (1657 - 1747)				
SOLIMENA, Francesco (Attrib.)	*P*	$10,450	$11,275	$12,100
Italian (1657 - 1747)				
SOLIMENA, Francesco (Circle)	*P*			$880
Italian (1657 - 1747)				
SOLIMENA, Francesco (Follower)	*D*			$605
Italian (1657 - 1747)	*P*	$605	$1,238	$1,870
SOLMAN, Joseph	*P*	$1,100	$1,925	$2,750
American (1909 -)	*W*			$193
SOLOMON, Abraham	*P*	$1,540	$10,670	$19,800
British (1824 - 1862)				

D=Drawing, P=Painting, S=Sculpture, W=Watercolor

		Low	Mean	High
		\multicolumn{3}{c}{Current Price Range}		

		Current Price Range		
		Low	Mean	High
SOLOMON, Frederick	*P*	$248	$509	$770
American (1899 - 1980)				
SOLOMON, Simeon	*D*			$16,500
British (1840 - 1905)				
SOLOMON, Solomon J.	*P*	$9,900	$22,550	$35,200
British (1860 - 1927)				
SOLOWEY, Ben	*P*			$165
American (1901 - 1978)				
SOMAINI, Francesco	*S*	$467	$1,471	$2,475
Italian (1926 -)				
SOMELLI, Guido	*P*			$2,750
Italian (1881 -)				
SOMER,	*P*			$770
(20th -)				
SOMER, Hendrick van	*P*			$71,500
Dutch (17th -)				
SOMERS, Guillaume	*P*			$1,540
Belgian (1819 -)				
SOMM, Henry	*D*			$220
French (1844 - 1907)				
SOMMER, Ferdinand	*P*			$468
Swiss (1822 - 1901)				
SOMMER, William	*D*	$193	$262	$358
American (1867 - 1949)	*P*	$550	$605	$660
	W	$165	$527	$1,760
SOMMERS, Otto	*P*	$2,750	$21,175	$39,600
American (19th -)				
SOMOGYI, D.	*P*			$1,650
(?)				
SON, Joris van	*P*	$22,000	$100,375	$242,000
Flemish (1623 - 1667)				
SONDAG, Alphonse E.	*P*	$248	$303	$358
American (1874 - 1971)				
SONDERBORG, Kurt	*P*			$20,900
German (1923 -)				

D=Drawing, P=Painting, S=Sculpture, W=Watercolor

		Current Price Range		
		Low	Mean	High

SONDERLAND, Fritz	*P*	$6,600	$9,567	$11,100
German (1836 - 1896)				
SONJE, Jan G.	*P*			$9,900
Dutch (1625 - 1707)				
SONNENSTERN, Friedrich S.	*D*			$9,350
Lithuanian (1892 -)				
SONNEVELD, Carl	*P*			$550
American (19th - 20th)				
SONNIER, Keith	*D*			$6,050
American (1941 -)	*P*			$19,800
	S			$41,250
SONNTAG, William L.	*P*	$3,520	$17,224	$55,000
American (1822 - 1900)	*W*	$1,320	$4,510	$7,700
SONNTAG, William L. (Attrib.)	*P*			$275
American (1822 - 1900)				
SONNTAG, William L. (Et al.)	*P*			$13,200
American (19th - 20th)				
SONNTAG, JR., William L.	*D*	$990	$4,345	$7,700
American (1870 -)	*P*			$1,155
	W	$990	$2,882	$4,950
SOONIUS, Louis	*P*			$880
Dutch (20th -)				
SORBI, Refaello	*P*			$28,600
Italian (1844 - 1931)				
SORBINI, A.	*P*			$16,500
Italian (19th -)				
SORENSEN, Karin	*P*			$3,300
Danish (19th -)				
SORENSEN, Y.	*P*			$110
Dutch (19th - 20th)				
SORENSON, Carl F. S.	*P*			$4,675
Swedish (1818 - 1879)				
SORGH, Hendryk M. (Circle)	*P*	$3,300	$3,438	$3,575
Dutch (1611 - 1670)				

D=Drawing, P=Painting, S=Sculpture, W=Watercolor

| | | Current Price Range | | |
		Low	Mean	High
SORIANO, Juan	D			$1,650
Mexican (1919 -)	P	$8,800	$24,933	$35,200
	W			$4,675
SORKAU, Albert	P			$605
French (1874 -)				
SORMAN, Steven	S			$880
(20th -)				
SOROLLA Y BASTIDA, Joaquin	P	$27,500	$450,542	$2.420M
Spanish (1863 - 1923)				
SORRI, Pietro	P			$880
Italian (1556 - 1621)				
SORTA, Salvador	S			$1,210
(20th -)				
SOTHERLAND,	P			$935
(20th -)				
SOTO, Jesus R.	P	$12,650	$31,036	$71,500
Venezuelan (1923 -)	S	$2,090	$19,821	$44,000
SOTTER, George W.	D	$500	$525	$550
American (1879 -)	P	$450	$9,052	$29,500
SOTTOCORNOLA, Giovanni	P			$35,200
Italian (1855 - 1917)				
SOUCY, Elizabeth	S			$495
American (20th -)				
SOUDEIKINE, Serge	D			$1,650
Russian (1883 - 1946)	P	$110	$678	$990
	W	$880	$1,155	$1,430
SOULACROIX, Frederic	P	$12,100	$52,261	$110,000
French (1825 -)				
SOULAGES, Pierre	D			$47,300
French (1919 -)	P	$20,900	$113,300	$242,000
SOULE, Carleton M.	P	$495	$578	$660
American (1911 -)				

D=Drawing, P=Painting, S=Sculpture, W=Watercolor

		Current Price Range	
	Low	Mean	High

		Low	Mean	High
SOULEN, Henry J.	P			$8,250
American (1888 - 1965)	W			$1,320
SOULES, Eugene	D			$248
French (? - 1876)				
SOUPLET, Louis Ulysse	P			$7,700
French (1819 - 1878)				
SOUTH GERMAN SCHOOL 15C,	P			$30,250
German (15th -)				
SOUTH GERMAN SCHOOL 17C,	D			$2,200
German (17th -)	P			$1,540
SOUTH GERMAN SCHOOL 18C,	D	$1,320	$2,805	$4,400
German (18th -)				
SOUTHER, J. K.	P			$935
American (1869 -)				
SOUTHERN, J. M.	P			$770
American (19th -)				
SOUTINE, Chaim	P	$165,000	$386,467	$880,000
Russian (1893 - 1943)				
SOUTMAN, Pieter (Circle)	P			$7,700
Dutch (1580 - 1657)				
SOUVIAK,	W			$495
American (20th -)				
SOUZA-PINTO, Jose G.	P	$24,750	$35,750	$46,750
Portuguese (1855 - 1939)				
SOWDEN, John	W			$220
British (1838 - 1926)				
SOWERBY, John	W			$550
British (19th - 20th)				
SOWINSKI, Jan	P			$330
American (1885 -)				
SOYER,	P			$138
American (20th -)				
SOYER, Avron	W			$220
American (?)				

D=Drawing, P=Painting, S=Sculpture, W=Watercolor

		Current Price Range		
		Low	Mean	High
SOYER, Isaac	*P*	$1,430	$12,210	$26,400
American (1907 -)				
SOYER, Moses	*D*	$220	$634	$1,320
American (1899 - 1975)	*P*	$440	$3,556	$9,350
	W	$220	$358	$468
SOYER, Moses (Manner)	*D*			$165
American (1899 - 1975)				
SOYER, Raphael	*D*	$165	$1,232	$4,675
American (1899 - 1987)	*P*	$935	$10,132	$46,750
	W	$248	$2,863	$16,500
SOYER, Raphael & Moses	*D*			$2,640
American (1899 -)				
SPADA, Lionella	*P*			$66,000
Italian (1576 - 1622)				
SPADINO, Giovanni P.	*P*			$29,700
Italian (17th -)				
SPAENDONCK, Cornelis van	*P*	$28,600	$69,300	$110,000
Dutch (1756 - 1840)				
SPAENDONCK, Cornelis van (Att)	*W*			$1,100
Dutch (1756 - 1840)				
SPAENDONCK, Gerard (Foll.)	*P*			$1,980
French (1746 - 1822)				
SPALATIN, Marko	*P*			$990
American (1945 -)				
SPAMPINATO, Clemente	*S*	$660	$2,609	$3,850
American (1912 -)				
SPANDORF, Lilly	*D*			$275
American (20th -)	*W*	$138	$226	$358
SPANG, Frederick	*P*			$1,650
American (1831 - 1909)				
SPANGENBERG, George	*P*			$880
American (20th -)				
SPANISH FORGER 19C,	*P*			$3,850
Spanish (19th -)				

D=Drawing, P=Painting, S=Sculpture, W=Watercolor

		Current Price Range		
		Low	Mean	High

		Low	Mean	High
SPANISH SCHOOL,	P			$1,430
Spanish (?)				
SPANISH SCHOOL,	P			$2,200
Spanish (18th - 19th)				
SPANISH SCHOOL,	P			$550
Spanish (19th - 20th)				
SPANISH SCHOOL 15C,	P	$11,000	$12,100	$13,200
Spanish (15th -)				
SPANISH SCHOOL 16C,	P	$2,200	$10,065	$23,100
Spanish (16th -)				
SPANISH SCHOOL 17C,	D	$1,100	$1,100	$1,100
Spanish (17th -)	P	$1,100	$20,378	$74,250
SPANISH SCHOOL 18C,	P	$1,210	$2,481	$4,950
Spanish (18th -)				
SPANISH SCHOOL 19C,	P	$1,100	$10,148	$52,800
Spanish (19th -)				
SPANYI, Bela von	P			$440
Hungarian (1852 - 1914)				
SPANZOTTI, Giovanni (Follower)	P			$35,200
Italian (15th - 16th)				
SPARKS, Will	P	$880	$1,245	$1,980
American (1862 - 1937)				
SPAT, Gabriel	P	$319	$1,883	$7,150
American (1890 - 1967)				
SPAULDING, Henry P.	W	$495	$509	$523
American (1868 -)				
SPAULDING, Warren D.	W			$110
American (1916 -)				
SPAZSALI, Luciano	P	$220	$248	$275
Italian (20th -)				
SPAZZAPAN, Luigi	P			$2,420
Italian (1890 - 1958)				
SPEAR, Arthur P.	D	$220	$495	$770
American (1879 - 1959)	P			$2,420

D=Drawing, P=Painting, S=Sculpture, W=Watercolor

		Current Price Range		
		Low	Mean	High
SPEAR, Ruskin	P			$6,600
British (1911 -)				
SPECK, Gene	P			$1,650
American (1954 -)				
SPEED, Ulysses Grant	S	$2,090	$3,410	$4,400
American (1930 -)				
SPEER, J. A.	P			$220
(?)				
SPEER, Will	P			$275
American (20th -)				
SPEICHER, Eugene E.	D	$220	$623	$1,430
American (1883 - 1962)	P	$165	$2,237	$4,950
	W			$880
SPENCE, Ernest	P			$3,300
British (19th -)				
SPENCE, Freida D.	P			$303
American (20th -)				
SPENCE, J.	P			$110
American (20th -)				
SPENCE, Thomas R.	P			$660
British (19th - 20th)				
SPENCELAYH, Charles	P			$3,300
British (1865 - 1958)				
SPENCER, A.	P	$550	$3,025	$5,500
British (19th -)				
SPENCER, Asa	P	$165	$623	$1,155
American (1847 -)				
SPENCER, Harry	W	$110	$110	$110
British (20th -)				
SPENCER, Howard B.	P	$440	$578	$715
American (20th -)				
SPENCER, John C.	P	$220	$880	$1,760
American (19th - 20th)				
SPENCER, Lilly M.	D	$110	$1,054	$9,350

D=Drawing, P=Painting, S=Sculpture, W=Watercolor

		Current Price Range		
		Low	Mean	High

		Low	Mean	High
SPENCER, Lilly M.	P	$5,500	$5,500	$5,500
American (1822 - 1902)				
SPENCER, Margaret F.	P			$523
American (1882 -)				
SPENCER, Niles	P	$5,500	$22,000	$47,300
American (1893 - 1952)				
SPENCER, R. B.	P	$3,025	$11,330	$44,000
British (19th -)				
SPENCER, Robert	P	$1,430	$39,133	$99,000
American (1879 - 1931)				
SPENCER, Stanley	D			$2,090
British (1891 - 1959)				
SPENGLER, H. A.	P			$138
American (19th - 20th)				
SPERLICH, Sophie	P			$2,530
German (19th -)				
SPERLING, Heinrich	P			$13,200
German (1844 - 1924)				
SPERLISH, L.	P			$413
(?)				
SPICUZZA, Francesco	D	$165	$712	$1,980
American (1883 - 1962)	P	$550	$578	$605
SPICUZZA, Francesco (Attrib.)	P	$300	$323	$350
American (1883 - 1962)				
SPIDELL, Enid Jean	W			$248
American (1905 -)				
SPIELBERGER, M. G.	P			$110
(?)				
SPIELTER, Carl J.	P			$5,500
German (1851 - 1922)				
SPIERS, Harry	W	$330	$509	$1,045
American (1869 - 1934)				
SPILIMBERGO, Lino Eneas	D			$3,080
(?)				
SPINELLI, Giovanni B.	D			$2,970
Italian (? - 1647)				

D=Drawing, P=Painting, S=Sculpture, W=Watercolor

		Current Price Range		
		Low	Mean	High

		Low	Mean	High
SPINELLI, Luca Italian (14th - 15th)	*P*			$104,500
SPINETTI, Mario Italian (19th - 20th)	*W*			$4,400
SPINKS, Thomas British (19th -)	*P*	$990	$1,815	$2,640
SPIRIDON, Ignace Italian (19th - 20th)	*P*			$9,900
SPIRO, George French (1909 - 1948)	*P*	$1,210	$2,145	$3,850
SPISANO, Vincenzo (?)	*P*			$3,300
SPITZER, Walter Polish (1927 -)	*P*	$790	$2,524	$8,800
SPITZWEG, Carl German (1808 - 1885)	*D*			$1,650
SPODE, John British (19th -)	*P*			$4,950
SPODE, Samuel British (19th -)	*P*			$2,090
SPOEL, Jacob Dutch (1820 - 1868)	*P*			$2,420
SPOERRI, Daniel Swiss (1930 -)	*P*			$1,650
SPOHLER, J. F. Dutch (1853 - 1894)	*P*	$4,400	$6,417	$10,450
SPOHLER, Jan J. Dutch (1811 - 1879)	*P*	$908	$16,835	$49,500
SPOHN, Clay E. (20th -)	*P*	$187	$1,456	$2,310
SPOLVERINI, Ilario Italian (1657 - 1734)	*P*			$44,000
SPRAGUE, Amelia B. American (1870 -)	*P*			$350
SPRAGUE, Curtiss American (19th -)	*W*	$110	$152	$193

D=Drawing, P=Painting, S=Sculpture, W=Watercolor

		Current Price Range		
		Low	Mean	High

SPRAGUE, Howard F.	*P*	$6,600	$8,250	$9,900
American (1871 - 1899)				
SPREAD, Harry F.	*P*			$275
American (1844 -)				
SPRINCHORN, Carl	*D*	$220	$504	$935
American (1887 - 1971)	*P*	$248	$1,169	$2,640
	W	$468	$651	$990
SPRING, Alfons	*P*			$5,225
German (1843 - 1908)				
SPRING, J. J.	*P*			$605
European (20th -)				
SPRINGER, Charles H.	*P*			$715
American (1857 - 1920)				
SPRINGER, Cornelis	*P*			$16,500
Dutch (1817 - 1891)	*W*			$715
SPRINGER, Sidonie	*P*			$1,430
Austrian (1878 -)				
SPRUCE, Everett F.	*P*	$2,310	$4,455	$6,600
American (1907 -)				
SPRUYT, Johannes (Attrib.)	*P*			$3,300
(? - 1671)				
SPUEHLER, Ernst A.	*P*			$660
American (1900 - 1973)				
SPULAK, A.	*P*			$4,400
(19th -)				
SQUIER, Donald G.	*P*	$110	$278	$2,640
(1895 - 1987)	*W*			$165
SQUIRES, C. Clyde	*P*			$1,210
American (1883 - 1970)				
SSUZEA, David de	*S*			$220
(?)				
ST. CLAIR, Norman	*P*			$550
American (1863 - 1912)				

D=Drawing, P=Painting, S=Sculpture, W=Watercolor

		Current Price Range		
		Low	Mean	High

STAATEN, Louis van	*W*	$440	$660	$880
Dutch (19th -)				
STACEY, Anna L.	*P*	$440	$1,251	$2,970
American (1871 - 1943)				
STACHOWSKI, Wladyslaw von	*P*			$385
Polish (1852 - 1932)				
STACK, Josef M.	*P*			$1,320
Swedish (1812 - 1868)				
STACKHOUSE, Robert	*D*			$3,850
American (1942 -)	*W*	$2,475	$4,538	$6,600
STACQUET, Henry	*W*			$990
Belgian (1838 - 1907)				
STADEMANN, Adolf	*P*	$11,000	$14,575	$18,150
German (1824 - 1895)				
STAEGER, Ferdinand	*P*			$182
(?)				
STAEHL, Albert	*P*	$275	$633	$990
American (1899 - 1974)	*W*			$1,870
STAEL, Nicolas de	*P*	$165,000	$523,600	$1.320M
Russian (1914 - 1955)				
STAGLIANI, J.	*P*			$358
Italian (19th -)				
STAGLIANO, Arturo	*P*			$6,600
Italian (1870 - 1936)				
STAHL, Benjamin	*D*			$605
American (1910 -)	*P*	$300	$590	$880
STAHL, Hans Von	*P*			$110
(?)				
STAHR, Paul	*P*			$850
American (1883 -)	*W*			$385
STAINFORTH, Martin (Attrib.)	*P*			$798
Australian (20th -)				
STALBEMT, Adriaen van	*P*			$12,100
Flemish (1580 - 1662)				

D=Drawing, P=Painting, S=Sculpture, W=Watercolor

		Current Price Range		
		Low	Mean	High
STAMOS, Theodoros	*D*			$2,310
American (1922 -)	*P*	$1,540	$20,213	$110,000
	W	$1,210	$3,603	$6,600
STAMPER, James W.	*P*			$1,320
British (1873 -)				
STANCZK, Julian	*P*			$1,430
American (20th -)				
STANDING, William	*P*	$880	$2,880	$7,700
American (1904 - 1951)	*W*			$990
STANDISH, Frank	*P*			$2,090
American (1860 - 1944)				
STANE, S.	*P*			$165
American (20th -)				
STANFIELD, Clarkson (Circle)	*P*			$1,760
British (19th -)				
STANFIELD, George C. (Attrib.)	*P*			$650
British (1828 - 1878)				
STANFIELD, William C.	*P*	$550	$1,531	$3,300
British (1793 - 1867)				
STANFIELD, William C. (Attrib.)	*P*	$770	$935	$1,100
British (1793 - 1867)				
STANI, G.	*W*			$110
Italian (20th -)				
STANISLAW, Ejsmond	*D*			$5,500
Polish (19th - 20th)				
STANKIEWICZ, Richard	*S*			$6,600
American (1922 -)				
STANNARD, Emily	*P*			$1,045
British (1875 - 1907)				
STANNARD, Henry	*W*			$9,350
British (1844 - 1920)				
STANNARD, Henry S.	*W*	$1,870	$5,632	$14,300
British (1870 - 1951)				
STANNARD, Lilian	*W*			$2,640
British (1884 -)				

D=Drawing, P=Painting, S=Sculpture, W=Watercolor

		Current Price Range		
		Low	Mean	High

STANNARD, Sylvester British (1898 -)	W			$1,100
STANNUS, Anthony British (19th -)	W			$2,420
STANTON, Gideon T. American (20th -)	P	$176	$563	$990
STANTON, John A. American (1857 - 1929)	P	$990	$1,210	$1,430
STANWOOD, Franklin American (1856 - 1888)	P			$1,210
STANZIONE, Massimo Italian (1585 - 1656)	P			$143,000
STANZIONE, Massimo (Circle) Italian (1585 - 1656)	P	$2,200	$28,600	$55,000
STAPLES, Elliott (?)	P			$132
STAPLES, John French (19th -)	P			$1,045
STAPLES, Sir Robert P. British (1853 - 1943)	W			$275
STAPRANS, Raymond American (1926 -)	P	$468	$564	$660
STARK, Jack G. American (1882 - 1950)	P			$358
STARK, James (Attrib.) British (1794 - 1859)	P			$8,250
STARK, Larry (?)	P			$550
STARK, Mel American (1904 -)	P			$700
STARK, Otto American (1859 - 1926)	W			$880
STARKWEATHER, William American (1879 - 1969)	P	$385	$1,650	$4,950
STARN TWINS,	D	$4,400	$20,763	$35,200

D=Drawing, P=Painting, S=Sculpture, W=Watercolor

		Current Price Range		
		Low	Mean	High
STARN TWINS,	*P*			$55,000
(20th -)	*S*	$19,800	$29,150	$38,500
STARRENBURG, Arent P. W. van	*P*			$220
Dutch (1874 - 1945)				
STAUDER, Karl	*P*			$3,300
German (18th -)				
STAUFFER,	*P*			$825
European (19th -)				
STAUNTON, JR., Phineas	*P*			$1,100
American (1817 - 1867)				
STAVROWSKY, Oleg	*P*	$770	$6,418	$20,000
American (1927 -)				
STAYTON, Bob	*S*			$1,250
American (20th -)				
STEARNS, Junius B.	*P*	$2,200	$2,475	$2,750
American (1810 - 1885)				
STEARS-THOMSON,	*P*			$193
(?)				
STEBBINS, Roland	*P*	$1,210	$1,925	$2,640
American (1883 - 1974)				
STEED, Robert	*W*			$110
(?)				
STEEL, Adolf	*P*			$46,200
German (1829 - 1907)				
STEEL, Annie (Attrib.)	*P*			$605
American (?)				
STEELE, Edwin	*P*	$770	$1,348	$1,650
British (19th -)				
STEELE, J.	*P*			$715
American (19th -)				
STEELE, Marion W.	*P*			$715
American (1916 -)				
STEELE, Theodore C.	*P*	$3,850	$5,500	$7,150
American (1847 - 1926)				
STEELE, Thomas S.	*P*			$330
American (1845 - 1903)				

D=Drawing, P=Painting, S=Sculpture, W=Watercolor

		Current Price Range		
		Low	Mean	High

		Low	Mean	High
STEELE, Zulma	*P*	$110	$293	$475
American (1881 - 1979)				
STEELINK, Willem	*W*			$1,320
Dutch (1826 - 1913)				
STEEN, Agustus van den	*P*			$2,750
Flemish (1803 - 1870)				
STEEN, Jan	*P*	$33,000	$1.501M	$2.970M
Dutch (1626 - 1679)				
STEEN, Jan (After)	*P*			$825
Dutch (1626 - 1679)				
STEEN, Jan (Attrib.)	*P*			$16,500
Dutch (1626 - 1679)				
STEEN, Jan (Follower)	*P*			$6,050
Dutch (1626 - 1679)				
STEEN, Jan (Manner)	*P*			$1,100
Dutch (1626 - 1679)				
STEEN, Jan (School)	*P*	$3,300	$4,400	$5,500
Dutch (1626 - 1679)				
STEEN, Lodwijk C. van der	*P*			$193
Dutch (19th - 20th)				
STEENWYCK, JR., Hendrick	*P*			$28,600
Flemish (1580 - 1649)				
STEENWYCK, JR., Hendrick (Att)	*P*			$6,600
Flemish (1580 - 1649)				
STEENWYCK, JR., Hendrick (Cir)	*P*			$6,325
Flemish (1580 - 1649)				
STEEPLE, John	*W*			$1,100
British (19th -)				
STEER, Philip W.	*P*			$4,290
British (1860 - 1942)	*W*	$660	$660	$660
STEFAN, Ross	*P*	$1,210	$2,656	$4,400
American (1934 -)				
STEFANI, Salvatore L.	*P*			$193
Italian (1827 - 1898)				
STEFFAN, Johann G.	*D*			$605
Swiss (1815 - 1905)				

D=Drawing, P=Painting, S=Sculpture, W=Watercolor

		Current Price Range		
		Low	Mean	High
STEICHEN, Edward	P	$17,600	$18,150	$18,700
American (1879 - 1973)				
STEIN, Georges	P			$8,800
French (19th - 20th)	W	$1,650	$5,775	$9,900
STEIN, Janos	P			$330
Hungarian (1874 - 1944)				
STEIN, William B.	D			$341
(?)				
STEINBACH, Haim	P	$13,200	$23,980	$29,700
(20th -)				
STEINBERG, Nathaniel P.	D			$275
American (1895 -)	P			$110
STEINBERG, Saul	D	$495	$19,169	$110,000
American (1914 -)	P	$14,300	$28,286	$44,000
	S	$7,150	$24,819	$38,500
	W	$13,200	$25,781	$55,000
STEINER, Agnes	P			$1,210
German (1845 - 1925)				
STEINER, G.	P			$165
Austrian (20th -)				
STEINER, Michael	P	$550	$697	$770
American (1945 -)	S	$2,200	$8,067	$17,600
STEINLEN, Theophile A.	D	$330	$1,345	$3,850
French (1859 - 1923)	P	$880	$1,797	$3,080
	S			$660
	W			$2,090
STEIR, Pat	P	$11,000	$22,000	$33,000
American (20th -)	W			$2,750
STELLA, Frank	D	$38,500	$179,667	$440,000
American (1936 -)	P	$9,900	$405,599	$5.060M

D=Drawing, P=Painting, S=Sculpture, W=Watercolor

		Current Price Range		
		Low	Mean	High
STELLA, Frank	*S*	$5,500	$73,573	$352,000
American (1936 -)	*W*	$66,000	$154,000	$242,000
STELLA, Jacques (School)	*P*			$3,300
French (1596 - 1657)				
STELLA, Joseph	*D*	$1,210	$4,705	$17,600
American (1880 - 1946)	*P*	$12,100	$37,675	$63,250
	S	$12,100	$12,650	$13,200
	W			$24,200
STENBERRY, Algot	*P*			$2,090
American (1902 -)				
STEPHAN, A.	*P*	$1,100	$1,513	$1,925
Dutch (19th - 20th)				
STEPHAN, Gary	*D*			$1,430
American (20th -)	*P*	$4,180	$7,095	$11,000
STEPHEN, A.	*P*			$110
French (20th -)				
STEPHENS, Alice B.	*D*			$3,850
American (1858 -)	*P*			$1,375
STEPOLE,	*P*			$248
(20th -)				
STEPPE, Romain	*P*			$2,200
Belgian (1859 - 1927)				
STERLING, J. O.	*P*			$770
American (20th -)				
STERN, Bernard	*P*	$14,300	$19,067	$26,400
American (20th -)				
STERN, Ignaz	*P*			$44,000
German (1680 - 1748)				
STERN, Ignaz (Attrib.)	*P*			$7,700
German (1680 - 1748)				
STERN, Lucia (Attrib.)	*P*			$105
American (20th -)				

D=Drawing, P=Painting, S=Sculpture, W=Watercolor

		Current Price Range		
		Low	Mean	High

		Low	Mean	High
STERN, Max	*P*	$3,300	$11,000	$16,500
German (1872 - 1943)				
STERNBERG, Frank	*P*			$440
British (1858 -)				
STERNBERG, Harry	*P*			$38,500
American (1904 -)				
STERNE, Hedda	*P*			$880
American (1915 -)				
STERNE, Maurice	*D*	$160	$411	$770
American (1878 - 1957)	*P*	$550	$3,878	$12,100
STERNER, Albert E.	*D*	$220	$1,344	$4,950
American (1863 - 1946)	*P*	$385	$1,485	$3,520
	W	$138	$152	$165
STETSON, Charles W.	*P*	$220	$1,547	$4,950
American (1858 - 1911)	*W*			$550
STETTHEIMER, Florine	*P*			$60,500
American (1871 - 1948)				
STEVENS, Aime	*P*			$41,250
Belgian (1879 -)				
STEVENS, Alfred	*D*	$110	$202	$275
Belgian (1823 - 1906)	*P*	$770	$93,683	$462,000
STEVENS, Alfred (Attrib.)	*P*			$440
Belgian (1823 - 1906)				
STEVENS, Alfred (Circle)	*P*	$10,450	$11,000	$11,550
Belgian (1823 - 1906)				
STEVENS, Beatrice	*P*			$330
American (1876 -)				
STEVENS, Edward J.	*W*			$550
American (1923 -)				
STEVENS, Gustav Max	*D*			$1,650
German (1871 -)	*P*			$440
STEVENS, Jack	*S*			$550
American (20th -)				

D=Drawing, P=Painting, S=Sculpture, W=Watercolor

| | | Current Price Range | | |
		Low	Mean	High
STEVENS, John C.	*P*	$935	$1,073	$1,210
American (1855 -)				
STEVENS, Lawrence T.	*S*			$1,100
American (?)				
STEVENS, Marjorie	*W*	$385	$468	$550
American (20th -)				
STEVENS, Peter	*P*	$110	$203	$400
American (?)				
STEVENS, Pieter	*D*			$35,200
Flemish (1567 - 1624)				
STEVENS, Will H.	*P*	$1,540	$2,695	$3,850
American (1881 -)				
STEVENS, William L.	*P*	$468	$2,531	$7,700
American (1888 - 1969)	*S*			$880
	W	$176	$763	$1,870
STEVER, Jorge	*P*			$770
German (1940 -)				
STEWART, A. M.	*P*			$660
British (19th -)				
STEWART, B. P.	*P*			$1,650
(19th -)				
STEWART, Brent	*D*			$440
American (20th -)				
STEWART, Charles E. (Attrib.)	*P*			$1,210
British (1890 - 1930)				
STEWART, E.	*P*			$3,300
British (19th -)				
STEWART, F.	*P*			$440
British (19th -)				
STEWART, Frank Algernon	*D*	$2,640	$10,120	$17,600
British (1877 - 1945)	*W*			$3,575
STEWART, G. M.	*P*			$110
(19th -)				
STEWART, Julius	*P*	$3,025	$14,355	$38,500
American (1855 - 1919)				

D=Drawing, P=Painting, S=Sculpture, W=Watercolor

| | | Current Price Range | | |
		Low	Mean	High
STEWART, Lizbeth	*P*			$3,740
(20th -)				
STEWART, Mary B. R.	*P*			$440
American (20th -)				
STEWART, N. Neale	*P*			$440
(19th -)				
STEWART, Robert W.	*P*			$5,000
American (?)				
STICHT, Jan	*P*			$605
American (20th -)				
STICK, Frank	*P*	$3,300	$3,300	$3,300
American (1884 - 1966)				
STICKS, C. B.	*P*			$2,420
(19th -)				
STIEBORSKY, Willy	*P*			$440
Austrian (1881 -)				
STIEPEVICH, Vincent G.	*P*	$3,850	$8,983	$17,600
Russian (1841 - 1910)	*W*			$715
STIFFER, Ferd	*P*			$1,155
(19th -)				
STIFTER, Moritz	*P*			$19,800
Austrian (1857 - 1905)				
STILKE, Hermann A.	*P*			$22,000
German (1803 - 1860)				
STILL, Clyfford	*P*	$38,500	$316,250	$1.100M
American (1904 -)				
STILLMAN-MYERS, Joyce	*P*			$4,180
(20th -)				
STILLWELL, Charles	*P*			$358
American (20th -)				
STILSON, Ethel M.	*D*	$132	$165	$198
American (20th -)				
STILSON, William W.	*W*	$550	$550	$550
American (19th -)				
STIMELING, Peter	*W*			$138
American (20th -)				

D=Drawing, P=Painting, S=Sculpture, W=Watercolor

		Current Price Range		
		Low	Mean	High
STINSKI, Gerald	*P*	$2,200	$2,933	$4,125
American (1929 -)				
STINSON, C. F.	*D*			$110
(?)				
STIRLING, Dave	*P*	$193	$330	$523
American (1889 -)				
STITES, Caribel	*P*			$1,540
American (19th - 20th)				
STITT, Hobart D.	*P*			$880
American (1880 -)				
STIX, Marguerite	*S*			$440
Austrian (1907 - 1975)				
STOBBE, Marie	*D*			$385
(?)				
STOBIOK, J.	*P*			$220
(?)				
STOCK, Ernest	*P*			$1,925
American (20th -)				
STOCK, Ignatius van der	*P*			$15,400
Dutch (17th -)				
STOCK, Joseph W. (Attrib.)	*S*			$6,710
American (1815 - 1855)				
STODDARD, Alice K.	*P*			$3,850
American (1884 - 1976)				
STOFFE, Jan J. van der	*P*	$4,400	$5,867	$6,600
Dutch (1611 - 1682)				
STOHR, Julie (Attrib.)	*P*			$110
American (1895 -)				
STOILOFF, Constantin	*P*	$1,760	$3,756	$6,600
Russian (1850 - 1924)				
STOILOFF, Constantin (Et al.)	*P*			$7,700
Russian (19th - 20th)				
STOITZNER, Josef	*W*	$303	$339	$385
Austrian (1884 -)				
STOJANOW, C.	*P*			$1,210
(?)				

D=Drawing, P=Painting, S=Sculpture, W=Watercolor

		Current Price Range		
		Low	Mean	High

		Low	Mean	High
STOJNOV, Joseph (?)	*P*			$18,700
STOKES, Adrian British (1854 - 1935)	*P*			$15,400
STOKES, Frank W. American (1858 -)	*P*			$990
STOLL, Rolf American (1892 -)	*P*			$2,090
STOLTE, B. D. American (19th - 20th)	*P*			$121
STOLTENBERG, Hans J. American (1880 - 1963)	*P*	$275	$731	$1,210
STOMER, Matthias Flemish (17th -)	*P*	$5,500	$68,750	$132,000
STOMER, Matthias (Follower) Flemish (17th -)	*P*			$1,650
STOMME, Maerten B. de (Attrib.) Dutch (17th -)	*P*	$55,000	$63,250	$71,500
STONE, A. British (19th -)	*P*	$1,650	$2,035	$2,420
STONE, Don American (1929 -)	*W*	$770	$990	$1,210
STONE, Eleanor (?)	*P*			$110
STONE, Fern C. American (20th -)	*P*			$275
STONE, Gilbert (1940 - 1984)	*P*			$800
STONE, Henry (Manner) British (1616 - 1653)	*P*			$1,430
STONE, Marcus British (1840 - 1921)	*P*	$33,000	$66,000	$99,000
STONE, Richard American (?)	*W*	$138	$219	$300
STONE, Robert Australian (20th -)	*P*	$880	$2,750	$4,620

D=Drawing, P=Painting, S=Sculpture, W=Watercolor

		Current Price Range		
		Low	Mean	High
STONE, Robert	*P*	$4,400	$13,750	$17,600
British (19th -)				
STONE, Sarah	*P*			$275
American (18th - 19th)				
STONE, William R.	*P*			$6,380
British (19th -)				
STONEY, Eleanor E.	*P*			$743
American (19th -)				
STOOP, Dirck	*P*			$11,000
Dutch (1618 - 1681)				
STOOP, Dirck (Manner)	*P*			$1,650
Dutch (1618 - 1681)				
STOOPS, Herbert M.	*P*			$2,000
American (1888 - 1948)	*W*			$1,595
STORCK, Abraham J.	*P*	$4,070	$14,410	$24,750
Dutch (1635 - 1710)				
STORCK, Abraham J. (Attrib.)	*P*			$1,100
Dutch (1635 - 1710)				
STORER, Charles	*P*			$385
American (19th -)	*W*			$193
STORIE, Jose	*P*			$11,000
Belgian (1899 -)				
STORK, Lisl	*P*			$880
American (1888 -)				
STORM, H. J.	*P*			$880
European (20th -)				
STORRS, Francis H.	*P*			$275
(19th - 20th)				
STORRS, John H.	*S*			$36,300
American (1885 - 1956)				
STORY, George H.	*P*			$13,200
American (1835 - 1923)				
STOTESBURY, Charles C.	*P*			$330
American (20th -)				

D=Drawing, P=Painting, S=Sculpture, W=Watercolor

		Current Price Range		
		Low	Mean	High
STOTHARD, Thomas	P			$2,090
British (1755 - 1834)				
STOTTLEMEYER, Margaret	P			$193
American (20th -)				
STOUT, Frank	P			$825
(?)				
STOVEHOUSE, Brian	D			$715
(?)				
STOWELL, James V.	W			$121
American (?)				
STRAATEN, Hendrick van der	P			$550
Dutch (1665 - 1722)				
STRACHAN, Claude	W	$4,400	$5,408	$6,600
British (1865 - 1929)				
STRADA, Vespasiano (Attrib.)	D			$2,750
Italian (16th -)				
STRADONE, Giovanni	P			$990
Italian (1911 -)				
STRAET, Jan van der	D	$11,000	$26,033	$47,300
Flemish (1523 - 1605)				
STRAET, Jan van der (Circle)	D			$1,650
Flemish (1523 - 1605)				
STRAETEN, George van der	S			$715
Belgian (1856 -)				
STRAHALM, F.	P			$495
(?)				
STRAIN, Daniel (Attrib.)	P			$2,310
American (19th -)				
STRAIN, John P.	W	$3,300	$4,290	$5,500
American (1955 -)				
STRANG, Ray	P			$4,400
American (1893 - 1957)				
STRANGE, A.	P			$275
American (19th -)				
STRANGE, Emil (Attrib.)	P			$110
Danish (1883 - 1943)				

D=Drawing, P=Painting, S=Sculpture, W=Watercolor

		Current Price Range		
		Low	Mean	High
STRANOVER, Tobias	*P*			$39,600
Czechoslovakian (1684 - 1724)				
STRANOVER, Tobias (Manner)	*P*			$2,090
Czechoslovakian (1684 - 1724)				
STRAOUTEN, B. V.	*P*			$4,125
Belgian (19th -)				
STRASSER, Arthur	*S*			$3,300
Austrian (1854 - 1927)				
STRASSER, Herb	*D*	$2,750	$3,125	$3,500
American (1929 -)				
STRASSER, Roland	*P*			$550
Austrian (1880 -)				
STRATHMANN, Carl	*W*			$1,100
German (1866 - 1939)				
STRATTON, Mary Chase	*D*			$330
American (1867 -)	*W*			$248
STRAUS, M.	*P*			$6,820
European (19th -)				
STRAUS, Meyer	*P*	$1,320	$2,585	$3,850
American (1831 - 1905)	*W*			$220
STRAUSER, Sterling	*P*			$175
(?)				
STRAUSS, Malcom A.	*W*			$330
American (1883 - 1936)				
STRAUSS, Raphael	*P*			$3,575
American (19th -)				
STRAWBRIDGE, Anne W.	*P*			$9,900
American (1883 - 1944)				
STRAWBRIDGE, Edward	*W*			$193
American (1903 -)				
STRAYER, Paul	*P*	$413	$605	$880
American (1885 - 1981)				
STREADBECK, Steve	*S*			$2,900
American (20th -)				

D=Drawing, P=Painting, S=Sculpture, W=Watercolor

		Current Price Range		
		Low	Mean	High

STREECK, Hendrik van	*P*			$60,500
Dutch (1659 - 1719)				
STREEFKERK, Carl A.	*P*			$688
Dutch (1894 -)				
STREET, Frank	*P*	$330	$1,765	$3,200
American (1893 - 1944)				
STREET, Robert	*P*	$2,475	$9,625	$16,500
American (1796 - 1865)				
STREET, Robert (Attrib.)	*P*			$413
American (1796 - 1865)				
STREIT, Robert	*P*			$6,380
Austrian (1883 -)				
STRETTON, Philip E.	*P*	$1,870	$3,410	$4,950
British (19th - 20th)				
STREVENS, Frederick	*P*			$1,320
British (1902 -)				
STRICKLAND, Charlotte	*W*	$352	$352	$352
British (18th - 19th)				
STRIDER, Majorie	*S*			$220
(20th -)				
STRINGER, Francis	*P*			$15,400
British (18th -)				
STROBEL, Christian	*P*			$1,018
Austrian (1855 - 1899)				
STROBEL, Oscar A.	*P*			$248
American (1891 - 1967)				
STROEBEL, Johann A. B.	*P*			$605
Dutch (1821 - 1905)				
STROITZNER, Josef	*P*			$1,320
Austrian (1884 - 1951)				
STRONG, Elizabeth	*P*	$193	$331	$468
American (1885 - 1941)				
STRONG, Joseph D.	*P*	$523	$2,599	$4,675
American (1852 - 1899)				
STRONG, Ray S.	*P*			$495
American (1905 -)				

D=Drawing, P=Painting, S=Sculpture, W=Watercolor

		Current Price Range		
		Low	Mean	High
STROOBANT, Francois Belgian (1819 - 1916)	P			$3,300
STROUD, Ida Wells American (1869 -)	W			$990
STROZZI, Bernardo Italian (1581 - 1644)	P	$88,000	$99,000	$110,000
STROZZI, Bernardo (Circle) Italian (1581 - 1644)	P			$44,000
STRUCK, Herman American (1887 - 1954)	P	$1,100	$1,155	$1,210
STRUTT, William British (1826 - 1915)	P	$5,500	$7,150	$8,800
STRUTZEL, Otto German (1855 - 1930)	P			$4,400
STRYDONCK, Guillaume van Belgian (1861 - 1937)	P			$24,200
STUART, (?)	P			$440
STUART, Charles British (19th -)	P	$2,475	$2,558	$2,640
STUART, Gilbert American (1755 - 1828)	P	$1,155	$68,970	$242,000
STUART, Gilbert (After) American (1755 - 1828)	P	$495	$3,740	$17,600
STUART, James A. (Attrib.) British (1713 - 1788)	D			$1,100
STUART, James E. American (1852 - 1941)	P	$165	$738	$3,300
STUART, Jane American (1816 - 1888)	P			$3,850
STUART, Jane (Attrib.) American (1816 - 1888)	P			$2,420
STUART, R. T. American (19th -)	P			$275
STUART, S. British (19th -)	P			$385

D=Drawing, P=Painting, S=Sculpture, W=Watercolor

		Current Price Range		
		Low	Mean	High

		Low	Mean	High
STUBBS, George	*P*			$1.210M
British (1724 - 1806)				
STUBBS, George (After)	*P*			$3,300
British (1724 - 1806)				
STUBBS, George (Attrib.)	*P*			$4,400
British (1724 - 1806)				
STUBBS, Kenneth H.	*P*	$1,500	$1,795	$2,090
American (20th -)				
STUBBS, Ralph	*P*			$1,100
British (19th -)				
STUBBS, William P.	*P*	$2,200	$4,926	$7,700
American (1842 - 1909)				
STUBER, Dedrick B.	*P*	$990	$2,090	$4,400
American (1878 - 1954)				
STUCK, Carl	*P*			$1,210
German (19th -)				
STUCK, Franz von	*D*			$1,100
German (1863 - 1928)	*P*	$3,300	$15,180	$27,500
	S			$1,870
STUEMPFIG, Walter J.	*P*	$385	$6,295	$18,700
American (1914 - 1970)				
STUHLMULLER, Karl	*P*	$8,800	$9,350	$9,900
German (1858 - 1930)				
STULL, Henry	*P*	$1,430	$7,747	$16,500
American (1851 - 1913)	*W*			$2,585
STURGESS, John	*P*	$2,860	$6,655	$10,450
British (19th - 20th)	*W*			$2,200
STURGIS, Allanson H.	*W*			$193
(?)				
STURM, W.	*S*			$11,000
(?)				
STURTEVANT, Elaine	*P*			$8,250
American (1926 -)				

D=Drawing, P=Painting, S=Sculpture, W=Watercolor

| | | Current Price Range | | |
		Low	Mean	High
STURTEVANT, Helena	*D*			$275
American (1872 - 1946)	*P*	$605	$9,662	$27,500
STUSSY, Jan	*W*			$550
American (20th -)				
STUVEN, Ernst	*P*			$93,500
German (1660 - 1712)				
SUBIT, Aline	*D*			$1,650
American (1819 - 1896)				
SUCHY, Adalbert	*W*			$770
Austrian (1783 - 1849)				
SUCUI, Edmond	*P*			$990
(?)				
SUDKOVSKY, Rufin	*P*			$2,420
(?)				
SUDRE, Raymond	*S*			$4,180
French (1870 -)				
SUDY, J. P.	*W*			$523
American (20th -)				
SUES, Jean J. (Attrib.)	*P*			$660
Swiss (1726 - 1802)				
SUEUR, Eustache le	*P*			$154,000
French (1617 - 1655)				
SUEUR, Eustache le (Circle)	*D*			$49,500
French (1617 - 1655)	*P*			$35,200
SUGAI, Kumi	*D*			$6,600
Japanese (1919 -)	*P*	$20,900	$72,783	$132,000
	W			$9,020
SUGARMAN, George	*S*			$1,100
American (20th -)				
SUGARS, Fanny	*P*			$385
British (?)				
SUHRLANDT, Carl	*P*			$27,500
German (1828 - 1919)				

D=Drawing, P=Painting, S=Sculpture, W=Watercolor

		Current Price Range		
		Low	Mean	High

SULLIVAN, Bill	*D*			$220
American (1946 -)				
SULLIVAN, Blanche	*P*			$1,430
American (19th - 20th)				
SULLIVAN, David	*P*			$165
American (20th -)				
SULLIVAN, Mary O.	*P*			$523
American (20th -)				
SULLIVAN, William H.	*P*			$18,700
British (? - 1908)				
SULLIVANT, Thomas S.	*D*			$700
American (1854 -)				
SULLY, Alfred	*W*			$2,200
American (19th -)				
SULLY, R. A.	*P*			$325
(?)				
SULLY, Thomas	*D*	$825	$825	$825
American (1783 - 1872)	*P*	$330	$22,371	$143,000
	W	$1,210	$6,105	$11,000
SULLY, Thomas (After)	*P*			$550
American (1783 - 1872)				
SULLY, Thomas (Attrib.)	*P*	$525	$1,733	$3,575
American (1783 - 1872)	*W*			$2,475
SULLY, Thomas (Manner)	*P*	$303	$372	$440
American (1783 - 1872)				
SULLY, Thomas (Style)	*P*			$1,870
American (1783 - 1872)				
SULTAN, Altoon	*P*			$3,300
American (1948 -)				
SULTAN, Donald	*D*	$4,400	$43,523	$115,500
American (1951 -)	*P*	$8,250	$122,068	$440,000
	S			$2,640
	W			$4,950

D=Drawing, P=Painting, S=Sculpture, W=Watercolor

		Current Price Range		
		Low	Mean	High
SULYON-PAPP, J.	P			$935
American (20th -)				
SUMERLIN, Mabel E.	P			$495
American (20th -)				
SUMMA, Emily B.	P	$303	$821	$1,760
American (1875 -)				
SUMMERS, Alick D.	P	$1,430	$1,485	$1,540
British (1864 - 1938)				
SUMMERS, Ivan	P	$880	$963	$1,045
American (? - 1964)				
SUMMERS, Robert	P	$4,510	$8,894	$17,600
American (1940 -)	S	$1,980	$5,564	$11,550
SUMMERS, Robert (Et al.)	S			$440
American (20th -)				
SUNDBLOM, Haddon	P			$358
American (1899 - 1976)	W			$3,575
SUNDQUIST, Th.	P			$400
(?)				
SURBER, Paul	W			$450
American (20th -)				
SURENDORF, Charles	W	$220	$385	$550
American (1906 - 1979)				
SURLS, James	P			$17,600
(20th -)	S			$16,500
SURTEES, John	P	$2,310	$2,530	$2,750
British (1819 - 1915)				
SURVAGE, Leopold	D	$1,760	$3,593	$5,500
French (1879 - 1968)	P	$2,640	$37,070	$71,500
	W			$1,430
SUSS, Johann	P	$220	$990	$1,980
Austrian (1857 -)				
SUSSWITCH, H. P.	P			$385
American (19th - 20th)				

D=Drawing, P=Painting, S=Sculpture, W=Watercolor

		Current Price Range		
		Low	Mean	High

SUSTERMANS, Justus	*P*			$4,180
Flemish (1597 - 1681)				
SUSTERMANS, Justus (Follower)	*P*			$2,970
Flemish (1597 - 1681)				
SUSTERMANS, Justus (Studio)	*P*			$7,150
Flemish (1597 - 1681)				
SUSTRIS, Lambert (Attrib.)	*P*	$18,700	$30,250	$41,800
Dutch (1540 - 1599)				
SUTHERLAND, A.	*P*			$125
(20th -)				
SUTHERLAND, Graham	*D*			$550
British (1903 - 1980)	*P*			$55,000
SUTTER, Joseph	*P*			$193
American (20th -)				
SUTTER, Samuel	*P*			$248
American (1888 -)				
SUTTON, Ruth H.	*P*	$110	$110	$110
American (1898 - 1960)				
SUTTON, JR., Harry	*P*	$165	$320	$605
American (1897 - 1964)	*W*			$6,600
SUVEE, Joseph B. (Attrib.)	*D*			$2,530
Italian (1743 - 1807)				
SUVERO, Mark Di	*D*	$1,045	$2,218	$3,850
American (1933 -)	*P*	$88,000	$181,500	$275,000
	S	$2,090	$74,309	$187,000
	W			$5,500
SUYDAM, James A.	*P*			$88,000
American (1819 - 1865)				
SUYKER, Reyer C.	*P*			$8,800
(16th - 16th)				
SUZUKI, James H.	*P*			$5,720
(20th -)				
SUZUKI, Taro	*P*			$385
Japanese (?)				

D=Drawing, P=Painting, S=Sculpture, W=Watercolor

		Current Price Range		
		Low	Mean	High
SVENDSEN, Charles	*W*			$220
American (1871 -)				
SVENDSEN, F.	*P*			$468
Danish (19th -)				
SVENDSEN, K. O.	*W*			$220
(?)				
SVENDSEN, Svend	*P*	$110	$941	$3,080
American (1864 - 1915)	*W*			$220
SVERTSCHKOFF, Nicolas G.	*P*	$2,420	$2,640	$2,860
Russian (1817 - 1898)				
SWAIN, William (Attrib.)	*P*			$9,900
American (1803 - 1847)				
SWAINE, Francis	*P*	$6,600	$8,983	$10,450
French (1740 - 1782)				
SWAN, John M.	*P*			$11,000
British (1847 - 1910)				
SWAN, Robert J.	*P*			$990
British (1888 -)				
SWAN, Russell	*P*			$440
American (1908 - 1963)				
SWANSON, Frank	*S*			$1,155
American (20th -)				
SWANSON, Glenn	*S*	$800	$2,160	$3,520
American (20th -)				
SWANSON, Mark	*P*			$3,300
American (20th -)				
SWANSON, Ray	*P*			$7,500
American (1937 -)				
SWANTEES, Ethel L.	*W*			$110
American (1896 -)				
SWEBACH, Edouard	*P*			$3,300
French (1800 - 1870)				
SWEDISH SCHOOL 17C,	*P*			$5,500
Swedish (17th -)				
SWEENEY, Gilberte	*P*			$330
(20th -)				

D=Drawing, P=Painting, S=Sculpture, W=Watercolor

		Current Price Range		
		Low	Mean	High

		Low	Mean	High
SWEERTS, Michiel (Circle) Dutch (1624 - 1664)	*P*	$4,400	$46,200	$88,000
SWEERTS, Michiel (Manner) Dutch (1624 - 1664)	*P*			$2,200
SWEET, American (?)	*P*	$165	$179	$193
SWEET, W. H. British (19th -)	*W*			$330
SWERINGEN, Ron Van American (20th -)	*P*	$440	$550	$605
SWERTZ, J. W. Dutch (20th -)	*P*			$440
SWETT, William O. American (1859 - 1938)	*P*	$358	$1,843	$4,730
SWIFT, C. A. American (20th -)	*W*			$193
SWIFT, Clemment N. American (1846 - 1918)	*P*			$605
SWIFT, George A. (19th - 1947)	*W*			$193
SWIGGETT, Jean American (1910 -)	*W*			$550
SWING, David American (1864 - 1945)	*P*	$248	$331	$413
SWINNERTON, James American (1875 - 1974)	*P*	$358	$2,386	$6,600
SWINTON, Marion American (?)	*P*			$1,045
SWISS SCHOOL 16C, Swiss (16th -)	*P*	$1,650	$6,233	$13,200
SWISS SCHOOL 18C, Swiss (18th -)	*P*			$6,875
SWISS SCHOOL 19C, Swiss (19th -)	*P*			$1,650
	W	$2,200	$3,190	$4,180
SWITZER, Scott (?)	*P*			$132

D=Drawing, P=Painting, S=Sculpture, W=Watercolor

		Current Price Range		
		Low	Mean	High
SWOPE, H. Vance	*P*			$300
American (1879 -)				
SWOPE, Kate F.	*P*	$165	$908	$1,650
American (19th - 20th)				
SWORD, James B.	*P*	$330	$2,860	$7,150
American (1839 - 1915)	*W*	$193	$372	$550
SYBORCK, R.	*P*			$1,980
(19th -)				
SYER, JR., John	*P*	$1,870	$3,245	$4,620
British (1815 - 1885)				
SYKES, Charles	*S*			$1,650
British (20th -)				
SYKES, Charles H.	*P*			$558
American (1882 -)				
SYKES, G. D.	*P*			$180
(20th -)				
SYLVESTER, Frederick	*P*	$330	$2,823	$9,350
American (1869 - 1915)				
SYLVESTER, Frederick (Attrib.)	*P*			$303
American (1869 - 1915)				
SYMES, John	*P*			$1,650
American (? - 1888)				
SYMONS, George G.	*P*	$330	$9,794	$52,250
American (1863 - 1930)	*W*	$330	$688	$1,045
SYMONS, George G. (Attrib.)	*P*			$660
American (1863 - 1930)				
SYNAVE, Tancrede	*P*			$715
French (1860 -)				
SYROP, D.	*P*			$413
American (20th -)				
SYVERSON, Judy	*P*			$500
American (20th -)				
SZAION, J. S. C.	*S*			$2,475
(?)				

D=Drawing, P=Painting, S=Sculpture, W=Watercolor

		Current Price Range		
		Low	Mean	High

		Low	Mean	High
SZANTHO, Maria	*P*	$165	$1,467	$3,850
Hungarian (1898 -)				
SZCZEBLEWSKI, V.	*S*			$1,540
(?)				
SZEWCZENKO, Taras	*P*			$220
(?)				
SZIRT, Attributed	*P*			$110
Hungarian (20th -)				
SZYK, Arthur	*D*			$1,155
Polish (1894 -)				
SZYKIER, Fiekierz	*P*			$7,150
Polish (19th -)				
SZYSZLO, Fernando de	*P*	$1,760	$12,877	$24,200
Peruvian (1925 -)				
TAAFFE, Phillip	*D*			$6,600
(20th -)	*P*			$49,500
TAANMAN, Jacob	*P*			$1,265
Dutch (1836 - 1923)				
TABACHNICK, Anne	*P*			$385
(20th -)				
TABER, I. Walton	*D*	$110	$504	$2,200
American (19th - 20th)				
TABER, I. Walton (Et al.)	*D*	$242	$700	$1,210
American (19th - 20th)				
TABON, Caesar	*W*			$385
(20th -)				
TACCA, Ferdinando	*S*			$550,000
Italian (1619 - 1686)				
TACCA, Pietro (After)	*S*			$16,500
Italian (18th -)				
TACK, Augustus V.	*P*	$6,380	$28,160	$49,500
American (1870 - 1949)				
TACK, Augustus V. (Attrib.)	*P*			$2,310
American (1870 - 1949)				
TADOLINI, Giulio	*S*			$14,300
Italian (1849 - 1918)				

D=Drawing, P=Painting, S=Sculpture, W=Watercolor

		Current Price Range		
		Low	Mean	High
TAGE, (20th -)	P			$550
TAGGART, Lucy M. American (19th -)	P			$1,430
TAIT, Agnes American (1897 -)	P			$880
TAIT, Arthur F. American (1819 - 1905)	P	$4,125	$26,246	$68,750
TAIT, Arthur F. (After) American (1819 - 1905)	P			$770
TAIT, John R. American (1834 - 1909)	P			$935
TAKIS, Vassilakis (20th -)	P	$1,540	$4,730	$7,920
TAKSAYI, A. Japanese (20th -)	P			$385
TAL-COAT, Pierre French (1905 -)	P			$8,250
TALBOT, Grace H. American (1901 -)	S			$3,520
TALBOT, Henry S. American (19th -)	P			$1,430
TALBOT, Jonathan American (20th -)	S	$413	$441	$468
TALBOT, Thomas (?)	P			$770
TALCOTT, Sarah W. American (1852 -)	P			$1,540
TALENGHI, Enrico Italian (1848 -)	W			$2,200
TALLANT, Richard H. American (1853 -)	P	$1,430	$1,650	$1,760
	W			$121
TALLONE, Guido Italian (1894 - 1967)	P	$1,100	$1,155	$1,210
TALMAGE, Algeron M. British (1871 - 1939)	P			$715

D=Drawing, P=Painting, S=Sculpture, W=Watercolor

		Current Price Range		
		Low	Mean	High
TAMARIZ, Eduardo	*P*			$935
Mexican (1945 -)				
TAMAYO, Rufino	*D*	$1,760	$12,964	$26,400
Mexican (1899 -)	*P*	$77,000	$286,250	$770,000
	W	$7,700	$28,862	$63,250
TAMBURINI, A.	*P*	$138	$454	$770
(20th -)				
TAMBURINI, Arnaldo	*P*	$1,100	$2,897	$4,400
Italian (1843 -)				
TANAKA, Akira	*P*			$6,325
Japanese (1918 -)				
TANAKA, Yasushi	*P*			$3,575
Japanese (1886 -)				
TANANCHI,	*W*			$330
Japanese (20th -)				
TANGHAUS, I.	*P*			$385
(?)				
TANGUY, Yves	*D*	$1,155	$12,991	$41,250
French (1900 - 1955)	*P*	$180,000	$353,333	$495,000
	W	$55,000	$134,063	$209,000
TANNER, Henry O.	*P*	$4,125	$10,588	$17,050
American (1859 - 1937)				
TANNER, O.	*P*	$550	$1,100	$1,650
(20th -)				
TANNER, P.	*P*			$468
(?)				
TANNERT, Volker	*P*			$3,300
(20th -)				
TANNING, Dorothea	*P*	$22,000	$27,500	$33,000
American (20th -)				
TANOUX, Adrien H.	*P*	$7,150	$7,425	$7,700
French (1865 - 1923)				
TANZI, Leon L. A.	*P*			$4,730
French (1846 - 1913)				

D=Drawing, P=Painting, S=Sculpture, W=Watercolor

		Current Price Range		
		Low	Mean	High
TAOIST SCHOOL,	*P*			$1,100
(20th -)				
TAPIES, Antonio	*P*	$3,740	$99,748	$165,000
Spanish (1923 -)				
TAPIRO Y BARO, Jose	*W*	$2,200	$2,310	$2,420
Spanish (1830 - 1930)				
TAPPERT, Georg	*P*	$187,000	$440,000	$638,000
German (1880 - 1957)				
TARAVAL, Guillaume	*P*			$38,500
French (1701 - 1750)				
TARAVAL, Hugues	*P*			$7,700
French (1729 - 1785)				
TARBELL, Edmund C.	*P*	$8,250	$86,625	$165,000
American (1862 - 1938)	*W*			$3,300
TARENGHI, Enrico	*P*			$1,650
Italian (1848 -)	*W*	$1,100	$1,650	$2,200
TARENNE, Roger	*P*	$358	$537	$715
(20th -)				
TARTAR, E.	*S*			$165
American (20th -)				
TASCA, Luigi (Attrib.)	*D*			$1,045
Italian (18th - 19th)				
TASHA, Carl	*S*			$660
American (20th -)				
TASKER, William (Attrib.)	*P*			$11,000
British (1805 - 1852)				
TASSI, Agostino	*P*			$4,400
Italian (1565 - 1644)				
TASSI, Agostino (Attrib.)	*D*			$1,650
Italian (1565 - 1644)	*P*			$5,500
TATE, Gayle B.	*P*	$1,760	$2,933	$3,740
American (1944 -)				
TATKA, L.	*P*			$110
British (19th - 20th)				

D=Drawing, P=Painting, S=Sculpture, W=Watercolor

		Current Price Range		
		Low	Mean	High

		Low	Mean	High
TAUBERT, Bertoldo	*P*			$770
French (1915 -)				
TAUBES, Frederick	*P*	$165	$1,452	$3,740
American (1900 - 1981)				
TAUBMAN, Frank M.	*P*			$1,155
British (1868 -)				
TAUNAY, Nicolas A.	*P*	$6,600	$14,300	$22,000
French (1755 - 1830)				
TAUNAY, Nicolas A. (School)	*P*			$1,650
French (1755 - 1830)				
TAUSZKY, David A.	*P*	$248	$317	$385
American (1878 - 1972)				
TAVELLA, Carlo A.	*P*			$10,450
Italian (1668 - 1738)				
TAVELLA, Carlo A. (Circle)	*P*			$1,760
Italian (1668 - 1738)				
TAVERNIER, Jules	*P*	$7,700	$43,817	$66,000
American (1844 - 1889)				
TAVERNIER, Paul	*P*			$990
French (1852 -)				
TAYLER, Albert C.	*P*	$330	$9,515	$18,700
British (1862 - 1925)				
TAYLOR,	*P*			$825
American (20th -)				
TAYLOR,	*P*			$1,155
British (19th -)				
TAYLOR, Charles J.	*D*			$220
American (1855 - 1929)				
TAYLOR, E. L.	*W*			$500
(20th -)				
TAYLOR, Edward R.	*P*			$8,800
British (1838 - 1911)				
TAYLOR, Frank	*W*			$110
American (1846 -)				
TAYLOR, Frank W.	*P*			$880
American (1874 - 1921)				

D=Drawing, P=Painting, S=Sculpture, W=Watercolor

		Current Price Range		
		Low	Mean	High

		Low	Mean	High
TAYLOR, H. W.	*P*			$110
American (?)				
TAYLOR, Henry F.	*P*			$248
American (1853 - 1925)				
TAYLOR, James	*P*			$1,540
American (20th -)				
TAYLOR, Jay C.	*P*	$440	$454	$468
American (19th - 20th)				
TAYLOR, John	*P*			$5,500
(20th -)				
TAYLOR, John	*P*			$1,540
American (20th -)				
TAYLOR, Loretta	*W*			$275
American (20th -)				
TAYLOR, Marie	*S*			$2,200
American (1904 -)				
TAYLOR, Ralph	*P*			$880
American (1897 -)				
TAYLOR, Rolla	*P*			$440
American (20th -)				
TAYLOR, Walter	*D*			$286
American (1894 -)				
TAYLOR, Will S.	*P*	$193	$423	$653
American (1882 -)				
TCHELITCHEW, Pavel	*D*	$440	$2,232	$6,600
American (1898 - 1957)	*P*	$4,950	$11,943	$17,600
	S			$2,640
	W	$495	$6,480	$34,100
TCHERIKOVA, Ludmilla	*W*			$1,100
Russian (?)				
TEAGUE, Donald	*P*			$7,150
American (1897 -)	*W*	$2,475	$10,269	$27,500
TEAL, Raymond	*W*			$825
American (20th -)				

D=Drawing, P=Painting, S=Sculpture, W=Watercolor

		Current Price Range		
		Low	Mean	High
TEED, Douglas A.	*P*	$880	$1,716	$2,970
American (1864 - 1929)				
TEEL, Lewis W.	*P*			$935
American (1883 -)				
TEIGEN, Peter	*W*			$1,650
American (20th -)				
TEIXLER, Dr. A. M.	*P*	$143	$215	$286
(20th -)				
TELARICK, A.	*P*			$660
(?)				
TELES, JR., Jose J.	*P*			$13,750
Brazilian (1851 - 1908)				
TELSIC, A.	*P*			$2,200
(?)				
TEMPEL, Abraham van (Attrib.)	*P*			$45,100
Dutch (1622 - 1672)				
TEMPEST, Cyril	*P*	$990	$1,265	$1,540
British (19th - 20th)				
TEMPESTA, Antonio	*D*			$2,640
Italian (1555 - 1630)				
TEMPESTA, Antonio (Attrib.)	*D*			$2,420
Italian (1555 - 1630)				
TEMPLE, Ruth A.	*P*	$660	$2,695	$6,600
American (1884 - 1939)				
TEN CATE, Hendrik G.	*W*			$990
Dutch (1803 - 1856)				
TEN KATE, Herman	*P*	$1,980	$9,790	$17,600
Dutch (1822 - 1891)	*W*			$1,320
TEN KATE, Johan M. H.	*P*			$3,300
Dutch (1831 - 1910)	*W*	$3,520	$6,435	$9,350
TENIERS, David	*P*	$5,225	$81,503	$231,000
Flemish (1610 - 1690)				
TENIERS, David (After)	*P*			$2,475
Flemish (1610 - 1690)	*W*			$440

D=Drawing, P=Painting, S=Sculpture, W=Watercolor

		Current Price Range		
		Low	Mean	High
TENIERS, David (Attrib.)	P	$330	$1,540	$2,750
Flemish (1610 - 1690)				
TENIERS, David (Circle)	P	$6,600	$7,425	$8,250
Flemish (1610 - 1690)				
TENIERS, David (Follower)	P	$2,475	$4,606	$7,700
Flemish (1610 - 1690)				
TENIERS, David (Manner)	P	$330	$1,794	$4,675
Flemish (1610 - 1690)				
TENIERS, David (School)	P	$990	$3,520	$8,800
Flemish (1610 - 1690)				
TENIERS, David (Style)	P	$330	$344	$358
Flemish (1610 - 1690)				
TENIERS, ELDER, David (After)	P			$5,500
Flemish (1582 - 1649)				
TENIERS, ELDER, David (Attrib.)	P			$3,850
Flemish (1582 - 1649)				
TENRE, Charles H.	P	$2,200	$4,620	$9,460
French (1864 - 1926)				
TEPPER, Irv	S			$1,650
(20th -)				
TEPPER, Saul	P	$220	$3,080	$5,170
American (1899 - 1987)				
TERBORCH, Gerard (Attrib.)	D			$2,640
Dutch (1617 - 1681)				
TERBORCH, Gerard (Circle)	P			$5,500
Dutch (1617 - 1681)				
TERBORCH, Gerard (Follower)	P			$24,200
Dutch (1617 - 1681)				
TERBORCH, Gerard (School)	P			$19,800
Dutch (1617 - 1681)				
TERBRUGGHEN, Hendrick (Foll)	P			$4,960
Dutch (1587 - 1629)				
TERECHKOVITCH, Kostia	P	$4,070	$24,732	$66,000
French (1902 - 1978)	W	$2,640	$2,695	$2,750
TERELAK, John C.	P	$248	$349	$523
American (20th -)				

D=Drawing, P=Painting, S=Sculpture, W=Watercolor

		Current Price Range		
		Low	Mean	High

		Low	Mean	High
TERESCZUK, Peter	S			$220
European (19th - 20th)				
TERESZCZUK, F.	S			$2,530
Austrian (19th - 20th)				
TERKEN, John	S			$330
(20th -)				
TERKLIKOWSKI, Vladimir de	P			$1,375
Polish (1873 - 1951)				
TERNI, A. L.	P			$275
Italian (19th - 20th)				
TERPNING, Howard A.	P	$17,600	$25,300	$33,000
American (1927 -)				
TERRELL, Allen	P			$1,100
American (1897 -)				
TERRY, Luther (Et al.)	D			$605
American (19th - 20th)				
TERUEL, Augustian S.	P			$2,475
Spanish (1871 -)				
TERUZ, Orlando	P			$26,400
Brazilian (1902 - 1984)				
TESSARI, Vittorio	P			$143
Italian (1860 -)	W			$193
TESSIER, Adam (Et al.)	S			$7,150
Spanish (1910 -)				
TESSIER, Louis	P			$6,600
French (1719 - 1781)				
TESSIER, Louis (Attrib.)	P			$71,500
French (1719 - 1781)				
TESSON, Louis	P			$4,950
French (1816 - 1872)	W			$352
TESTA, Pietro	D	$5,500	$14,667	$29,700
Italian (1611 - 1650)				
TESTA, Pietro (Attrib.)	D			$11,000
Italian (1611 - 1650)				

D=Drawing, P=Painting, S=Sculpture, W=Watercolor

| | | Current Price Range | | |
		Low	Mean	High
TESTA, Pietro (Circle)	D			$1,540
Italian (1611 - 1650)				
TESTU, Paul	P	$468	$1,751	$4,180
French (19th - 20th)				
TETES, Sister Mary Chris	D			$413
French (19th -)				
TEUBER, Hermann	P			$2,640
(20th -)				
TEUFEL, Ernst Baron von	P			$440
German (19th - 20th)				
TEYRAL, Austin	P			$110
(?)				
TEYRAL, Hazel	P	$440	$688	$935
American (1918 -)				
TEYRAL, John	P			$220
American (20th -)				
THACKERAY, William M.	D			$275
British (1811 - 1863)				
THAL, Sam	D			$495
American (1903 - 1964)				
THALEN, Wilhelm	P			$303
(?)				
THALINGER, E. Oscar	P	$110	$358	$1,100
American (1885 - 1965)				
THAULOW, Frits	P	$4,400	$43,450	$101,200
Norwegian (1847 - 1906)	W			$3,150
THAXTER, Edward R.	S	$4,400	$4,400	$4,400
American (1857 - 1881)				
THAYER, Abbott H.	P	$605	$11,261	$39,600
American (1849 - 1921)				
THAYER, Abbott H. (Attrib.)	P			$660
American (1849 - 1921)				
THAYER, Albert R.	P			$1,210
American (19th - 20th)				
THAYER, E. T.	S			$550
(?)				

D=Drawing, P=Painting, S=Sculpture, W=Watercolor

		Current Price Range		
		Low	Mean	High
THAYER, Karen	P	$2,310	$2,555	$2,800
American (20th -)				
THAYER, V.	S			$605
(?)				
THEK, Paul	P			$8,800
American (1933 -)				
THEMMEN, C.	P	$1,925	$2,613	$3,300
German (19th -)				
THEMMEN, Charles	P	$550	$1,100	$1,650
American (19th -)				
THEOBOLD, JR., Samuel	P	$350	$840	$1,320
American (1872 -)				
THERKILDSEN, Michael	P			$6,600
Danish (1850 - 1925)				
THEROUX, Carol	D	$330	$443	$500
American (20th -)				
THERRIEN, Robert	P	$7,700	$19,250	$30,800
(20th -)				
THEUERKAUF, Christian	W			$231
Alsatian (1831 - 1911)				
THEUERKOFF, Carl R.	P			$495
American (1875 - 1926)				
THEUNISSON, Corneille (After)	S			$935
Dutch (1553 -)				
THIBAULT, Pierre	W	$165	$193	$220
(?)				
THIBON, Jean	P			$550
(?)				
THIEBAUD, Wayne	D	$2,420	$33,132	$143,000
American (1920 -)	P	$17,600	$247,622	$495,000
	W			$44,000
THIEBAULT, Henri L.	P			$5,500
French (1855 -)				
THIEBLIN, Reine J.	P	$3,575	$5,638	$7,700
French (19th - 20th)				

D=Drawing, P=Painting, S=Sculpture, W=Watercolor

| | | Current Price Range | | |
		Low	Mean	High
THIELE, Hans (Attrib.)	*P*			$3,850
Austrian (1850 -)				
THIELE, Leo E.	*P*			$303
American (20th -)				
THIELENS, Gaspard	*P*			$74,250
Flemish (17th -)				
THIEM, Herman C.	*P*			$138
American (1870 -)				
THIEME, Anthony	*D*			$2,475
American (1888 - 1954)	*P*	$468	$5,435	$26,400
	W	$1,045	$1,549	$2,530
THIERRIAT, Augustin A.	*W*			$1,760
French (1789 - 1870)				
THINSEN, C.	*P*			$1,540
(?)				
THIRION, Victor C.	*P*	$5,500	$11,092	$19,800
French (1833 - 1878)				
THOLANDER, August	*P*			$715
Swedish (1835 - 1910)				
THOM, J.	*P*			$1,760
British (19th -)				
THOM, James C.	*P*	$440	$1,494	$3,520
American (1842 - 1898)				
THOM, James C.	*P*			$440
British (1785 -)				
THOMA, Hans	*P*			$19,800
German (1839 - 1924)	*W*			$2,200
THOMAS, Alain	*P*			$358
(?)				
THOMAS, Barry	*P*			$4,300
American (1961 -)				
THOMAS, G.	*P*			$1,265
British (19th -)				
THOMAS, Gilbert	*W*			$248
French (20th -)				

D=Drawing, P=Painting, S=Sculpture, W=Watercolor

		Current Price Range		
		Low	Mean	High

		Low	Mean	High
THOMAS, J.	*P*			$440
American (19th -)				
THOMAS, Lloyd S.	*P*			$2,090
American (?)				
THOMAS, Norman	*W*			$220
American (1915 -)				
THOMAS, P.	*P*			$880
British (19th -)				
THOMAS, Pat	*P*			$990
American (20th -)				
THOMAS, Paul K. M.	*S*			$1,320
American (1875 -)				
THOMAS, Reynolds	*W*			$660
American (1927 -)				
THOMAS, Stephen S.	*P*	$165	$645	$1,100
American (1868 - 1956)				
THOMASON, Jim	*W*			$700
American (20th -)				
THOMASSE, Adolphe	*P*			$1,980
French (1850 - 1930)				
THOMASSIN, Desire	*P*	$3,850	$6,142	$7,700
Austrian (1858 - 1933)				
THOMM,	*P*			$176
(?)				
THOMPKINS, F. H.	*P*			$110
(?)				
THOMPSON, Albert	*P*			$798
American (1853 -)				
THOMPSON, Alfred	*P*	$2,475	$13,509	$44,000
American (1840 - 1896)				
THOMPSON, Alfred (Attrib.)	*P*			$495
American (1840 - 1896)				
THOMPSON, Bob	*P*	$3,520	$4,400	$5,280
American (1936 - 1966)				
THOMPSON, C. L.	*P*	$220	$440	$660
American (19th -)				

D=Drawing, P=Painting, S=Sculpture, W=Watercolor

		Current Price Range	
	Low	Mean	High

THOMPSON, Cephas G. American (1809 - 1888)	*P*			$990
THOMPSON, Frederick L. American (1868 -)	*P*	$303	$605	$1,100
THOMPSON, G. American (20th -)	*W*			$220
THOMPSON, G. British (19th -)	*P* *W*	$275	$317	$358 $413
THOMPSON, George A. American (1868 - 1938)	*P*	$165	$605	$880
THOMPSON, Guy H. American (19th - 20th)	*P*			$880
THOMPSON, J. Leslie European (19th - 20th)	*P*			$2,200
THOMPSON, Jerome American (1814 - 1886)	*P*	$18,700	$20,350	$22,000
THOMPSON, Jerome (Attrib.) American (1814 - 1886)	*P*			$1,870
THOMPSON, John S. British (19th - 20th)	*P*			$880
THOMPSON, Leslie P. American (1880 - 1963)	*P*	$468	$2,269	$4,070
THOMPSON, Malcolm American (1901 -)	*P*	$193	$289	$385
THOMPSON, Marvin F. American (1895 -)	*P*			$358
THOMPSON, Virgil (?)	*D*			$770
THOMPSON, Walter W. American (1881 - 1945)	*P*	$275	$358	$440
THOMPSON, William John British (1771 - 1845)	*P*			$248
THOMPSON, Wordsworth American (?)	*P*			$26,400
THOMSEN, Carl C. Danish (1847 - 1912)	*P*			$15,400

D=Drawing, P=Painting, S=Sculpture, W=Watercolor

		Current Price Range		
		Low	Mean	High

		Low	Mean	High
THOMSON, Chandler British (20th -)	W			$413
THOMSON, Henry G. American (1850 - 1937)	P	$4,675	$9,488	$14,300
THOMSON, W. Taylor (?)	W			$770
THORBURN, Archibald British (1860 - 1935)	W	$20,900	$34,100	$47,300
THOREN, Otto von Austrian (1828 - 1889)	P			$4,400
THOREN, Van (?)	P			$132
THORENFELD, Anton E. C. Danish (1839 - 1907)	P			$17,600
THORNAM, Emmy M. C. Danish (1852 - 1935)	P			$1,430
THORNDIKE, C. A. American (?)	P			$3,960
THORNE, Diana American (1895 -)	P	$319	$875	$1,430
THORNE-WAITE, Robert British (1842 - 1935)	W			$220
THORNHILL, James (Attrib.) British (1676 - 1734)	P			$2,750
THORNLEY, G. W. (?)	P			$1,100
THORNTON, Alfred H. R. British (1863 - 1939)	W			$303
THORNTON, R. British (20th -)	W			$715
THORPE, American (19th -)	P			$165
THORS, Joseph British (19th -)	P	$660	$3,311	$9,350
THORTON, Thomas H. European (19th - 20th)	P			$825

D=Drawing, P=Painting, S=Sculpture, W=Watercolor

		Current Price Range		
		Low	Mean	High

		Low	Mean	High
THRASH, Dox American (1892 - 1965)	W			$440
THRASHER, Leslie American (1889 - 1936)	P			$3,600
THULDEN, Theodor van Dutch (1606 - 1669)	P			$49,500
THULSTRUP, Thure de American (1848 - 1930)	D			$1,540
	W	$275	$313	$350
THURBER, James American (1894 - 1961)	D			$1,870
THWAITES, Charles American (20th -)	P			$550
THYSEN, Carolus J. Dutch (1867 -)	P			$1,980
TIARINI, Alessandro Italian (1577 - 1668)	D			$55,000
TIBALDI, Pellegrino (Et al.) Italian (15th - 16th)	W			$4,125
TIECHMAN, Sabina American (20th -)	P			$440
TIEDEMANN, Berthold (1916 -)	D			$165
	P			$440
TIELENS, Alexandre Belgian (1868 - 1959)	P			$1,210
TIEPOLO, Giovanni B. Italian (1696 - 1770)	D	$7,700	$26,053	$126,500
	P			$71,500
	W			$22,000
TIEPOLO, Giovanni B. (Circle) Italian (1696 - 1770)	D			$3,025
TIEPOLO, Giovanni B. (Follower) Italian (1696 - 1770)	P			$13,750
TIEPOLO, Giovanni B. (Manner) Italian (1696 - 1770)	D			$248

D=Drawing, P=Painting, S=Sculpture, W=Watercolor

		Current Price Range		
		Low	Mean	High

TIEPOLO, Giovanni D.	*D*	$9,075	$22,354	$82,500
Italian (1727 - 1804)				
TIFFANY, Louis C.	*D*	$330	$440	$550
American (1848 - 1933)	*P*	$1,650	$7,700	$11,000
	W	$1,210	$2,651	$4,675
TIGLIO, M.	*P*			$495
Argentina (20th -)				
TILBORCH, Gillis van	*P*	$38,500	$74,250	$110,000
Flemish (1625 - 1678)				
TILBORCH, Gillis van (Manner)	*P*	$8,250	$10,175	$12,100
Flemish (1625 - 1678)				
TILCHE, H. O.	*W*			$990
(?)				
TILGNER, Victor O.	*S*			$1,320
Austrian (1844 - 1896)				
TILLY, Vilhelm	*P*			$138
Danish (1860 - 1935)				
TILOT, H.	*P*			$495
French (19th - 20th)				
TILTON, John R.	*P*			$3,300
American (1828 - 1888)				
TILTON, John R. (Attrib.)	*P*			$110
American (1828 - 1888)				
TIMEN, F.	*P*			$220
French (19th - 20th)				
TIMKE, Frieda	*P*			$150
(20th -)				
TIMMINS, Harry L.	*W*			$413
American (1887 - 1963)				
TIMMONS, Edward J.	*P*	$330	$543	$880
American (1882 - 1960)				
TIMOCK, George	*S*			$1,100
(20th -)				
TING, Walasse	*P*	$3,520	$6,820	$10,120
Chinese (1929 -)				

D=Drawing, P=Painting, S=Sculpture, W=Watercolor

		Current Price Range		
		Low	Mean	High
TINGUELY, Jean	P	$132,000	$161,333	$198,000
Swiss (1925 -)	S	$4,180	$4,840	$5,500
TINKLEMAN, Murray	D			$100
(1933 -)				
TINTORE, Simone del (Attrib.)	P			$28,600
Italian (17th -)				
TINTORE, Simone del (Manner)	P			$44,000
Italian (17th -)				
TINTORETTO, Domenico R.	D			$11,000
Italian (1560 - 1635)				
TINTORETTO, Il (Follower)	P			$825
Italian (18th -)				
TINTORETTO, Jacopo R.	D			$25,300
Italian (1518 - 1594)	P	$8,800	$53,900	$99,000
TINTORETTO, Jacopo R. (After)	P	$1,210	$1,540	$1,870
Italian (1518 - 1594)				
TINTORETTO, Jacopo R. (Attrib.)	P			$66,000
Italian (1518 - 1594)				
TINTORETTO, Jacopo R. (Foll.)	P	$2,200	$4,767	$9,350
Italian (1518 - 1594)				
TIPPETTS, Linda	P			$1,150
American (20th -)				
TIRATELLI, Aurelio	P			$6,600
Italian (1842 - 1900)				
TIRELLI, Umberto	D			$2,310
(20th -)				
TIRONI, Francesco	P			$60,500
Italian (? - 1800)				
TIRONI, Francesco (Circle)	P	$9,900	$10,450	$11,000
Italian (? - 1800)				
TIRONI, Francesco (Follower)	P			$5,500
Italian (? - 1800)				
TISHBEIN, Johann (Circle)	P			$3,080
(1750 - 1812)				

D=Drawing, P=Painting, S=Sculpture, W=Watercolor

		Current Price Range		
		Low	Mean	High

		Low	Mean	High
TISI, Benvenuto	*P*			$126,500
Italian (1481 - 1559)				
TISSOT, James J. J.	*D*	$16,500	$558,250	$1.100M
French (1836 - 1902)	*P*	$198,000	$514,250	$1.375M
	W	$5,775	$104,555	$198,000
TISSOT, James J. J. (Follower)	*P*			$4,950
French (1836 - 1902)				
TISSOT, James J. J. (School)	*P*			$3,520
French (1836 - 1902)				
TITCOMB, Mary B.	*D*			$1,650
American (1856 - 1927)	*P*	$7,700	$19,983	$33,000
	W	$550	$1,173	$1,870
TITI, Tiberio	*P*			$18,700
Italian (1573 - 1627)				
TITIAN,	*P*			$2.640M
Italian (1477 - 1576)				
TITIAN, (After)	*P*	$165	$3,513	$9,900
Italian (1477 - 1576)				
TITIAN, (Circle)	*P*			$82,500
Italian (1477 - 1576)				
TITIAN, (Follower)	*P*			$3,575
Italian (1477 - 1576)				
TITIAN, (Studio)	*P*			$9,350
Italian (1477 - 1576)				
TITLE, Christian	*P*	$3,080	$3,190	$3,300
American (20th -)				
TITO, Ettore (Attrib.)	*P*			$28,600
Italian (1859 - 1941)				
TITO, Santi di	*P*			$187,000
Italian (1536 - 1603)				
TITTLE, Walter E.	*P*	$440	$1,160	$2,200
American (1883 - 1966)	*W*			$385
TOBAR, Alonso M. de	*P*			$3,850
Spanish (1678 - 1758)				

D=Drawing, P=Painting, S=Sculpture, W=Watercolor

		Current Price Range		
		Low	Mean	High
TOBEY, Mark	D	$1,100	$28,050	$55,000
American (1890 - 1976)	P	$770	$22,173	$68,750
	W	$1,980	$23,816	$55,000
TOBIASSE, Theo	P	$2,090	$19,234	$41,800
Israeli (1927 -)	S			$13,200
	W	$9,350	$9,900	$10,450
TOBIN, George T.	D			$550
American (1864 - 1956)				
TOBUENA, Romeo V.	P			$770
Mexican (20th -)				
TOCQUE, Louis	P			$20,900
French (1696 - 1772)				
TODAHL, John O.	P	$275	$289	$303
American (1884 -)				
TODD, Henry G.	P			$8,800
British (1847 - 1898)				
TODESCHINI, Giacomo F.	P			$3,300
Italian (17th - 18th)				
TODESCHINI, Giacomo F. (Attrib.)	P			$14,300
Italian (17th - 18th)				
TODHUNTER, Francis A.	P			$550
American (1884 - 1963)	W	$660	$1,100	$1,540
TODHUNTER, Norman	W			$550
American (20th -)				
TOECHE, Carl J. F.	P			$2,420
German (1814 - 1890)				
TOEPUT, Lodewijk (Attrib.)	D			$1,760
Flemish (1550 - 1610)				
TOESCHI, G.	P			$3,300
European (19th - 20th)				
TOFELER, C.	P			$275
(19th -)				
TOFT, Peter	W			$110
British (1825 - 1901)				

D=Drawing, P=Painting, S=Sculpture, W=Watercolor

		Current Price Range		
		Low	Mean	High
TOJETTI, Domenico	*P*	$770	$3,685	$6,600
American (1806 - 1892)				
TOJETTI, Eduardo	*P*	$1,045	$1,623	$2,200
American (1852 - 1930)				
TOJETTI, Virgilio	*P*	$880	$7,381	$14,300
Italian (1851 - 1901)				
TOLEDO, Francisco	*D*	$5,500	$12,742	$25,300
Mexican (1940 -)	*P*	$5,500	$48,000	$308,000
	S			$30,800
	W	$1,320	$10,626	$57,750
TOLGYESSY, Artur	*P*			$1,650
Hungarian (1823 - 1920)				
TOLLEY, Edward	*P*			$3,190
British (19th -)				
TOLMAN, Stacy	*D*	$165	$263	$375
American (1860 - 1935)	*P*	$275	$490	$770
	W	$138	$431	$935
TOM, Jan Bedys	*W*			$825
Dutch (1813 - 1894)				
TOM OF FINLAND,	*D*	$2,200	$3,227	$4,400
(20th -)				
TOMANEK, Joseph	*P*	$242	$794	$1,650
American (1889 -)				
TOMASO, Rico	*P*			$3,000
American (1898 -)				
TOMBA, Casimiro	*W*			$2,200
Italian (1857 - 1929)				
TOMBROS, Michael	*S*			$1,100
(?)				
TOMBU, Leon	*P*			$550
Belgian (1866 - 1958)				
TOMINZ, Alfredo	*P*			$8,800
Italian (1854 - 1936)				

D=Drawing, P=Painting, S=Sculpture, W=Watercolor

| | | Current Price Range | | |
		Low	Mean	High
TOMIOKA, Saichiko	P			$1,100
Japanese (20th -)				
TOMLIN, Bradley W.	P	$3,300	$196,075	$572,000
American (1899 - 1953)				
TOMLINSON, Lorena	W			$6,600
American (19th -)				
TOMLINSON, R.	P			$3,080
(?)				
TOMMASI, Publio de	W			$3,080
Italian (1849 -)				
TOMMASO,	P			$7,700
(15th -)				
TOMMI, Alberto	P	$110	$138	$165
American (20th -)				
TOMPKINS, Frank H.	P	$600	$2,378	$7,700
American (1847 - 1922)				
TONER, Thomas	P	$110	$330	$550
American (1941 -)				
TONEY, Anthony	P			$165
American (1913 -)				
TONGE, Lammert van der	P	$2,420	$3,758	$4,675
French (1871 - 1937)				
TONGIANI, V.	P			$2,200
European (19th - 20th)				
TONSBERG, Gertrude	P	$880	$1,925	$3,575
American (20th -)				
TOOKER, George	D			$20,900
American (1920 -)	P	$28,600	$247,720	$396,000
TOOR, Nishan	P			$165
American (1888 -)				
TOORENVLIET, Jacob	P			$44,000
Dutch (1635 - 1719)				
TOORENVLIET, Jacob (Attrib.)	D			$1,540
Dutch (1635 - 1719)				
TOPANELIAN, Fanny N.	W			$275
American (20th -)				

D=Drawing, P=Painting, S=Sculpture, W=Watercolor

		Current Price Range		
		Low	Mean	High

TOPHAM, Frank W. W.	*P*	$2,530	$9,277	$19,800
British (1838 - 1924)				
TOPHAM, J.	*P*			$935
British (19th -)				
TOPOR, Roland	*W*			$990
French (20th -)				
TOPPING, James	*P*	$605	$880	$1,155
British (1879 - 1949)				
TORAN, A. T.	*P*			$275
American (20th -)				
TORBIDO, Francesco (Attrib.)	*D*			$15,400
Italian (1482 - 1562)				
TORDI, Sinibaldo	*P*	$1,650	$4,593	$11,000
Italian (1876 - 1955)				
TORDOFF, Fred	*P*	$193	$317	$440
American (20th -)	*W*	$176	$185	$193
TORETTI, P.	*P*			$220
Italian (19th -)				
TORGERSON, William	*P*			$22,000
American (19th -)				
TORLAKSON, James	*W*			$1,760
American (1951 -)				
TORMA, Karoly	*P*			$550
Hungarian (19th -)				
TORO, Atillio	*P*	$1,430	$1,925	$2,420
Italian (1892 -)				
TORRALBA, Master	*P*			$26,400
Mexican (?)				
TORRE, Giulio del	*P*			$6,600
Italian (1856 - 1932)				
TORRE, M. N. F. de la	*P*			$20,900
Spanish (1888 - 1938)				
TORREANO, John	*P*	$1,100	$3,355	$5,060
American (20th -)	*S*	$3,960	$5,170	$6,600

D=Drawing, P=Painting, S=Sculpture, W=Watercolor

		Current Price Range		
		Low	Mean	High
TORRENS, Monserrat Spanish (1933 -)	P			$303
TORRES, Horatio American (20th -)	P	$55,000	$57,750	$60,500
TORRES-GARCIA, Joaquin Uruguayan (1874 - 1949)	D	$6,600	$8,525	$11,000
	P	$24,200	$80,000	$187,000
	S			$4,620
	W	$18,700	$20,350	$22,000
TORREY, Elliot American (1867 - 1949)	P	$193	$1,210	$3,025
	W			$880
TORRIGLIA, Giovanni B. Italian (1858 -)	P			$7,150
TORRINI, Pietro Italian (1852 -)	P			$12,100
TORSLEFF, August Danish (1884 - 1968)	P			$4,950
TORSSLOW, Einar Swedish (19th - 20th)	W			$248
TOSCANI, Giovanni di F. Italian (? - 1430)	P			$77,000
TOSI, Italian (20th -)	P			$550
TOSINI, Michele Italian (1503 - 1577)	P	$6,930	$17,893	$30,250
TOSINI, Michele (Follower) Italian (1503 - 1577)	P			$8,800
TOSINI, Michele (School) Italian (1503 - 1577)	P			$2,200
TOTH, A. (?)	P			$165
TOTI, Lewis C. American (20th -)	P			$110
TOUCHE, Gaston de la French (1854 - 1913)	P			$660

D=Drawing, P=Painting, S=Sculpture, W=Watercolor

		Current Price Range		
		Low	Mean	High

TOUDOUZE, Edward French (1848 - 1907)	*P*	$3,850	$11,550	$20,900
TOULMOUCHE, Auguste French (1829 - 1890)	*P*	$11,000	$25,300	$41,800
TOULOUSE-LAUTREC, Henri de French (1864 - 1901)	*D*	$1,650	$16,496	$49,500
	P	$3,300	$2.792M	$12.980M
	W	$17,600	$1.527M	$3.080M
TOURNACHON, Gaspard F. European (19th -)	*D*			$5,500
TOURNIER, A. (?)	*P*			$121
TOURNOVA, Natasha Russian (1957 -)	*P*			$2,860
TOUSS, Herb American (1929 -)	*P*			$165
TOUSSAINT, Fernand French (1873 - 1955)	*P*	$5,500	$6,875	$8,250
TOUSSAINT, Louis German (1826 -)	*P*			$990
TOUSSAINT, Pierre J. Belgian (1822 - 1888)	*P*			$7,700
TOUTENEL, Lodewuk J. P. Belgian (1819 - 1883)	*P*			$3,300
TOVAR, H. Burston American (20th -)	*D*			$523
TOVAR, Ivan Dom. Rep. (1942 -)	*P*	$7,150	$8,250	$9,350
TOWNE, Charles British (1781 - 1854)	*P*	$10,450	$10,817	$11,000
TOWNSEND, Diane (20th -)	*D*			$5,500
TOWNSEND, Harry American (1879 - 1941)	*P*			$440
TOWNSEND, Lee	*P*			$330

D=Drawing, P=Painting, S=Sculpture, W=Watercolor

		Current Price Range		
		Low	Mean	High

TOWNSEND, Lee American (1895 - 1965)	W			$605
TOWNSHEND, James British (19th - 20th)	W			$385
TOWNSLEY, Channel P. American (1867 - 1921)	P			$1,900
TRACY, (Attributed) (?)	P			$121
TRACY, John M. American (1844 - 1893)	P	$1,100	$12,650	$27,500
TRAFELI, M. (?)	S			$1,430
TRAIES, William (Attrib.) British (1789 - 1872)	P			$935
TRAMKA, European (20th -)	P			$743
TRAVER, George A. American (1864 - 1928)	D P	$495	$660	$495 $825
TRAVERSE, Charles de la (Attrib.) (1726 - 1780)	D			$3,300
TRAVIS, Olin H. American (1888 -)	P			$385
TRAVIS, Paul B. American (1891 -)	W			$275
TRAYER, Jules French (1824 - 1908)	P	$7,700	$9,900	$12,100
TRAYNER, John C. American (20th -)	P			$1,430
TRE, Howard B. (?)	S			$5,500
TREBILCOCK, Paul American (1902 - 1981)	P			$1,540
TREDUPP, Charles F. F. A. American (1864 - 1936)	P			$300
TREFETHEN, Jessie B. (19th - 20th)	P			$770

D=Drawing, P=Painting, S=Sculpture, W=Watercolor

| | | Current Price Range | |
	Low	Mean	High
TREIMAN, Joyce *P*			$935
American (1922 -)			
TREMBATH, James *W*			$1,210
American (?)			
TRENHOLM, William C. *P*			$11,000
American (1856 - 1931)			
TRENK, F. *W*			$275
American (20th -)			
TREPICCION, A. *P*			$385
British (?)			
TREUX, Van D. *D*	$660	$1,045	$1,430
European (20th -)			
TREVISANI, Francesco *D*			$1,430
Italian (1656 - 1746) *P*			$18,700
TREVISANI, Francesco (Follower) *P*			$3,850
Italian (1656 - 1746)			
TREVOR, Jean P. *P*			$550
French (20th -)			
TRIBE, George T. *W*			$523
American (19th - 20th)			
TRIBOULET, *S*			$1,320
(?)			
TRICKER, Florence *P*			$440
American (20th -)			
TRIGGS, Floyd W. *P*			$330
American (1872 - 1919)			
TRINQUESSE, Louis R. (Attrib.) *P*			$22,000
French (1746 - 1800)			
TRIPET, Alfred *P*			$16,500
French (19th -)			
TRIRUM, Johannes W. van *P*			$825
Dutch (1924 -)			
TRISCOTT, Samuel *W*	$275	$660	$1,430
American (1846 - 1925)			
TROEKES, Heinz *W*			$1,650
(20th -)			

D=Drawing, P=Painting, S=Sculpture, W=Watercolor

		Current Price Range		
		Low	Mean	High

		Low	Mean	High
TROMP, Jan Z.	P	$16,500	$32,010	$52,250
Dutch (1872 - 1947)				
TROMPIZ, Virgilio	P			$13,200
Venezuelan (20th - 1972)				
TROOST, Cornelis (Circle)	P			$18,700
Dutch (1697 - 1750)				
TROPP, P.	P			$880
American (20th -)				
TROPPA, Girolamo	P			$37,400
Italian (17th -)				
TROSSARELLI, Gaspare	P			$990
Italian (1763 - 1825)				
TROTTER, Newbold H.	P	$1,045	$2,823	$4,950
American (1827 - 1898)				
TROUBETZKOY, Paul	P	$1,980	$4,290	$8,800
American (1866 - 1938)	S	$3,300	$10,796	$18,700
TROUBETZKOY, Paul (After)	S			$2,200
American (1866 - 1938)				
TROUILLEBERT, Paul D.	P	$6,600	$16,050	$29,700
French (1829 - 1900)				
TROUILLEBERT, Paul D. (Mann.)	P			$660
French (1829 - 1900)				
TROVA, Ernest	D			$550
American (1929 -)	P	$990	$2,049	$3,520
	S	$770	$14,347	$110,000
TROWBRIDGE, Sherman	W			$138
(?)				
TROY, C	P			$358
French (18th - 19th)				
TROY, Jean-F. de	D			$7,700
French (1679 - 1752)	P	$7,700	$78,925	$132,000
TROYA, Rafael	P			$4,400
Lat. Amer. (19th -)				

D=Drawing, P=Painting, S=Sculpture, W=Watercolor

		Current Price Range		
		Low	Mean	High

		Low	Mean	High
TROYE, Edward	P	$6,050	$16,940	$33,000
American (1808 - 1874)				
TROYON, Constant	P	$935	$28,985	$110,000
French (1810 - 1865)	W			$770
TRUCHET, Abel	P	$3,190	$5,372	$9,350
French (1857 - 1918)				
TRUE, David	D	$1,100	$1,155	$1,210
American (1942 -)	P	$12,100	$13,200	$14,300
	S			$2,420
TRUESDELL, Gaylord S.	P			$3,520
American (1850 - 1899)				
TRUFFAUT, Georges	P			$660
French (19th -)				
TRUIJEN, Johannes P. F.	P			$880
Dutch (1928 -)				
TRUITT, William H.	P			$193
American (?)				
TRUJILLO, Guillermo	P			$1,760
Lat. Amer. (20th -)				
TRUMBALL, Edward	P	$825	$1,128	$1,430
American (20th -)				
TRUMP, Petronella	P			$1,870
Dutch (19th - 20th)				
TRUPHEME, Auguste J.	P	$22,000	$24,200	$26,400
French (1836 - 1898)				
TRYON, Benjamin F.	P			$770
American (1824 -)				
TRYON, Dwight W.	P	$4,400	$16,844	$55,000
American (1849 - 1925)				
TSCHACBASOV, Nahum	P	$825	$935	$1,210
(1899 -)				
TSCHAGGENY, Charles P.	P	$825	$3,163	$5,500
Belgian (1815 - 1894)				
TSCHAGGENY, Edmond J. B.	P			$16,500
Belgian (1818 - 1873)				

D=Drawing, P=Painting, S=Sculpture, W=Watercolor

		Current Price Range		
		Low	Mean	High
TSCHAPLOWITZ, E.	*P*	$154	$174	$193
German (19th - 20th)				
TSCHOPP, Stanley D.	*P*			$385
American (20th -)				
TSCHUDI, R.	*P*			$495
(?)				
TSCHUDY, Herbert B.	*W*			$330
American (1874 - 1946)				
TSEREGOTY, N. G.	*P*			$3,300
Russian (19th -)				
TSINAJINIE, Andrew Van	*P*			$165
American (1918 -)				
TSUCHIYA, Tilsa	*D*			$1,100
(20th -)				
TUCKER, A. P.	*W*			$110
American (20th -)				
TUCKER, Allen	*P*	$1,100	$6,566	$13,200
American (1866 - 1939)	*W*	$468	$864	$1,540
TUCKER, Arthur	*W*	$1,045	$1,348	$1,650
British (1864 - 1929)				
TUCKER, Charles E. (Attrib.)	*P*			$2,200
British (19th -)				
TUCKER, E.	*P*			$165
British (19th -)				
TUCKER, John W.	*P*			$3,850
British (18th - 19th)				
TUCKER, M.	*W*			$165
American (?)				
TUCKER, Raymond (Attrib.)	*P*			$264
British (19th -)				
TUCKER, William	*D*			$2,860
Egyptian (20th -)				
TUDGAY, Frederick	*P*			$22,000
British (19th -)				
TUER, Herbert	*P*			$2,420
Dutch (17th -)				

D=Drawing, P=Painting, S=Sculpture, W=Watercolor

		Current Price Range	
	Low	Mean	High

		Low	Mean	High
TULLIDGE, J.	*P*			$715
American (19th - 20th)				
TUNISON,	*D*			$138
American (20th -)				
TUNISON, Thompson	*P*			$330
(?)				
TUNNARD, John	*P*	$110	$10,303	$22,000
British (20th -)				
TURCAN, Jean	*S*			$3,190
French (1846 - 1895)				
TURCATO, Giulio	*P*			$5,500
Italian (1912 -)				
TURCHI, Alessandro	*D*			$29,700
Italian (1578 - 1649)	*P*			$88,000
TURENGHI, Enrico	*W*			$550
Italian (19th -)				
TURGENOFF, Paul	*S*			$4,950
Russian (19th -)				
TURGOT, F.	*P*			$2,750
French (19th -)				
TURNBULL, William	*P*			$1,100
British (1922 -)	*S*			$8,250
TURNER, A. D.	*P*			$1,430
(?)				
TURNER, Alan	*P*			$1,320
(20th -)				
TURNER, Alfred	*W*			$1,320
American (1851 - 1932)				
TURNER, Charles H.	*P*	$220	$1,013	$4,510
American (1848 -)	*W*			$132
TURNER, Charles Y.	*P*	$220	$1,320	$2,420
American (1850 - 1919)				
TURNER, Charles Y. (Attrib.)	*P*			$550
American (1850 - 1919)				

D=Drawing, P=Painting, S=Sculpture, W=Watercolor

		Current Price Range		
		Low	Mean	High
TURNER, E.	*P*			$2,090
(?)				
TURNER, Francis C.	*P*	$3,300	$17,507	$44,000
British (1795 - 1865)				
TURNER, Francis C. (Attrib.)	*P*			$4,400
British (1795 - 1865)				
TURNER, Francis C. (Manner)	*P*			$6,050
British (1795 - 1865)				
TURNER, Frank	*P*			$1,100
British (19th -)				
TURNER, G. A.	*P*			$495
American (19th - 20th)				
TURNER, George	*P*	$770	$1,943	$4,400
British (1843 - 1910)				
TURNER, Helen M.	*P*	$3,300	$4,400	$5,500
American (1858 - 1958)				
TURNER, J. A.	*P*			$1,320
British (19th -)				
TURNER, J. M. H. (Style)	*P*			$110
(?)				
TURNER, James A.	*P*			$550
Australian (19th - 20th)				
TURNER, Joseph M. W.	*D*	$74,250	$78,375	$82,500
British (1775 - 1851)	*P*			$165,000
	W	$3,575	$94,394	$231,000
TURNER, Joseph M. W. (After)	*P*	$440	$1,210	$1,980
British (1775 - 1851)				
TURNER, Joseph M. W. (Attrib.)	*P*			$1,760
British (1775 - 1851)				
TURNER, R. W.	*P*			$110
(?)				
TURNER, Raymond	*S*			$1,100
American (1903 -)				
TURNER, Robert	*S*	$2,200	$2,567	$3,300
(20th -)				

D=Drawing, P=Painting, S=Sculpture, W=Watercolor

		Current Price Range		
		Low	Mean	High

		Low	Mean	High
TURNER, Ross S.	*W*	$495	$1,063	$1,485
American (1847 - 1915)				
TURTLE, Ranold	*P*			$330
American (20th -)				
TUTTLE, Emma	*P*			$200
(19th -)				
TUTTLE, Lena A.	*P*			$160
American (?)				
TUTTLE, Richard	*D*			$3,850
American (1941 -)	*P*	$4,400	$8,250	$12,100
	W	$2,860	$3,740	$4,620
TVETEN, Connie	*S*			$770
American (20th -)				
TWACHTMAN, John H.	*D*	$6,600	$9,900	$13,200
American (1853 - 1902)	*P*	$6,875	$52,464	$132,000
TWACHTMAN, John H. (After)	*P*			$660
American (1853 - 1902)				
TWACHTMAN, John H. (Attrib.)	*D*			$2,420
American (1853 - 1902)	*P*			$3,025
TWARDOWICZ, Stanley	*P*			$440
American (1917 -)				
TWARDZIK, Henryk	*P*			$935
American (1900 -)				
TWELVETREES, C.	*D*			$935
American (19th - 20th)				
TWINING, Yvonne	*P*	$5,170	$7,260	$9,350
American (1907 -)				
TWOMBLY, Cy	*D*	$15,400	$443,483	$1.705M
American (1929 -)	*P*	$110,000	$1.060M	$5.500M
	S			$150,000
	W	$88,000	$289,667	$561,000
TWORKOV, Jack	*D*			$880

D=Drawing, P=Painting, S=Sculpture, W=Watercolor

		Current Price Range		
		Low	Mean	High
TWORKOV, Jack	P	$2,200	$17,906	$40,700
American (1900 -)				
TYLER, Bayard H.	P	$413	$1,260	$2,200
American (1835 - 1931)				
TYLER, George W.	P			$825
American (1803 - 1833)				
TYLER, Hugh	P			$275
(19th - 20th)				
TYLER, James G.	P	$440	$3,104	$16,500
American (1855 - 1931)	W			$770
TYLER, William R.	P	$3,080	$4,455	$6,160
American (1825 - 1896)				
TYNE, Peter van	P			$220
Eurpoean (20th -)				
TYSON, Carroll S.	P	$440	$2,241	$4,675
American (1877 - 1956)				
TYTGAT, Edgard	W			$7,150
Belgian (1879 - 1957)				
UBEDA, Augustin	P	$550	$3,153	$14,300
Spanish (1932 -)				
UBERTINI, Francesco	P			$66,000
Italian (1494 - 1557)				
UDEN, Lucas van (School)	P			$3,520
Flemish (1595 - 1672)				
UFER, Walter	P	$29,700	$58,536	$104,500
American (1876 - 1936)				
UFERT, Oskar	S			$550
German (1876 -)				
UHL, Jerome	P			$358
American (1842 - 1916)				
UHLMANN, Hans	S			$2,310
German (1900 -)				
ULEN, Paul	W			$495
American (1894 -)				
ULFT, Jacob van der	D			$1,650

D=Drawing, P=Painting, S=Sculpture, W=Watercolor

		Current Price Range		
		Low	Mean	High

ULFT, Jacob van der	*P*			$50,600
Dutch (1627 - 1689)	*W*			$36,300
ULKE, Henry (Attrib.)	*P*			$660
German (1821 - 1910)				
ULNITZ, E. C.	*P*			$4,950
Danish (19th -)				
ULP, Clifford	*P*	$385	$729	$1,100
American (1885 - 1957)				
ULREICH, Edward	*P*			$303
American (20th -)				
ULYSSE-ROY, Jean	*P*			$7,150
French (19th -)				
UMBRIAN SCHOOL 15C,	*P*			$12,100
Italian (15th -)				
UMBRIAN SCHOOL 16C,	*P*			$15,400
Italian (16th -)				
UMLAUF, Charles	*S*			$154
American (20th -)				
UNDERHILL, George E.	*P*			$1,320
American (19th - 20th)				
UNDERWOOD, Clarence	*P*			$900
American (1871 - 1929)	*W*	$660	$825	$990
UNGER, Hans	*P*			$1,100
German (1872 - 1936)				
UNSWORTH, Edna G.	*P*			$2,200
American (1890 -)				
UNTERBERGER, Franz R.	*P*	$2,200	$26,150	$63,250
Belgian (1838 - 1902)				
UNTERBERGER, Franz R. (Mann)	*P*			$3,850
Belgian (1838 - 1902)				
UNTERBUSCH, W.	*P*			$385
British (19th -)				
UPELNICKS, Arthur	*P*			$605
American (1911 -)				

D=Drawing, P=Painting, S=Sculpture, W=Watercolor

		Current Price Range		
		Low	Mean	High

		Low	Mean	High
UPJOHN, Anna M.	*P*			$385
American (20th -)				
URBAHN, O.	*P*			$2,530
German (19th -)				
URBAN, Humberto	*P*	$3,300	$3,438	$3,575
(20th -)				
URBANN, O.	*P*			$880
(?)				
UREN, John C.	*W*			$825
British (20th -)				
URIBE-HOLIGUIN, Santiago	*P*			$1,320
Colombian (1957 -)				
URLAUB, Georg A. A.	*P*			$23,100
German (1744 - 1788)				
URLAUB, R.	*P*			$4,400
German (19th -)				
URUETA, Cordelia	*P*	$16,500	$21,450	$26,400
Mexican (1908 -)				
URY, A. Muller	*P*			$1,210
German (19th -)				
URY, Lesser	*D*	$4,950	$51,906	$126,500
German (1861 - 1931)	*P*	$13,750	$52,470	$110,000
	W			$6,050
USSINGER,	*D*	$176	$198	$220
(?)				
UTRECHT SCHOOL 17C,	*P*			$3,300
Dutch (17th -)				
UTRILLO, Maurice	*D*	$10,450	$21,450	$38,500
French (1883 - 1955)	*P*	$35,750	$267,622	$990,000
	W	$49,500	$96,897	$181,500
UTRILLO, Maurice (After)	*P*			$605
French (1883 - 1955)				
UTTER, Andre	*P*	$4,950	$6,197	$6,820
French (1886 - 1948)				

D=Drawing, P=Painting, S=Sculpture, W=Watercolor

		Current Price Range		
		Low	Mean	High

UTZ, Thornton	*P*			$550
American (1914 -)				
VACCARO, Andrea	*P*			$3,520
Italian (1598 - 1670)				
VACCARO, Andrea (Attrib.)	*P*			$36,300
Italian (1598 - 1670)				
VACCARO, Lorenzo	*S*			$55,000
Italian (1655 - 1706)				
VACCARO, Nicola	*P*			$20,900
Italian (1637 - 1717)				
VACCHI, Sergio	*P*			$110
European (20th -)				
VACHELL, Arthur H.	*P*			$385
American (1864 -)				
VADDER, Lodewyk de	*P*			$24,200
Flemish (1605 - 1655)				
VAERE, Jean-Antone de	*S*			$60,500
Flemish (1755 - 1828)				
VAGA, Perino del (Attrib.)	*D*			$6,600
Italian (1500 - 1547)				
VAGA, Perino del (Circle)	*D*	$440	$715	$990
Italian (1500 - 1547)				
VAGO, Alex	*P*	$248	$262	$275
American (20th -)				
VAGO, Sandor	*P*	$440	$759	$1,320
Hungarian (1887 -)				
VAIL, Eugene L.	*P*	$605	$1,302	$2,420
American (1857 - 1934)				
VAILLANT, Louis D.	*P*			$660
American (1875 -)				
VAJDA, Zsigmond	*P*			$1,980
Hungarian (1860 - 1931)				
VALADE, Gabrielle M. M.	*P*			$12,100
French (19th -)				
VALADON, Suzanne	*D*	$990	$20,937	$57,200

D=Drawing, P=Painting, S=Sculpture, W=Watercolor

		Current Price Range		
		Low	Mean	High

		Low	Mean	High
VALADON, Suzanne	P	$79,750	$133,375	$187,000
French (1865 - 1938)				
VALAPERTA, F.	P			$715
European (19th -)				
VALBUENA, Ricardo	D			$13,200
Lat. Amer. (20th -)				
VALDENUIT, Thomas B. de	D			$1,155
American (1763 - 1846)				
VALE, J. W.	P			$495
American (20th -)				
VALE, R.	P			$15,400
(?)				
VALENCIA, Manuel	P	$660	$2,233	$6,050
American (1856 - 1935)	W			$330
VALENCIAN SCHOOL 15C,	P			$9,350
Italian (15th -)				
VALENKAMPH, Theodore V. C.	P	$303	$2,234	$4,180
American (1868 - 1924)				
VALENSI, Henry	P			$1,870
French (1883 - 1960)				
VALENTE, Paolo	P			$3,300
Italian (19th -)				
VALENTINE, Janet H.	P			$121
American (1866 -)				
VALENTINI, Va	P			$2,860
Italian (19th -)				
VALERI-PREVOT, Andre	P			$880
French (1890 -)				
VALERIO, Pietro	P			$990
American (19th - 20th)				
VALERIO, Theodore	D			$660
French (1819 - 1879)				
VALERO, G.	P			$550
(?)				
VALKENBORCH, Lucas van (Cir)	P			$71,500
Flemish (1535 - 1597)				

D=Drawing, P=Painting, S=Sculpture, W=Watercolor

		Current Price Range		
		Low	Mean	High

VALKENBORCH, Lucas van (Sc)	P			$6,050
Flemish (1535 - 1597)				
VALKENBORCH, Lucas van (St)	P			$13,200
Flemish (1535 - 1597)				
VALKENBORCH, Martin van	P			$20,350
Flemish (? - 1612)				
VALKENBURG, Dirk (Attrib.)	P			$11,000
Dutch (1675 -)				
VALKENBURG, H.	P			$1,100
Dutch (20th -)				
VALLAYER-COSTER, Anne	P			$341,000
French (1744 - 1818)				
VALLEE, Etienne M.	P			$880
(?)				
VALLES, Lorenzo	P			$1,870
Spanish (1830 - 1910)				
VALLET, Jean E. P.	P	$413	$1,857	$3,300
French (? - 1889)				
VALLET-BISSON, Frederique	D			$16,500
French (1865 -)				
VALLIN, Jacques A. (Attrib.)	P			$5,500
French (18th - 19th)				
VALLOIS, Paul	P	$385	$1,238	$2,090
French (19th - 20th)				
VALLOTTON, Felix	P	$12,100	$58,300	$104,500
Swiss (1865 - 1925)				
VALLY,	P			$1,760
European (19th - 20th)				
VALMIER, Georges	S	$5,280	$10,193	$16,500
French (1885 - 1937)	W			$19,800
VALPEY, M.	S			$138
(?)				
VALTAT, Louis	D			$3,850
French (1869 - 1952)	P	$3,025	$48,836	$242,000

D=Drawing, P=Painting, S=Sculpture, W=Watercolor

		Current Price Range		
		Low	Mean	High
VALTAT, Louis	*W*	$8,800	$9,075	$9,350
French (1869 - 1952)				
VALTON, Charles	*S*	$2,860	$2,970	$3,080
French (1851 - 1918)				
VALUTIN,	*W*			$495
(?)				
VALVERANE, L. Denis	*P*			$1,650
French (19th - 20th)				
VAN BEAN, Carolyn	*W*			$110
(?)				
VAN BRUSSEL, Anneke	*W*			$7,700
(20th -)				
VAN BUREN, Albert A.	*P*			$138
American (20th -)				
VAN BUREN, Stanbery	*P*			$110
American (?)				
VAN CAULAERT, J. D.	*P*			$4,675
(20th -)				
VAN DE VEENE, Adriaen	*P*			$9,900
Dutch (1589 - 1680)				
VAN DER HOT,	*P*			$880
(?)				
VAN DER LAMEN, Christoffel	*P*			$28,600
Flemish (1615 - 1651)				
VAN DER MYN, Herman (Circle)	*P*			$4,950
(1684 - 1741)				
VAN DER VAART, W.	*P*			$660
Dutch (19th - 20th)				
VAN DER VELDE, Hanny	*P*			$1,320
American (1883 -)				
VAN DER WEYDEN, Harry	*D*			$248
American (1868 -)	*P*			$8,800
VAN DIJK, Wim. L.	*P*			$963
Brazilian (20th -)				
VAN ELK, Ger	*D*			$33,000
(20th -)				

D=Drawing, P=Painting, S=Sculpture, W=Watercolor

		Current Price Range		
		Low	Mean	High

		Low	Mean	High
VAN GORDER, Luther E.	*P*	$248	$2,324	$4,400
American (1861 - 1831)				
VAN LEIVEN,	*P*			$575
Dutch (19th - 20th)				
VAN STEENSEL, Jan	*P*			$1,100
Belgian (19th -)				
VAN STRY, Jacob	*P*			$27,500
Dutch (1756 - 1815)				
VAN TONGEREN, Herk	*S*			$1,430
American (1943 -)				
VAN WYK, Henri	*P*			$4,180
Dutch (1833 -)				
VAN ZANDT, William G.	*P*	$220	$399	$578
(20th -)				
VANDENBERGE, Peter	*P*			$1,980
(20th -)	*S*	$550	$2,475	$4,400
VANDERBANK, John (Attrib.)	*P*			$1,760
British (18th -)				
VANDERBANK, John (School)	*P*			$6,050
British (18th -)				
VANDERHOOF, Charles	*D*	$154	$449	$1,100
American (? - 1918)				
VANDERHOOF, Charles (Et al.)	*D*	$1,650	$1,650	$1,650
American (20th -)				
VANDERLAAN, S.	*P*			$385
American (20th -)				
VANDERLYN, John (Attrib.)	*P*	$880	$9,460	$13,750
American (1755 - 1852)				
VANDERLYN, John (Manner)	*P*			$605
American (1755 - 1852)				
VANDERVAART, John (Attrib.)	*P*			$6,050
(1653 - 1727)				
VANKA, Max	*P*			$633
American (1889 -)				
VANNUCCI, Pietro di C.	*P*			$22,000
Italian (?)				

D=Drawing, P=Painting, S=Sculpture, W=Watercolor

		Current Price Range		
		Low	Mean	High

VANTUEVAN, Paul	P			$330
European (19th - 20th)				
VARADY, Frederick	W			$1,400
American (1908 -)				
VARELA, Abigail	S	$3,850	$15,767	$52,800
Venezuelan (1948 -)				
VARGAS, Alberto	W			$2,500
American (1926 - 1983)				
VARI, Sofia	S			$8,800
(20th -)				
VARIA, Felix	P			$220
(?)				
VARIAN, George E.	W			$990
American (1865 -)				
VARLEY, John	P			$1,045
British (1778 - 1842)				
VARLEY, John (Attrib.)	W			$330
British (1778 - 1842)				
VARLEY, JR, John	P			$358
British (? - 1899)	W			$715
VARO, Remedios	D			$4,400
Spanish (1900 - 1963)	P	$198,000	$473,000	$825,000
	W	$20,900	$31,075	$46,750
VARO, Remedios (Attrib.)	P			$4,675
Spanish (1900 - 1963)				
VART, Cauldon	W			$176
American (20th -)				
VASA, Velizar	P			$825
Yugoslavian (1933 -)	S			$770
VASARELY, Victor	P	$990	$25,640	$77,000
Hungarian (1908 -)	S	$2,530	$4,418	$6,600
VASARELY, Victor (After)	S			$11,000
Hungarian (1908 -)				

D=Drawing, P=Painting, S=Sculpture, W=Watercolor

| | | Current Price Range | | |
		Low	Mean	High
VASARI, Giorgio	D			$110,000
Italian (1511 - 1574)	P			$77,000
	W	$41,800	$92,400	$143,000
VASARI, Giorgio (Attrib.)	P			$77,000
Italian (1511 - 1574)				
VASILIEFF, Nicolai	P	$1,540	$2,063	$2,640
American (1892 - 1970)				
VASQUEZ, J.	P			$100
(?)				
VASSILIEFF, Marie	P			$20,900
Russian (1894 - 1955)				
VASSILOFF, Boris	P	$165	$381	$495
American (20th -)				
VASTAGH, Geza	P			$550
Hungarian (1866 - 1919)				
VASZARY, Janos (Attrib.)	P			$440
Hungarian (1867 - 1939)				
VAUNES, A. du	P			$440
French (19th -)				
VAUX, Jules E.	P			$3,025
French (1837 -)				
VAYANA, Nunzio	P	$193	$702	$1,210
American (1887 - 1960)				
VEA, Van	P			$825
European (20th -)				
VECCHI, Giovanni de	D			$3,300
Italian (1536 - 1615)				
VECCHIA, Pietro Della	P			$5,500
Italian (1605 - 1678)				
VECELLIO, Tiziano (Studio)	P			$44,000
Italian (15th - 16th)				
VED, T.	P			$2,750
(?)				
VEDDER, Elihu	D	$220	$10,523	$24,200

D=Drawing, P=Painting, S=Sculpture, W=Watercolor

		Current Price Range		
		Low	Mean	High
VEDDER, Elihu	P	$2,750	$11,090	$55,000
American (1836 - 1923)	S			$33,000
	W	$1,430	$2,200	$2,970
VEDDER, Simon H.	P			$413
American (1866 -)				
VEDURA, Fulco	W			$1,650
(?)				
VEEGAN, Anna	P			$3,520
Belgian (19th - 20th)				
VEEN, Otto van (Circle)	P			$2,640
Dutch (1556 - 1629)				
VEEN, Stuyvesant van	P			$138
American (1910 - 1977)				
VEERENDAEL, Nicolaes van	P			$165,000
Flemish (1640 - 1691)				
VEERKAMP,	P			$275
Dutch (20th -)				
VEGA, Jose de la	P			$1,980
Spanish (19th -)				
VEGA, Manolo de la	P			$16,500
(?)				
VEGA Y MUNOZ, Pedro	P	$4,675	$4,858	$4,950
Spanish (19th -)				
VEILLON, Aguste L.	P			$8,250
Swiss (1834 - 1890)				
VEJERANO, Gustavo	P			$1,650
Colombian (1952 -)				
VELA, Vincenzo	S	$2,420	$4,473	$7,150
Italian (1820 - 1891)				
VELASCO, Jose M.	P			$341,000
Mexican (1840 - 1912)				
VELASQUEZ, Diego R. (After)	P	$770	$1,210	$1,650
Spanish (1599 - 1660)				
VELASQUEZ, Diego R. (Attrib.)	P	$12,100	$41,800	$71,500
Spanish (1599 - 1660)				

D=Drawing, P=Painting, S=Sculpture, W=Watercolor

		Current Price Range		
		Low	Mean	High

		Low	Mean	High
VELASQUEZ, Jose A. Honduran (1906 - 1985)	*P*	$3,025	$5,163	$11,000
VELDE, Adriaen van de Dutch (1636 - 1672)	*P*			$4,400
VELDE, Bram van Dutch (1910 -)	*P*			$19,800
VELDE, Esaias van de Dutch (1587 - 1630)	*D*			$15,400
VELDE, Esaias van de (After) Dutch (1587 - 1630)	*D*			$715
VELDE, Esaias van de (Attrib.) Dutch (1587 - 1630)	*D*			$3,080
VELDE, Geer van Dutch (1898 -)	*P*			$28,600
VELDE, Peter van de (Attrib.) Dutch (1634 - 1687)	*P*			$550
VELDE I, Willem van de (Manner) Dutch (1611 - 1693)	*P*			$4,070
VELDE I, Willem van de (School) Dutch (1611 - 1693)	*P*			$8,250
VELDE II, Willem van de Dutch (1633 - 1707)	*D*	$1,210	$81,483	$462,000
VELDE II, Willem van de (Cir.) Dutch (1633 - 1707)	*D* *P*	 $2,640	 $5,170	$440 $7,700
VELDE II, Willem van de (Studio) Dutch (1633 - 1707)	*P*			$16,500
VELDHUIJZEN, Johannes Dutch (1831 - 1910)	*P*			$4,400
VELTEN, Wilhelm Russian (1847 - 1929)	*P*	$1,100	$7,425	$15,400
VELVA, R. European (20th -)	*P*			$110
VELY, Anatole French (1838 - 1882)	*P*			$715
VENARD, Claude French (1913 -)	*P*	$495	$8,606	$46,200

D=Drawing, P=Painting, S=Sculpture, W=Watercolor

		Current Price Range		
		Low	Mean	High
VENDITTI, Jerry	P	$5,500	$10,833	$16,000
American (1942 -)				
VENET, Gabriel	P			$880
French (1884 -)				
VENET, ET AL., Bernard	S			$3,850
(20th -)				
VENETIAN SCHOOL 16C,	D			$4,620
Italian (16th -)	P	$1,760	$3,978	$6,050
VENETIAN SCHOOL 17C,	D	$1,320	$4,813	$8,250
Italian (17th -)	P	$4,180	$8,608	$13,200
VENETIAN SCHOOL 18C,	D	$1,430	$1,562	$1,650
Italian (18th -)	P	$3,300	$8,464	$16,500
VENETIAN SCHOOL 19C,	P	$1,100	$3,960	$6,820
Italian (19th -)	W			$9,900
VENETO SCHOOL 15C,	P			$55,000
Italian (15th -)				
VENETO SCHOOL 18C,	P	$3,300	$8,800	$16,500
Italian (18th -)				
VENETO SCHOOL 19C,	P			$10,450
Italian (19th -)				
VENTNER, D.	P			$578
American (19th -)				
VENTURRI, Achille	P			$5,775
Italian (1826 - 1897)				
VENUSTI, Marcello (Attrib.)	P			$11,000
Italian (1512 - 1579)				
VENUTI, Filippo	W			$1,870
Italian (19th -)				
VERA,	P			$880
Spanish (19th - 20th)				
VERBECK, Frank	D			$1,100
(1858 - 1933)				
VERBOECKHOVEN, Charles L.	P	$990	$4,664	$10,450
Belgian (1802 - 1875)				

D=Drawing, P=Painting, S=Sculpture, W=Watercolor

| | | Current Price Range | | |
| --- | --- | Low | Mean | High |

		Low	Mean	High
VERBOECKHOVEN, Eugene	*P*	$605	$14,343	$105,600
Belgian (1798 - 1881)				
VERBOECKHOVEN, Louis	*P*			$12,100
Belgian (1802 - 1889)				
VERBOOM, Adriaen	*P*			$4,400
Dutch (17th -)				
VERBRUGGEN, Gaspar P.	*P*	$9,350	$29,563	$71,500
Flemish (1664 - 1730)				
VERBRUGGEN, Gaspar P. (Circle)	*P*			$17,600
Flemish (1664 - 1730)				
VERBRUGGEN, Gaspar P. (Sch.)	*P*	$7,150	$13,475	$19,800
Flemish (1664 - 1730)				
VERBRUGGEN, ELDER, Gaspar	*P*	$9,350	$11,275	$13,200
Flemish (1635 - 1681)				
VERBRUGGHE, Charles	*P*			$1,650
Dutch (1877 -)				
VERBURGH, Dionys	*P*	$12,100	$12,100	$12,100
Dutch (? - 1722)				
VERDEVOVE, P.	*W*			$110
European (20th -)				
VERDI,	*P*			$330
European (19th -)				
VERDI, A.	*P*			$4,125
Italian (19th -)				
VERDIER, Francois	*D*	$990	$990	$990
French (1651 - 1730)				
VERDIER, Francois (Circle)	*D*			$440
French (1651 - 1730)				
VERDIER, Gene	*P*			$358
(20th -)				
VERDIER, Maurice	*P*	$220	$248	$275
French (20th -)				
VERDURA, Fulco	*W*	$1,430	$1,595	$1,760
Italian (20th -)				
VERDUSSEN, (School)	*P*			$3,300
Flemish (1700 - 1763)				

D=Drawing, P=Painting, S=Sculpture, W=Watercolor

		Current Price Range		
		Low	Mean	High

		Low	Mean	High
VERELST, Simon Dutch (1644 - 1721)	*P*	$49,500	$272,250	$495,000
VERELST, William British (17th -)	*P*			$12,100
VERES, T. Zoltan Hungarian (1868 - 1935)	*P*			$935
VEREY, A. French (19th -)	*P*			$1,650
VEREY, Johanna L. A. Dutch (1886 - 1966)	*P*			$1,320
VERGER, Carlos Spanish (1872 - 1929)	*P*			$715
VERHAECHT, Tobias (1561 - 1631)	*P*			$38,500
VERHAEREN, Carolus American (20th -)	*P*			$440
VERHAERT, Piet Dutch (1852 - 1903)	*P*			$1,100
VERHAGEN, Carlos (Attrib.) Dutch (20th -)	*P*			$100
VERHAS, Frans Belgian (1827 - 1897)	*P*			$19,800
VERHEUL, G. Dutch (20th -)	*P*			$110
VERHEYDEN, Francois Belgian (1806 - 1890)	*P*			$2,750
VERHOESEN, Albertus Dutch (1806 - 1881)	*P*	$770	$3,669	$7,150
VERKOLJE, Jan (Circle) Dutch (1650 - 1693)	*P*			$4,400
VERLAT, Charles M. M. Belgian (1824 - 1890)	*P*	$5,775	$5,913	$6,050
VERLEUR, Andries Dutch (1876 - 1953)	*P*			$495
VERLOT, O. French (19th - 20th)	*P*	$3,300	$4,125	$4,950

D=Drawing, P=Painting, S=Sculpture, W=Watercolor

		Current Price Range	
	Low	Mean	High

VERMEHREN, Johan F. N.	*P*			$15,400
Danish (1823 - 1910)				
VERMEHREN, Otto	*P*			$1,320
German (19th -)				
VERMEHREN, Sophus	*P*			$3,410
Danish (1866 -)				
VERMEULEN, Andries	*P*	$5,500	$12,650	$19,800
Dutch (18th - 19th)				
VERMEULEN, Andries (Manner)	*P*			$1,100
Dutch (18th - 19th)				
VERNARD, Claude	*P*			$853
French (1913 -)				
VERNEER, Abraham	*P*			$2,200
Dutch (19th -)				
VERNET, Carle	*D*			$8,800
French (1758 - 1836)				
VERNET, Carle (Attrib.)	*W*			$935
French (1758 - 1836)				
VERNET, Claude J.	*P*	$132,000	$353,833	$880,000
French (1714 - 1789)				
VERNET, Claude J. (Attrib.)	*W*			$935
French (1714 - 1789)				
VERNET, Claude J. (Circle)	*P*			$12,100
French (1714 - 1789)				
VERNET, Claude J. (Follower)	*P*			$9,900
French (1714 - 1789)				
VERNET, Claude J. (Manner)	*P*	$2,420	$25,960	$49,500
French (1714 - 1789)				
VERNET, J. C. (Attrib.)	*P*			$303
French (1712 - 1782)				
VERNIER, Emile	*P*			$3,520
French (1829 - 1887)				
VERNIER, J.	*P*			$495
French (19th -)				
VERNIER, L.	*P*			$1,045
French (1829 - 1887)				

D=Drawing, P=Painting, S=Sculpture, W=Watercolor

		Current Price Range		
		Low	Mean	High
VERNILE,	*P*			$4,400
Italian (19th -)				
VERNON, Emile	*P*	$7,700	$32,945	$68,750
French (19th - 20th)				
VERNON, Emile (Attrib.)	*P*			$1,650
French (19th - 20th)				
VERNON, Jules	*P*			$1,045
(19th -)				
VERNON, W.	*P*			$4,400
British (19th -)				
VERON, Alexander R.	*P*			$4,180
French (1826 - 1897)				
VERON-FARE, Jules H.	*P*			$1,430
French (19th -)				
VERONESE, After	*P*			$16,500
Italian (16th -)				
VERONESE, Bonifazio (Circle)	*P*	$1,100	$8,250	$15,400
Italian (16th -)				
VERONESE, Bonifazio (School)	*P*			$12,100
Italian (16th -)				
VERONESE, Paolo C.	*P*			$2.970M
Italian (1528 - 1588)				
VERONESE, Paolo C. (Circle)	*D*			$1,100
Italian (1528 - 1588)				
VERONESE, Paolo C. (Follower)	*P*			$11,000
Italian (1528 - 1588)				
VERONESE, Paolo C. (School)	*D*	$2,200	$4,950	$7,700
Italian (1528 - 1588)	*P*	$3,850	$89,925	$176,000
VERPOEKEN, Hendrik	*P*			$7,700
Dutch (1791 - 1869)				
VERRIER, Maurice	*P*			$138
French (20th -)				
VERROCCHIO, Andrea del (Foll.)	*D*			$2,090
Italian (?)				
VERSARI, G.	*P*			$468
Italian (19th - 20th)				

D=Drawing, P=Painting, S=Sculpture, W=Watercolor

		Current Price Range		
		Low	Mean	High

		Low	Mean	High
VERSCHAFFELT, Edward Belgian (1874 -)	*P*			$11,000
VERSCHUUR, Wouter Dutch (1812 - 1874)	*P*	$6,600	$47,300	$88,000
VERTANGEN, Daniel Dutch (1598 - 1684)	*P*	$4,400	$7,700	$11,000
VERTES, Marcel French (1895 - 1961)	*D*	$330	$743	$1,650
	P	$770	$4,077	$13,200
	S	$275	$513	$715
	W	$330	$756	$1,650
VERTES, Marcel (Studio) French (1895 - 1961)	*D*			$193
VERTIN, Pieter G. Dutch (1819 - 1893)	*P*	$3,410	$4,730	$6,050
VERUTTI, A. American (?)	*W*			$220
VERVEER, Salomon L. Dutch (1813 - 1876)	*P*	$7,150	$8,250	$9,350
VERVOORT, M. Flemish (19th -)	*P*			$2,090
VERWEE, Louis P. Belgian (1807 - 1877)	*P*			$2,200
VERY, Marjorie American (20th -)	*D*	$248	$427	$605
VESIN, Jaroslav Bulgarian (1859 - 1915)	*P*			$7,150
VESSELY, Boris-Theo French (19th - 20th)	*P*			$6,600
VESTCHILOFF, C. (?)	*P*			$193
VESTER, Willem Dutch (1824 - 1871)	*P*			$33,000
VESTIER, Antoine (Attrib.) French (1740 - 1822)	*P*	$248	$7,691	$16,500

D=Drawing, P=Painting, S=Sculpture, W=Watercolor

		Current Price Range		
		Low	Mean	High
VESTIER, Antoine (Circle)	P			$2,200
French (1740 - 1822)				
VEYRASSAT, Jules J.	P	$6,050	$7,150	$8,250
French (1828 - 1893)				
VEZIEN, Elie	S			$770
French (1890 -)				
VEZIEN, V.	P			$413
French (19th - 20th)				
VEZIN, Charles	P	$770	$2,228	$4,840
American (1858 - 1942)				
VIANA, Raul	P			$286
(20th -)				
VIANDEN, Heinrich	P			$2,475
American (1814 - 1899)				
VIANELLO, Cesare	P			$3,520
Italian (19th -)				
VIANI, Giovanni M.	P			$16,500
Italian (1636 - 1700)				
VIARD, Georges	P			$15,400
French (19th -)				
VIAVANT, George L.	W			$1,100
American (20th -)				
VIBERT, Jean G.	P	$2,750	$17,600	$44,000
French (1840 - 1902)	W	$3,300	$103,400	$203,500
VICAJI, R.	W			$110
American (?)				
VICENTE, Esteban	D			$3,850
American (1906 -)	P			$7,700
	S			$5,500
VICENTINO, Andrea	D			$8,250
Italian (16th -)				
VICHI, F.	S	$550	$4,840	$13,200
Italian (19th -)				
VICKERS, Alfred	P	$286	$869	$1,540
British (1786 - 1868)				

D=Drawing, P=Painting, S=Sculpture, W=Watercolor

		Current Price Range		
		Low	Mean	High

		Low	Mean	High
VICKERS, Alfred (Attrib.)	*D*			$2,860
British (1786 - 1868)				
VICKERS, C.	*P*			$1,045
British (19th -)				
VICKERS, Henry H.	*P*			$1,100
(?)				
VICTORS, Jacobus	*P*	$6,600	$6,783	$7,150
Dutch (1640 - 1705)				
VICTORYNS, Anthonie	*P*			$4,400
Dutch (15th -)				
VIDAL, Couce	*P*	$220	$344	$468
American (20th -)				
VIEIRA DA SILVA, Maria E.	*D*			$8,250
French (1908 -)	*P*	$165,000	$225,500	$286,000
VIEN, YOUNGER, Joseph M.	*P*			$9,900
French (1762 - 1848)				
VIERIN, Emmanuel	*P*	$1,100	$2,750	$4,400
Belgian (1869 -)				
VIERKANT, Brigitte	*P*			$4,950
German (1942 -)				
VIGEE-LEBRUN, Marie	*D*			$33,000
French (1755 - 1842)	*P*	$16,500	$89,833	$198,000
VIGEE-LEBRUN, Marie (After)	*P*	$4,180	$5,115	$6,050
French (1755 - 1842)				
VIGEE-LEBRUN, Marie (Attrib)	*P*			$9,350
French (1755 - 1842)				
VIGEE-LEBRUN, Marie (Circle)	*P*	$6,050	$9,625	$13,200
French (1755 - 1842)				
VIGEE-LEBRUN, Marie (Foll.)	*P*			$38,500
French (1755 - 1842)				
VIGEE-LEBRUN, Marie (Manner)	*P*			$440
French (1755 - 1842)				
VIGEE-LEBRUN, Marie (School)	*P*			$17,600
French (1755 - 1842)				

D=Drawing, P=Painting, S=Sculpture, W=Watercolor

		Current Price Range		
		Low	Mean	High

		Low	Mean	High
VIGNARI, John T.	*P*			$110
American (20th -)				
VIGNAUD,	*P*			$1,540
European (19th -)				
VIGNERON, Pierre R.	*P*			$12,100
French (1789 - 1872)				
VIGNET, Henri	*P*			$3,850
French (20th -)				
VIGNOLES, Andre	*P*	$550	$2,255	$3,575
French (20th -)				
VIGNON, Claude	*D*			$41,250
French (1593 - 1670)	*P*			$22,000
VIGNON, Claude (Attrib.)	*D*			$3,575
French (1593 - 1670)	*P*			$10,450
VIGNON, Claude (Circle)	*P*			$66,000
French (1593 - 1670)				
VIGNON, Victor	*P*	$5,500	$13,544	$24,200
French (1847 - 1909)				
VIGNY, Sylvain	*W*			$660
French (1902 - 1970)				
VIGON, Louis J.	*P*			$275
French (20th -)				
VIKOS, K.	*P*			$165
(?)				
VILATO, Javier	*P*			$4,400
French (1921 -)				
VILLA, Hernando	*D*	$248	$399	$550
American (1881 - 1952)	*P*	$303	$1,040	$2,475
	W	$715	$1,348	$1,980
VILLACRES, Cesar A.	*P*			$1,980
Ecuadorian (1880 -)				
VILLANDS, P.	*P*			$1,980
French (19th - 20th)				

D=Drawing, P=Painting, S=Sculpture, W=Watercolor

		Current Price Range		
		Low	Mean	High

		Low	Mean	High
VILLANIS, Emmanuele	S	$825	$853	$880
French (19th - 20th)				
VILLANUEVA, Leoncio	P	$8,800	$10,450	$12,100
Lat. Amer. (20th -)				
VILLEGAS Y CORDERO, Jose	P	$19,800	$270,233	$770,000
Spanish (1848 - 1922)				
VILLEON, Emmanuel de la	P	$6,600	$12,467	$22,000
French (1858 - 1944)				
VILLETTE, P.	S			$440
French (19th - 20th)				
VILLIERS, T.	P			$1,650
(?)				
VILLON, Eugene	W			$1,540
French (1879 -)				
VILLON, Jacques	D	$825	$2,736	$4,950
French (1875 - 1963)	P	$19,800	$90,907	$363,000
	W	$1,650	$9,598	$30,800
VILOT, Cesar	P			$605
French (20th -)				
VINCELET, Victor	P			$1,210
French (? - 1871)				
VINCENT, George	P			$1,650
British (1796 - 1831)				
VINCENT, Harry A.	P	$220	$3,674	$8,250
American (1864 - 1931)				
VINCENT, W.	P			$440
British (19th - 20th)				
VINCENZA,	P			$5,500
(?)				
VINCENZINA, Giuseppe (Circle)	P			$16,500
Italian (18th -)				
VINCINTINI,	W			$330
American (?)				
VINCKEBOONS, David (School)	P			$38,500
Flemish (1576 - 1629)				

D=Drawing, P=Painting, S=Sculpture, W=Watercolor

		Current Price Range		
		Low	Mean	High
VINE, J. British (19th -)	P	$2,200	$2,475	$2,750
VINEA, Francesco Italian (1845 - 1902)	P			$2,860
VINO, G. (?)	S			$1,320
VINTON, Frederick American (1846 - 1911)	P	$770	$1,503	$2,420
VIOLLET LE DUC, Victor French (1848 - 1901)	P	$1,320	$3,699	$6,600
VIORENTINO, E. Italian (20th -)	W			$385
VIRY, Paul French (19th -)	P	$8,140	$11,770	$15,400
VISCONTI, Alphonse A. F. French (1850 - 1924)	P			$7,700
VISKI, Janos Hungarian (1891 -)	P	$330	$633	$935
VISKOLATY, W. E. French (19th -)	P			$660
VISSER, Peir J. de Dutch (19th - 20th)	P			$385
VISSO, Paolo da Italian (?)	P			$46,200
VITAL-CORNU, Charles French (1851 - 1927)	S			$9,350
VITALI, E. Italian (19th -)	W	$330	$367	$403
VITERBO, A. (?)	P	$248	$248	$248
VITERBO, Lorenzo da (Circle) Italian (15th -)	P			$88,000
VITIELLO, Pasquale Italian (1912 - 1962)	P			$121
VITOLLO, A. (?)	P			$1,100

D=Drawing, P=Painting, S=Sculpture, W=Watercolor

		Current Price Range		
		Low	Mean	High

VITY, A. D.	*P*			$275
French (20th -)				
VIVANT-DENON, Baron D.	*D*			$770
French (1747 - 1825)				
VIVAR, Juan C. de	*P*			$9,900
(16th -)				
VIVARINI, Alvise	*P*			$143,000
Italian (1445 - 1503)				
VIVARINI, Alvise (Manner)	*P*			$3,520
Italian (1445 - 1503)				
VIVARINI, Alvise (School)	*P*			$46,200
Italian (1445 - 1503)				
VIVIAN, Calthea	*P*	$413	$729	$1,045
American (1857 - 1943)				
VIVIAN, G.	*P*			$1,760
(19th -)				
VIVIAN, John	*P*	$1,650	$2,035	$2,420
British (19th -)				
VIVIN, Louis	*P*	$1,210	$8,103	$16,500
French (1861 - 1936)				
VIZKELETI, W. E.	*P*	$950	$1,233	$1,650
Hungarian (1819 - 1895)				
VIZZOTTO, Alberti G.	*W*			$2,200
Italian (1862 - 1931)				
VLAMINCK, Maurice de	*D*	$20,900	$39,325	$52,250
French (1876 - 1958)	*P*	$41,800	$358,148	$7.150M
	W	$18,700	$44,895	$99,000
VLAMINCK, Maurice de (Style)	*P*			$220
French (1876 - 1958)				
VLIEGER, Simon de	*P*			$770,000
Dutch (1600 - 1653)				
VLIET, Don van	*P*			$1,760
(20th -)				
VLIET, Willem van der	*P*			$18,700
Dutch (1583 - 1642)				

D=Drawing, P=Painting, S=Sculpture, W=Watercolor

		Current Price Range		
		Low	Mean	High
VOCKE, F. H.	*S*	$330	$468	$605
(20th -)				
VOERMIBURGH, V.	*S*			$1,320
(?)				
VOGEL,	*P*			$330
German (19th - 20th)				
VOGEL, Cornelis J. (Et al.)	*P*	$3,850	$7,975	$12,100
Dutch (19th -)				
VOGEL, Cornelius J.	*P*			$1,045
Dutch (1824 - 1879)				
VOGEL, E.	*P*			$550
British (19th -)				
VOGEL, Valentine	*P*			$385
American (? - 1965)				
VOGELAER, Karel van	*P*	$35,200	$50,600	$66,000
Dutch (1653 - 1695)				
VOGELI, Felix	*W*			$660
French (18th -)				
VOGELSANG, Christian R.	*P*			$1,650
Danish (1824 - 1911)				
VOGSTAD, Austin E.	*W*			$138
American (20th -)				
VOGT, Louis C.	*P*	$220	$1,173	$2,420
American (1864 -)	*W*			$484
VOILLEMOT, Charles	*P*	$1,320	$1,320	$1,320
French (1823 - 1893)				
VOIRIN, Leon J.	*P*			$148,500
French (1833 - 1887)				
VOIRIOT, Guillaume	*P*			$52,800
French (1713 - 1799)				
VOISARD-MARGERIE, Adrien G.	*P*			$12,100
French (19th -)				
VOISIN, Charles	*P*			$440
French (19th -)				
VOLAIRE, Jacques P. de	*D*	$1,100	$1,595	$2,090
French (18th - 19th)				

D=Drawing, P=Painting, S=Sculpture, W=Watercolor

		Current Price Range		
		Low	Mean	High

		Low	Mean	High
VOLCKER, Robert German (1854 - 1924)	*P*			$1,320
VOLEKER, Rob (?)	*P*			$1,045
VOLK, Douglas American (1856 - 1935)	*P* *W*			$605 $220
VOLK, Leonard American (1828 - 1895)	*S*	$1,980	$5,940	$9,900
VOLKERS, Emil German (1831 - 1905)	*P*	$1,650	$7,150	$11,000
VOLKERT, Charles (?)	*W*			$268
VOLKERT, Edward C. American (1871 - 1935)	*P* *W*	$770	$2,383	$4,950 $605
VOLKMER, Bernard American (1865 - 1929)	*D* *P*	$110	$413	$715 $550
VOLKMER, Hans German (19th - 20th)	*P*			$660
VOLKOV, Sergei Russian (1956 -)	*P*	$8,250	$10,725	$13,200
VOLLERDT, Johann C. German (1708 - 1769)	*P*			$11,000
VOLLET, H. French (19th -)	*P*			$1,870
VOLLMER, Grace L. American (1884 - 1977)	*P*			$880
VOLLMERING, Joseph American (1810 - 1887)	*P*	$550	$1,650	$3,300
VOLLON, Alexis French (1865 -)	*P*			$5,500
VOLLON, Antoine French (1833 - 1900)	*P*	$550	$10,529	$44,000
VOLLRATH, Kelly American (20th -)	*D*	$600	$650	$700

D=Drawing, P=Painting, S=Sculpture, W=Watercolor

		Current Price Range		
		Low	Mean	High
VOLLWEIDER, Johann J.	*P*	$3,300	$3,850	$4,400
German (1834 - 1891)				
VOLPE, Vencenzo	*P*	$770	$5,610	$10,450
Italian (1855 - 1929)				
VOLPER, Israel	*P*			$143
American (1889 - 1985)				
VOLTI, Antoniucci	*D*			$165
French (1915 -)	*S*			$7,700
VOLTOLINA, Pierd	*D*			$3,850
Italian (19th - 20th)				
VOLTZ, Friedrich	*D*			$1,210
German (1817 - 1886)	*P*	$20,900	$30,433	$37,400
VOLTZ, Friedrich (Attrib.)	*P*			$605
German (1817 - 1886)				
VON LUERZER, F.	*P*			$880
Dutch (19th -)				
VONNOH, Bessie P.	*S*	$550	$21,822	$143,000
American (1872 - 1954)				
VONNOH, Bessie P. (After)	*S*	$3,300	$3,988	$4,675
American (1872 - 1954)				
VONNOH, Robert W.	*P*	$605	$12,931	$37,400
American (1858 - 1933)				
VONNOH, Robert W. (Attrib.)	*P*			$248
American (1858 - 1933)				
VOOGD, Hendrick	*P*			$33,000
Dutch (1768 - 1839)				
VOORBAES, J.	*P*			$2,200
European (19th -)				
VOORDECKER, Henri	*P*			$4,400
Belgian (1766 - 1839)				
VOORHEES, Clark G.	*P*	$2,200	$5,537	$12,100
American (1871 - 1933)				
VOS, Gerrit	*P*			$495
Dutch (1794 - 1840)				

D=Drawing, P=Painting, S=Sculpture, W=Watercolor

		Current Price Range		
		Low	Mean	High
VOS, Hubert	*P*	$1,100	$1,540	$1,980
American (1855 - 1935)				
VOS, Izaak de	*P*			$413
Flemish (?)				
VOS, Maerten de	*D*			$5,225
Flemish (1532 - 1603)				
VOS, Maerten de (Circle)	*D*			$1,100
Flemish (1532 - 1603)				
VOS, Paul de	*P*			$10,450
Flemish (1596 - 1678)				
VOS, Paul de (School)	*P*			$46,750
Flemish (1596 - 1678)				
VOS, Simon de	*P*			$4,180
Flemish (1603 - 1676)				
VOSEHER, Leopold	*P*			$3,025
Austrian (1830 - 1877)				
VOSMAER, Jan W.	*P*			$8,800
Dutch (1584 - 1641)				
VOSS, Carl L.	*P*			$8,250
German (1856 - 1921)				
VOSS, Franklin B.	*P*	$2,090	$5,748	$12,100
American (1880 - 1953)				
VOUET, Jacob F. (School)	*P*			$4,400
Flemish (1639 -)				
VOUET, Simon	*P*			$104,500
French (1590 - 1649)				
VOUET, Simon (Circle)	*D*	$2,640	$6,545	$10,450
French (1590 - 1649)	*P*			$2,200
VOUET, Simon (School)	*P*			$2,200
French (1590 - 1649)				
VOULKOS, Peter	*S*	$1,650	$12,391	$55,000
American (1924 -)				
VRANCX, Sebastian	*P*	$31,900	$37,950	$44,000
Flemish (1573 - 1647)				
VRANCX, Sebastian (Circle)	*P*	$4,950	$35,200	$99,000
Flemish (1573 - 1647)				

D=Drawing, P=Painting, S=Sculpture, W=Watercolor

		Current Price Range		
		Low	Mean	High

		Low	Mean	High
VREEDENBURGH, Cornelis Dutch (1880 - 1946)	P	$3,850	$5,298	$6,820
VREELAND, F. van Dutch (19th -)	W	$308	$374	$440
VREELAND, Francis W. American (1879 - 1954)	W			$385
VREELAND, Harriet E. (19th -)	P			$1,000
VREL, Jacob (Circle) Dutch (17th -)	P			$31,900
VRIES, Paul V. de Flemish (16th - 17th)	P			$52,250
VRIES, Roelof van Dutch (1631 - 1681)	P			$7,150
VRIES, Sjoerd de Dutch (20th -)	P	$550	$605	$660
VRIES, Sophia de Dutch (1915 -)	P			$880
VROOM, Hendrik Attrib.) Dutch (1566 - 1640)	P			$16,500
VU, Michel (1941 -)	P			$880
VUCHT, Gerrit van Dutch (? - 1699)	P			$22,000
VUILLARD, Edouard French (1868 - 1940)	D	$2,475	$60,257	$550,000
	P	$33,000	$677,486	$7.700M
VUKOVIC, Marko American (1892 -)	P	$138	$317	$495
VULLIAMY, Gerard French (1909 -)	P			$1,210
VYTLACIL, Vaclav American (1892 -)	P	$880	$1,914	$2,530
	W	$660	$1,568	$2,475
WAAY, Nicolaes van der Dutch (1855 - 1936)	P			$12,100

D=Drawing, P=Painting, S=Sculpture, W=Watercolor

		Current Price Range		
		Low	Mean	High
WACHSMUTH, Ferdinand	*P*			$8,800
French (1802 - 1869)				
WACHSMUTH, Maximilian	*P*			$4,400
German (1859 - 1912)				
WACHTEL, Elmer	*P*	$1,760	$9,785	$27,500
American (1864 - 1929)	*W*	$1,100	$1,485	$1,870
WACHTEL, Marion K.	*P*	$2,090	$5,093	$8,250
American (1876 - 1954)	*W*	$2,200	$29,229	$66,000
WACK, Henry W.	*P*	$220	$358	$495
American (1875 - 1955)				
WACONER, H. B.	*P*			$165
(20th -)				
WADE, Pearl S.	*P*	$385	$385	$385
American (19th - 20th)				
WADE, Robert	*P*			$110
American (1882 -)				
WADE, William	*W*			$440
(19th -)				
WADSWORTH, Frank R.	*P*			$880
American (1874 - 1905)				
WADSWORTH, Myrta M.	*P*			$385
American (19th - 20th)				
WAEL, Cornelis de	*D*			$1,320
Flemish (1592 - 1669)				
WAEL, Cornelis de (Attrib.)	*D*			$770
Flemish (1592 - 1669)				
WAGMANS, Pieter J.	*P*			$1,100
Dutch (1879 - 1955)				
WAGNER,	*S*			$990
(?)				
WAGNER, F.	*P*			$220
(?)	*S*			$4,400
WAGNER, Fred	*D*			$495
American (1864 - 1940)				

D=Drawing, P=Painting, S=Sculpture, W=Watercolor

| | | Current Price Range | | |
		Low	Mean	High
WAGNER, Fritz	P			$4,950
Swiss (1872 -)				
WAGNER, George	S			$4,125
American (19th - 20th)				
WAGNER, Hans	P			$176
(?)				
WAGNER, Helene	P			$3,300
German (19th -)				
WAGNER, Jacob	P	$1,210	$4,547	$8,800
American (1852 - 1899)				
WAGNER, Karl	P			$4,950
German (19th -)				
WAGNER, T. H.	P			$770
(19th -)				
WAGNER, SR., Ferdinand	P			$49,500
German (1819 - 1881)				
WAGONER, Harry B.	P	$550	$688	$825
American (1889 - 1950)				
WAHLISS, Ernst	S	$220	$935	$1,650
(?)				
WAHLQVIST, Ehrnfried	P			$9,900
Swedish (1815 - 1895)				
WAINWRIGHT, G.	P	$440	$454	$468
(?)				
WAINWRIGHT, Thomas F.	W			$1,980
French (19th -)				
WAINWRIGHT, William J.	W			$9,350
British (1855 - 1931)				
WAIT, Blanche E.	P			$523
American (1895 - 1934)				
WAITE, M. C.	P			$138
American (20th -)				
WAITE, R. T.	W			$220
(?)				
WAKEFIELD, M. B.	P			$825
American (20th -)				

D=Drawing, P=Painting, S=Sculpture, W=Watercolor

		Low	Mean	High
			Current Price Range	

		Low	Mean	High
WALBOURN, Ernest	P	$2,750	$6,875	$11,000
British (19th - 20th)				
WALCOTT, Harry M.	D			$24,200
American (1870 - 1944)	P	$1,980	$22,990	$44,000
WALDE, Alfons	P	$29,700	$35,475	$41,250
Austrian (1891 -)				
WALDECK, Nina V.	P			$220
American (1868 - 1943)				
WALDEGG,	P			$275
(?)				
WALDEIM, Auguste	P			$1,485
German (19th -)				
WALDEN, Lionel	P	$468	$894	$1,320
American (1861 - 1933)	W			$248
WALDMULLER, Ferdinand G.	P			$198,000
Austrian (1793 - 1865)				
WALDO, J. Frank	P	$193	$399	$605
American (19th -)	W			$330
WALDO, Samuel L.	P	$1,650	$3,025	$4,400
American (1783 - 1861)				
WALDO, Samuel L. (Et al.)	P			$5,500
American (18th - 19th)				
WALES, Susan M. L.	W			$110
American (1839 - 1927)				
WALKER, Addison	P			$1,045
American (20th -)	W			$523
WALKER, Barvo	S	$990	$2,214	$4,125
American (20th -)				
WALKER, C. C.	P			$358
(19th - 20th)				
WALKER, Charles A.	P			$1,320
American (1848 - 1920)	W			$303

D=Drawing, P=Painting, S=Sculpture, W=Watercolor

		Current Price Range		
		Low	Mean	High
WALKER, Charles H.	*D*			$2,640
American (1857 - 1936)				
WALKER, Frank H.	*W*			$1,540
British (19th -)				
WALKER, Frederick	*P*			$1,980
American (20th -)				
WALKER, Frederick	*W*			$248
British (1840 - 1875)				
WALKER, Harold E.	*P*	$350	$437	$523
American (1890 -)	*W*			$110
WALKER, Henry O.	*P*			$1,760
American (1843 - 1929)				
WALKER, Hobart A.	*P*			$220
American (1869 -)				
WALKER, J. H.	*P*			$165
British (19th -)				
WALKER, James A.	*P*	$2,750	$51,150	$132,000
British (1841 - 1898)				
WALKER, Jeff	*P*	$650	$902	$1,155
American (20th -)				
WALKER, John	*D*	$1,980	$2,090	$2,200
British (20th -)	*P*	$4,950	$24,658	$35,750
WALKER, John R.	*P*			$935
British (1796 - 1873)				
WALKER, Joseph F.	*P*			$63,250
British (19th -)				
WALKER, M.	*P*			$143
British (19th -)				
WALKER, R. Hollands	*W*	$440	$2,558	$4,675
British (19th - 20th)				
WALKER, Robert (School)	*P*			$8,800
British (1607 - 1659)				
WALKER, T. Dart	*D*			$1,540
American (1869 - 1914)	*W*			$1,760

D=Drawing, P=Painting, S=Sculpture, W=Watercolor

		Current Price Range		
		Low	Mean	High
WALKER, W.	*P*			$1,100
(?)				
WALKER, William A.	*P*	$550	$7,051	$14,850
American (1839 - 1921)				
WALKER, William A. (Attrib.)	*P*			$2,200
American (1839 - 1921)				
WALKLEY, David B.	*P*			$2,090
American (1849 - 1934)				
WALKOWITZ, Abraham	*D*	$385	$1,116	$3,520
American (1880 - 1965)	*P*	$1,540	$7,453	$22,000
	W	$220	$1,265	$2,310
WALL, A. Bryan	*P*	$1,650	$3,612	$6,325
American (20th -)				
WALL, Alfred S.	*P*	$440	$537	$633
American (1809 - 1896)				
WALL, Bernhardt	*P*			$165
American (1872 -)				
WALL, W.	*P*			$715
(19th - 20th)				
WALL, William Allen	*W*			$1,760
American (1801 - 1855)				
WALL, William G.	*P*			$15,400
American (1792 - 1864)				
WALLACE, David	*W*			$880
American (20th -)				
WALLACE, Donald	*P*			$495
American (?)				
WALLACE, James	*P*			$605
British (1911 -)				
WALLACE, Lilly	*P*	$248	$372	$605
American (20th -)				
WALLACE, Raymond L.	*P*			$385
American (20th -)				
WALLBURG, Egon	*W*			$385
(?)				

D=Drawing, P=Painting, S=Sculpture, W=Watercolor

		Current Price Range		
		Low	Mean	High
WALLER, Frank	P	$275	$622	$1,210
American (1842 - 1923)				
WALLIN, Carl E.	P	$413	$1,601	$3,300
American (1879 -)				
WALLIS, Alfred (Attrib.)	P			$1,210
British (1855 - 1942)				
WALLIS, George A. (Attrib.)	P			$1,320
British (1811 - 1891)				
WALLIS, S.	P			$187
British (19th - 20th)				
WALLS, William	W			$440
British (1860 -)				
WALMSLEY, J. M. (Attrib.)	P			$660
British (20th -)				
WALRAVEN, Jan	P			$4,180
Dutch (1827 -)				
WALSCAPELLE, Jacob van	P			$181,500
Dutch (1644 - 1727)				
WALSH, A. A.	P			$935
American (19th - 20th)				
WALT DISNEY STUDIOS,	D			$248
American (20th -)				
WALTENSPERGER, Charles	P	$303	$829	$2,420
American (1871 - 1931)				
WALTENSPERGER, Charles (Att)	P			$715
American (1871 - 1931)				
WALTER,	P			$275
American (19th -)				
WALTER, E. Barstow	P			$138
American (?)				
WALTER, Emma	P	$1,045	$1,073	$1,100
British (19th -)				
WALTER, Martha	P	$242	$11,154	$44,000
American (1875 - 1976)				
WALTER, Valerie H.	S	$3,850	$5,775	$7,700
American (20th -)				

D=Drawing, P=Painting, S=Sculpture, W=Watercolor

		Current Price Range		
		Low	Mean	High

		Low	Mean	High
WALTER, W. G. Dutch (20th -)	P			$1,540
WALTERS, Emile American (1893 -)	P	$523	$791	$1,100
WALTERS, George S. British (1838 - 1924)	W	$303	$644	$1,210
WALTERS, S. European (19th -)	P			$193
WALTERS, Samuel British (1811 - 1882)	P			$79,750
WALTERS, Samuel (Attrib.) British (1811 - 1882)	P			$4,400
WALTERSBERG, (?)	P			$1,540
WALTHER, Charles American (1879 - 1938)	P			$4,400
WALTHER, J. Dutch (?)	P			$330
WALTMANN, Harry F. American (1871 - 1951)	P			$495
WALTON, Edward A. (?)	P			$440
WALTON, Frank British (1840 - 1928)	P			$3,520
WALTON, Henry British (1746 - 1813)	P			$96,250
WALTON, James (18th -)	W			$165
WALTON, Jay C. American (19th -)	P			$275
WAN, J. C. American (20th -)	P			$715
WANING-STEVELS, Marie van Dutch (1874 -)	P			$1,320
WANKIE, Wladyslaw Polish (1860 - 1925)	P			$4,400

D=Drawing, P=Painting, S=Sculpture, W=Watercolor

| | | Current Price Range | | |
		Low	Mean	High
WARD, Arthur E.	*P*	$248	$303	$358
American (19th - 20th)				
WARD, C. M.	*P*	$154	$270	$385
American (19th - 20th)	*W*			$110
WARD, Charles C.	*W*	$1,320	$1,595	$1,870
American (1831 - 1896)				
WARD, Edmund F.	*P*	$550	$1,875	$3,200
American (1892 -)				
WARD, Edward M.	*P*			$33,000
British (1816 - 1879)				
WARD, Enoch	*P*			$550
British (1859 - 1922)				
WARD, J. Stephen	*P*			$660
American (1876 -)				
WARD, James	*D*			$110
British (1769 - 1859)	*P*	$7,150	$75,130	$297,000
	W			$440
WARD, John Q. A.	*S*	$385	$15,593	$30,800
American (1830 - 1910)				
WARD, Keith	*P*			$358
American (20th -)	*W*			$275
WARD, JR., William	*P*	$150	$526	$1,210
American (19th - 20th)				
WARDLE, Arthur	*D*			$5,500
British (1864 - 1949)	*P*	$2,750	$14,994	$46,750
	W			$495
WARDLEWORTH, J. L.	*P*			$330
British (19th -)				
WARE, G. S.	*P*			$220
American (19th -)				
WARHOL, Andy	*D*	$990	$15,353	$77,000
American (1930 - 1987)	*P*	$2,310	$238,049	$4.070M

D=Drawing, P=Painting, S=Sculpture, W=Watercolor

		Current Price Range		
		Low	Mean	High
WARHOL, Andy	S	$715	$29,091	$63,250
American (1930 - 1987)	W	$2,200	$10,869	$28,600
WARHOL, Andy (Et al.)	D			$17,600
American (20th -)	S	$11,000	$15,767	$18,700
WARNEKE, Heinrich	S			$1,210
American (1895 -)				
WARNER, Justine A.	P			$495
American (20th -)				
WARNER, Mary E.	P			$248
American (20th -)				
WARNER, Nell W.	P	$440	$1,425	$4,400
American (1891 - 1970)				
WARNER, Olin L.	S	$770	$825	$880
American (19th - 20th)				
WARREN, Andrew W.	P			$1,210
(?)				
WARREN, Bonomi	W			$440
American (20th -)				
WARREN, Elisabeth B.	W	$275	$358	$440
American (1886 -)				
WARREN, Harold B.	W	$121	$281	$440
American (1859 - 1934)				
WARREN, Melvin C.	P	$17,600	$30,910	$45,100
American (1920 -)				
WARREN, Russ	P	$715	$1,128	$1,540
American (20th -)				
WARSHAW, Howard	P	$1,430	$1,998	$2,475
American (1920 -)				
WARSHAW, Howard (Attrib.)	D			$440
American (1920 -)				
WARSHAWSKY, Abel G.	P	$220	$2,930	$15,400
American (1883 - 1962)				
WARVILLE, Felix S.	P	$2,090	$4,950	$10,450
French (1818 - 1892)	W			$495

D=Drawing, P=Painting, S=Sculpture, W=Watercolor

		Current Price Range		
		Low	Mean	High

		Low	Mean	High
WASCH, Jeanne	*P*			$440
American (1886 -)				
WASEY, Jane	*S*			$308
American (20th -)				
WASHBURN, Mary N.	*P*			$3,850
American (1861 - 1932)				
WASHBURN, Philip (Attrib.)	*P*			$550
American (1624 - 1700)				
WASHINGTON, Elizabeth F.	*P*	$523	$805	$1,430
American (1871 - 1953)				
WASHINGTON, Georges	*P*	$7,810	$18,902	$30,800
French (1827 - 1910)				
WASHURN, J. M.	*P*			$165
American (19th -)				
WASLEY, J.	*P*			$495
British (19th -)				
WASMULLER, J. H.	*P*			$11,000
American (19th -)				
WASSENBURG, Matthieu	*P*			$1,100
Belgian (1939 -)				
WASSERMAN, Shirley S.	*P*			$100
American (20th -)				
WASSERMAN-LEVY, Margaret	*S*			$9,900
(20th -)				
WASSON, George S.	*P*			$1,210
American (1855 - 1926)				
WATER, Leonard	*P*			$330
(?)				
WATERALL, Ruella Volte	*P*			$100
(20th -)				
WATERLOO, Anthonie	*D*	$2,200	$6,600	$11,000
Flemish (17th -)	*P*			$1,210
WATERLOW, Ernest A.	*W*			$110
British (1850 - 1919)				
WATERMAN, Marcus	*P*	$523	$1,054	$1,980
American (1834 - 1914)				

D=Drawing, P=Painting, S=Sculpture, W=Watercolor

		Current Price Range		
		Low	Mean	High
WATERMAN, Marcus (Attrib.)	*P*			$1,210
American (1834 - 1914)				
WATERS, Alfred A.	*W*	$138	$399	$550
British (19th -)				
WATERS, George W.	*P*	$193	$922	$1,650
American (1832 - 1912)	*W*			$550
WATERS, Ray K.	*P*			$500
American (1887 -)				
WATERS, Susan C.	*P*	$908	$8,154	$15,400
American (1823 - 1900)				
WATERS, Susan C. (Attrib.)	*D*			$1,485
American (1823 - 1900)				
WATKINS, E. F.	*P*			$138
British (20th -)				
WATKINS, Franklin C.	*P*	$2,805	$6,353	$9,900
American (1894 -)				
WATMAN,	*P*			$165
(?)				
WATROUS, Harry W.	*P*	$1,540	$4,721	$18,700
American (1857 - 1940)				
WATSON, Adele	*P*			$2,090
American (1873 - 1947)				
WATSON, Amelia M.	*W*	$358	$399	$440
American (1856 - 1934)				
WATSON, C. A.	*P*			$204
(?)				
WATSON, Colin	*S*			$468
Italian (?)				
WATSON, Dawson	*P*			$8,250
American (1864 - 1939)				
WATSON, Edgar M.	*P*			$330
American (1877 - 1956)				
WATSON, Elizabeth V. T.	*P*			$413
American (20th -)				
WATSON, George (Attrib.)	*P*			$9,900
British (1767 - 1837)				

D=Drawing, P=Painting, S=Sculpture, W=Watercolor

		Current Price Range		
		Low	Mean	High
WATSON, Harry S. British (1822 - 1911)	P			$248
WATSON, Homer R. Canadian (1855 - 1936)	P			$2,475
WATSON, Jessie N. American (1870 - 1963)	W			$303
WATSON, Nan American (20th -)	P			$100
WATSON, P. Fletcher British (1842 - 1907)	W			$990
WATSON, Robert British (19th - 20th)	P	$132	$710	$1,265
WATSON, Syd British (1892 -)	P			$1,925
WATSON, W. (?)	P			$3,575
WATSON, Walter J. British (1879 -)	P			$2,090
WATSON, William British (? - 1921)	P W	$385	$3,465	$7,150 $385
WATTEAU, Jean A. (After) French (1684 - 1721)	D			$770
WATTEAU, Jean A. (Attrib.) French (1684 - 1721)	D	$6,050	$148,683	$385,000
WATTEAU, Jean A. (Circle) French (1684 - 1721)	D P			$2,475 $23,100
WATTEAU, Jean A. (Follower) French (1684 - 1721)	P			$3,300
WATTEAU, Jean A. (Manner) French (1684 - 1721)	P	$2,750	$24,750	$46,750
WATTEAU, Jean A. (School) French (1684 - 1721)	P			$8,800
WATTEAU, Louis J. French (1731 - 1798)	P			$71,500

D=Drawing, P=Painting, S=Sculpture, W=Watercolor

		Current Price Range		
		Low	Mean	High
WATTEL,	*P*			$358
European (19th -)				
WATTER, Joseph	*P*			$4,125
German (1838 - 1913)				
WATTNAUD, Jean	*P*			$550
(?)				
WATTS, D.	*P*			$330
British (20th -)				
WATTS, Frederick W.	*P*	$4,290	$17,197	$36,300
British (1800 - 1862)				
WATTS, George F.	*D*			$7,700
British (1817 - 1904)	*P*	$2,200	$17,600	$33,000
WATTS, Sidney	*P*			$688
British (19th - 20th)				
WATTS, William C.	*P*			$1,950
British (1752 - 1851)	*W*			$770
WATTS, William Clothier	*W*			$1,540
American (1869 - 1961)				
WATZELHAN, Carl	*P*			$6,820
German (1867 - 1942)				
WAUD, Alfred R.	*D*	$770	$2,530	$3,520
American (1828 - 1891)	*W*	$238	$3,489	$6,050
WAUD, Alfred R. (Et al.)	*D*	$990	$2,035	$3,080
American (19th -)	*P*			$3,575
WAUGH, Coulton	*W*			$495
American (1896 - 1975)				
WAUGH, Frederick J.	*D*			$990
American (1861 - 1940)	*P*	$770	$5,425	$28,600
	W			$550
WAUGH, Frederick J. (Attrib.)	*D*			$110
American (1861 - 1940)	*P*			$495

D=Drawing, P=Painting, S=Sculpture, W=Watercolor

		Current Price Range		
		Low	Mean	High
WAUGH, Henry	D	$138	$202	$275
American (19th -)	W			$138
WAUGH, Ida	P			$3,960
American (? - 1919)				
WAUGH, Samuel B.	P			$660
American (1814 - 1885)				
WAUTERS, Camille	P	$11,000	$11,000	$11,000
Belgian (1856 - 1919)				
WAY, A. H. (Attrib.)	P			$248
(?)				
WAY, Andrew J. H.	P	$660	$7,439	$18,700
American (1826 - 1888)				
WAY, Charles J.	P			$3,630
British (1834 - 1919)				
WAY, George B.	P			$880
American (1854 -)				
WAY, Tom Robert	D			$990
British (1862 - 1913)				
WAY, William C.	P			$385
British (19th - 20th)				
WAYCOTT, Hedley	P			$880
American (1865 - 1937)				
WAYNE, June C.	P	$715	$743	$770
American (20th -)				
WEARE, Shane	D			$330
American (20th -)				
WEARSTLER, Albert M.	W			$110
American (1893 - 1955)				
WEATHERBEE, George F.	P	$4,950	$4,950	$4,950
American (1851 - 1920)				
WEATHERHEAD, William H.	P			$3,850
British (19th -)				
WEAVER, Harold	P			$303
American (20th -)				
WEAVER, Rene	P			$248
American (1898 - 1984)				

D=Drawing, P=Painting, S=Sculpture, W=Watercolor

		Current Price Range		
		Low	Mean	High

		Low	Mean	High
WEAVER, Thomas	*P*			$14,300
British (1774 - 1803)				
WEAVER, Thomas (Attrib.)	*P*			$6,875
British (1774 - 1803)				
WEBB, A. C.	*D*			$121
American (1888 -)				
WEBB, Charles M.	*P*	$2,475	$5,170	$7,260
British (1830 - 1895)				
WEBB, James	*P*	$880	$6,710	$14,300
British (1825 - 1895)				
WEBB, William	*P*	$3,410	$11,055	$18,700
British (18th - 19th)				
WEBB, William (Circle)	*P*			$8,250
British (18th - 19th)				
WEBB, William E.	*P*			$6,600
British (1862 - 1903)				
WEBBER, Charles T.	*P*	$468	$591	$714
American (1825 - 1911)				
WEBBER, Ottis S.	*P*			$2,420
(?)				
WEBBER, Wesley	*P*	$468	$1,381	$2,970
American (1841 - 1914)				
WEBBER, Wesley (Style)	*P*			$385
American (1841 - 1914)				
WEBER, Anton	*W*			$1,870
German (1833 - 1909)				
WEBER, C. Phillip	*P*	$440	$889	$1,430
American (1849 - 1921)	*W*	$110	$477	$1,100
WEBER, Carl	*P*	$440	$1,694	$4,125
American (1850 - 1921)	*W*	$110	$813	$2,145
WEBER, Fred W.	*P*			$715
American (1890 -)				
WEBER, Frederick	*D*	$220	$330	$440
American (1883 - 1956)	*P*			$358

D=Drawing, P=Painting, S=Sculpture, W=Watercolor

		Current Price Range		
		Low	Mean	High

WEBER, Heinrich	*P*	$770	$2,108	$4,125
German (1843 - 1913)				
WEBER, Heinrich	*P*			$825
Swiss (1892 -)				
WEBER, Louis	*P*			$154
American (?)				
WEBER, Max	*D*	$2,970	$3,548	$4,125
American (1881 - 1961)	*P*	$3,520	$12,980	$30,800
	S			$9,350
	W	$990	$11,183	$52,800
WEBER, Otis	*P*	$385	$2,053	$4,675
American (19th -)	*W*	$165	$281	$413
WEBER, Paul	*P*	$3,300	$11,594	$38,500
American (1823 - 1916)	*W*			$110
WEBER, R.	*P*	$275	$688	$1,100
(20th -)				
WEBER, Rudolf	*P*	$1,320	$1,650	$1,980
Austrian (1872 -)				
WEBER, Theodor A.	*P*	$1,100	$5,618	$16,500
French (1838 - 1907)				
WEBER-FULOP, Elizabeth	*P*			$138
American (1883 -)				
WEBSTER, Bernice M.	*P*			$165
American (1895 -)				
WEBSTER, Herman A.	*W*			$248
American (1878 -)				
WEBSTER, Hutton	*P*	$440	$495	$550
American (1910 - 1956)				
WEBSTER, Thomas	*P*			$4,180
British (1800 - 1886)				
WEBSTER, Thomas (Attrib.)	*P*			$495
British (1800 - 1886)				
WEEDEN, Eleanor R.	*P*			$825
American (1898 -)				

D=Drawing, P=Painting, S=Sculpture, W=Watercolor

		Current Price Range		
		Low	Mean	High

		Low	Mean	High
WEEKES, Henry	P			$5,500
British (19th -)				
WEEKES, Herbert W.	P			$11,000
British (19th -)				
WEEKES, William	P	$1,430	$6,343	$10,450
British (19th -)				
WEEKS, Arthur	P			$110
(?)				
WEEKS, Edwin L.	P	$440	$44,669	$242,000
American (1849 - 1903)				
WEEKS, Edwin L. (Attrib.)	P			$1,760
American (1849 - 1903)				
WEENIX, Jan	P			$539,000
Dutch (1640 - 1719)				
WEENIX, Jan B.	P	$20,900	$29,700	$38,500
Dutch (1621 - 1663)				
WEENIX, Jan B. (Circle)	P			$5,500
Dutch (1621 - 1663)				
WEENIX, Jan B. (Manner)	P			$28,600
Dutch (1621 - 1663)				
WEGER, Marie	P			$468
American (1882 -)				
WEGMAN, William	D	$1,100	$2,640	$4,180
(20th -)	P			$82,500
WEICHBERGER, Philip	P	$110	$293	$440
American (20th -)				
WEICKUM, Louis	P			$1,100
American (20th -)				
WEIDEL, Seff	D			$110
(?)				
WEIGALL, Arthur H.	P	$990	$3,520	$6,050
British (19th -)				
WEIGAND, Gustave	P	$770	$880	$990
American (1870 - 1957)				
WEIGAND, K.	P			$110
German (20th -)				

D=Drawing, P=Painting, S=Sculpture, W=Watercolor

		Current Price Range		
		Low	Mean	High
WEIGHORST, Olaf	*P*	$1,760	$4,730	$7,700
American (1899 - 1975)	*W*			$1,540
WEILENBECK, G.	*P*			$275
(?)				
WEILER, Casper	*P*			$440
American (19th - 20th)				
WEINDORF, Arthur	*P*			$715
American (1885 -)				
WEINDORF, Paul	*P*	$330	$385	$440
American (20th -)				
WEINGARTNER, Hans	*P*			$880
(20th -)				
WEINMAN, Adolph A.	*S*	$550	$7,810	$22,000
American (1870 - 1952)				
WEINRICH, Agnes	*D*	$220	$457	$750
American (1873 - 1946)	*P*	$825	$1,733	$3,300
	W	$110	$481	$770
WEINSTEIN, M.	*P*			$187
American (?)				
WEIR, Julian A.	*D*	$990	$5,170	$9,350
American (1852 - 1919)	*P*	$2,310	$29,728	$56,100
	W	$1,430	$2,805	$4,180
WEIR, Julian A. (Attrib.)	*P*	$385	$706	$935
American (1852 - 1919)				
WEIR, M.	*P*			$400
(?)				
WEIR, Robert W.	*D*	$660	$715	$770
American (1803 - 1889)	*P*	$3,960	$32,230	$88,000
	W			$24,200
WEIROTTER, Franz E.	*D*			$1,045
Austrian (1730 - 1771)				
WEIS, John E.	*P*	$1,320	$2,035	$2,750
American (1892 -)				

D=Drawing, P=Painting, S=Sculpture, W=Watercolor

		Current Price Range		
		Low	Mean	High

		Low	Mean	High
WEISE, Alexander Russian (1883 -)	*P*			$550
WEISE, Robert German (1870 - 1923)	*P*			$440
WEISMAN, William H. American (19th - 20th)	*P*	$550	$825	$1,100
WEISS, Emil R. German (1875 - 1942)	*P*			$3,080
WEISS, Georges French (1864 -)	*P*			$4,950
WEISS, H. American (20th -)	*P*			$825
WEISS, Jose British (1859 -)	*P*	$220	$4,290	$11,000
WEISS, Lee American (1928 -)	*W*			$468
WEISS, Lee (Attrib.) American (1928 -)	*W*			$250
WEISSE, Rudolph Austrian (1869 -)	*P*	$44,000	$57,750	$71,500
WEISZ, Adolphe French (1868 -)	*P*			$27,500
WELCH, E. M. (19th -)	*P*			$248
WELCH, Jack (1905 -)	*P*			$3,400
WELCH, Ludmilla P. American (1867 - 1925)	*P*	$330	$646	$990
WELCH, Rosemary S. European (?)	*P*			$110
WELCH, Thaddeus American (1844 - 1919)	*D* *P*	$825	$2,277	$523 $5,500
WELEY, A. American (20th -)	*P*			$138
WELEY, V. American (20th -)	*P*			$303

D=Drawing, P=Painting, S=Sculpture, W=Watercolor

		Current Price Range		
		Low	Mean	High
WELL, John S.	D			$3,300
British (19th - 20th)				
WELLER, C.	W			$193
(19th -)				
WELLIVER, Neil	P	$3,410	$17,301	$38,500
American (1929 -)				
WELLS,	P			$176
British (20th -)				
WELLS, Amy W.	P			$413
American (1888 -)				
WELLS, George	P			$1,650
British (1842 - 1888)				
WELLS, J.	W			$143
American (?)				
WELLS, John S.	P	$1,870	$8,140	$15,400
British (1872 - 1911)				
WELLS, Lynton	P	$385	$2,393	$4,400
American (1940 -)				
WELLS, Newton A.	P			$660
American (1852 -)				
WELLS, T.	P			$143
American (?)				
WELLS, William L.	P	$413	$867	$1,320
American (20th -)				
WENDEL, Theodore	D	$1,540	$4,730	$7,700
American (1857 - 1932)	P	$2,750	$4,125	$5,500
WENDLING, Gustav	P			$1,650
German (1862 -)				
WENDT, W. L.	P			$330
American (19th -)				
WENDT, William	P	$2,200	$24,613	$55,000
American (1865 - 1946)	W			$3,850
WENGENROTH, Stow	W	$523	$1,176	$1,760
American (1906 - 1978)				

D=Drawing, P=Painting, S=Sculpture, W=Watercolor

		Current Price Range		
		Low	Mean	High
WENGLEIN, Joseph	*P*	$2,640	$21,963	$46,750
German (1845 - 1919)				
WENK,	*S*			$770
European (19th -)				
WENKEBACH, L. W. R.	*P*			$1,650
European (19th - 20th)				
WENNER, C.	*P*			$400
American (19th -)				
WENTWORTH, Almond H.	*P*	$138	$166	$193
American (1872 - 1953)				
WENTWORTH, Daniel F.	*P*	$523	$606	$688
American (1850 - 1934)	*W*			$286
WENTWORTH, John	*W*			$138
(20th -)				
WENZELL, Albert	*P*	$165	$1,027	$1,980
American (1864 - 1917)	*W*			$9,900
WERFF, Adriaen van	*W*			$880
Dutch (1659 - 1722)				
WERFF, Adriaen van (After)	*P*			$7,150
Dutch (1659 - 1722)	*S*			$2,640
WERFF, Pieter van der	*P*	$16,500	$55,000	$93,500
Dutch (1665 - 1722)				
WERKEL, C.	*P*			$440
British (19th -)				
WERNER, W.	*P*			$495
German (19th -)				
WERTHEIMER, Gustav	*P*			$11,000
Austrian (1847 - 1904)				
WERVEKE, George van	*D*			$400
(?)				
WESSEL, Herman H.	*P*			$605
American (1878 - 1969)	*W*	$358	$427	$495
WESSELMANN, Tom	*D*	$3,850	$24,416	$93,500

D=Drawing, P=Painting, S=Sculpture, W=Watercolor

		Current Price Range		
		Low	Mean	High

		Low	Mean	High
WESSELMANN, Tom	*P*	$12,650	$80,074	$528,000
American (1931 -)	*S*	$33,000	$174,350	$495,000
	W	$9,350	$29,242	$60,500
WESSELS, Albert	*P*			$440
Dutch (20th -)				
WESSELS, Glenn	*W*			$2,200
American (20th -)				
WESSLEY, Anton	*P*			$5,500
Austrian (1848 -)				
WESSON, Robert	*P*	$303	$605	$990
American (19th - 20th)				
WEST, Benjamin	*D*	$495	$1,925	$4,400
British (1738 - 1820)	*P*			$24,200
WEST, Benjamin (Attrib.)	*D*	$660	$770	$880
British (1738 - 1820)	*W*			$715
WEST, Benjamin (Circle)	*D*	$220	$605	$990
British (1738 - 1820)	*P*			$1,320
WEST, Helen	*P*			$1,100
American (20th -)				
WEST, Levon	*W*			$1,100
American (1900 - 1968)				
WEST, Louise	*P*			$220
American (1878 - 1952)				
WEST, Raphael L.	*D*	$550	$3,850	$7,150
American (1769 - 1850)				
WEST, Walter J.	*P*			$2,090
British (19th - 20th)				
WESTCHILOFF, Constantin	*P*	$330	$1,448	$3,025
Russian (1880 - 1945)				
WESTERBEEK, Cornelis	*P*			$990
Dutch (1844 - 1903)				
WESTERBURG, Gus P. (After)	*P*			$495
Dutch (1791 - 1873)				

D=Drawing, P=Painting, S=Sculpture, W=Watercolor

		Current Price Range		
		Low	Mean	High
WESTERMANN, H. C.	*D*			$11,000
American (1922 -)	*P*			$110,000
	S	$4,180	$22,176	$38,500
	W			$132,000
WESTERMEIER, Clifford P.	*W*			$550
(1910 -)				
WESTFALL, William (Manner)	*W*			$132
(20th -)				
WESTON, Dell	*S*	$143	$147	$154
American (20th -)				
WESTON, F.	*P*			$176
(20th -)				
WESTON, Harold	*P*			$220
American (1894 - 1972)	*W*			$660
WESTON, James	*P*			$715
American (19th - 20th)				
WET, Jacob W. de	*P*	$4,400	$6,875	$9,350
Dutch (1610 - 1671)				
WETERING DE ROOY, Johannes	*P*			$1,430
Dutch (1877 -)				
WETHERBEE, George F.	*P*			$8,350
American (1851 - 1920)				
WETHERILL, Edith B.	*P*			$350
(?)				
WETHERILL, Elisha K. K.	*P*	$1,100	$4,895	$14,300
American (1874 - 1929)				
WETZEL, Richard	*P*			$1,045
American (20th -)				
WEXIER, George	*P*			$247
(?)				
WEYDEN, Harry van der	*P*	$413	$669	$825
American (1868 -)				
WEYDEN, Roger van der (After)	*P*			$550
Flemish (1399 - 1464)				

D=Drawing, P=Painting, S=Sculpture, W=Watercolor

		Current Price Range		
		Low	Mean	High
WEYGANDT, John H.	*P*			$193
American (? - 1951)				
WEYGOLD, Frederick P.	*P*			$385
American (1870 - 1941)				
WEYL, Max	*D*			$495
American (1837 - 1914)	*P*	$578	$1,945	$3,575
WEYMOUTH, Frolic	*D*			$825
American (20th -)				
WEYRICH, Joseph L.	*P*			$264
American (1889 - 1918)				
WHALLEY, F.	*P*			$413
British (19th -)				
WHARTON, Elizabeth M.	*W*			$303
American (20th -)				
WHEAT, John	*P*			$825
American (1920 -)				
WHEATLEY, Francis	*P*	$5,225	$10,542	$15,400
British (1747 - 1801)				
WHEATLEY, Francis (After)	*P*			$935
British (1747 - 1801)				
WHEATLEY, Francis (Attrib.)	*P*			$440
British (1747 - 1801)				
WHEATLEY, G. H.	*P*	$440	$495	$550
American (20th -)				
WHEATON, Francis	*D*			$990
American (1849 -)	*W*			$385
WHEELER,	*P*			$5,500
German (20th -)				
WHEELER, C. L.	*S*			$6,600
American (20th -)				
WHEELER, Hughlette T.	*S*	$880	$1,815	$2,750
American (20th -)				
WHEELER, James T.	*P*			$2,420
British (1849 - 1888)				

D=Drawing, P=Painting, S=Sculpture, W=Watercolor

		Current Price Range		
		Low	Mean	High

		Low	Mean	High
WHEELER, John A.	*P*	$880	$3,878	$9,625
British (1821 - 1877)				
WHEELER, L. F.	*P*			$990
American (19th -)				
WHEELER, William R.	*P*	$660	$2,420	$4,180
American (1832 -)				
WHEELER, JR., John	*P*			$4,180
British (1875 - 1930)				
WHEELWRIGHT, Rowland	*P*	$33,000	$35,750	$38,500
British (1870 - 1955)				
WHEELWRIGHT, W. H.	*P*			$22,000
British (19th -)				
WHEETE, Treva	*P*			$1,045
American (1890 -)				
WHIPPLE, Charles A.	*P*			$1,100
American (1859 - 1928)				
WHIPPLE, Seth A.	*P*			$4,400
American (1855 - 1901)				
WHISTLER, James A. M.	*D*	$605	$29,294	$99,000
American (1834 - 1903)	*P*			$176,000
WHISTLER, James A. M. (Attrib.)	*W*			$275
American (1834 - 1903)				
WHISTLER, Rex	*W*			$1,760
British (1905 - 1944)				
WHITAKER, George W.	*P*	$330	$765	$1,650
American (1841 - 1916)	*W*			$1,870
WHITAKER, William	*D*	$2,200	$2,338	$2,475
American (1943 -)	*P*	$1,210	$3,145	$4,620
WHITCOMB, Jon	*D*			$1,300
American (1906 - 1988)	*W*	$220	$614	$1,300
WHITCOMBE, H.	*P*			$3,300
British (19th -)				
WHITCOMBE, Mark	*P*			$193
(?)				

D=Drawing, P=Painting, S=Sculpture, W=Watercolor

		Current Price Range		
		Low	Mean	High
WHITE, Alvin A.	*P*	$165	$385	$660
American (20th -)				
WHITE, Belle	*P*			$633
American (? - 1945)				
WHITE, Clarence S.	*D*			$220
American (1872 -)	*P*			$413
	W			$358
WHITE, Edith	*P*	$495	$1,994	$5,225
American (1855 - 1946)				
WHITE, Edwin	*P*			$2,200
American (19th -)				
WHITE, Fritz	*S*			$7,150
American (1930 -)				
WHITE, H. Dennison	*W*			$110
American (20th -)				
WHITE, Henry C.	*P*	$1,980	$2,225	$2,495
American (1861 - 1952)				
WHITE, J. H.	*P*	$440	$495	$550
(19th -)				
WHITE, Jacob	*P*			$523
American (1895 -)				
WHITE, Joseph	*P*	$330	$825	$1,320
American (20th -)				
WHITE, Nelson	*P*			$1,760
American (1900 -)	*W*			$275
WHITE, Newton H.	*P*	$825	$1,082	$1,210
American (19th -)				
WHITE, Orrin A.	*P*	$200	$2,004	$5,225
American (1883 - 1969)	*W*			$1,045
WHITE, Roy M.	*P*			$248
American (20th -)				
WHITE, Sydney W.	*P*			$770
(20th -)				

D=Drawing, P=Painting, S=Sculpture, W=Watercolor

		Current Price Range		
		Low	Mean	High

		Low	Mean	High
WHITE, T.	*P*			$9,625
British (19th -)				
WHITE, Verner	*P*			$176
American (19th - 20th)				
WHITE MOUNTAIN SCHOOL,	*P*	$131	$836	$1,540
American (19th -)				
WHITEHEAD, Frederick W. N.	*P*			$4,400
British (1853 - 1938)				
WHITEMAN, Samuel E.	*P*			$440
American (1860 - 1922)				
WHITEMORE, A.	*S*			$176
American (19th - 20th)				
WHITING, L. Maria	*D*			$1,430
American (1833 -)				
WHITING, Lillian V.	*P*			$330
American (1876 - 1949)				
WHITLEY, H. C.	*P*			$990
American (20th -)				
WHITMORE,	*P*			$330
American (20th -)				
WHITMORE, Charlotte	*P*			$220
American (20th -)				
WHITMORE, Coby	*P*	$1,000	$1,600	$2,200
American (1913 -)	*W*	$138	$436	$935
WHITMORE, Helen	*P*			$1,200
American (20th -)				
WHITMORE, R. H.	*P*			$165
American (20th -)				
WHITMORE, William R.	*P*			$440
American (19th - 20th)				
WHITNEY, Charles F.	*W*			$250
American (1858 -)				
WHITNEY, E. S.	*P*			$660
American (19th -)				
WHITNEY, Helen R.	*P*	$138	$146	$154
American (1878 - 1942)				

D=Drawing, P=Painting, S=Sculpture, W=Watercolor

		Current Price Range		
		Low	Mean	High
WHITNEY, Richard (?)	*P*			$110
WHITTAKER, James British (1828 - 1876)	*P*			$5,280
WHITTAKER, John B. British (1836 - 1926)	*P*	$154	$290	$385
WHITTEMORE, William J.	*D*			$1,760
American (1860 - 1955)	*P*	$550	$935	$1,650
	W	$660	$3,630	$6,600
WHITTLEY, T. (?)	*P*			$990
WHITTREDGE, Worthington American (1820 - 1910)	*P*	$2,750	$220,381	$1.870M
WHITTREDGE, Worthington (Att.) American (1820 - 1910)	*P*			$660
WHORF, John	*P*	$385	$2,681	$4,950
American (1903 - 1959)	*W*	$528	$2,928	$9,350
WHORF, Marjorie (1927 -)	*W*	$248	$248	$248
WHYMPER, Charles (?)	*W*			$2,640
WIAI, N. V. Dutch (20th -)	*P*			$286
WICHERA, Raimund Austrian (1862 -)	*P*	$880	$5,060	$7,150
WICKENDEN, Robert J. British (1861 -)	*P*			$358
WICKER, (20th -)	*P*			$132
WICKER, Mary H. Irish (20th -)	*P*	$275	$275	$275
WICKES, E. M. (?)	*W*			$165
WIDDAS, Richard D. British (1826 - 1885)	*P*	$7,700	$20,900	$34,100

D=Drawing, P=Painting, S=Sculpture, W=Watercolor

| | | Current Price Range | | |
		Low	Mean	High
WIDER, Wilhelm	*P*			$16,500
German (1818 - 1884)				
WIDFORSS, Gunnar	*W*	$1,210	$6,910	$16,500
American (1879 - 1934)				
WIDFORSS, Gunnar (Attrib.)	*W*			$550
American (1879 - 1934)				
WIDGERY, Frederick J.	*P*			$523
British (1861 - 1942)	*W*	$385	$413	$440
WIDGERY, William	*P*			$825
British (1822 - 1893)				
WIECK, Johann	*P*			$825
German (1855 -)				
WIEGAND, Charmion von	*P*			$17,600
(?)				
WIEGAND, Gustave A.	*P*	$110	$1,640	$5,500
American (1870 - 1957)				
WIEGANDT, Bernhard	*W*			$17,600
German (1851 - 1918)				
WIEGHORST, Olaf C.	*D*	$500	$7,584	$40,700
American (1899 - 1975)	*P*	$1,430	$15,895	$57,200
	S			$1,760
	W	$2,420	$3,685	$4,950
WIELAND, F.	*P*			$605
(19th -)				
WIER, Julian A.	*P*			$4,950
American (1852 - 1919)				
WIERINGEN, Cornelis C. van	*D*			$6,600
Dutch (16th - 17th)				
WIERIX, Johan	*D*	$4,400	$7,425	$10,450
Flemish (16th - 17th)				
WIERUSZ-KOWALSKI, Alfred	*P*	$8,800	$18,700	$28,600
Polish (1849 - 1915)				
WIESENTHAL, Franz	*P*	$4,125	$5,408	$7,700
Austrian (1856 -)				

D=Drawing, P=Painting, S=Sculpture, W=Watercolor

		Current Price Range		
		Low	Mean	High
WIESNER, Hella	*P*			$7,700
German (20th -)				
WIGEL, Archie P.	*P*			$330
(?)				
WIGGINS, Carleton	*D*			$385
American (1848 - 1932)	*P*	$606	$2,061	$6,050
	W			$4,400
WIGGINS, Guy C.	*P*	$990	$11,909	$40,700
American (1883 - 1962)	*W*			$2,090
WIGGINS, Guy C. (Attrib.)	*P*			$750
American (1883 - 1962)				
WIGLE, Archie P.	*P*	$110	$303	$495
American (20th -)				
WIJSMULLER, Jan H.	*P*			$5,500
Dutch (1855 - 1925)				
WIJSMULLER, Jan H. (Attrib.)	*P*			$275
Dutch (1855 - 1925)				
WIKSTROM, Bror A.	*P*			$1,045
American (? - 1909)				
WILBER, Lawrence N.	*W*			$468
American (1897 -)				
WILBUR, Isaac	*P*			$1,650
American (19th -)				
WILBUR, J. B.	*W*			$2,750
(?)				
WILBUR, Lawrence	*P*			$4,125
American (19th - 20th)				
WILCOX, Frank	*W*			$385
American (1887 -)				
WILCOX, Leslie A.	*P*	$2,970	$5,748	$8,525
British (1904 -)				
WILCOX, Ray	*P*			$550
American (1883 -)				
WILCOX, W. H.	*P*			$275
(19th -)				

D=Drawing, P=Painting, S=Sculpture, W=Watercolor

		Current Price Range		
		Low	Mean	High
WILDE, John	P	$4,400	$8,800	$13,200
American (20th -)				
WILDE, John (Attrib.)	P			$4,200
American (20th -)				
WILDENS, Jan	P			$24,200
Flemish (1586 - 1653)				
WILDENS, Jan (Circle)	P			$8,250
Flemish (1586 - 1653)				
WILDER, Arthur B.	P			$523
American (1857 - 1945)				
WILDER, J.	P	$1,045	$2,668	$4,290
American (19th - 20th)				
WILDER, Louise H.	S			$2,475
American (1898 -)				
WILDER, T. B. M.	P			$110
(?)				
WILDHABER, Paul	P	$165	$403	$660
American (20th -)				
WILES, Irving R.	D			$302
American (1861 - 1948)	P	$1,430	$14,735	$77,000
WILES, Lemuel M.	P	$2,200	$3,575	$5,775
American (1826 - 1905)				
WILEY, J. G.	P			$660
American (20th -)				
WILEY, William T.	D			$1,210
American (1937 -)	P	$4,400	$15,400	$26,400
WILFORD, Loren	P			$110
American (1892 - 1972)	W			$275
WILHELM, Genevieve B.	W			$242
American (20th -)				
WILHELMI, Heinrich	P			$20,900
German (? - 1902)				
WILHER, A. R.	P			$198
(19th -)				

D=Drawing, P=Painting, S=Sculpture, W=Watercolor

| | | Current Price Range | | |
		Low	Mean	High
WILKE, Sir David (School)	P			$770
British (1783 - 1841)				
WILKIE, Robert D.	P	$1,870	$6,974	$17,600
American (1828 - 1903)				
WILKINS, John G.	P			$1,760
(?)				
WILKS, Maurice C.	P	$825	$1,082	$1,540
British (19th -)				
WILL, August	D			$880
American (1834 - 1910)	W			$1,320
WILL & GROTH, August & John	D			$550
American (19th - 20th)				
WILLAERTS, Isaac	D			$33,000
Dutch (1620 - 1693)				
WILLANER, Ive	P			$220
American (20th -)				
WILLARD, Archibald	P	$330	$715	$1,100
American (1837 - 1918)				
WILLARD, J.	P			$550
(19th -)				
WILLARD, Stephen	P			$605
American (20th -)				
WILLCOX, W. H.	P			$2,640
American (1831 -)				
WILLE, Johann G.	D			$6,270
German (1715 - 1808)				
WILLEMS, Florent	P			$3,850
Belgian (1823 - 1905)				
WILLENBORG, H. A.	W			$440
Dutch (19th -)				
WILLERS, William	S			$825
American (20th -)				
WILLETT, J.	P			$330
(?)				
WILLETTE, Charles E.	D			$440

D=Drawing, P=Painting, S=Sculpture, W=Watercolor

| | | Current Price Range | | |
		Low	Mean	High
WILLETTE, Charles E.	*P*	$165	$275	$330
American (1895 - 1979)				
WILLIAM, John H.	*P*			$11,000
British (19th -)				
WILLIAMS,	*D*			$440
(?)				
WILLIAMS, Annabelle	*P*			$413
American (20th -)				
WILLIAMS, Con	*S*			$1,700
American (20th -)				
WILLIAMS, Dwight	*D*			$165
American (1856 - 1932)				
WILLIAMS, Edward	*P*			$2,750
British (1782 - 1855)				
WILLIAMS, Edward C.	*P*	$3,575	$4,785	$5,500
British (1807 - 1881)				
WILLIAMS, Edward K.	*P*			$2,090
American (1870 -)				
WILLIAMS, Esther	*P*			$550
American (1901 -)				
WILLIAMS, Ewart L.	*P*			$990
(20th -)				
WILLIAMS, F.	*P*	$275	$605	$935
British (19th -)				
WILLIAMS, F. H.	*P*			$1,100
British (19th -)				
WILLIAMS, F. O.	*W*			$253
(19th -)				
WILLIAMS, Florence W.	*P*	$341	$1,405	$4,510
American (? - 1953)				
WILLIAMS, Frederick B.	*P*	$660	$1,451	$2,090
American (1871 - 1956)				
WILLIAMS, Frederick D.	*P*	$550	$1,540	$1,980
American (1829 - 1915)	*W*			$715
WILLIAMS, George A.	*D*			$633

D=Drawing, P=Painting, S=Sculpture, W=Watercolor

		Current Price Range		
		Low	Mean	High
WILLIAMS, George A. American (1875 - 1932)	P			$550
WILLIAMS, George A. British (1814 - 1901)	P	$2,475	$3,713	$4,950
WILLIAMS, Graham British (19th -)	P	$770	$1,306	$2,090
WILLIAMS, J. L. British (19th -)	P	$1,100	$1,430	$1,760
WILLIAMS, John A. American (1869 -)	W			$138
WILLIAMS, Keith S. (?)	P			$193
WILLIAMS, Mary Belle American (1873 - 1943)	P	$275	$941	$3,025
WILLIAMS, Mary E. G. American (1825 - 1902)	W			$2,750
WILLIAMS, Mary R. American (? - 1907)	D			$330
WILLIAMS, Micah (?)	D	$4,730	$12,128	$19,525
WILLIAMS, Mildred E. American (1892 -)	P	$110	$165	$220
WILLIAMS, Paul A. American (1934 -)	P	$468	$2,894	$12,100
WILLIAMS, Penry British (1798 - 1885)	P	$1,210	$2,805	$4,400
WILLIAMS, Robert F. American (20th -)	P			$1,265
WILLIAMS, S. (?)	P	$220	$220	$220
WILLIAMS, T. J. American (19th - 20th)	P			$138
WILLIAMS, Terrick British (1860 - 1937)	D P	$1,870	$14,190	$5,500 $30,800
WILLIAMS, Virgil American (1830 - 1886)	W			$1,650

D=Drawing, P=Painting, S=Sculpture, W=Watercolor

		Current Price Range		
		Low	Mean	High

		Low	Mean	High
WILLIAMS, Walter British (1835 - 1906)	*P*	$550	$2,943	$8,800
WILLIAMS, Wheeler American (1897 - 1972)	*S*	$4,400	$7,792	$14,300
WILLIAMS, William British (18th -)	*P*			$8,800
WILLIAMS-LYOUNS, Herbert F. British (1863 -)	*P*			$220
WILLIAMSON, Arthur T. American (20th -)	*P*			$110
WILLIAMSON, E. E. American (19th -)	*P*			$715
WILLIAMSON, Frederick British (19th -)	*P*			$1,595
WILLIAMSON, John American (1826 - 1885)	*P*	$1,050	$3,503	$7,700
WILLIAMSON, T. British (19th -)	*P*			$330
WILLIAMSON, William H. British (1820 - 1883)	*P*			$495
WILLIGEN, Jan C. van der Dutch (15th -)	*P*			$6,050
WILLIOT, P. French (19th -)	*P*			$330
WILLIS, Edmund A. American (1808 - 1899)	*P*	$1,100	$2,200	$3,300
WILLIS, Henry B. British (1810 - 1884)	*P*	$1,375	$10,432	$27,500
WILLIS, Richard Irish (1853 - 1905)	*P*			$1,100
WILLIS, Thomas American (1850 - 1912)	*P*	$1,980	$2,090	$2,200
WILLISON, T. J. American (20th -)	*P*	$143	$226	$385
WILLMANN, Michael L. L. German (1630 - 1706)	*P*			$6,600

D=Drawing, P=Painting, S=Sculpture, W=Watercolor

		Current Price Range		
		Low	Mean	High

		Low	Mean	High
WILLOUGHBY, W.	*P*			$715
British (19th -)				
WILLROIDER, Ludwig	*P*	$4,400	$4,583	$4,950
German (1845 - 1910)				
WILLS,	*P*			$2,200
British (19th -)				
WILLS, William	*P*			$495
(?)				
WILLSON, John J.	*P*			$550
British (1836 - 1903)				
WILLY, C. A.	*P*			$330
(20th -)				
WILMARTH, Christopher	*D*	$18,700	$19,250	$19,800
American (1943 -)	*P*	$13,200	$27,225	$41,250
	S	$66,000	$82,500	$99,000
WILMARTH, Lemuel Everett	*P*			$1,760
American (1835 - 1918)				
WILSON, A.	*P*			$220
(?)	*W*			$138
WILSON, Bryan	*P*			$935
American (20th -)				
WILSON, C.	*P*			$358
(?)				
WILSON, Charles E.	*W*			$3,850
British (1934 -)				
WILSON, Charles J. A.	*W*			$660
American (1880 - 1965)				
WILSON, D. P.	*P*			$275
American (20th -)				
WILSON, David F.	*P*			$5,225
British (1873 - 1950)				
WILSON, Francis V.	*D*			$165
American (1874 - 1938)				
WILSON, Frederick	*P*			$880
American (19th - 20th)				

D=Drawing, P=Painting, S=Sculpture, W=Watercolor

		Current Price Range		
		Low	Mean	High

WILSON, H.	*P*			$385
American (20th -)				
WILSON, J.	*P*	$1,320	$2,457	$3,850
British (19th -)	*W*			$440
WILSON, J. Coggeshall	*P*			$770
American (19th -)				
WILSON, Jane	*P*	$715	$1,526	$2,090
American (1924 -)				
WILSON, Mary Loomis	*P*			$4,620
(20th -)	*S*			$165
WILSON, Melissa A.	*S*	$2,200	$2,823	$3,520
American (1968 -)				
WILSON, Mortimer	*P*	$3,200	$4,200	$5,200
American (1906 -)				
WILSON, Nelson	*P*	$220	$234	$248
American (1880 -)				
WILSON, Nevada	*P*			$138
American (20th -)				
WILSON, Norman B.	*P*			$605
American (20th -)				
WILSON, Ray	*W*	$880	$1,045	$1,210
American (1906 - 1972)				
WILSON, Ray (Attrib.)	*P*			$330
American (1906 - 1972)				
WILSON, Richard	*P*	$495	$1,073	$1,650
British (1714 - 1782)				
WILSON, Richard (Attrib.)	*D*			$660
British (1714 - 1782)	*P*			$3,850
WILSON, Richard (Circle)	*P*	$1,540	$1,870	$2,200
British (1714 - 1782)				
WILSON, Richard (School)	*P*			$7,150
British (1714 - 1782)				
WILSON, Robert B.	*D*	$187	$286	$385

D=Drawing, P=Painting, S=Sculpture, W=Watercolor

		Current Price Range		
		Low	Mean	High

		Low	Mean	High
WILSON, Robert B. American (1851 - 1916)	*W*	$330	$440	$495
WILSON, Sol American (1894 -)	*P* *W*	$110	$582	$1,100 $425
WILSON, Ubediah American (19th -)	*P*			$440
WILSON, W. American (20th -)	*P*			$209
WILSON, William British (19th -)	*P*			$9,350
WILSTACH, George L. American (1892 -)	*P*	$154	$162	$187
WILTON, Olive M. British (20th -)	*P*			$2,090
WIMPERIS, Edmund M. British (1835 - 1900)	*W*			$880
WINANS, Walter American (1852 - 1920)	*S*	$6,600	$12,100	$17,600
WINCHELL, (?)	*P*			$385
WINCK, Christian German (1738 - 1797)	*P*			$2,420
WINCK, Johann A. German (1748 - 1817)	*P*			$16,500
WINDMAIER, Anton German (1840 - 1896)	*P*			$6,050
WINDT, Chris Van Der Dutch (1877 -)	*P*			$385
WINDT, Phillip P. Dutch (1847 - 1921)	*P*			$2,750
WINES, James American (1932 -)	*S*			$1,540
WINFIELD, Rodney M. American (1925 -)	*S*			$2,750
WING, George F. American (20th -)	*P*			$110

D=Drawing, P=Painting, S=Sculpture, W=Watercolor

		Current Price Range		
		Low	Mean	High

WINGFIELD, James D.	*P*			$2,420
British (? - 1872)				
WINHART, A.	*P*			$935
German (?)				
WINK, Johann C. T. (Circle)	*P*			$3,850
German (1738 - 1797)				
WINKELBERG, G.	*P*			$121
(?)				
WINKLER, K.	*P*			$440
American (19th - 20th)				
WINT, Peter de	*D*			$4,400
British (1784 - 1849)	*W*	$468	$1,224	$1,980
WINT, Peter de (Follower)	*P*			$6,875
British (1784 - 1849)				
WINTER, Alice B.	*D*	$220	$440	$660
American (1877 - 1970)	*P*	$165	$862	$1,650
WINTER, Andrew	*P*	$468	$2,468	$7,150
American (1893 - 1958)				
WINTER, Charles A.	*P*	$110	$1,128	$3,080
American (1869 - 1942)				
WINTER, Ezra	*P*			$1,100
American (1886 - 1949)				
WINTER, Frederik	*P*			$1,045
Danish (1853 - 1916)				
WINTER, Fritz	*P*			$17,600
German (1905 - 1976)				
WINTER, H. Edward	*P*			$825
American (1908 -)				
WINTER, Heinrich	*P*			$330
German (1843 - 1911)				
WINTER, Robin	*W*			$880
(20th -)				
WINTER, Thelma	*S*			$110
American (20th -)				

D=Drawing, P=Painting, S=Sculpture, W=Watercolor

		Current Price Range		
		Low	Mean	High

WINTER-SHAW, Arthur	*P*			$4,125
British (1869 - 1948)				
WINTERBERG,	*P*			$165
American (20th -)				
WINTERBURN, George T.	*P*			$358
American (1865 -)				
WINTERHALTER, Franz X. (Sc.)	*P*			$4,620
German (1806 - 1873)				
WINTERINGHAM, A. P.	*P*			$468
British (20th -)				
WINTERMOTE, Mamie W.	*P*			$495
American (1885 - 1945)				
WINTERS, Robin	*P*			$4,950
American (20th -)				
WINTERS, Terry	*D*	$3,850	$11,629	$26,400
American (20th -)	*P*	$25,300	$38,133	$60,500
WIREMAN, Eugenie M.	*P*			$990
American (19th - 20th)				
WIRTH, Paul	*P*			$7,700
(16th -)				
WISBY, Jack	*P*	$330	$1,166	$1,760
American (1870 - 1940)				
WISEMAN, Robert	*P*			$165
(1891 -)				
WISSING, William (Attrib.)	*P*			$9,900
Dutch (1653 - 1687)				
WISSING, William (School)	*P*			$3,080
Dutch (1653 - 1687)				
WISTEHUFF, Revere F.	*P*			$3,000
(1900 - 1971)				
WIT, Jacob de	*D*	$2,420	$2,970	$3,520
Dutch (1695 - 1754)	*P*			$16,500
WIT, Jacob de (Circle)	*D*			$3,300
Dutch (1695 - 1754)				

D=Drawing, P=Painting, S=Sculpture, W=Watercolor

		Current Price Range		
		Low	Mean	High

		Low	Mean	High
WITHAM, Joseph	*P*	$3,300	$5,088	$6,875
British (1832 - 1901)				
WITHEMS, J.	*P*			$1,540
European (19th - 20th)				
WITHERINGTON, William F.	*P*	$3,850	$16,225	$28,600
British (1785 - 1865)				
WITHERSTINE, Donald	*P*			$1,320
American (1896 - 1961)				
WITHOOS, Alida	*W*			$1,320
Dutch (17th - 18th)				
WITHOOS, Franz	*P*			$14,300
Dutch (1657 - 1705)				
WITHOOS, Matthias	*P*	$7,150	$11,550	$15,400
Dutch (1627 - 1703)				
WITHROW, Evelyn A.	*P*			$1,540
American (1858 - 1928)				
WITJENS, Willem	*P*			$990
Dutch (1884 - 1962)				
WITKIN, Isaac	*S*	$1,540	$2,145	$2,750
American (1936 -)				
WITKIN, Jerome	*D*			$1,100
American (20th -)				
WITKOWSKI, Karl	*P*	$1,100	$6,160	$14,300
American (1860 - 1910)				
WITMAN, C. F.	*P*			$2,475
American (19th -)				
WITT, John H.	*P*			$605
American (1840 - 1901)				
WITTE, Pieter de	*P*			$15,400
Flemish (1548 - 1628)				
WITTEL, Gaspar van	*D*	$13,200	$23,100	$37,400
Dutch (1653 - 1736)	*P*			$242,000
	W			$22,000
WITTEL, Gaspar van (Circle)	*P*	$4,400	$5,775	$7,150
Dutch (1653 - 1736)				

D=Drawing, P=Painting, S=Sculpture, W=Watercolor

		Current Price Range		
		Low	Mean	High
WITTEL, Gaspar van (Manner)	*P*			$44,000
Dutch (1653 - 1736)				
WITTKAMP, Johann B.	*P*			$3,300
German (1820 - 1885)				
WITTMACK, Edgar F.	*P*			$1,540
American (1894 - 1956)				
WODNASKY, Wilhelm	*P*			$1,100
Austrian (1876 -)				
WOELFLE, Arthur W.	*P*	$550	$990	$1,430
American (1879 - 1936)				
WOERFFEL, C. F. (After)	*S*			$1,100
Russian (19th -)				
WOFFORD, Phillip	*S*			$176
American (20th -)				
WOHL, Millie	*P*	$275	$930	$1,980
American (20th -)				
WOICESKE, Ronau W.	*P*			$220
American (1887 - 1953)				
WOJNAROWICZ, David	*P*	$3,300	$4,290	$5,280
(20th -)	*S*			$4,400
WOLCOTT, Harold C.	*P*			$2,750
American (20th -)				
WOLF, A.	*P*			$2,640
European (19th -)				
WOLF, Franz X.	*P*			$5,500
(?)				
WOLF, H.	*P*			$248
(?)				
WOLF, Jacques	*P*			$1,100
French (19th - 20th)				
WOLF, S. R.	*P*			$121
(20th -)				
WOLFE, Byron B.	*W*			$660
American (20th -)				
WOLFE, Edith G.	*P*			$3,080
British (1888 - 1970)				

D=Drawing, P=Painting, S=Sculpture, W=Watercolor

		Current Price Range		
		Low	Mean	High

		Low	Mean	High
WOLFE, Edward	*P*			$6,050
American (20th -)				
WOLFENSBERGER, John J.	*W*	$3,300	$3,300	$3,300
Swiss (1797 - 1850)				
WOLFERT, C.	*P*			$935
(?)				
WOLFF, Gustave	*P*	$358	$625	$1,155
American (1863 - 1935)				
WOLFF, H.	*P*			$308
German (19th - 20th)				
WOLFF, Joseph (Attrib.)	*P*			$1,100
British (1820 - 1899)				
WOLFLE, Franz X.	*P*			$3,300
Austrian (1896 -)				
WOLFROM, Friedrich E.	*P*			$825
German (1857 -)				
WOLHAUPTER, Helen P.	*P*			$193
American (1897 -)				
WOLINS, Joseph	*P*	$605	$715	$935
American (19th - 20th)				
WOLKIN, F. L. H.	*W*			$550
American (19th -)				
WOLLNER,	*P*			$303
(?)				
WOLMARK, Alfred A.	*P*			$2,640
British (1877 - 1961)				
WOLMUET, Paulus	*D*			$9,350
German (16th -)				
WOLRUNG, F.	*D*			$3,850
(19th -)				
WOLSTENHOLME, SR., Dean	*P*	$2,640	$23,247	$49,500
British (1757 - 1837)				
WOLTER, Hendrik J.	*P*			$13,200
Dutch (1873 - 1952)				
WON, Jack C.	*P*			$1,760
American (20th -)				

D=Drawing, P=Painting, S=Sculpture, W=Watercolor

		Current Price Range		
		Low	Mean	High

		Low	Mean	High
WONTNER, William C. British (19th -)	*P*	$12,100	$22,367	$33,000
WOOD, American (20th -)	*P*			$165
WOOD, A. M. American (19th -)	*P*	$825	$825	$825
WOOD, Beatrice American (20th -)	*S*	$2,750	$2,750	$2,750
WOOD, Bertha R. (?)	*P*			$2,750
WOOD, Charles H. British (1856 - 1927)	*P*			$26,400
WOOD, Charles K. American (19th - 20th)	*W*			$110
WOOD, Christopher British (1901 - 1930)	*D*			$138
WOOD, Frank W. British (1862 - 1953)	*W*			$2,750
WOOD, George A. American (1845 - 1910)	*P*			$110
WOOD, Grant American (1891 - 1942)	*D* *P*	$55,000 $2,750	$101,750 $5,317	$148,500 $8,800
WOOD, Grant (Attrib.) American (1891 - 1942)	*P*			$2,090
WOOD, Gretchen K. American (20th -)	*P*			$248
WOOD, Hunter American (1908 -)	*P*	$413	$1,311	$2,970
WOOD, Hunter (Attrib.) American (1908 -)	*P*			$750
WOOD, J. British (19th -)	*P*			$220
WOOD, James L. American (20th -)	*P*			$303
WOOD, John British (18th - 19th)	*P*			$1,650

D=Drawing, P=Painting, S=Sculpture, W=Watercolor

| | | Current Price Range | | |
		Low	Mean	High
WOOD, Julia S.	*P*	$193	$289	$385
American (1890 -)				
WOOD, Lewis J.	*P*	$1,210	$2,695	$4,125
British (1813 - 1901)				
WOOD, Nan	*P*			$193
American (1874 -)				
WOOD, Ogden	*P*	$880	$1,403	$1,925
American (1851 - 1912)				
WOOD, Robert	*P*	$880	$3,840	$13,200
American (1889 - 1979)	*W*	$1,100	$1,155	$1,210
WOOD, Sara L.	*P*			$165
American (?)				
WOOD, Silas	*P*			$14,850
American (19th -)				
WOOD, Stanley	*P*			$440
American (1894 -)				
WOOD, Thomas W.	*D*			$8,520
American (1823 - 1903)	*P*	$110	$10,021	$35,200
	W			$3,520
WOOD, William R. C.	*P*	$440	$1,045	$1,650
American (1875 - 1915)				
WOOD, Worden	*W*	$248	$399	$550
American (20th -)				
WOODARD, M. T.	*P*			$660
American (20th -)				
WOODBURN,	*P*			$154
American (20th -)				
WOODBURY, Charles H.	*D*	$110	$130	$150
American (1864 - 1940)	*P*	$220	$4,069	$82,500
	W	$550	$1,188	$1,540
WOODBURY, Susan M. O.	*D*			$358
American (1865 - 1913)				
WOODCOCK, Hartwell L.	*W*	$132	$259	$413
American (1853 - 1929)				

D=Drawing, P=Painting, S=Sculpture, W=Watercolor

		Current Price Range		
		Low	Mean	High

		Low	Mean	High
WOODFORDE, Samuel	*P*			$2,750
British (1763 - 1817)				
WOODLEIGH, Alma	*P*			$2,090
Tasmanian (19th - 20th)				
WOODMAN, Betty	*S*	$1,045	$1,962	$2,750
(20th -)				
WOODMAN, Tim	*P*			$1,540
(20th -)	*S*			$1,870
WOODROW, Bill	*P*			$33,000
(20th -)	*S*			$13,200
WOODRUFF, G. M. Leanard	*P*			$330
American (20th -)				
WOODSIDE, John A.	*P*	$1,045	$4,923	$8,800
American (1781 - 1852)				
WOODVILLE, Richard C.	*P*			$12,100
British (1825 - 1855)	*W*			$990
WOODWARD, Dewing	*P*			$550
American (1856 -)				
WOODWARD, Ellsworth	*P*	$1,100	$1,925	$2,750
American (1861 - 1939)	*W*	$248	$1,902	$6,600
WOODWARD, Helen	*P*			$110
American (1902 -)				
WOODWARD, Hildegard H.	*W*			$440
American (19th - 20th)				
WOODWARD, J. D.	*D*	$110	$176	$242
American (1848 - 1924)				
WOODWARD, J. D. (Et al.)	*D*	$660	$880	$1,100
American (19th - 20th)	*W*			$990
WOODWARD, Laura	*P*			$1,870
American (19th -)	*W*			$275
WOODWARD, Mabel M.	*P*	$330	$4,139	$14,850

D=Drawing, P=Painting, S=Sculpture, W=Watercolor

		Current Price Range		
		Low	Mean	High

		Low	Mean	High
WOODWARD, Mabel M. American (1877 - 1945)	W	$770	$1,100	$1,430
WOODWARD, Robert S. American (1885 - 1960)	D P	$825 $660	$853 $1,705	$880 $2,750
WOODWARD, Stanley W. American (1890 - 1970)	P W	$303 $193	$1,011 $303	$2,475 $440
WOODWARD, William American (1859 - 1939)	P W	$165	$1,257	$3,740 $4,400
WOOG, Raymond French (1875 -)	P			$6,600
WOOL, (?)	P			$1,870
WOOL, Christopher (20th -)	S			$26,400
WOOLF, Samuel J. American (1880 - 1948)	P	$880	$2,090	$3,300
WOOLLETT, Henry British (19th -)	P	$1,320	$2,585	$3,850
WOOLLEY, Virginia American (1884 - 1971)	P			$385
WOOLMER, Alfred J. British (1805 - 1895)	P	$413	$2,851	$5,500
WOOLRYCH, F. H. W. American (1868 -)	P	$358	$1,169	$1,980
WOOLSEY, Wood W. American (1899 -)	P	$500	$965	$1,430
WOOSTER, Austin C. American (19th - 20th)	P	$715	$3,804	$7,700
WOOTTON, Frank British (1914 -)	P			$2,530
WOOTTON, John British (1683 - 1764)	P	$10,450	$30,663	$44,000
WOPFNER, Joseph Austrian (1843 - 1927)	P			$23,100

D=Drawing, P=Painting, S=Sculpture, W=Watercolor

		Current Price Range		
		Low	Mean	High

		Low	Mean	High
WORDEN, J.	*W*			$110
(?)				
WORDEN, Laicita	*P*			$220
American (1892 -)				
WORES, Theodore	*D*			$3,850
American (1859 - 1939)	*P*	$1,760	$4,703	$7,150
	W			$1,100
WORMAN, Eugenia A.	*P*			$605
French (20th -)				
WORMS, Jules	*P*			$990
French (1832 - 1924)	*W*			$3,850
WORTH, Thomas	*D*			$220
American (19th -)				
WOSZINOWSKI, W.	*P*			$143
(?)				
WOTRUBA, Fritz	*D*			$715
Austrian (1907 - 1975)	*S*	$5,500	$8,800	$11,000
WOU, Claesz C.	*P*			$20,900
Dutch (1592 - 1665)				
WOU-KI, Zao	*P*	$8,250	$60,331	$104,500
French (1921 -)	*W*	$3,850	$6,600	$9,350
WOUDE, Elzard van der	*P*			$286
Dutch (1859 - 1922)				
WOUTERS, Frans	*P*			$17,600
Flemish (1614 - 1659)				
WOUTERS, Frans (Attrib.)	*P*			$6,050
Flemish (1614 - 1659)				
WOUTERS, Jan	*P*			$3,300
Dutch (1599 - 1663)				
WOUTERUS, Verschuur	*P*			$880
Dutch (1812 - 1874)				
WOUWERMANS, Philips	*P*			$638,000
Dutch (1619 - 1668)				

D=Drawing, P=Painting, S=Sculpture, W=Watercolor

		Current Price Range		
		Low	Mean	High

		Low	Mean	High
WOUWERMANS, Philips (After)	*P*			$6,600
Dutch (1619 - 1668)				
WOUWERMANS, Philips (Circle)	*D*			$1,980
Dutch (1619 - 1668)	*P*	$1,650	$2,970	$5,500
WOUWERMANS, Philips (Mann.)	*P*	$550	$1,302	$2,750
Dutch (1619 - 1668)				
WOUWERMANS, Philips (School)	*P*			$4,950
Dutch (1619 - 1668)				
WRAG, Carl	*P*			$165
American (20th -)				
WREFORD, Denis	*W*			$1,320
British (1910 -)				
WRIGHT, Charles L.	*P*			$1,210
American (1876 -)				
WRIGHT, Emma	*P*			$385
American (20th -)				
WRIGHT, George	*P*	$1,540	$7,047	$19,800
British (1860 - 1942)	*W*	$330	$330	$330
WRIGHT, George H.	*D*	$248	$1,224	$2,200
American (1872 - 1951)	*P*			$1,320
	W			$600
WRIGHT, Gilbert S.	*P*	$22,000	$25,300	$28,600
British (1880 - 1958)				
WRIGHT, H. A.	*P*			$1,100
British (19th -)				
WRIGHT, H. Boardman	*P*			$110
American (19th - 20th)				
WRIGHT, James C.	*W*	$550	$733	$880
American (1906 - 1969)				
WRIGHT, Joseph	*P*			$71,500
British (1734 - 1797)				
WRIGHT, Louise Wood	*P*			$440
American (19th -)				

D=Drawing, P=Painting, S=Sculpture, W=Watercolor

		Current Price Range		
		Low	Mean	High
WRIGHT, Mason	P			$330
American (20th -)				
WRIGHT, P. J.	P			$4,400
British (19th -)				
WRIGHT, R. Stephens	P			$468
American (20th -)				
WRIGHT, Redmond	P			$660
American (1903 -)				
WRIGHT, Richard (Attrib.)	P			$4,400
British (1735 - 1774)				
WRIGHT, Richard H.	W			$1,100
British (1857 - 1930)				
WRIGHT, Robert C.	P			$330
American (20th -)				
WRIGHT, Stanton	D			$990
American (1890 - 1974)	P			$2,200
WROBEL, Stephen	W	$303	$344	$385
Dutch (20th -)				
WSSEL, Manuel	W			$1,650
Spanish (19th -)				
WTEWAEL, Joachim	P			$220,000
Dutch (1566 - 1638)				
WUERMER, Carl	P	$990	$6,123	$8,800
American (1900 - 1983)				
WUERPEL, Edmund	P	$110	$204	$248
American (1866 - 1958)				
WUJIK, Theo	S			$385
American (1936 -)				
WUNDERLICH, Paul	P	$5,280	$13,493	$18,700
German (1927 -)	S			$5,280
	W	$5,500	$6,783	$8,250
WUNNENBERG, Carl	P			$3,410
German (1850 - 1929)				
WURTELE, Isobel K.	P			$605
American (1885 - 1963)				

D=Drawing, P=Painting, S=Sculpture, W=Watercolor

| | | Current Price Range | | |
		Low	Mean	High
WUST, Alexander	*P*	$1,045	$1,412	$2,090
American (1837 - 1876)	*W*			$1,650
WUTTKE, Carl	*P*			$11,000
German (1849 - 1927)				
WYANT, Alexander H.	*P*	$275	$3,828	$11,000
American (1836 - 1892)	*W*	$1,980	$3,850	$6,600
WYANT, Alexander H. (Attrib.)	*P*	$523	$812	$1,100
American (1836 - 1892)				
WYATT, A. C.	*P*			$495
American (? - 1933)				
WYATT, Kenneth	*P*	$165	$413	$660
American (20th -)				
WYCK, Thomas	*D*			$715
Dutch (1616 - 1670)				
WYCK, Thomas (Attrib.)	*P*			$880
Dutch (1616 - 1670)				
WYCK, Thomas (Style)	*W*			$495
Dutch (1616 - 1670)				
WYDEVELD, Arnoud	*P*			$1,045
Dutch (19th -)				
WYETH, Andrew	*D*	$35,200	$177,100	$319,000
American (1917 -)	*P*			$275,000
	W	$13,200	$106,700	$187,000
WYETH, Jamie	*P*	$22,000	$38,683	$52,250
American (1946 -)	*W*	$9,350	$18,563	$24,200
WYETH, John A.	*P*			$1,320
American (20th -)				
WYETH, Newell C.	*D*	$1,980	$5,390	$8,800
American (1882 - 1945)	*P*	$11,000	$36,239	$77,000
WYETH, Newell C. (Attrib.)	*P*			$715
American (1882 - 1945)				
WYGAERD, A. W.	*P*			$1,650
Dutch (19th -)				

D=Drawing, P=Painting, S=Sculpture, W=Watercolor

		Current Price Range		
		Low	Mean	High
WYGANT, Bob	P	$3,960	$7,893	$11,000
American (1927 -)				
WYGRZYWALSKI, Feliz K.	P			$220
Polish (1875 -)				
WYLD, William	P			$6,050
British (1806 - 1889)				
WYLE, Florence	S			$2,200
American (18th - 19th)				
WYLLIE, William L.	P			$440
British (1851 - 1931)				
WYMAN, William	S			$4,180
(20th -)				
WYMANN, M. R.	P			$121
American (19th - 20th)				
WYNANTS, Jan	P			$46,750
Dutch (? - 1684)				
WYNANTS, Jan (Attrib.)	P			$7,700
Dutch (? - 1684)				
WYNGAERDT, Antoine J. van	P	$165	$275	$385
Dutch (1808 - 1887)				
WYON, Allan G.	S			$4,400
British (1882 -)				
WYSMULLER, Jan H.	P			$1,980
Dutch (1855 - 1925)				
XCERON, Jean	W			$3,850
American (1890 - 1967)				
XUMAIA, Barbara	P			$154
Brazilian (20th -)				
YAEGER, Edgar	P			$187
American (1904 -)				
YALE, J. S.	D			$248
American (20th -)				
YALE, Leroy M.	D	$154	$275	$396
American (1841 - 1906)				
YAMAGUCHI, Kaoru	W			$220
Japanese (1907 - 1968)				

D=Drawing, P=Painting, S=Sculpture, W=Watercolor

		Current Price Range		
		Low	Mean	High

		Low	Mean	High
YANDELL, Enid	S	$1,540	$6,270	$11,000
American (1870 - 1936)				
YANG-HUI, Huang	D			$110
Chinese (?)				
YANKILEVSKY, Vladimir	P			$19,800
Russian (1938 -)				
YAO, C. J.	P			$8,800
(20th -)				
YARBER, Robert	D	$3,575	$4,744	$6,050
American (1948 -)	P	$16,500	$18,700	$23,100
YARD, Sydney J.	D			$1,430
American (1855 - 1909)	P			$660
	W			$1,045
YARNALL, Anna C.	P			$330
American (20th -)				
YARNELL, Agnes	S			$440
American (20th -)				
YARNOLD, B.	P			$1,045
British (19th -)				
YARROW, William H. K.	W			$220
American (1891 - 1941)				
YATES, Cullen	P	$248	$4,310	$18,700
American (1866 - 1945)				
YATES, Fred	P			$275
British (1854 - 1919)				
YATES, Thomas	P			$49,500
British (? - 1796)				
YATES, William H.	D			$193
American (1845 - 1934)	P	$248	$446	$990
YAUSS, G.	P			$1,320
European (19th - 20th)				
YAZZ, Beatin	W			$220
American (20th -)				

D=Drawing, P=Painting, S=Sculpture, W=Watercolor

		Current Price Range	
	Low	Mean	High

		Low	Mean	High
YDEMA, Egnatius	*P*			$1,100
Dutch (1876 - 1937)				
YEAGER, Edgar	*P*	$132	$292	$440
American (1904 -)	*W*			$220
YEAGER, Ira	*P*	$413	$1,032	$1,650
American (20th -)				
YECKLEY, Norman	*P*			$330
American (20th -)				
YEKTAI, Manoucher	*P*			$1,100
American (1922 -)				
YELLAND, Raymond D.	*P*	$1,210	$3,520	$5,500
American (1848 - 1900)				
YENIL, Nahum B.	*P*			$8,250
Mexican (1947 -)				
YENS, Karl H.	*D*	$220	$275	$330
American (1868 - 1945)	*P*	$248	$2,018	$5,225
	W			$550
YEPES, Tomas	*P*	$319,000	$668,250	$1.017M
Spanish (1600 - 1674)				
YEPES, Tomas (Circle)	*P*			$55,000
Spanish (1600 - 1674)				
YEPEZ, Arteaga	*P*			$385
(?)				
YEWELL, George H.	*P*	$1,870	$2,695	$3,520
American (1830 - 1923)				
YIEREVELT, Michael van (Circle)	*P*			$3,300
Dutch (1567 - 1641)				
YIP, Richard	*W*			$303
American (1919 - 1981)				
YOAKUM, Joseph E.	*D*	$1,320	$2,365	$3,960
American (1886 - 1973)				
YOHN, Frederick C.	*P*			$3,600
American (1875 - 1933)	*W*			$440

D=Drawing, P=Painting, S=Sculpture, W=Watercolor

		Current Price Range		
		Low	Mean	High

		Low	Mean	High
YONG, Joe De	*D*	$275	$358	$440
American (1894 - 1975)	*P*	$110	$495	$1,210
YORKE, William H.	*P*	$1,870	$7,618	$13,200
British (19th -)				
YOSHIDA, Hiroshi	*W*			$1,760
Japanese (1876 -)				
YOUNG, Art	*D*			$605
American (1866 - 1943)				
YOUNG, B. Y.	*P*			$1,210
American (19th -)				
YOUNG, Charles M.	*P*	$1,100	$1,815	$2,530
American (1869 - 1964)				
YOUNG, Florence U.	*P*	$275	$317	$358
American (1872 -)	*W*			$358
YOUNG, Grace	*P*			$385
American (1874 -)				
YOUNG, H. DeM.	*W*			$110
American (20th -)				
YOUNG, Harry	*P*			$2,310
American (19th -)				
YOUNG, Harvey O.	*P*	$1,403	$1,967	$2,530
American (1840 - 1901)				
YOUNG, Henry D.	*W*			$440
(19th -)				
YOUNG, J. P.	*P*			$3,300
European (19th -)				
YOUNG, Mahonri M.	*D*			$220
American (1877 - 1957)	*S*			$4,950
	W	$660	$729	$798
YOUNG, Phillip de	*P*			$468
(20th -)				
YOUNG, William	*P*	$3,300	$4,950	$8,250
American (1874 -)				

D=Drawing, P=Painting, S=Sculpture, W=Watercolor

| | | Current Price Range | | |
		Low	Mean	High
YOUNG, William S.	*P*			$1,760
American (19th -)				
YOUNGERMAN, Jack	*P*	$2,310	$4,290	$6,050
American (1926 -)	*S*	$522	$564	$605
YOUNGLOVE, Ruth Ann	*W*			$440
American (1909 -)				
YRISARRY, Mario	*P*			$660
(20th -)				
YVARAL, Jean P.	*S*			$330
French (1934 -)				
YVON, Adolphe (Attrib.)	*P*			$770
French (1817 - 1893)				
ZABALETA, Vladimir	*P*	$9,350	$11,825	$14,300
(20th -)				
ZABARIAS,	*P*			$330
(?)				
ZABEL, H.	*P*			$275
American (20th -)				
ZACH, Bruno	*S*			$550
American (20th -)				
ZACH, Bruno (Attrib.)	*S*			$385
American (20th -)				
ZACHARIE, Ernest P.	*P*			$8,525
French (1849 - 1915)				
ZADKINE, Ossip	*D*			$8,800
French (1890 - 1967)	*S*	$11,000	$79,200	$297,000
	W			$22,000
ZADOROJNY, Vasiliy	*P*			$1,650
Russian (20th -)				
ZAIS, Giuseppe	*P*			$46,750
Italian (1709 - 1784)				
ZAIS, Giuseppe (Follower)	*P*			$11,000
Italian (1709 - 1784)				
ZAIS, Giuseppe (School)	*P*			$3,300
Italian (1709 - 1784)				

D=Drawing, P=Painting, S=Sculpture, W=Watercolor

		Current Price Range		
		Low	Mean	High
ZAK, Eugene	*D*			$2,750
Polish (1884 - 1926)				
ZAKANITCH, Robert	*P*	$440	$5,156	$11,000
American (1935 -)				
ZAKHAROV, Feodor	*P*	$990	$990	$990
American (1882 - 1935)				
ZAKHAROV, Vadim	*P*	$20,900	$24,750	$28,600
Russian (1959 -)				
ZALTZA, Philip von	*P*	$1,320	$1,375	$1,430
(?)				
ZAMACOIS Y ZABALA, Eduardo	*P*	$25,300	$64,900	$104,500
Spanish (1842 - 1871)				
ZAMORA, Mario	*S*			$3,740
(?)				
ZAMPIERI, Domenico (Attrib.)	*D*			$12,100
Italian (1581 - 1641)				
ZAMPIGHI, Eugenio	*P*	$825	$14,498	$39,600
Italian (1859 - 1944)	*W*	$715	$2,819	$4,400
ZAMPIGHI, Eugenio (Manner)	*P*			$303
Italian (1859 - 1944)				
ZANAZIO, G.	*P*			$880
Italian (19th - 20th)				
ZANCHI, Antonio (Circle)	*P*	$2,200	$3,300	$4,400
Italian (1631 - 1722)				
ZANDOMENEGHI, Federico	*D*			$165,000
Italian (1841 - 1917)				
ZANETTI-ZILLA, Vettore	*W*	$440	$935	$1,430
Italian (1864 - 1946)				
ZANG, John J.	*P*	$1,650	$2,145	$2,640
American (19th -)				
ZANIN, Francesco	*W*			$1,650
European (19th -)				
ZANPAGIN, D.	*P*			$176
(?)				
ZANSTZINGER, M. G.	*W*			$440
American (20th -)				

D=Drawing, P=Painting, S=Sculpture, W=Watercolor

		Current Price Range		
		Low	Mean	High
ZARITZKY, Joseph	*P*			$9,900
Israeli (1891 -)				
ZARRAGA, Angel	*P*	$46,200	$67,925	$88,000
Mexican (1886 - 1946)				
ZATZKA, Hans	*P*	$880	$9,793	$17,600
Austrian (1859 - 1945)				
ZAWISKI, Edouard	*P*			$1,650
French (19th - 20th)				
ZBINOWSKY, J.	*P*			$440
American (20th -)				
ZEEBROECK, Van	*P*			$2,200
Dutch (? - 1844)				
ZEHME, Werner	*P*			$33,000
German (1859 -)				
ZEIGLER, William J.	*W*			$100
(?)				
ZELLINSKY, C. L.	*P*	$1,650	$5,500	$9,350
American (19th -)				
ZEMSKY, Jessica	*W*	$1,650	$1,803	$2,100
American (20th -)				
ZENO, Jorge	*P*	$3,850	$4,538	$5,225
American (1956 -)				
ZEPPENFELD, Victor	*P*			$358
German (19th -)				
ZERBE, Karl	*D*			$165
American (1903 - 1972)	*W*			$935
ZEROLO, Martin	*P*			$770
(20th -)				
ZETSCHE, Eduard	*P*	$770	$1,210	$1,650
Austrian (1844 - 1927)	*W*	$1,100	$1,485	$1,870
ZETTEL, Josephine	*D*			$413
American (20th -)	*P*			$275
	W			$176

D=Drawing, P=Painting, S=Sculpture, W=Watercolor

	Current Price Range		
	Low	Mean	High

		Low	Mean	High
ZEVENBERGHEN, Georges A. van Belgian (1877 -)	P			$7,150
ZEWY, Karl Austrian (1855 - 1929)	P			$4,400
ZEZZOS, G. French (20th -)	P			$605
ZHENYU, Hu Chinese (20th -)	P	$303	$358	$413
ZICK, Januarius J. R. German (1730 - 1797)	P			$6,600
ZICKENDRAUGHT, Bernhard German (1854 - 1937)	P			$660
ZIEGLER, Eustace P. American (1881 - 1969)	P W	$605	$8,457	$41,250 $2,500
ZIEGLER, Nellie American (1874 - 1948)	P	$990	$2,402	$4,675
ZIEL, George (20th -)	P			$700
ZIEM, Felix F. French (1821 - 1911)	P W	$2,530	$15,558	$60,500 $1,760
ZIEM, Felix F. (Attrib.) French (1821 - 1911)	P	$385	$454	$523
ZIER, Francois E. French (1856 - 1924)	P	$3,850	$9,167	$18,700
ZIER, Victor Polish (1822 -)	P			$1,045
ZIGLIARI, Eugene L. French (1873 - 1918)	P			$1,760
ZILLER, European (19th - 20th)	P			$1,980
ZIMMER, Wilhelm C. A. German (1853 - 1937)	P			$33,000
ZIMMERMAN, Carl American (19th - 20th)	P W	$660	$825	$1,100 $248

D=Drawing, P=Painting, S=Sculpture, W=Watercolor

		Current Price Range		
		Low	Mean	High
ZIMMERMAN, Charles B.	P			$358
American (?)				
ZIMMERMAN, Frederick A.	P	$385	$1,522	$2,750
American (1886 - 1974)				
ZIMMERMAN, Karl	P			$17,600
German (1796 - 1857)				
ZIMMERMANN, Jan W. G.	P			$5,500
Dutch (1816 - 1887)				
ZINKEISEN, Doris C.	P	$770	$1,100	$1,430
British (1898 -)				
ZINOVIEV, Andre	W			$880
(?)				
ZLOTNIKOV, Yuri	W	$1,100	$1,458	$2,090
Russian (1930 -)				
ZLOWE, Florence	P			$413
American (20th -)				
ZMURKO, Franciszek	P			$4,400
Polish (1859 - 1910)				
ZOBEL, B.	P			$4,125
British (18th - 19th)				
ZOELLNER, Richard	P			$248
American (1908 -)				
ZOFFANY, Johann J. (Circle)	P			$3,080
German (1733 - 1810)				
ZOFFOLI, A.	P			$8,250
Italian (19th -)				
ZOGBAUM, Rufus F.	W	$1,980	$2,200	$2,420
American (1849 - 1925)				
ZOIR, Emil	P			$1,100
Swedish (1867 -)				
ZOLAN, Donald J.	P	$165	$330	$522
American (20th -)				
ZOMPINI, Gaetano G. (Attrib.)	P	$2,750	$14,575	$26,400
Italian (1700 - 1778)				
ZONARO, Faust	P			$1,650
Italian (1854 - 1929)				

D=Drawing, P=Painting, S=Sculpture, W=Watercolor

		Current Price Range	
		Low	Mean	High

		Low	Mean	High
ZOPPI, Antonio	*P*			$6,600
Italian (1860 - 1926)				
ZORACH, Marguerite	*P*	$825	$12,595	$28,600
American (1887 - 1968)	*W*	$4,950	$6,875	$8,800
ZORACH, William	*D*	$440	$917	$1,650
American (1887 - 1966)	*P*	$715	$4,070	$10,450
	S	$1,100	$8,467	$33,000
	W	$1,150	$4,383	$12,100
ZORACH, William (Et al.)	*P*			$38,500
American (19th - 20th)				
ZORKOCZY, Gyula	*P*			$880
Hungarian (1873 - 1932)				
ZORN, Anders	*D*			$4,950
Swedish (1860 - 1920)	*P*	$154,000	$740,300	$1.375M
	W	$11,000	$246,400	$704,000
ZORNES, Milford	*D*			$330
American (1908 -)	*P*			$4,675
	W	$165	$1,528	$3,575
ZOX, Larry	*P*	$825	$1,939	$3,300
American (1936 -)				
ZUBER, Henri	*P*			$14,300
French (1844 - 1909)				
ZUBER-BUHLER, Fritz	*D*			$495
Swiss (1822 - 1896)	*P*	$3,520	$20,955	$55,000
ZUBIAURRE, Ramon de	*P*	$3,300	$6,050	$8,800
Spanish (1882 -)				
ZUBIAURRE, Valentin de	*P*	$8,800	$12,980	$20,900
Spanish (1879 - 1963)				
ZUCCARELLI, Francesco	*D*			$63,250
Italian (1702 - 1788)				
ZUCCARELLI, Francesco (Attrib)	*P*	$7,700	$9,350	$11,000
Italian (1702 - 1788)				

D=Drawing, P=Painting, S=Sculpture, W=Watercolor

		Current Price Range		
		Low	Mean	High
ZUCCARELLI, Francesco (Foll.)	P	$2,200	$2,750	$3,300
Italian (1702 - 1788)				
ZUCCARELLI, Francesco (Mann.)	P	$2,420	$2,723	$3,025
Italian (1702 - 1788)				
ZUCCARELLI, Francesco (Sch.)	P			$4,400
Italian (1702 - 1788)				
ZUCCARO, Federico	D	$7,975	$352,584	$2.530M
Italian (1543 - 1609)	W	$15,400	$81,180	$159,500
ZUCCARO, Federico (Attrib.)	P			$8,250
Italian (1543 - 1609)				
ZUCCARO, Federico (Circle)	D			$15,400
Italian (1543 - 1609)				
ZUCCARO, Taddeo	D	$63,250	$132,000	$319,000
Italian (1529 - 1566)	W	$16,500	$66,220	$137,500
ZUCCARO, Taddeo (Attrib.)	W	$8,800	$11,367	$15,400
Italian (1529 - 1566)				
ZUCCARO, Taddeo (Studio)	D			$1,100
Italian (1529 - 1566)	W			$3,300
ZUCCHI, Antonio P.	D			$3,080
Italian (1726 - 1795)				
ZUCKER, Jacques	P			$138
(?)				
ZUCKER, Joe	D			$467
American (20th -)	P	$3,080	$9,636	$17,600
ZUCKERMAN, M.	S	$110	$152	$193
American (20th -)				
ZUGEL, Heinrich	P			$33,000
German (1850 - 1941)				
ZUGNO, Francesco (Circle)	P			$44,000
Italian (1709 - 1787)				
ZUHR, Hugo	D			$550
Swedish (1895 - 1971)				
ZUILL, Abbie L.	P			$358
American (1856 - 1924)				

D=Drawing, P=Painting, S=Sculpture, W=Watercolor

| | | Current Price Range | | |
		Low	Mean	High
ZULOAGA Y ZABALETA, Ignacio	*D*			$6,050
Spanish (1870 - 1945)	*P*	$16,500	$130,167	$341,000
ZUNIGA, Francisco	*D*	$3,080	$6,666	$22,000
Mexican (1913 -)	*S*	$5,500	$26,159	$66,000
	W	$3,575	$11,283	$19,300
ZURBARAN, Francisco	*P*	$121,000	$203,500	$286,000
Spanish (1598 - 1664)				
ZURBARAN, Francisco (Circle)	*P*			$55,000
Spanish (1598 - 1664)				
ZURBARAN, Francisco (Manner)	*P*			$1,100
Spanish (1598 - 1664)				
ZURBARAN, Francisco (School)	*P*			$15,400
Spanish (1598 - 1664)				
ZURBARAN, Francisco (Studio)	*P*	$26,400	$34,100	$41,800
Spanish (1598 - 1664)				
ZURBARAN & STUDIO, Francisco	*P*			$253,000
Spanish (1598 - 1664)				
ZUTTER, Jonathan	*P*	$170	$239	$330
French (1938 -)				
ZUYDERLAND, Siet	*P*			$770
(20th -)				
ZWAAN, Cornelis C.	*P*	$110	$894	$4,675
American (1882 - 1964)				
ZWART, A. J.	*P*			$1,485
Dutch (19th -)				

D=Drawing, P=Painting, S=Sculpture, W=Watercolor

About the Authors

Rosemary and Michael McKittrick are art and antique appraisers and dealers in Pittsburgh, Pennsylvania. The couple are certified members of The International Society of Fine Art Appraisers, and their company has been in existence for fourteen years.

In addition to compiling *The Official Price Guide to Fine Art*, the McKittricks write a self-syndicated weekly art and antique advice column called "Ask Our Advice." They have also authored numerous magazine articles dealing with the arts and have lectured and taught courses in the art and antique field.

About the Author

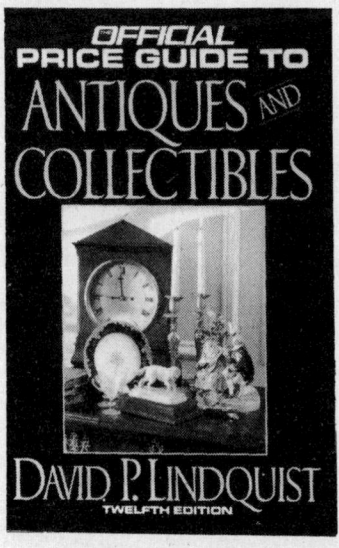